CONTENTS

The Neston Collieries, 1759–1855:

An Industrial Revolution
in Rural Cheshire

First published 2019
Reprinted with minor revisions 2020
Second edition 2023
by University of Chester Press
University of Chester
Parkgate Road
Chester CH1 4BJ

Printed and bound in the UK by the
LIS Print Unit
University of Chester

Cover designed by the
LIS Graphics Team
University of Chester

A catalogue record for this book is available
from the British Library

ISBN 978-1-910481-22-6

The Neston Collieries, 1759–1855:

An Industrial Revolution
in Rural Cheshire

Anthony Annakin-Smith

University of Chester Press

LIST OF FIGURES

LIST OF TABLES

List of Tables

PREFACES

Preface to the First Edition

The extraordinary story of the two early colliery businesses at Neston, in west Cheshire, has been largely overlooked by historians. As an incomer to this leafy, residential part of Cheshire in the 1990s, I was surprised to discover that the area had a history of coal mining – yet the longest-running of these two mines operated for almost a century, between 1759 and 1855 (as well as there being a later half-century of operations which falls outside the scope of this book). Even today, I encounter local people who do not know that mining was ever carried out in the area.

Few books or other studies on the history of coal mining, or on industry in this part of Britain, give Neston's collieries more than a passing mention, if they say anything at all. When reference is made, some of them give incorrect information on, say, the start date of coal working or the extent of production and trade. Mentions of the mines generally ignore facts which made them noteworthy or even extraordinary. I was keen, therefore, to put the record straight and to ensure that the mines' history was properly recorded.

My research into the collieries has been spread, on and off, for about thirteen years. From the outset, my aim was to try to answer questions about much more than just the mines themselves and their operation. Coal mines – indeed any industry – sit within a range of contexts. The workers had personal lives and families; they joined existing communities and developed their own. What, then, were the social conditions and connections surrounding the colliers? The mines had customers, suppliers, distributors and competitors – a network of individuals, businesses and institutions with whom they interacted in one way or another. Who and where were they, how were they involved in the trade and what was the nature of the relationships? At a national level, were events happening economically, politically or scientifically which influenced what went on at the mines? More generally but very importantly, the mines were operating during the period which is widely known as the Industrial Revolution. How did what was happening in this 'revolution' manifest itself at Neston's collieries? Did the works have any connections with other contemporary so-called 'revolutions' – in agriculture and transport for example? The collieries also fitted into a range of geographical contexts, relating not just to the Wirral Peninsula on which Neston sits, but also to Chester and North Wales, and to markets in Ireland, Europe and even the Americas. How did what was happening at the mines fit with what was happening in these other locations at the time? For me, these multiple contexts are a key part of the mines' story. I have been surprised to find that there appear to be very few histories of individual mining areas during this period which go into similar detail. My wish to answer the many questions about the mines and their contexts has led me on a search at dozens of British archives and the occasional one overseas. Every researcher knows that the extent of information which survives from 200 years or so ago is highly serendipitous. Nevertheless, sufficient diverse sources of valuable information have been found on Neston's mines to piece together what I hope is an acceptably comprehensive picture of a rural English colliery of the time. I hope, too, that this account will prove of interest to historians and researchers of industrial history, as well as those interested in history at a more local level. In addition, many families may find reference to ancestors scattered amongst the pages, or on the accompanying website. This variety of groups with a potential interest in this work is testament to the current resurgent interest in Britain's past. I hope this book will play a part, however small, in advancing our knowledge of a fascinating era.

Preface to the Second Edition

The need to reprint this book in 2023 due to continuing demand has presented an opportunity to introduce a significant new piece of information to the story of the Neston collieries. I recently identified a reference to a colliery in the area in the pre-industrial age, before the establishment of the two businesses which are the focus of the book. Whilst the information on this early operation is scant and does not significantly change anything that has been written about the later businesses, it does add an important new dimension to Neston's coal mining history. It is also the first substantiation of claims about pre-industrial working at Neston which have appeared in various places over the years but without sound supporting evidence. More information is given in Chapter 2.

As well as the significant new information noted above, the opportunity has been taken to add other, smaller pieces of information in this edition and to update various points which have been the subject of new research.

Over the past couple of years I have become increasingly aware of the use of microhistory as a technique for approaching historical subjects. Whilst the term 'microhistory' was not explicitly in my mind when I first wrote *The Neston Collieries* that is, in effect, what the book became. Microhistories use a highly focused approach to address a narrow subject such as a person, business or constrained period of time. A concentration on detail allows exploration of the lived experience of those involved and sheds light on how large events – such as the Industrial Revolution – were experienced in ways which more generalised, high-level approaches might mask. I have always viewed the use of information at a 'micro' level – about, say, individual colliers or specific ships' voyages – to see how it fits into a wider context as a critically important aspect of the book. Thus, as one writer has said, microhistories allow us to 'gain insight into how the large [was] felt by the small'.[1] I would be delighted to share further thoughts on the microhistorical approach with anyone who wishes to contact me (see page 2 for contact details).

ACKNOWLEDGEMENTS

Many people have assisted over the years with my research into the Neston collieries. I have endeavoured to keep a note of those who have helped, sometimes giving just a useful snippet and other times more substantially. I sincerely apologise to anyone whose name is omitted from this list. Thanks, then, to Keith Atkinson, Tony Barratt, Sallie Bassham, Paul Booth, Val Bowker, John Boyle, Peter Carrington, Alison and David Caldwell, John Cartlidge, Mike Clarke, Mike Curtis, Alan Davies, Greg Dawson, Gordon Emery, Mike Gill, Maurice Handley, Edward Hilditch, Gavin Hunter, Ray Jones, Patricia Jonker-Cholwe, Peter Kelsall, Jacqui Kenton, David Kitching, Michael Lewis, Peter Mason, the late Hilary and David Morris, Susan Nicholson, Ian Norris, Victoria Owens, Jonathan Pepler, Rob Philpott, Phil Pritchard, Emily Schofield, Renie and Malcolm Verity, Geoff Wright and Stella Young. I should also mention the late Geoffrey Place who was a great inspiration for research into the history of Parkgate and Neston.

Numerous staff have assisted at various record offices and archive centres around Britain and abroad. Those at Cheshire Archives and Local Studies deserve special mention given my frequent enquiries and demand for multiple documents. Jennifer Kelly at North of England Institute of Mining and Mechanical Engineers (NEIMME), and Helen Simpson and Coryn Reynolds at the Coal Authority were also especially helpful.

Special thanks to Susan Chambers who, as well as being an extraordinary fount of local knowledge, gave valuable comments on the draft text, as did the ever-helpful and inspirational Rodney Wright. Also, thanks to my son James for his great assistance with database work and additional help from my daughter Claire. Sarah Griffiths at the University of Chester Press needs a special mention for her enduring patience and relaxed attitude to my constantly deferred deadlines! Thanks too to Gary Martin with his great help with the graphics. I must also mention Paul Dixon for his great work on the website accompanying the book.

Finally, thanks to my wife Ruth for allowing me the time to undertake this mammoth task.

TIMELINE

A summary of the main events at the Neston collieries

1634	Latest date of establishment of small-scale pre-industrial coal-working at Ness
1757–8	First known boreholes dug at Ness
1759	Ness Colliery opens, owned by John Stanley Massey, George Clarke, Richard Richardson (also the manager) and two others. Probably has a steam engine, the first in west Cheshire. First lease granted to Ness Colliery to mine on the Cottingham family's land in Little Neston
1761–2	James Brindley visits Ness Colliery – to discuss building a canal to Chester?
1765	Emy Lyon, future Lady Hamilton, Nelson's mistress, is born at Ness, probably to the colliery blacksmith
1769–70	Richard Richardson dies. Major rejuvenation at the colliery
1775	First lease granted to Ness Colliery to mine on the Earl of Shrewsbury's land in Little Neston
1776–7	Producing over 22,000 tons of coal in twelve months
1777	Four men killed in an accident
1786	Ness Colliery enquires about acquiring a newly-invented winding engine from Boulton and Watt
1780s–90s	Ness Colliery probably has a near-monopoly on the coal trade from Chester to Ireland (several Flintshire collieries have very limited sea access)
1789–90	Thomas Stanley Massey takes over the business
1790	Underground canals ('navigations') opened
1791	Building of Denhall Quay begins
1795	Thomas Stanley Massey dies – ownership of Ness Colliery in hands of executors for eighteen years
1795	Advertisement for 'Coal Mines to Let' in Neston (possibly at Parkgate)

1796	Ness Colliery advertised to let
1806	The 'very valuable colliery at Parkgate' advertised to let
1812	Ness Colliery advertised to let again
1813	Sir Thomas Stanley and Charles Stanley jointly acquire the business; some colliery assets sold
1819	First letter from George Stephenson to Joseph Cabry at Ness Colliery
c.1820	Little Neston Colliery opens, owned by Thomas Cottingham senior
1821	Sabotage of Little Neston Colliery steam engine. First Cottingham v Stanley court case for trespass – Stanley loses
1822	Second Cottingham v Stanley court case for trespass and wilful damage – Stanley loses
1822–3	Sales at Ness Colliery apparently at all-time low
1823	Thomas Cottingham junior takes over Little Neston Colliery. Forced to abandon main pit following deliberate flooding by Ness Colliery
1826	Attempted sale of Little Neston Colliery – fails
1826–31	John Watson, leading colliery viewer (surveyor/engineer), advises Ness Colliery
1828	'Lancashire System' of coal working introduced at Ness to increase the volume of coal obtained
1830	George Stephenson proposes to bring a Chester–Liverpool railway close to the collieries (later rejected)
1841	Sir Thomas Stanley dies; Charles Stanley now sole proprietor
1842	John Buddle, leading colliery viewer (surveyor/engineer) advises Ness Colliery
1845	Four proposals made to bring a railway to Neston, two to the colliery area
c.1845	Little Neston Colliery closed
1847– c.1852	Boreholes dug in Great Neston (Parkgate) to find coal

Timeline

1851–3   Auction sales of Little Neston Colliery

1852   Attempted sale of Ness Colliery

1854   Rowland Errington becomes proprietor of Ness Colliery

1855   Ness Colliery closed; equipment sold

ABBREVIATIONS

A & P   Accounts & Papers (Parliamentary Papers)

BGS   British Geological Survey
BPP   British Parliamentary Papers (published by Irish University Press)
BPR   Burton Parish Registers

ch.   chaldron
CALS   Cheshire Archives and Local Studies
CMLBA   Cheshire Marriage Licence Bonds and Allegations
CSLH   Chester Society for Landscape History
CRGN   Common Room of the Great North
CAS   Cumbria Archive Service
cwt   hundredweight

d.   (pre-decimal) penny/pence
DRO   Durham Record Office

FHSP   *Flintshire Historical Society Publications*
FHSJ   *Flintshire Historical Society Journal*
FMP   findmypast (findmypast.co.uk)

IJHET   International Journal for the History of Engineering and Technology

IUP   Irish University Press
JRL   John Rylands Library (University of Manchester)

LA   Lancashire Archives
Liv. RO   Liverpool Record Office
LMA   London Metropolitan Archive

N/A   Not available
Nch.   Newcastle chaldron
n.d.   no date (stated)
n.p.   no place (stated)

Abbreviations

NEIMME   North of England Institute of Mining and Mechanical Engineers
NEWA   North East Wales Archives
NLW   National Library of Wales
NPL   Neston Public Library
NPR   Neston parish registers*

OED   *Oxford English Dictionary* (online)

OS   Ordnance Survey

PA   Parliamentary Archives
PR   Parish register(s)

s.   shilling(s) – 5p in modern terms. Sometimes expressed as '/–', e.g. '3/–' is three shillings (15p)

T&WA   Tyne & Wear Archives
TCWAAS   *Transactions of the Cumberland and Westmorland Antiquarian and Archaeological Society*
THSLC   *Transactions of the Historic Society of Lancashire and Cheshire*
TNA   The National Archives
TNS   *Transactions of the Newcomen Society*

* The Neston parish registers consulted at CALS were:
P 149/1/1–5 Early Registers (1559–1812)
P 149/2/1–3 Register of Christenings (1813–86)
P 149/3/1–5 Register of Marriages (1754–1891)
P 149/4 Register of Banns (1823–1904)
P 149/5/1–3 Register of Burials (1813–88)
EDB/154 – Bishops' Transcripts of Register entries
Transcripts of the register entries are available at http://cprdb.csc.liv.ac.uk/

NOTES

Place Names

English and Welsh place names have been spelt in their modern form regardless of the form of the original, unless indicated otherwise. Similarly, modern county names have been used unless the context demands otherwise.

Measurements

As the original sources used in researching this material invariably used imperial measures and are often quoted here, these have been used as the basis for weight, distance and area. Where appropriate, metric equivalents have been added.

The lack of standardisation of measures, particularly the quantity of coal in a 'ton' and in a 'chaldron', presents problems at times with accurate statements of the amount of coal involved and of equivalent metric amounts.

A ton commonly comprised twenty hundredweight (cwt) but, when measuring coal, it could often vary between 21 and 36 cwt usually depending on the amount of other material mixed with it (e.g. stone or slack).[1] Thus, for example, a 'collier ton', by which Neston workers' productivity might be measured, was typically 32 cwt. Meanwhile, other places such as Aberystwyth or Newcastle had their own measures of 'ton', making comparisons challenging. To add to the complexity, a hundredweight usually comprised 120 lbs rather than the modern 112 lbs.

Where known, in this book the quantities used in the original are stated. In all other cases, a ton of coal (or other goods) is assumed to comprise 20 cwt of 120 lbs, i.e. 2,400 lbs or 1,089 kg. This is about 7% more than the current meaning of 'ton' (2,240 lbs or 1,016 kg). Tons of 2,400 lbs were also in use in Lancashire.[2]

The 'burthen' (carrying capacity) of a ship was usually quoted in tons but, both before and after an attempt to bring standardisation in 1786, the measure was often variably applied. For simplicity in this book, quoted ship 'tons' have been converted to metric as if they were modern measures but they should be recognised as being approximate at best.

A chaldron of Winchester Measure was the most widely used measure at Chester of coal sold to the sea trade. It has been assumed here to be equivalent to about 28 hundredweight of 120 lbs, or 1.4 tons (1.5 tonnes). A Newcastle chaldron, generally used for European and transatlantic business, was substantially larger at 53 hundredweight (2.9 tonnes). More information on the interpretation of 'chaldron' is given in Chapter 10, note 53.

Cheshire had its own definition of 'acre' which was often used locally up to the nineteenth century. Various referenced sources in this book mention acres but the contexts generally imply that these were the normal, statutory acres not the customary Cheshire ones. Conversions to hectares have been calculated accordingly.

Notes

Further Information

A website has been established to accompany this book. This will be used to a) offer additional information which there has been no room to accommodate here. This includes expansion on some of the endnotes and, in particular, two databases of known colliers at Neston; b) to add information or make any corrections which come to light as a result of my continuing research or from readers' comments.

Web address: *nestoncollieries.org* Email: anthony@nestoncollieries.org

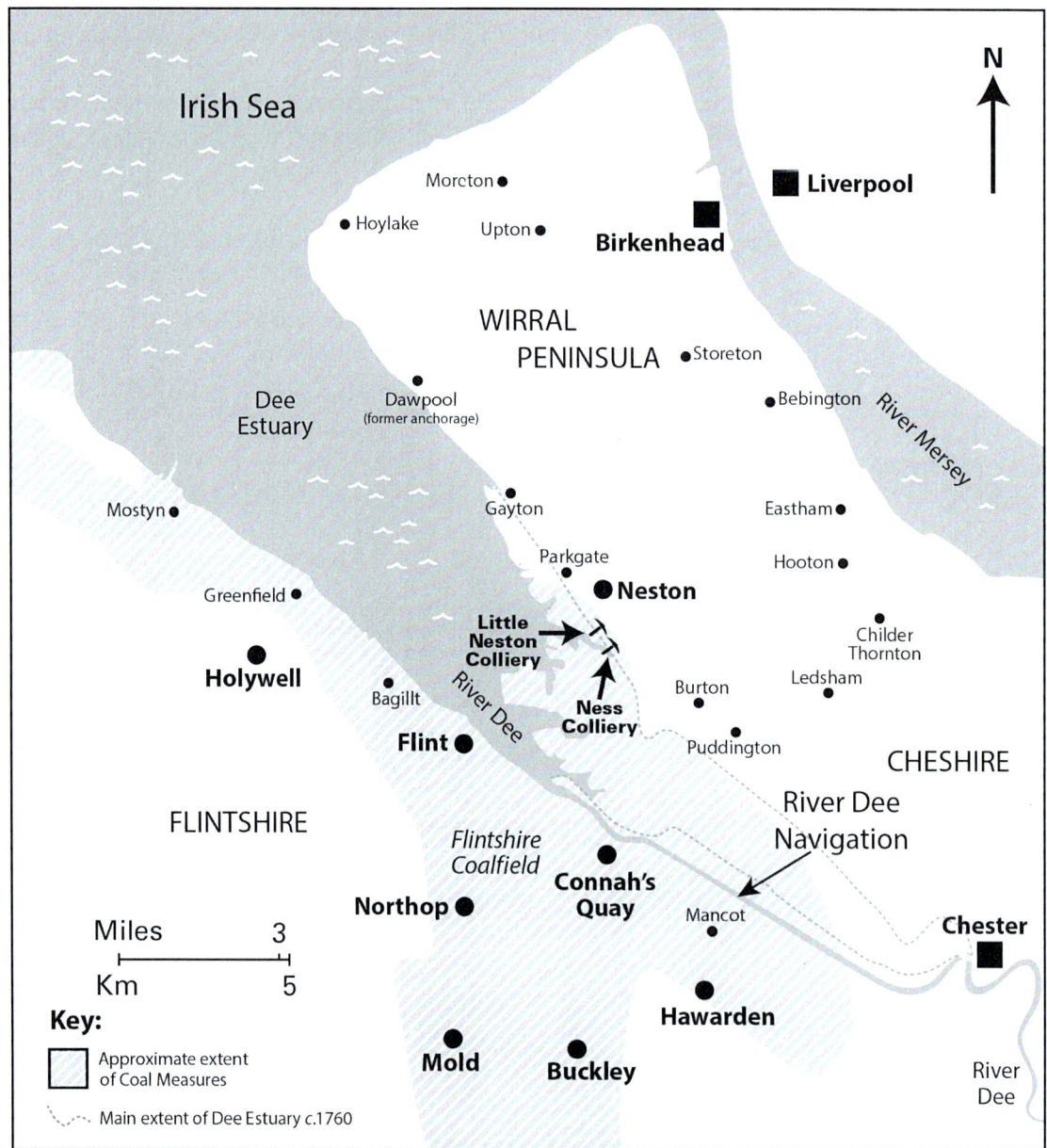

Figure 1.1: The Wirral Peninsula and the Flintshire Coalfield. Main sources: extent of Dee Estuary *c*.1760 – Emanuel Bowen, 'An Accurate Map of the County Palatine of Chester Divided into its Hundreds', 1760 (CALS, PM 12/3); extent of Coal Measures – principally BGS, 1:250,000, 'Liverpool Bay' (1978). N.B. there are variations in the boundary of the Coal Measures on different geological maps, not least on the English side of the estuary.

CHAPTER 1

THE NESTON COLLIERIES –
A SIGN OF THEIR TIMES

The year 1759 was anticipated with fear by many in Britain. Five decades earlier the astronomer, Edmond Halley, had realised that a comet was visible from the earth at roughly seventy-six year intervals and would next be seen in the night skies by the beginning of 1759.[1] Even if many people were, by then, discarding age-old superstitious beliefs about comets, they were still fearful of apparently more rational warnings – for example from founding Methodist John Wesley that the comet could collide with the earth and 'burn it to coal'.[2]

The end of the world would, to say the least, have put rather a brutal stop to the hopes of the people of Neston in west Cheshire who – comet aside – had every reason to be optimistic about what 1759 held. Indeed, it was said that the discovery of extensive coal deposits in recently dug boreholes had led 'all Cheshire' to rejoice.[3] The find ushered in what has become known as the Industrial Revolution to a corner of the county previously untouched by significant industrialisation. It came with the prospect of employment for many and a new source of wealth for a few. Nevertheless, for some, the comet's menacing portent would prove all too true as the realities of coal mining led to appalling living and working conditions, injury and even death.

Halley's prediction early in the eighteenth century of the comet's return was indicative of an evolving Age of Enlightenment. Science and reason were replacing superstition and dogma, paving the way for discovery, invention and innovation which were the bedrocks of the new industrial age. There has been much discussion about the appropriateness of the term 'Industrial Revolution' to describe this period of change and, indeed, debate over the period which it encompasses.[4] We will return to some of these arguments in the final chapter of this book. Suffice to say at this stage that the period over which the collieries at Neston were to operate – 1759 to 1855 – forms all or a substantial part of what has generally been viewed as the main span of the Industrial Revolution.[5] This 'revolution' was about much more than technological change, also bringing new ways of working, living and doing business. One of the other remarkable features of the period was the enormous growth in population – for example, in England, from an estimated 6.3 million in 1761 to 17.8 million in 1856.[6] The commensurate growth in demand for coal for domestic use and for manufacturing was a key driver of the Neston mines' trade.

Two collieries were to be opened near Neston in the period under discussion: one – the larger and longer-lasting – was at Ness; the other was adjacent to it in Little Neston (Figure 1.2 on p. 4). The mines introduced a totally new way of life and of work to west Cheshire. A large new workforce and community was created which was centred, initially, on a single employer; such an arrangement was unparalleled on the

Wirral Peninsula or, almost certainly, anywhere else in west Cheshire. Practices at the mines reflected the great innovations of the age including the introduction of steam engines and horse-drawn rail roads, as well as social developments such as workers' healthcare. There was also the construction of underground canals – an inspirational solution to try to solve a major problem – and the involvement of several of the leading mine engineers of the day, with new working methods introduced. But the mines' arrival brought the darker side of life too – for example, the extraordinary sight of an English baronet successfully prosecuted in court for deliberately wrecking his neighbour's mine; and 100-hour working weeks and the use of child labour which were wretched features of the newly industrialising British economy. Thus, the story of the Neston collieries is fascinating not only for the extraordinary things that went on there but also because it was, for a time, the pre-eminent local manifestation of the changes brought on by industrialisation which were sweeping Britain from the eighteenth century. What was going on at Neston reflected, one way or another, so much else that was happening in Britain at this time – not just in mining but also in, say, transport, entrepreneurship, the economy, trading relationships, demographics and social conditions.

Today, Neston is a pleasant market town, considerably dwarfed by other population centres on the Wirral. Its relative significance was much greater in the mid-eighteenth century, when the first local colliery of the industrial era opened. With roots going back to Anglo-Saxon times, Neston was by far the largest area of settlement on the Wirral and was the nearest large English town to the city of Chester.[7] A sign of Neston's status was that it had even acquired its own market in 1728, being 'the largest and best town' on the Wirral.[8]

As in most of Britain, agriculture was a leading form of local employment with many labourers and farmers listed in the parish registers – but Neston's real importance had come from the sea. Mariners had been using the River Dee and its estuary for centuries.[9] It gave access to fishing waters and opportunities for trade between Chester and ports in the British Isles and further afield.[10] Neston is known to have been a participant in this trade since the Middle Ages and, as ships' access to the port of Chester became increasingly difficult due to silting of the Dee, a plan was adopted in 1541 to site the city's main quay at Neston.[11] The adjacent port of Parkgate grew from the seventeenth century and, for a time, was a main access point between England and Ireland (as well as becoming a fashionable bathing resort).[12] When the first colliery business began near Neston in the mid-eighteenth century, sea-borne routes to market were to be crucial to its success.

There was very little local industry in the mid-eighteenth century: small-scale ship-building and supporting trades were to be found in Parkgate and there were a few domestic weavers in Neston.[13] Nevertheless, the town was bustling and thriving, keeping busy the innkeepers, wig-makers, horse-hirers and many other service trades alongside the mariners, ropemakers and shipwrights.

Notwithstanding the prospect of the returning comet, when the coal reserves were discovered in boreholes made in 1757 and 1758, the excitement would have compounded a wider prevailing mood of self-confidence and optimism. Nationally, Britain's status was in the ascendancy. In 1759, there were decisive victories over the French in the Seven Years' War; great national institutions were founded such as Kew Gardens and the British Museum; and commerce was flourishing with the establishment of what would prove to be long-standing businesses such as Wedgwood and Guinness.[14] As a turning point in the Seven Years' War, some commentators went on to term 1759 an *annus mirabilis* – 'year of miracles';[15] one recent author called it 'The Year Britain Became Master of the World'.[16] Regionally, the North West was growing in importance with Liverpool a dominant British port, not least due to the slave trade. Chester's maritime trade had been eclipsed by Liverpool but there was still a thriving economy centred on the River Dee and its estuary.[17] There were, admittedly, perennial problems with navigation of the river but such concerns would surely not have been at the forefront of minds in the area. The talk in the local parlours and taverns would have been of the discovery of the new coal reserves, and the business and employment opportunities this geological good fortune presented. It also meant that coal – the upcoming fuel of choice for modern households – would be on the doorstep, making it both convenient and relatively inexpensive.

The Neston Collieries

The 1757–8 discovery of the local coal seams was probably first made in the corner of the township of Ness, in the hamlet of Denhall, 1¾ miles (2.8 km) from the centre of Neston (Figure 1.2). At the time, each English parish was divided into a number of townships: the parish of Neston comprised eight townships which included Great Neston (where the town itself was situated) and Ness. Between them lay the township of Little Neston. The resultant first mine, opened in 1759, was at Ness and sited on the bank of the Dee Estuary; it became known as Ness Colliery. The manor of Ness was held by the Stanley family and they were involved as owners of the colliery throughout its life. The coal seams stretched into neighbouring Little Neston, a manor held jointly by the Earl of Shrewsbury and the Cottingham family. Ness Colliery's owners obtained a series of leases to work the coal there for almost all of the next sixty years.

In about 1820 the Cottinghams established their own mining operation in Little Neston – 'Little Neston Colliery'. These new works were also adjacent to the estuary, and accessed the coal previously worked by Ness Colliery. It was thus in direct competition with the Ness business, giving rise to the extraordinary acts of sabotage by the Stanleys against their smaller rival. Both collieries were closed by 1855. These two collieries, then – Ness Colliery and Little Neston Colliery – are the principal

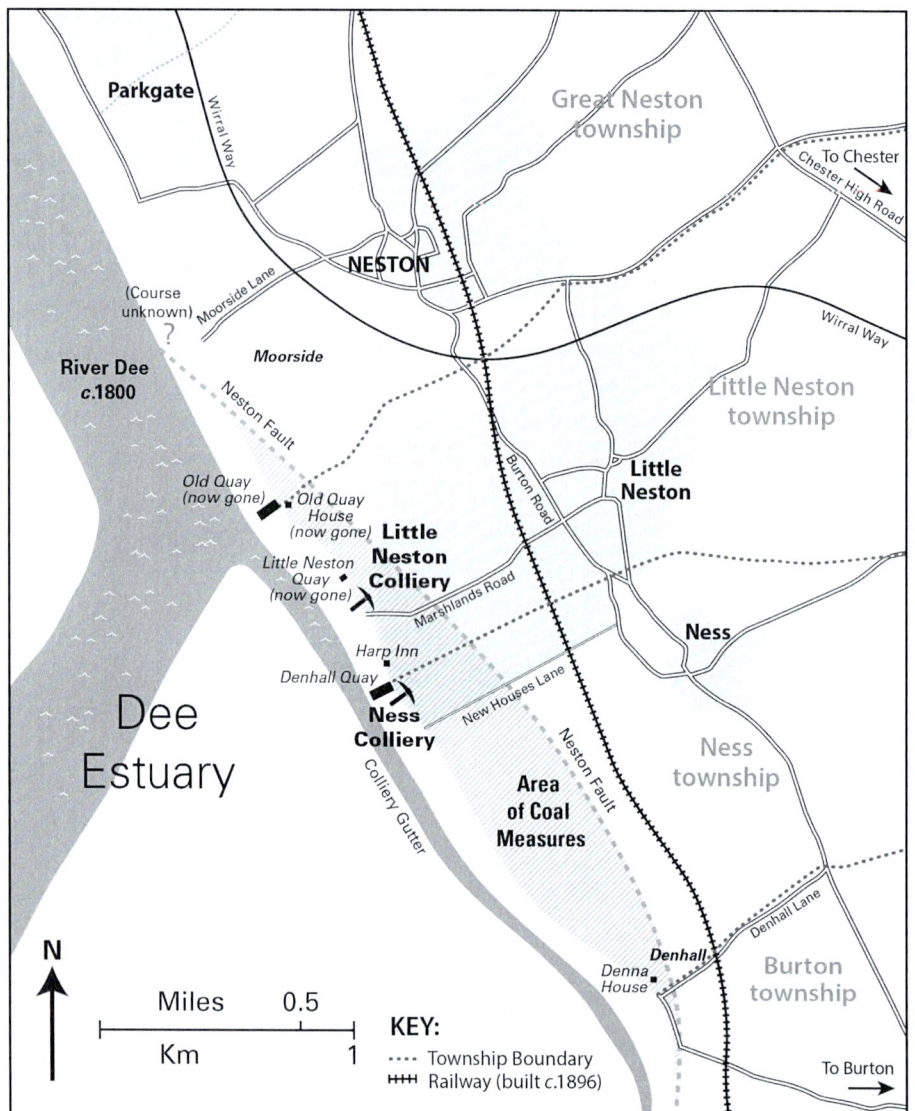

Figure 1.2: The Neston area showing the location of the former Neston collieries. The map includes modern features to assist orientation as well as the names and boundaries of the townships applicable at the time the Neston collieries were operating. The course of the River Dee is shown as it was from when Ness Colliery first opened until about 1800. Principal sources: CALS, PM 11/7, 'A Plan of So Much of the Lands of the River Dee Company'; the tithe maps for Great Neston, Little Neston, Ness and Burton (CALS, EDT 176/2, 241/2, 286/2 and 78/2; OS, two inches to one mile, Sheet 345 (1836); Coal Measures from OS Geological Survey of Great Britain, Sheet 96, Liverpool, Solid (1974) and Sheet 108, Flint, Solid (1974).

'Neston collieries' referred to in this book. While they were in operation, unsuccessful attempts were also made to start a colliery near Parkgate and these attempts are discussed here too. Many photographs, and even a painting, exist of the colliery at Neston but these date from a later period of mining, starting in 1875, which is outside the scope of this book (brief details are given in the Epilogue, page 248).[18]

The proximity of the town of Neston was to be a major benefit to the collieries, giving immediate access to a large market of individual households as well as coal-using businesses. Twelve miles (19 km) away by river lay Chester with a population of over 16,000 in 1801 and its own dedicated coal market.[19] The collieries' riverside location meant that other customers – in Wales, Ireland and occasionally even continental Europe and America – could initially also be reached with ease. However, Neston's coal was an extension of a much larger presence of the resource in Flintshire, separated by the Dee Estuary which is about 3 miles (4.8 km) wide at Ness. The many collieries of Flintshire became a serious source of competition to the Neston works, especially when deliberate changes to the course of the Dee moved it in the Welsh mines' favour. Collieries further afield, in Lancashire, Cumbria and South Wales, were also competitors in the variety of markets accessible from Neston. For a time, though, Ness Colliery was one of the largest and most successful of the many mines amongst its regional neighbours in Flintshire and south-west Lancashire.

The colliery at Ness remained in business for ninety-six years. Its early years were the most successful but, despite geological challenges, reducing market opportunities and national economic fluctuations, it was kept going by continuous innovation and adaptation. Eventually it had extracted almost all the accessible coal in the township. Little Neston Colliery was less fortunate. The Stanleys' aggression and various legal fights with other parties dogged the Cottinghams and, within thirty years, the business collapsed. The story of these Neston collieries is the subject of this book.

* * *

Readers may find it helpful to have a background understanding of two topics which are relevant to much of the discussion. One of these is the local geology which, of course, evidences the local coal and is particularly important in relation to where and how the coal seams were worked, discussed in Chapters 4 to 6. The other topic is the main families involved in the colliery businesses. The names of the individuals concerned can sometimes be confusing – often members of different generations shared the same names; sometimes people changed their names – so charts have been included which it is hoped will help clarify the relevant relationships.

The Geology of the Mine Area
The coal seams worked in the Neston area are an extension under the Dee Estuary of the coalfields of North Wales, specifically the Flintshire Coalfield. The coalfield covers

some 60 sq. miles (155 sq. km) and was extensively worked on the Welsh side of the river (Figure 1.1).[20] The coalfield comprises strata from both the Lower and Middle Coal Measures of the Carboniferous period, both of which can be found at Neston.[21] The coal was formed from vegetation which decayed in swampy, equatorial conditions around 300 million years ago.

Coal Measures do not consist of solid coal but, instead, comprise seams of coal of varying thickness between layers of other rocks including sandstones, mudstones and clays. The Coal Measures at Neston are the only occurrence of Carboniferous rocks in west Cheshire and the Wirral and, in relation to the land surface they underlie, form a roughly lens-shaped area 1.9 miles (3.0 km) long, by 550 yards (503 metres) at its widest point (Figure 1.2 on p. 4).[22] The rocks are bounded to the east by a geological fault (a vertical displacement due to ancient shifts in the land) lying north-west/south-east, beyond which lies Triassic sandstone.[23] Thus there was no accessible coal east of this line, variously known as the 'Neston Fault' or 'Wirral Colliery Fault'.[24]

The Neston seams dip – i.e. slope downwards – generally to the north-west at a gradient of about one-in-six, extending under the Dee Estuary towards North Wales.[25] Thus, with only sandstone accessible to the east, a notable feature of the colliery was the extended workings westward under the clay-lined bed of the estuary. On at least one occasion the workings at Neston were said to have reached the bed of the river although without serious consequences.[26] The furthest workings at Ness Colliery went out under the estuary 'upwards of 2,000 yards' (1,830 metres).[27] There is, though, no evidence of the workings ever meeting their counterparts bored from the Welsh side of the river.[28]

A feature of the Coal Measures at Neston was that they contained many faults. These movements were very localised so that the characteristics of the rock in one location might be very different from the characteristics surveyed a short distance away. This is well illustrated in two detailed vertical geological sections from 1876 of the two main shafts which were just 57 yards (52 metres) apart at Neston Colliery, on the site of the earlier Little Neston Colliery.[29] These show a different number of seams of coal at varying depths and of different thicknesses; for example, the depth below ground of one seam, the Six-Foot, differed by 19 yards (17 metres) between the sections (and the Five-Foot seam below it was missing altogether in one case).[30] A plan of workings of the Five-Foot seam in Ness shows eleven faults of various sizes and orientations spanning the area.[31] In Little Neston, two shafts were sunk which presumably straddled a fault – one shaft, on land, did not find coal; the other, sunk abreast of the first but a few yards into the estuary, did find coal 21 yards (19 metres) below the surface.[32] A generalised depiction of the faulting is shown in Figure 1.3.

The great variation in local conditions presented immense challenges in both finding and then following worthwhile coal seams which could end abruptly. While seams of reasonable quality up to 7 feet (2.1 metres) thick occurred in places, in one of

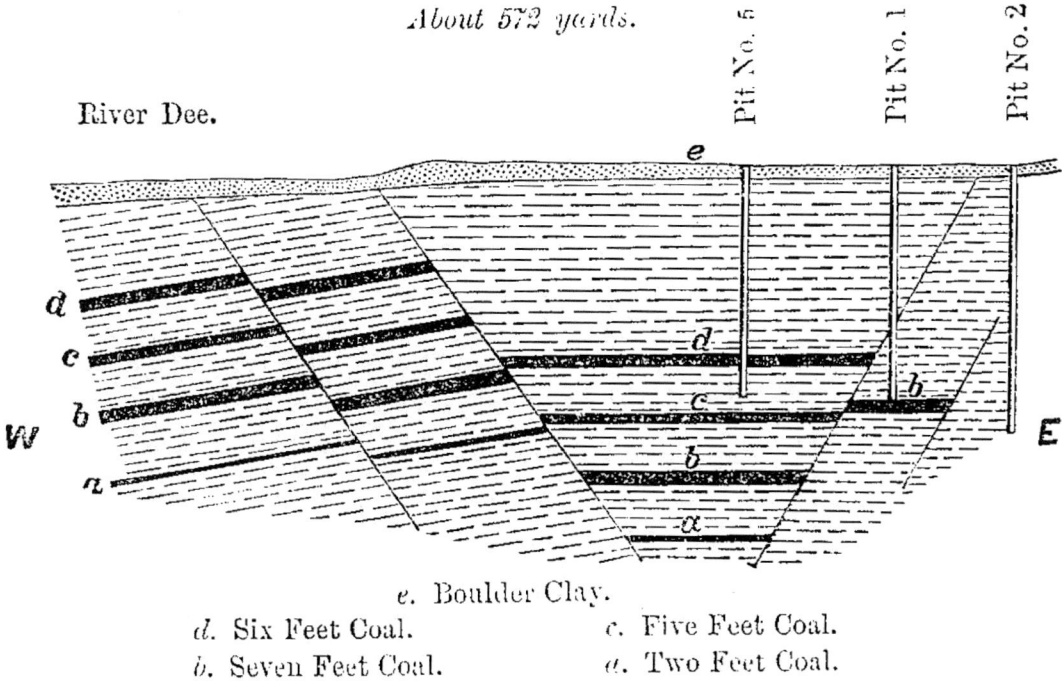

Figure 1.3: Simplified geological section at Little Neston. The section was drawn for Wirral Colliery in the late nineteenth century and illustrates well the succession of coal seams and how faulting could disrupt them. 'Boulder clay' was a former term to describe glacial drift. Source: George Morton, *The Geology of the Country Around Liverpool* (London: George Philip, 1897), p. 37.

three boreholes made south-east of Denhall Quay only 3 feet 7 inches (1.1 metres) of coal was found in 170 yards (155 metres) of boring – all of it very deep and none of it in seams thick enough to have been worth exploiting.[33] This may be one of the reasons why there were so many shafts at Ness, at least thirty, as new ones were sunk to pick up fresh seams.[34]

A record survives from 1797 complaining about the extent of faulting at Ness Colliery and many documents from the period 1819–31 evidence frustration at the disappearance of the Six-Foot and Five-Foot seams at faults.[35] It was necessary to undertake various forms of exploration to try to find them again; these searches were time-consuming and costly, and were sometimes in vain.

Before boreholes or shafts could reach the solid rock they first had to penetrate the overlying clay soil. The geologist Charles Wedd noted that the Coal Measures 'are entirely concealed by Glacial Drift' (i.e. till, or unsorted glacial deposits, laid down around 10,000 years ago).[36] The 1876 geological sections show drift thicknesses of about 42 feet (13 metres) and 58 feet (18 metres) with the first coal seams within the Measures at 108 feet (33 metres) and 92 feet (28 metres) below the surface respectively.

The depths of this drift and then rock above the coal were not unusual, although coal seams were reported at just 37 feet (11.3 metres) and 45 feet (13.7 metres) below the surface in a couple of locations.[37]

The depth of the material above the coal, known as the 'overburden', precludes opencast mining, which was practised in parts of Flintshire, and probably also means that bell-pits – an early form of mining using single shafts – were never a viable option in Ness.[38] It also means that coal could only have been found by boring, either specifically for coal or, perhaps, by chance when sinking a well. In terms of depth, Ness Colliery was reported to have worked seams down to about 146 yards (134 metres), with the deepest known borehole sunk to 197 yards (180 metres).[39]

The northern extent of the coalfield was the subject of much interest over the years. The issue was significant, not only because it influenced the extent of activities in Little Neston township, but also in the next township north too, Great Neston. This was largely owned by the Mostyn family of North Wales who made attempts over several decades to encourage extraction of coal from beneath the estuary off Parkgate, claiming the presence of significant quantities of coal. As late as 1874 there was a reference to 'Gayton Coal Field' in Mostyn correspondence, referring to a township even further north than Parkgate.[40] Interestingly, the earliest geological map of Britain (and, indeed, the world's first national geological map) was published in 1815 and shows coal-bearing rocks all the way up the Wirral's west coast.[41] How this was arrived at is unclear as it is incorrect: in reality, the lens-shaped exposure at Neston curved into the estuary near the Old Quay, heading towards North Wales.[42] Perhaps the map's surveyor was influenced by the presence of sea-coal – pieces of coal washed up on the coast from seams elsewhere, in this case from across the estuary. The occurrence of sea-coal was indicated at Ness in 1788.[43]

The Mostyns were right, though, in claiming that the coal seams stretched into part of Great Neston. Thus, when Edward Lloyd Mostyn sunk a line of four boreholes starting about 230 yards (210 metres) from the shore near Moorside in the mid-nineteenth century he was able to evidence the presence of various coal strata.[44] However, their quantity, quality and accessibility did not merit the establishment of the mine which Mostyn sought. The post-1875 works based at Little Neston were to mine under the estuary in some of these northern exposures, though never venturing as far as Mostyn's line of boreholes.[45]

The Neston Coal Seams – Quantity and Quality
Through the randomness of geological circumstances, Neston never had the quantity or thickness of coal seams that were enjoyed in the Flintshire Coalfield. The most important seam in North Wales was the 'Five Yard' or 'Main Coal', described as 'being generally the best in quality and everywhere a thick seam' – up to sixteen feet (4.9 metres).[46] However, this seam is not found at Neston, whose seams originated below

the Main Coal.[47] Given that the costs of working coal fell steeply in proportion to the thickness of the seam, this was a considerable disadvantage.[48]

Neston also had fewer seams: in total, the geologist Charles Wedd described fourteen seams which could be found in the Middle Coal Measures in various parts of the Flintshire Coalfield, above and below the Main Coal; the early Neston colliery businesses found only four worthwhile seams (with one other worked in the later period of mining at Neston).[49] Fate dealt another bad hand to Neston with the Six-Foot seam which was of 'fair quality' at Mostyn Colliery on the Flintshire coast but had dwindled to being 'thin and inferior' by the time it was at Neston.[50] All these geological problems were to be significant contributors to the ongoing difficulties and ultimate demise of the colliery workings. The mine-owners at Neston could only have dreamed of the conditions in Flintshire where, for example, the author Thomas Pennant reported twelve seams of coal with a total thickness of 65 feet (19.8 metres) in a 615-feet (187-metre) section at Bychton, near Holywell in 1796.[51]

The four seams worked at the Neston collieries are shown in Table 1.1. The three lower seams were to be found in both Little Neston and Ness.[52] The top-most seam, the Six-Foot, was found only in Little Neston and was worked by Ness Colliery while it held the lease there.[53] Little Neston Colliery subsequently worked it, later accessing the Five-Foot too.[54] As well as the Six-Foot, Ness Colliery worked the Five-, Seven- and Two-Foot seams over the years.[55] The depths in the table are only indicative. Faulting and the dip of the rocks mean that the same seam could be found at different depths in differing locations.

Table 1.1: The seams mined at the Neston collieries. The stated depths were as described in relation to Pit. No. 14 in 1826.[56]

Seam	Quality	Use	Depth at Which Found Yards (Metres)	Worked by
Six-Foot	'Very inferior'	Steam coal	56 (51)	Ness Colliery, in Little Neston, to c.1820; thereafter by Little Neston Colliery
Five-Foot	'Best'	House coal	86 (79)	Ness Colliery and Little Neston Colliery
Seven-Foot	'3rd best'	House coal	117 (107)	Ness Colliery
Two-Foot	'2nd best'	House coal	146 (134)	Ness Colliery

As the Six-Foot seam was also the lowest quality, it was the least valuable. This was considered to be 'steam coal' and one use for it would have been in the colliery's own engines; it was also useful in furnaces and for smelting.[57] The quality of the coal made a substantial difference in price – the best house coal was selling for 38% more than the lowest grade in 1828.[58] Slack (small pieces of coal) would have sold for even less.

In places the coal was only inches thick and the names of the more substantial seams were not necessarily accurate descriptors of their thickness – for example the 'Seven-Foot' at Ness was described in one document as having a 'height of workable coal' of 'three feet nine inches' (1.1 metres).[59] It was also said that 'in some parts the [Two-Foot] seam was so thin that with their elbow resting on the floor [the miners] could touch the roof with their fingers'.[60]

Other coal seams were reported at Neston but were not worked by the early (or later) collieries. For example, an 1823 report on Thomas Cottingham's mine reported the availability of 'Yard Coal', i.e. a three-foot seam, between the Six-Foot and Five-Foot but reported it was of 'little value'.[61]

As well as coal, other resources were to be found in the Coal Measures.[62] Perhaps the most valued at Neston was fireclay, used for making bricks to be used in high temperature environments such as kilns. There were several fireclay seams at Neston, one being specifically offered as an attraction when Ness Colliery was advertised to let in 1812.[63] Some seams of cannel, a hydrogen-rich form of coal, were also found in the local strata.[64] Cannel was much valued for lime burning and was also said to be burnt by the Irish in small quantities mixed with other coals.[65] Lying between seams of the ordinary coal the local cannel was presumably mined and sold although no explicit evidence for this appears to have survived. However, when Edward Lloyd Mostyn was trying to sell the supposed 'colliery' at Parkgate, the alleged presence of valuable cannel was used as a selling point.[66] Bands of ironstone, formed in stagnant swamp conditions in the Carboniferous, were also scattered in the coal seams but there is no evidence the mineral content was ever exploited locally.

The Landowners of Ness and Little Neston

The story of coal mining at Neston centres on two townships – Ness and Little Neston. The land within a township usually formed a manor held by a single family. In the case of Ness, this family was the Stanleys. Little Neston was unusual in being divided between two families, the Talbots, Earls of Shrewsbury, who held three-fifths of the manor and the Cottinghams who had the remainder. As these families feature extensively in this book it is worth briefly describing them and explaining the relationships involved.

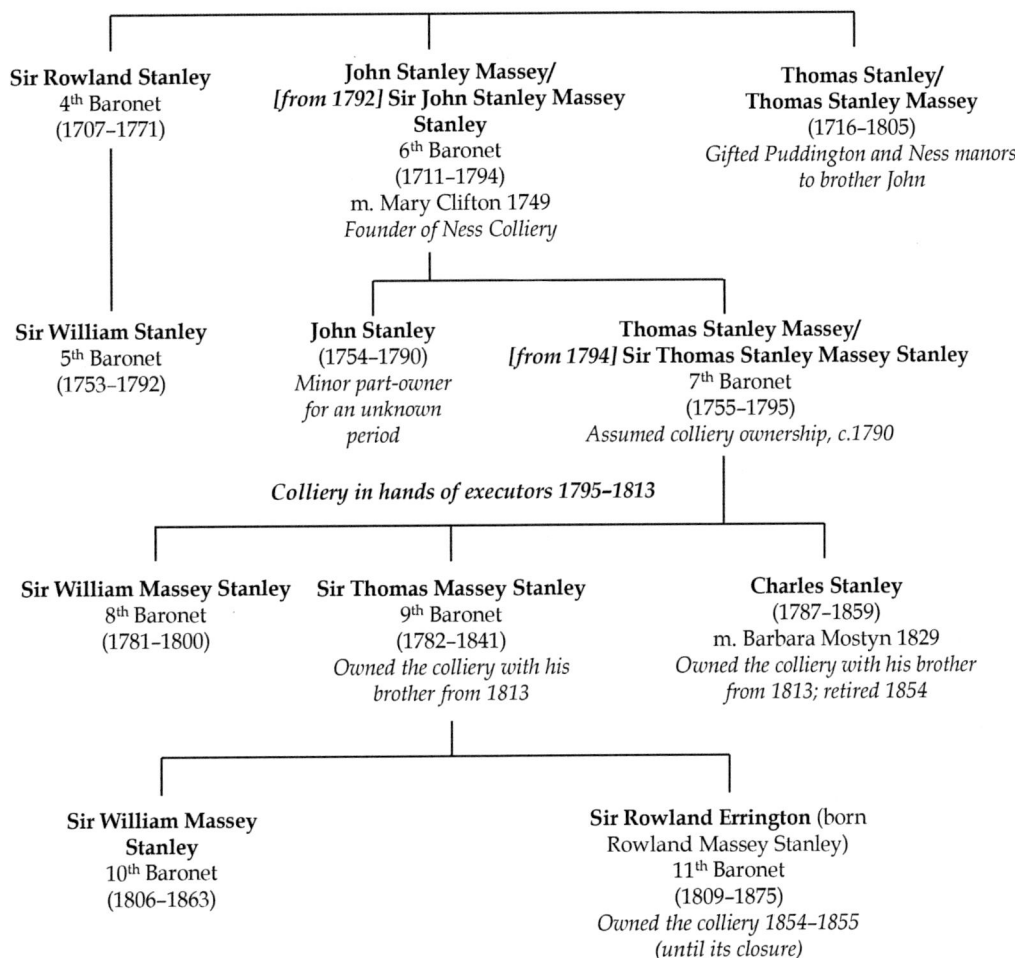

Figure 1.4: The Stanley Family during the time of Ness Colliery (selected information only).

Ness: the Stanleys (Figure 1.4)[67]

The Stanley family has played a prominent part in the history of England for centuries. There have been many branches of the family, which includes the Earls of Derby, and they had been a significant (and, on occasion, malevolent) presence on the Wirral since the Middle Ages. The instigator of Ness Colliery, John Stanley Massey, came from the branch of the family which had its seat at Hooton. When the colliery was founded in 1759, his elder brother Sir Rowland Stanley, 4th Baronet was head of the family.

John Stanley Massey had been born as John Stanley. The manor of Ness came into his hands when he was granted it, as well as the manor of Puddington, by his younger brother, Thomas, who in 1741 chose to become a Jesuit priest. This brother had inherited the two manors from Sir William Massey, the Masseys having been a long-standing, high status, Catholic family on the Wirral like the Stanleys. Thus, on receiving Puddington, John Stanley chose to add the Massey surname to his own. On inheriting the title to Hooton in 1792, and thus uniting the manors of Hooton, Puddington and Ness under his baronetcy, John assumed the further surname of Stanley, becoming Sir John Stanley Massey Stanley, 6th Baronet until his death two years later.[68] He held other Wirral manors too – Storeton, Eastham and Ledsham.

Sir John was succeeded as head of the family by his son Thomas, 7th Baronet, and then *his* sons William, 8th Baronet and Thomas, 9th Baronet. The manors of Hooton, Eastham and Storeton had to be sold off in 1849 following the profligacy of the 10th Baronet, Sir William Massey Stanley who squandered the money on gambling and high living. Meanwhile the manor in which the colliery lay, Ness, as well as Ledsham and Puddington, passed to Rowland Massey Stanley who had changed his name by licence to Rowland Errington. He closed down the colliery in 1855.

As well as the manors mentioned above, the Stanleys had parcels of land of various sizes in several other places – on the Wirral Peninsula (such as at Upton, Willaston, Childer Thornton and Bebington), elsewhere in Cheshire, and in Lancashire and Flintshire.[69] The Wirral estates were particularly important in relation to Ness Colliery as the tenants were customers for its coals as well as for other products which the works produced such as lime for agricultural use. Interests in Lancashire included Bickerstaffe, near Ormskirk, where there was a Stanley Gate Colliery though there is no evidence the Stanleys of Hooton ever had any direct involvement in its operation.[70] In Flintshire, the Stanleys sold leases to their land at Hawarden for others to mine coal;[71] they also benefited from royalties from several lead and zinc mines in the county.

Little Neston: the Cottinghams and the Talbots, Earls of Shrewsbury

As indicated above, the manor of Little Neston was, unusually, split between two families. The two-fifths of the manor of Little Neston held by the Cottinghams had been in their hands after purchasing it, probably in 1628. The three-fifths owned by the Talbots, Earls of Shrewsbury, had been in the family somewhat longer having passed through generations of forebears.

The land in the township had been divided between the Cottinghams and Shrewsburys in scattered parcels but, when a survey was undertaken in 1788, the Earl of Shrewsbury was by far the largest landowner (1,200 acres/486 hectares) with the Cottinghams owning 196 acres (79 hectares); 183 acres (74 hectares) were now in third parties' hands.[72] To the Cottinghams' good fortune, though, the land under which coal was discovered was more evenly split between their family and the Shrewsburys.

Furthermore, they were to claim exclusive rights to the coal won under the estuary, offshore from Little Neston. The issue of what proportions the Cottinghams and Shrewsburys held in Little Neston, and the rights that went with them, were to be a bone of contention between the families in the eighteenth and nineteenth centuries leading to lengthy court cases.

The Cottinghams

(Figure 1.5)[73]

The family's involvement with local coal mining was, initially, passive – simply granting a lease in 1759 for the Stanleys to mine for coal under their land. A document written several decades later mentions only Charles Cottingham in connection with this lease.[74] However, his brother, Theodore, was the Cottingham lord of the manor in 1759, and it may actually have been he who granted that

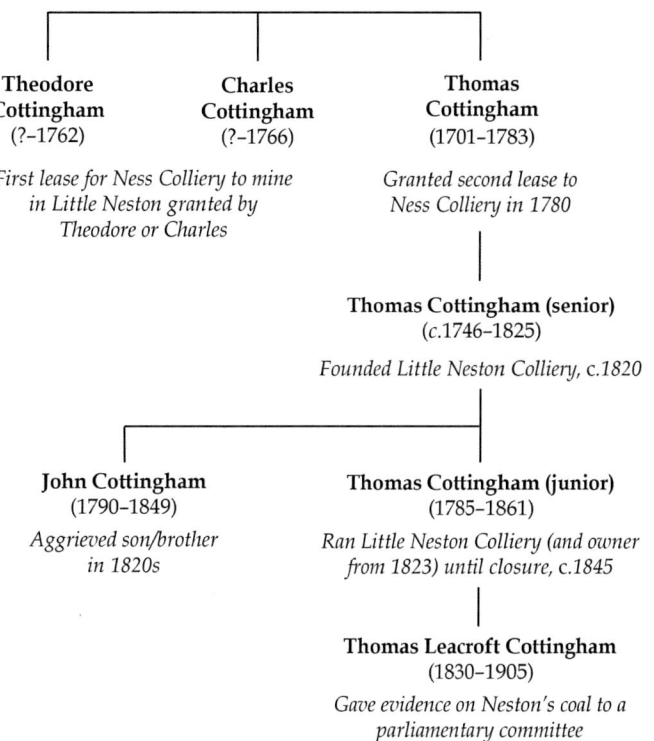

Theodore Cottingham (?–1762)

First lease for Ness Colliery to mine in Little Neston granted by Theodore or Charles

Charles Cottingham (?–1766)

Thomas Cottingham (1701–1783)

Granted second lease to Ness Colliery in 1780

Thomas Cottingham (senior) (c.1746–1825)

Founded Little Neston Colliery, c.1820

John Cottingham (1790–1849)

Aggrieved son/brother in 1820s

Thomas Cottingham (junior) (1785–1861)

Ran Little Neston Colliery (and owner from 1823) until closure, c.1845

Thomas Leacroft Cottingham (1830–1905)

Gave evidence on Neston's coal to a parliamentary committee

Figure 1.5: The Cottingham Family during the time of Ness Colliery and Little Neston Colliery (selected information only).

first lease, though he died just three years later. He was childless and intestate, and his estate passed to his childless brother Charles who also soon died, in 1766.[75] His estate largely went to his surviving brother, Thomas, although two nieces were granted the income for their lifetimes from the coal raised from Bank Hey – a field in Little Neston under which much early mining was undertaken.[76]

There was a succession of further Thomas Cottinghams – the first Thomas's son and then *his* son. The first son, born about 1746 and termed 'Thomas Cottingham senior' here, took the decision around 1820 to establish his own colliery in Little Neston after the Stanleys' lease to mine there expired. His own son ('Thomas Cottingham junior'), an injured veteran of the Battle of Waterloo, ran the business and soon took over ownership, seeing the colliery through to its end in the 1840s. He too had a son Thomas, adding the middle name Leacroft. Thomas Leacroft Cottingham had no direct involvement with the Neston collieries but became a mining engineer and colliery manager elsewhere, giving evidence to a parliamentary committee on the former state of the works at Neston.

The Talbots, Earls of Shrewsbury[77]

The Earls of Shrewsbury, who owned three-fifths of the Manor of Little Neston, comprised members of the Talbot family. Unlike the Stanleys and Cottinghams they never lived in the local area. They played a relatively minor role in the story of the Neston collieries, never actively engaging in local mining. Instead the Earls' role was as landowner, granting leases for coal to be won under their various parcels of land.

When the colliery at Ness was founded the family was headed by Sir George Talbot, 14th Earl of Shrewsbury. In 1775, he granted a twenty-one year lease to Ness Colliery to mine under his land. The lease gave rise to acrimony with both Ness Colliery and the Cottingham family and was not, apparently, renewed. George was succeeded in 1787 by his nephew Charles Talbot, 15th Earl who, in 1824, granted a lease to allow the Little Neston Colliery to mine there. Charles was succeeded by his nephew John Talbot, 16th Earl, from 1827. Again, there was dispute over the leasing arrangements with the Cottingham family as well as other legal challenges. It seems these bankrupted Thomas Cottingham junior and led to the closure of Little Neston Colliery.

* * *

The following chapters consider diverse aspects of the mines. Chapters 2 and 3 look at the mines as businesses, considering, for example, their size, ownership and degree of success. The following three chapters take a more operational perspective, discussing the mining methods used and the working conditions that the colliers experienced. This section also includes a review of the evolving role of new technologies. Chapters 7 to 11 consider the various markets which the collieries sought to access and how they did so. There is discussion of the trade with Chester as well as analysis of the collieries' important sea-borne business. A short section has been added looking at marketing practice at the collieries, a topic which generally has received little attention. Chapter 12 looks at the social conditions faced by those who lived and worked at the mines including the colliers' families, much of it based on extensive analysis of data on individuals taken from a variety of sources. The final chapter reflects on the significance of the Neston collieries from national, regional and local perspectives and asks to what extent they reflected what was happening elsewhere in Britain during the Industrial Revolution.

CHAPTER 2

NESS COLLIERY:
A NEAR-CENTURY OF BUSINESS

This chapter and the next focus on how the two colliery businesses operating at Neston during the Industrial Revolution were conducted – who established and owned them, their size and profitability, the key business decisions made, levels of competition and the general pattern of success or failure. Chapter 2 focuses on the larger and longer-running of the businesses, Ness Colliery. This was established by a five-man consortium in 1759 and later owned and operated solely by the Stanley family. It was to be a long-running business – ninety-eight years from conception to closure. From about 1820 a rival works owned by the Cottingham family, Little Neston Colliery, operated on adjacent land in Little Neston for twenty-five years or so. This colliery, and the extraordinary and discreditable tactics used by the Stanleys to damage it, form the subject matter of Chapter 3. There were also unsuccessful attempts over several decades to establish a colliery on the edge of the nearby port, resort and fishing village of Parkgate; discussion of this activity has been included in Chapter 3 too.

The Search for Coal

It was in 1757 that the first known systematic exploration for coal was undertaken in the Neston area. Details survive of three boreholes sunk in that year and the next in the southern part of the township of Ness, at Denhall.[1] The work would have been instigated by the then lord of the manor of Ness, John Stanley Massey.

It is not known what prompted Massey's commission of the boreholes at that time. However, in the mid-eighteenth century landowners across the country were increasingly keen to bore for coal, often for purely speculative reasons. The principles of geology were little understood in the 1750s but with growing industrialisation the presence of coal could increase land values forty-fold.[2] Other landowners were to bore elsewhere on the Wirral (including John's grandson, Thomas, at Puddington) but without success.[3]

In any event, John Stanley Massey would have had better reason than most to undertake a search for coal seams as there is a record of prior coal-working in the township of Ness. A recently-identified 1634 estate survey records the existence of 'Collery way Butts' [sic] – apparently a plot of land adjoining a lane leading to a coal works.[4] The word 'colliery' (with later variants such as 'collery') is recognised as being used from the seventeenth century to describe such works.[5] There is, however, no reference in the apparently comprehensive estate survey to a colliery per se. Thus we do not know when the works began, nor can we be sure that they were operating in 1634.

A few writers have previously suggested that there was local coal mining in the seventeenth and early eighteenth centuries but this author has seen no unequivocal evidence to support their assertions. There has also been an intriguing suggestion that the coal from Neston was used during the period of Roman occupation – a conclusion reached following analysis of a coal sample from a known Romano-British site at Irby on the Wirral Peninsula.[6] However, there are several question marks concerning the evidence so far presented for this. Fuller discussion of all these claims can be found elsewhere.[7]

It seems likely that the pre-industrial 'collery' was in the Denhall area of Ness which crossed into the adjoining township of Burton. Denhall is where the shallowest local coal was to be found, at just 37 feet (11.3 metres).[8] The area had been the site of a medieval hospital as well as being an anchorage;[9] coal might have been discovered when, for example, a well was being sunk. Several lanes led to the area which may account for the 'Collery way' reference in the 1634 survey. Moreover, the name 'Denhall' and variants was used in connection with Ness Colliery from its earliest days, continuing throughout its life and beyond.[10] The name was often applied even when the workings were away from that area suggesting that the name was ingrained in local consciousness regarding coal working. These early works may also account for the mention of a 'pit' at Denhall which, in 1790, was described as 'old'.[11]

The nature of these early workings is unknown but it seems unlikely that they were of any great scale. They appear to have left no surviving record of their operation and coal at a relatively shallow depth was still to be found there in 1757. Denhall appears to have been the first area where John Stanley Massey chose to sink boreholes suggesting he believed the reserves there were not exhausted. The records from that time label the boreholes numbers 'Two' to 'Four'; nothing is known of number 'One' but it may have been where a shaft was later recorded. They were up to 71 yards (65 metres) in depth and the geology in each one varied significantly. Coal seams ranged in thickness from just two inches (51 mm) to 5 feet 8 inches (1.7 metres).

The coal strata stretch into a narrow coastal fringe in Burton and there is a suggestion that holes had been sunk there at some time – maybe boreholes or even bell-pits.[12] Bell-pits were an early method of coal mining but if they were used at Burton they would have been at about the limit of depth for the technique.[13] There is also a 1619 record in Burton of a field called 'coale pitt Hay'.[14] However the word 'coal[e]' was sometimes applied to charcoal, with the 'pit' being where it was made; this was the case at nearby Saughall where there is a Coalpit Lane.[15] As for other references in Neston, there is mention in parish church records to 'The coal' and 'The cole' as local locations in 1711;[16] in the light of evidence of pre-industrial local coal-working, it seems plausible that these relate to these early coal works.

As well as the 1757–8 boreholes at Denhall there are likely to have been others further north at what would become the main colliery site; there was probably also one or more in the adjacent township of Little Neston. There the land was mainly owned by the two joint lords of the manor, the Earl of Shrewsbury and Theodore Cottingham.

Boreholes in Little Neston would have identified the continuation of the coalfield into the township. If asked, the landowners would surely have been keen to co-operate with this exploration but there is no indication that any coal on Shrewsbury's land was actually worked until 1775.[17]

The 1757–8 boreholes evidently uncovered previously-unknown coal mining opportunities. The excitement this caused is indicated in a 1760 letter from the Rev. John Prescot of Chester who, with some hyperbole, wrote:

> 'All Cheshire is happy in the discovery of a rich vein of coals, made near two years ago, that reaches, they say, from Park-yate [Parkgate] almost to this town [Chester].'[18]

It is possible that another leading figure in Chester society, Richard Richardson, prompted John Stanley Massey's search for new coal in 1757. As the Ness manor-holder was, himself, a senior local figure it is quite probable that the two men already knew each other; in any event Richardson and Massey were to be two of the initial five co-investors in the colliery. Richardson had enormous experience of mining – albeit for metal ores rather than coal – having extensive interests in mines across North Wales and as far afield as Scotland.[19] The men may have met at Pentrobin (Flintshire) where the Stanley family had land and Richardson owned a smelting works.[20] Richardson knew the value that the discovery of valuable minerals could bring. He was one of the leaseholders in a lead mine at Minera, near Wrexham – an undistinguished piece of agricultural land left in a legacy to the Chester Companies until lead was discovered and the income from the land soared.[21] Richardson would surely have gleaned some knowledge of coal mining through his many Flintshire connections. The commodity was being successfully won at several places on or close to the Dee Estuary (and had been since the thirteenth century).[22]

The Early Years

It would have taken a couple of years after the new coal deposits were discovered for the colliery to commence production. It may have been necessary to clear land, and time was certainly needed to acquire equipment and machinery, recruit men and sink shafts. There are several indications that, by 1759, coal was being raised at Neston. One such indication involved Richard Richardson a leading member of the City of Chester Assembly (the city's ruling corporation). He petitioned the Assembly on 30 November asking to be granted a thirty-one-year lease of the Old Quay at Neston to ship coals. The quay was a long-standing structure, 900 yards (823 metres) from the main colliery site, which had fallen into disuse; Richardson undertook to repair it.[23] He also indicated that he wished to lease a patch of ground by the Dee in Chester 'for the landing of coals and taking the same into a coal yard'. A decision was deferred by the Assembly and there was no significant progress on the matter until 1763.[24]

There are indications, though, that the colliery was already operating in 1759 as just a month after Richardson's request to the Assembly, there came the first entry for a coal-worker in Neston parish registers: on 26 December 1759 the son of 'William Bramhall, Collier of Nesse' was buried.[25] In addition, shipping records suggest production started from the middle of that year, with a dedicated customs official to oversee activities appointed from 5 July and a sudden increase in shipments from the area to Ireland.[26]

Landowners who found themselves in the fortunate position of possessing coal deposits had a number of options. Some took on the role of entrepreneur, exploiting the asset themselves. Others preferred to stand back, granting a lease to allow others to take on the work. John Stanley Massey went for an intermediate option, setting up his own business but bringing in four co-investors. This arrangement shared the substantial costs of establishing a new colliery – digging shafts, erecting buildings and buying equipment, especially very expensive steam engines – while also sharing the risks and rewards. The earliest known detailed reference to ownership of the business dates from 1763, and, rather than recording it under the Stanley Massey name, describes it as 'George Clarke & Company of colliers'.[27] The list of owners is given as 'John Stanley Massey Esq., George Clarke Esq., Richard Richardson, John Oxton, Thomas Whittle'. It seems probable that all five men were involved from the time of the initial decision to establish the colliery in 1757 or 1758.

Whilst the first-known full list of colliery owners dates from 1763, there are previous references to George Clarke and Co., the earliest-known being as the merchants for a shipload of local coal bound for Dublin in November 1760.[28] The identity of Clarke is a little uncertain – it was either a father or his son who shared the same name, or it was possibly both of them. George Clarke senior had been colonial lieutenant-governor of the province of New York from 1739 to 1743.[29] 'Governor Clarke', as he was known even after his return to England in 1745, was shrewd, sometimes ruthless, and very wealthy, investing in an estate at Hyde, in east Cheshire. He later lived in Chester and would surely have known the senior figures in Chester society, one of whom was Richard Richardson. Clarke may well have been one of the initial owners of Ness Colliery but, if so, his interest was short-lived as he died in January 1760. He was buried at Chester Cathedral where a marble memorial tablet installed in his honour can still be seen. Nevertheless, the name 'George Clarke' continued to be associated with the colliery at least until 1763, suggesting his son had the interest in it, possibly even living in Neston for a while.[30] When he died in 1777, his will indicated he had an interest in a colliery at Hyde and it seems probable that he had divested himself of any involvement in Ness Colliery many years before.[31]

Richard Richardson was a wealthy and well-connected individual being a leading figure in the life of Chester. His civic roles included being an alderman (i.e. member of the ruling Assembly of the city) from 1754, city mayor in 1757–8 and a magistrate.[32] In a business context Richard Richardson was the second man of that name in a wealthy family dynasty of goldsmiths and silversmiths, with premises in Eastgate Street.[33] He was a leading member of Chester's Goldsmiths' Company and became Assay Master of Chester in July 1761 with his 'RR' mark appearing on numerous items of gold and silver plate, still popular with collectors today.[34] Richardson may have had a financial interest in the Mostyn and Bychton collieries in Flintshire too.[35]

John Oxton was steward (i.e. business and administrative manager) of the Hooton estate, working for Sir Rowland Stanley, 4th Baronet.[36] Thomas Whittle, of nearby Childer Thornton, was described as a 'yeoman' and 'gentleman'.[37] Oxton described Whittle as his 'kinsman' in his will.[38] They probably took smaller shares in the new colliery than the other parties.

John Stanley Massey had no industrial or business background so bringing in the expertise of an experienced operator like Richard Richardson would have made good sense. Richardson was highly savvy about the new advances of this era and, he may even have investigated the possibility of bringing a canal to Neston – this would have been one of the first in the country, but it never materialised.[39] The coal works were 'principally under [his] direction and management', presumably due to his extensive business experience, until his sudden death in 1769.[40] He owned one quarter of the business and it is almost invariably his name, rather than that of the other owners', which is found in early documents concerning its operation.[41] By contrast, the Stanley Massey name is entirely absent from surviving colliery-related records in the 1760s. Like many of his contemporary landowners, it seems John had little interest in being directly involved with day-to-day management of a mining business.

The coalfield stretched north into the manor of Little Neston which adjoined Ness. The manor was divided between the Cottingham and Talbot families who owned two-fifths and three-fifths of the manor respectively. There was no apparent desire by the Cottingham family to work the coal on their land themselves; instead one of the Cottinghams, probably Theodore, granted Ness Colliery a lease to extract coal under his lands.[42] The thirty-year lease was apparently dated 21 May 1759, thus marking the earliest date from which coal could begin to be mined from land which was to be very important in the colliery's early years.[43] Cottingham was entitled to a 10% royalty (or 'farm-rent') on the value of the coal sold which was gained from under his territory.[44] This royalty was an average rate in the North Wales coalfields, and the same rate was paid to John Stanley Massey as landowner of Ness (on top of any share of colliery profits).[45] Further leases were agreed by succeeding generations of the families.[46]

Although a substantial amount of mining was undertaken in Little Neston, it seems probable that from Ness Colliery's earliest days its operational and administrative centre was in Ness township where John Stanley Massey was lord. However, no specific name was given to the new coal works. Prescot's 1760 letter, cited earlier, did not state a name; and newspaper reports of nearby drownings in 1760 and 1761 merely refer to 'the new colliery in Wirrall' [sic] and 'the new Wirral Colliery' respectively.[47] When the engineer James Brindley visited in 1761 and 1762 he referred to 'Parkgate Colliery' – Parkgate being the best-known nearby location – and just 'Neston' (in poorly spelled variants).[48] The first known use of the name 'Ness Colliery' comes in 1761 but this term was not used consistently.[49] For example, Thomas Boydell's map, surveyed in 1770–1, refers simply to 'Denna Coal works' (Figure 4.2 on p. 52).[50] It was not until 1779 that 'Nesse Colliery' [*sic*] first appeared on a published map.[51]

Over the decade to 1769, the business appears to have thrived under Richardson's guidance. From 1759 there are hundreds of records of ships departing the Dee Estuary with local coals, most of them probably emanating from Ness Colliery.[52] The number of shafts sunk at the colliery grew to twenty.[53] There were also large and growing numbers of colliery workers – maybe 170 or more at its peak (see Chapter 6). This was almost certainly the largest single workforce anywhere in west Cheshire. However, Richard Richardson died unexpectedly, aged fifty-eight, in September 1769 and this seems to have been the catalyst for a new phase in the story of Neston's mining.[54]

One of the changes that occurred was to the ownership of the business. John Stanley Massey, as well as Thomas Whittle and John Oxton, continued as proprietors. However, Thomas Clifton of Lytham, Stanley Massey's brother-in-law, was a partner in the business by 1775 and had perhaps joined some years earlier.[55] Meanwhile, Richardson's interest was now in the hands of his sister, Ellinor Farrington.[56] There is no indication of any involvement by George Clarke junior who may have relinquished his interest years before.[57]

There was also much new operational activity at the mine. During 1770 two new shafts were started, and completed in the following year; a new sailing vessel, the *Stanley Massey*, was built to carry coals to Ireland; seven new horses were acquired, probably to increase winding capacity in the shafts; there were signs that new buildings and a steam engine were erected; and the subscription to the Chester Infirmary for medical treatment of colliers was started in the colliery's name.[58] These changes may have been driven by new owners but there was also a new manager who probably brought fresh ideas; he was Joshua Small who had worked with Richard Richardson at Chester's Foundling Hospital.[59] Additional activities at the colliery included the identification of the previous business's debtors, who were no doubt chased for what they owed; traders were told that they would need 'ready money' to obtain coal as there would be no credit facilities.[60] All this activity coincided with a substantial spike in the area's coal sales to the shipping trade (see Figure 10.3 on p. 159).[61]

It appears that 2 December 1769 was a significant date in the reorganisation as a new financial accounting period was started. The accounts have survived, covering the ten months to the company's year-end of 29 September (i.e. Michaelmas) 1770, and are a valuable source of information on colliery activity at the time.[62] They show ten-month sales of £5,993 and an apparent profit of £720.[63] The profit appears to be a very respectable figure, especially as there would have been many increased costs during

Table 2.1: Ness Colliery's output and sales for the twelve months to 27 September 1777.[64] The average price per ton was 7s. 9d. (38p) for coal and 2s. 2d. (11p) for slack. For simplicity, conversion to tonnes has not been included: one ton of 2,400 lbs equated to 1.089 tonnes (see Glossary).

Quarter-Year	Coal raised (Tons)	Slack raised (Tons)	Coal sold (Tons)	Slack sold (Tons)	Slack used in colliery engines (Tons)	Coal sold (£)	Slack sold (£)
1776 Q4	4,611	1,093	4,230	322	621	1,634	38
1777 Q1	4,347	1,186	4,251	166	705	1,611	20
1777 Q2	3,788	1,189	4,692	930	621	1,811	96
1777 Q3	4,375	1,486	3,983	1,092	600	1,565	120
12-month sub-totals	17,121	4,954	17,156	2,510	2,547	6,621	274
12-month totals	22,075		19,666		2,547	6,895	

the period such as boatbuilding and sinking of new shafts.[65] It is more than any of the limited number of comparators in Britain offered by coal historian, Michael Flinn, and better than most in Lancashire in the 1760s and 70s given in a study by John Langton.[66]

From the ten-month sales value figure in 1769–70 it is possible to estimate the volume of annual sales – around 20,549 tons (22,378 tonnes).[67] The figures are consistent with fuller data gleaned from other accounts covering fifteen months of operation between October 1776 and December 1777.[68] These show twelve-month sales of almost £7,000 and the total volumes of coal and slack raised of 22,075 tons (24,039 tonnes) (Table 2.1). These figures suggest that Ness Colliery was one of the largest collieries in this part of Britain. Of the many south-west Lancashire mines, starting just 16 miles (25 km) away from Ness as the crow flies, only Parr, Ravenhead and Thatto Heath are likely to have been larger (there were probably dozens of others, though, which were smaller).[69] As for the Flintshire collieries, output at Ness was probably more than the combined output of the three collieries in the Hawarden area at the time – about 20,000 tons (21,780 tonnes).[70] Comparative figures are not available for the other Flintshire mines. The evidence suggests that the works at Mostyn and nearby Bychton were not producing large quantities of coal, but nothing is known of volumes at Bagillt, or Coleshill near Flint.[71] In any event, the Flintshire mines were suffering from loss of access to the River Dee and, with it, little opportunity to exploit the lucrative Irish trade.[72] This gave Ness Colliery a near-monopoly in that business against its Welsh rivals, helping it to flourish. All things considered, Ness Colliery's owners must have felt very satisfied with their large and profitable enterprise.

The 1776–7 accounts were produced to record royalties payable to landowners. Royalties were calculated on the value of coal sold which had been taken from under a landowners' property. The rate of royalty was usually stated as a proportion of the sales value and would vary depending on local circumstances.[73] In Ness Colliery's early years the figure was 10% but in the next century, as the mining became more challenging, the rate was reduced to one-fifteenth and there was talk of it going lower still.[74] The 1776-7 accounts indicate that, in the latter calendar year, about 40% more coal was being taken from Little Neston than Ness. In particular, the Cottingham estate was doing very well: that year Thomas Cottingham received well over three times the royalties of the Earl of Shrewsbury (£285 vs. £81) – the Earl having granted Ness Colliery a twenty-one-year lease two years earlier.[75]

This difference between the rewards to the Cottingham estate and the Earl of Shrewsbury was to become a serious issue between the two parties. The Earl was soon dissatisfied with the 1775 lease, apparently believing that the Cottinghams were benefiting unfairly.[76] Shrewsbury demanded to see details of royalties which had been paid to the Cottingham estate – but the request was refused.[77] By 1788 the newly installed 15th Earl was taking legal action, complaining that Thomas Cottingham (senior) was receiving royalties which were due to the Shrewsbury estate relating to coal gained from under and on the 'pebly shore' of the Dee.[78] He had a point as the 1776-7 royalty accounts show (the first) Thomas Cottingham benefiting from 'coals disposed of from his Lordship' (i.e. from the shore and under the estuary, or 'waste') but no similar credit to Shrewsbury; the Cottingham estate was eventually forced to concede the issue.[79] A few years later the Earl was concerned that Ness Colliery was not working the pits on his land for the minimum of three months per annum stipulated in the 1775 lease, thus failing to generate sufficient royalties for himself.[80] There is no record of a subsequent lease by Shrewsbury to Ness Colliery for working under his land although he did receive some royalties for coal won under the estuary.[81]

Royalty figures enable the value of sales to be calculated but, sadly, only incomplete figures have survived in relation to most of the 1770s and 1780s (Appendix I). While it is therefore impossible to be certain, the indications are that these were good years at Ness Colliery. The 1770s were probably the best in the colliery's life; sales in the following decade were lower but still reasonably healthy. More workers were sought in 1778 and employment levels remained relatively high judging by the number of entries mentioning colliers in the Neston parish register.[82] Trade was still good enough in 1786 to motivate the colliery owners to enquire about acquiring one of the recently-invented Boulton and Watt rotary steam engines.[83] However, there was a shadow hanging over the works which was to have an increasing effect until its eventual closure. As the works inevitably extended further under the estuary, more and more time was spent hauling coals from distant workfaces to the shaft. This was an unproductive use of time and added costs which negatively impacted profits. The issue was to be a constant source of frustration to the mine-owners who sought various solutions to the problem. There is an apparent trend in the 1780s of a reduction in the coal won offshore at Little Neston and also a trend towards increasing amounts of coal being mined at Ness in that decade and the next (Appendix I) – one explanation is that these were moves towards mining more accessible, and thus less costly, coal.

Although other investors retained interests in the business, in late 1789 or early in the following year, principal ownership of Ness Colliery passed from the seventy-eight-year-old John Stanley Massey to his son Thomas.[84] Land Tax returns from 1790 record 'Thomas Stanley Massey Esq. & Co.' as occupier of the colliery lands.[85] This change marked the start of another period of rapid and extraordinary innovation at the colliery. Developments included new exploratory activity, marked by the digging of at least one new borehole, and the construction of a substantial new shipping quay.[86] The colliery farm, described in Chapter 4, may have been established around this time and there also seems to have been a plan to bring two new roads to the colliery area from Neston.[87] Most remarkable was the introduction of two underground canals, or 'navigations', to transport the coal to the shafts from the distant coal face. There have been very few such arrangements in British coal mines; the topic is considered in more detail in Chapter 5. The new activity appears to have been funded, in part at least, by a loan of £600 from the retiring John Stanley Massey.[88] It appears the innovations quickly yielded results, evidenced by a rapid upturn in royalty payments to the Stanley estate (Appendix I).

Uncertainty and Decline

Thomas Stanley Massey was able to enjoy the business's success for only a few years as he died in February 1795. His father Sir John Stanley Massey Stanley, co-founder of Ness Colliery, had died the previous year (he had added a second 'Stanley' to his name after becoming 6th Baronet in 1792, also automatically acquiring the honorific 'Sir'; Thomas also took on the additional name, and became 7th Baronet on John's death).[89] A memorial tablet to them both, erected by Sir Thomas's widow in 1797, can be seen in the church of St Nicholas in Burton, the parish in which the Stanleys' Puddington estate lay.[90]

Shortly before he died, Sir Thomas Stanley Massey Stanley was having to fight off a legal challenge from the River Dee Company which was potentially critical to the future of the colliery. The Company, represented by the Attorney General, claimed rights to the saltmarsh, soil and ground of the Dee Estuary off the Wirral coast.[91] The case went to appeal after Stanley's death but the Dee Company's claim was rebuffed, establishing the Stanleys' rights to the estuary up to the former course of the River Dee which had been diverted in 1737. This boundary lay some way offshore and, for geological and operational reasons, it is unlikely that mining would have gone that far. Nevertheless, if the case had been lost, the colliery would not have been able to work under the Dee where most of its coal was being won.

Sir Thomas's death left no suitable family members to carry the colliery business on so it was advertised to let.[92] Two advertisements appeared during late 1795 and in 1796 but they were worded very differently from each other and only the later one specifically referred to Ness Colliery.[93] It is possible that the earlier, more ambiguous, advertisement actually related to an attempt to start a colliery at nearby Parkgate; it is discussed in the next chapter. The later notice mentioned the 'valuable work of Ness Colliery' with its engines and other equipment as well as the 'considerable' colliery farm, the shipping pier and 'rail roads'. However, despite the advertisement running over several weeks, no new lease resulted.

The two deaths in quick succession were followed by a third, in 1800, of Sir Thomas's eldest son Sir William Massey Stanley, 8th Baronet, who was a minor when he died. Sir Thomas's second son, also Thomas, thus succeeded, becoming 9th Baronet. He too was a minor. This succession of owners of the Stanley estate, complicated by the young ages of two of those involved and the curious terms of the late Sir Thomas's will, seems to have left the colliery without a figurehead and in the hands of executors for many years.[94] Thus, a printed 'Ness Colliery' receipt, dated 1809, is sub-headed 'Bought of the surviving Executors of the late Sir Thomas Stanley Massey Stanley, baronet, Deceased', even though he had died fourteen years earlier.[95] The position was complicated yet further by there having been other co-proprietors of the colliery in the family.[96]

The death of Sir Thomas in 1795 and the subsequent lack of clear leadership may well have created some turbulence at the colliery. In the year of his death the colliery made a significant loss (£562) and did not make a profit for two years. These figures are revealed in summary accounts which survive for the period 1795 to 1811 (Table 2.2). These show years when substantial profits were made (up to £2,115) but also two further years of losses, 1807 and 1808 – and with no particular upward trend over the period. This was over a time, during the French Wars, when British colliery profits generally showed a 'marked rise' as coal prices soared.[97] Indeed, the profits at Ness in 1809–11 are likely to have simply been a function of the more-than-doubling of sales prices between those years, mirroring a national trend, rather than any other factor.[98] Whatever profits were being made, they were being enhanced by diversification in the colliery's activities. While coal production was the principal form of business, like similar mining operations Ness was producing or selling a range of other products. Most of these were derived from, or made using, coal or slack (small pieces of coal). In the early nineteenth century lime, coke, bricks and charcoal were all being sold. Slate, imported from Wales, was also being offered. The production activity underlines the very industrialised – and therefore exceptional – character of this corner of Cheshire at that time. The range of products is considered more fully in Chapter 7.

Table 2.2: Ness Colliery's annual profit/loss, 1795–1811.
Source: LA, DDBL 54/55.

12 Months to 26 September	Profit/Loss (£)
1795	(562)
1796	(5)
1797	304
1798	1,220
1799	689
1800	1197
1801	159
1802	293
1803	1,975
1804	2,115
1805	818
1806	241
1807	(282)
1808	(278)
1809	576
1810	682
1811	106
Four years of the colliery manager's salary omitted from the above (years unspecified)	(300)
Total for 1795–1811	**8,948** **Average: 526 p.a.**

A significant source of information on production at Ness Colliery from 1800 to 1838 comes from the financial accounts of the Stanleys' Hooton and Puddington estates.[99] These show royalties received for almost all of those years and enable sales levels of coal to be calculated (Appendix IIa). Coupled with the 1795–1811 accounting data, they show that the highest profits coincided with years of highest sales values, with possible sales volumes of around 20,000 tons (21,780 tonnes) in 1804.[100] This would have made Ness Colliery roughly comparable in size with some of the Flintshire collieries, such as Northop, which was producing about 25,000 tons (27,225 tonnes) in 1811.[101] However, the production level at Ness in 1804 was exceptional and, generally, the colliery was not growing. Indeed, by the early nineteenth century, it was relatively small compared to many other mining operations: in Flintshire, sales volumes at Hawarden had risen to 75,000 tons (81,675 tonnes) and nearby Aston was raising 72,000 tons (78,408 tonnes) soon after 1800.[102] In south-west Lancashire, there had been considerable growth in the size of collieries in the last quarter of the eighteenth century. Many of the Lancashire mines were now larger than Ness including Ravenhead and the collieries at Whiston; Orrell was producing 48,120 tons (52,403 tonnes) in 1800, most of it going to Liverpool.[103] Collectively, these collieries posed strong competition to Ness Colliery so that it was effectively blocked from the Liverpool market and faced increased challenges in the overseas and coasting trades (i.e. principally trade to Ireland and Wales). More significantly, Ness was losing its ability even to participate in sales via shipping as the course of the waters of the Dee was being steered away from the works by deliberate action in North Wales by the River Dee Company.[104]

The colliery's ownership position remained unresolved for many years. The executors of the late Sir Thomas, 7th Baronet, sought other buyers. These may have included William Blundell of Crosby Hall, Lancashire who had married Sir Thomas's daughter, Catherine, in 1809 – a union of two staunchly Catholic families.[105] The accounts cited in Table 2.2 are lodged in Blundell family papers but, if William had any interest, nothing came of it. In any event, in 1812 the colliery was again advertised to let, over several weeks (Figure 2.1).[106] The offer included steam engines, the colliery farm of ninety acres (36.4 hectares), a smithy, a large lime kiln and twelve workers' cottages. There was also a newly built boat. However, again, there were no takers. The colliery was not a particularly attractive proposition with its relatively poor geology, high underground haulage costs and weak profits.

The ownership issue was finally settled in 1813. The exact sequence of events is unclear but the decision may have been linked to the executors' power to withhold distribution of the troublesome Stanley estate until beneficiaries reached the age of thirty. In any event, the thirty-year old Sir Thomas Stanley, 9th Baronet, appears to have made up his mind not to sell the business.[107] Instead, a series of exchanges between various parties including Sir Thomas, his younger brother Charles and the executors of Sir Thomas Stanley Massey Stanley, 7th Baronet, who had died in 1795 seems to have led to both brothers acquiring a share of the business, probably half each.[108] Its three steam engines, machinery and other equipment were valued at £3,169.[109] The new arrangement led to Charles running the business and being entitled to all its profits.[110] Sir Thomas was to benefit from the royalties on coals raised from his manor of Ness although at a reduced rate of one-fifteenth of sales, presumably reflecting the various difficulties the colliery was facing.[111] The name 'Ness Colliery' remained but subsequent records often refer to the business as 'Charles Stanley & Co.' Nevertheless, as part-owner, Sir Thomas continued to take an active interest in the business for some time.

It seems that as part of the new arrangement, a decision was made to sell off much of the colliery's farming stock; Sir Thomas paid £107 for a half-share of the remaining horses and equipment. [112] In addition, the colliery's large boat, the *Hooton* built just a few years earlier, was sold for a small loss and a smaller one, the *Puddington*, purchased.[113] It seems probable that this exchange was in response to the rapid changes in the course of the Dee which were making it increasingly difficult for vessels to reach the colliery, leading to loss of its important Irish trade. However, within little more than a year, the brothers were seeking to sell the *Puddington* too.

It is possible that Thomas's brother, Charles, had had some earlier involvement with the colliery as, from 1811, he began to build Denna House at Denhall, one mile (1.6 km) from the main colliery site.[114] The house was constructed over the next couple of years and he was recorded as the occupier from 1813, the year of the agreement about Ness Colliery between the Stanley brothers.[115] He remained there for several decades.[116] Thus, he was almost 'living above the shop' allowing him to keep a close eye on the business. In 1829 he married Barbara, the daughter of Sir Edward Mostyn Baronet, of Talacre (Flintshire).[117] The Mostyn families, with baronetcies in

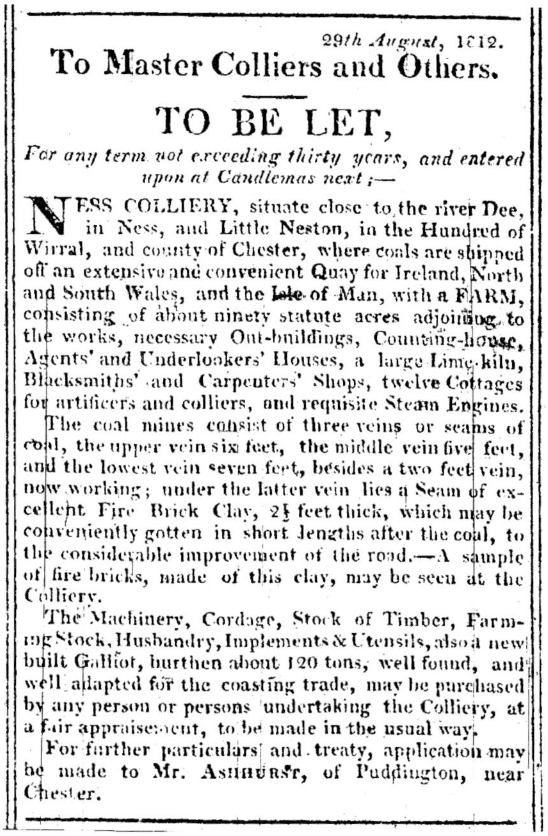

29th August, 1812.

To Master Colliers and Others.

TO BE LET,

For any term not exceeding thirty years, and entered upon at Candlemas next ;—

NESS COLLIERY, situate close to the river Dee, in Ness, and Little Neston, in the Hundred of Wirral, and county of Chester, where coals are shipped off an extensive and convenient Quay for Ireland, North and South Wales, and the Isle of Man, with a FARM, consisting of about ninety statute acres adjoining to the works, necessary Out-buildings, Counting-house, Agents' and Underlookers' Houses, a large Lime-kiln, Blacksmiths' and Carpenters' Shops, twelve Cottages for artificers and colliers, and requisite Steam Engines.

The coal mines consist of three veins or seams of coal, the upper vein six feet, the middle vein five feet, and the lowest vein seven feet, besides a two feet vein, now working; under the latter vein lies a Seam of excellent Fire Brick Clay, 2½ feet thick, which may be conveniently gotten in short lengths after the coal, to the considerable improvement of the road.—A sample of fire bricks, made of this clay, may be seen at the Colliery.

The Machinery, Cordage, Stock of Timber, Farming Stock, Husbandry, Implements & Utensils, also a new built Galliot, burthen about 120 tons, well found, and well adapted for the coasting trade, may be purchased by any person or persons undertaking the Colliery, at a fair appraisement, to be made in the usual way.

For further particulars and treaty, application may be made to Mr. Ashhurst, of Puddington, near Chester.

Figure 2.1: The letting advertisement for Ness Colliery, 1812. Source: *Chester Courant*, 1 September–27 October 1812.

Talacre and Mostyn, owned much of Flintshire and had substantial indirect coal mining interests through the grant of numerous leases to work their land.[118]

The timing of Charles's and Thomas's decision to take on the colliery business in 1813 seems to have been very unfortunate. Coal prices had soared and were probably at their highest in that year and the next.[119] If the brothers' assumption was that such prices were to continue they were to be disappointed. Nationally, coal prices collapsed at the end of the Napoleonic Wars in 1815 and there was widespread economic depression.[120] From the limited data available it seems that the national trend in prices was mirrored at Ness.[121] The annual value of sales at the colliery drifted downward and then tumbled to a nadir in 1822-3 (Appendix IIa). At this time Neston coal was selling at the same price it had been in 1806;[122] the heady peak of ten years earlier was just a memory. The problem of falling prices was compounded by rising haulage costs as the colliery spent more and more time transferring coal won from under the Dee

Estuary to the shafts where it could be raised. Sir Thomas Stanley was later to complain that the works had made cumulative losses of £800 in the period 1813–22.[123] To add to these woes, the rapid decline in sea access, mentioned above, meant that as the 'teen years moved into the 1820s there was little opportunity for coal exports. Instead there would have been increasing reliance on the local market, but this would have been in a sorry state. Income from the sea trade was dying in Parkgate, and the rest of the local economy was based on agriculture which would have suffered from the widespread and deep collapse in grain prices.[124] As happened elsewhere, local landowners no doubt struggled to cover the costs of production, labourers were laid off and tenants defaulted on their rents or abandoned their leases;[125] there would have been little spare money available to pay for coal.

Ness Colliery's lease to mine on Thomas Cottingham senior's land in Little Neston, which had expired in 1811, was renewed for five years in 1814, soon after the Stanley brothers took over ownership.[126] Little mining had gone on there for a decade or more but Ness Colliery wanted access to the Six-Foot seam to try to find its hoped-for continuation across the township boundary into Ness.[127] Also, one of the very useful underground canals ran through the edge of Little Neston before passing back into Ness.[128] The prospect of the lease expiring in 1819 was the catalyst for several actions. In 1818 the Stanleys engaged a viewer from the North East, John Henderson, to survey the colliery (a 'viewer' was a surveyor and engineer specialising in colliery design and development); he counselled against renewing the lease.

As we will see in the next chapter, Henderson would be blamed for many of the colliery's troubles over the next few years. Also, Nicholas Wood, who was to become a renowned mining and civil engineer, was asked to come from Killingworth Colliery, near Newcastle, to make recommendations as to how the how the Six-Foot seam might be found in Ness and how the colliery should subsequently be worked.[129] The seam had been accessed only from Little Neston in the immediately preceding years but there is no evidence that it ever went on to be worked at Ness. Surprisingly, despite the colliery's problems, the owners took action to install a new winding engine, making use of the services of the Cabry family, friends of the renowned engineer George Stephenson.[130]

In 1819 the Stanleys negotiated a one-year extension to their agreement to allow use of a pit in Little Neston but, after that period, continued to venture into Cottingham's manor without permission.[131] They were found out, thanks to Henderson, leading to Cottingham successfully suing Sir Thomas Stanley for trespass in 1821. The subsequent inability to access the coal and canal in Little Neston would have been another factor in the fall in sales at Ness in 1822 and 1823. By this time the colliery was probably selling little more than 100 tons (109 tonnes) of coal each week, the lowest figure so far that century and, probably, since inception.[132] It was claimed that 'Most of the Colliers were aged men, and Sir Thomas carried on the works for their support.'[133] Despite this alleged philanthropy, Stanley was an irascible man and his anger at the poor prospects for his mine coupled with his neighbour's victory in the trespass case prompted him to take extraordinary action to sabotage Cottingham's newly opened colliery. As a result, Cottingham again took the baronet to court, this time claiming £10,000. This shocking episode is covered in more detail in the next chapter.

Despair ... and Recovery

Despite Stanley's complaint about losses in the decade to 1822, the mine was generally yielding worthwhile profits after the court cases (Table 2.3, overleaf). They represent, perhaps, a few tens of thousands of pounds annually in today's money but, in at least one year, they fell to nothing. There was renewed activity and at least one new borehole was dug, in 1825–6, although this found only a poor-quality seam.[134] Possible impetus for the exploration may have come from the potential construction of a ship canal from the Dee Estuary to Manchester passing through the colliery site. This could have given access to markets in both industrialised Manchester and around the Irish Sea but, in the end, the canal scheme was abandoned.[135] Output did, however, pick up as the decade progressed but it was still only one-third to a half of what it had been in the 1770s.[136]

Accounts from the 1820s show that the method of calculating the colliery's profitability was straightforward at this time, being simply the value of sales minus the total of expenses. The largest expense was workmen's wages which, in the mid-1820s, represented about two-thirds of the value of sales.[137] Other expenses included the salary of the manager-cum-accountant, royalty payments and operational costs. The latter routinely included timber for underground propping, oil and grease for engines and other machinery, candles, horse feed, ropes, and hazel rods for weaving baskets to hold the coal. Other less common expenses included surveying charges, colliers' welfare payments, iron for wheels and boring rods, and flannel to be used in the repair and maintenance of engine parts.[138]

Profits would have been enhanced by sales of products other than coal – bricks, lime, slate and so on. However, the surviving nineteenth-century accounts make no specific reference to these sales. They are likely to have been a valuable additional profit stream but their significance cannot be accurately assessed.

An extensive set of correspondence and other papers survives from the period 1826–31 and reveals much about the state of the colliery over the period, including the multiplicity of problems it faced.[139] Haulage costs remained a key, and growing, issue. Most of the colliery's output had to be transported a long distance from the coalface to the shaft – over a mile (1.6 km) for the Seven-Foot seam in Pit No. 1, and 600 yards (549 metres) for the Two-Foot seam (the third seam being worked, the Five-Foot, was

Table 2.3: Known sales volumes and profits for Ness Colliery, 1823–30. Less comprehensive data is available for other years from 1801 – see Appendix IIa. Figures marked * are imputed sales – see note to the Appendix. Figures for estimated profits were anticipated by manager James Gregory. For simplicity, conversion to tonnes has been excluded.
Sources: NEIMME/Wat/3/71/4, 11, 13, 15, 16, 17, 19, 21.

Time Period	Tons Sold	Value of Sales (£)	Full-Year Profit (£)	Profit as Percentage of Sales
Oct. 1823–Sept. 1824	7,608	2,866	350	12.2
Oct. 1824–Sept. 1825	9,634	3,924	613	15.6
Oct. 1825–Sept. 1826	7,690	3,439	403	11.7
1827: Jan.–May and Oct.–Dec. (34 weeks)	4,387 (12 months pro rata: 6,709)	3,150 (12 months)*	Not known	–
1828: Jan.–May and Sept.–Nov. (32 weeks)	3,730 (12 months pro rata: 6,061)	2,925 (12 months)*	'No profit'	0.0
Oct. 1828–Sept. 1829	9,300	3,420*	Est. 300	8.8
Oct. 1829–June 1830 (34 weeks)	6,857 (12 months pro rata: 10,487)	3,645 (12 months)*	Est. 400	11.0

relatively close to the shaft).[140] This transportation was time-consuming and incurred high underground haulage costs whether horses or manpower were used. The Stanleys engaged another noted colliery viewer, John Watson, to look at options to increase efficiency and reduce costs.[141] The Seven-Foot seam produced coal of relatively low value and was hardly profitable but it delivered about half of the colliery's total output. Consideration was given to closing this part of the works but it would have meant transferring some overhead costs, such as the colliery accountant's salary and other surface costs to the other seams, making them less profitable.[142] Larger collieries, such as at Mostyn across the Dee which had access to more and thicker seams, were in a better position to spread such costs across all their output, gaining economies of scale.[143] Sadly for the owners of Ness Colliery, they were not able simply to pass on the costs to customers as it was in competition both with the neighbouring Little Neston Colliery and also with the Flintshire mines. Thus, in 1828 – a year in which the colliery made no profit – James Gregory, the colliery's accountant and manager, wrote,

> We have been under the necessity of lowering the price of coals a 2nd time. For several weeks our sales have been very bad and as the spring advanced we saw no hope of their recovery without following the example of our welsh neighbours, who reduced their

prices a penny a cwt. and were sending coals to be sold at Gayton Lane end [a Wirral location almost 3 miles (4.8 km) from Ness colliery]. The first reduction I made was ... a halfpenny a cwt., which produced a trifling reaction in our favor, but was soon lost by Mr. Cottingham reducing a penny.[144]

There was a wider reason for keeping the highest possible levels of production and not closing the unprofitable seam: it benefited Sir Thomas Stanley's estates scattered across the Wirral. Thus, John Watson talked of Stanley having 'an ultimate interest in prolonging the duration of the colliery, for the purpose of supplying his tenantry on the estates with coals at a moderate and convenient rate, not only for household purposes, but for burning lime for agricultural purposes.'[145] In other words a ready supply of coal meant happy, continuing rent-payers who would find it easy to improve the soil using lime, helping to keep both rents and land values high.

As coal prices fell, wages at the colliery had to be cut too in a downward spiral which saw discontent spread amongst the workers. Some of them left, with too few remaining to raise all the available coal.[146] The paternalism which Stanley claimed he had shown towards his 'aged men' was giving way to the stark realities of business and the British economy.[147] This was a period of increasing militancy amongst colliers nationally, discussed in Chapter 6, and there was at least one strike at Ness. Sometimes the manager, James Gregory, struggled to bite his tongue at the Stanley brothers' orders: 'I have said all I could with propriety on the impolicy of reducing these wages' he wrote in 1827, adding 'It would be madness to reduce the price of coals and put forth advertisements [for reduced price coal] without any means of raising them'.[148]

The Watson correspondence explored many options to resolve the colliery's problems by increasing efficiency, reducing costs and finding new coal. Detailed assessments were made of the role of different methods of underground transport such as 'rail roads' and 'tram ways', and the use of manpower (which included boys) for hauling versus horse power.[149] The underground canal at Ness had fallen out of use by this time, although brief consideration was given to reopening it.[150] Other options included sinking new linking shafts ('staples') between tunnels and repositioning equipment such as horse gins (discussed in Chapter 5). It was also suggested that Sir Thomas Stanley could reduce the royalty he took, but there is no further reference to this idea![151]

Potential salvation for Ness Colliery lay in finding the continuation of the Five-Foot seam, which was first reported to disappear at a geological fault about 96 yards (88 metres) south-west from the shaft.[152] This seam yielded the best quality and therefore highest value coal; it was also a relatively short distance from the coal face to the shaft and thus cheap to transport. The ability to exploit the seam continuously would have delivered a handsome reward to the colliery but the quest to follow it was constantly frustrated by the presence of geological faults. This quest featured in the first letter in the Watson correspondence in 1826 and still featured in the last, in 1831.

In the intervening years Watson suggested a variety of ways to seek the seam which kept disappearing; these included tunnelling forward, and boring upwards and downwards. This work was expensive with seven men working a 'stone drift' (i.e. cutting through rock, not coal) at one point.[153] The seam did yield *some* useful coal and the correspondence is characterised by moments of great optimism when a breakthrough was anticipated. But, in the end, James Gregory talked of beginning to 'dispair' [*sic*] at finding coal beyond the 'great fault' at the end of the workings.[154]

The problems with costs and supply were compounded by limited opportunities for sales. Alterations to the course of the River Dee since the start of the century had led to rapidly decreasing access for vessels and a corresponding loss of most of the colliery's vital ship-borne trade. The low volumes of coal output meant, somewhat ironically, that the colliery had no difficulty in selling all it produced (at the market price), with little if any stock held on site.[155] Watson wrote that 'All hands [were] employed' but, nevertheless 'very limited sales' could be made, and these were largely restricted to the local, landsale trade.[156]

Despite all its problems the colliery survived for over two more decades. Cost efficiencies were identified and, very importantly, a new way of working introduced which extracted a greater proportion of the available coal. Known as the 'Lancashire System', this major development is discussed in Chapter 4. There was also much focus on the thin Two-Foot seam which was extended from 650 yards (594 metres) in 1830 to almost 2,000 (1,828 metres) by 1839.[157] In addition to all this, there was much disruption at neighbouring Little Neston Colliery while Cottingham fought legal battles and dealt with operational problems. This would have worked in Ness Colliery's favour, with the reduction and eventual elimination of immediate local competition. These factors help account for the increase in sales at Ness from the late 1820s although there is no indication they ever regained the levels of the operation's first few decades. Nor was Ness able to match the volume of production at the collieries across the Dee at Mostyn and Flint which were said, in 1833, to be producing respectively 300 tons (327 tonnes) daily and 1,500 tons (1,634 tonnes) weekly – at least five times Ness's output.[158] Thus, Ness did not get its share of the voracious growth in British demand for coal which rose more than three-fold between 1816 and 1855.[159] Nevertheless the collieries of west Cheshire were said by a Poor Law commissioner in 1837 to be 'in full employ and thriving'.[160]

Sir Thomas Stanley continued to hold his share of the colliery, and benefited from royalties generated by it, but for how long he retained any operational interest is unclear. He and his brother Charles were both said to be 'anxious' about the future of Pit No. 1 in 1828, and they were joint addressees of a long letter from John Watson, the viewer, about colliery operations the following year.[161] But Sir Thomas Stanley was devoting a considerable amount of time to field sports to which he was said to be 'addicted', practising 'hunting and shooting every day' (Figure 2.2).[162] He bred and raced horses – three were named *Dennah, Hooton* and *Wirral* – as well as sponsoring races.[163] In June 1830 John Watson commented that it was the Liverpool Races which would bring Sir Thomas back from a six-week visit to 'the North'.[164] Another man with passionate racing interests was Sir Edward Mostyn,

Figure 2.2: 'Regent, a Favourite Horse of Sir Thomas Stanley of Hooton, Cheshire' (1814) by Charles Towne. Towne was a celebrated painter of animals, and a founder of the Liverpool Academy. The horse was probably used for hunting. Reproduced with permission from the National Museums, Liverpool.

Charles's father-in-law, and it seems likely that Mostyn and Sir Thomas Stanley enjoyed the sport together. Indeed, Stanley was very well connected and used his pastimes as a way of maintaining his social network. For example, around 1831, he took his hounds to Hawarden for a hunting party attended by, amongst others, future prime minister William Gladstone, Sir Stephen Glynne (who had extensive local coal mining interests), Robert Grosvenor who was Lord Lieutenant of Flintshire and shared Stanley's love of racing, and Sir Philip Egerton, politician and renowned palaeontologist.[165]

As well as owning Ness Colliery, the Stanley family had long-standing interests in industries in North Wales and elsewhere which were sources of income through royalties. For example, the Puddington estate held land at Pentrobin in the parish of Hawarden, which had been leased by the owner of nearby Sandycroft Colliery, Sir John Glynne, in 1770.[166] From 1801 the leading Flintshire industrialists, William Rigby and William Hancock, took over Little Mountain Colliery at Pentrobin and began to pay royalties to Sir Thomas Stanley's estate seven years later.[167] In some years, royalties from this source, paid at one-eighth of the sales value, exceeded those payable to Stanley by Ness Colliery.[168] Sir Thomas Stanley's difficult attitude again reveals itself in the royalty accounts, with his insistence in 1814 that several years' retrospective royalties be paid to him in respect of coals raised at Pentrobin which had been used to power the colliery engines rather than being sold for profit.[169] There was, though, sometimes some reciprocity for the Flintshire men. Their extensive industrial interests included iron founding as well as brick and tile making, and their goods were sometimes bought for the Stanley estates. Items included cast iron window frames and fittings for the new Denna House built for Charles Stanley.[170]

The royalty incident above is just one of numerous episodes in Stanley's life which paint him as being the most awkward – even unpleasant – of men. Yet he clearly had some charms. At one hunt, in the late 1830s, he was described as follows:

> Of the middle size, and filled out to the proper bulk which so much becomes one who has passed the middle period of life. ... his age about 50, his countenance mild and benevolent, and his whole bearing that of a gentleman.[171]

The Final Years

Sir Thomas Massey Stanley died in August 1841, leaving the colliery, its equipment and farm in the hands of his brother Charles for as long as he lived.[172] The will provided for Rowland Errington, Sir Thomas Stanley's second son, to inherit the manors of Puddington, Ness and Ledsham and to receive the colliery after Charles's death.[173] In the meantime Errington was to benefit from all royalties on the coal raised at Ness. He was soon unhappy about how his income source and future inheritance was being managed. The year after Sir Thomas's death he indicated that he believed the colliery was 'ill conducted' by his uncle Charles, complaining that the 'Coal owners in North Wales are able to undersell the produce of [Ness] colliery' – although they, of course, benefited from thicker more accessible seams.[174] Sir Thomas Stanley's will had allowed for up to £1,500 to be provided for new investment in the colliery, such as sinking pits or erecting engines. Given this opportunity, Errington's land agent, Thomas Donkin, and the renowned colliery viewer John Buddle were invited to survey the works.[175] Buddle made new borings, but his report has not survived.[176]

Details of the colliery's output are not available after 1838 but it was said to be employing 120 men in 1851;[177] one contemporary source described the collieries as 'extensive'.[178] Estimated output per man-year in the North Wales coalfields that year was 271 tons (295 tonnes) which, if it could have been replicated at Ness, would have meant about 35,000 tons (38,115 tonnes) in total.[179] But Ness had several disadvantages, in particular its geology and long-distance haulage, and there is no indication that productivity matched that of North Wales. Profits at Ness were probably also very low even though immediate competition disappeared when the neighbouring Little Neston Colliery closed in the 1840s. The valuations ascribed to the mine in the church rate assessments – indicative of the mine's fortunes – suggest a pattern of decline from about 1848 with very low valuations from 1851–2.[180]

The colliery was offered to let in 1852 as 'the present company ... wish to retire' apparently indicating sixty-five-year-old Charles Stanley's desire to step down.[181] As well as the business said to be 'abounding with excellent coal and fire brick clay', evidenced by the borings undertaken by John Buddle and others, the offer included 'a good shipping pier', and 'extensive lime and brick works'. The colliery's advisers were said to have described it as a 'promising plant'. However, no one was convinced to buy the business and within a couple of years it had passed to Charles's nephew Rowland Errington.[182] In 1854, a final, unsuccessful, attempt was made to find the Five-Foot seam which, again, seems to have been lost.[183] Coal was still being sold the following year.[184] Nevertheless, the decision was taken to put all the colliery's equipment up for sale by auction in July, bringing an end to operations (Figure 2.3).[185] At least £888 was raised.[186]

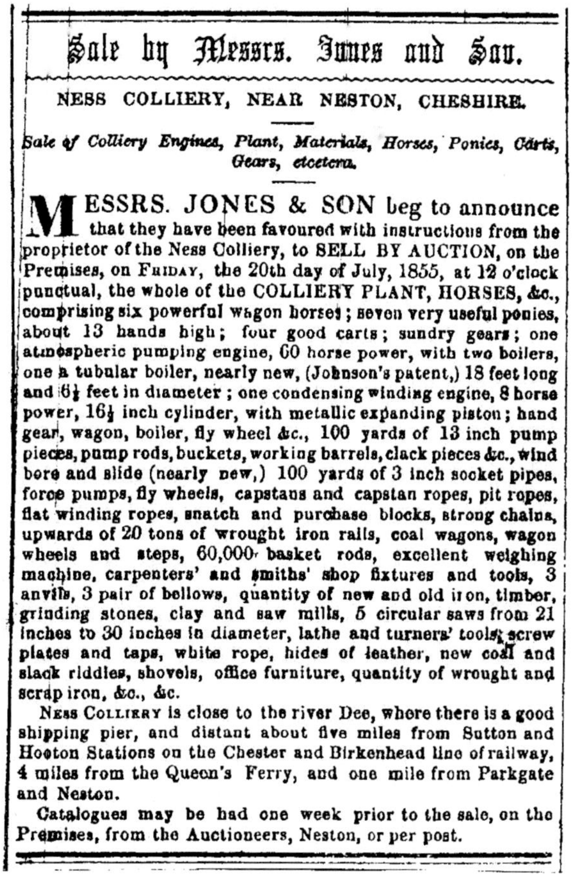
Sale by Messrs. Jones and Son.

NESS COLLIERY, NEAR NESTON, CHESHIRE.

Sale of Colliery Engines, Plant, Materials, Horses, Ponies, Carts, Gears, etcetera.

MESSRS. JONES & SON beg to announce that they have been favoured with instructions from the proprietor of the Ness Colliery, to SELL BY AUCTION, on the Premises, on FRIDAY, the 20th day of July, 1855, at 12 o'clock punctual, the whole of the COLLIERY PLANT, HORSES, &c., comprising six powerful wagon horses; seven very useful ponies, about 13 hands high; four good carts; sundry gears; one atmospheric pumping engine, 60 horse power, with two boilers, one a tubular boiler, nearly new, (Johnson's patent,) 18 feet long and 6½ feet in diameter; one condensing winding engine, 8 horse power, 16½ inch cylinder, with metallic expanding piston; hand gear, wagon, boiler, fly wheel &c., 100 yards of 13 inch pump pieces, pump rods, buckets, working barrels, clack pieces &c., wind bore and slide (nearly new,) 100 yards of 3 inch socket pipes, force pumps, fly wheels, capstans and capstan ropes, pit ropes, flat winding ropes, snatch and purchase blocks, strong chains, upwards of 20 tons of wrought iron rails, coal wagons, wagon wheels and steps, 60,000 basket rods, excellent weighing machine, carpenters' and smiths' shop fixtures and tools, 3 anvils, 3 pair of bellows, quantity of new and old iron, timber, grinding stones, clay and saw mills, 5 circular saws from 21 inches to 30 inches in diameter, lathe and turners' tools, screw plates and taps, white rope, hides of leather, new coal and slack riddles, shovels, office furniture, quantity of wrought and scrap iron, &c., &c.

NESS COLLIERY is close to the river Dee, where there is a good shipping pier, and distant about five miles from Sutton and Hooton Stations on the Chester and Birkenhead line of railway, 4 miles from the Queen's Ferry, and one mile from Parkgate and Neston.

Catalogues may be had one week prior to the sale, on the Premises, from the Auctioneers, Neston, or per post.

Figure 2.3: Advertisement in 1855, offering Ness Colliery's equipment for sale. Source: *Chester Chronicle*, 23 June 1855.

Mining engineer Thomas Leacroft Cottingham, the son of the final owner of Little Neston Colliery, gave parliamentary evidence in 1869 in which he was asked about Ness Colliery. He said that 'Ness Colliery was given up as it was ... presumed to be exhausted, as far about the two-feet [seam], the seven feet, and the five feet.'[187]

This exhaustion of the seams had been confirmed by a surveyor eight years after the mine closed although, if Errington had been so-minded, he might have turned his attention to Little Neston where there was still much unwrought coal;[188] he could have sought a lease to work it. However, the silting of the estuary was also a critical factor, hindering the ability to shift coal by water and almost wholly limiting markets to those most immediately accessible by land. Thus, an 1864 trade directory stated about the once 'extensive collieries' at Ness that 'a considerable quantity of coal' used to be raised there 'but in consequence of the sandbanks having obstructed the passage to the Dee, they have fallen into disuse'.[189] As it was, within a few years of abandonment, the workings at Ness became completely flooded.[190]

*

It was ninety-eight years from when the first boreholes were dug at Ness until the colliery's closure – a near-century which saw remarkable change. The works would have been launched with a sense of optimism and entrepreneurship which was characteristic of the age and which brought a union of men who contributed the land ownership, capital and knowledge that the new business required. It swiftly rose to being both successful and regionally significant. However, the colliery was to be buffeted by forces outside its control – economic factors such as the fluctuation in the national economy and coal prices; market factors as regional competitors sought to exploit the growing opportunities that coal presented and actions were taken which almost wholly deprived the colliery of access to the Dee; and natural forces such as the constant battle with the uncertainties of local geology. Innovation was central to setting the business up and was equally important in coping with the vicissitudes it faced. The use of steam engines, rail roads and underground canals, together with the engagement of leading mine consultants who brought knowledge of best practice such as how the Lancashire System of working could be used, all reflected evolving ideas in the period and were essential to the business's survival. Although Ness Colliery necessarily experienced much change there was also considerable continuity, with ownership by a single family to a greater or lesser extent throughout its life. Thus, there is no sign that the business was subject to the 'improvidence' that, for example, saw wasteful practices in North Wales as mine-owners came and went seeking 'get rich quick' schemes.[191] This did not mean that Ness was exemplary though, and, in particular, the bullying by Sir Thomas Stanley – an English aristocrat resorting to naked sabotage – is a remarkable feature of the colliery's story. Ness Colliery's main successes came early but its survival for almost a century is testament to the willingness of its management to adapt and innovate in whatever way they thought necessary.

CHAPTER 3

LITTLE NESTON COLLIERY
AND THE 'COLLIERY' AT PARKGATE

Until about 1820 the Cottingham family, who were joint lords of the manor of Little Neston and owned scattered lands there, were passive participants in the coal business. A series of leases granted to Ness Colliery since 1759 meant that it was the Stanley family and their co-investors who worked the coal under the Cottinghams' land. But, after sixty-one years, things were to change with the establishment of a new business – a rival to the Stanleys' one – which was to experience little but turbulence over its few decades of life.

The Stanleys' third lease to mine on Thomas Cottingham senior's land expired in 1819. In anticipation of this and in order to pay off very substantial debts, Cottingham advertised his 'coal mines' for sale or lease in 1817.[1] The offer comprised 30 acres (12.1 hectares) of enclosed land as well as the coal situated under the adjoining 'waste' (uncultivated land such as the shore). There was a promise of 'very great profit' for suitable 'Adventurers' due to 'the high price of coals here, the cheapness of labour and the lands lying [next] to the river' but there was little interest and no takers.[2] Instead, Cottingham allowed the Stanleys' business to continue to use the main pit on his land, No. 21, for one more year in exchange for a small rent.[3] The agreement did not specify that use could be made of the underground canal on Cottingham's land – a point which would soon become important.

Although the exact timing is uncertain, it seems that it was when the Stanleys finally abandoned their mining interest in Little Neston in 1820 that the ageing Cottingham decided to establish his own business, Little Neston Colliery.[4] The new business would mine the area of his township previously worked by Ness Colliery and be run by the eldest of his seven sons, also named Thomas.[5] Thomas senior presumably hoped to build a valuable asset to eventually sell and pay off his debts. The first surviving record of coal being raised is in March 1821.[6] However, the Cottinghams quickly encountered problems as the establishment of the business gave rise to a series of extraordinary and malevolent actions by Sir Thomas Stanley, acting on behalf of his colliery.

The Court Cases

Trouble was already brewing during the one-year extension to Ness Colliery's access to the pit in Little Neston. Legal threats were being made by both Thomas Cottingham senior and the Stanleys against each other in February 1820, demanding monies owed.[7] Cottingham's claim probably related to his concern that Ness Colliery had been using one of the two of the underground canals which had been built in 1790 to convey coal

Figure 3.1: Poster offering a reward for information on malicious damage to Little Neston Colliery's winding engine, May 1821. Source: TNA, J 90/82. Reproduced with permission.

from distant working faces even though this had not been in the one-year extension agreement.[8] Although one of the canals was unequivocally in Ness township, Cottingham claimed at least part of the other was within his township so Ness Colliery was therefore trespassing.

The matter had been brought to Cottingham's attention the previous summer via a viewer, John Henderson, employed by Ness Colliery from July 1818.[9] Spurning loyalty to those who had employed him, Henderson supplied a map of the Ness works to Cottingham's attorney, Thomas Dicas, when he requested one; this showed the location of the canal. The opinion of John Buddle, the leading colliery viewer from the North East, was sought and he stated that the trespass looked to be 'serious' (nevertheless, as we have seen, he was also to give advice at Ness a couple of decades later).[10] The Stanleys, however, paid no attention to Cottingham's claim so, in September 1821, the matter came to court. It may be no coincidence that, four months earlier, Little Neston Colliery's winding engine was deliberately damaged one night (Figure 3.1). This would have required a bold and purposeful perpetrator, willing to risk seven years' transportation to achieve his goal. There is, however, no record of the culprit being found.

At the court hearing at Chester Assizes concerning the canal, Cottingham brought evidence to show that the waterway was within his township, that the Ness works was still using it even though their lease had expired, and that Stanley knew that they were trespassing.[11] There was much argument over where the township boundary was, but Henderson confirmed he had warned Sir Thomas Stanley and his associates that the canal was on Cottingham's property by up to 96 yards (91 metres), and was sacked for informing Cottingham about this.[12] The case was quickly found in favour of Cottingham who was awarded £100 damages for trespass. Stanley's legal fees and other expenses added very substantially to the cost of the affair to him.[13]

Henderson clearly had a deep dislike for his former employer and it is worth reproducing the words he wrote immediately after the case to John Buddle:

> I was subpoenaed to attend Chester assizes on the 10th, in the cause Cottingham against Sir Thomas Stanley. The Trial commenced on the 13th and lasted 2 ½ days, being a cause of great importance. Cottingham won in a Canter notwithstanding a more iniquitous defence was never attempted to be set up by Sir Thos and his Agents, which has reduced Sir Thos's Character still lower if possible than it was before. My friend [Robert] Johnson was there attempting with others to get Sir Thos out of the scrape – but I shall give you a full account at some future opportunity. Sir Thos's Colliery being knocked up [finished], I was detained giving directions for the Cottinghams, in working some of their own Coal to supply the immediate wants of the neighbourhood as a landsale which they are now doing.[14]

As well as enraging Stanley by warning Cottingham about his trespass, Henderson was blamed for advising the baronet not to renew the lease to mine on Cottingham's land, leaving him access to allegedly inadequate coal supplies and creating the problem with the canal.[15] Henderson was a respected colliery viewer but seems to have subsequently been blacklisted by others in his profession for whistle-blowing on his employer.[16]

Besides Sir Thomas Stanley's conduct in this affair there is plenty of other evidence for his unpleasant character; he was not a man to be beaten. A racing incident from a few years' earlier gives a glimpse into his win-at-any-cost character. In 1815 Sir Thomas took a man to court for failing to honour a bet. Each man had wagered that he had the fastest horse and they bet 100 guineas, with the winner to be decided at Chester races. The defendant's horse died before the race but Stanley still pursued the winnings, taking the issue to court, as his horse had not been beaten! His claim was upheld.[17]

It is unsurprising therefore that Stanley did not take the trespass case lying down. This led to another court case, in 1822. This was far more serious than the earlier one and led to the extraordinary spectacle of the English baronet standing trial in Cheshire Assizes for sabotaging a rival coal mine. Cottingham senior was again suing Stanley for trespass as he had continued to use the canal, but also for wilful damage to his mine. His total claim was for £10,000, representing lost sales and a punitive element reflecting Stanley's alleged malicious intent.[18] Stanley pleaded not guilty.

The incident to which this case related started just two days after the end of the 1821 case – the timing can have been no coincidence. Stanley's men were seen to start bringing up all their mining equipment, boats and horses through No. 6 Pit; they took other materials down into the mine. The following week Joseph Cabry and his sons erected tall boards on the surface, preventing Cottingham from seeing what was going on. Stanley's men also hid their faces; one was even masked. Sir Thomas Stanley himself was seen to be present on at least two occasions around this time. Over the course of four nights the noise of pickaxes, the boring of holes for gunpowder and explosions were heard underground. When Cottingham went to investigate, he found that the tunnel, or 'road', leading from Pit No. 21 on his land to the underground canal had been wrecked; his works were 'a heap of ruins' and 'he could not get any coal now'. Stanley's men were seen to celebrate, cheering and enjoying 'a barrel of ale carried from the public house' – presumably the nearby Welch Harp [sic] as it was then known.

The loss of the road was devastating to Cottingham's newly established business. It was used for ventilation and also gave access to '200 yards of coal, seven feet high perpendicular on both sides of the road'. It was stated that perhaps 5,000 to 8,000 tons (5,445 to 8,712 tonnes) of coal could have been obtained in a year, delivering about 5s. (25p) profit per ton – maybe £2,000 profit per year.

Richard Blundell, who had worked on the surface at Ness but had moved to the rival colliery by the time of the court case, gave evidence that the colliers had been instructed by Robert Johnson, a leading viewer and Sir Thomas's adviser, to progress as far down Cottingham's tunnel as they could and to 'break it down'. If Cottingham's men tried to stop them they had to 'break their heads or otherwise they might expect no more jobs from him'. Threats of violence do not seem to have been unusual at Ness; in one instance a surveyor appointed by Thomas Cottingham was threatened with murder if he ventured beyond an underground doorway guarded by two of Stanley's men.[19]

John Henderson was also called to appear. He turned up against his wishes, saying he had been 'dragged' there. Having testified against Stanley in the first trial he was 'much abused' by the defence team, being ridiculed for his 'shuffling and quibbling' manner, and was blamed for being 'the sole author of these disputes'.[20]

Various legal defences to the trespass were put up by Stanley's lawyers including questioning whether Cottingham had any right to the coal in the estuary as opposed to the Crown or Lord Shrewsbury. Robert Johnson did not deny that Stanley's men had destroyed the tunnel. However, he justified the damage done as being part of a scheme to manage the ventilation of the more distant parts of Ness Colliery's underground work; without the action 'men would be suffocated and have no air' (a point which Henderson then contradicted). Destroying the roadway was also intended to 'prevent Cottingham's men destroying the canal'. As well as justifying the actions, Stanley's counsel sought to gain sympathy from the jury saying that the colliery was making losses and that Stanley only kept it going for the sake of the 'aged labourers' to enable them 'to get their bread'.

Cottingham's lawyer also played for sympathy. He made much of the social differences between Stanley and Cottingham: the 'powerful', 'opulent and wealthy Baronet' versus a man of 'comparatively limited income' who was significantly affected by the country's low agricultural prices; he talked of an 'act of high-handed violence to trample down an inferior by wealth' and of Cottingham's simple wish: 'I ask, gentlemen, only for my rights'.

The foreman of underground operations at Cottingham's colliery, Thomas Roberts, claimed that prior to the sabotage the business 'Had plenty of customers, as many as they could serve and sometimes more, and got from 10 to 12 tons a day'.[21] This did not seem to be reflected in the business's accounts, though, which showed sales for almost ten months of 1821 – over six months of it before the sabotage – of just £250; this represents no more than about 667 tons (726 tonnes).[22] Perhaps Cottingham had been exaggerating, although the report of a surveyor in 1823 complained that Little Neston Colliery's book-keeping was 'so very imperfect' that the writer could not understand aspects of its accounts;[23] it seems from this comment and later actions that the Cottinghams were not natural business people.

The judge discussed with the jury the motives for the Stanley mine's action. He said they would have to have clear evidence if they believed Stanley acted out of spite or ill will – in which case the damages would be higher than if no such motive was involved. The judge expressed his own, very partial, view: there was no malevolence involved and Stanley, knowing nothing about mining, merely acted on his agent's suggestions which were made with the best of intentions. The jury then retired and returned within half an hour to deliver a verdict of just £2,000 for the plaintiff adding, no doubt to the judge's approval, that no motive of malice could be attributed to Stanley. Again, legal costs added substantially to the bill.[24] Cottingham was ecstatic, treating the witnesses to dinner and tying flying ribbons to the coaches that carried them.[25]

Despite the relative leniency of the 1822 verdict, an appeal was made by Sir Thomas Stanley the following year, but it was not upheld.[26] There had been a measure of recovery at Little Neston Colliery evidenced by sales of £1,393 in 1822, but Stanley was determined not to be outdone. Once again he took overtly malevolent action: stopping operation of the engine which pumped water from Ness Colliery. This can have done his mine no good but it is clear from various sources that he was doing so to allow the water level to rise so that it eventually flowed down into Cottingham's works to ruin them. Cottingham was forced to act quickly: he knew that Stanley was deliberately 'drowning us out'.[27] The surveyor, writing in 1823 about Little Neston Colliery, commented that:

> [Sir Thomas Stanley], having ceased to work his mine engine, it is expected the water will rise up and injure the works; Messrs Cottingham and Co. are therefore using their utmost exertions to raise all the coal they can before that time arrives.[28]

Stanley's motive was never in doubt. A later report on Ness stated:

> The water has been allowed to rise within 36 yards of the surface for the purpose of affecting the colliery adjoining which lies to the dip of this, wrought by [Cottingham].[29]

And, from a later memorandum, it is clear Ness Colliery had even sacrificed access to a coal seam to flood the neighbouring works: [30]

> [We have] opened out the original Road to work the 7 foot Coal, which was given up formerly in consequence of the water being allowed to rise to such a height as would effect Cottingham & Co.'s works.

In the same year as the flooding, vandalism was again occurring locally to Cottingham property. Thomas junior's brother, John, was having a new home built locally (despite having large debts) and found one day that timber had been stolen and the windows smashed.[31] Again, there is no available evidence of a link to the Stanleys. However, one other episode does illustrate the vindictiveness of Sir Thomas Stanley. A man, Samuel Kendrick, and his wife had occupied a house on Stanley's estate based on an informal rental agreement. When Stanley heard that Kendrick had gone to work at Little Neston Colliery, the baronet ordered his men to remove the roof, windows and door from the property. Stanley was reported as 'saying "Samuel Kendrick will be warm and comfortable this [February] weather" and he grinned when he said this'.[32]

Decades of Struggle

The acts of sabotage and court cases seem to have been enough for the elderly Thomas Cottingham who, in 1823, gave ownership of the business to his son Thomas who had been running the operation, granting him a thirty-one year lease.[33] The son had been severely injured as a lieutenant in the 52nd Regiment of Foot at the Battle of Waterloo in 1815. He was invalided out of the army with a foot injury, thereafter receiving 'half pay'.[34] He worked with his cousin, Thomas Dicas, who had been Cottingham senior's attorney in the two court cases.[35]

Cottingham and Dicas worked frantically to mine the Six-Foot and Five-Foot seams of coal until the flooding overtook them. Soon, though, the seams had to be abandoned. Other pits were sunk, only one of which was successful and served the colliery for the remainder of its life.[36]

Meanwhile, Cottingham sought expansion opportunities. He was, surprisingly, keen to acquire the lease to Ness Colliery, which was at a low ebb, but the plan came to nothing.[37] He also sought a lease to exploit the minerals under the land of the Earl of Shrewsbury, joint manor-holder of Little Neston who owned several fields adjacent to Cottingham's.[38] A thirty-one-year lease was agreed in 1824; it involved payment of both rent and royalties and allowed the Earl's holdings to be exploited to any depth both on land and also in his 'waste' under the estuary.[39] The Earl insisted that the lease be granted to Thomas Cottingham senior, even though he was not running the business.[40]

The Shrewsbury lease was a significant contributor to what was an extraordinarily acrimonious relationship between two sons of the ageing Thomas Cottingham, John and Thomas. John expected that the lease would be granted to his father and himself, but he was excluded from it.[41] Bitter and emotional correspondence followed from John, who was highly indebted – so much so that Thomas eventually had his brother thrown into jail for money he owed to him.[42] Things did not get any better for John when he was also effectively excluded as a beneficiary in his father's deathbed will executed in 1825, leaving him determined to mount a legal challenge to it.[43] All this must have been a great distraction for Thomas Cottingham junior who cannot have given the business the attention it deserved, probably impacting production. He later claimed in court that Little Neston Colliery had raised just £3,796 worth of coal from the low-value Six-Foot seam in three years from 1824 (although some scepticism was expressed at how low the figure was).[44]

A requirement of the late Thomas Cottingham senior's will had been that the primary beneficiary – Thomas junior – paid off substantial mortgages attached to the estate which his second son, John, had taken on.[45] Thus, in July 1826, an auction was held comprising the interest in the Manor of Little Neston and twenty-eight lots of property. These included fifteen acres (6.1 hectares) of land with 'valuable seams of coal' beneath, and 'New Coal Works'. They were said to be in 'full work' coming with a machine house, a lime kiln and a smithy with dwelling above.[46] Yet again, though, circumstances militated against Cottingham for the timing was unfortunate. Britain experienced a major financial crisis in late 1825 and 1826. Many banks collapsed, bankruptcies reached an all-time high, and confidence in the financial system plummeted.[47] At the same time coal prices were probably the lowest they had been for years.[48] It was not a good time to be seeking new investors in a business, particularly one with a neighbour with a track record of antagonism, and the colliery as well as several other lots went unsold.[49] Most of the lots were re-auctioned in 1827 – the estate's debts were almost £12,000 by then – but Cottingham decided to retain the colliery this time.[50] He hoped that the debts could be 'liquidated by the profit from the colliery'.[51] He continued to run the works in partnership with his cousin, Thomas, who had changed his surname from Dicas to Leacroft.[52]

As well as struggling to find a buyer, the colliery was probably also struggling to find customers. Some sales to the sea- and river-borne trades did take place through the 1820s but access to the rapidly receding waters of the estuary would have become increasingly intermittent via the short quay which the colliery used.[53] The colliery became more and more dependent on land sales – the market that John Henderson was helping them to exploit in 1821 but in which they were always in direct competition with the Ness mine. Some years after the mine closed, one of Thomas Cottingham junior's sons, Thomas Leacroft Cottingham, commented that 'we were dependent entirely upon local sale in those days which was very small'.[54]

The business probably ticked over passably for a year or so, but more calamity was just around the corner for Cottingham who was to become embroiled for years in litigation with the Earl of Shrewsbury. The first of these actions was a little-reported case in 1828 at Chester Assizes, followed by another at the Sheriff's Court the following year.[55] Shrewsbury's argument was straightforward: Cottingham and Leacroft had failed to fulfil their obligations under the mining lease granted in 1824 which included requirements to sink a new shaft on his land and erect an engine. The defendants admitted this failure, acknowledging they were working slowly pending the manufacture of the engine. As part of their defence, they claimed that they had tried to sink two pits on Shrewsbury's land over the years but had to abandon them due to flooding.

The hearings were found in Shrewsbury's favour and he was awarded nominal damages. The cases seem to have spurred Cottingham and Leacroft into recklessness to prove they were complying with Shrewsbury's requirements: they spent up to £1,500 on an engine, engine house and shafts only to find sandstone rather than coal in the location they had chosen.[56] This expenditure was very substantial for a small concern like Little Neston Colliery and it is astonishing that they did not check first that there was coal by sinking a borehole.

The legal case was back in Chester Assizes in 1830. One of Cottingham's lame defences in the 1828 case had been that the whole of the manor of Little Neston belonged to him, with Lord Shrewsbury having no part of it and thus having no claim to royalties.[57] Now Cottingham's argument shifted, arguing that the coal was being won from *his* portion of the shared waste (the shore and estuary) and if anyone else was entitled it was the Crown; this echoed an argument made in the 1821 and 1822 court cases between Cottingham and Stanley. Although there are some suggestions of rapprochement between the Stanleys and Cottinghams a couple of years after their legal fights, there can be little doubt that the Stanleys would have been very happy to see the difficulties and distractions at Cottingham's works which competed with their own.[58]

A letter sent in 1830 by Ness Colliery's viewer, John Watson, said:

> I am given to understand [Cottingham and Leacroft] have been at law with the Earl of Shrewsbury as to the right of some part of the coalmines [where] they have been working the coal, wherein it appears a verdict has been given in favour of [the Earl].[59]

The last phrase was an oversimplification of the complex verdict. With questions raised about manorial rights and who owned the 'waste', the case had moved to the Vice-Chancellor's Court, a division of the Court of Chancery in London, by 1832.[60] Meanwhile a separate highly complex case had begun, involving Thomas Cottingham, Lord Shrewsbury and many others over the Cottingham estate's long-standing debts. There are many subsequent references to these court cases through the 1830s and 1840s.[61] Chancery cases were notorious for their longevity – a theme central to Dickens' contemporary novel *Bleak House*. The legal battles would have involved Cottingham in much time and expense, perhaps taking him away for an extended period to London.[62]

These issues must have led to him paying considerably less attention to his colliery than was desirable.

Despite the distractions, the colliery continued to work two seams from its single pit. In 1829, the access tunnel for the Six-Foot seam had been described as running at least 550 yards (502 metres) and Sir Thomas Stanley's advisers suspected it was within the boundary of his manor.[63] They were quite possibly right although there is no record of anything being done about it.[64] In any event, Cottingham was struggling to sell his coal, stacks of which were 'always' piled high, despite being low-priced.[65] There was a fillip for the mine for a couple of years when its coal became a preferred choice of fuel for the very substantial smelting works of Mona Mine Company in Amlwch, Anglesey.[66] However, river access continued to present problems and Cottingham's coal fell from favour.

Cottingham's business partner, Thomas Leacroft, died in 1836 but the business continued.[67] Fresh borings were said to have been made by Cottingham in 1839 though there is no evidence for their success and they may just have been trials.[68] Eventually, though, some time in the next decade the workings ground to a halt, perhaps in 1845. The last known significant sales by the colliery were three years earlier, to the parish church, and a plan of the workings records their state in 1845 implying this was a significant point in time.[69] By the same year, land belonging to the aged and invalid Cottingham had been seized by creditors and by 1849 his estate was in the hands of the Court of Chancery, with no mention of a colliery in the tithe apportionment that year.[70] When Cottingham's son gave evidence to the 1869 parliamentary committee he was asked what had happened to the colliery. He replied, 'Owing to a chancery suit in which my ancestors were concerned it was sold, and was never revived'.[71]

The only land Cottingham was occupying in 1849 besides his 'house and garden' was an area, rented from the Earl of Shrewsbury, which included the short quay at Little Neston on which a pit had once been sunk.[72] Isaac Jackson, who had been the colliery manager, also rented a plot nearby on which there had been pits.[73] Cottingham was blind by 1851 and it seems that Jackson was being kept on to watch over the former works while they were being prepared for sale.[74] It was presumably he who recorded several 'crownings' – collapse of the material above the mine up to the bed of the estuary – in 1845, 1851 and 1852.[75] However, Jackson had debts by 1848, perhaps a sign that his earnings were now minimal.[76]

The trustee in bankruptcy sought to dispose of Cottingham's estate but, like so much of Cottingham's torrid business history, the process was not straightforward. An auction was held in 1851 to sell 140 acres (57 hectares) of the estate including the coal beds under the land.[77] It was reported that 'the shares in the colliery were knocked down to Mr. J. Laurence Butler of the Moss-Hall Coal Company, for £8,600'.[78] However, Butler failed to complete the sale and so sixty acres (24.3 hectares) were re-auctioned the following year.[79] The final lot comprised the 'Old Colliery banks' which contained a 'Machine-House, limekiln and smithy' (the same buildings as were offered in 1825) and the 'New Colliery Banks' but the lot was withdrawn from sale at the last minute.[80] The auction advertisement had promised great opportunities for 'capitalists' and, to add to the colliery's appeal, mentioned a newly proposed railway from which sidings could be built for a 'trifling outlay'. The withdrawal was to enable this 'projected railway from Chester to Birkenhead via Neston and Parkgate' to be built.[81] However, like predecessor schemes, this railway failed to materialise and the final tranche of 20 acres (8 hectares) of the estate, once again offering the 'colliery' including a machine house and rights to the coal under the land, was auctioned in 1853.[82] Isaac Jackson, the 'resident manager' was still there to show interested parties around. The buyer appears to have been a Benjamin Chandler who had also acquired the right to mine under neighbouring Great Neston.[83] The purchase may have led to trial borings on the site in 1854 but there is no evidence for any raising of coal; the early phase of mining in Little Neston was over.[84]

Thomas Cottingham, one-time war hero and luckless mine-owner, died in Little Neston in 1861, aged seventy-seven. He was buried in the grounds of Neston parish church.[85]

The 'Colliery' at Parkgate

Soon after Ness Colliery began its long period of uncertainty over ownership following the death of Sir Thomas Stanley Massey Stanley in 1795, an advertisement appeared in several newspapers for 'Coal Mines to be let'.[86] The stated location was curious – 'the Township of Neston' which did not exist – and the wording was quite generalised: it focused on the availability of 'valuable beds of coal and cannel' rather than on the 'coal mines' as a going concern with any supporting infrastructure of pits, engines, machinery, buildings, quay, etc. It is *possible* that this poorly-worded advertisement related to Ness Colliery. However, within a few years, there was to be attempted mining activity in the township of Great Neston on land belonging to the Mostyn family. It is therefore quite plausible that the advertisement related to a quest by Sir Roger Mostyn to interest 'an adventurer' (as the notice put it) in coal which he believed lay under his land. Advertisements of the time could be quite liberal with the truth – see, for example, the 1806 example below – so the mention of 'coal mines' should not be taken as confirmation that there were works in progress.

There are various reasons to think the advertisement could have related to Mostyn's interest. If it had been about Ness Colliery, one might have expected enquiries to be directed to someone on that site or to someone connected with the Stanley estates. Instead interested parties were referred to a William Briscoe Davies. He had been a manager at Ness Colliery until a few years previously but at the time of the advertisement was a grocer in Neston.[87] Perhaps, then, Mostyn was basing his belief in the availability of coal on knowledge gained from Davies. The grocer would have known about the nature and extent of the seams in Little Neston (where Ness Colliery had had leases to work) and thus how they might be expected to continue into Great Neston.

In addition, the 1795 advertisement stated that there was great demand locally and in Ireland for the available coal. Three years earlier Sir Roger Mostyn had been in negotiation to buy the stone from the disused and dilapidated Old Quay from its owners, the Chester Corporation.[88] Maybe he was contemplating building his own quay which would have supported the advertisement's claim for the 'very advantageous' situation of the mines by the sea from where coals could be shipped at 'trifling expense'.

Regardless of the origin of the advertisement, some time in the following decade a long lease must have been granted to work the coal in Great Neston: the holder of the lease was trying to sell it on by 1806 when an advertisement appeared in Chester, Newcastle and national newspapers for 'The very valuable Colliery of Parkgate'.[89] The lease would have to have been granted by Sir Thomas Mostyn who owned all of Parkgate at the time;[90] 'above thirty-five' years of the lease were unexpired. One of the contacts for anyone wanting more information was Robert Bowers, a Chester goldsmith and future city mayor, but whether he was part of a mining consortium is not known.[91] The 1806 advertisement contained more information than the one in 1795, stating the 'proved' depth and thickness of the coal. Such information may have been gleaned from a borehole – or maybe it was just made up! The notice claimed that the coal ran to within a short distance of Flint Castle – which was certainly unproven and, in any event, irrelevant as it would not have been operationally or legally accessible. Regardless of these points the coal could, it was said, be had 'with comparative facility' making the colliery 'capable of being … one of the most profitable undertakings of its class'. There was other hyperbole – for example claiming that vessels of '4 or 500 tons' could reach Parkgate when this would not have been possible then or, probably, ever.

There is no evidence that anyone fell for the hype and took over the lease; nor, indeed, is there evidence that a single lump of coal was ever raised at the 'colliery'. Any efforts to do so seem to have been largely abandoned by 1809 as, in December that year, an eight-horsepower colliery steam engine 'lately worked for a short time' was offered for sale at Moorside, to the south of Parkgate.[92] The sale also included 'a counting house [i.e. office], smithy, stable with sundry other serviceable articles used in the colliery business'. The ropes were described as 'little worse than new'. It is not known who bought the engine and equipment; it was possibly Ness Colliery but uncertainty about the ownership and future of Ness works may have deterred those controlling the business at the time from making such purchases.

Interestingly, as was stated in Chapter 1, the earliest geological map covering the Wirral, published in 1815, does show a coalfield stretching all the way up the peninsula's west coast. We know today that this is incorrect and we cannot say how the map-maker, William Smith, reached his view. Clearly, though, Mostyn was not alone in believing in the potential for mining in Parkgate and quite possibly beyond; maybe he even influenced Smith's thinking. As late as 1874 there were references in Mostyn correspondence to a 'Gayton Coal Field'.[93]

Following the early failures to establish a colliery in Parkgate nothing further appears to have been done about the issue for some time. However, in 1847, Edward Mostyn Lloyd Mostyn, then lord of the manor of Great Neston, sunk two new boreholes to prove the availability of coal in the township.[94] These showed several seams, the shallowest at 69 feet below the estuary-bed. Widespread newspaper reports excitedly exclaimed that there were 'scenes of considerable rejoicing' in Parkgate and Neston at the finding of 'an extensive field of coals' (just as it had been said that 'All Cheshire' had rejoiced when significant coal reserves were first found at Ness).[95] This was good news for Mostyn who was keen to realise value from his land, having £100,000 of debts to pay.[96] Several more boreholes were dug in the next few years, under the sand and mud of the estuary up to 800 yards (732 metres) from the shore.[97] Some of the findings were reported to the press, gaining yet more publicity for Mostyn's benefit.[98] The most comprehensive series of boreholes – four over almost half a mile between 230 and 480 yards (210 to 439 metres) from the shore – were dug by mining engineer, John Lancaster.[99] These revealed seams at various depths from 69 to 417 feet (21 to 127 metres), and up to 6 feet thick. An attempt was made in 1848 to interest 'capitalists, coal merchants and others' in Parkgate's 'very extensive and valuable coal-field'.[100] Liverpool and Birkenhead, which had grown rapidly in the previous decades, were said to be potential markets allowing the purchaser of the lease to compete with suppliers from the mines at St Helens and elsewhere. Birkenhead alone was said to be demanding 60,000 tons (65,340 tonnes) of coal per annum in 1845.[101]

In 1849 Mostyn auctioned off most of his estates in Neston and elsewhere to pay off his debts and to provide funds to develop a resort at Llandudno.[102] The opportunities presented by a possible coal mine, together with plans for new local roads and a railway for which parliamentary approval had been obtained, must have boosted the sale proceeds significantly.[103] Local historian Geoffrey Place commented that Mostyn's long-standing interest in the welfare of Parkgate may have been intended to 'fatten it for sale' and his actions around this time support that suggestion.[104] In a further shrewd move, Mostyn retained the mineral rights over the foreshore and some of the land. He thus re-advertised the coalfield in 1851, and the following year was able to grant a forty-year mining lease to a Robert Wynne Williams who soon sold the lease to Benjamin Chandler – but still no mining was undertaken.[105] Seven years later, the 'Coal and Ironstone Mines' – which still did not exist – were said to be valued at £11,683 5s. 5d.: a nice price if Mostyn could get it.[106] 'Capitalists', though, were deterred by the 'obnoxious' terms of Mostyn's proposed lease and the estimated

£30,000–£40,000 cost of getting the mine into action.[107] On top of all this, silting in the Dee meant that there was no sea outlet for the coal, and the roads and railway which Mostyn had planned did not materialise – thus the coal would not only have been expensive to access but also hard to shift.[108] Unsurprisingly the leaseholder, Chandler, seems to have disappeared from the scene within a few years.[109] In summary, no coal was ever mined at Parkgate – or any part of Great Neston – while Ness Colliery was open.

*

It is hard to read the story of Little Neston Colliery, and Thomas Cottingham junior's involvement in particular, without feeling a sense of sympathy. The injured war veteran struggled against a barrage of adversities – presented variously by family, neighbour, creditors and joint lord of the manor, not to mention competitors and market forces – to establish and operate a viable business. There is no evidence, though, that he ever really succeeded. Nevertheless, if for no other reason, the tale of Sir Thomas Stanley's sabotage of Cottingham's mines by explosion and flooding will surely ensure that the story of Little Neston Colliery will live on.

By contrast, the story of the 'colliery' at Parkgate is characterised by opportunism and hyperbole. In particular, Edward Lloyd Mostyn's claims and promises to would-be entrepreneurs and to local people came to nothing. No doubt to Mostyn's chagrin, he could not convince anyone to put spade into ground for coal at Parkgate.

CHAPTER 4

COAL MINING AND SUPPORTING OPERATIONS

Mining for coal was, of course, at the heart of the Neston colliery businesses and Chapters 4 to 6 look at the physical and human resources needed to carry out this activity, as well as the mining methods used. This chapter looks at the surface arrangements needed to support the collieries' workings, including Ness Colliery's farm, a leading role of which was to provide fodder for the mine's horses. It also considers the systems used underground to access the coal and some of the problems the mine-owners faced in doing so. A key driver of the Industrial Revolution was technological development reflected in, amongst other things, the invention of steam engines and advances in transport. In mines, these directly influenced how underground drainage and haulage were carried out – the subject of Chapter 5. Chapter 6 considers the roles and working conditions of the men and boys employed at the collieries and the evidence in relation to female employment.

Much of the focus here is on Ness Colliery, being substantially the largest and longest-running of the early colliery businesses at Neston, and about which most information survives. Where possible, the limited available information on Little Neston Colliery has been included too.

Surface Arrangements at the Collieries

It appears that, from its earliest days, coal working at Ness Colliery spanned over a mile along the shore of the Dee Estuary. The concentration of boreholes dug at Denhall which helped to initiate the works and the subsequent persistence of the name Denhall, Denna, etc. in connection with the colliery, suggests that there was activity in the extreme south-westerly corner of the township. In addition, further north, through the grant of a lease, the works extended into the adjoining township of Little Neston at least as far as a field called Bank Hey[s] (Figure 4.1).[1] It is probable that the operational, administrative and sales centre of the colliery was at the north-western corner of Ness township, near to what is known today as Denhall Quay. This was certainly the later centre for such activities and was relatively close to the important population centres of Neston and Parkgate. Much of the mining was carried out around this point too.

The coal was worked via a series of circular shafts, termed a 'pit'. These were scattered across several fields in the colliery area and, where required, would have had winding gear above. Each pit was numbered. Logic suggests that the numbering started in 1759 with 'No. 1' which was located in Ness township about 70 yards (64 metres) south-east of where Denhall Quay was later to be built, close to the Dee's high

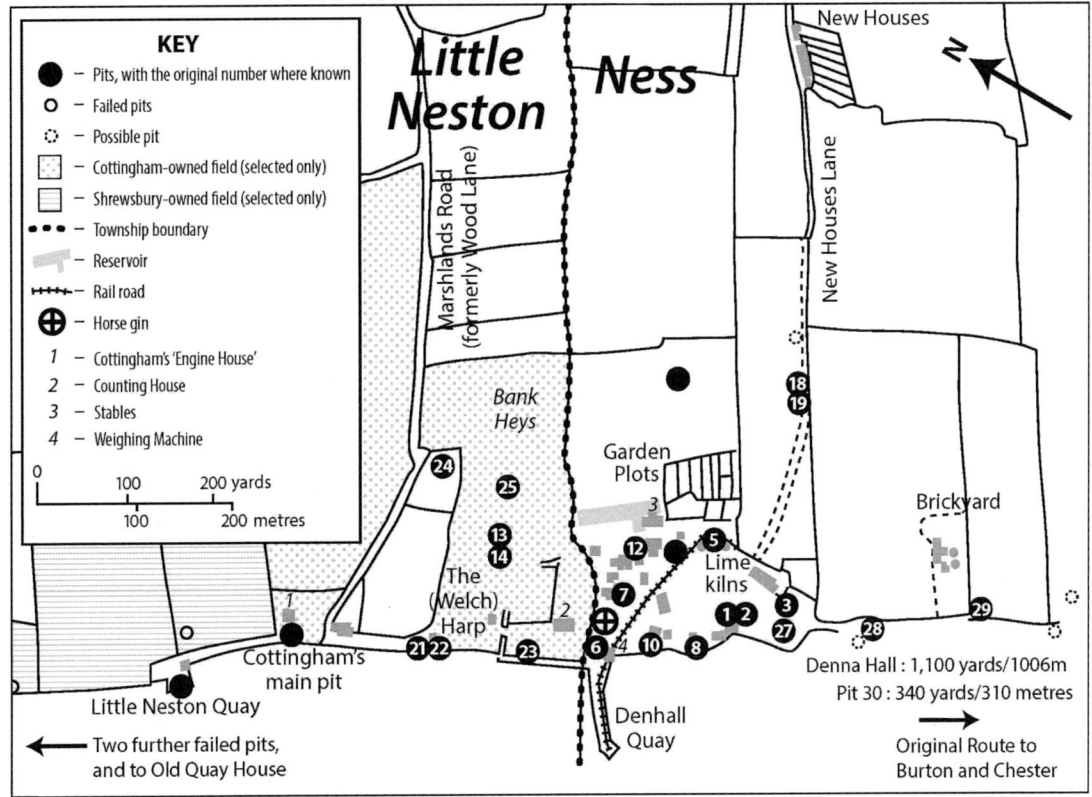

Figure 4.1: Surface features at the sites of Little Neston Colliery and Ness Colliery. The map is based on the tithe maps of Little Neston (1849) and Ness (c.1845) but does not represent the workings at any one time. In particular, the numbered pits were in use at different times. Some pit numbers and locations are unknown. Other sources: see endnote.[2]

water mark.[3] The highest known pit number was '30', sunk by 1826, but the numbering of some pits is unknown.[4] Pits 21 and 22 were said to have been sunk in 1770–1 which

implies that more than two-thirds of the total known pits were completed within twelve years of the colliery's opening.[5] This relative lack of expansion of pits over the following fifty or so years was indicative of the mine's position – the surface operations were sandwiched between the Dee Estuary and the Neston Fault and the colliers necessarily had to work outwards, under the river, from a limited number of access points. The location and numbering of any pits in the Denhall area is unknown. There was an 'Old Pit' there in 1790 and 'old pits' were being filled in by 1813 in the grounds of Charles Stanley's newly built house.[6] One of the shafts in Little Neston was in an unusual position, having been sunk in the mine's early days on a 'pier' or quay projecting into the estuary. This is discussed more fully in Chapter 10.

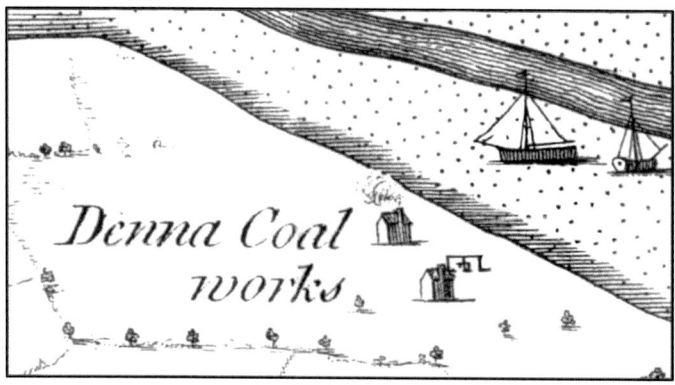

Figure 4.2: Detail from Boydell's map of the Dee Estuary, published in 1772. 'Denna Coal works' (i.e. Ness Colliery) includes a horse gin (to the right of the lower building) and the probable engine house (with smoke). Source: CALS, PM 11/7, 'A Plan of So Much of the Lands of the River Dee Company' (with courtesy of CALS).

Various buildings were needed to support the mining work. Two are shown on the first map showing the colliery site, surveyed in 1770–1 by Thomas Boydell (Figure 4.2), although these are probably indicative rather than necessarily being an actual count.[7] One of the structures was almost certainly the engine house.

More buildings appear on the many other maps and plans which cover the colliery area over its decades of operation. Four are depicted on an estate map in 1788;[8] a colliery plan from 1839 shows twenty structures including kilns (Figure 4.3).[9]

With few exceptions, the exact role of each mapped structure is unclear but buildings which were likely to have been needed from an early stage include the engine house, an office for administration and accounting, stables for the horses working above ground, a smithy and a storage shed. The 1769–70 accounts mention many items which would have required storage including ropes, wire riddles, candles, tools, iron, nails, horse feed and basket rods (the last being used to make wicker baskets to hold the coal).[10] When lime was made at the colliery, a sound storage place would have been needed to keep it dry as, when wet, it would be highly corrosive.

Some of the small buildings on maps will simply have been cabins used for shelter, especially by the 'browman' who oversaw winding operations at the top of a shaft. One, at the top of Pit. No. 6, was described as 'a cabin of sods' (i.e. made from lumps of turf).[11] The same account mentioned that it was also a place for the colliers 'to dry their cloaths in'. There was another 'Cabin' on the quay in Little Neston on which there was a shaft.[12] The 1812 letting offer at Ness mentions several buildings at the colliery:[13]

> Necessary outbuildings, a Counting-house, Agents' and Underlookers' Houses, Blacksmiths' and carpenters' Shops, twelve cottages for artificers and colliers.

This is the first known explicit reference to colliery workers' housing locally ('Agents and Underlookers' are the managers and their assistants; artificers are skilled craftsmen). These cottages were probably a few hundred yards from the main site but men were certainly living at the heart of the colliery from the 1820s and, probably from its earliest days.[14]

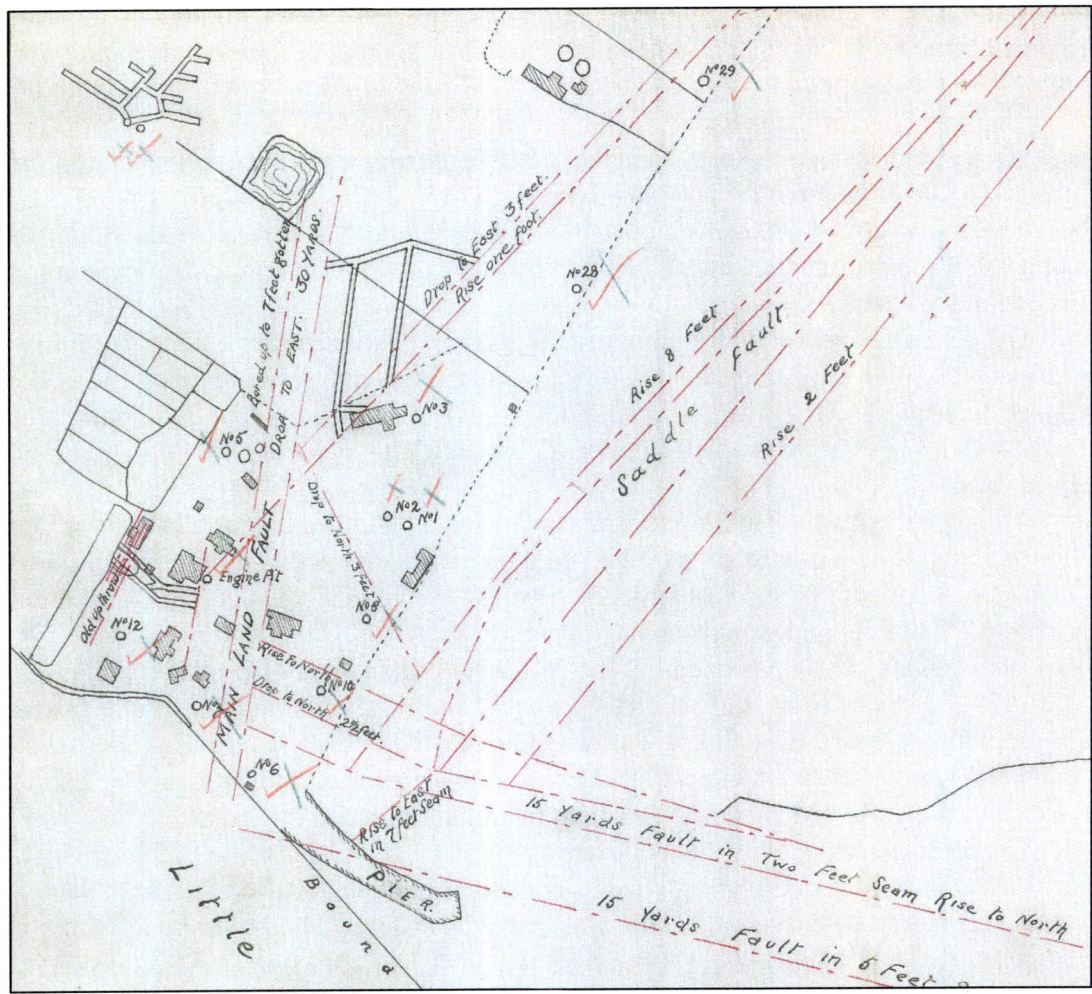

Figure 4.3: The site of Ness Colliery, 1839. Source: © Coal Authority 3808/1, detail from 'Tracings of the Workings in the Two Feet Mine', with kind permission.

The 'Counting house', or office, appears to have been in Little Neston, just over the boundary from Ness, probably on a small piece of land owned by Sir Thomas Stanley.[15] The office was to be the scene of a crime in June 1837.[16] It was broken into by thieves who 'ransacked every part of the building' looking in vain for valuables. They then forced from the floor an iron chest which was bolted to the ground and weighed between 200 lbs and 300 lbs (90–136 kg). They carried it outside and broke it open, stealing '£9 in gold'. Curiously they 'carefully rapped' the papers in the chest and left them in a heap of straw in the field. They then went on to break into the machine house and steal five shillings (25p) in copper.

A prominent feature at the colliery was a reservoir, measuring about 93 x 13 yards (88 x 12 metres). It provided the power source via a canal for a bucket engine and would also have supplied water for the colliery's steam engines, both discussed later.[17] A further use was for the slack mill which was used 'to wash slack instead of riddling it' (a riddle being a coarse sieve).[18] Slack comprises small pieces of coal and the milling process would have separated out the dust. Ness Colliery's stables were situated close to the reservoir giving access for animals' drinking water.[19] A statement in 1821 adds a little scenic colour mentioning a tinker 'idling about [by the reservoir] and swimming his dog in the canal'.[20]

The colliery consumed large amounts of timber, particularly for use as pit props; stacks of it would have laid on site. There were at least two saw-pits used to cut the timber to size. These presumably included covered sheds as the two had been converted into a warehouse and 'cowhouse' by 1821;[21] a 'New Saw Pit' was shown on a later plan.[22]

A marked feature of the landscape would have been the coal stocks that lay on 'the bank' waiting for land or sea sale. This coal was mentioned frequently in Ness correspondence and, in accounts, represented the difference between coal raised and coal sold.[23] The coal made an attractive target for theft, discussed in Chapter 12.

Other goods sold at, or used by, the colliery would have been stacked on site. In 1770, 120,000 bricks were lying there – probably to line shafts, discussed later in this chapter.[24] Over its life, the colliery would sell bricks, tiles, slates, lime and sand, as well as charcoal and coke (see Chapter 7). There was a 'slate yard' and, from about 1826, a 'brick and tile yard' 400 yards (366 metres) from the main site.[25]

The area of Ness Colliery was not a pretty place. The 1821 and 1822 court cases included much reference to the township boundary between little Neston and Ness. It was once marked by a ditch but there was uncertainty as to where it lay:

> Every trace of [the boundary] had for the last 50 years been obliterated, and the whole covered with rubbish, ten, fifteen, or twenty feet deep … Men were to dig deep holes to find out the old ditch.[26]

The 'rubbish' presumably included mining spoil and also operational detritus such as damaged bricks and worn out tools and equipment; an 'old empty boiler' was amongst the debris.[27] The surrounding area was covered in scrub – gorse, briar and 'thorn bushes'.[28] On the shore of the estuary, old pieces of timber, as well as tree roots, were thrown up by the tide.[29]

When Ness Colliery was sold in 1855, a comprehensive equipment list was included in the sale advertisement.[30] In many ways little had changed from the listings in the colliery accounts eighty-five years earlier: there were 60,000 basket rods, carpenter's and smith's shop fixtures, tools, riddles and ropes as well as wrought and scrap iron. The most significant additions were a wide range of pumping and winding engines with associated equipment, and iron rails and coal waggons – the use of these items is discussed in the next chapter.

The presence of the Cottinghams' Little Neston Colliery was relatively insignificant compared to Ness Colliery's. Despite operating from about 1820 it was not referred to on any published map until 1836; even then it was just 'Colliery'.[31] A few colliery-related buildings are shown on earlier maps and plans, but generally with little detail.[32]

When Thomas Cottingham senior established the business he took over Ness's Pit No. 21, and presumably adjacent No. 22, which had been sunk in 1770–1.[33] These gave access to the two uppermost seams – the Six-Foot and the Five-Foot. However, these pits soon had to be abandoned following Stanley's sabotage of the new mine. The area became known as the 'Old Colliery Banks' and the 1826 Little Neston estate sale particulars listed a 'Machine House, Lime Kiln, Smithy, Dwelling over the Smithy, and other appurtenances' there.[34] At least two of the buildings feature on a later plan which shows an 'Old engine house' and an unlabelled structure, as well as a nearby 'machine house'.[35] It seems likely the buildings were originally erected when Ness Colliery had a lease to operate in that area.

After Thomas Cottingham junior took on ownership of the business he sank (or reopened) a Pit 'No. 1' on the 'pier' projecting into the estuary in Little Neston but this also soon had to be abandoned.[36] By 1826 another pit had been sunk in one of his fields, close to the shoreline.[37] This initially accessed solely the low quality Six-Foot seam.[38] It later reached the Five-Foot too and would serve the colliery for the remainder of its life.[39] Cottingham never went lower than the Five-Foot, restricting the operation to the low-value steam coal seam and one house coal seam. One plan survives which labels an 'Engine house' by this pit.[40]

Just two of the buildings depicted on any pre-1855 map covering the area of the Neston collieries survive today: both appear on the 1788 'Plan of Little Neston'.[41] One is a building at the bottom of today's Marshlands Road, now much extended. The other is today's Harp Inn, also now considerably enlarged. Being close to the centre of Ness Colliery's operations, it is possible that the pub building was constructed in connection with the works.

The Colliery Farm

It was common in the period under review for collieries to have their own farms. Their principal role was to provide the means to feed and pasture the works' horses and ponies. If Ness Colliery had a farm in its early years then it was not able to supply all the business's needs as it was buying in horse feed: the 1769–70 accounts show £284 spent on hay, oats and bran over ten months.[42] The earliest-known written indications of a farm come from about 1790.[43] It was described as 'considerable' in 1796 and, more specifically, consisted of about 90 acres (36.4 hectares) in 1812.[44] The farmland appears to have consisted of about eleven fields, mostly fronting the estuary.[45]

The horses and ponies were used for hauling coal both above and below ground and also powered the gins used for winding, working on a shift system (gins are discussed more fully on pages 73–4). In addition donkeys were used for small deliveries of coal.[46] There were twenty-five horses at Ness Colliery in 1770, valued at £4 each, and it still had 'six powerful wagon horses' and 'seven very useful ponies about thirteen hands high' when it closed in 1855.[47] The farm buildings were located on the central site of the colliery and, according to the 1845 tithe map, included a large barn with a 'fold-yard' (farm-yard) and adjacent 'stack yard' (for hay ricks).[48] The colliery stables for horses used on the surface were located close by;[49] there would also have been stables underground.

A good description of the stock of a colliery farm was given in 1813 when much of the operation's 'Farming-Stock and Colliery Horses' was offered for sale after the Stanley brothers took on the business.[50] The items comprised:

> Eleven stout Draught HORSES, nine sets of horse geers [for yoking horses to carts and machinery], a timber carriage with six inch [wide] wheels, cone carts with broad wheels [cone is a type of wheat], three ploughs, three pairs of harrows, a straw cutter, pan and steaming tub, eight fodder cribs, eighteen sacks, and a variety of husbandry utensils.

The auction raised £415.[51] To keep the colliery running, six horses, a cart, a timber carriage and supporting equipment were retained, valued at £214.[52] At Ness, the term 'horses' seems to have been used interchangeably with 'ponies' a few years later so it is quite possible that some of the six 'horses' here were underground ponies.[53]

The main produce of a colliery farm was hay for horse feed but, as the 1813 advertisement indicates, other produce might be grown such as wheat as well as oats, beans and turnips.[54] The items could be used for horse feed, or sold to the miners and their families or to outside buyers. In 1814 a medal was awarded to 'The Proprietors of Ness Colliery' in a Wirral and West Cheshire Agricultural Society competition for 'the best crop of wheat'. It can surely only be coincidence that the chairman of the judges was … Sir Thomas Stanley (who, himself, won a prize for best sheep; two of his estate employees also won prizes)![55] As well as arable produce, livestock was kept and the animals or their produce sold to colliers or to others in the area.[56] A 'cowhouse' had been introduced by 1821 and there is a later reference to 'colliery beef'.[57]

An economic argument for maintaining a colliery farm was that it gave the business a degree of insulation at times when grain prices were high, as they were during the Napoleonic Wars, for example.[58] Later, in 1816, with many of its horses sold, the colliery was in a position to offer for sale 20 tons (21.8 tonnes) of 'superior hay', said to be 'part of the growth of 1814, and the rest of 1815' (1815 was a year of bumper harvests but 1816 was to become known as the 'Year Without a Summer' when harvests failed nationally after a volcanic eruption in what is present-day Indonesia causing climate disruption).[59] However, with a sharp downward trend in grain prices from 1814, albeit with occasional respite, the farm was valued in 1818 at just £172 and Sir Thomas Stanley allowed a rebate of the rent the colliery paid him for it.[60] The farm was mentioned in Thomas's 1841 will and was still in use in 1846 when a ploughing competition was held there.[61] Several agricultural labourers are recorded as living at the colliery in the 1851 census.[62]

There is little if any evidence of females working in the mine at Neston but the farm provided a potential source of employment for the colliers' wives. At times of peak need some of the colliers themselves, or surface labourers, may have been brought on to the farm to work, as happened elsewhere.[63] The mining historian Thomas Ashton noted:

> The colliers themselves were close the soil; it was usual for them to leave the pits for work on the land in the months of harvest; and the methods of hiring, and relations with employers, were very similar to those of the agricultural labourer.[64]

This synergy between land and colliery was reflected at, for example, County Durham's Newbottle Colliery where records from 1749–50 list eleven men working as 'collier and farm'.[65] Lancashire, too, had men recorded as 'farmer and collier'.[66] At Holywell (Flintshire) it was said in 1837 that 'Most of the Harvest Labourers work in the collieries throughout the Winter'.[67]

There is no particular evidence in the limited available data relating to Ness Colliery of seasonal variation in coal production while men did agricultural work.[68] However, there are several instances of individuals having involvement in both types of work, going from collier to farmer or vice versa.[69] To give just two examples, Richard Kelsall was the manager at Ness Colliery in 1763 and, up to the 1750s, had been connected to the coal mining towns of Audley and Madeley in Staffordshire, and Flint and Buckley in Flintshire.[70] However, the Neston parish register describes him as a 'farmer' in 1760.[71] And James Stock was recorded as an 'Underground steward' (i.e. manager) at Ness Colliery between 1786 and 1790 but was a 'farmer' thereafter.[72] Many colliers at Ness were, at times, also described as 'labourer' in parish registers but we cannot say whether they were labouring at the mine or, perhaps, doing temporary agricultural work.

Reference was made earlier to the sale of the farm's produce to outside buyers. An important role for the colliery farm was as a buyer from, and seller to, the Stanley estates, a topic discussed in Chapter 8.

Accessing the Coal

The collieries' existence depended, of course, on obtaining coal. So what methods were used to reach and win that precious commodity?

Figure 4.4: The remains of adjacent mine shafts at Ness Colliery. These are Pit Nos. 13 and 14. Each was about 6 feet (1.8 metres) in diameter. The shafts are no longer visible. Source: NPL, 'Mines' file.

Access to the coal seams came via the shafts or 'pits' – reference has already been made to the thirty or more which were sunk at Ness Colliery as well as those sunk by Little Neston Colliery. Sinking shafts was time-consuming and expensive. It was claimed in 1829 that a shaft down to the Two-Foot seam at Little Neston, probably well over 100 yards (91 metres) deep, would take about twelve months to complete.[73] The decision to sink a shaft was therefore usually preceded by the sinking of at least one borehole and generally more. At least four were sunk at Ness in the two years before the colliery opened and records survive of several later ones.[74] The boring was undertaken using a rotating bit or chisel a few inches in diameter with the excavated material lifted to the surface for analysis.[75] The depth, thickness and quality of coal found in the boreholes were all critical factors in assessing the viability of a possible pit. Boreholes were sometimes dug at Ness starting underground; these could go upwards as well as downwards, looking for seams lost amongst the geological faults.[76]

When boreholes indicated that it would be worth sinking a shaft, specialist 'pit sinkers' were often brought in to make it, paid by the distance they cut. No records are available about the identity of sinkers used at Ness but, for example, in the 1770s at Lord Molyneux's mines in south-west Lancashire, sinkers from Northumberland were contracted.[77] Sinkers' costs varied significantly depending on the nature of the strata to be dug through and the depths involved. In the 1760s and '70s, when Ness Colliery was sinking the majority of its own shafts, costs of between 8s. 6d. and 18s. per yard (46–98p per metre) were quoted in Lancashire.[78] Another variable which influenced cost was the shaft's diameter. The pits at Ness seem to have been about 6 feet (1.8 metres) across (Figure 4.4). It was usual to make the shaft size as narrow as possible to keep costs down although some larger shafts would probably have been needed for bulky equipment and horses or ponies.[79] Thomas Cottingham was reckoned to have paid £120 to sink two 'large' (in diameter) pits in 1829. These were said to have been about 12–15 yards (11.0–13.7 metres) in depth before being abandoned.[80]

The price for sinking Cottingham's shafts included lining of the shaft's walls. Lining was needed to protect against the fall of loose rock, and ingress of water. The lining would also have been essential to give stability to the shaft as it penetrated the clay at Neston between the surface and the start of the underlying Carboniferous rock. In 1770, 120,000 bricks were stacked at Ness Colliery and many of them may have been intended to line the shafts the colliery was sinking at that time.[81] Sandstone blocks were also used for lining as evidenced by photographs of surviving shafts; these were probably used to give added strength through the clay.

The thirty shafts at Ness were not all in use simultaneously but were opened, closed and occasionally reopened, depending on working requirements.[82] The large number of shafts reflects the fact that they were used for various purposes – for drawing coal to the surface, for lowering and raising men and equipment, for ventilation and also for pumping water from the mine. Each of these uses will be considered in this and the following chapter. However, another key reason was simply that the coal seams needed to be worked in different locations.

The local seams stretched for about 1.5 miles (2.4 km) in Ness and Little Neston and across that area the geology varied substantially: the extent of local faulting and other geological factors, meant that a shaft sunk in one location might encounter seams at very different depths and of different thicknesses to ones elsewhere. The decision about how to access these different coal strata depended upon the vertical and horizontal distances involved. As a general rule, if the horizontal distance was relatively small, it was preferable to dig underground stone drifts (i.e. tunnels cut through bare rock) from an existing shaft rather than sink a new one. Thus, in 1819 for example, colliery viewer Nicholas Wood commented in relation to seeking to trace the lost Six-Foot seam at Ness that a 'stone drift will be considerably cheaper than to sink another pit'.[83] If, however, the selected working areas were far apart or the seams were shallow a new shaft might be preferable. Extra shafts could also reduce underground haulage distances and their associated labour costs – but the river meant there were no realistic westward opportunities to sink shafts.

Four seams were worked at Ness Colliery – in descending order of depth, the Six-Foot, Five-Foot, Seven-Foot and Two-Foot. The Six-Foot seems only to have been found in Little Neston and could not be worked by the Stanleys after Cottingham's colliery was opened. Because of the Neston Fault east of the shoreline, the main direction that the mine 'levels' (long tunnels through the mine, also known as 'roads') extended was south-west, under the Dee Estuary. Thomas Leacroft Cottingham (the son of the final owner of Little Neston Colliery, and a mining engineer) was asked to give evidence to a parliamentary committee in 1869 on 'Waste in Working [coal mines]'. In answer to a question about the local mines he reckoned that the workings extended 'upwards of 2000 yards' (1,829 metres) for the Two-Foot seam, and 'upwards of 1000 yards' (914 metres) for the Six-Foot.[84] A plan of Ness Colliery, dated 1839, shows the Two-Foot seam extending about two thousand yards (1,829 metres).[85]

Working the coal so far out under the estuary gave rise to practical problems, one of which was ventilation (another was haulage, discussed in the next chapter). As the works extended it became increasingly difficult to arrange ventilation to the furthest parts. In the 1830 court case involving Thomas Cottingham, it was mentioned that there was a risk of a tunnel becoming of such an 'extreme length' that 'the working of a mine at the end of it [would be] precarious, if not impossible, for want of ventilation'.[86]

This problem was one of the several reasons for the multiplicity of shafts at Ness Colliery. As the network of underground tunnels grew, more shafts would have been needed to admit the necessary volume of fresh air required by the underground workers and animals and to expel the dangerous gases which occur naturally in mines. Several pits can be found in pairs, just a few yards apart, for example Nos. 1 and 2, and 21 and 22 (Figure 4.1).[87] These pairings were almost certainly to provide an efficient ventilation system. Coal historian, Michael Flinn states,

> Already by the beginning of the eighteenth century … it was becoming usual, in all except the very smallest of mines, to provide two shafts to an underground working, one a downcast shaft to admit fresh air, and the other an upcast shaft to draw out the dangerous gases. The upcast shaft was normally also the working shaft for winding and pumping (the 'engine shaft'). Circulation of air was achieved by placing a fire either suspended in a brazier at the top of the shaft, or in a hearth at the foot of the shaft, and the updraught was assisted by the tall chimney at the pithead that is a feature of so many prints of eighteenth and early nineteenth-century coal-mines.[88]

There was certainly a chimney by Pit Nos. 21 and 22, and there may have been others.[89] Figure 4.4 shows two adjacent mine shafts revealed during building work in 1988. The photographer described them as '6 ft. in diameter and apparently 80 ft. deep'.[90] From information with the photos it would appear these are the shafts numbered 13 and 14 and in the middle of 'Bank Heys'.[91] If creating two shafts was too costly it was possible to use just one, divided by a brattice to make two sections.[92]

Some of the colliery plans show 'Air roads' – long tunnels apparently dug specifically for ventilation to remote parts of the works; these were an expensive undertaking.[93] It may have been to avoid such a necessity that a shaft was dug 1,320 yards (1,207 metres) into the estuary near Mostyn Colliery (presumably with a high parapet to protect it from inundation by the sea).[94] Shafts are depicted offshore at Ness on some plans but these all seem to have been underground 'staples' – shafts which linked one area of the mine to another, rather than descending from the surface.[95] Staples could be used for ventilation – at least one was situated on an 'Air road'; they could also be used for winding operations between tunnels at different depths.

Fans were eventually introduced to assist ventilation in British mines but they came late in the life of Ness Colliery and there is no indication they were ever used there.[96]

Underground Working Systems

Much of the working during the Neston collieries' operational life used the 'pillar and stall' (or 'pillar and board') method, used in many parts of northern England and Wales.[97] Passages were cut through the coal, both lengthwise and crosswise; these passages were the 'stalls' or 'boards' (Figure 4.5). Support was needed for the rock above the workings – the overburden – and this came from leaving substantial

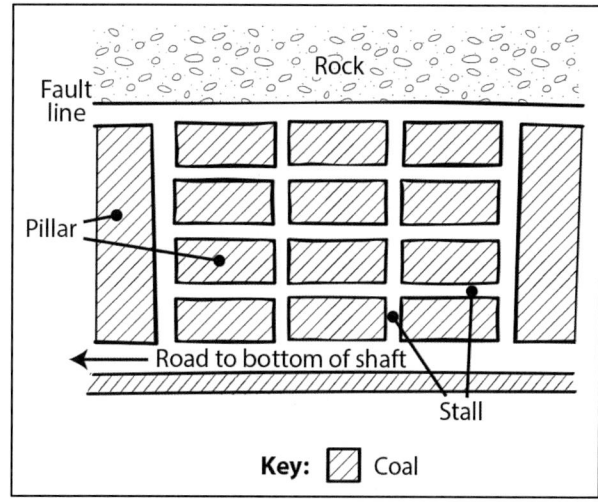

Figure 4.5. Illustration of the pillar and stall coal-working system as used at the Neston collieries, depicted as if viewable from above. Source: adapted from Church, Fig. 4.2, p. 331.

'pillars' of rock untouched between the stalls. At Neston the weight of the tidal waters of the estuary was an added factor when assessing the need for support: an advantage of the pillar and stall method was that it was more likely than other mining techniques to leave the surface intact. This was an important consideration when collapse of the river bed (known as 'crowning') might bring catastrophic results.

By working this system, a complex grid of tunnels was formed; one contemporary poet termed this type of arrangement a 'City of subterraneous streets'.[98] Part of the system at Ness is illustrated in Figure 4.6 (overleaf). The dimensions of the pillars varied with depth and geological conditions; in the Figure the pillars near the 'pier' (quay) average about 28 x 8 yards (25 x 7 metres).

Many plans of the colliery workings in both Ness and Little Neston have survived, and all show evidence of the grid-like pillar and stall system. Thomas Leacroft Cottingham produced an illustration of pillar and stall at Neston in his evidence to the 1869 parliamentary committee (Figure 4.7 on p. 63). The pillar and stall method was, however, wasteful as it left much coal behind. The system was used across the estuary at Mostyn Colliery and it was said in 1844 that 'Nearly one half of this coal is left in pillars to guard against the waters of the Dee.'[99] There was inevitable temptation for mine-owners to seek to whittle away at the pillars or even eliminate them altogether. This gave rise to a system of secondary working where the pillars were removed or 'robbed'.[100] The removal could take place pillar by pillar, or along a

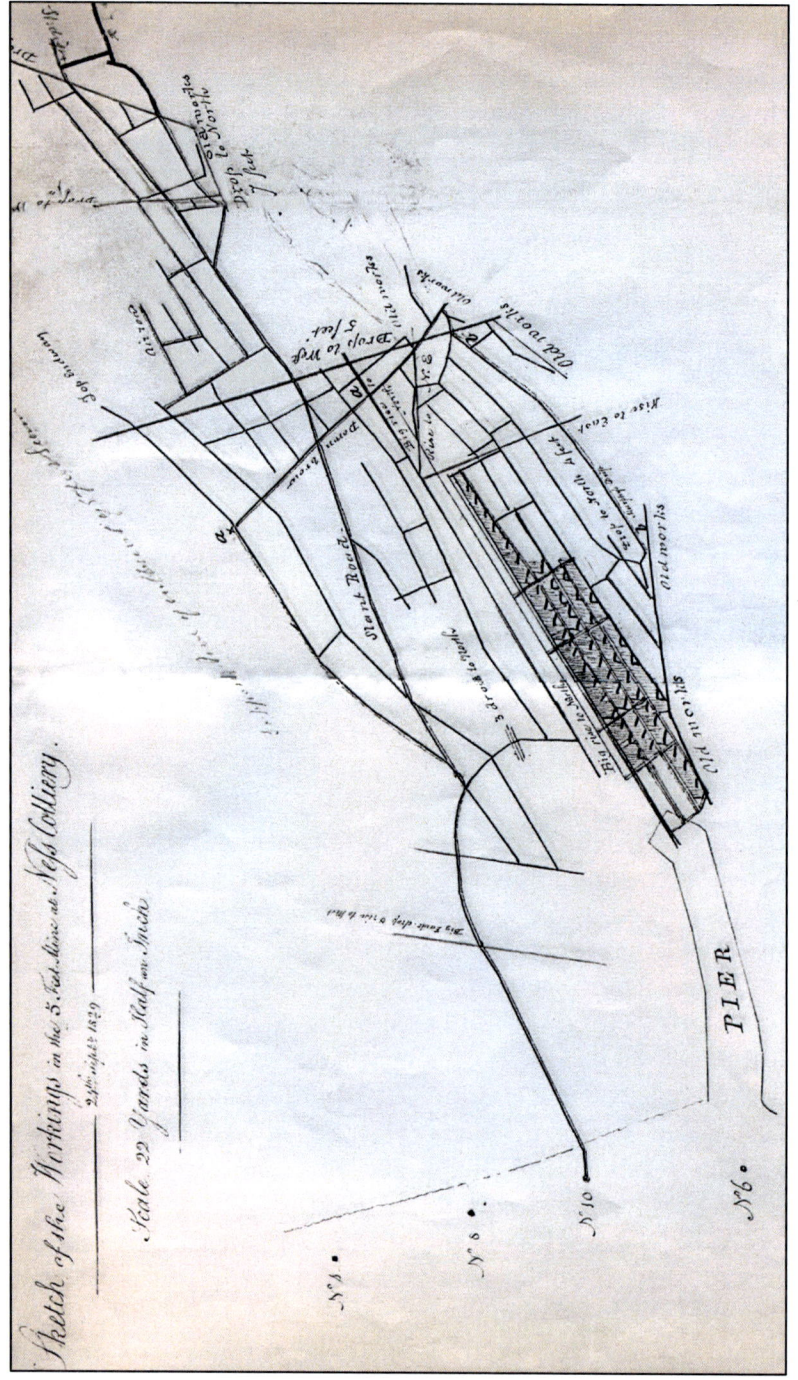

Figure 4.6: 'Sketch of the Workings in the 5 Feet Mine' at Ness Colliery, 1829. The shore and line of pits are to the left, with Denhall Quay ('Pier') projecting to the right. The sketch mentions 'air roads' (for ventilation), an 'endway' (a tunnel driven through a coal seam) and 'old works', most notably at the boundary with Little Neston. The hatched area is probably secondary working, characteristic of the 'Lancashire System'. Source: NEIMME/Wat/3/71/18 with permission of NEIMME and CRGN.

line of pillars and termed 'longwall' working.[101] Initially, wooden props were used to support the area being worked but waste could be used to partially fill the gap (known as a 'goaf') and, after the props were moved forward, the roof would be allowed to collapse into the remaining space.[103] This method was referred to by Thomas Leacroft Cottingham in his 1869 evidence.[104] Speaking of the Six-Foot seam in Little Neston, he said:

> The pillars [were] on the average 20 yards wide, and the boards [or stalls] 9 feet wide. The length of the pillars varied from 40 to 50 yards. They were cut through at intervals of perhaps 30 yards, and subsequently worked back. The depth of the strata reached was 55½ yards from the surface, and the coal was reached under the river at that depth and worked to the rise, to within about, say, 30 yards of the surface.

The combination of pillar and stall and the subsequent working-back of the pillars was used at, amongst others, Jonathan Blundell's Orrell and Pemberton Collieries and became known as the 'Lancashire System' (Figure 4.8, overleaf).[105]

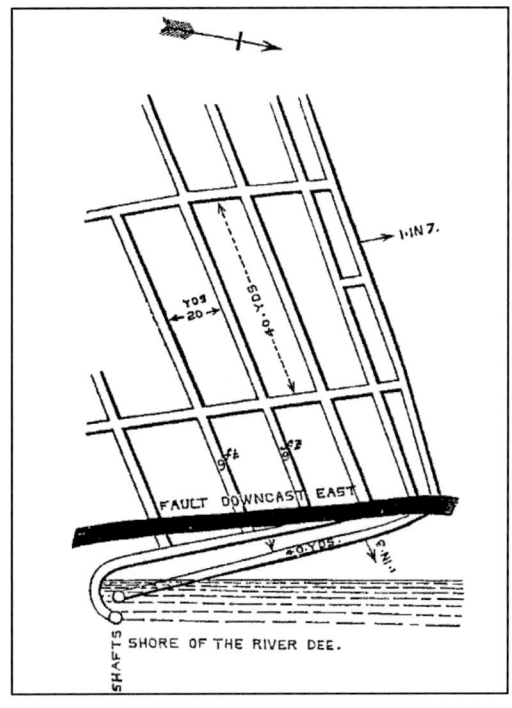

Figure 4.7: Thomas Leacroft Cottingham's illustration of coal workings for the 1869 parliamentary committee on 'Waste in Working [coal mines]' showing stalls (the tunnels) and pillars (the remaining rock). Source: BPP [1871], p. 374. With kind permission of IUP.

The introduction of the Lancashire System at Ness Colliery came in about 1828. A colliery surveyor had recommended 'stripping the walls back [in the Seven-Foot seam] instead of cutting them across and leaving a large proportion of coals'.[106] His view was that, as the coal seam being worked was 'thin', and the overburden thick and strong, the excavated area would simply be 'choaked up' by limited roof falls 'without endangering the works'; there was 'no risk'. Ness Colliery's manager, James Gregory, said he was willing to 'experiment' with the system but said he would 'return to our old way of working if there should be any appearance of danger'. There are subsequent indications of the system being used in all the seams worked at Ness, either from correspondence or in plans of the workings.[107] Sometimes all the coal could be removed;[108] on other occasions some support was left, for example 'small pilasters of a triangular form'.[109] By this method it appears that the then viewer to the colliery,

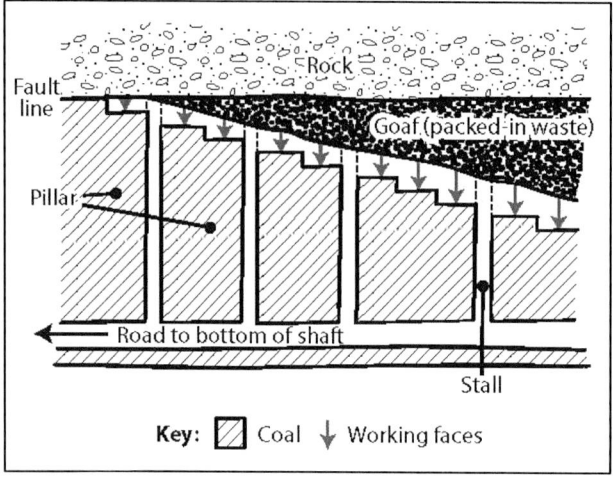

Figure 4.8: The 'Lancashire System' of coal-working used at the Neston collieries, depicted as if viewable from above. Source: adapted from Church, Fig. 4.6, p. 332.

John Watson, was hoping the colliery would be able to extract 'all' the coal from the Two-Foot seam and two-thirds from the Seven-Foot.[110]

With the possible exception of the Two-Foot, surviving plans do not show the final extent to which cutting back of the pillars was implemented but Thomas Leacroft Cottingham later claimed in relation to the seams worked at both Ness and Little Neston that 'the whole of the coal was extracted as nearly as could be by the then system of working'.[111] It seems, then, that the adoption of this new method was a significant factor in enabling Ness Colliery to continue for a further twenty-seven years after the surveyor's recommendation. It would also help account for the later claim that Ness Colliery was sold because its seams were believed to be exhausted.[112]

One of the principal dangers underground was of roof falls, and correspondence shows that the colliery's advisers took safety into account and sought to minimise risk.[113] Much attention was paid to supporting the ground above the tunnels even where pillar and stall was used. Large quantities of timber were bought by Ness Colliery, often from the Stanley estates, to make pit props;[114] equipment could be used too. It was suggested that a horse gin, 'at least six yards in breadth' and intended for underground winding, would also be 'a strong safeguard' as a roof support (Figure 5.6 on page 75); 'old pumps' could be re-used for this purpose too.[115]

The coal seams dipped (i.e. sloped downwards) towards the north-west at a gradient of roughly one in six. The general direction of the tunnels in the workings was south-westerly, at right angles to the dip of the coal seams, suggesting the works followed horizontally along the line of these seams (i.e. running along their geological 'strike'). The long tunnels were kept as level as possible to make haulage easily – hence they were often known as 'levels'. As new stalls were dug to the side it was usual to try to work up the slope of the seam where possible.[116] This avoided working in water which drained to the bottom of the workings, and made it easy to move the extracted coal downhill to the level from where it could be transported to the shaft for raising to the surface. Hauling the coal underground was known as 'putting' so that working upslope was said to make 'easy putting for the boys'.[117] In 1830, when an account was given of Thomas Cottingham's workings in the Six-Foot seam, he was said to have worked a series of 'up-brows', each 100 yards (91 metres) long.[118]

A perennial problem in collieries was water. Every mine suffered from rainwater and water from underground sources percolating into shafts and tunnels. Dealing with water problems is a feature of much of the surviving correspondence at Ness. Water prevented efficient working – or any working at all. It was also costly as men had to be paid more for digging in wet conditions.[119] It is not surprising that water was described as 'very troublesome and expensive'.[120]

The main solution at the Neston collieries was to raise the water from the mine (other options were available at mines elsewhere, depending on local geography). In the early days of British mining all such lifting was via winding machinery, usually horse-powered gins which brought single buckets of water, or chains of them, up the shafts.[121] However, by the time Ness Colliery opened in 1759, steam-powered atmospheric engines were available to undertake the task. These forms of technology are covered more fully in the next chapter. Whatever the solution, though, one or more shafts was needed as a conduit for the necessary equipment, giving another likely reason for the large number of shafts found at Ness.

Various other water-management measures were implemented or proposed at Ness Colliery including the creation of a sump to contain water; the use of long 'water-levels' (drainage tunnels) to channel water to the shaft where it could be removed; and the sinking of boreholes to allow water to flow from one seam to a lower one where the engine pump was working.[122]

The water problem does not appear to have been exacerbated by inundation from the Dee Estuary – the clay bed of the river provided an effective seal.[123] On one occasion Ness Colliery's workings actually reached the bed but with no serious consequences.[124] There was clearly caution about implementing the Lancashire System of coal working but, when addressing the 1869 parliamentary committee, Thomas Leacroft Cottingham said that roof falls generated only minor ingress of water on 'one or two' occasions, and only at Ness Colliery, not Little Neston.[125] There were reports of 'crownings' – collapse of the land or estuary-bed above leading to roof falls – at Little Neston Colliery, but at least two of these came after the colliery closed.[126] There was always the additional risk, though, of boring into abandoned, long-forgotten flooded workings as happened on at least one occasion in the later period of colliery working at Neston – fortunately without catastrophic consequences.[127] The rapid flooding of Ness Colliery when it closed is indicative of the importance of fighting the battle against water while the mine was operating.[128]

*

In many ways the Neston collieries were like other coal mines around the country. All had to have surface infrastructure to support underground working; all had to adopt appropriate systems for working the coal seams; and all had to deal with the constant ingress of water. Many had colliery farms, too. However, the location and geology of the Neston collieries led to particular challenges. The multiple shafts were constrained to the edge of the land, and the underground working systems needed to take careful account of the weight of the estuarine waters and the potentially catastrophic consequences of breaching the estuary-bed. Ness Colliery's management were understandably cautious in adopting the new Lancashire System of working but it was a gamble which paid off, extending the colliery's life for over twenty years.

CHAPTER 5

INNOVATION: UNDERGROUND TRANSPORT
AND TECHNOLOGY

One of the notable features of the Industrial Revolution was the introduction and continual development of equipment and machines. These reduced the labour required from humans and animals or enhanced their capabilities. Ingenuity and invention, coupled with enhanced understanding of materials and manufacturing processes, meant that there were constant incremental steps and, sometimes, great leaps in productivity. In relation to coal mining in the period under review, these advances were probably most evident in relation to the evolution of underground transport and in connection with two processes fundamental to mining – winding and pumping. Steam engines were to play a major part in improving the efficiency of those two processes. How these important developments were manifested at the Neston collieries forms the subject of this chapter.

Underground Transport

The previous chapter described the large extent to which the workings at the Neston collieries were carried out under the Dee Estuary. As well as the ventilation problems this caused, the other main challenge was transportation, giving rise to pressing problems regarding cost-efficiency. As the works extended from the shore, more and more time, energy and expense were incurred in bringing coal (and, probably, some waste too) from the face to the shaft – this was a fundamental problem which directly impacted the economics of the colliery operations.[1] Thus, in 1829, Stanley was considering abandoning No. 1 Pit because of,

> The problems of the lowness of the selling price and the expense in working No. 1 pit in consequence of the great distance the coals have been obliged to be conveyed underground to the shaft.[2]

It was therefore critical that efficient forms of underground haulage were used; several methods were introduced over the collieries' life.

In Ness Colliery's earliest days, transport of the coal was probably undertaken using sledges, as was commonplace elsewhere.[3] Corves full of coal were placed on the sledges which had iron runners; these were dragged and sometimes also pushed, often by children, along planking to the shaft – a process often known as 'putting' (Figure 5.1, overleaf).

Corves ('corf' in the singular) were baskets made of long, sturdy wooden sticks, usually hazel, which were woven together by skilled craftsmen. In 1770 at Ness, 90,000 'basket rods' were held, presumably waiting to be used to make baskets. The basket rods would be placed in a cylinder into which steam was blown to make them pliable for bending into the shape of the basket.[4] The capacity of corves varied with tunnel

Figure 5.1: A collier hauls a sled, loaded with a wooden corf, over planking, 1842. This basic hauling technique was still in widespread use in Lancashire at that time, and quite possibly at the Neston collieries too. Source: *Report of the parliamentary Children's Employment Commission, BPP* [1842a], pp. 81, 104. With kind permission of IUP.

size and how they were being moved; filled corves in Lancashire around this time, drawn by women or children wearing harnesses, weighed one-and-a-half hundredweight (82 kg). Wicker corves were gradually replaced by sturdier wooden boxes in British collieries.[5] A visitor commented on the two wicker corves being used at Little Neston Colliery in 1829, comparing them to the stronger wooden ones used at Yorkshire collieries (presumably because production levels were higher there so the corves had to be more robust).[6]

Due to the frictional inefficiency of sledges, improved haulage methods were developed. Sometimes wheels were added to the sledges making them easier to pull over the planking.[7] Also, during the eighteenth century, waggon ways came into use with wheeled waggons or 'rolleys' running on wooden rails.[8] These could carry heavier loads. By 1786 corves at Ness weighed up to four hundredweight (217 kg), suggesting that horses were being used to pull the sledges or that it had adopted rail technology.[9] Four-hundredweight baskets were still being used at Ness in 1828.[10]

Pit ponies began to be used in British mines in the first half of the eighteenth century, but the economics of their use were complex.[11] They could move heavier loads than boys, who were the usual alternative source of labour for underground haulage. However, they were expensive to buy, and came with high maintenance costs in terms of feed when compared to a boy's wages.[12] Extra horses were needed to cover long shifts and handlers had to be paid too. In addition, tunnels need to be made large enough to allow the animals to work. In 1828 Ness had seven ponies working in one of its pits, each pony costing ten shillings (50p) per week to keep; this was twice what a fourteen-year old boy was paid.[13] The animals used underground were kept there permanently and were usually stabled in the driest part of the works.[14] Rats and mice were a common problem that went with keeping the ponies: their bedding and feed attracted the rodents.

Rails made of cast iron were slowly introduced in Britain in the final decade or so of the eighteenth century. Sometimes these took the form of plate-ways where waggons with flangeless iron wheels ran on L-shaped iron rails which were said to be more efficient than the earlier waggon ways.[15] Horses could pull ten or more large corves along such rails but they were not adopted at all collieries.[16] The 1796 letting offer for Ness Colliery indicated it had 'rail roads' although it is not clear if these were below ground as well as above.[17]

It was common for more than one form of underground haulage to operate at the same time within mines.[18] Ness Colliery correspondence in the late 1820s refers to several types of transport being in use, as well as cranes to transfer corves between them. For example, a record from 1827 states:

Length of putting in [No. 1 Pit working the 7-feet seam]

	yds.
Rail road from shaft to crane	1460
Tram way from crane to face of working	100
Total distance of putting	1560

Six Horses are now employed leading the
present quantity of coals to the shaft.[19]

It seems that the 'tram way' in the quotation was used in the sloping tunnels through the seams to take the hewn coal up or down the relatively short distance to the long rail roads which led back to the shaft. The term refers to the hauling of either sledges or wheeled containers on planking – the term 'tram' could be used for either.[20] Upslope haulage could have been assisted by cranes.

Horses were the preferred form of power where long distance haulage was involved. Those working the Seven-Foot seam were walking 8 miles (12.9 km) per day over four return journeys pulling their baskets along the rail road. They hauled four baskets at a time, carrying 1,920 lbs (871 kg) coal on each journey.[21] Horses could also use their power to haul up slopes.[22]

At the two other pits in use at Ness in around 1827, labourers, not horses, were being used for haulage.[23] There was a 500-yard (457-metre) 'Rollway' [sic] in the Two-Foot seam, the seam being too small for animals to work.[24] It was recommended in 1829 that the Stanleys cease 'Waggoning [the coal] by labourers' there; to reduce costs it was proposed to hoist the coals via an underground shaft (a 'staple') to where the horses were already using the more efficient rail roads.[25] In the Five-Foot seam it was said that costs could also be saved by improving the waggon road to make it suitable for use by ponies, not just labourers.[26]

The transport systems in the Two-foot or Five-Foot seams do not appear to have been using iron rails in 1827 but there may have been later enlargement of the railway system as George Mortimer, writing in 1847, stated that Ness Colliery had railways (plural) extending under the Dee, 'upon which carriages with the coal are drawn by ponies',[27] while '20 tons of wrought iron rails' were offered for sale when the colliery closed.[28]

The Cottinghams' works also extended a considerable distance under the estuary and they would have faced similar problems to those at Ness Colliery. Much less information is available about the Little Neston mine but it was later claimed that the main level extended over 1,000 yards (914 metres), although no plans show any evidence of this.[29] Haulage by men and boys as well as by horses or ponies was presumably used there but no reference to any particular methods has yet been found.

The Underground Navigations

While development of wheeled transport at Ness largely appears to have mirrored what was going on elsewhere in British coal mining, one very exceptional approach – albeit a low-tech one – was taken to the problems of long-distance underground haulage. In 1790, Ness Colliery's owners initiated an extraordinary solution by establishing two underground canals or 'navigations'.[30] Using these, coal could be carried on boats from distant coalfaces to the shafts which led to the pithead. The use of navigations took advantage of what was normally an enemy of the mine-owner – water – with the level of the water in the canals having to be carefully controlled through pumping and other means. Both navigations started at pits near Denhall Quay which was built at about the same time under the stewardship of the new principal proprietor of Ness Colliery, Sir Thomas Stanley Massey. The fact that the owners of Ness Colliery saw the need for such an unusual arrangement at Ness underlines the challenging position the colliery was facing – it was becoming increasingly time-consuming to bring coal to the shafts, and this problem could only get worse as working ventured further under the estuary.

The canals were wholly underground, unconnected in any way to the surface other than via the shafts, making Ness one of the very few locations in the country to have operated such an arrangement. There were a small number of 'navigable levels' recorded at collieries in other parts of the country around this period, but almost all were connected one way or another with the evolving surface canal system or acted as a drain with an associated outflow point.[31]

One of the few exceptions was the country's largest underground canal system at Worsley Colliery, Lancashire. Work was started on these canals in 1759 by the Duke of Bridgewater and, when complete, 46 miles (74 km) of waterway ran underground.[32] The system consisted of four tiers of canal and, while most were linked directly or indirectly to the Bridgewater Canal which ran on the surface, the Lower Canal Levels were self-contained, for the first few decades at least.[33]

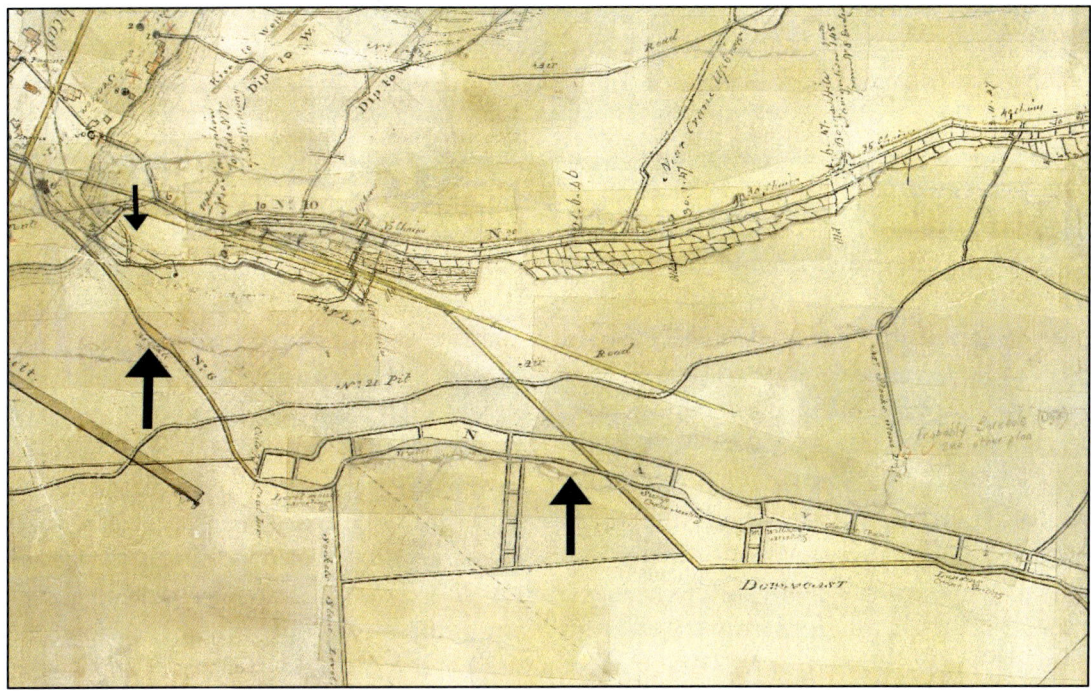

Figure 5.2: Plan showing part of No. 6 Pit Navigation. The canal starts underground near Denhall Quay (small arrow, top) and initially passes through rock (lower left arrow); it then forms the lower of two parallel tunnels (right arrow) cut through the coal. There are short, wider sections for passing places. Source: Coal Authority, 14923/4, with kind permission.

Worsley was a popular tourist attraction and may have been the model for Ness's canals but there was also a navigable level, accessible from the surface, just across the Dee Estuary from Ness in the mineral workings at the Holywell Level Lead Mine at Holywell (Flintshire).[34] This would have been well known in Neston. Local figures were investors in the Welsh mine and, from 1788, it was also a tourist attraction – it even had a cavern provided with tables and chairs where visitors could have a picnic.[35] Thus, it may well have been visited by Sir Thomas Stanley Massey.

As for the depth of the Neston canals, George Mortimer, writing in 1847, stated that one was at a depth of '60 yards' (55 metres), the other at '94 yards' (86 metres). Both appear to have served the extensive Seven-Foot seam, the difference in depth being accounted for by the downward slope of the seam towards the north-west. Mortimer added that the canals ran for 'more than a mile' under the Dee.[36] This distance is borne out by plans of the workings where the extent of the more northerly canal – 'No. 6 Pit navigation' – is about 2,120 yards (1,939 metres) including bends.[37]

The first 330 yards (302 metres) of the canal was cut through bare rock, not coal – an expensive undertaking (Figure 5.2).[38] Where the coal started, two parallel tunnels were cut through the rock about 22 yards (20 metres) apart. They were each cut horizontally, heading through the sloping seam of coal with the navigation downslope of the dry tunnel. Every 100 yards (91 metres) or so, a short cross-tunnel linked the canal to the parallel working. These points also had passing places for boats and a crane was situated there to transfer the loaded corves on to the boats. The boats were 'each carrying four baskets, containing four hundredweight each [basket]' (218 kg).[39] The boats may have been 'starvationers' of the type used at Worsley – so-named because of the prominent ribs which gave strength to their structure (Figure 5.3). However, assuming Mortimer's measurements are correct, each of the long, narrow boats carried only around one-tenth of the load of one of the Worsley vessels; this would have avoided the need for large tunnels and kept construction costs down.[40] Four or five boats were attached together and were then propelled by a boatman lying on his back pushing – or 'legging' – against the roof of the tunnel.[41]

No. 6 Pit navigation was the subject of the trespass case brought by Thomas Cottingham senior against Sir Thomas Stanley in 1821.[42] The canal was accessible from Ness Colliery as well as from the new Little Neston Colliery and Cottingham alleged Stanley's men used it illegally. Even after the trial, it seems that Ness Colliery was willing to use it, as it formed part of Cottingham's damages claim in the 1822 case too.[43] One of Stanley's defences was that the canal was not in Cottingham's land. Uncertainty over the line of the township boundary, coupled with the difficulty of underground surveying, is illustrated in two plans, one of which shows the canal as fully within the boundary of Ness, the other showing it running into Little Neston.[44] The courts, though, had little doubt about the matter, finding in Cottingham's favour each time. There was no question about the location of the other canal, from Pit No. 10: this was wholly within the boundary of Ness township and was about 1,980 yards (1,813 metres) long (Figure 5.4).[45]

It seems unlikely that Sir Thomas Stanley's men continued to use the more northerly canal after 1822. He had already found himself in court twice for doing so; it would not have been worth risking a third damages claim.[46] Instead it probably became a key target for Stanley's deliberate flooding of Cottingham's works. In any event, the main disadvantage of the legging method was that it was very slow, running at no more than one mile

Figure 5.3: A 'starvationer' boat. Photographed here in about 1980, it is now on display at the National Waterways Museum, Ellesmere Port. It came from Worsley Colliery. A similar type is likely to have been used at Ness Colliery. Picture credit: Ken Howarth.

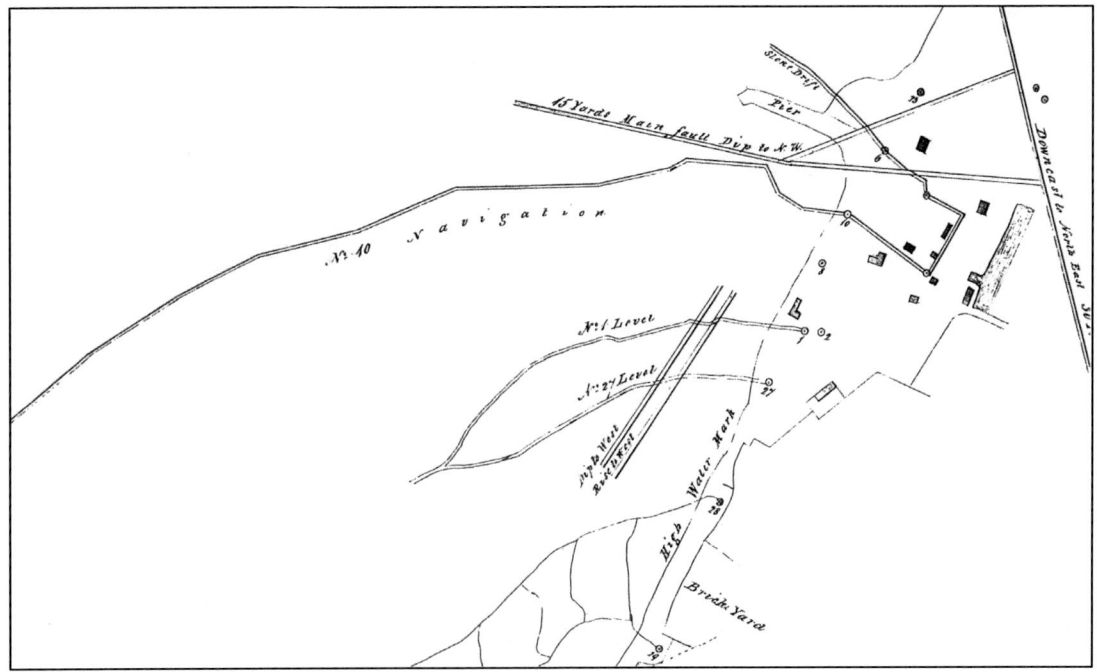

Figure 5.4: Detail from a colliery plan showing the line of 'No. 10 Navigation', *c*.1826, after its abandonment. To assist reader orientation, Denhall Quay is top right, jutting left into the estuary and marked 'Pier'. Source: NEIMME/Wat/35/14.

per hour. For this reason the more southerly No. 10 Navigation was abandoned in about 1824 in favour of the horse-drawn waggon ways.[47] Two years later there was talk of reopening this canal. Some preliminary pumping work was done but nothing further came of the idea, with the 'rail road' continuing to be used instead.[48]

Mechanisation in Winding

Winding had always been fundamental to mining operations – men, materials and, as mining developed, horses needed to descend into the mine. Coal needed to be brought up, as well as the returning men. Winding could also provide a solution to the perennial problem of water in mines, removing it in single or multiple buckets as mentioned previously.

From the 1780s steam engines were able to do the job of winding but, before then, various mechanical methods were used in mines, the main one being the horse gin. The gin, or 'whimsey', was a large but simple rotary machine powered by one or more horses walking in a circle (Figure 5.5, overleaf). This wound or unwound a rope encircling a large wooden drum, causing the rope and whatever was attached to it to ascend or descend the shaft as required. A gin would have been in use at Ness Colliery

Figure 5.5. A horse gin. One or more gins was used at Ness Colliery from its opening until at least 1829. Henry Davies, *Coal Mining: A Reader* (Cardiff: Educational Publishing Co., 1912), p. 22.

from its earliest days. Thomas Boydell illustrated one there in 1772 (Figure 4.2), the only depiction of such a device this author has seen on a contemporary map.[49] The presence of a whimsey next to Pit No. 6 was recalled by men giving statements for the 1821 court case; they said it needed a diameter of about 15 yards (13.7m) in order to operate.[50]

Horse gins had limitations. In its best years Ness Colliery may have been raising 71 tons (77 tonnes) or more of coal per day, requiring at least 353 four-hundredweight (217 kg) basket-loads.[51] This would have stretched the capacity of a single shaft as winding using gins was slow. To give one example of a gin's lifting capacity, at a pit in South Wales twelve horses working in relays were required in order to raise 80 tons of coal from 300 feet (87 tonnes from 91 metres) every twenty-four hours.[52] As well as coal, operations to raise or lower the colliers, mining equipment and, occasionally, boats and horses would have put additional pressure on the use of shafts at Ness. The various needs for winding would be a further explanation for the large number of shafts at the colliery.

Horse gins could be found underground at Ness as well as on the surface. They would operate in a staple – a shaft between underground tunnels – and could be supervised cheaply by a boy.[53] They had the additional benefit of providing a means of roof support (Figure 5.6).[54] Other methods of lifting could be used at mines. There is one account which describes a bucket engine at Ness (different to the type described on page 65).[55] This used a barrel, filled with water channelled to the pithead via the canal from the reservoir. The weight of the water in the barrel made it descend a shaft, raising a basket of coals in a nearby shaft as a counterweight. Communication between the shafts was usually via a rope, using pre-agreed signals. The water used was presumably then pumped from the mine.

Figure 5.6: An underground horse gin for winding, also providing roof support. Source: *Report of the parliamentary Children's Employment Commission, BPP* [1842c], p. 160. With kind permission of IUP.

Iron blocks containing heavy sheaves of brass could also be used as counterweights for lifting and were used when the colliery's engine was under repair.[56] These substantial metal items presented an opportunity for theft. In 1828 two illiterate local men (neither of whom were colliers) were accused of stealing two blocks of sheaves – weighing four or five hundredweight in total.[57] The items, valued at £4, were taken from Ness Colliery's engine house and offered for sale to a brazier, Francis Massey, at his shop in Chester. In a comical twist, it was reported that Massey at first denied to a policeman that he had bought the metal from the men. But when a witness reported that he had seen the material in Massey's shop, Massey told the policeman he had 'forgotten' he had bought these enormously heavy and bulky items from the men within the previous few days; furthermore, somehow the deal in which he had paid them 30 shillings (£1.50) had not been entered in his transaction book! It was decided not to bring charges against Massey, a member of the Corporation of Chester, but the thieves were found guilty at Chester Assizes and sentenced to seven years' transportation to Australia.[58]

The Engine to raise Water by Fire

Figure 5.7: An early Newcomen atmospheric engine. The engine is shown within a cut-away engine house. A fire, lower left, heats water in the hemispherical boiler above. Steam is drawn into the cylinder above the boiler, where it condenses and creates a partial vacuum. The change in air pressure moves a piston in the cylinder which, in turn, shifts the heavy wooden beam, top. Rods descend from the right-hand end of the beam to pump water from the base of the mine shaft. Source: *The Universal Magazine*, September 1747.

The Coming of Steam Engines

The use of coal-powered steam engines was to revolutionise the process of winding in British mines. However, they were first devised and used as a solution for pumping water. The first steam engine was patented by Thomas Savery in 1698.[59] Known as his 'pump' it was described as using 'an engine to raise water by fire'; steam engines were often subse-quently known as 'fire engines'. The technology was developed further by Thomas Newcomen whose creations were termed 'atmospheric engines' as the greatest pressure used in their operation was near to atmospheric pressure (Figure 5.7). A key driving force for these early engines was the need to drain mines and one of Newcomen's engines is believed to have first been installed in a coal mine in 1712. There were continuous improvements in size and pumping capacity over the following decades so that, by the time Ness Colliery was opened, the Newcomen engine was established technology, and had already been in use in the coal mines on the other side of the Dee Estuary since 1714.[60] The engines were 'considerably cheaper per gallon of water raised than the old method of horse-gins' and, at collieries, could use readily-available fuel. It seems likely that Ness Colliery had a steam engine when it opened in 1759 given the need to compete effectively against the Welsh mines and the capital available from the wealthy early investors in the business. It certainly had one or more within four years of opening. Elizabeth Edwards, the wife of one of the colliers, was found guilty of stealing a large lump of coal, weighing about 25 lbs (11 kg), from the engine house there in March, 1763.[61] Two months earlier, Ralph Pearson, who was getting married in Neston, was recorded in the parish register as being an 'engineer' – a term which could be applied to both a constructor and an operator of engines.[62] Pearson's new wife was from Flint and it is possible that he had previously been contracted to build or operate one of the several engines in the Flintshire coal and lead mines.[63] He does not appear in Neston parish registers again that decade but he is referred to in the 1769–70 Ness Colliery accounts in which he is listed as a creditor, owed a small amount of salary.[64] These accounts also refer to the employment of 'Edward Smith engine tenter' (i.e. the engine minder) and indicate that the valuation made of the colliery was exclusive of 'engines'. Smith was still described as an 'engineer' from Ness when he was buried on Christmas Day in 1783.[65]

It is worth mentioning here that James Brindley, the great Staffordshire engineer, visited Ness Colliery in early 1761 and 1762. His engineering interests were diverse and, while he would no doubt have taken an interest in any engine the colliery had, the evidence suggests his visit was more probably connected with surveying for a canal, discussed on page 148.

The presence of an atmospheric steam engine at Ness no later than 1763 makes it the first such engine in the west of Cheshire – the next would not be installed until 1785, in Chester.[66] It seems likely that only the mine at Norbury, near Poynton on the easternmost fringe of the Cheshire Plain, had an earlier engine in the county.[67] Locals drawn to view the extraordinary new contraption at Ness must have been awe-struck as it clanked and heaved, shifting a great horizontal timber arm in its specially constructed engine house. Cartographic evidence for the building comes in Thomas Boydell's map, surveyed in 1770–1 which shows two structures at 'Denna Coal works' (Figure 4.2 on p. 52).[68] One has a chimney from which emanates clear puffs of smoke. The Denna buildings are larger than those shown elsewhere on the map, and no others have smoke coming from them, so this presumably depicts the engine house (Figure 5.8).

It seems that the probable builder of the engine at Norbury came to work at Ness for a while. John Serjeant was described as an 'engineer' at Norbury in 1755 and nine years later was responsible for selling its existing steam engine which was to be replaced.[69] The engine and the pit where he worked were named after him – 'Sargants Old Engine Pit' [sic].[70] He fell out of favour at Norbury in 1768 and at some point afterwards came to Ness, perhaps as part of the major renewal activities after Richard Richardson died. He may have built an engine at Ness: as mentioned above, there was apparently more than one engine at the colliery by 1770 and he was certainly capable of building one, as he erected a 'fire engin' [sic] near Wrexham within the next five

Figure 5.8: A surviving eighteenth-century engine house in North Wales. This was erected by famed industrialist John Wilkinson for his coal mine at Penrhos (Wrexham). Ness Colliery would have had a very similar building.

years.[71] He doesn't seem to have been a very pleasant character. At Norbury, he was described as a 'Rascail' [*sic*] who wrote a 'villainous letter', and in 1775 an advertisement was placed in a Chester newspaper warning tradesmen against trusting him with money he was supposed to be collecting on behalf of his former Wrexham employer.[72]

More detailed evidence of engine use at Ness comes in the surviving accounts of 1776–7.[73] Their first entry each quarter related to 'Engine slack consumed'. Slack – small pieces of coal – was a useful fuel. It was readily available on site either from poor quality seams or as a by-product of mining for larger lumps of coal and was a low-value commodity to use up.[74] The accounts show that in 1777 Ness was consuming just under seven tons (7.6 tonnes) of slack per day. Average fuel consumption in steam engines at the time was about 30 lbs (13.7 kg) per horsepower per hour so, assuming twelve hours' pumping per day, the level of slack consumption would suggest about 46 horsepower was being delivered.[75] Typical engine sizes in Ness's early days were 20–32 horsepower so a plausible conclusion is that Ness had two engines operating each day.[76]

Newcomen engines solved the problems of pumping but their reciprocal action was not suited to the rotary motion required for winding hewn coal up shafts – hence

Figure 5.9: 'A Pithead near an Estuary' (undated) by John Laporte (1769–1831). A scene from a typical rural colliery around 1800, with a horse gin to the right of the engine house. Source: The Sir Arthur Elton Collection, The Ironbridge Gorge Museum Trust. With kind permission.

the need for horse gins which operated alongside the pumping engines (Figure 5.9). However, horses were expensive to buy, maintain and handle and several were needed to cover shift working. Where British mines were shallow – 30 yards (27 metres) or so – horses provided a practical solution but as mines reached greater depths the difficulties also increased.[77] Developments in steam power would lead to an alternative approach.

From the 1760s significant improvements were made to the early Newcomen engines by James Watt, later in partnership with Matthew Boulton. First, he introduced a separate condensing cylinder which dramatically improved atmospheric engines' efficiency and, thus, substantially reduced their coal consumption; secondly, from the 1780s, he (as well as other engineers) was able to make engines capable of rotary action, suitable for winding.[78] There was immediate interest in this new type of engine and 130 were in use for winding in British collieries by the end of the century.[79] The owners of Ness Colliery were clearly interested in being amongst these users. In February 1786 Joshua Small, acting for the mine's owners, wrote to Boulton and Watt at their Soho works in Birmingham, saying:

The proprietors of this Colliery, have been inform'd you have contrived and erected fire engines for raising coals at any depths up to the Pitts upon the Banks. They wish to know the Expences of erecting one upon a Pitt of eighty or ninety yards deep, to bring up their Baskets of Coals weighing from three & a half to four hundred weight each, of clear coals and with what expedition.[80]

Small also enquired where any of Boulton and Watt's new engines had already been installed so that they could be viewed in action – something Boulton and Watt were keen to encourage.[81] Ness Colliery's proprietors were clearly unfamiliar with this new technology for Small wrote a second letter the following month.[82] It reads:

[The Proprietors] desire to know what kind of gin you intend for winding the coals, whether by a Horizontal wheel somewhat resembling a common Gin, or a Vertical Truck or Barrel to turn over the top of the Pitt with a Chain and a shallow Pitt to balance the difference in the weight of the Ropes going down the Pitt, whether you chuse to have more Pitts than one, with the distance between them, and to be informed in particular of the Diameter of the Ground which will contain the Pitts, Engine Gin etc.

Small went on to reveal the difficulties of the position where the colliery was sited.

The reason for being so particular about the space of Ground necessary for the above purposes, is, that they are intended to be fixed where the Tide of the Sea rises to the perpendicular height of 15 feet, and that they may know what distance of Ground to take in to secure them from the violence of the Waves which in stormy weather are very boisterous.

Today, tides still occasionally cover some of the land once used by the collieries and their workings.[83]

He adds a 'P.S.':

Can the Basket of Coals when brought to its particular height, be instantly stop'd and the motion inverted for resting it upon the bank, or top of the Pitt and what time it will require [?].

Sadly, Boulton and Watt's replies do not appear to have survived. There is no indication, though, that the colliery acquired one of their engines. The proprietors may have turned to one of the many other potential suppliers who soon became available.[84] One likely source of parts is John Wilkinson whose famed ironworks at Bersham, near Wrexham, supplied collieries in Flintshire.[85]

Little further information on engine use is available for some time although it appears a large new boiler was built in about 1796.[86] The letting advertisements of the colliery in that year and 1812 both mentioned an unspecified number of steam engines as part of their offer but, in 1813, it is known that Ness Colliery had three engines.[87] The split between use for pumping and winding is not known but it is worth commenting that Ness Colliery was extraordinary in using steam-powered pumping engines in three ways: most obviously to enable tunnels and shafts to be negotiated, and seams to be worked, without their becoming waterlogged. Secondly, they would have been used to assist in regulating water levels in the underground navigations while they were in use. The third application was to use the pumps *offensively*, enabling deliberate flooding of the neighbouring Little Neston Colliery in the 1820s, as described in Chapter 2.

George Stephenson and the Cabry Family

Correspondence between 1819 and 1825 sheds interesting light on the people operating the engines at Ness. Four letters survive which show that Joseph Cabry, the progenitor of a renowned family of railway engineers, worked at the mine.[88] Of particular interest is the fact that this correspondence is from George Stephenson, the renowned engineer (Figure 5.10). When the correspondence started, Stephenson was already well known for inventing a safety lamp for mines, and was supervising various mine-engine operations in the North East, as well as experimenting with locomotive designs.[89] Durham-born Cabry had worked with Stephenson at Killingworth Colliery, near Newcastle, and they had become good friends. Cabry had come to Ness in 1819 with his eldest son, Thomas, aged eighteen. Stephenson's son, Robert, added a chatty note to Thomas in one of the letters – clearly they were good friends. The Cabrys had come to install a new winding engine, apparently at the instigation of Robert Johnson, a mine-owner in Northumberland and a coal viewer for Sir Thomas Stanley.[90] Stanley drew heavily on expertise from the North East, the pre-eminent area of coal output in the UK. He had previously engaged Killingworth-based mining engineer Nicholas Wood; John Henderson who probably served his apprenticeship under Johnson's father and then managed several North East collieries; and mining engineer Thomas Storey who was a colleague of George Stephenson and later worked on the pioneering Stockton and Darlington Railway.[91] Later, Stanley would use the services of another North East viewer, John Watson.[92]

The first letter from Stephenson, in December 1819, refers to young Thomas Cabry having been unwell, and implies that Sir Thomas Stanley was penalising him financially for it:

> I have talked a good deal to Mr Johnson about Thomas Wages [*sic*]. I hope Sir Thomas will not Behave so mean as you mention in your letter ...

Figure 5.10: George Stephenson (1838). Source: National Portrait Gallery, with permission.

> I think if you can possibly finish the Lifting Engine it will be better – I hope they will lay meanness aside – I will provide work for you and Thomas when you return – I intend setting you both with my brother Robert to assist in erecting the large engine at Tyne Main Colliery.

It is odd that the Stanleys were choosing to install a new engine at a time when the colliery was not doing well financially and producing relatively low volumes of coal. Perhaps it was a replacement for one that had broken.

Cabry was still at Ness in March 1820, and the colliery management were still being awkward. Stephenson wrote:

> I think you have had your troubles with the Cheshire Gents. I am astonished to hear of Mr Ashhurst [the colliery manager at the time] finding fault with you for accompanying [mining engineer] Mr Storey down the pit.

The letter goes on to suggest that Stephenson was hoping to visit Ness that month.

By the time of the third surviving letter, in June 1824, Stephenson was writing from Liverpool, working on the proposed Liverpool–Manchester railway.[93] Joseph Cabry was still tending the engines at Ness. His second son, also Joseph, had joined him in about 1821 but the eldest son, Thomas, had left, with Stephenson promising to help in advancing his career.[94]

Joseph senior must have appreciated his life in the Neston area for, despite an earnest invitation from Stephenson in 1825 for him to return to the North East, contained in the fourth surviving letter, he continued to work locally for many years.[95] His circumstances, though, are unclear. In 1827, only one Cabry is recorded as working at Ness Colliery.[96] The following year it was Joseph Cabry junior who was called to give the required engineer's evidence for the prosecution in the court case involving the theft of brass sheaves from Ness Colliery, and he stated that he lived opposite the engine house there.[97] Meanwhile, Cabry senior had moved to Little Neston.[98] It seems possible, then, that as there seems to have been some rapprochement between the Stanleys and the Cottinghams in the mid-1820s, Cabry senior was now working for Thomas Cottingham, not least to help him erect a new engine. The father still had access to Ness Colliery's engine house, though, suggesting he was still assisting there or, at least, was a trusted visitor.[99]

The Cabrys were keen to please Sir Thomas Stanley – even if it meant getting up to no good. In 1822 Joseph (probably the father) had complied with Stanley's instructions to help sabotage the neighbouring colliery.[100] The following year both father and son participated in an act of thuggery, making uninhabitable the house of one of Stanley's tenants who had dared to go to work for Thomas Cottingham.[101] In a more peaceable example, in 1831 Cabry senior was invited to oppose proposed parliamentary reforms – the major political issue of the day – but said he would not do so without first consulting Sir Thomas Stanley, who Cabry seems to have classed as a 'friend'.[102] Stanley was said to be a 'jealous advocate' of the measures which were championed by the Whig party which he supported.

The sixty-nine-year-old Joseph Cabry senior was still an engineer in 1841, living at Little Neston Colliery, but when his wife died six years later he returned to the North East.[103] Meanwhile, from 1829, Cabry junior had become the occupier of the property which had been the Wheat Sheaf [sic] public house in Ness and it appears to have continued to be run as a pub.[104] At that time, it was near the top of the lane leading to the colliery (New Houses Lane today) and would no doubt have been popular with the colliers.[105] It may have been run by his wife, Anne, as Cabry junior was still described as an engineer, like his father, in the 1841 census.[106] His willingness to remain at the colliery, despite the many other engineering jobs available in Britain at the time, suggests he enjoyed his work and it is surely no coincidence that four of his children were given the same Christian names as the Stanley brothers and their wives.[107] He remained an engineer, maybe part-time, until at least 1851 and, after the mine closed, described himself as a 'publican and farming 50 acres, employing two men and a boy'.[108]

Ness Colliery's link with the Stephenson family continued after the surviving correspondence ended, because an order for equipment – mostly metal buckets, bucket attachments and rods, presumably for use in a rotary-motion engine for pumping water – is recorded as being placed with Robert Stephenson & Co. in May 1827.[109] The order was worth £27, a very small amount considering that the goods had to be sent across the country. Other orders in the same accounts were for thousands of pounds, and Ness's order was one of only two sent to collieries outside the North East in the period 1823–9. Later that year James Gregory at Ness received a cask of grease from 'Mr Stephenson'.[110] These minor orders indicate the continued close relationship between Ness Colliery and the Stephensons; it is perhaps also indicative of the Stephenson company's desperation to get *any* business as it was struggling badly at that time.[111]

While no specific record has yet been found of George Stephenson visiting Ness Colliery it is highly likely that he did so, even if only on the surface. He had plenty of opportunity and motivation to do so. He hoped to visit his friend Joseph Cabry in 1820 and Cabry was still in his thoughts when Stephenson was staying at nearby Chester in the autumn of 1824.[112] From that year Stephenson also spent much time working in Liverpool, on the new Liverpool–Manchester Railway. The first proposal for a railway on the Wirral, in 1830, was surveyed by Stephenson and passed through the colliery area.[113] This did not proceed but his later proposal for a railway on the Mersey side of the Wirral, was carried out. We know he visited Sir Thomas Stanley's other major industrial concern on the Wirral, Storeton Quarry (and may have been instrumental in the establishment of a tramway from the quarry to Bromborough Pool, on the Mersey).[114] The tone of his correspondence to Cabry indicates he knew Sir Thomas

Stanley, and those who surrounded him, well. They appear also to have socialised together; for example, newspapers in 1834 reported that Stephenson attended a formal dinner in Liverpool with Sir Thomas and his brother Charles.[115] It seems likely that Stanley used his closeness to Stephenson to encourage the engineer's 1830 railway plan to go past his two Wirral industrial sites at Ness and Storeton.

In evidence to an 1835 parliamentary Select Committee on Accidents in Mines, Stephenson confirmed he had visited a colliery belonging to Sir Thomas Stanley, although the exchange was confusing.[116] He was asked 'Have you visited the mines in North Wales in Flintshire, on the banks of the Dee?'; he responded, 'On the south side I have, belonging to Sir Thomas Stanley'. This could, arguably, refer to the mine at Pentrobin in Flintshire, on which Stanley had granted a lease and which was towards the southern end of the county.[117] However, unlike Ness Colliery, it was some distance from the banks of the Dee and, for the reasons given in the previous paragraph, it seems more likely that Stanley would have invited Stephenson to visit the Ness works in which the baronet had a direct interest. Nicholas Wood, Stephenson's close associate, gave evidence to the same committee and said, in answer to a question asking if he had visited 'any coal works in North Wales', 'I have been in a mine at Ness, Sir Thomas Stanley's'.[118] It is possible the questioner was confused about Ness's location, it being an extension of the Flintshire Coalfield which was the topic of the line of enquiry. It should also be borne in mind that Wood and, maybe, Stephenson were speaking many years after their visits.

Later Engine Use

There are many references to engine use in surviving sources from Ness Colliery's final thirty years, although detail is often lacking. By the mid to late 1820s there appears to have been just two engines in use at the colliery. One was the 'sawney', a Staffordshire term applied to the winding gear and associated engine.[119] For example, in 1828 it was mentioned that Joseph Cabry junior used to 'clean the sawney engine at No. 1 pit' on Sundays.[120] It was not able to do all the lifting work, though, as a horse gin was still also in use in 1829.[121]

A little more detail survives regarding the pumping engine: one document from 1826 mentions that a 56-inch (1,422 mm) engine cylinder was in use 'working at present 2 setts of pumps 60 yards in length – one 13" in diameter, the other 12" which draw the water from the 7' feet seam.'[122] This was the only pumping engine in use at the time and the water from the seam above had to be channelled to it in order to be extracted.[123] It was often reported around this time that the pumping engine was in operation twelve hours per day, seven days per week with a man constantly superintending it.[124] The colliery bought quantities of flannel, probably to be soaked in tar and used in the repair or maintenance of engine parts.[125]

Local maps and colliery plans from the 1820s and '30s often included reference to the engines or the 'engine pit' – the shaft served by the pumping engine.[126] Three men tended the colliery's engines – the Cabrys and a Stephen Sharp who was the 'fire man', shovelling coal to fuel the hungry machines.[127]

The costs of an engine and associated equipment and buildings were considerable. John Watson, the experienced colliery viewer, estimated the costs of the unsuccessful operation in Little Neston by Cottingham and Leacroft to find coal in 1829 as follows:

	£
Engine House & other buildings	200
Engine	480
Pumps etc.	40
Spears etc.	40
Sinking 15 yards of walling	40
Sinking two large pits	80
Labouring work and boring	40
Sundries	80
	1,000[128]

The engine involved was small at 24-horsepower but would nevertheless have represented a substantial investment for struggling Cottingham. Other sources suggested the costs involved were even higher.[129] At least the engine was reusable – after the failure, Cottingham intended to move it to a new site.[130] A later report said that drainage at the mine was achieved fully effectively by using 'a 9-inch pump, working at very moderate speed' – presumably powered by the same 24-horsepower engine.[131]

With the relatively low production levels at Ness Colliery from the 1820s there was no need to increase engine capacity nor, probably, money to do so should it have been needed. It therefore seems likely that the two engines at the colliery in the 1820s survived until its demise. When the colliery was put up for sale in 1855, the machinery included (Figure 2.3):

> One atmospheric pumping engine, 60 horse power, with two boilers … [and] one condensing winding engine, 8 horse power, 16½ inch cylinder.[132]

A Newcomen-type atmospheric engine had lasted until the colliery's closure; the machines were noted for their reliability, durability and ease of maintenance.[133] Another advantage was that they burned the low-value, or unsaleable, slack – of which the Neston collieries apparently had plenty. This was one of the main reasons these engines often remained in use so long after the more efficient Watt engines were available.[134] However they were old technology by the time Ness Colliery closed and it was said later that the colliery's machinery had been 'very imperfect'.[135]

*

The themes of innovation and adaptation, identified in Chapter 2, have been further evidenced in Chapters 4 and 5 on operational aspects of the mine. These document, amongst other things, the introduction of the atmospheric engine, the rotary-action engine, underground railways and secondary working of pillars (the Lancashire System). Perhaps most extraordinary was the introduction of subterranean canals, of which there were very few in British collieries. Apart from these canals, the advancements mirrored what was happening elsewhere in the mining industry and were no doubt driven by necessity – the need to operate efficiently just to compete. However, the developments show that the proprietors embraced the spirit of the age, being willing to adopt new ideas and to invest to drive the business forward. Even so, the account of the business in Chapter 2 shows that, after the first thirty years or so, this quest for innovation appears to have meant only that Ness Colliery managed to keep its head more or less above water for several decades, rather than delivering significant growth or financial returns.

CHAPTER 6

THE COLLIERIES' EMPLOYEES AND
THEIR WORKING CONDITIONS

The previous two chapters reviewed the methods and equipment used to work the coal seams at the Neston collieries. But what of the workers who gave their labour, their sweat, their health, and sometimes their lives to obtain the coal? This chapter discusses the colliers who worked at Neston – how many there were and their origins, roles and working conditions. Many tragic accidents occurred at the mines, some involving children – these accidents and the general use of child labour are covered here, as is the evidence for the use of females at the mine. Several contemporary local sources are available to explore these topics and these have been supplemented with information from the coalfields of North Wales and Lancashire which were geographically close and, as we will see, were the place of origin for many of the Neston colliers.

The Early Colliers

The decision to exploit the newly-found coal seams at Neston from 1759 meant that there was a need to recruit men with the necessary skills. There is no evidence for any recent mining in the area before then, so who were these men? A valuable starting point to answer this question is Neston's parish registers for the period which generally recorded occupations of those involved in baptisms and sometimes in the case of marriages and burials too. A small number of other documents have also yielded useful information. Collectively, these give the names of 159 different men known to have worked at Ness Colliery in the first twenty years after it opened – all men termed 'collier' or with other direct links to the works such as its engineers (Appendix III).[1] For various reasons parish registers are not a perfect record of particular groups, most obviously because they exclude those not involved with any baptisms, marriages or burials.[2] As a result, the figure of 159 inevitably understates the true figure. Nevertheless, the available information tells us much about the early recruits.

It is clear, first of all, that very few of the colliers were local. This author has been able to identify only two individuals recorded as working as a collier in the first ten years of Ness Colliery's operation who had been living in the area previously – John Burrows, previously a mariner and labourer (and who died in a colliery accident in 1769), and Christopher Evans who lived at Denhall.[3] However, it is possible that some Neston men were taken on to do unskilled and low-paid labouring jobs at the colliery such as shovelling coal on the surface. Men doing such jobs were often just termed 'labourer' in records making them potentially indistinguishable to researchers from labourers working in agriculture or other physical roles away from the mines.[4] In any event, it is clear that the skilled work was almost wholly done at Ness by incomers. These were largely drawn from the two closest areas of mine working to Ness – North Wales and south-west Lancashire. A few may also have come from Staffordshire.

It is striking how many of the early colliers' names were of Welsh origin. Sixty of the 159 men (38%) had surnames which were amongst the most common in Wales such as Jones, Williams, Davies and Thomas.[5] Several others had less common Welsh names.[6] North Wales is only about 3 miles (5 km) from Ness and had a well-established coal mining industry in both Flintshire and, a little further south, in Denbighshire.[7] Furthermore, Richard Richardson, co-founder of Ness Colliery and who was active in its early management, had strong industrial connections with North Wales. It would be surprising, therefore, if the area was not the first place where experienced colliers were sought.

It is possible to identify some specific incomers to Ness from Flintshire; two of these instances relate to men who originally hailed from north Staffordshire. As mentioned in Chapter 4, the manager of Ness Colliery in 1763, Richard Kelsall, was born in the mining parish of Audley, later moving to Flintshire. And the maternal uncle of the future Emma, Lady Hamilton, William Kidd, is believed to have come as a child from the north Staffordshire mining village of Madeley to Hawarden in Flintshire by 1743.[8] The coal needs of the developing Buckley potteries brought many Staffordshire men to Flintshire – management as well as workers who were often 'hackneyed in vicious habits'.[9] The Hawarden area would become 'in the main, a Staffordshire colony'.[10]

Other early workers at Ness from Flintshire included Peter Robinson, an apprentice basketmaker from Bagillt; Ellis Kendrick (a relatively common North Wales surname), who became an engineer at Ness Colliery, and was almost certainly born in the mining village of Hope; and John Parry, collier, who married a woman at Hawarden in 1768 before moving to Neston.[11] Another collier from Hawarden, Charles Duckworth, married Sarah Thornton of Little Neston at Neston parish church in January 1763.[12] Their first child was baptised at Hawarden later that year, suggesting that Duckworth's association with Neston was not permanent.[13] It is possible that he, and four 'miners' mentioned in the parish registers around this time – all with Welsh places of residence or surnames – were pit sinkers, temporarily brought in to dig shafts. The Welsh origins of many of Neston's colliers would go on to be recognised in the naming of the Harp public house (also called the Welch Harp [sic]) adjacent to the main colliery site, although the earliest surviving record of this name is in 1822.[14]

The other main area of recruitment appears to have been from south-west Lancashire, notably the colliery district of Prescot. Prescot's mines were undergoing upheaval due to the 1757 opening of the Sankey Brook Navigation which affected the epicentre of mining activities in southern Lancashire.[15] In the year Ness Colliery opened, 1759, sales were said to be 'very slack' at Prescot Hall Colliery, and 'a monstrous quantity' of coal had piled up.[16] These Lancashire mines would largely recover within a few years but for a while there must have been insecurity in the workforce, if not layoffs; this would have made the men there a useful target for Ness's recruitment activities.

From today's perspective, the most notable Lancashire recruit was Henry Lyon, from Whiston, a township within Prescot parish, who almost certainly became the blacksmith at Ness Colliery. He was to be father of the future British belle, Emma Hamilton, and is discussed more fully below. There was also collier William Swift who married a Little Neston woman the following March, describing his residence as Prescot.[17] They went on to have six children in Neston. It is not always possible to connect unequivocally other names between parishes, but there are several other likely candidates including William Bramhall, John Manchester, Henry Skeath, George Marsh and Thomas Ashbury.[18] The first two both apparently died in accidents at Ness, in 1761 and 1762 respectively. Marsh soon returned to Prescot;[19] another man, Hugh Maddison, moved there in about 1784 after leaving his job at Ness.[20] The connection with the Prescot area continued for decades. To give just three of many possible later examples: coal miners Joseph Jones and Thomas Jones – perhaps brothers – moved between Whiston and Neston around 1840, having children in both places;[21] and James Pie, described as a collier from Whiston, fathered an illegitimate daughter who was baptised at Neston in 1842.[22] Men came from other parts of Lancashire too – for example, Richard Mug moved from Eccles bringing his pregnant wife with him.[23]

Some men may have come directly to Ness from south Staffordshire. The surname 'Gellico' (later 'Jellico' and several variants) first appears in the Neston parish registers in late 1758, when a labourer from Ness had his daughter baptised.[24] This was just as preparations would have been being made for the opening of the new colliery and, by 1762, the man was recorded as a 'collier'.[25] The surname was most often found in south Staffordshire at that time, on the western edge of a coalfield, and suggests one or more people moved from there at the start of Ness Colliery's life.[26]

There is little indication that men came from the North East, despite this being the largest area of British coal production at the time.[27] The writer, Thomas Pennant, indicated that in the mid-eighteenth century the colliery at Bagillt (Flintshire) had 'engaged a number of colliers from Newcastle'.[28] It seems more likely that this referred to Newcastle upon Tyne in the North East rather than Newcastle-under-Lyme in Staffordshire as the latter had no pits within the then borough boundary.[29] However, only one uncertain connection has been found between Ness Colliery and the northern pits in the twenty years after it opened – Ralph Pearson, the engineer mentioned in Chapter 5.[30]

It would have been interesting to observe the dynamics between the workers. The incoming men from Wales, Lancashire and Staffordshire were probably having to work alongside Neston men hired to do the non-specialist labouring jobs. There would

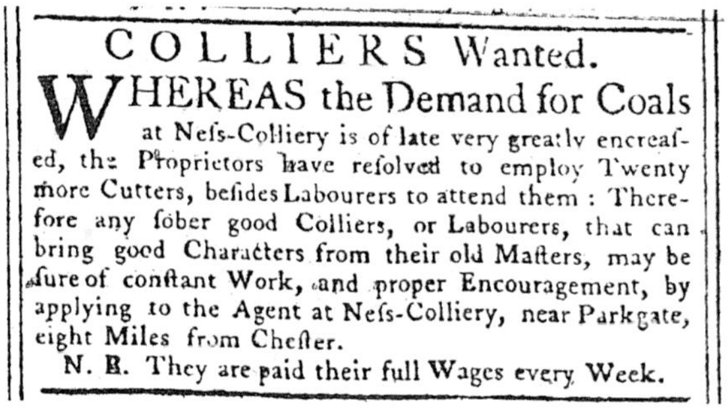

COLLIERS Wanted.

WHEREAS the Demand for Coals
    at Nefs-Colliery is of late very greatly encreaf-
ed, the Proprietors have refolved to employ Twenty
more Cutters, befides Labourers to attend them : Therefore any fober good Colliers, or Labourers, that can
bring good Characters from their old Mafters, may be
fure of conftant Work, and proper Encouragement, by
applying to the Agent at Nefs-Colliery, near Parkgate,
eight Miles from Chefter.
    N. B. They are paid their full Wages every Week.

Figure 6.1: Recruitment advertisement for Ness Colliery workers, 1767. Source: *Adams's Weekly Courant*, 21 July.

have been a mix of cultures, terminology and even language; such mixtures did not always work well, with an inherent suspicion amongst some colliers of 'strangers'.[31]

As alluded to above, disruption in south Lancashire may have prompted men to seek new opportunities elsewhere. An early recruitment advertisement may give a clue to what attracted men from there and elsewhere to come to work specifically at Ness Colliery. A notice in Chester's newspaper in 1767 sought '20 more cutters besides labourers to attend them' to work at Ness. They had to be 'sober, good' men, who brought 'good Characters [i.e. testimonials] from their old Masters'. In return they were promised 'constant work … [and] … proper encouragement' and would be 'paid their full wages every week' (Figure 6.1).[32] While the former phrases were not uncommon in a recruitment advertisement, the reference to 'full wages' was unusual, and suggests that no deductions would be made for the overhead costs of their work such as supporting labour.[33] This could have been a significant incentive and is discussed more fully below when considering pay. By 1770 medical care was also available for workers at the colliery; this was highly innovative and there is an indication it may have been offered from the colliery's earliest days.[34]

A similar recruitment advertisement to the 1767 one was placed in a Chester newspaper in 1778, although without the promise of 'full wages'.[35] This author has found no similar advertisements in Lancashire newspapers. Their placement suggests that it was mainly Welshmen who were now being targeted – the early Chester newspapers covered North Wales too – and indicates that Ness Colliery's management expected that word of mouth would ensure the news spread from readers to the colliers who were largely illiterate.[36]

The Size of the Workforce

Very limited information is available on the number of men working at the Neston collieries, especially in its early days. As mentioned above, 159 names are known from the first twenty years. However, not all would have been working there at the same time – some died, others moved on. Conversely, for reasons previously stated, the available sources do not list all the men working at the mines.

However, a surviving ten-month record of £3,209 for 'workmen's wages' at Ness in 1769–70, plus £121 for 'salaries', enables an estimate of worker numbers to be made based on a comparison with the number of men employed at nearby Hawarden at that time.[37] While some assumptions must be made, the figures suggest that about 172 men were working at Ness around this time including a small number of salaried officials.[38] Even if this number is only an estimate, there can be no doubt that there was a substantial workforce there, almost certainly unparalleled anywhere in west Cheshire which had no large-scale industry at this time.[39]

The estimated workforce number is supported by comparison with productivity data from other collieries. Annual output at Ness was approximately 20,549 tons (22,378 tonnes) at the time, suggesting average output of about 119 tons (130 tonnes) per man.[40] This appears to be reasonably consistent with production at Hawarden in the same period and at some other British collieries.[41] However, mines in the richly endowed Lancashire coalfield appear to have had considerably higher productivity (and, quite possibly therefore, profitability).[42]

It is not until 1827 that specific information on worker numbers at Ness Colliery becomes available, discussed more fully later in this chapter (no overall information is available at any time for Little Neston Colliery). However, the appearance of references to colliery workers in Neston parish church's baptism records helps give an indication of the relative numbers of men involved both before and after that year. The data is shown in Figure 6.2 (overleaf) and the pattern largely helps to confirm what we know of the collieries' fortunes.

Baptism numbers soared in the 1760s and '70s as young, fertile men came to the colliery bringing their wives or finding local women to marry. The numbers slip in the 1780s, just as Ness Colliery's fortunes had apparently also previously peaked.[43] This falling off in baptism numbers does not necessarily mean there were fewer employees though; it could well mean that, as the colliery was no longer expanding, few, if any, men were being recruited and the older workers were no longer having children. There is then largely a downward trend in baptisms reaching a low in the early 1820s, despite Thomas Cottingham's Little Neston Colliery having opened by then. It was said of Ness Colliery at this time that 'The company found themselves with a great number of aged men.'[44]

During the 1820s there was a measure of recovery at Ness Colliery and the 1827 letter gives the first certain figure for employee numbers there – sixty-nine. Thereafter, new working methods were introduced with a concomitant rise in recruitment. This was reflected in a doubling over ten years in the number of Ness households depending on non-agricultural work and in increased baptism numbers.[45] In 1837 the collieries were said to be in 'full employ and thriving'.[46] Despite these positive indicators the graph shows a decline in baptisms of colliers' children recorded in the parish church register after the 1830s. In fact, the register had been under-recording such children for some time as parents turned to other religions or dismissed baptism altogether. These trends are discussed further in Chapter 12.

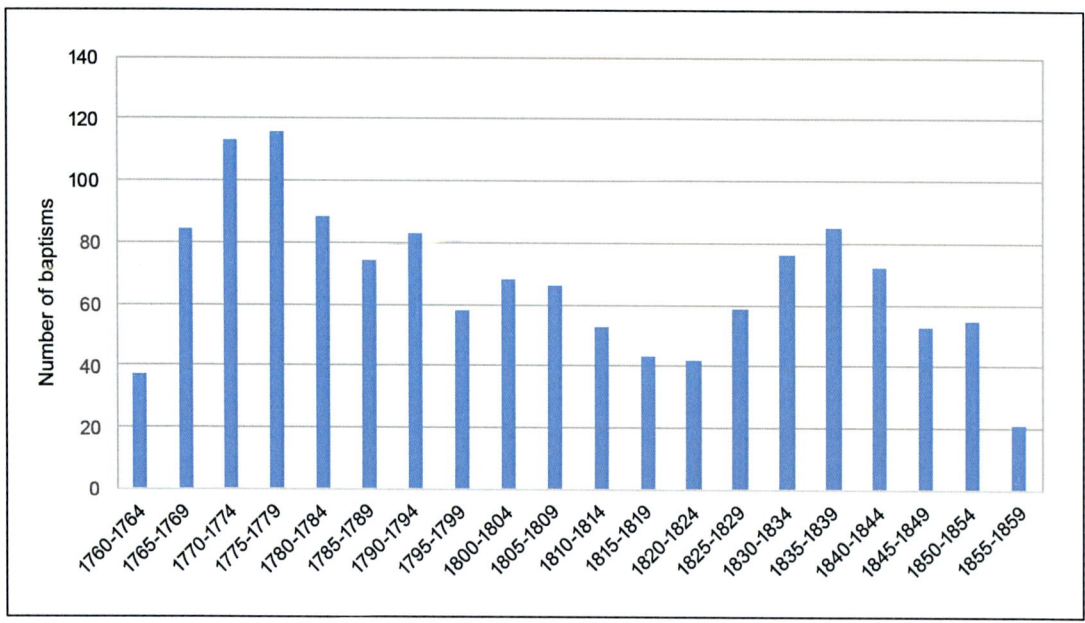

Figure 6.2: Baptisms of children of colliery workers over five-year periods, 1760–1859, as recorded in the Neston parish registers. Only entries where men were recorded as 'collier', 'coal miner' or similar occupations have been included. Full details: *nestoncollieries.org*

Ninety-eight 'colliers' and 'coal miners' were employed in Ness and Little Neston according to the 1841 census (the occupational terms seem to have been used interchangeably by this time).[47] Sixteen others were almost certainly directly or indirectly connected with the mines. These included colliery agents (managers), engineers, brickmakers, a basketmaker and at least one of the five locally-recorded blacksmiths; some of the many local labourers probably worked there too.[48] Ten years later the number of local coal miners (or similar terms) had grown to 106 despite the closure of Little Neston Colliery; again, there were several other workers with specialist skills (and just a single labourer).[49] The manager at Ness, James Gregory claimed to be employing 120 men.[50] Table 6.1 summarises the available data about worker numbers.

The census data enables us to revisit the topic of the origins of the miners at Neston. Whereas in the early days there were many incomers, by the census years the mining community was largely composed of local men and boys. In 1841, when respondents simply had to say whether or not they were born in Cheshire, only ten of the colliers indicated they were born outside the county. More detail is available from 1851 when fifteen of the 106 colliers and miners (14.2%) indicated origins elsewhere – almost all from Lancashire or North Wales (Table 6.2 overleaf).

Table 6.1: Known or approximate numbers of workers at the Neston collieries on all dates for which information is available, 1759–1855. The figure for 1841 includes men at both Ness Colliery and Little Neston Colliery. Sources: see text.

Year	Number of Colliery Workers
1770	Est. 172
1827	69 + manager/accountant
1841	c.114 (+ labourers?)
1851	120 + manager/accountant

Table 6.2: Place of birth of Neston colliers and coal miners, 1851. Source: census – Little Neston, Great Neston and Ness (nil in adjacent Burton and Puddington).

Birthplace	Number of Colliers/Miners
Neston area	91
North Wales	10
Lancashire	4
Other (Ireland)	1

Censuses and other sources also reveal that there was considerable migration from the Neston collieries to those of south Lancashire, and sometimes back again. Movement from Neston during the lean times of the 1810s and 1820s may well have been one reason, but the trend continued strongly in later decades too. To give just a few of many possible examples: collier Peter Thomas and his wife had six children in Neston in the years before and after 1800 but moved to Tarbock, becoming infirm there by 1838.[51] Similarly, Daniel Briscoe moved to Lancashire with his wife and children some time after 1814 and was eventually deported to Clatterbridge workhouse on the Wirral when he was aged and infirm.[52] Neston-born coal miner-turned-labourer John Standish was another man who went to Tarbock, evidenced by the 1851 census there; five other miners shared the household, all born at Ness.[53] In one very sad case, collier Robert Anglesey and his family moved to Wigan from Ness shortly before the 1851 census. He was injured in a roof fall there in March 1852, returned to work but died of burns following an explosion eight months later.[54]

At least 127 people (including seven females), who had lived or been born in Neston, were recorded as working at Lancashire mines in the 1851 and/or 1861 censuses (Figure 6.3, overleaf). Eleven other former Neston colliers were recorded in the censuses for Staffordshire, but many of those who ended up in Lancashire had worked in Staffordshire first, particularly at Golden Hill a few miles north of Stoke-on-Trent.

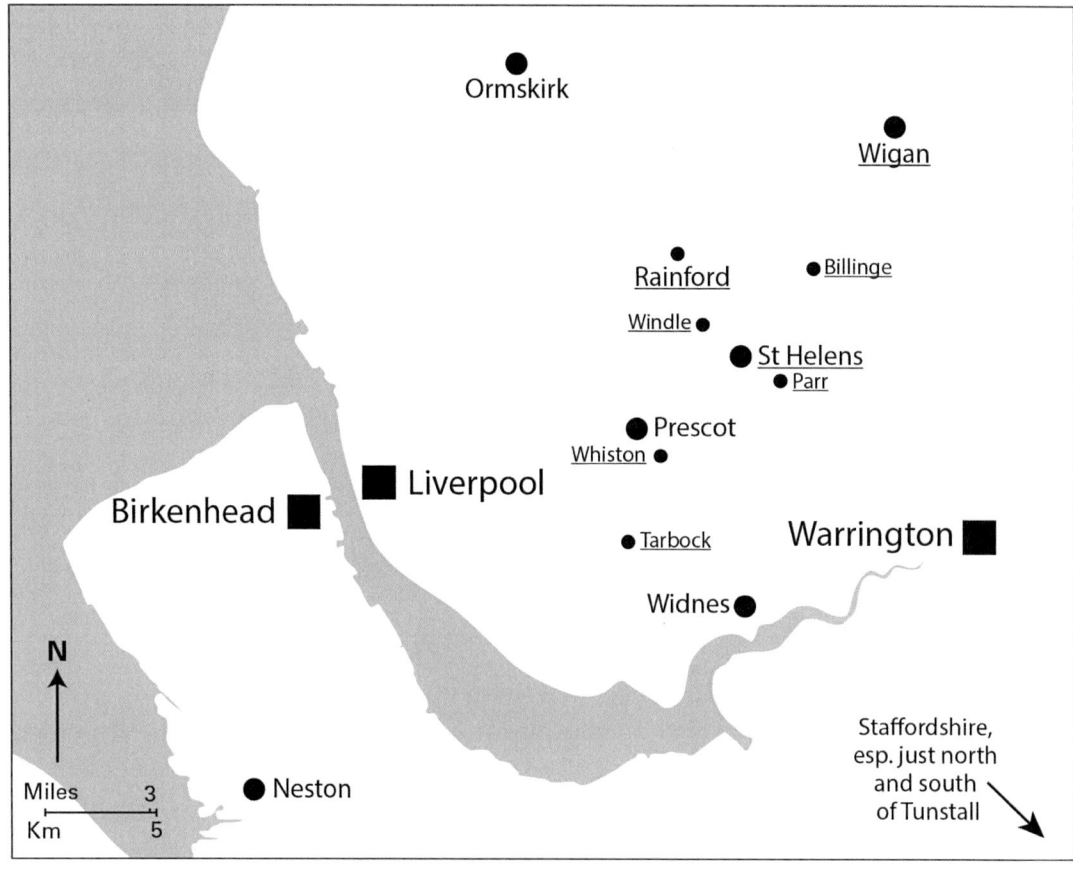

Figure 6.3: Principal locations of ex-Neston colliers 1840s to 1860s. The main such locations are underlined. Sources: 1851 and 1861 censuses. Full details at *nestoncollieries.org*

Curiously, despite the Neston collieries' long connections with Wales, it has been possible to trace few men who left Neston to go to the Flintshire mines.[55] The issue of mobility is looked at further in Chapter 12.

The Workers' Roles

The workforce at the colliery was divided between those who worked above ground and those who worked below it. Underground workers were split into teams, each responsible for a specific seam which was worked from a particular pit (i.e. shaft). At the surface, or 'brow', men were responsible for receiving the coal, separating out the dust and slack, and piling it all 'on the bank'. There were also a number of specialist roles performed on the surface – carpenter, engineers and so on. The surface workers represented around one quarter of the workforce at Ness.[56] Over all these men was the chief officer of the mine, usually termed the 'agent', who was often also the business's accountant or 'auditor'.[57]

There are few surviving references to individual roles within the colliery workforce during the eighteenth century although there are mentions of an 'Underground Agent', who was in charge of activities within the mine workings.[58] Considerably more information is available in 1827. The source is a letter from James Gregory, Ness Colliery's manager and accountant, sent to Robert Johnson, a senior adviser to the

Figure 6.4: A typical nineteenth-century underground scene. Cutters using hand tools attack the coal, to be taken away on a rail waggon. The pony is tended by a boy. Source: *The Graphic*, 28 January 1871, p. 77.

Stanleys on their mining business. The letter was written following Sir Thomas Stanley's demand to cut costs to deliver more profits.[59] It includes references to wages, working hours, production levels and child labour. The letter also sets out the reductions in pay that Gregory had been forced to introduce but makes clear his dismay at Stanley's requirements. Parts of the letter, detailing arrangements over the fortnight ending 3 October, are set out in Table 6.3 (overleaf) which lists sixty-nine working men. This was at a time when the colliery was producing around 7,000–9,000 tons (7,623–9,801 tonnes) of coal per year.[60]

The letter mentions a number of different underground roles. These include the twelve *cutters*, also often termed hewers – the men at the coalface cutting it from the seam. This was very physical work as, during the period of operation of the Neston mines, only hand tools were available such as picks, chisels, hammers and shovels (Figure 6.4). Explosives were widely available at this time (Stanley used them to sabotage Cottingham's mine) but they carried the risk of causing an uncontrolled explosion of easily-ignited gases, and also damaged the coal, leaving more of the low-value small pieces.[61] The use of gunpowder was therefore probably largely restricted to driving stone drifts (blasting through rock, not coal) and, perhaps, to sinking shafts.[62]

Cutters (or hewers) have been described as 'the aristocracy of the colliery labour force', usually having high wages and status (Figure 6.4).[63] Their work was not only physically hard and dangerous but they also needed the mental ability to assess how

Table 6.3: Workers' wages over two weeks at Ness Colliery, to 3 October 1827. The information is extracted from a long letter from James Gregory at Ness Colliery written in relation to Sir Thomas Stanley's demands to cut pay costs. A total of sixty-nine workers are mentioned specifically; there are also at least two individuals termed 'pensioners'. The stated total quantity of coal raised (293 tons) does not equate to the stated quantities from the individual pits. This is probably because of differences in the definition of a 'ton', the collier's ton weighing considerably more than the ton used for sales (see Glossary). Source: NEIMME/Wat/3/71/9, 19 November 1827.

	£	s.	d.
No. 1 Pit			
Williams & Littlemore, Eccles & D. Williams, Ashbrook and Bartley, Swift and Minshull, W. Williams & Bryan, Maylor and Standish	16	2	3
[12 men, working in pairs as cutters. Each pair worked 11 days in the fortnight, averaging 14 yards of tunnelling and 17 tons of coal produced. Paid by the ton *and* the yard]			
Reduced by 2*d*. per yard.			
3 waggoners and a drawer earned that fortnight.	6	6	5
Reduced 1*d*. per ton			
2 Ostlers & drivers who work from 2 o'clock in the morning to 6 at night and 4 hours on Sunday have together.	2	14	–
Reduced 1/– per fortnight			
Another driver 15 years old allowed 1/– per day, 2 of 14 years allowed 10*d*. per day, and four about 11 years old 8*d*. per day from which no reduction can be made. The hanger-on, 19 years old, has 18*d*. a day [all – no reductions]	3	16	8
Two load men have 2/– a day each one and one 20*d*. A door tenter at 6*d*. [no reductions]	3	5	6
No. 10 Pit			
4 cutters and three waggoners in 12 days earned for 24 tons of coal. Paid by the yard and the ton [no reductions]	9	12	8
No. 28 Pit			
Ten cutters and 8 waggoners raised 58 tons coals and a lot of [fire]clay; and a door tenter. Reduced 2*d*. per ton.	21	–	2
[On the Surface]			
Jones, Thomas, Cabry, Webster the blacksmith & Gin driver 'whose wages cannot be reduced'	10	16	0
Others reduced 1/– per fortnight:			
Engine tenter – hours from 4 o'clock in the morning to 8 at night	1	8	–
Sawney man – from 2 o'clock to 6 – and attend Ostlers on Sunday	1	8	–
Basket maker 'common hours'	1	10	–
No. 1 [pit] Browman from 2 o'clock to 6 and occasionally on Sunday	1	8	–
No. 28 [pit] Browman from 6 o'clock to 6 and occasionally on Sunday	1	4	–
No. 10 [pit] Browman from 6 o'clock to 6 but not on Sunday	1	2	–
Driver of a one horse cart to supply engine and Limekiln	1	1	–

Assistant Browman – jobber and Slack Riddler	1	1	–
Assistant weigher – to attend asses, 16/–; and pensioners 20/–	1	16	–
Cost of raising 293 tons of coal is	**85**	**11**	**8**

best to extract coal from a seam and how to minimise risks from flooding or gas. Little is known about worker numbers at Little Neston Colliery but they had at least six cutters in 1822.[64]

Cutters were supported by a team of people to ensure the coal was carried to the bottom of the shaft. In Ness's Pit Nos. 10 and 28 the cutters outnumbered the assistants. However, in Pit No. 1, where the coal needed to be carried over a mile there were eighteen support workers for the twelve cutters. Such a ratio was not customary in the industry.[65] The assistants at Ness included *waggoners* who used their own strength to haul the waggons on the rail roads and *drivers*, mostly listed as children, who drove ponies which pulled the waggons, walking up to 8 miles (12.9 km) per day.[66] There is also reference here to a *drawer* and the distinction with waggoners suggests he may have been dragging wheel-less sleds over planking, rather than wheeled waggons on rails (Figure 6.5; also 5.1). This was another job often undertaken by children and was still practised widely in Lancashire at the time.[67] The *load men* were probably responsible for filling the corves with the freshly hewn coal – they were termed 'fillers' in some collieries.[68] On the way to the shaft, *door tenters* (often known as trappers) waited at ventilation doors, ready to open or close them as necessary – a simple job which was not physically demanding and was therefore often undertaken by very young children. At the shaft, the *hanger-on* attached each loaded corf to a rope for raising to the surface.[69] *Ostlers* tended the ponies which were kept permanently in the underground stables.

Figure 6.5: Drawing a corf of coal uphill on a wheel-less sled, 1842. Source: *Report of the parliamentary Children's Employment Commission, BPP* [1842a], p. 84. With kind permission of IUP.

The conditions underground would have been appalling. Limited ventilation led to poor air quality, constant dust and, often, 'oppressive' heat away from the main passages.[70] Cold water percolating through the rock was also a constant problem, dripping from ceilings and down walls, pooling on the floor. In addition, there were claustrophobic conditions in tunnels which would have been no larger than were needed to do the job in order to keep costs down. Men probably just lay on their sides to hack away at the thin seams such as the Two-Foot (see Figure 6.10 on p. 111).[71] There was also, of course, a complete lack of natural light. A mining inspector described the scene at a coal face in north Staffordshire in 1842: the sight of several near-naked men 'in their peculiar posture' and dimly lit by a handful of candles gave them a 'hideous and Satanic appearance and prompted me to ask myself – Can these be human creatures?'. He described the heat and odour as 'intolerable'.[72]

Responsibility for bringing the coal to the surface rested with the *sawney man*, operating the winding engine. The loaded corves were received by the *browmen*, one assigned to each pit. The *assistant browman's* duties included acting as slack riddler to separate out the small coal from the larger, more valuable, lumps. Often, those on the surface were simply termed 'labourers'. It was common for men to move between working as a collier and a labourer during their working lives – one fifth of the Neston colliers did so although, as indicated earlier, it is not possible to be certain what kind of labouring work they were doing.[73]

Joseph Cabry junior, discussed in the previous chapter, was the *engineer* with overall responsibility for the colliery's engines; the *engine tenter*, or 'fire man', Stephen Sharp, kept the pumping engine fed with fuel during its twelve-hours-per-day, seven-days-per-week operation.[74] There was also a *cart driver* and two men with unspecified roles, Jones and Thomas, one of whom perhaps had a supervisory role while the other was, maybe, a carpenter – an important specialist role missing from the list. Two other roles are mentioned in the letter, *basketmaker* and *blacksmith*.

Basket making was a long-standing job at the colliery. A total of 90,000 basket rods were waiting to be woven into corves at the colliery in 1770.[75] This was skilled work and a nine-year old child, Peter Robinson, was apprenticed to the colliery basket maker in 1773 to learn the 'art or mystery of a Coal Basket-maker' (see page 214 for a copy of his apprenticeship indenture).[76] A basket maker was still employed at the colliery in 1853.[77]

The duties of the colliery blacksmith would have included farriery services for the horses and ponies, as well as supplying, repairing and maintaining metalwork for the business such as hooks, chains, hinges and tools. Thirteen blacksmiths are recorded at Ness or Denhall during the period under review, three of whom were specifically mentioned as being at Ness Colliery.[78]

An intriguing name in local records in the years after Ness Colliery opened was Henry Lyon, father to the future Emma, Lady Hamilton, the mistress of Lord Nelson (Figure 6.6). She was born at Ness and her father was very probably the colliery blacksmith until his premature death in 1765. Lyon first appears in the Neston parish registers on 11 June 1764 when he married Mary Kidd. She was born at Hawarden and had travelled to Ness, perhaps to help with the birth of a child to another Mary, wife of her brother William who was a collier at Ness.[79] No occupation was stated for Lyon in the register and he and his wife each made their mark, 'X', suggesting they were illiterate (William Kidd, however, was able to sign his name elsewhere very neatly).[80] The following year, on 12 May, 'Emy', the later Emma Hamilton, was baptised, with Lyon recorded as a 'Smith' of Ness.[81] However, within weeks he was dead, the burial register entry for 12 June 1765 again indicating that he had been a 'Smith', this time of Denhall. The cause of his death is unknown; there is no record of a coroner's inquest and no spike in burials in the parish register at that time which might have suggested a major colliery accident or disease epidemic. Henry's occupation and stated places of residence (especially Denhall, a name much associated with the early colliery), does strongly suggest that he was indeed a smith at the colliery. However, there was another blacksmith recorded at 'Ness', and nearby, between 1759 and 1771, Thomas Longley (also 'Langley'); he was apparently providing services to the colliery in 1769–70, being one of its creditors.[82]

Figure 6.6: Emma Hart, *c.*1785 later Emma, Lady Hamilton. She adopted the name Hart between 1782 and her marriage to Sir William Hamilton in 1791. Portrait by George Romney. Source: National Portrait Gallery, with permission.

Emma later indicated that her father came from Lancashire, where the Lyon surname is relatively common.[83] A Henry Lyon was born to a George and Alice Lyon on 17 June 1740 at the colliery village of Whiston, near Prescot.[84] George was recorded as a blacksmith in the parish register of St Mary the Virgin, Prescot on ten occasions from the date of Henry's birth until 1758. Several connections between Prescot and Ness Colliery were discussed earlier in this chapter and it seems that Henry Lyon was one of the men to make the move to Ness. When he married he was almost twenty-four – old enough to have picked up valuable blacksmith's skills and to take twenty-one-year old Mary as his bride. George Lyon was to have another son at Whiston, Thomas, born in 1747;[85] a collier of this name was living in Ness by 1770 and, as a blacksmith, baptised his son with the name Henry at Neston in 1773, having married there the previous year (with an 'X' as his mark).[86] He was specifically recorded as the colliery blacksmith in 1787 and remained in the area until he died in 1826.[87]

Emma Hamilton was to become celebrated for her vivacity, beauty and social standing, and internationally famous for her relationship with Nelson – extraordinary accomplishments for one born into such humble, inauspicious surroundings. Yet, after Nelson's death, she fell into massive debt and died penniless in a flat in Calais in 1815.[88] It is a great irony that, despite her years of living at the apex of society, she was to die in conditions closer to those that surrounded her at birth in Ness.

Turning to the other smiths at Ness, the 1827 letter from James Gregory shows that the smith he mentions had a secondary role as gin driver. Another record suggests he was also occasionally contracted out by the colliery to do work elsewhere.[89] As well as the blacksmiths at Ness, six blacksmiths or farriers were recorded in Little Neston during the life of its colliery.[90] These included Thomas Forshall who lived at one of the oldest properties in the area, close to the pits, and which, in the twentieth century, was called Colliery Farm.[91]

On occasions, one gets a glimpse of career progression at the colliery. For example, in 1761 to 1767 John Richard(s) was a 'collier' at Ness in the parish register.[92] By 1769 he had risen to 'Steward', overseeing men at the colliery.[93] But he appears to have somehow fallen from grace; within a year he was 'late agent' (i.e. ex-manager), owing the colliery the substantial sum of £96, subsequently appearing in the parish register as just a labourer in Neston.[94]

Pay and Working Conditions

The issue of pay at British collieries can be a complex one. There were many different ways of determining pay depending on the type of job, working conditions and whether the workers were adults or children; sometimes teams of men were paid collectively so that individual rates cannot be determined. Geological conditions could vary greatly at a single colliery and, of course, between different collieries, affecting working conditions and productivity. As a result, pay comparisons between locations, or extrapolation of data from one period to another, need to be treated with caution.

However, one record from Hawarden in 1770 suggests that, at that time at least, the payment method was simple: all the workers (except senior officials) were paid a day rate. It seems probable that the practice at Ness, just 6 miles (10 km) away, was similar. The figures for Hawarden are set out in Table 6.4.

The stated lack of pay differential between the cutters and labourers is unexpected. Generally in British collieries the cutters' skills meant that they were the best paid workers (other than salaried management), frequently also working shorter hours than their colleagues.[95] To give two examples of pay from Lancashire, the hewers were the best paid men at Orrell in 1776; and at Worsley the following year 'miners' were paid two shillings (10p) per day and labourers half of this amount.[96]

Hawarden was also unusual, according to the 1770s figures, in apparently paying a simple day rate, although more detailed accounts for following years suggest a slightly more nuanced approach: while many men did get a day rate, sometimes pairs of individuals were paid jointly, at a higher rate.[97] These pairs often consisted of a named man and an unnamed drawer or the named man's son. In any event, it was common elsewhere for cutters to be paid based on piece work, i.e. according to the volume of coal they obtained or by the distance of the drift (a passage through the coal) they cut.[98] More than fifty years later, James Gregory's 1827 letter shows that in at least two seams at Ness the men were rewarded by a combination of these measures (Table 6.3). Thus, for example, the first pair of cutters on the list – Williams and Littlemore – were paid for driving 18 yards (16 metres) of tunnel at 18*d*. (7.5p) per yard as well as for producing 20½ tons (35.7 tonnes) of coal at 18*d*. per ton.[99] This combined approach suggests that the quantity of usable coal in the seam was variable and the men were not being unduly penalised for failing to obtain coal when driving through less productive rock.[100] It was expensive for the colliery to be rewarding men for cutting anything other than coal and, in particular, this must have been a major factor in the lack of profitability of the distant Seven-Foot seam. Unsurprisingly, the poor geological conditions meant that the men appear to have been less productive than cutters at other mines for which comparative information is available.[101]

Other variables might affect the cutters' rate of pay, for example they received higher pay when working conditions were wet.[102] And, when being paid by the yard for cutting drifts, different rates applied for cutting a main drift, which would allow animals and waggons to pass, as opposed to a smaller air drift.[103]

Table 6.4: Daily wages of colliery workers at Hawarden, October 1770. The 194 individuals all apparently worked at Hawarden, although the names of their colliery/collieries was/were not stated. The Hawarden collieries were producing around 20,000 tons (21,780 tonnes) of coal annually at this time, making them of a similar size to Ness Colliery.[104] Source: NEWA, 'The Explanation of the Colliers' Procession at Hawarden Wakes on Monday the first of October 1770' contained within W. Bell Jones's copy of R. R. Rawson's 1941 article (see Bibliography).

Description	Daily Wage	Number of Workers
Cutters	18*d*. (7.5p)	68
Underground labourers	18*d*. (7.5p)	42
Underground stewards (managers)	18*d*. (7.5p)	10
'Engineers, smiths, carpenters, sawyers, basket makers, banksmen and labourers of all denominations above ground'	16*d*. (7p)	42
'Boys. Gin lads, horse drivers and of various employment'	6*d*. (2.5p)	26
'Stewards and accountants of the works'	Not stated	6
Total		**194**

The cutters at Ness worked for eleven days in the fortnight in question and averaged 2s. 5d. (12p) pay per day. As at Hawarden, despite the usual high status of cutters elsewhere, this meant they were not the best paid men at the colliery. The waggoners and drawer in No. 1 Pit earned about 2s. 8d. (13p) per working day, albeit almost certainly working far more hours per week.[105] Even worse for the cutters, they had subsequently had their pay cut by 2d. per yard driven. On this evidence it is unsurprising that Gregory said that two men had left and that trying to recruit new men was 'hopeless'. He went on to make clear his dismay at Stanley's insistence on wage reductions, though his concern was not altruism. He feared he would lose more men, and thus coal production. He commented, '12 months back the wages I have been giving were rejected outright by a regular Turn-out [i.e. a strike] so other men were obtained [in replacement] who did us no good.'

The waggoners and drawers above appear to have been paid by the weight of coals they hauled as Gregory had reduced their pay by 1d. per ton. The '2 Ostlers & drivers' and the 'No. 10 brow man', however, seem to have been paid a day rate, and were less well paid then the cutters;[106] the 'load men' also received a daily amount. Children were an attractive labour source for less physical jobs such as driving, with a very low day rate for the youngest, rising with age.[107] Wages and the proposed reductions for men above ground were expressed per fortnight but may also have been calculated as day rates.

A group rate seems to have applied to the workers in Pit No. 28, which served the Two-Foot seam, as the 1827 letter refers to the cutters and waggoners together being measured and rewarded per ton. Similarly, correspondence two years later mentioned that a group of men were being paid a rate per ton for 'cutting, Waggoning and hanging on … also [keeping] roads in repair'.[108] More generally, labour costs and the value of coal won were calculated separately for each pit so that, after deducting other expenses, including a proportionate allowance for surface costs, the mine-owners could assess the profitability of each one.[109]

James Gregory's 1827 letter makes no reference to any salaries for senior positions. In 1769–70, a 10-month 'Salaries' figure of £121 was stated (about £145 annually) which would have been enough to cover two, possibly three, people – to include a colliery manager, a clerk-cum-book-keeper and, perhaps, the man superintending underground activities.[110] In the early 1800s, the salary of Ness Colliery's manager, William Taylor, was stated to be £75 p.a.[111] The temporary manager, Richard Ashhurst, was paid £50 p.a. during Ness Colliery's poorest years around 1820; a similar annual sum was paid to the accountant a few years later.[112] In the 1827 letter, 'Jones, Thomas, Cabry and Webster' were clearly relatively senior men, averaging about 4s. 6d. (22.5p) per day, around twice what many others received.[113]

It seems that some of the Ness workers feared they would not find alternative work if they left as James Gregory said of the eighteen men in No. 28 Pit, whose pay had been reduced by 2*d*. per ton, that they 'submit quietly altho' they have in fact the most reason to complain'. Others apparently had more bargaining power: the wages of the four senior men 'cannot be reduced'. In addition, the children's already-low wages were not cut. It seems the other reductions went through, however, as in April 1828 it was said that 'the men have handsomely agreed to work for reduced wages across the establishment'.[114] The wage reduction allowed coal prices to be reduced with a consequent rise in sales.

In addition to pecuniary wages many collieries gave men a free, or reduced price, allowance of coal.[115] Two baskets per week were allowed at Orrell Fire Engine Colliery, Lancs., and it seems likely that a similar arrangement operated at the Neston works.[116] Men at Ness were apparently prepared to work just for beer too. Joseph Cabry junior, the colliery engineer, and Stephen Sharp, the 'fire man', spent an hour or so each Sunday morning cleaning one of the boilers, at No. 1 Pit, for which 'they have each a pint of ale allowed for their labour'; there was no mention of money.[117] The coal industry historians, Ashton and Sykes, commented that 'Almost any departure from routine operations was marked by the provision of ale and sometimes of food'.[118] A small bonus went to the colliers in 1805, when Sir Thomas Stanley got married. A gift of 6*d*. was given to 693 'labouring and poor people and their families living on [his] estate and [those] employed at the colliery'.[119]

Wages were often subject to deductions at British collieries.[120] For example, at Orrell in 1771 several deductions were made from the quantity of coal for which the men underground had been credited with producing.[121] These included amounts for the costs of all support staff, including the winders, engineer, basketmaker and auditor, as well as for coal used on the workmen's fire and the candles used underground. However, surviving accounts from the pits at Hawarden in the 1770s suggest that no deductions were being made there for candles, axe sharpening or the transport of men and coal.[122] The early recruitment advertisement for Ness promised 'full wages' and the very limited other sources available on pay at the Neston collieries give no indication of deductions being made. Candles were generally just listed as an expense for the colliery at Ness, both in its early and later years.[123] It seems, then, that a more generous expenses regime applied at collieries around the Dee than in Lancashire (and many other places). However, without knowing more about other factors such as pay rates, rent arrangements and food subsidies it would be wrong to draw conclusions about overall relative benefits between locations.

Some of the working hours set out in the 1827 letter are extraordinary, even by the poor and unregulated standards of early nineteenth-century mines. The ostlers and drivers in Pit No. 1, where horses had to haul long distances, as well as the sawney man at the surface, worked from two a.m. to six p.m. – sixteen hours. Reports on hours at other British collieries are fragmentary but show they could vary significantly by location and over time. Nevertheless, twelve-hour shifts (including meal breaks) were fairly common, with fourteen hours in some places.[124] Ness's sixteen hours was therefore unusually demanding, apparently matched in few places – one was Killingworth (George Stephenson's former place of employment) where, in 1831, pitmen were lobbying for their assistants' working day to be reduced from fifteen or eighteen hours to twelve; they succeeded in their aim.[125] Another man at Ness with very long hours was the 'engine tenter', or 'fire man', Stephen Sharp.[126] His stated hours were four a.m. till eight p.m. – again, a sixteen-hour shift. The engine was in operation twelve hours per day, seven days per week so it seems likely he had some responsibility for running it on Sundays too.[127] As for the shift times referred to in the 1827 letter, nationally a two a.m. start was 'not unknown, and three or four a.m. was usual' to allow miners some daylight at the end of their shift – but even this pleasure would have been denied the early starters at Ness in the winter months.[128]

Turning to the length of the working week, the figures from Hawarden in 1770 suggest that men worked about 261 days that year – an average of just five days per week.[129] The proximity of Ness to Hawarden suggests that working arrangements at the two locations may have been similar at that time. However, the number of days worked at a colliery per week could fluctuate with business need, seasonal factors, a worker's role, and absenteeism and sickness rates so one needs to be careful in reading too much into a single figure.[130]

The number of days worked is clearer in the 1827 letter relating to Ness Colliery which detailed 'an average pay bill'.[131] The cutters are stated as working eleven days in the fortnight. For the rest, the references to Sundays as being non-routine indicates that six-day working was the norm, with several having to do more. Having to work more than six days was not unknown in Britain, although this was atypical; the national pattern was very variable but six days was common, with five-and-a-half the average in larger collieries.[132] It is clear from the foregoing information that some of the workers at Ness – those working sixteen-hour days and four hours or more on a Sunday – were working at least 100 hours per week in total.

Many collieries allowed their workers breaks around Christmas or New Year but it seems no such practice occurred at Ness.[133] Production data early in the colliery's life, in 1776–7, as well as fifty years later, shows no lessening in activity during the festive season.[134] This appears to reflect practice in North Wales where there were no fixed holidays although work usually stopped 'on occasions of public rejoicings' which might have included coronations and victories in war.[135]

Dreadful as working hours were for many workers at Ness, such hours were not exceptional in other industries, and even longer hours were common amongst children working in Lancashire mills.[136] The mining historian Michael Flinn said that 'By the standards of working hours in other industries in the eighteenth and early nineteenth centuries, miners, even when they worked up to twelve hours, enjoyed a comparatively short working day'. However, if the hours in collieries were better than in factories, the conditions were not. A government inspector commented in 1833, after viewing 'the best mine' at Worsley (Lancs.), 'I cannot much err in coming to the conclusion ... that the hardest labour in the worst room in the worst-conducted factory is less hard, less cruel, and less demoralizing [sic] than the labour in the best of coalmines.'[137]

Many contemporary commentators suggested that colliers were better off than those labouring elsewhere. For example, it was said of the men in the pits of North Wales in 1842 that, compared to agricultural and other labourers, 'They had better wages, they live better, their houses are better furnished, and their clothing, if not superior, is at least equal; nor do they work more hours'.[138] This made sense: as another contemporary observer put it, 'Few would undergo the slavery of a coal-pit who could obtain nearly equal wages in more secure and congenial employment'.[139] Unfortunately, little evidence is available to make worthwhile comparisons between colliers' and others' wages at Neston. However, in 1825, local agricultural labourers were typically being paid 1s. 9d. to two shillings (9–10p) which seems little different to most of the colliers two years later.[140] The colliers, though, potentially had regular work and thus continuity of pay whereas agricultural labouring was seasonal; colliers also usually had a free fuel allowance and, sometimes, free or subsidised housing – a topic discussed in Chapter 12.

Industrial Relations

There is very little surviving evidence of miners at Neston combining to lobby for better conditions and none relating to union membership. However, it seems unlikely that local men failed to participate in the trend towards collectivism which was evident in North Wales, Lancashire and beyond in the early nineteenth century. Indeed, as we have seen, there was at least one strike at Ness Colliery – in 1826, perhaps in the same wave of unrest that had seen 'disturbances' amongst Flintshire colliers which led to troops being placed on standby.[141] The men at Neston had long-held connections with the colliers of North Wales and the latter had a track record of being restive.

In the previous century, a system of bonds had been in use in many British coal mines; they were common in Lancashire and it is possible they were in use at Ness too although no evidence has survived for this.[142] The bond was an annual occasion for wage bargaining with a view to establishing a commitment binding the collier to work for the mine-owner for the following twelve months. The security of labour supply worked to both parties' advantage and was especially useful in relation to skilled workers.

The bond system encouraged men to combine to negotiate collectively. However, growing concern over workers' power led to Parliament passing the Combination Acts of 1799 and 1800. These outlawed collective action but men still found ways to combine and there was a riot by colliers in Bagillt, just across the Dee Estuary from Neston, in

1819.[143] There was also unrest in Lancashire mines around this time.[144] The Acts were repealed in 1824 although restrictions remained in place and attempts at more followed. Nevertheless, the repeal led to an increase in collective action by colliers, agitating for higher wages. The manager at Ness Colliery, James Gregory, referred to the industrial action at Ness in 1826 as a 'regular turn-out' of his men (i.e. a strike within the rules).[145] Men who were brought in as replacements 'did us no good'. It may be that these strike-breakers were subject to intimidation and violence as was sometimes the case elsewhere.[146]

The years 1830–1 brought disturbance amongst miners across the nation, and the Flintshire colliers were heavily involved.[147] Sir Stephen Glynne (who socialised with Sir Thomas Stanley) called for the assistance of troops after rioting amongst workers at his Hawarden coal pits in late 1830.[148] The men were members of the newly formed Bagillt Branch of the Friendly Associated Coal Miners Union Society of Lancashire which coordinated successful strike action.[149] The workers returned to work with higher wages in early January 1831 after a stoppage characterised by mysterious fires and intimidation of potential 'blacklegs'.[150] However, further unrest was to follow that year with strikes at Mostyn, Flint, Bagillt and Greenfield, hitting local industries which depended on the coal. In a view quite possibly shared by Sir Thomas Stanley, the Welsh mine-owners were in no doubt about the new 'clubs' which were, they said, 'in the highest degree detrimental to the best interest of the labourer, and opposed to all the best interests of society'.[151] There was further unrest during 1842 to 1844, following years of national economic difficulties;[152] the Hawarden mine-owners alleged that their colliers were averaging earnings of 18s. to 25s. (90p–£1.25) per week at this time but this may have been exaggerated.[153]

The extent to which the Neston collieries participated in all this later industrial unrest is not known. Welsh collectivism was certainly visible locally in 1829 when men from the Mostyn mine came to Parkgate as part of a Mayday celebration 'bearing a flag with the insignia of their calling' – perhaps a precursor to the Union Society's arms?[154] That year the manager at Ness, James Gregory, complained that 'strangers' – workers coming from elsewhere – were sowing seeds of discontent amongst the colliers about their wages or 'working prices'.[155] The following year the Union Society were known to be sending 'missionaries' to North Wales, and maybe Neston too, to recruit miners.[156] It seems unlikely that the Neston collieries did not get caught up in this regional and national disquiet; however, there is a suggestion that, for a while at least, the Neston men did not join the strike which affected Flintshire in 1831.[157] Whatever their direct involvement, Neston men would have indirectly benefited from the increased wages which were the focus of much of the Welshmen's actions, with any significant pay differentials risking encouraging men to defect across the Dee.

Mention was made above of a friendly society. Such societies were formed in many mining communities from the late eighteenth century as a form of insurance in case of accident and illness; they also became a means to try to circumvent the Combination Acts.[158] There is evidence of friendly societies in Neston from the 1790s, the best known being the Neston Female Friendly Society. This was formed in 1814 and continues today but no link has yet been identified between that society and the Neston collieries.[159] It seems likely, though, that the colliers were members of the Ness Friendly Society which had been formed by the 1850s.[160]

Colliery Accidents

No formal reporting on mine-working was required of mine-owners until the 1850s, although any accidental death should have been recorded by coroners and this is one of the principal sources of information in Table 6.5 (on pp. 112–13).[161] A total of twenty-seven certain or almost certain accidental deaths have been identified in the period under review. Newspapers are of limited use when researching this topic during the period in question; only three accidents involving Neston colliers found their way into the local press. Early records of paupers – men or their families receiving financial relief under the Poor Law system – are also an occasional source of explicit or implied information on colliers' accidents.

Gases were one of the main hazards faced by colliers in any mine, notably 'firedamp' and 'chokedamp' ('damp' being a word of German origin for a noxious gas). Firedamp was an easily-ignited methane gas mixture (Figure 6.7, overleaf) whilst chokedamp was high in carbon dioxide and led to unconsciousness and death through suffocation.[162] Such gases are characteristic of the bituminous coal which predominated at the Neston collieries.[163]

One of the ways of dealing with firedamp was to send a 'fireman' down the pit before each shift to deliberately ignite the accumulated gas – a hugely risky practice which was said to have originated at Mostyn Colliery across the Dee from Ness.[164] Despite, or maybe because of, this practice explosions led to dozens of deaths at Mostyn Colliery, and firedamp became closely associated with the Flintshire pits.[165] There can be no doubt that it affected the Neston mines too. Several coroners' inquests into local colliers' deaths were attributed to 'a sulphurous explosion'. One inquest, on William Armstrong's death in 1837, specifically stated that 'foul air' was ignited by his colleague's candle. Armstrong was fatally injured and his colleague severely burnt.[166] The problem was long-standing: four men were 'burnt in the colliery' in an incident in 1773 though none died.[167] Three years later John Berry was less fortunate after also being 'burnt in the colliery', dying soon afterwards in Chester Infirmary.[168] The largest cause of admissions of Ness colliers to Chester Infirmary around this time was burns (Table 12.4 on p. 203). One man, Edward Taylor aged twenty-seven, needed treatment there for burns in 1774, recovered and then died in an explosion three years later (his new baby was baptised a month afterwards).[169] Curiously, Nicholas Wood, the colliery and steam locomotive engineer known to have visited Ness in 1819, indicated to an

Figure 6.7: A nineteenth-century depiction of a firedamp explosion in a coal mine. Source: L. Simonin, *Underground Life; Or Mines and Miners*, trans. H. W. Bristow (London: Chapman and Hall, 1869).

1835 parliamentary committee investigating accidents in mines that there was 'little or no danger' there from inflammable gases.[170] Maybe conditions were more favourable at the time. The engineer George Stephenson, a friend of Wood's, also suggested that firedamp had not been a particular problem when he visited Stanley's unnamed mine, presumed to be Ness.[171] Nevertheless, data compiled a few years later for Parliament showed the mines of Lancashire, Cheshire and North Wales collectively having higher accident rates than almost every other area of Britain and more than double the accident rate from explosions of any area.[172]

Chokedamp seems to have been much less of a problem at Neston than firedamp. There are no explicit mentions of it in records although it may have been the cause of death for James Glaves and Edward Davis who both 'suffocated in the coal pits' in 1790.[173] Alternatively they may have been smothered in a rock fall. The collapse of underground spaces such as tunnels was a common cause of accidents in British mines. William Cottrell was smothered in a roof fall at Ness in 1815 and it was said he left a wife (who was apparently newly pregnant) and nine children.[174] The *Chester Courant*, reporting on the death, said:

The compassion of the whole neighbourhood [of Neston] is most strongly excited by [his family's] truly pitiable situation, and the most laudable exertions are making [*sic*] to procure them some present relief and assistance.[175]

The newspaper set up a collection for the family to which they encouraged the people of Neston, 'so characterised by its prompt benevolence', to contribute.

The limited surviving records of Chester Infirmary in the eighteenth century indicate two fracture cases, as well as bruising or 'sores' to limbs sufficient to warrant medical attention; roof falls are one plausible cause of these incidents too.[176] Wirral Union Poor Law records also indicate colliers being 'disabled' from time to time. The cause is usually unstated but on one occasion an accident at work was mentioned.[177]

Another danger colliers faced was falling into or within shafts. This cause of death is cited in several cases at Ness Colliery, although the exact circumstances are seldom known. There

Figure 6.8: Logo depicting a collier on Ness Colliery stationery, 1788. Source: NLW, Powis MSS, 18650. Reproduced with the kind permission of the Trustees of the Powis Castle Estate.

were probably few if any barriers to prevent trips into pits which were in use, and derelict shafts may well have been left unfenced at Ness, as was the case across the Dee and elsewhere.[178]

In addition, ascending or descending the shafts led to many falls. It was common practice in British mines for men simply to hang on to loops in a rope which was wound up or down and this presumably happened at Ness too.[179] Many accidents occurred in the North Wales pits when the limited safety rules concerning ascents and descents were ignored.[180] It was said that 'Both adults and boys seem thoroughly careless and incautious; and the master and their agents little less so.'[181] Workers might also descend in baskets, sometimes with tragic consequences. In 1838 two deaths occurred at Ness in one incident. The Death Certificates recorded:

Both accidentally killed by factures and convulsion received by them falling to the bottom of a coal shaft, out of a basket in which they were descending to there [*sic*] work in the [coal pit at Ness].

One of those killed was James Lewis, thirty-eight, whose funeral took place at Neston parish church on the same day as his two-month old son was baptised there. The other occupant of the basket was Joseph Taylor who was just ten years old.[182]

Figure 6.9: A collier in Yorkshire, *c*.1813, in similar dress to the figure depicted on Ness Colliery stationery. Behind him is a steam locomotive, used successfully at some mines (though not Neston) from around 1812. Source: George Walker, *The Costume of Yorkshire* (London: 1814).

A similar incident had occurred in 1814 when nine-year-old Thomas Bartley, a collier's son, and Thomas Davies, 44, died when the rope broke which was holding the basket in which they were descending. They fell 84 yards (77 metres) sustaining terrible injuries but, miraculously, a third collier was said to have survived incurring just a broken thigh and bruising.[183]

Despite the risks associated with coal mining the men had little protection. A collier depicted on Ness Colliery's printed sales stationery in 1788 wore basic clothing: shoes rather than boots, and a brimmed hat, not a helmet (Figure 6.8). In addition, he wore a jacket, breeches and gaiters, like colliers elsewhere (Figure 6.9). In some mines, because of heat or discomfort, toiling colliers discarded much of their clothing, offering no protection against abrasions or burns (Figure 6.10).[184]

The 1788 stationery shows the scene lit by a candle which was the principal form of illumination at the time. The fatal explosion at Ness which killed William Armstrong almost fifty years later, mentioned above, was attributed to a candle and suggests things had not really moved on in the intervening years.[185] Safety lamps, which

Figure 6.10: A near-naked cutter works at a thin seam of coal. Source: *Report of the parliamentary Children's Employment Commission, BPP* [1842c], p. 158). With kind permission of IUP.

guarded against the accidental ignition of gases, had been introduced by early 1816 but, if the men of Neston reacted like those of North Wales, there was scepticism and even fear concerning these new-fangled devices.[186] It would not have helped that the men probably had to pay for their own lamps if they wanted them.[187]

The two accidents involving children descending in baskets do not appear to have been the only ones where children were killed at the Ness works. The Burton parish register records that Thomas Coterall [*sic*], buried there in 1769, was the 'son of Thomas Coterall', implying he was a child.[188] Another child, Anne Jones, was said in the register to have 'died from a scald in the water from the engine at the Colliery' in 1802. This was probably the girl of that name baptised in July 1791, a collier's daughter from Ness. She would have been ten when she died although it is unlikely she was doing colliery work (see 'Female Employment' below).

Despite the lack of consistent record-keeping at the time, the death of many of Neston's colliers, both young and old, can be traced (discussed in Chapter 12). Those known to have died in accidents are listed in Table 6.5 (overleaf) but there are several other instances of burials of two or more men on the same day or within a few days of each other. In many such instances the men were relatively young, making accidents or, possibly, virulent contagious disease the likely causes of death.[189] In one instance, there were four burials between 17 and 19 May 1777. Three are listed in the table on the basis of information from coroner's inquests on 17 May which found that each man died as the result of a 'sulphurous explosion'. However, there was a fourth burial, on the day of the coroner's visit, of another collier, William Prestwood, who was recently married and whose wife was probably pregnant.[190] Given the timing and his relative youth, this man has been included in the table as well (although it is unclear why the

Table 6.5: Accidental deaths recorded at the Neston collieries. The table records all known deaths at the collieries from accidental causes. It is apparent that some deaths did not result in either a locally recorded burial or a surviving coroner's record. Key to sources: NPR = Neston Parish Registers; CA = Coroner's Account, after attending to view the body, in Quarter Session Records (same year as death unless stated; CALS, QJF series); DC = Death Certificate; Inf = Chester Infirmary record (CALS, Z HI 52).

Name (and occupation/status and age, if recorded)	Date of Death (or earliest record of it)	Cause of Death	Source(s)
John Manchester, collier	26/4/1762	'Killed in a coalpit'	NPR; CA
William Griffith	17/2/1765	'Accidentally killed in a coal pit'	NPR; CA
John Tatlock, collier	9/7/1765	'Killed in a coalpit'	NPR; CA
John Burroughs	11/10/1769	'A fall into a coalpit'	CA
Thomas Coterall Son of Thomas Coterall	27/11/1769	'By a sulphurous explosion in a cole pit'	Burton St Nicholas PR; 'Cotterell' in CA
James Brundrett	18/2/1771	'A fall into a coal pit'	CA
George Smith	7/1/1774	'Accidentally killed in a coal pit'	NPR; CA
John Berry, collier age 27	17/1/1776	'Burnt in the colliery'	NPR; Inf. (as James Berry)
Robert Williams, collier	31/3/1777	'Accidentally killed by falling into a coal pit'	NPR; CA (1778; visited 31/3/77)
John Rowlands (or Rollin), collier	17/5/1777	'Killed in a sulphurous explosion in a coal pit'	NPR (as Rollin); CA (1778; visited 17/5/77)
Thomas Roberts, collier	17/5/1777	'Killed in a sulphurous explosion in a coal pit'	NPR; CA (1778; visited 17/5/77)
Edward Taylor, collier	17/5/1777	'Killed in a sulphurous explosion in a coal pit'	NPR; CA (1778; visited 17/5/77)
William Prestwood, collier	17/5/1777	[Assumed related to three deaths above]	NPR
John Cottrell	11/3/1779	'Killed by a sulphurous explosion in a coal pit'	CA
James Glaves, pauper	5/5/1790	'Suffocated in the coal pit'	NPR; 'Gleaves' in CA
Edward Davis, pauper	5/5/1790	'Suffocated in the coal pit'	NPR; CA
William Griffiths	15/6/1794	'Fell into a coalpit'	NPR (as Griffith); CA
Ellis Kendrick of Ness Colliery, age 65	22/1/1799	'Falling to the bottom of the [fire] engine'	Burton St Nicholas PR; CA

Name (and occupation/status and age, if recorded)	Date of Death (or earliest record of it)	Cause of Death	Source(s)
Anne Jones, a child (probably age 10)	16/4/1802	'Died from a scald in the water from the engine at the Col[lier]y'	NPR
Thomas Bartley, age 9	18/2/1814	Basket's rope broke while descending, at Little Neston	NPR; *Chester Courant* 22/2/14 re inquest
Thomas Davies, age 44	18/2/1814	Basket's rope broke while descending, at Little Neston	NPR; *Chester Courant* 22/2/14 re inquest
William Cottrell, age 43	7/6/1815	Smothered when supports gave way while digging underground.	NPR; *Chester Courant* 20/6/15 (as Thomas Cottrell)
William Armstrong, collier, age 50	6/7/1837	'The candle of his colleague Hugh Messam ignited foul air and there was an explosion'	NPR; *Chester Chronicle* 7/7/37
James Lewis, collier, age 38	5/7/1838	Fell from a basket while descending a shaft	NPR; DC
Joseph Taylor, age 10, son of Daniel Taylor	5/7/1838	Fell from a basket while descending a shaft	NPR; DC
Thomas Jones, age 37	18/3/1844	'Accidentally killed in the mine'	NPR; DC
Joseph Bartley, age 52 (brother of Thomas, above)	1/5/1855	'Accidentally killed by a fall'	NPR; DC

coroner did not inspect the body – maybe he was buried before he should have been). The surviving Ness Colliery royalty accounts show the week of these four deaths as the only one in the fifteen months of records when the colliery engine did not run and when no details of coal sales are logged.[191] It seems likely that the mine operators were preoccupied with the incident, although it was unreported in contemporary newspapers.

In another instance four colliers in their early fifties, and one of their wives, were buried within nineteen days of each other in 1834.[192] There are no surviving coroner's records and there was no spike in other burials at the time which might indicate disease was the cause of the deaths. There was a claim made a few months afterwards that Ness Colliery had experienced a flood but it has not been possible to verify the story, told by a couple of beggars.[193] If this *is* what caused the deaths (with burials spread over a few days as the bodies were slowly recovered) then it would indicate that a woman was working underground.

The recorded deaths of just six men and two boys in six incidents after 1799 looks surprisingly low given the prior record, albeit that there were some years of relatively low mining activity at Neston during that time. This may be because of a lack of surviving records, rather than due to any increase in safety levels. The *Report of the parliamentary Select Committee on Accidents in Mines* in 1835 said that the Cheshire coroners had notified just seven lives lost in the coal mining industry in the previous twenty-five years – yet there were many pits in the east of the county, as well as those at Neston in the west.[194] Whilst not mentioning Cheshire specifically, the committee's report strongly suspected under-reporting of accidents associated with the British coal industry.

Child Labour

The deaths in accidents of at least three working children at Ness Colliery, in 1769, 1814 and 1838, have already been described. The use of children in mines was common practice across Britain and would have occurred at the Neston works throughout the period of operation although surviving records tell us little about them until 1827. As we have seen, in that year a letter by manager James Gregory mentions seven under-sixteens at Ness including four children 'about eleven years old'. The censuses of 1841 and 1851 show that child labour was still in use in later years.

Although there was a general improvement in British industrial working conditions during the nineteenth century, a landmark 1842 parliamentary report by the Children's Employment Commission identified that those as young as four years old were working in British pits.[195] There is no evidence for children this young working at Ness but, in the coal mines of North Wales, children were employed as young as five years old and it was 'common' for children aged seven to be working there.[196] An article written in 1899 indicates that boys of seven had worked at the Neston pits too, although no original source is given.[197]

A statement proposing the setting up of a school in Little Neston in about 1840 said that as 'a large portion of the children in this locality procure employment in the collieries at a very early age it is intended that the school be open to children of two years old and upwards' – but what was meant by 'a very early age' was not stated.[198] The children who are known to have died underground at Neston included a nine-year old and a ten-year old. The 1841 census data shows that seventeen workers at the Neston collieries were aged under sixteen; there were fifteen in that age bracket in 1851, six of whom were aged twelve or less (Table 6.6). These children were mostly described as colliers or coal miners but several were 'waggoners' who would have hauled loaded waggons underground. The Mines and Collieries Act of 1842 had prohibited the use of children underground under ten years of age but the law was

Table 6.6: Numbers of under-sixteens employed at the Neston collieries in the 1841 and 1851 censuses. The figures include two coal carriers and two children who were 'assisting', one a girl. Full details: *nestoncollieries.org*

Age	1841	1851
9	–	2
10	–	1
11	–	2
12	1	1
13	1	4
14	5	3
15	10	2
Total	**17**	**15**

widely flouted including, quite possibly, by Ness Colliery.[199] Two pairs of brothers, each aged nine and eleven and with 'coal miner' fathers, were recorded as working in the local coal trade in the 1851 census – one pair were 'coal carriers', probably making local deliveries from Ness Colliery by donkey, but the others were described as 'coal miners'.[200]

Child labour was used in a variety of ways. Young children could be used as 'door tenters' or 'trappers', waiting by the underground doors which managed ventilation flows, opening and closing them as necessary; this was a long and lonely vigil (Figure 6.11). A mine inspector in Lancashire commented in 1842:

> This employment is the one to which children are generally put on first entering the mines; and it is one of the most pitiable in the coal pit, from its extreme monotony. As these little fellows are always the youngest in the pits, I have generally found them very shy and they never have anything to say for themselves. Their whole time is spent sitting in the dark for

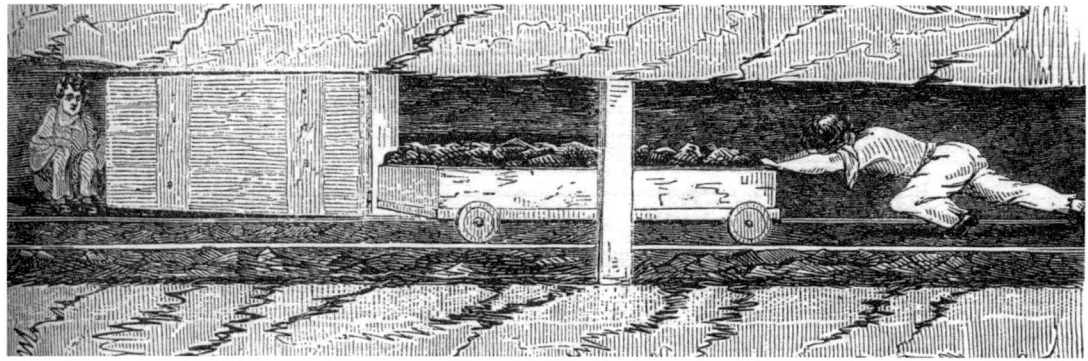

Figure 6.11: A young door tenter ('trapper'; crouching left) opens an air-door for a passing coal load. Source: *Report of the parliamentary Children's Employment Commission, BPP* [1842a], p. 81. With kind permission of IUP.

twelve hours; and were it not for the passing and repassing of the wagons, it would be equal to solitary confinement of the worst order.[201]

Older children were often employed to drive horses as indicated in James Gregory's 1827 letter, where seven drivers between eleven and fifteen were mentioned. Older boys could also be used in pushing or hauling underground waggons – often known as 'putting' or 'drawing' (Figure 6.12).[202] The boy pulling the waggon – a drawer – would have a leather girdle around his waist attached to which was a chain linked to the coal waggon; he would then crouch down and heave the waggon along.[203] Inevitably, terrible chafing ensued for boys new to the task but they soon got used to their 'wretched fate'.[204] Other children might help by pushing the waggon, using their hands and forehead, which could leave them with a bald patch on their crown.[205] It must have been very welcome when Ness Colliery's viewer, John Watson, proposed a mode of working one seam in 1827 which would make 'easy putting for the boys'.[206]

Boys could also be used to operate horse gins, used underground for winding;[207] another job for them was to manually operate pump handles for hours at a time.[208] Employing children in roles that did not need a man's strength saved costs for mine-owners. In 1827 the 'door tenter' at Ness – almost certainly a very young child – was paid just 6d. (2½p) per day; other children were paid just 8d. (3p).[209] Men might cost two shillings (10p) or more – three or four times as much. Children could be used in tasks above ground too such as Peter Robinson, probably aged nine, who, as described earlier, was taken on to learn the 'art or mystery of the Coal Basket-maker'.

The conditions in which children worked shocked the mine inspector writing about the North Wales pits in the 1842 parliamentary report. He commented, 'The work of the children is a grievous subject for reflection and a sad spectacle to behold. The air they breathe is full of dust and noxious gases and dangers surround them on all sides. Pitiable indeed is their sad condition'.[210]

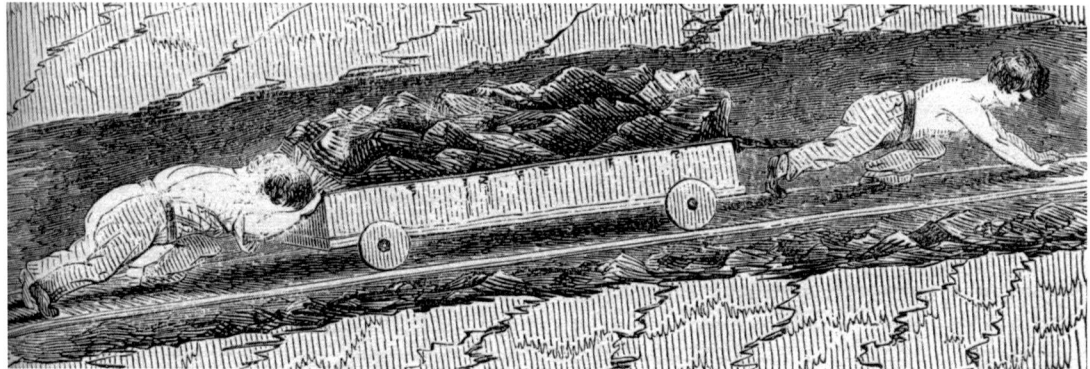

Figure 6.12: Three boys strain to draw an underground waggon. Source: *Report of the parliamentary Children's Employment Commission, BPP* [1842c], p. 165. With kind permission of IUP.

Table 6.7: Occupations of the father, or head of household, of child workers at the Neston collieries in the 1841 and 1851 censuses. No occupations were given for the six females in 1841. The 1851 female head of household was Ann Tunstall, charwoman, widow of a former collier. Source: censuses for Ness, Little Neston and Great Neston.

Occupation of Father/ Head of Household	Number of Child Workers	
	1841	1851
(Coal) miner or collier	9	12
Labourer	1	–
Engine tenter	1	–
Other (bricklayer's labourer, clockmaker)	–	2
Female head of household	6	1

Despite the dangers and unpleasantness of the mine, it was common for boys to follow in their father's footsteps – figuratively and literally, as children would often work with their parent.[211] It is common to see generation after generation of the same surnames appearing in the lists of known Neston colliers – Swift, Jellicoe and Cottrell (or variant spellings) are just some of the less common names that span many decades. All of the children who died at Ness had collier fathers, and the census data in Table 6.7 shows that most of the children who worked at the colliery had fathers who worked there too. In some households the children may have been the sole breadwinners – in all the instances in the 1841 Neston census where there was no stated male head of household the children were listed as the only earners.[212]

The 1842 Employment Commission's report gave one reason why fathers took their children down the mine: 'Lured by the wages, [the parents] are never backward in sending their children to the pits, as soon as they can get them into employ'.[213] The young children, too, were often keen to go underground, having grown up knowing nothing but a mining environment.[214]

Female Employment

There are many instances of females being employed in British mines in the eighteenth and nineteenth centuries though the practice was far from being general.[215] In 1795, a widely-distributed pamphlet told the apparently true morality tale of a 'Lancashire Collier Girl' who accompanied her father into a Wigan mine at the age of about nine and continued to labour there to support her family after his death in a mining accident.[216] Several females left Neston after the collieries closed and became colliery workers in Lancashire; one was a girl, Ann Tunstall, a 'collier' in the 1861 census for Windle, aged twelve years (she was the daughter of the woman, also Ann, mentioned in the Table 6.7 description).[217] As for North Wales, females were employed on the surface in the Denbighshire coalfield, including girls under eighteen, but the practice seems to have been much less widespread in Flintshire.[218]

Whilst the evidence from Lancashire shows that females who had come from Neston were not averse to working in coal mines there is little, if any, explicit evidence of this happening at Neston itself. The possible death of a collier's wife in an underground flood, mentioned above, is one instance but the circumstances are very uncertain. In addition, two daughters of a collier, aged nineteen and fifteen, were described as 'Assisting' in the 1841 census for Ness, just as the fifteen-year-old son of another collier was also 'Assisting'. The children's exact roles are unclear, though. There are, however, other indirect connections between females and the mines (besides obvious familial relationships).

As mentioned earlier, Anne Jones, a collier's daughter probably aged ten, died after being scalded by water from an engine at the colliery. The circumstances behind the accident will never be known but women sometimes took hot water from colliery engine houses to do washing – and Anne was old enough to do this kind of work.[219] In a different context, three women were treated at Chester Infirmary on the recommendation of the proprietors of Ness Colliery.[220] Whilst this might simply be because they may have been colliers' wives, it could also be evidence that they were working at the colliery in some way, perhaps on the farm. There are also several records of women being paid by the Stanleys to cart heavy loads of coal and other goods from Ness Colliery to the Stanley estates, at least one of whom, Mary Price, was a collier's wife;[221] Neston parish church also bought coal delivered by women.[222]

*

The place of origin of the miners changed over the course of the ninety-six years of the Neston collieries. From a reliance on labour and skills from elsewhere, particularly North Wales, over time the local mines created their own largely home-grown workforce. There were also the beginnings of a shift in power in the coal industry in the Neston collieries' final thirty years. Collective action and unionisation brought better wages, and government began to take an interest in how mines were run. Little else changed, though. Conditions in the North Wales pits in 1842 were described as follows: 'In many mines in this district the roads are low and narrow, the air foul, and the places in which people work dusty, dirty, and damp. The ventilation in general is very imperfect'.[223] There is no reason to believe that the Neston collieries were any different from those across the estuary at that time, nor that conditions had been any better in any of the previous decades. The men, boys and maybe girls and women always worked long hours for little pay, risking their health and lives in the process.

CHAPTER 7

THE NESTON COLLIERIES' PRODUCTS

While coal was, of course, the principal produce of the Neston collieries, like many other coal works of the period, the mines sold a variety of additional heavy goods. Some of these were coal-based, such as slack and coke. Other goods were manufactured on site taking advantage of immediately available raw materials; in some cases goods were imported for onward sale.

This range of goods sold by the Neston collieries is the subject of this short chapter. The collieries' proximity to the Dee Estuary was a considerable advantage when raw materials or finished goods had to be imported. More generally, the production or sale of these goods took advantage of synergies available to mine-owners – synergies in transport or in the ready availability of fuel and labour. The revenues from these ancillary activities would have been a valuable supplement to those from mining operations, especially in the collieries' leaner years.

There is no indication that the Cottinghams' Little Neston Colliery produced anything other than coal, slack and lime and most surviving documents on this topic relate to Ness Colliery. Discussion in this chapter is therefore largely focused on the latter.

Coal-Based Products
Coke

Some of the higher quality coal obtained at Neston was converted into coke. Coke is made by pyrolysis of coal (baking it at high temperatures in a low oxygen environment), a process which drives out impurities and leaves a compact substance which is high in carbon.[1] Coke was much used for smelting metal ores but had other industrial uses where lack of smoke and fumes was important.[2]

There is evidence that coke was being produced at Ness: a 1790 letter from John Carter of Powis Castle records his order for 'coaks for the slaghearth' from 'Denna Colliery'.[3] Slag hearths reheated metal slag to extract further metal and relied on the use of coke, which does not produce the sulphur that weakens the material.[4] The coke which Carter ordered was to go to the Anchor Smelting Co. which had been established near Aberystwyth four years previously to produce lead and silver.[5] The business had bought coal from Ness in 1788.

At the time of Carter's order, coke was typically made in 'beehive' coking ovens made from firebricks; from the mid-eighteenth century these ovens were replacing open air production in smouldering heaps.[6] Ness Colliery may not have been producing coke for long – it does not appear as a standard item on pre-printed sales dockets which survive from 1808–9 (Figure 7.1, overleaf).[7]

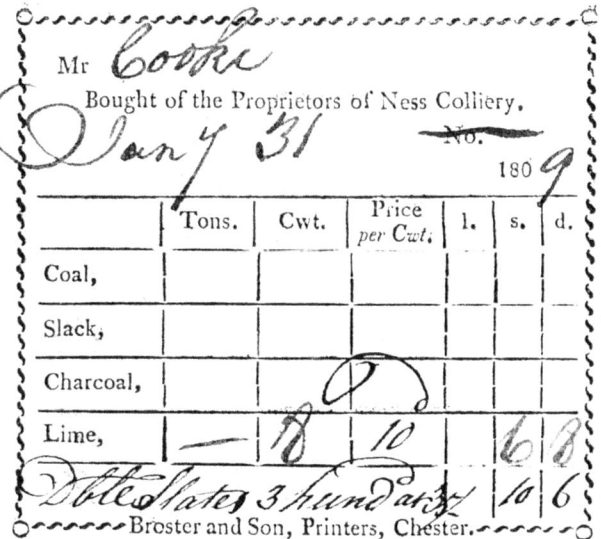

Figure 7.1: A pre-printed sales voucher from Ness Colliery, dated 1809. Standard items for sale are coal, slack, charcoal and lime. Here, a Mr Cooke bought 8 cwt of lime at 10*d*. per cwt, and also three hundred 'double slates' for 10*s*. 6*d*. Source: CALS, DHL 54C/45 (with courtesy of CALS).

Slack

Slack, sometimes known as culm, consists of small pieces of coal and is a by-product of coal mining.[8] It might simply break off as the coal was being hewn from the coalface, especially from poorer quality seams, or separate from larger lumps during handling of the coal prior to sale. Slack riddling was an important job at the colliery, using a wire mesh to separate out the small pieces:[9] customers would complain if they found slack when they thought they were getting coal. A slack mill, used to wash away coal dust, was also used.[10] Being of lower quality, slack was also of lower value. In 1805 and 1806 it was advertised for sale from Ness Colliery at 3*s*. 4*d*. (17p) per ton – 40% of the price of coal.[11]

The Ness Colliery royalty accounts of 1776–7 show slack was accounted for separately and represented about 20–25% of the total tonnage raised.[12] Some of this was consumed to power the colliery's engine(s) with 2,529 tons (2,754 tonnes) used for this purpose in 1777; a similar quantity was sold.[13] Surviving pre-printed sales dockets from both Ness Colliery and Little Neston Colliery show 'Slack' as a standard item of sale.[14] Slack was used in kilns on the Wirral built to burn lime and bake bricks. Large quantities were used on the Stanley estates for these purposes, discussed later, and records survive of leading local figure Joseph Lyon using Ness coal and slack to make bricks in nearby Willaston.[15]

Cannel

Reference was made in Chapter 1 to this commodity, a hydrogen-rich form of coal. This was presumably exploited at Ness although records of sales have not survived.

Non-Coal Products
Charcoal

Charcoal was the main source of fuel for industrial use in the eighteenth century, being rich in carbon and capable of reaching high temperatures when burnt.[16] Charcoal was first produced at Ness Colliery no later than 1776.[17] The accounts covering that year have an entry for the costs of slack burnt in producing the charcoal. An average of eight tons (8.7 tonnes) of slack per month were used but sales volumes and revenues for the charcoal are not given. Charcoal's relative lack of impurities may have been valued locally in, for example, brewing, baking and dyeing, or the fuel might have been exported via the Dee to other regional or overseas industrial users.[18] It was also used to make lime, discussed in the next section.

The wood to make the charcoal – usually hardwood such as oak and ash – was probably obtained from plantations on the Stanleys' own estates, discussed on page 137. At the colliery, the timber would have been slowly combusted in carefully arranged clay- or turf-covered stacks.[19] The pre-printed sales dockets used by Ness Colliery in 1808–9 show that charcoal was still a standard product available from them at that time (Figure 7.1). However, it was becoming much less widely used by the early 1800s, with coke having become the fuel of preference for many purposes.[20]

Lime

Quicklime – usually just termed lime – was of considerable social importance in the period of the collieries' operation. Made from burning limestone in a kiln (Figure 7.2), it was used by the rapidly growing population as a key ingredient in mortar for buildings. However, most lime was used in agriculture as an improver for the soil to boost yields or to help convert waste land to productive use.[21]

The first known reference to lime at Ness Colliery is in the accounts for 1769–70, showing it as an expense, perhaps for building.[22] However, by 1785 the colliery was selling its own lime.[23] It was well placed to meet the demand for the product – limestone was readily available from quarries just across the estuary in North Wales and, of course, coal to fire the kilns was immediately at hand. The lime burning process could use slack rather than coal – a handy way to extract benefit from this fuel which had a low retail price. Charcoal was an alternative fuel source. One of the few advertisements put out by Ness Colliery, in 1806, was for 'lime burnt with charcoal'.[24] Lime appears as a standard item on the colliery's pre-printed sales vouchers surviving from 1808–9, and there are many other references to sales of it, typically selling at around 10d. per hundredweight, until the colliery's closure.[25] Pre-printed sales dockets from the 1820s for Little Neston Colliery also show it as a standard item for sale and its ready availability was promoted as an advantage when Thomas Cottingham senior sought to sell his dairy farm in 1823.[26]

The 1785 reference mentioned above was to the purchase from Ness Colliery of lime and bricks, and the juxtaposition of these materials suggests they were for building use. A hand-written note in June 1809 refers to the purchase of bricks and lime as well as sand, all supplied by Ness Colliery.[27]

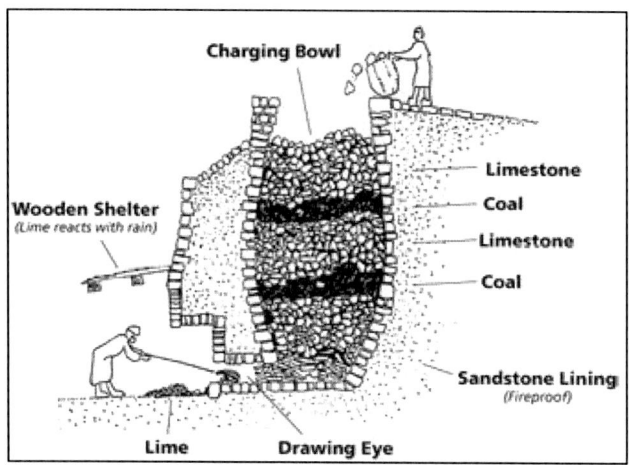

Figure 7.2: The features of a lime kiln. Source: National Stone Centre, with kind permission.

In relation to agriculture, the use of lime was one of many improvement techniques increasingly adopted in the eighteenth century as part of the long period which some have termed the Agricultural Revolution.[28] It boosted fertility of the soil and was generally applied to fallow land, prior to arable planting, and to the county's plentiful grassland used for dairy farming, though the latter required good drainage to make the lime effective.[29] When used with root crops like turnips, it helped turn uncultivated areas such as heath into productive land.[30] Ness Colliery's move into production of the commodity reflected a general trend of increasing demand for it in the decades after the colliery opened as food prices rose.[31] It was also indicative of the need over time to bring more marginal land into agricultural use.[32] There were many other lime kilns on the Wirral, especially around the coast where the limestone could be easily unloaded and processed.[33] British demand for lime peaked during the Napoleonic Wars when high crop prices guaranteed quick returns on the outlay;[34] nevertheless demand for it from Ness continued as long as it operated.

Limestone was burnt in lime kilns and 'a large Lime-kiln' was included in Ness Colliery's offer to let of 1812; a single kiln was again mentioned in 1827.[35] Little Neston Colliery also had a kiln, listed in the 1826 sale particulars.[36] As with coal, local competition such as this put downward pressure on the price Ness Colliery could charge for lime, at a time when the colliery was struggling.[37] By 1839 Ness had two adjacent kilns, depicted on a colliery plan and specifically labelled on the tithe map of c.1845.[38] A final reference to the production facility comes in the 1852 colliery letting advertisement which talked of 'extensive lime-works'.[39] That year there was, apparently, still a kiln on the site of the former Little Neston Colliery too.[40]

Most of the limestone used in the kilns would have come from North Wales – numerous quarries were made in the various limestone areas near the North Wales coast, and Conwy's chief export was said to be 'mountain stones', i.e. limestone.[41] Ships in the coasting trade taking coal to North Wales could return with loads of limestone which, as well as having commercial value, acted as ballast. Relatively few records of limestone shipments to the local area survive after 1769 but in 1814 the *Jane* carried a load of the stone from Caernarfon to 'Parkgate' – there was a lime kiln at each end of the village but it could equally have been destined for Ness Colliery (Parkgate being the official port to which vessels would have been cleared).[42] In 1819 Ness Colliery advertised that:

> Six shillings a ton will be paid for red Wharf [on Anglesey] Limestones, on delivery, in the usual way, at this colliery.[43]

On a few occasions, vessels are known to have brought limestone from Ireland. The Parkgate customs accounts for 1776 record four vessels bringing the stone as their sole cargo, arriving from Drogheda (two vessels), Larne and Newry – all known destinations for Chester's coal and all locations with long-standing limestone quarries nearby.[44] Vessels from the Isle of Man may have brought limestone too.

After the building of Denhall Quay in the 1790s the imported limestone would have been unloaded there. Maps show two narrow parallel lines from the quay to the kilns – evidence of a 310-yard (283-metre) rail road, the only certain record of a rail road above ground in the mines' history.[45] As late as 1851 a vessel, the *Mary* with two Welsh crew, was recorded as bringing limestone to Ness.[46]

Slate

Another import from North Wales which was sold at the colliery was slate. Slates from several Welsh ports were regularly shipped up the Dee, reflecting the need to meet the demand for housing and other buildings as the region's population grew rapidly.[47] In particular, Caernarfon saw huge exports of slate from the Penrhyn Quarry.[48] There are records of slates being shipped from Caernarfon to 'Parkgate' in the early nineteenth century and it seems likely that some or all of them were destined for Ness.[49] The colliery presumably bought the slates in at wholesale prices and sold them on from its 'slate yard'.[50] Coal would have made a useful return cargo for the visiting vessels.

The accounts of Neston's Joseph Lyon show him buying slate from the colliery on several occasions. For example, slates were bought for the herring curing house in Parkgate which was being refurbished in 1803–4, for the Old Quay House (the former House of Correction) which he had owned for many years, as well as for his own home, Ashfield House.[51] The Stanley family estates were also major customers; the Cottinghams bought Ness slates too, as did the parish church for steeple repairs.[52] Slates were still being sold at the colliery until it closed in 1855.[53]

Brick and Tile Making

The manufacture of bricks and, later, tiles was a useful complement to Ness Colliery's other activities. It made use of readily available resources and fed demand for new and better quality buildings to support an expanding population. However, hefty duties on bricks from 1784 to 1850 suppressed demand nationally and, in areas such as

Neston and elsewhere on the Wirral, the ready availability of duty-free sandstone from local quarries would often have made stone the material of choice for most buildings.[54]

A large quantity of bricks – 120,000 – were on site at the colliery in 1770.[55] It is not clear if they were made there, nor what they were for.[56] However, bricks could be used to line shafts and two were being sunk at the time.[57] As with the manufacture of lime, a decision was made at some point to start making bricks at the colliery using the readily available local clay soil and coal for firing kilns on site. The earliest record of bricks being sold there is in 1785 when Joseph Lyon bought bricks, as well as lime, from Ness Colliery. He also bought coal and slack to make his own bricks in Willaston.[58] Bricks presumably continued to be made at the colliery over the following thirty years or so – there are certainly references to brick sales in 1810 and 1813.[59]

Although purchases from Ness Colliery were not always fully itemised, there is at least one surviving record of firebricks also being supplied, in 1827.[60] Firebricks were used to line high-temperature environments such as kilns, furnaces and ovens and were made from fireclay. Four hundred were used to make a lime kiln on one of the farms on the Stanley estates.[61] Unlike conventional brickmaking clay, fireclays are mined at depth, often occurring beneath coal-bearing strata – they once formed the soil in which the vegetation grew which decayed and became coal. The geological sections at Neston show various seams of fireclay at the colliery.[62] We do not know from what date the clay was extracted and processed but the *Venus*, a regular visitor to the colliery, was exporting firebricks from 'Parkgate' in 1767.[63]

More information about the fireclay comes in the 1812 letting particulars:

> Under the [two feet coal] vein lies a Seam of excellent Fire Brick Clay, 2½ feet thick, which may be conveniently gotten ... A sample of fire bricks, made of this clay, may be seen at the Colliery.[64]

Prior to the 1820s, brickmaking at Ness Colliery seems to have been integrated with other activities on the colliery site, using the business's labourers; references are sporadic and there is no indication of dedicated resources.[65] However, it appears a decision was then made to set up a specific brick and tile operation. This may have been motivated by the Stanleys' continued problems with the coal mining business. The colliery was regularly supplying bricks and tiles from about 1820; trade in the latter would have been spurred by the abolition in 1826 of all duty on tiles used for field drainage, supporting the move for agricultural improvement.[66] The colliery made floor and ridge tiles too (duty remained on these until 1833 and on bricks until 1850).[67]

The occupation of 'brickmaker' first occurs in parish registers in 1826.[68] In the same year the colliery was buying in brick clay and a 'Brick Yard' is first depicted on a plan, showing it located 250 yards (229 metres) south-east of Denhall Quay.[69] The later tithe map shows it in more detail, comprising two buildings (one very small) and two circular kilns.[70] The accompanying tithe apportionment describes the area as a 'Brick and Tile Yard' owned by Charles Stanley.[71]

Ness Colliery was still making bricks in its final year, selling them to the Stanley estates.[72] The brickyard probably closed soon after, having lost its ready supply of coal to fire the kilns (as well as fireclay if firebricks were still being made).[73] Eight different individuals are recorded as 'brickmaker' in Ness township between 1826 and the colliery's closure.[74]

*

The Neston collieries were not unusual amongst British mine operations in integrating other production and sales activities on to their site.[75] Nevertheless, the importance of these activities should not be underestimated. At the very least, they would have contributed to the viability of the colliery and may have made the difference between survival and closure when, in much of the first three decades of the nineteenth century, Ness Colliery's future was uncertain. Beyond this, they were an important source of much-needed materials to local people looking to improve and invest in their buildings and land – a theme which is explored further in the next chapter.

CHAPTER 8

LOCAL TRADE: THE LANDSALE BUSINESS

Newly mined coal could be carried from the colliery by land or water, the trades being known as 'landsale' and 'seasale'. This chapter reviews the landsale markets for the Neston collieries' coal and other products – who was using them, why, and how the products reached them. The relationship with the Stanley family and their local estates is a particularly interesting aspect of the landsale trade as they were not only owners of the colliery, but also important customers of it and suppliers to it. As this chapter will show, Ness Colliery was of great value to the development of the Stanleys' estates, and the estates were critical to the collieries. The landsale trade was dependent on local roads and, like so much in Britain at the time, these evolved rapidly during the life of the collieries – the subject of the final part of this chapter.

Whether the collieries' goods were moved by land or sea, customers needed to be found and communicated with. Today we term this 'marketing' but the word was not used at the time and its techniques were in their infancy. Little has been written about marketing in the early coal trade but it is an interesting topic and one in which Ness Colliery was quite remarkable in one respect. As these marketing activities spanned both the landsale and seasale businesses, material on both facets has been included in a single section at the end of Chapter 11.

Local markets

Land sales were an important market for the Neston collieries though scope for them was relatively limited. Coal is bulky and heavy so, as a general rule, 10 to 12 miles (16–19 km) was considered the limit for overland coal carriage.[1] This would have been a significant distance for heavy carts over the rough and often poorly maintained routeways of the time. The local agricultural economy meant that roads were often churned up by cattle and, as we will see, improvements to the Wirral's road network came slowly, spread over decades.[2]

The limitation on the distance coal could be conveyed by land effectively restricted land sales to the Wirral Peninsula – Chester, which was almost 10 miles (16 kilometres) away, was better served by river-borne coal. As there were no significant large-scale industries on the Wirral for most of the period in which the Neston collieries operated this meant that the trade was largely serving the domestic market. The market town of Neston, with adjacent Parkgate, was by far the largest population centre on the Wirral for the first sixty years or so of the collieries' existence and was the natural focus for most of their sales.[3] Thus, with Neston nearby as well as access for shipping, Ness Colliery had ready markets all year. By contrast, until 1770, coal from the inland Denbighshire mines had to be stacked in fields in winter until better weather made the roads passable.[4]

During the eighteenth century, demand for coal as a domestic fuel for cooking and heating grew due to its efficiency compared to alternatives and because of its increasing availability. In 1808 Henry Holland wrote that 'a few years ago' wood was the fuel of preference for ordinary folk in Cheshire, along with peat where it was available, but 'pit coal is now the general article of use'.[5] He added that it was 'conveyed … by land carriage immediately from the collieries in the hundred of Wirral' as well as from surrounding counties (a hundred was an ancient subdivision of a county). Hanshall, writing in about 1823, said that 'for a number of years [Ness Colliery had] furnished a plentiful supply for a great part of the Hundred of Wirral'.[6]

Three of the seams worked at Ness were said to be 'house coal'.[7] A diarist writing at one of Parkgate's lodging houses in 1829 mentioned that local house coal came chiefly from the 'Denna coal works'. He described it as burning 'extremely well' and reducing 'to a white ash which on stirring the fire rises and settles on the furniture'.[8] Parkgate was a significant sea port and bathing resort for much of the time the mines were open and local inns, lodging houses and meeting places would have been important customers for the mines.

The availability of coal at Ness was seen as a marketing advantage locally. In 1766, the handsome Gayton Hall, then in possession of Sir Ellis Cunliffe Baronet, Liverpool MP, merchant and former slave trader, was advertised to let.[9] One of its selling points was that it was 'Within two miles of good coals'.

The viable distance for carriage of coal potentially put all of the Wirral Peninsula within reach of Ness – although whether the more distant parts wanted it, given the availability of water-borne coals from Wales or Lancashire, was another matter. Ness supplied its landsale coal by cart and perhaps also by packhorse – at least in the colliery's early years. Packhorse was the main method used at the Duke of Bridgewater's mine at Worsley, Lancashire until the much more convenient canal was built.[10] Ness had twenty-five horses in 1770 some of which, presumably, could have performed this role.[11] The record from that year also shows that one of the largest expenses at the time was 'carriers'. These were individuals who supplied cart, waggon or pack animal services for conveying goods. Local carriers formed the bedrock of Britain's road distribution network at the time, making journeys within relatively confined areas.[12] Donkeys kept by the colliery were another form of carriage, delivering small loads. In the 1820s – and maybe earlier – a man at the colliery had the job of looking after them.[13] Making donkey deliveries was quite possibly the modus operandi of two brothers, a collier's sons aged nine and eleven, who were described as 'coal carriers' in the 1841 Ness census. There was also a 'colliery carter'; this term was used for one man, named Jellico, in 1834 when the Ness works had to pay four shillings (20p) for a gate and post he damaged when delivering to the Stanley estate.[14]

Although twelve miles was usually about the limit for coal delivery, a surviving rental agreement from 1768 required a somewhat longer journey.[15] A Wirral yeoman,

John Dawson, obtained a lease for land at Moreton from Philip Egerton of Oulton, Cheshire. The agreement stipulated a rent of £82 p.a. and also required Dawson to arrange the annual delivery of a waggon load of coal from Ness to Oulton House, the Egertons' family seat in Cheshire, which is about 24 miles (39 km) by today's roads; a waggon-load also had to be supplied to an unspecified location – perhaps Leasowe Castle, on the north Wirral coast, which the Egertons occupied for a time in the eighteenth century.[16]

It seems that, unlike in Chester where various independent intermediaries were involved with coal sales, around Neston the collieries mostly sold directly to the public, albeit often contracting locals to make the deliveries. The use of carriers is evidence for this as was, probably, the engagement of local man, William Peters in 1810. He drowned in the estuary and was described as 'a poor man, who had been in the habit of drawing coals in a one-horse cart to Neston and Parkgate'.[17] The first suggestion of an independent coal merchant in the Neston area appears in Pigot's 1822 *Commercial Directory* where George Edwards of Parkgate is recorded as 'joiner and coal dealer', apparently unable or unwilling to specialise.[18]

Delivery costs depended upon the distance the coal was to be carried. Even for short distances the costs were a significant proportion of the total order. In the early nineteenth century, senior Neston figure Joseph Lyon was paying 2s. 6d. (12.5p) for each cartload of coal to be delivered locally.[19] Each cart carried about one-and-a-quarter tons (1.4 tonnes), costing around 10s. (50p) – so the delivery charge added 25%. In 1837 Thomas Cottingham charged the local parish church 3s. 5d. (17p) for the delivery of just over two tons (2.2 tonnes) of coal worth 17s. 1d. (85.5p) – the carriage was 20% of the cost of the coal for little more than a mile.[20]

Surprisingly, the Cottingham family were buyers of materials from Ness Colliery for their Neston estates in the 1820s – not just of tiles, slate and bricks which there is no record of their own colliery ever selling but also of lime, coals and slack even though they produced these items.[21] An earlier buyer of coal from Ness was Joseph Lyon, mentioned above, with many such purchases recorded in his estate's accounts between 1785 and 1812.[22] They were not only for his personal use. Several loads were for the benefit of others, for example being described as 'distributed in charity at Neston' or to supply 'poor housekeepers'.[23] One of Lyon's records, in December 1797, details a payment of 4s. 4d. (22p) 'For coals and potatoes distributed among Neston paupers being a severe snow'.[24] Sir Thomas Stanley, too, made gifts of coal – seventeen tons (18.5 tonnes) for the poor of Eastham and Hooton in the severe winter of 1815–16.[25] Annual gifts by him of coal and other items became customary.[26]

The poor were also to be found at the Neston House of Correction, located at the Old Quay, a few hundred yards along the shore north of Neston's pits. The building was mainly used to temporarily house 'vagrants' – often migrant Irish labourers who had sought seasonal work – until they could be returned to their homeland on an

Ireland-bound ship.[27] An average of 500 men, women and children passed through its doors each year, usually staying a week or so. Fifty years of detailed quarterly accounts record the House's expenses which included regular purchases of coals required in the 'frosty and cold weather'.[28] There were few comforts at the House of Correction for the inmates and in summer reduced quantities of coal were purchased solely for 'the benefit of sick people and children'.[29]

Other institutional buyers of coal included the workhouse at Clatterbridge, completed in 1837, which bought from both Thomas Cottingham and Ness Colliery, and Neston parish church.[30] The church needed to warm the main body of the building and also fuel the fire in the vestry. Relevant churchwardens' accounts are available from 1803 and for the first couple of decades make explicit mention of payment for coals only occasionally. In April 1828 the wardens thanked Thomas Cottingham for his 'liberal offer' to supply coal to the church. They undertook to explore ways to heat the church including using a 'cockle' – a form of cast iron stove. The following month they resolved to buy a 'Howden's Hot Air Dispenser' – an early form of central heating, fuelled by coal, which was becoming widely used in churches and public buildings.[31] It appears that Cottingham was offering his coal for free but he became increasingly embroiled in lawsuits and it seems his offer lapsed.[32] From 1837 he re-started supplies, on normal terms, stopping in 1842. Meanwhile, Ness Colliery was a regular supplier from the 1830s, also occasionally supplying slate, lime and bricks for repairs.[33] The church often bought coal by the 'ass load', brought by various individuals who were paid about 7*d.* each. One of these was described as 'Parry's boy';[34] another was a woman, Nancy Matthews, one of the rare records in this period of a female being paid locally for anything other than domestic work or teaching.[35] The church looked to update its heating system in 1849 when a loan of £50 was offered by the vicar to invest in the 'hot air apparatus of Mr Bennett of Liverpool' which appears mainly to have been fuelled by coke brought from Chester.[36] Ness Colliery continued to supply coal to the church, presumably for the vestry, until the works closed in 1855.

Meanwhile, there was increasing competition locally with the Parkgate Coal Company setting up near the Boat House inn [*sic*] in 1852.[37] Despite the proximity of Welsh coal they prided themselves on offering the 'best' Lancashire coal. It could be delivered locally for 'free' … but was cheaper if collected in one's own cart! After the collieries closed, local people seem to have been dependent on coal brought in by boats but the supply seems to have been unreliable. A Chester coal trader, William Booth, solved the problem when he opened a coal yard in Neston in 1858, saying he '… trusts the undertaking will be well supported as hitherto the Supply of Coal in these districts (by vessels) has been very uncertain, the Neston Collieries now being Closed'.[38] Booth had another yard in Hooton which, being situated on the railway, had easy access to Welsh coal brought via Chester. Alternatively, Lancashire coal could be brought in by rail from the Birkenhead docks.[39]

Although the domestic market was the principal target for the Neston collieries' landsale trade, there were small-scale local industries which would have required heat from fires, such as brewing, baking and smithy-work.[40] A number of local farms probably had their own bakehouses and malt kilns too.[41] Some users may have preferred charcoal or, later, coke to coal.[42] However, the major 'brewing and malting' concern in Neston, owned by Joseph Lyon, was certainly buying coal from Ness in the 1780s (and Ness Colliery appears to have been buying significant quantities of ale in return, as it was often used in lieu of pay).[43] As discussed in the previous chapter, another non-domestic use for coal and slack was to fire lime and brick kilns.

The growing number of heavy industries on the Mersey side of the Wirral in the nineteenth century were, though, never going to be realistic outlets for Neston coal. The well-developed canal network which brought plentiful supplies of coal to Liverpool was in a much better position to meet that need – even Sir Thomas Stanley himself took advantage of it.[44] However, this did not stop Birkenhead, which had grown extremely rapidly from the 1820s, from being promoted as an attractive market for Neston coal in later years: 'Birkenhead will be enabled to derive … the extensive supplies of coal required for the use of the rising port' claimed the *Liverpool Mercury* and other newspapers when Lord Mostyn announced the 'discovery' of coal at Parkgate in 1847.[45] Advertisements in 1848 and 1851 relating to the find made even more of Birkenhead's market potential, claiming that 60,000 tons (65,340 tonnes) of coal had been consumed there in 1845.[46] The possibility of a railway coming to the Neston area, led to further excited speculation about access to Birkenhead. An 1852 advertisement for the sale of Thomas Cottingham's assets, including the colliery, stated that:

> … a siding might, at a trifling outlay, be constructed … to connect it to the main line, by which the transit of coal to the thriving town of Birkenhead may be accomplished in a few minutes while the consumption and requirements of so populous a district must necessarily ensure a continued and uninterrupted demand … The quality of the coal is excellent and is held in the highest estimation, and [it] has preference over other coal now being consumed in Birkenhead and the locality.[47]

There is no evidence, though, that Birkenhead was ever actually a significant market for the Neston collieries' coal.

Ness Colliery and the Stanley Estates

A particularly interesting aspect of Ness Colliery's history is its relationship with the Stanley family estates. The estates were a major user of goods from the colliery and, at the same time, were a significant supplier of items to it, creating a symbiotic relationship. This relationship is largely revealed in the detailed accounts for the family's estates of Hooton and Puddington.[48] The accounts include information on activities on the large demesne farms in those manors (i.e. farms for the Stanleys' own use) and also cover activities on Stanley property elsewhere on the Wirral, and in Flintshire, Lancashire and other parts of Cheshire. Much of the income and expenditure in these wider areas relates to property rented out by the Stanleys. As well as agricultural land which was mainly for pastoral use, the estates included tree plantations, heathland and dwellings for local people. There were also the grounds of the Stanleys' Hooton and Puddington Halls – at Hooton the grounds were called the 'Park'.

The Hooton Hall estate accounts survive from 1801–31 and 1834–9, all in the period of Sir Thomas Massey Stanley's baronetcy. They relate to Hooton itself as well as to activity in many other parts of the Wirral where land was held (including the manors of Eastham and Storeton), with further holdings in North Wales, south Cheshire and Lancashire.[49] The Puddington Hall estate accounts are available for the same period as for Hooton and also for 1784–1800 (i.e. in the time of Sir Thomas's predecessors; these mainly relate to the manors and estates of Puddington, Ness and Ledsham, as well as lands in Flintshire and east Cheshire) and 1844–56 when the estate was in the hands of Rowland Errington with his uncle, Charles Stanley, owning the colliery).[50] The two sets of accounts do not specifically relate to Ness Colliery but do record royalties and other income to the estates from the colliery and, conversely, payments to the colliery by the estates. From these details it is clear that the colliery's products were extremely important in the development and maintenance of the estates, as well as being a source of income to them. Equally, the estates were almost certainly the colliery's largest customers in the nineteenth century.

Many products were involved in this two-way exchange. As far as the Stanley estates were concerned the primary role of the colliery's products was to facilitate their improvement, either by supplying materials for new building or by enhancing the productivity of farmland in various ways. For the colliery, the estate's produce supported both its mining operations and, on occasion, the colliery farm.

The Use of Coal and Slack
From the earliest days of the nineteenth-century estate accounts, coal was being bought from the colliery; slack was also a routine purchase. Not only are the purchases mentioned in the accounts but there are references to hundreds of journeys by local people paid to cart the coals to different parts of the estates.

Some of the coal was for domestic use: there was a coal yard at Hooton Hall and there are several references to coal being used in the building, for example to heat the bed chambers.[51] In addition, the carting of coals to the Hall enabled Stanley to pursue an interest in horticulture. Humphry Repton, the great landscape designer, had visited Hooton in 1802 and proposed new designs for the Park.[52] Repton was a proponent of hothouses – artificially heated glasshouses – and in 1805 had included them in a grand landscaping scheme he designed for Woburn Abbey.[53] This may have been the spur to

Figure 8.1: The proposed forcing garden at Woburn, drawn by Humphry Repton in 1805.
Note on the left the chimney for the fire used for heating the hothouses. Source: Woburn Abbey
Collection, Humphry Repton's Red Book. Used with kind permission.

Sir Thomas Stanley who, the following year, built his own large hothouses, requiring
'5006 feet of hothouse lights', i.e. glazed units.[54] Hothouses enabled exotic fruit to be
grown such as oranges, pineapples, melons and grapes and could be used as part of a
'forcing garden' where fruit, flowers and vegetables could be grown out of season
(Figure 8.1).[55] The usual method of heating in hothouses, and used at Hooton, was
from a fire with the heat conducted via air flues made of brick and tile.[56]

Coal and slack had, however, a more strategic use on the Stanley estates: fuelling
kilns to make bricks. Although bricks were made at Ness Colliery, the weight when
transporting them meant that they were primarily used close to the point of
production. In areas further from the colliery, the bricks were generally made close to
where they were needed, using the readily available local clay as well as fuel carted
from the colliery.[57] The estates' accounts record the construction of many brick kilns
over four decades, at Hooton, Puddington, Childer Thornton, Eastham and near
Ledsham.[58] Some of the kilns were presumably made using some of the firebricks
bought by the estates from the leading industrialist, William Hancock at Buckley
(Flintshire).[59] Buckley was well known for its potteries and, particularly, its fireclays.[60]
Firebricks were also made at Ness Colliery and bought by the estate.[61] After the main

Figure 8.2: One of the two pairs of Grade II listed cottages on Hooton Green. They were probably built during the great period of brickmaking at the start of the nineteenth century.

structure of the kiln was formed, it was covered with sods of earth to help retain its heat.[62] Brickmaking required several steps, often detailed in the accounts – preparing the ground, 'feighing' the clay (i.e. scooping it up from the agreed area), casting it into moulds and baking it in the kiln.[63]

The estates' kilns produced large quantities of bricks, sometimes on a massive scale. The accounts often do not indicate what the bricks were used for, whether for agricultural buildings, houses or walls, and quite often the place of production is not stated, although related entries may give clues. Whatever the place and purpose, the effect would have been to enhance, and maybe occasionally transform, the estates over the period; many structures visible today must date from this period. For example, from 1804 to 1809 over two million bricks were made at Hooton Green.[64] Three pairs of cottages on Hooton Green today, two pairs of which are Grade II listed, were probably built in this period (Figure 8.2).[65]

One property specifically mentioned in the accounts was occupied by the Stanleys' Catholic priest who presided over the Hall's chapel; works there included bricklaying and slating.[66] In addition, brick outbuildings were constructed for the Hall and there are occasional references in the accounts to bricklaying for the 'park wall'.[67] It is perhaps during this first decade of the nineteenth century that substantial works were undertaken on the wall enclosing Hooton Hall's rectangular horticultural garden. These massive and impressive walls still stand about 16 feet (4.9 metres) high, with a perimeter of 117 by 60 yards (107 x 55 metres), enclosing an area of 1.4 acres (0.6 hectares). An existing 'Kitchen Garden' at Hooton, roughly square in shape, was sketched on a plan of the estate by Repton in 1802. It may subsequently have been reshaped and enlarged, with enhancements to the walls providing added protection for Stanley's new hothouses.[68] There are other records of episodes of brickmaking at Hooton over the years as well as of instances which probably, but not certainly, relate to Hooton.[69]

At Puddington, over 500,000 bricks were made in 1803 and tens of thousands of others in 1800, 1808, 1811, 1813 and 1822.[70] Puddington today is an attractive village with Conservation Area status. A local authority character appraisal in 2008 attributed the village's 'feeling of solid continuity from an earlier age' partly to the fact that most of its long-standing buildings were made of brick (Figure 8.3).[71] It seems highly likely that many of these buildings date from the period when coal is known to have been supplied from Ness. Several new brick structures are mentioned in the Puddington estate's accounts. Again, one was a priest's house, on today's Chapel Lane (since demolished).[72] Others included a range of buildings made for the estate manager's farm including a milk-house, stable, cart house, granary and shippons (cowsheds) as well as at least one new house.[73] Jessamine Cottage, a 'landmark house' made of brick which still stands in the village centre, almost certainly dates from this period.[74]

Elsewhere on Sir Thomas Stanley's Wirral estates, there were notable periods of brickmaking recorded at Eastham (1809–10 and 1818);[75] Childer Thornton (1802, 1811, 1813, 1818 and 1826);[76] and Ledsham (1813, 1854 and 1855).[77]

Figure 8.3: A Grade II listed dovecote at Puddington. Built in red brick in English garden wall bond, the listing details state it to be 'later eighteenth century'.[78] The bricks were almost certainly made at Ness Colliery or made on site using coal (or slack) from the colliery.

Bricks made at Puddington were carted to Little Sutton in 1805 and used at the lodges there.[79] Shippons were built at Caughall near Chester in 1807.[80] To complement all the brickmaking, slates were routinely supplied by Ness Colliery, used in both roofing new-builds and for repairs.[81] As noted in the previous chapter, the colliery also supplied various types of tile from the 1820s.

The amounts of coal bought by the estate were not usually separated out in the accounts. However, figures are given for twelve months from October 1836 showing the Hooton estate alone bought 483 tons (526 tonnes) of coal (with more bought for Puddington).[82] In terms of value, this represented almost 7% of the colliery's total estimated sales that year.[83]

It seems that the estates' demand for coal and slack – for making bricks and lime, as well as for domestic and garden use – was almost inexhaustible to the extent that the fuel would often also be imported from Lancashire mines. Many records exist of such deliveries from 1810 until the end of the available accounts.[84] In particular, supplies came from Ashton and Rushey Park collieries near St Helens.[85] They were transported on flats (sailing barges) via the Sankey Canal and the River Mersey, and unloaded on the shore at Hooton or Eastham.[86] The firm of Eccles and Stock, whose owners had undertaken various underground surveys of the Neston collieries, were frequent suppliers.[87]

It is interesting to compare the costs of different ways of taking coal to Hooton. In the mid-1830s the carriage of coal by cart from Ness Colliery to Hooton cost 4s. 2d. (21p) per ton.[88] An alternative was freighting it by sea from the colliery, around the Wirral to the shore at Hooton. This cost 2s. 6d. (12.5p) per ton.[89] The problem with this, though, was the increasing difficulty in accessing the colliery quay following diversion of the Dee. Another option, obtaining deliveries from Lancashire, was more expensive – the carrier's cost was the same at 2s. 6d. per ton but there were additional canal dues of 1s. (5p) per ton.[90] This was still cheaper than carting, though. There is little evidence that Sir Thomas Stanley made much use of the round-Wirral shipping route, apparently taking advantage of the simpler or cheaper alternatives.

Agricultural Improvement
The importance of lime to British agriculture was discussed in the previous chapter. It is unsurprising, therefore, that the Stanley estates were substantial users of the commodity. In 1776 the Hooton estate had its own kiln on the shore of the Mersey but this had gone by 1802.[91] Instead, purchases from Ness Colliery are recorded in almost every year from 1801 until the colliery closed.[92] The quantities involved were often not detailed but the largest stated amount was 338 tons (368 tonnes) used in the twelve months from October 1835.[93] The important relationship between lime and coal production was evidenced by the 1829 letter from John Watson, Ness Colliery's viewer,

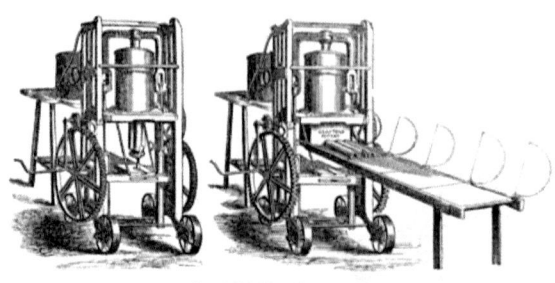

Clayton's Brick, Tile, and Pipe-making Machine.

Figure 8.4: Henry Clayton's patent 'Brick, Tile and Pipe-making Machine', a prizewinning exhibit at the 1851 Great Exhibition. Source: *Official Descriptive and Illustrated Catalogue of the Great Exhibition of the Works of Industry of All Nations*, Part II, Class IX, (London: Royal Commission, 1851), p. 360.

quoted on page 31. He argued that it was important to keep the colliery open so that Sir Thomas Stanley's tenants would be able to access inexpensive coal to make their own lime.[94] The tenants were, presumably, making the lime in semi-permanent field kilns.[95] In addition, the leases granted by the Stanley estates allowed for farm tenants to be reimbursed for the cost of lime used on the land when they had had to buy it.[96] As well as agricultural use, lime would have been used on the estates for mortar for building or repairing both brick and stone structures.

The colliery occasionally sold dung to the Stanley estate, as well as another form of fertiliser that was finding favour in the early nineteenth century (and recommended by the Board of Agriculture) – soap waste, also known as soap ashes.[97] Soap ashes were being bought from Ness Colliery by the Stanley estates from 1817 in quantities of up to 158 tons (161 tonnes) at a time.[98]

As the term implies, soap waste was a by-product of soap manufacture. The waste consisted of ashes which had been boiled in water to make an alkaline solution – lye. Lye was used in bleaching and, when combined with rendered fat, made soap. The material was often described in the Stanley accounts as 'Irish soap ashes' and the large quantities involved suggest it was exported from Ireland on vessels coming to Ness for coal. Ireland had a large soap industry. The ashes could come from burning hardwood but kelp and ferns, of which Ireland had plenty, could also be used. Vessels from Ireland sometimes brought similarly large quantities direct to the Hooton estate via the Mersey.[99] The waste ashes were usable as a fertiliser and were scattered on various parts of the Stanley estates.[100] As with lime, Sir Thomas Stanley sometimes paid for his tenants' use of it.[101] The supply from Ness Colliery appears to have ceased after 1829 – by this time access up the Dee had become very problematic.[102]

Another important form of agricultural improvement in this period was field drainage. Drainage tiles, shaped like an upside-down horseshoe, were laid in lines to assist in removing excess quantities of water from the clayey Cheshire soil;[103] it was said that land values could be 'at least doubled' by such a measure.[104] The criticality of bringing wet land into use to feed a growing population was recognised by successive governments. As noted in the previous chapter, they reduced and, by 1826, eliminated the duty which had applied to tiles used for field drainage.[105]

For many years the Stanley estates bought their tiles from Buckley.[106] In 1817 Sir Thomas Stanley decided to bring in a specialist from Staffordshire to make both bricks and various kinds of tiles at Hooton; a kiln was specially built for the purpose.[107] By 1821 tiles were being supplied by Ness Colliery.[108] In particular, thousands of drainage tiles – which had to be stamped 'DRAIN' to avoid the duty – were being bought from Ness Colliery from the 1820s, with particularly large numbers in the 1830s. These were used on various parts of the Stanley estates. To give just one example, a single farm, Lowfields in Eastham, used at least 41,300 colliery-produced tiles in 1834 to 1838 (and had also benefited from at least 46 tons (56 tonnes) of lime).[109] As well as being used to drain fields, the estate used the tiles in woodland and in the park of Hooton Hall.[110]

The estate's kilns, used for making bricks, were sometimes also used to make drainage tiles.[111] A dedicated tile yard was established near Ledsham in 1836.[112] In 1845, £53 was paid to acquire a recently-invented machine for turning out *cylindrical* 'pipe tiles' – probably similar to that shown in Figure 8.4.[113] A new tile oven was also installed and the yard began to produce large quantities of this new form of drainage aid. A steam engine was installed to assist production three years later.[114] Pipe sales generated valuable revenue for the estate, and the oven and steam-powered machinery provided a ready market for Ness Colliery's coal.[115] There was a large leap in drainage activity across Cheshire from the 1840s, reflected locally in extensive pipe-laying on the Stanley estates and elsewhere.[116] In addition, as with lime and soap ashes, tenants were often reimbursed for laying draining pipes or were, presumably, given favourable rates to buy them as landlords were keen to encourage drainage activity to enhance land values.[117]

Timber and Other Goods

The most useful resource supplied by the Stanley estates to Ness Colliery was timber from the tree plantations on various parts of its estates.[118]

One use of the timber was to make charcoal. As mentioned previously, it is not known for how long Ness Colliery made charcoal but cordwood was being supplied from the Stanley estates to the colliery as late as 1837.[119] Cordwood comprised lengths of wood of roughly uniform thickness and length which were ideal for arranging in circular stacks. These could be covered in turf or soil and slowly combusted for several days to make charcoal.

The timber had several practical uses above ground, including building and fencing, but a particular need below ground was for pit props. There were therefore frequent sales of 'propwood' to the colliery and sometimes, more specifically, naturally curved pieces of wood known as 'knee timber'. Large quantities were involved – for example '926 feet' (282 metres) of propwood paid for in January 1814 and almost 110 tons (120 tonnes) used in 1836–7.[120] The costs to the often loss-making colliery were not insignificant – £121 in 1812, for example.[121] Larger sums were spent on timber from the 1830s as production grew and, perhaps, as increasing use of the Lancashire System of coal extraction led to a greater need for underground propping.[122]

A variety of types of wood was supplied, each with different properties and uses, including ash, elm, oak, alder, abele (poplar) and withen (willow). This trade complemented the peeling of bark from felled oaks on the estates.[123] The bark was sold, presumably to tanners, as in the early nineteenth century there was considerable demand for it in leather-making.[124] It also seems the colliery had its own fishery on the Dee as wooden stakes for nets were sometimes supplied for this purpose.[125] In return, occasionally fish, as well as wild ducks, were sold to the estate.[126] Curiously, the colliery also occasionally sold timber to the Stanleys even though they clearly had plenty.[127]

Another product sold by the estates to Ness Colliery was fat (occasionally listed as 'grease'), presumably obtained from slaughtered livestock – up to 616 lbs (279 kg) in a year.[128] The fat would have had to have been rendered, i.e. melted to remove the meat tissues, in an extremely smelly process which would no doubt have been fuelled by colliery coal. The primary use would probably have been as a lubricant for machinery. However, rendered fat – tallow – had another potential use: to make (foul-smelling) candles which were, of course, essential for the colliers. Soap was also made from tallow when boiled with lye. However, there are no known specific references to such uses at the colliery.

The colliery had its own farm, discussed on pages 55–7, and sometimes the Stanley estates would buy from it – wheat, oats, hay and potato sets were sometimes purchased.[129] So was straw which may have been used for thatching; 'thatch' itself was specifically mentioned on occasions.[130] Conversely, when the colliery farm couldn't meet its own need for hay, presumably used as animal fodder, it had to buy it from the estates.[131] The Hooton estate also sometimes supplied the colliery with wheat and seeds as well as the occasional horse.[132]

The Local Impact

The supply of coal, lime and other goods to the Stanley estates required hundreds – and more probably thousands – of loaded carts to be brought from Ness Colliery by scores of different individuals over the years. To give just one of numerous possible examples, Joseph Robbins was paid to cart 175 tons (191 tonnes) of coal in 1838 to Puddington, to brick and tile kilns at Ledsham, and to Hooton for brickmaking and the 'garden' (presumably the hothouses in the forcing garden).[133] Goods were carted several miles across and up the Wirral, including to Storeton, Bebington and Upton.[134] Carting was the only role where local records explicitly mention women in connection with the coal business: the estate accounts record several instances of them transporting cartloads of coal to the Stanley estates.[135] Sir Thomas Stanley had a way to avoid paying for carting work. There are many references in estate accounts to his tenants performing 'boon-work' – occasional labour required of tenants, without charge, by their landlords.[136]

It is hard to overstate the importance of the Stanley estates to Ness Colliery. They were regular customers for a wide and growing range of goods and the revenue to the colliery was substantial. For example, in 1828, the colliery made no profit on its coal mining activities (Table 2.3 on p. 30). However, in respect of that year it gained £665 in revenue from the estates, helping to prevent a loss on coal production and probably generating a worthwhile profit on non-coal products.[137] Similarly, the total revenue from the estates in the two years to the end of September 1808 was at least £561;[138] without this sum the total loss of £560 in those years (Table 2.2 on p. 25) would presumably have been much greater. This financial information, viewed alongside John Watson's exhortation to keep the colliery open to help tenants obtain inexpensive lime (page 31), evidences the crucial role the estates played at critical times in the colliery's life.

Although the Stanley estates can have formed only a small part of the Wirral's total economic activity, nevertheless the local people and the area's economy benefited in many ways from the relationship between Ness Colliery and the Stanley estates. Employment came from the manufacturing or reselling of goods at the colliery and from transporting them; and supplies of goods *to* the colliery also gave work, particularly associated with timber. Meanwhile, the productivity of the land would have increased through the use of lime and by land drainage, both facilitated by colliery products. This would have helped to feed a growing population which provided the labour force for the many industries which developed on the Mersey side of the Wirral from the early nineteenth century.[139] This increase in agricultural productivity would have been critical in a period which saw, for example, the Wirral's population grow from 10,764 in 1801 to over 59,000 fifty years later.[140]

While the focus of this section has been on the Stanley estates, it is worth underlining that the benefits mentioned above also accrued in respect of activity directed at customers other than the Stanley estates – there would have been many folk living away from the estates who would have bought coal, lime, drainage tiles and so on. There are a number of late eighteenth- and early nineteenth-century buildings still standing locally. Many of these will have been built with the direct or indirect contribution of materials from the Neston collieries – bricks, tiles, slate, lime for mortar, or coal to make bricks on site (see, for example, Figure 12.7 on p. 227). It is probable that, even now, local people unknowingly see a legacy of the collieries' activities every day.

The Developing Road Network

The landsale trade relied upon the local area's roads and tracks for distribution. At the time that Ness Colliery opened in 1759, the Wirral's roads were said to be 'deplorably

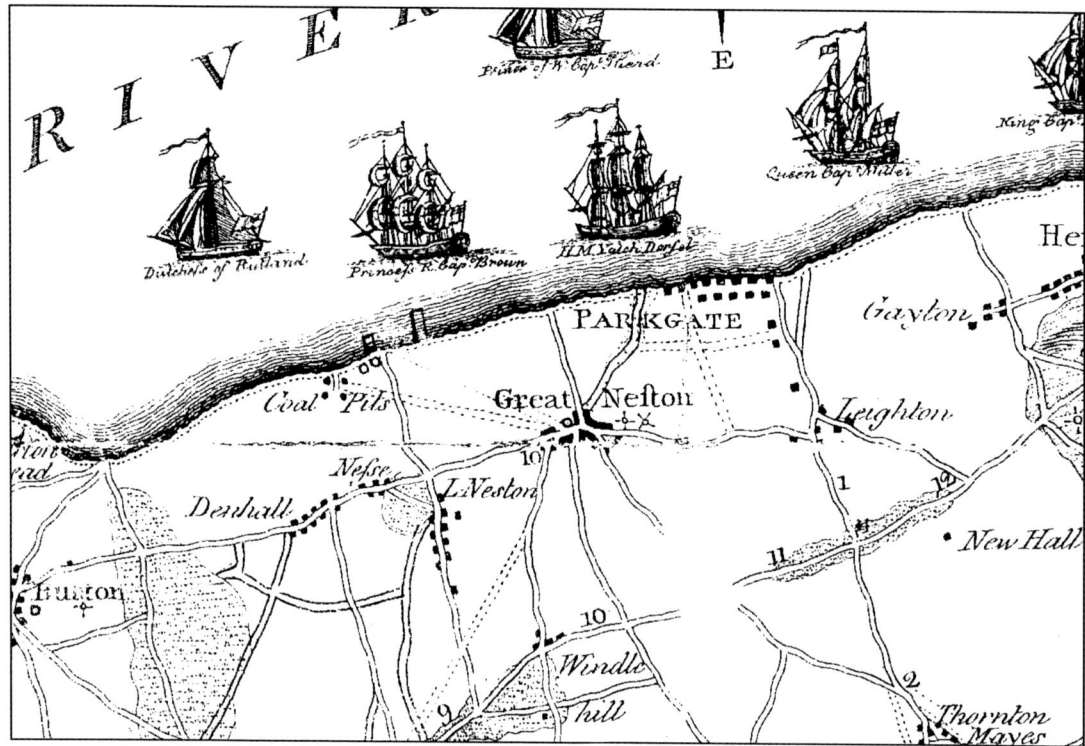

Figure 8.5: A detail from Hunter's map of *c.*1790, showing the 'proposed roads' between the area of 'Coal Pits' and Neston. The parallel strips of dotted lines are the 'proposed roads' (the upper one is rather faint). Source: CALS, PM 11/10 (with courtesy of CALS).

bad'.[141] The practice locally and elsewhere was that the burden of maintaining roads, or building new ones, fell to local communities. They had little incentive to do so if it would merely help passing travellers. The situation was, however, to improve with the introduction of turnpike roads. Their development in the eighteenth century and beyond was designed to meet the growing demands for transport of goods and people in an increasingly prosperous country. Under the turnpike system, groups of interested individuals formed trusts who maintained, upgraded and, where necessary, built roads in return for tolls levied on users.

In 1787, what has become known as the Wirral Turnpike Act brought several such roads to the peninsula. This largely led to upgrading of existing routes, and focused on established shipping locations: the Woodside and Eastham ferries on the Mersey side of the Wirral, and the port of Parkgate on the Dee side.[142] Turnpikes brought clear advantages to mine-owners with interests in land sales in terms of delivery speeds and productivity and it was common for them to invest in the new roads.[143] On the other side of the Dee Estuary, a turnpike road was built along the Flintshire coast by about 1769, specifically to carry coal from the various mines to their customers, in particular the growing number of smelting houses.[144] Unsurprisingly, then, John Stanley Massey was one of those who lent money to build the Wirral network, his estate receiving interest on the investment from 1788 onwards.[145] He was also a trustee of the scheme, alongside other members of the Stanley family and many other local figures, whose responsibility was to oversee the effective introduction and operation of the roads. While trustees were not allowed to gain direct financial benefit from the roads' tolls, it was to the benefit of those with business or significant agricultural interests to ensure the roads were well maintained and operated efficiently.[146]

Toll gates (where the barrier or 'turnpike' was situated) were positioned at various strategic locations on the Wirral, and levied a toll on road users: for horse-drawn waggons such as might be used for coal deliveries, the maximum charge allowed by the Act was 1½d.; horses or donkeys, laden or not, were usually charged one halfpenny.

Curiously, the road which led from the Stanley family's seat of Hooton Hall to Neston was authorised by the 1787 Act to be turnpiked but only subject to agreement by the majority of the 360 trustees; all the other roads merely needed five to agree. Presumably as a result of the terms of the Act, no gate appears to have been erected until about 1808.[147] The road was seen by the Stanleys as an important link from their mansion to the colliery.[148] As their interests dominated the eastern side of the Wirral served by the road – which included not only Hooton but also the village of Eastham and the important cross-Mersey Eastham ferry – maybe there was general antipathy to developing a road for the benefit of so strong a private interest (and, to the many at the time who had strong feelings on the matter, a *Catholic* interest too!).[149]

It seems that the improved roads precipitated plans for further road-building in the area. A map of the Wirral by James Hunter shows five 'proposed roads' in the Neston area including two leading to the collieries (Figure 8.5). The map is undated but was probably surveyed around 1790 – just after the turnpikes had been introduced.[150] Thus, the proposed colliery roads not only led directly to the Wirral's largest population centre at the time, Neston – thus reducing the gradient of the sloping land between the colliery and the town – but also gave onward access to other parts of the Wirral via the nascent turnpike network. The apparent timing for the road development fits with this being another of several initiatives undertaken, or intended, by Thomas Stanley Massey, later the 7th Baronet, after he took over the colliery. One of the proposed roads was linked to a quay near the colliery but, assuming this was Denhall Quay, it was misplaced on the map as it was only in the planning stage.[151] The quay was built soon after but the 'proposed roads' were never constructed, maybe for financial reasons or perhaps because of Sir Thomas's death in 1795.[152]

The many roads on the Wirral which were not turnpiked in 1787 remained in poor condition but further Acts the next century expanded the network considerably.[153] These would have facilitated the movement of coal from Neston for use in the domestic market and for local manufacturing such as brickmaking. The Act of 1826 was possibly the most important to the Neston collieries of these later Acts as it improved access to the north of the peninsula. However, ship-borne coal from North Wales or Lancashire was always a potential alternative to road traffic in more distant locations from the colliery.

*

The landsale trade was the bread and butter of the Neston collieries. It provided constant demand for the collieries' products from locals, and benefited from limited competition and being unaffected by the vagaries of the Dee. It is unsurprising that the Stanley family took an interest in the new turnpikes to make the trade easier. However, their interest went beyond road investment and the wide-ranging relationship between the Stanley estates and Ness Colliery is an enlightening example of the mutual benefits that could be derived by rural collieries and estates from each other.

CHAPTER 9

CHESTER: TRADE AND THE DEVELOPING TRANSPORT NETWORK

Whilst the landsale trade was necessarily focused on the Wirral, Chester presented an additional regional market for the coal from Ness Colliery – for domestic, institutional and industrial use. This chapter reviews the conduct of this trade, undertaken via shipping on the Dee.

Although shipping was a key way to move coal, during the lifetime of the Neston collieries important new methods for the bulk movement of heavy goods emerged – canals and railways. These offered potential opportunities for Neston's coal to reach Chester and further afield, thus generating interest by current or potential colliery owners as well as by investors in the new transport schemes – a subject looked at later in this chapter.

Trade with Chester

The large population of the city of Chester, relative to the Neston area, made it an attractive proposition for coal sales. In 1774 the city's population was said to be 14,713.[1] It had grown to over 16,000 by 1801 (Neston's was 2,353) and almost doubled over the following fifty years.[2] This drove direct consumer demand for coal for home consumption, to use for heating and cooking, as well as indirect demand to make goods including bricks to meet the growing need for housing.[3]

The economy of Chester in the late eighteenth century was built on its role as a retail, trading and social centre, acting as a transport node and with significant visitor numbers.[4] It was never a city with large amounts of heavy industry, instead having a diverse economy with over one hundred trades in the 1780s.[5] Besides brickmaking, other small-scale industries which would have driven the demand for heating fuel as part of their manufacturing process included malting, brewing, clay pipe-making, sugar-boiling, farriery and other metalworking involving gold, silver, pewter, brass and tin.[6] Coal would have suited some purposes although other fuels produced at Ness and elsewhere, such as charcoal and coke would have been preferred in some instances, having fewer impurities.[7]

By the early nineteenth century, the only heavy industries to have become established in Chester were an iron foundry and two lead-works.[8] Walker and Ward's lead-works had a steam engine by 1799, as did the Chester Roodee Iron Foundry and Paper Mill by 1800.[9] Both were possible users of the steam coal which Ness Colliery was able to supply. These were not the first engines in the city, though: this came at the Walker and Ley Flour Mill in 1785 which had acquired one of the recently patented Boulton and Watt rotative steam engines.[10]

With the growing demand for coal, a network of tradesmen evolved, variously termed merchants and dealers. Several of these intermediaries had their own coal yards by the river or in the city, some with weighing facilities.[11] One, George Lindsey, also had his own 'mark' or loading point on the Dee, at the end of a railed road from Mancot Colliery one-and-a-quarter miles (2.8 km) away, but there is no evidence that any dealer had a similar exclusive arrangement at Ness.[12] Ness Colliery had a strong advantage in being located adjacent to the estuary but several Welsh collieries used tram or rail roads to ease river access, for example at Aston, Bagillt, Northop and Buckley.[13]

Chester had had its own coal market since the seventeenth century.[14] By the time Ness Colliery was established in 1759 there were already coal landing and storage facilities in the city adjacent to the Dee, as well as a weighing machine.[15] In the 1760s several new parties sought similar land for coal yards, including Richard Richardson, co-proprietor of Ness Colliery, and John Champion, the principal owner of Bagillt Colliery.[16] The River Dee Company set up their own coal landing and weighing facility near the House of Industry (i.e. workhouse) in about 1769.[17] The growing importance of coal to the city over the following century is reflected in local directories: in 1782, four intermediaries were listed; by 1850 the number was fifteen plus six agents acting for various Denbighshire collieries.[18] There was a large informal set of suppliers, too, made up of the masters and merchants in the coasting trade. Many different individuals were paid by the City treasurer for coal including 'Thomas Ladmore for landing coals on the wasteland [of Chester]' – Ladmore being a Parkgate mariner.[19]

Although coal reached the city from collieries in Denbighshire and, from 1757, overland via an inadequate turnpike from Flintshire across Saltney marsh, much of Chester's coal came up the Dee.[20] Sadly, though, specific records by collieries or ships' masters of coal shipments to the city are scant in the decades following the opening of Ness Colliery. The most comprehensive source is the 'Register of Vessels Entering and Leaving the Port of Chester 1740–1769', which was introduced to allow calculation of the levy due from vessels using the River Dee Navigation which had been opened in 1737.[21] The register records coal sent to Chester as well as loads exported from the region by collier ships using the Navigation. The recording of coal movements is curiously incomplete in the register with no records between March 1757 and February 1764.[22] However, there are records of coal shipments from a single named colliery – Ness – in the late 1760s (Table 9.1). Most of the vessels involved were known operators in the coasting or overseas trades.[23] Another vessel known to have headed for Chester, having loaded at Ness, was the Conwy-registered *Seahorse* in 1767. She was, however, 'much damaged' in a storm and many of her coals were washed out.[24]

In addition to individual entries in the Register of Vessels there are quarterly records of a bulk figure for the 'tonnage of coals brought up the River by Ponts and other vessels'. Ponts were large, flat-bottomed boats whose small draught was suited to the shallow waters of the Dee and its estuary. This trade is recorded from 1755 – before the colliery at Ness opened – and the general trend in coal volumes carried to 1769 is upwards, reflecting growth in both demand and supply. In the final twelve months of the records almost 11,000 tons (11,979 tonnes) of coal reached Chester this way. It is impossible to say to what extent Ness Colliery was involved in these movements. There is evidence that the collieries along the Dee Navigation were involved in the 'river trade' and they were well located to do so.[25] However, that does not exclude the possibility that the ponts also visited Ness.

The records, then, of coal being transported up the Dee from Ness are very limited. Surviving records of coal purchases also give few clues – the generally intermediated nature of the trade means that they usually give no information on the original source of the fuel. There is, though, occasional evidence for Ness Colliery directly supplying the institutions and industry of Chester in its first few decades.

In 1763 Chester's Foundling Hospital bought coal from 'Mr Clarke & Co', a name used by Ness Colliery.[26] The Chester hospital took children from the overburdened Foundling Hospital in London which, since 1741, had been taking in babies – often illegitimate – from destitute mothers who were unable to care for them.[27] Much work was done to fit out the new Chester hospital, situated in the Blue Coat school, including brickwork, glazing and paving as well as 'attending the fires before the children come in'.[28] Given its young occupants, the hospital consistently bought large quantities of coal for heating, the 'cheapness' of which was one reason for establishing the institution in the city.[29] Richard Richardson, co-owner at Ness, was the hospital's treasurer; Joshua Small who later became manager at Ness, was the secretary.[30] Most of the coal came through middlemen, who had to arrange for shipments to be weighed

Table 9.1: Named vessels in the 'Register of Vessels Entering and Leaving the Port of Chester 1740–1769' carrying coal from Ness Colliery to the city. Parkgate was the official customs station for clearing coals from Ness. Source: CALS, QDN 1/5.

Date	Ship's Name, Master	Stated Place of Origin	'Burthen'
26 July 1766	*Swan*, Gother	Denna	30 tons (30.5 tonnes)
21 November 1766	*Nancy*, Davies	Ness	30 tons (30.5 tonnes)
11 April 1767	*William & John*, Cowley	Denna	10 tons (10.2 tonnes)
21 June 1768	*John*, Leather	Parkgate	40 tons (40.7 tonnes)
5 April 1769	*Pitt*, Ormandy	Ness	27 tons (27.4 tonnes)

at the 'Chester machine'.[31] Occasionally other collieries are mentioned in the hospital's records including Mostyn in which Richardson probably had a financial interest, Mancot and Sandycroft.[32] Some of the older children at the hospital were placed into apprenticeships: in 1768 one ten-year-old was apprenticed to a weaver at Willaston in Neston parish along with an eighteen-year-old given a one-month 'tryal'.[33] However, no apprenticeships were offered at collieries, working either above or below ground.

Another institutional buyer was Chester Infirmary which used about 150 tons (163 tonnes) of coal each year.[34] Again, there was a link with Alderman Richard Richardson who was an occasional board member there.[35] In the 1760s he was often paid by the Infirmary for coal and it seems very probable this was sourced from Ness Colliery. Between 1782 and 1792, the colliery was certainly the principal supplier to the Infirmary.[36] However, the institution was always under financial pressure and was sensitive to paying the best price for its coal. Thus, Ness did not have a monopoly of supply, with the Infirmary reviewing its coal contract periodically, sometimes putting it out to tender.[37] In 1806–7 Sir Thomas Stanley was nominated the Infirmary's president and in recognition of this he gifted it fifty guineas.[38]

Many other institutions are referred to in eighteenth-century city records as coal users. Locations include the city's key meeting and administrative buildings, the Pentice and the Exchange (the latter having eight chimneys: 'two kitchen chimneys, two chimneys in the assembly room, two in the drinking room, one in the room that keeps the sweet meats and one in the Regus room'), Chester Castle, Northgate Gaol, Chester workhouse and the cathedral – the last had its own coal yard and used coal in its school (the future King's School) as well as, occasionally, giving some to the poor.[39] Other users included judges' lodgings, the 'charity school' (the Blue Coat), and almshouses.[40]

As mentioned above, one local industry that was a user of coal was sugar-making; the fuel was needed to boil the cane juice as part of the refining process. It is possible that Ness Colliery directly supplied at least one of the several Chester businesses in the trade as the largest debt referred to in the colliery accounts of 1769–70 was £500, owed by Chester sugar-maker John Hincks.[41] Hincks was a Chester merchant and former investor in the slave trade who, in 1757, had formed a partnership with two Liverpool merchants to 'bake sugar' in a newly erected refining 'workhouse' in Chester.[42] The sugar partnership eventually broke up but Hincks continued in the business. When he died in 1772 his stock of 'syrups, coals etc.' was said to be valued at just £198 but he must, nevertheless, have been using large quantities of coal as his sugar stocks were often valued at thousands of pounds and his annual turnover was extraordinarily high at tens of thousands of pounds.[43] Another possible explanation for the £500 debt is that he had bought an old boat from the colliery – vessels were often valued in round numbers, and the colliery had just built a new one.[44]

Figure 9.1: 'Chester Castle and Skinner's Yard' by Francis Nicholson. The view is of Chester between about 1815 and 1830. The painting is centred on a flat – the type of vessel which Thomas Cottingham used to bring his coal to sell from a wharf here in 1823. The chimneys of nearby small industrial users – maybe a lime kiln and chemical works – belch smoke into the city air. Reproduced with kind permission of the Grosvenor Museum, Chester. (See also plate 44 in Herson.)

The various advertisements for the sale or lease of the actual or proposed Neston collieries between 1795 and 1825 make no reference to Chester as a potential market, preferring to focus on the landsale and overseas trades. Nevertheless, it seems likely that coal continued to be supplied to Chester for some time. John Aikin, writing in 1790, had mentioned solely Chester as the market for coals dug on the Wirral.[45] In 1823 Thomas Cottingham junior used a coal wharf on Skinner Street in Chester as an outlet for Little Neston Colliery's coal. He supplied it using a flat which he had bought for about £600.[46] Flats were sailing barges whose shallow draughts were well suited to the river trade to Chester (they were much used on canals and the Mersey too) (Figure 9.1).[47] Cottingham was 'always' at the wharf, and advertised his coals in the local papers.[48] How long this continued is not clear. However, records show that Ness Colliery retained river access to a greater or lesser extent until the 1850s and coasting vessels still unloaded and loaded there. A 'flatman' was recorded as living in Little Neston in the 1851 census. There was, though, no shortage of collieries in Flintshire close to the Dee, as well as in Denbighshire, which were well able to meet Chester's demand.

James Brindley and the Prospect of Canals

The opening of Ness Colliery in 1759 coincided with the dawning of an important era in the history of British transport – the canal age. The desire to create new waterways came from the need to move heavy, bulky materials such as coal as well as manufactured goods, around the country. Over the lifetime of the collieries, several schemes were put forward which could have linked the Neston collieries to Chester or even Manchester – indeed it is possible that one of the very first canals in the country may have been under consideration at Neston.

The evidence comes from the notebooks of James Brindley, the great canal engineer, who is known to have visited the colliery area at least four times in 1761 and 1762.[49] Brindley was the consulting engineer on the Bridgewater Canal, often cited as the Britain's first true canal, the initial stretch of which was opened in 1761.[50] It had been commissioned by the Duke of Bridgewater, keen to improve the efficiency of transporting coal from his colliery at Worsley to Manchester. Not all of Brindley's notebooks survive and those that do are often poorly written and lacking in detail, so they cannot give a complete picture of his activities or motives. However, he records visiting 'Par[k]Gat' in November 1761, 'Par[k]Gat Coollery' (colliery) in early April 1762, 'Parr or Neaston' (Parkgate or Neston) later in April and 'Neaston' again in July, each visit lasting one day. (Throughout Ness Colliery's life it was not unusual for it to be described in connection with nearby Parkgate which was a nationally-known location.)

Brindley was involved with other canal or river navigation schemes and, with the introduction of the Bridgewater canal, his reputation was growing swiftly.[51] He went to Chester before or after each visit to the Neston area and it appears, based on his notes and other records, that he was also investigating a possible canal connection between Chester and Shropshire.[52] Later that decade he arranged the survey preceding the first, unsuccessful, petition to Parliament to build a canal eastward from the city.[53] Brindley's main contact in Chester appears to have been Ness Colliery co-founder, Richard Richardson.[54] Brindley's visionary engineering genius and Richardson's entrepreneurship and interest in new developments of the age would have made a good match. There is, thus, plausible circumstantial evidence that Richardson had tasked Brindley with investigating the feasibility of building a canal to take coals and other goods from the new colliery at Ness to Chester and potentially beyond. Like the Duke of Bridgewater, Richardson may have wanted to improve the efficiency of the colliery's coal transport, especially given the difficulties with navigating the tidal Dee. Brindley's deliberations might explain why Richardson was in no rush to progress his 1759 request to the Chester Assembly to develop the Old Quay for coal shipments.[55]

As well as wanting to know whether the nascent Neston mining venture would make it worth the cost of building a canal, Richardson may have wanted to see how the Worsley project turned out. He may also have been waiting for the potential new inland canal from Chester – but this did not materialise in his lifetime. Whatever the issue was, it seems that things did not work out as Richardson had hoped, for no Neston-to-Chester canal ever ensued.

However, the Chester Canal, from the city to Huxley near Beeston, opened in 1775 and it was the creation in the following year of the link between the canal and the Dee which offered the possibility of inland carriage of coal mined from around the Dee Estuary.[56] In recognition of the potential for trade between river and canal, the Chester Canal Company commissioned a number of flats, modelled on boats built by the Duke of Bridgewater for his canal.[57] The first company flat was launched in 1776 and the *Chester Chronicle* of 13 December reported,

> For the first time one of the Canal barges, of the burden of about 60 tons, navigated out of the canal, thro' the five-fold lock lately compleated [*sic*] at this city, into the River Dee, to proceed on her voyage to the colliery, to load coals for the use of the interior parts of the country.

Sadly, the report did not state which colliery the barge was heading for. It could have been Ness, although the collieries near to the River Dee Navigation were closer and so, perhaps, more likely candidates.

The construction of canals presented apparent opportunities to the Neston collieries but they also created threats from competitors. For example, when the section of canal from the Mersey to Chester opened in 1796 the first commodity to be brought to the city was Lancashire coal which, it was said, 'cannot fail to be of considerable advantage to this city'.[58] It is ironic that in the decades after Sir Thomas Stanley became co-owner of Ness Colliery, he often found it more appropriate to import Lancashire coal, brought via the canal network to his estates fronting the Mersey, than to cart it across the Wirral from Ness.[59]

Proximity to the canal network was nevertheless put forward as an advantage for the Neston collieries. Trade directories from the 1830s and 1840s said:

> There are some productive coal mines worked in [Neston] parish, and the canal between the Mersey and the Dee, which passes near the town, affords the means of distributing their produce.[60]

In reality, though, the principal inland coal users such as the Cheshire saltworks were perfectly satisfactorily served by the well-developed canal network from Lancashire or, for those near the Trent and Mersey Canal, from Staffordshire.[61]

Several canal schemes were proposed in the 1820s, '30s and '40s which, if carried out, would have led to vessels passing through the area of the Neston collieries but none came to fruition.[62] Some, such as the Manchester and Dee Ship Canal in 1825, may have prompted renewed activity at Ness.[63] However, this author has found no reference to the collieries in any of the proposals and it seems that, by this time, they were of insufficient importance to give weight to the business case for the schemes.

The Promise of Railways

The final decades of Ness Colliery coincided with the introduction and development of Britain's railways. By the time the colliery closed, there were over 7,000 miles (11,265 km) of railway across Britain.[64] Railways presented a new opportunity for moving coal in bulk and it is unsurprising therefore to find that local plans for railways sought to exploit synergies with the Neston collieries.

The Wirral's first railway, the Birkenhead and Chester Railway, was formally proposed as early as 1830 by George Stephenson – just a year after his trial of the Rocket at Rainhill – and the first plans indicated it could run through Neston, benefiting from the colliery trade.[65] The possibility of using this innovative technology to transport coal must have been an exciting prospect for the owners of the Neston mines, offering a new way to reach inland markets economically and quickly. Despite this, the 'western line' was unpopular and not deemed viable even with the expected trade from the Ness and Little Neston collieries (as well as Sir Thomas Stanley's quarry at Storeton).[66] Instead a preferred eastern route, nearer the Mersey, soon emerged.[67]

There were no further serious proposals to develop local railways for several years, but in 1845 four schemes were put forward to build lines to the Neston area, linking with others running to Chester and the new town of Birkenhead. This period was the peak of 'railway mania', a speculative bubble in which numerous schemes were proposed across the country, many of which did not come to fruition.[68]

Connections to the collieries featured in two of the new propositions, both of which involved Edward Mostyn Lloyd Mostyn who was preparing to sell his extensive interests in the Neston area. One of the schemes was the Liverpool, Birkenhead, Parkgate and Holyhead Junction Railway.[69] The aim was to create a route which ran across the Wirral from Birkenhead, passed a few hundred yards from the Neston collieries and crossed the Dee Estuary to meet the Chester–Holyhead line, which was under construction. Claims that the intended railway went 'through the extensive coal field' at Denhall (which wasn't strictly true) and would bring cheap coal to the large, new town of Birkenhead were amongst the attractions offered to investors.[70] The company was to undergo various amalgamations but the plan was never executed.

Perhaps more significant to Mostyn was the Parkgate and Chester and Birkenhead Junction Railway, proposed in 1845.[71] This was to run from Parkgate across the Wirral to meet the Chester–Birkenhead Railway at Bebington. Again, there was evidence of a willingness to mislead the public with the announcement stating cheekily that the route went through Little Neston and Ness: this was untrue but was presumably included to attract investors.[72] In the original proposal the station was to be located just a quarter of a mile from what is today The Parade at Parkgate. However, in 1847 boreholes were sunk in the estuary off Mostyn's Great Neston estate, resulting in the finding of coal which was widely reported with excitement.[73] Apparently as a result of this, the location of the station was moved to the top of today's Moorside Lane (Figure 1.2 on p. 4), convenient for the proposed colliery at the bottom of the road, as well as for access to Neston and Parkgate (Mostyn also proposed a new road between Parkgate and Neston, running across Moorside Lane, which would have enabled heavy coal-carts to bypass a climb into the town).[74]

An Act for the railway's construction was given royal assent in 1847 and gave up to five years for the works to be completed.[75] It allowed the railway owners to charge tolls for goods carried including coal, coke, charcoal, fireclay, bricks and lime. It also gave the company the right to sell or lease the line to the Chester and Birkenhead Railway Company, which would enable investors to realise a valuable return quickly. Work appears to have started on the line in 1849 when the first sod was said to have been dug.[76] This was nicely timed to precede by just a few months the principal sale of Mostyn's Neston estate, for which the railway was an important part of the proposition – sale advertisements stated that the railway was 'in the course of formation'.[77] Perhaps unsurprisingly, after the sale of the estate, the Mostyn-led railway plan lost impetus; there also seems to have been a legal disagreement with the Irish building contractor.[78] Ultimately, the Parkgate and Chester and Birkenhead Junction Railway, like so many others in the country around this time, was never built.

Two other 1845 schemes proposed railways to the Neston area and more were to follow in the 1850s.[79] Two of these later schemes, both called the 'Hooton and Neston Railway', were proposed by Cynric Lloyd, nephew to Lord Mostyn, and were intended to have their terminus at the bottom of Moorside Lane from where the proposed coalfield was to be worked.[80] It seems likely that it was the first such proposal, in late 1851, which raised hopes for the sale of Thomas Cottingham's colliery at Little Neston to the extent that the auction was postponed to enable plans for the impending railway to be confirmed.[81] Would-be investors in the colliery were told that a branch line to the new railway could be constructed for a 'trifling outlay', opening up new markets for the coal.[82] The proposed railway did not, however, proceed.

The scheme was resurrected in 1858 and proved attractive to two proposed local mining businesses. Mostyn was still trying to get a mine open at Parkgate and an 1859 report on it said (after referring to the possibility of an 'enterprising colliery owner' cleaning out the silted-up shipping channel at a 'very small cost'): 'There is a prospect of an additional and even more desirable means of transit for these mines being provided by means of a railway'.[83] Around this time the Anglican Smelting, Reduction and Coal Company Limited, whose shareholders included Cynric Lloyd, was established on the site of the old Little Neston Colliery, primarily to process gold and lead ore.[84] It also intended to mine coal, taking it to Birkenhead and Liverpool, and the directors saw the proposed railway as a considerable advantage. The parliamentary bill for the line passed its early stages but the railway did not materialise and little, if anything, came of the smelting and mining works.[85]

It was not until 1866 that a railway reached the Neston area, following a proposal first made in 1861.[86] This was too late to be of any benefit to the Ness or Little Neston collieries. It was to be almost another decade before a mineral line was constructed from Parkgate to the newly opened Neston Colliery, enabling coal to be transported economically in bulk.[87]

As a footnote, it should be mentioned that it is very unlikely that the Neston collieries ever helped to power the region's early steam locomotives. They used coke as fuel until about 1860 and there is no evidence that the local collieries were still making coke by the time steam trains were introduced.[88]

*

The scale of Chester – its population and range of institutions and industries – made it a natural market for the Neston collieries' products for as long as the city remained accessible to them. However, competition from the closer Welsh mines meant that the Neston works were seldom if ever the automatic choice of supply source. The River Dee was key to access but, as explored in the next chapter, changes to the river's course meant shipping access became increasingly difficult. It seems this led to a concomitant decline in the trade in Neston's coals to Chester.

The previous chapter discussed how the evolving road network improved land access for coal supplies. The Industrial Revolution was a period of great advances in transport – some have dubbed it a 'transport revolution'.[89] The Neston collieries were not immune from excited exploration of how canals and, later, railways could make it easier to shift the works' bulky output to Chester and elsewhere. However, even in this age of heady development, economic reality won out and neither canal nor railway came to the aid of Neston's increasingly troubled mines.

CHAPTER 10

THE SEASALE TRADE – AN INTRODUCTION

The trade in coals shipped to sea was highly valuable to Ness Colliery for the first sixty years of its existence (as we will see, it was of much less use to Little Neston Colliery). Indeed, the colliery's role has been widely misunderstood and understated by writers and researchers who have generally attributed most, if not all, of the coal business from the port of Chester at this time to the Flintshire collieries.[1] This chapter and the next seek to explain the nature of this trade and to clarify the Neston collieries' role in it. The operation of the local customs stations and the quays from which coal was shipped will also be considered.

Background to the Seasale Trade

Coal was a very heavy commodity in relation to its value and this had a considerable influence on the economics of coal operations. Coal industry historian, Michael Flinn, has said 'It was customarily assumed in the eighteenth century, that land carriage of coal doubles its pithead price in ten miles' and that 'coal could be carried twenty times as far by water as by land for the same unit cost'.[2] Adam Smith, often called the 'father of economics', who was writing during Ness Colliery's heyday, said 'By means of water-carriage, a more extensive market is opened to every sort of industry than what land-carriage alone can afford it'.[3]

The Neston collieries had an advantage over many other coal mines in that they were adjacent to the sea, so it was natural that the owners sought to exploit this good fortune. Indeed, the ability for coal to be easily carried in bulk to widely dispersed customers was Ness Colliery's principal competitive advantage.

In order to understand this form of business – the seasale trade – and to appreciate the nature and extent of the collieries' involvement in it, it is essential to comprehend two closely related issues. Firstly, the different types of seasale trade – covered relatively briefly below as we will return to it in the next two chapters. Secondly, the state of the Dee Estuary insofar as it affected the ability of vessels to navigate it and to access the collieries. This latter point, in turn, influenced the degree of competition Ness Colliery faced. These issues are covered in later sections of this chapter.

The British seasale business during the period under review can be divided into two main types: the coasting trade and the overseas trade (there was additionally the river-borne trade to Chester, discussed in the previous chapter). In the former (sometimes also termed the 'coastwise' or 'coastal' business) vessels confined themselves to working their way around the British coast. As far as the collieries in the Dee Estuary were concerned, this usually meant journeying to the towns of North Wales but occasionally vessels ventured further south, or went north to Lancashire and beyond. The 'overseas' trade, on the other hand, involved transportation of coal across any sea or ocean. This included trade to Ireland and the Isle of Man as well as further afield to Europe or even across the Atlantic. There were several differences between the two types of business which will be explored later but, most importantly in the context of the navigability of the estuary, coasting vessels tended to be smaller and of shallower draught, carrying lighter loads.

Knowing the destination of a coal-carrying vessel makes it simple to identify whether it was involved in the coasting, overseas or river trades. It is, however, much less straightforward to identify at which colliery on the Dee or its estuary the vessel loaded – whether at Ness or at one of the several Flintshire collieries on or near the coast, stretching from the Hawarden area in the south to Mostyn near the mouth of the estuary. The problems arise from the nature of the surviving records.

In order to organise customs activity, the Exchequer had appointed various head-ports around the coast of England and Wales. The Port of Chester was one of these, its jurisdiction spanning from Barmouth in west Wales to the River Duddon in today's Cumbria.[4] Despite this geographical breadth of responsibility, officials at Chester were responsible for maintaining records relating only to shipping at Chester itself or in the Dee Estuary – not the various subordinate 'member-ports' and 'creeks' along the rest of the coastline, such as Liverpool or Caernarfon. However, Chester's importance was such that, when talking of a vessel carrying coal from anywhere situated up to the mouth of the Dee Estuary, it was common practice in official records, contemporary news accounts and other sources merely to indicate that a shipping movement was to or from 'Chester' or 'The Port of Chester', regardless of the specific place of arrival or departure. The phrases 'Chester Water' or 'Chester River' were also sometimes used, generally when referring to the estuary itself. This means that, when a record of a coal shipment from, say, 'Chester' is found, it is generally not obvious whether it was loaded at Ness or on the Flintshire coast from one of the nearby collieries. (For the avoidance of doubt, in this book all such places of loading and unloading on the Dee Navigation and in the estuary, as well in the city itself will be taken to comprise the 'port of Chester'; all these locations fell within coverage of the King's Remembrancer Port Books for Chester, as discussed below and illustrated in Figure 10.1.)

Another problem regarding the surviving records is that a great deal of seasale trade was conducted through merchants who bought the coal from a colliery at a riverside quay and then sold it where they could find an attractive market. Thus, records of coal movements are seldom attributed to a specific colliery; instead, frequently only the names of the merchant and ship's master (who were often, but not always, the same person) were recorded. Few records of the transactions between the merchant and a colliery survive. To further complicate things, coal-carrying vessels – frequently termed 'colliers' – were sometimes so plentiful that, for example, the Irish newspapers would simply report that a certain number of colliers had entered a port without even naming the vessel or its master.[5] Finally, the availability of surviving

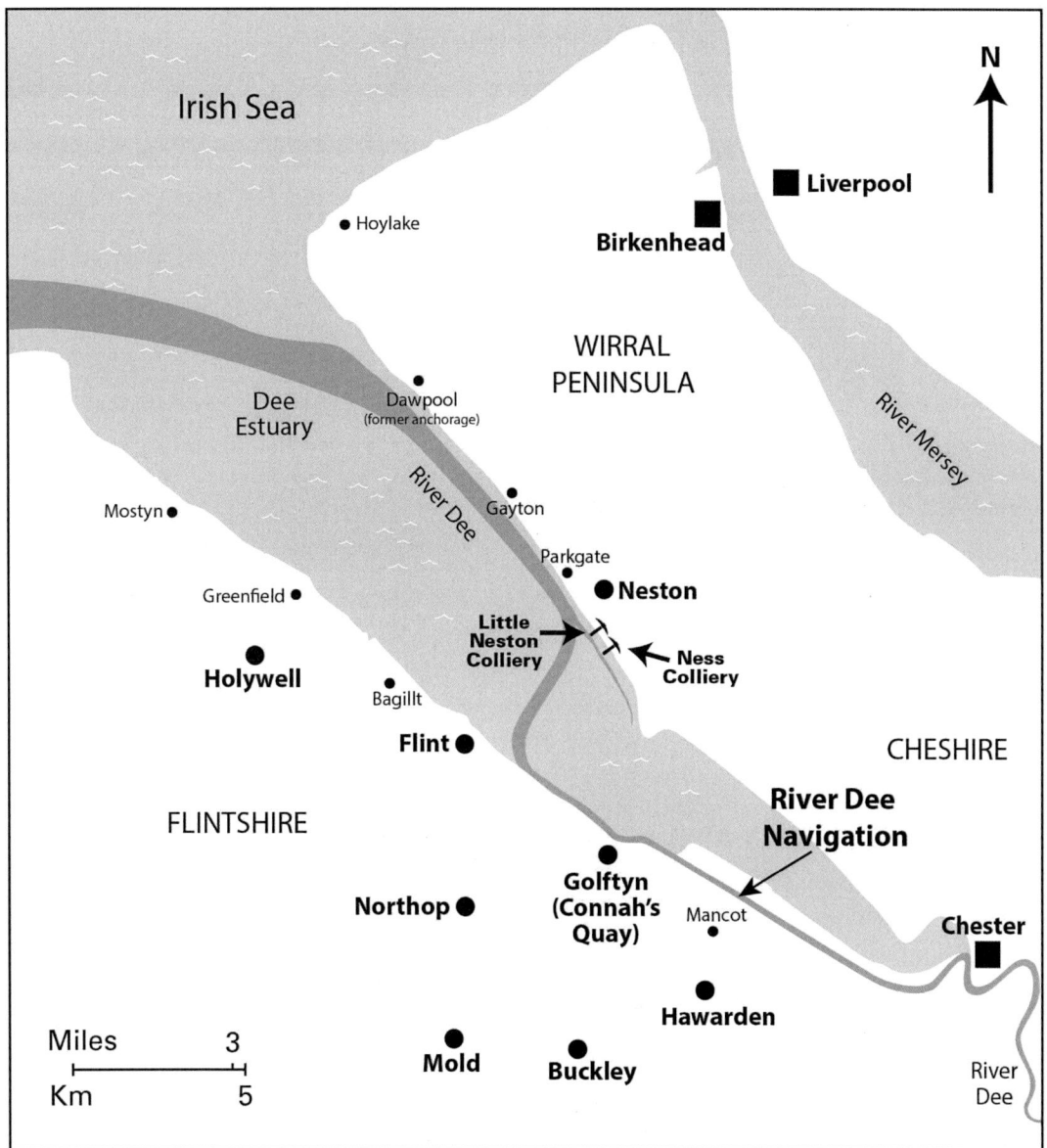

Figure 10.1: Chester, the River Dee Navigation and the Dee Estuary – the area covered by the Chester customs officials' port books. The course of the River Dee is shown here as it was in the first few decades of Ness Colliery's operation. The most important locations for shipping varied with the course and state of the River Dee over the years.

records is very hit-and-miss: for example, comprehensive Exchequer records survive for Chester's overseas trade during the first fifteen years of Ness Colliery's operation (in the King's Remembrancer Port Books kept by Chester customs officials, hereafter

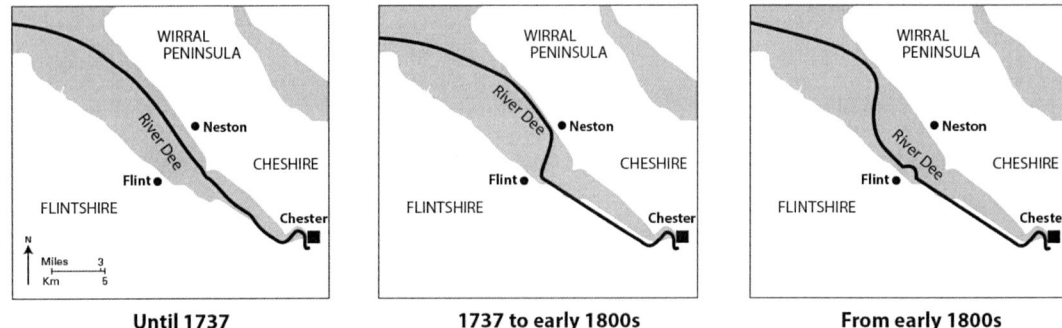

Until 1737 **1737 to early 1800s** **From early 1800s**

Figure 10.2: Changes to the main course of the Dee over time. The maps should be treated as indicative as there were variations in the course as well as other channels branching off. In particular the post-1800 position was very variable. Sources: National Maritime Museum, Greenwich, G221:4/2, Greenvile Collins, 'A New & Exact Survey of the River Dee or Chester' (1689); CALS, D3968/1, John Evans's 'North-East Wales and the Dee Estuary' (1794); OS, one-inch LXXIX (1840).

termed the 'port books'); however, the availability of information on the coasting trade is not as good during that period (see Appendix IV).[6] From the mid-1770s the surviving records are wholly serendipitous; there are no detailed customs records of outbound trade, and other sources – principally newspaper reports – occur only occasionally and are much less comprehensive. Despite these various problems, an understanding of the state of the local waters does help to give greater clarity about the origins of many of the coal vessels leaving the Dee Estuary and the extent to which the Neston collieries were involved.

The Navigation of the Dee

Siltation of the River Dee and its estuary had been a problem for centuries. It presented navigational challenges due to shifting sands, limiting access by large vessels to destinations along the coast up to Chester.[7] In an attempt to address the problem, the River Dee Navigation was opened in 1737. Whereas, until then, the river almost wholly flowed along the English coast, from that year the river ran from Chester in a canalised section for almost 8 miles (12.9 km) along the Welsh side of the estuary until Golftyn (now Connah's Quay).[8] At that point the river swung across the estuary to rejoin its old route just south of the well-established port of Parkgate, then continuing its previous course (Figure 10.2). The scheme created thousands of acres of land for reclamation and in terms of navigability of the river, was intended to guarantee sixteen feet of water at Chester at a moderate spring tide.[9] However, even after the Dee Navigation was open, problems remained. One source described the new course of the river across the estuary as so unstable that it was impossible to give a worthwhile description of it to ships' masters.[10] The frequent need to use lighters (typically, flat-bottomed barges) to transfer goods between Parkgate and the city of Chester indicates continued access problems throughout the second half of the eighteenth century.[11] Despite this, the city was able to function as an active port and even developed its dock infrastructure.[12] However, the aim of achieving sixteen feet depth of water in the Dee Navigation was never achieved and vessels might have to wait a week or more before a suitable tide arose to allow access.[13]

Although improved access to the collieries around Hawarden was one of the implied aims of the Dee Navigation, this access could still be difficult and the situation was to worsen;[14] fortunately for the colliery owners there, they had other options. They had ready markets for river sales to Chester, and increasing industrialisation on their doorstep – firms which were hungry for coal.[15] Thus, for example, Sandycroft Colliery saw a thirty-three-fold increase in land sales between 1757 and 1778.[16] Furthermore, these collieries were unlikely to be the first choice as a place of loading for merchants wishing to ship coals, especially overseas: why choose to load from one of the collieries on the Dee Navigation, incurring the levy applied for using the waterway of up to 18*d*. (7.5p) per ton, if there were opportunities to load without this additional charge at collieries situated on or near the Dee Estuary?[17] The 'Register of Vessels Entering and Leaving the Port of Chester' shows just eleven vessels using the Dee Navigation to export coals overseas in the period June 1764 to September 1769.[18] The coastwise trade was more active but the loads were small, averaging about ten tons (10.9 tonnes).[19] In any event, only a small proportion of coastwise coal traffic appears to have used the Navigation – about 18% in a sample year of 1767.[20] By implication, the bulk of coal shipments must have come from one or more collieries in the estuary which did not have to use the Navigation – but which one(s)?

It is clear that any coal shipped from the port of Chester prior to the opening of Ness Colliery in 1759 must have come from one of the many collieries on or near the coast of Flintshire. The main ones close to the open estuary were located near Flint, Bagillt and Mostyn (Figure 10.1). However, the Irish trade from the North Wales collieries had been in more or less continuous decline throughout the eighteenth century, compared to export volumes in the seventeenth;[21] this decline was even more marked in the decade before the Ness operation opened. According to the Chester port books, in 1750, sixty-four coal-carrying vessels left the Welsh quays, sixty-one of which were bound for Ireland (Appendix V). However, by 1758 only nineteen did so (fourteen for Ireland), with no vessels sailing for almost six months between October 1758 and April 1759. One possible contributory factor could have been the Seven Years' War, which started in 1756 and brought risk of attack by French vessels on British shipping; however, it does not appear to have affected non-coal trade from Chester considerably (including exports of lead, calamine, indigo and cochineal).[22] Thus, not only was there an absolute decline in coal exports but there was also a relative one – in 1750, 80% of exporting vessels carried coals; in 1758 it was half that figure. Another factor which may have distorted the market around this time was the 'discovery' of a large stockpile of coal at Bagillt (Flintshire) in 1756 which, it was said, subsequently made its way to the Irish market. However, the impact, if any, on Chester's shipping volumes is far from clear.[23] The state of the Dee would have been a factor as well, though – part of a long, slow decline in the Flintshire seasale business because of the receding local waters.

The 'Register of Vessels Entering or Leaving the Port of Chester' during the 1750s make specific mention only of 'ponts' (flat-bottomed boats) and 'small boats' carrying coals to Chester from the Welsh collieries by the estuary which might suggest that larger vessels were generally struggling to gain access.[24] Thomas Pennant, writing later that century, remembered only 'small vessels' loading at Mostyn Quay.[25] He commented that whereas craft of 200 tons could access the collieries of Mostyn and nearby Bychton at the start of the eighteenth century, in the 1770s 'vessels of sixty or seventy [tons] cannot approach nearer than two miles' due to the deterioration in the state of the shipping channels.[26] This left the Welsh collieries in a 'low state'. A few larger vessels must still have reached the collieries on the highest tides at that time, as Pennant reported that 'we load a few vessels for Ireland and some parts of North Wales'.[27] However, even this small Irish trade seems to have died altogether by 1796 when he commented that Mostyn's seasale trade consisted of just 'a few small vessels for the neighboring [sic] coasts of North Wales'.[28] Things seems to have been no better at Flint where, in the 1770s, the Dee was 'some distance' from the walls of the castle, despite having formerly flowed beneath them.[29]

The situation was considerably better on the English side of the estuary. While access to Parkgate was not without its difficulties, relatively large vessels were able to reach the port throughout the eighteenth century and could navigate an offshoot of the main channel, which became known as the Colliery Gutter, as far as the quays which were built at the Neston collieries.[30] A 1794 mariners' chart shows water near to the collieries no less than 2½ fathoms deep (15 feet; 4.6 metres) at the lowest tide.[31] However, this chart, and a contemporary map, give little, if any, indication of navigability which might enable large vessels to reach the Welsh coast north of Flint.[32] The Welsh collieries' problems worked to Ness Colliery's advantage: it was able to capitalise on the most important market – Ireland – while the Welsh competition could only watch impotently.

All these factors mean that, when considering coal exports to Ireland and other overseas markets from the port of Chester from around 1760 to the start of the nineteenth century, we can be increasingly confident that this coal emanated from Ness Colliery. This conclusion appears to be reflected in the port books recording exports from Chester. As discussed, the general trend in exports of coal to Ireland from the port of Chester in the early eighteenth century had been downwards, with a significant low in the 1750s – these exports must have emanated from Flintshire as Ness Colliery

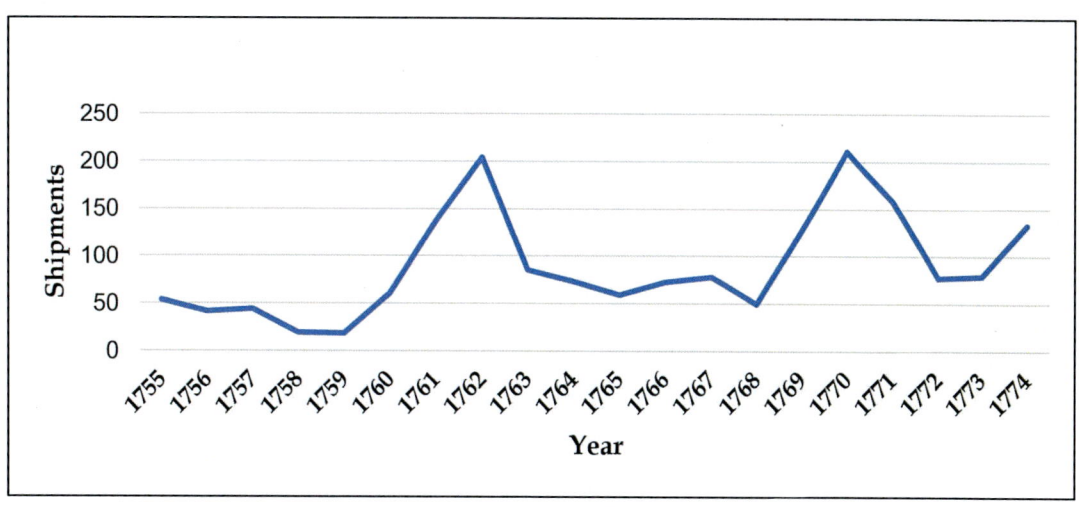

Figure 10.3: Number of overseas shipments of coal recorded in the Chester port books in the years before and after the opening of Ness Colliery in 1759. Source: TNA, E 190 series (see Appendices IV and V).

was not open.[33] Figure 10.3 shows the number of vessels exporting coals overseas from the port of Chester in the period 1755–74; this shows a sharp rise immediately following Ness Colliery's opening. In 1760, the colliery's first full year of operation, sixty coal-carrying vessels left the port and two years later the number reached 204, representing 81% of all of Chester's overseas shipping movements – a substantial absolute and relative increase on previous years. Such growth just as Ness Colliery opened seems unlikely to be mere coincidence.[34] There was also a peak in shipments in 1769–70, just as the colliery was going through a period of major rejuvenation. The intervening years were somewhat quieter but this largely mirrors the pattern of shipments of *all* goods from the port of Chester, not just coal, suggesting other factors were in play.[35]

There is considerable further supporting evidence for the dominance of coal from Ness over its Welsh counterparts, as far as the Irish trade was concerned. As noted above, the place of loading for coal was not routinely reported in customs or other records. However, when on occasions it was, in all but one instance found to date the reference is to coal being loaded at Ness, not at a Flintshire colliery (the single exception is in 1762, when the Flintshire coast was presumably still just about accessible at times).[36] Many of these cases are discussed in the next chapter. A further point of corroboration is the appointment of a dedicated customs official at Ness Colliery in 1759 – discussed more fully below – which reflected the immediate importance of the colliery upon its opening; no Flintshire colliery appears to have merited a similar appointment.[37] Customs receipts at Parkgate in the 1790s also suggest that most, if not all, coal exports from the port of Chester, came from local coal.[38] One additional piece of evidence is that many of the vessel and masters' names in the port books were well known traders out of nearby Parkgate in the 1760s and later, based upon a variety of contemporary sources.[39]

There are fewer surviving records for the coastwise coal trade and many that do survive are in poor condition; it is therefore not possible to create a meaningful series of continuous data similar to that underlying Figure 10.3. Nevertheless, patterns are discernible, with indications of spikes similar to those in the overseas trade. Coastwise coal traffic rose from 153 departures in 1760 to 241 in 1762 – a 58% increase (Appendix V).[40] The next highest number of coastwise sailings based on the data available was in 1770 with 208. It seems that the new source of coal, at Ness, with apparent easy access for shipping, stimulated the coastwise trade as well as the overseas one.

It can reasonably be concluded that the state of the Dee meant that for several decades there was little competition in the Irish trade between Ness Colliery and the Flintshire collieries – the conditions which favoured the former disadvantaged the latter. There was, though, likely to have been more competitive pressure in the coasting business where vessels with shallow draughts experienced fewer access difficulties (in addition there was plenty of competition in both trades from collieries elsewhere on the west coast of Britain, discussed later in this chapter). Even as late as 1803 there were still said to be 'numerous vessels' travelling between Ireland and Ness Colliery.[41] But the situation did not last, and the fortunes of the English and Welsh collieries were to be reversed.

It seems the changes were precipitated by actions by the River Dee Company to shift the course of the Dee to continue to follow the Flintshire coast, rather than swinging across the estuary towards Parkgate. The first such actions appear to have been taken by 1771 and others were to follow over the next few decades involving leading engineers of their time.[42] These included, from 1817, Thomas Telford but even before his involvement, alterations to the course of the river were noticeable.

An early sign may have been the coming of the Irish Coal Company to Northop in 1798 and the subsequent building of a tramway from their inland collieries to the Dee.[43] Maybe they were responsible for the uplift in coal exports from the port of Chester in 1799.[44] A decade later, Thomas Norbury, a Holywell man and prolific letter writer, recorded how the course of the Dee was swinging from the Cheshire side of the estuary to the Flintshire one.[45] In early 1816 he wrote that 'There is now a depth of water sufficient [off the coast between Flint and Bagillt] to swim one of the largest ships in the navy'. The change was so marked that Norbury noted that the owner of Bagillt colliery, Edward Roscoe, built a jetty from which he could load his coals. There were other significant investments in Flintshire's riverside industry around this time including the construction of large wharves in 1812 to access a smelting works at Flint, and moves from 1816 to improve the dock serving the Mostyn coal works and river access to it.[46] This decade seems to have seen the most significant alterations in the course of the river and, even though this movement faltered on occasions, the trend was unmistakable.[47] In 1820, Thomas Telford reported that, following the carrying out of work he had previously recommended, the course of the river no longer turned 'at nearly a right angle' towards the Cheshire coast but now headed towards the middle of the estuary.[48] He later added that the river was 'daily moving into the desired direction'.[49] But the 'desired direction' for those with interests in Flintshire industries was a disastrous direction for the people of the Neston area as the waters were receding ever further.

As early as 1806, a Ness Colliery advertisement felt it necessary to seek to reassure ships' masters that the works remained accessible, claiming that 'There is sufficient water in the channel to the colliery for vessels not drawing more than 10 feet of water, at a moderate spring tide'.[50] In 1814, forty collier ships managed to sail to Ireland from Parkgate (Ness Colliery's official customs station) but, by then, they represented less than one fifth of the total coal sailings from the port of Chester.[51] The decline in shipping on the English side of the estuary was unstoppable: the following year, the well-established packet ship sailings to Ireland ceased operating out of Parkgate; Holyhead and Liverpool could offer a much better service.[52] Coal exports to Ireland from Chester reached nearly 13,000 chaldrons in 1818 (as well as 14,000 shipped coastwise; a chaldron was about 1.4 tons or 1.5 tonnes).[53] Whereas, in the late eighteenth century, the majority of such overseas exports would have come from Ness, in 1818 the large majority would have come from Flintshire. The infrequency of the waters coming to Ness is even implied by a surveyor's suggestion in 1819 that a borehole to seek coal could be sunk from the bed of the river – an idea which does not appear to have been worth suggesting previously as it would have been rapidly overwhelmed by the tides.[54]

The rapid deterioration in Neston's seasale coal trade was noted by John Hanshall, writing in late 1822 or early 1823, who said:

> For a number of years [Ness Colliery] furnished a plentiful supply [of coal] for a great part of the Hundred of Wirral, beside encouraging a considerable export trade to Ireland. The late encroachment of the sands, however, prevents the approach of vessels of burden; the trade in consequence has considerably decreased, and it is now carried on in flats and barges, when the tides afford facility for approach.[55]

The flats and barges Hanshall mentions were designed for coasting and inland waters, not overseas business.[56] The Irish trade had collapsed and, while the odd vessel may have crossed the Irish Sea in the 1820s from Ness or the newly opened Little Neston Colliery, no records of any such sailings have yet been found. The collieries became increasingly dependent on the coasting trade which continued to a small extent until their close.

Reports from Thomas Telford throughout the 1820s reveal his considerable satisfaction with changes to the course of the Dee.[57] In 1828 he believed the river 'was in as perfect a state as it is capable of'. The course's transfer, however, had not only damaged Neston's coal business but was also detrimental to the important local tourist trade. Writing in Parkgate in 1829, map-maker and diarist William Holden recorded that 'The channel is now made on the Welch [*sic*] side [so that] Flint has become a much pleasanter residence than this'.[58]

Despite the diversion of the river, the problems of the Flintshire mines were not over. Welsh historian Arthur Dodd, writing a century after the event, was fairly downbeat about the early nineteenth-century Flintshire mines.[59] Continued problems with river access, exhausted pits, increasing competition and the economic slump following the 1825–6 financial crisis all took their toll. Nevertheless, the owners of the Neston collieries must have looked on with envy. By the 1830s, up to 100,000 tons (108,900 tonnes) of coal were routinely being shipped coastwise from Flintshire each year (Appendix VI). In 1832 alone, Flint – which was said to be becoming '*The* Port of Chester' (author's italics) – recorded 570 coasting vessels leaving with coal, as well as seventy-four bound for Ireland.[60] Over 36,000 tons (39,204 tonnes) of coal were reported as shipped from the town that year.[61] Flint later struggled for river access but, in 1844, there was said to be good access to the dock at Mostyn which could take vessels of 300 tons (327 tonnes), carrying away '50 or 60,000 tons' (54,450–65,340 tonnes) of coal per annum.[62] There is, though, absolutely no indication of any significant volumes of coastwise or overseas sales from Neston during this period.

Customs Activity

The rise and fall of shipping of Neston's coal was reflected in the activities of the customs service. The sea-borne carriage of coal – both overseas and coasting – attracted the attention of successive governments who saw it as a valuable opportunity to raise taxes; a complex and often-changing set of duty rates evolved.[63] The customs officers' main role was thus to ensure that the correct duty was applied and to check that there was no evasion of duty or smuggling of other goods. When Ness Colliery opened, the prevailing rate of duty of one shilling (5p) applied to every chaldron of coal exported to Ireland.[64] This rate was later increased by twopence (1p) but was still substantially less than the hefty duty of 5s. 6d. (27.5p) per chaldron on the coastwise trade at that time.[65]

It seems that the establishment of a new colliery at Ness was viewed as so significant by the customs service that a dedicated customs officer was appointed there, probably in July 1759 when the colliery was first opened.[66] The appointee was John Humphreys whose title was 'waiter and searcher', a relatively junior rank. Humphreys lived and had an office in Ness township for a number of years, although Parkgate was the 'legal quay' for customs purposes and was where coal-carrying vessels were often stated to originate.[67] From about 1795 Humphreys seems to have been based in Parkgate, though still having responsibility for clearing the colliery's ships out of the port.[68]

Humphreys died in 1812 aged eight-two (after sixty-five years' service 'without an hour's illness' it was said) and the decision was made not to replace him – presumably as colliery and other shipping was in decline.[69] His duties were to be carried out by the Parkgate customs officials, at a saving of £30 per annum to the Treasury.[70] The continued deterioration in trade – albeit with evidence of *some* Irish traffic – is indicated in a Customs service report in 1820 recommending a further reduction in local staff, 'as the foreign trade at Parkgate is solely coals exported and cattle from Ireland'.[71]

After Humphreys' death, the absence of a dedicated customs official to clear coals outwards from Parkgate gave problems to the local coal works. In 1819 Richard Ashhurst, acting for the proprietors of Ness Colliery, made a request to Chester officials that vessels loaded at Ness be cleared outwards from Parkgate, implying this had not been the case over the previous few years.[72] A similar request was made by Thomas Leacroft on behalf of Little Neston Colliery in 1823, about three years after it had opened – his petition indicated that vessels were having to travel up to Chester to be cleared.[73] His request was in respect of the coasting trade implying that the overseas trade was, by now, of little if any consequence. Both collieries' requests were approved. After the customs station at Parkgate was officially closed in 1828, the proprietors of Ness Colliery again complained as officials were charging travelling expenses to come from Chester to oversee the unloading of goods there.[74] The unloading may have related to limestone and slate imported from North Wales; sometimes oats were brought in from Beaumaris on Anglesey.[75] The appeal was allowed.

Wider Competition

The changing nature of the rivalry between the Neston collieries and their Flintshire counterparts has been discussed above. It is important to recognise, though, that all these coal works within the boundaries of the port of Chester were in competition with coalfields elsewhere. Over the life of the Neston collieries this competition increased markedly.

The growing town of Liverpool was supplied by coalfields in Lancashire and ease of access increased as the canal network evolved: first the Sankey Brook Navigation, the initial section of which was opened in 1757, and then the Leeds and Liverpool Canal in 1774.[76] Thus Liverpool was never a realistic market for Neston's coal, receiving 70–80,000 tons (76,230–87,120 tonnes) of coal per year from the St Helens coalfield alone in the early 1770s.[77] Moreover, the Lancashire collieries also shipped their coals *from* Liverpool, becoming increasingly active in both the coasting and overseas trades. In 1770, 2,134 chaldrons were said to have been sent to Ireland from

Liverpool, considerably less than the 8,832 chaldrons from the port of Chester from which Ness would almost certainly have been the main supplier (further quantities were shipped to other overseas destinations from Liverpool, mostly across the Atlantic).[78] Twenty-two years later, almost fourteen times that quantity was sent from Liverpool to Ireland while exports from Chester over the same period had fallen. Table 10.1 gives data for four years showing the rise of the Liverpool seasale coal trade in the late eighteenth century and indicating some recovery for the port of Chester's equivalent trade by 1819 – although sea sales from Ness Colliery itself were in severe decline by this time.

Table 10.1: Coal shipped from the ports of Chester and Liverpool, 1770, 1792, 1819 and 1828, measured in Winchester chaldrons. The years are ones in which most comparable data is available. For further comparison, Whitehaven shipped 217,972 chaldrons in 1828, 86% of it to Ireland. The ports of South Wales shipped considerably more than that in the same year.

Sources: Chester (1770) – TNA, E 190 1440/7, 1440/8, 1440/12; Liverpool (1770 and coastwise 1792) – Liv. RO, Holt Gregson Papers, xix, 49; Liverpool (overseas) and Chester (1792) – Parl. Papers, *Report from the Committee Appointed to Consider of the Coal Trade* [sic] *of the United Kingdom*, Appendix 42, HOCP Vol. 132 (1800); Liverpool and Chester (1819 and 1828): Parl. Papers, Report from the Select Committee of the House of Lords Appointed to Take into Consideration the State of the Coal Trade, Paper 9 (1830), pp. 106–9 and 126–7. To ease comparability, original figures have been adjusted, where necessary, to convert them into Winchester chaldrons, assuming one ton equals 20 cwt, a Winchester chaldron is 28 cwt, and a Newcastle chaldron is 53 cwt.

	Coastwise (chaldrons)		Overseas (chaldrons)		Total (chaldrons)	
	Chester	Liverpool	Chester	Liverpool	Chester	Liverpool
1770	2,586	2,188	8,894	3,692	**11,189**	**5,880**
1792	Not available (but almost certainly still relatively low)[79]	30,889	5,323	45,182	**5,323 + coastwise**	**76,071**
1819	26,312	18,501	9,362 (96% to Ireland)	49,115 (62% to Ireland)	**35,674**	**67,616**
1828	26,146	18,067	6,371 (92% to Ireland)	68,947 (46% to Ireland)	**32,517**	**86,701**

Coal from Whitehaven had dominated the trade to Ireland for almost a century by the time Ness Colliery opened and, despite Liverpool's ascendancy, Cumberland exports continued to do so throughout the eighteenth century.[80] Thus, while Liverpool was exporting around 45,000 chaldrons in 1792, and Chester about 5,300, the total for the Port of Whitehaven, which included Whitehaven itself as well as Workington, Maryport and Harrington, was almost 170,000.[81] There were few other sales opportunities for Cumberland coal so some attempt was made to develop coastwise trade too, reaching as far as mid-Wales.[82] Meanwhile vessels working from ports close to the extensive South Wales coalfield could work their way up the Welsh coast with ease as well as taking their loads to southern Ireland. Whitehaven continued to dominate the Irish trade in the early nineteenth century (over 170,000 chaldrons in 1819) with Cardiff a substantial second (99,700) and several other ports of South Wales contributing significant amounts to both the overseas and coastwise trades.[83] In addition, coal from Scotland presented growing competition in the Irish trade.[84] By 1828, the port of Chester contributed just 1.1% of Irish coal imports.[85]

Table 10.2 illustrates the strength of competition facing the port of Chester in the coastwise trade at one of the North Wales ports, Beaumaris, in a sample period of six months in 1789. By this time Liverpool dominated the trade but there was also competition from South Wales. Vessels taking coal to Amlwch on the northern Anglesey coast could return to Swansea taking copper mined from Parys Mountain.[86] In summary, in the decade following Ness Colliery's opening, the port of Chester was more important than Liverpool in the seasale coal trade; Whitehaven trumped them both. However, Liverpool soon grew and despite a later measure of recovery at Chester, especially in the coastwise trade, its total output was always eclipsed by the multiple sources of competition it faced.

Table 10.2: Port of origin of vessels taking coal (or culm) to Beaumaris, Anglesey, 6 January– 5 July 1789. The source is the Exchequer port book for Beaumaris which also covered Holyhead and Amlwch. Ten of the fifteen vessels from South Wales brought culm (small coal). The St Ives vessel presumably collected its coal in South Wales. Source; TNA, E 190 1446/2.

Port of Origin	Number of Vessels
Liverpool	111
Chester	11
South Wales (Carmarthen, Swansea, Pembroke, Milford [Haven], 'Llanelly')	15
Other (St Ives)	1
Total	**138**

The Colliery Quays

Three quays were associated with the Neston collieries over their lifetime. One of them, Denhall Quay, is the most prominent surviving feature of the coal works today, situated 120 yards (110 metres) south of the Harp Inn, and known to have projected into the estuary by about 110 yards (101 metres).[87] There was also a quay at Little Neston and, before that, there was brief interest in using the Old Quay.

The Old Quay, situated about 900 yards (823 metres) north-west of the main site of Ness Colliery (Figure 1.2 on p. 4), had been built in the sixteenth century as a mooring place for ships serving the city of Chester which, even then, was proving difficult for them to reach. Known originally as the New Haven, and then Neston Key, it was made of sandstone blocks built into the estuary.[88] However, long before Ness Colliery opened in 1759 the quay had fallen into disrepair, becoming known as the Old Key (or Old Quay).[89]

In the November after Ness Colliery started operating, co-owner Richard Richardson asked the Chester Assembly (of which he was a member) for permission to restore the quay to transport coals to Chester.[90] Separately, he enquired about buying the adjacent 'Key House' which was being used as the Neston House of Correction.[91] His offers for the building were rejected and the Chester Assembly twice deferred a decision about the quay; it was not until January 1763 that the Assembly agreed to Richardson repairing and leasing it.[92] He was also given permission to erect warehouses and other buildings each side of the quay and to construct a harbour 'for the encouragement of the Trade and Navigation within the Port of this City of Chester'. The rent was to be £1 1s. payable annually, with no term specified. The decision was contingent upon the preparation of a report on the construction of a cart road to bring the coals into the city from Richardson's proposed unloading facility along a 21-yard (19 metre) stretch of riverbank between the city's workhouse and Wilcox Point (where, today, the railway crosses the Dee by the Roodee race course). As we saw in Chapter 9, it seems probable that around the time that Richardson was enquiring about the quay, James Brindley was investigating the possibility of building a canal linking the colliery to Chester. Richardson's suggested harbour with warehouses at the Old Quay would have made a useful transfer point for goods coming to or from Chester; such goods were often having to be transferred to or from lighters at Parkgate.[93] However, it seems Richardson's plan never came to fruition for there is little, if any, evidence of building at the Old Quay, nor any record of the agreed rent being paid.[94]

Natural caution by Richardson about the success of the new colliery and of Brindley's other innovative canal projects may account for the lengthy delays in progressing his plans for the Old Quay. He was probably also wanting to see where in the coalfield most coal would be found. The quay was at the very northern end of the coalfield so, if most coal was going to be obtained further south at, say, Denhall then it

Figure 10.4: The remains of Denhall Quay today. Two centuries of silting have buried all but the uppermost two or three courses of the sandstone blocks used to form the quay.

would make little sense to haul it 1.5 miles (2.5 km) to the quay; instead, there would be more justification for building a canal which would pass close to the pit-head. In any event, for whatever reason, there was no progress regarding the Old Quay. Instead, a decision was made by the colliery proprietors to build a new quay in Little Neston closer to where much of the coal was being won.

The new quay – called here 'Little Neston Quay' although no actual reference to any name has yet been found – was situated 200 yards (183 metres) north of the bottom of today's Marshlands Road and is depicted on the earliest surviving detailed map of the area, dated 1788, although it was quite possibly built in the 1760s.[95] It was accessed via the side channel through the estuarine sand and mud from the then main course of the Dee and which became known as the Colliery Gutter.[96] Ships could approach the collieries via the channel but loading could take several tides and so they needed to be able to rest on the mud when there was no water. Thus, ships suited for the Neston colliery trade were described as needing to be able to 'take the ground well'.[97]

The square-shaped quay served a dual purpose as it also appears to have housed a pit, enabling coal to be raised and loaded directly on to vessels.[98] However, the quay was probably not in use for long: by 1790, a decision was made to erect a new, longer 'pier' which later became known as Denhall Quay (Figure 10.4). It was one of several initiatives taken when Thomas Stanley Massey took over the colliery. An enquiry was made to the Chester Assembly about buying the 'ashlers [*sic*] and other stone' which made up the dilapidated Old Quay.[99] The Assembly agreed to the sale but for some reason the purchase did not proceed; it seems the stone for the new quay was instead newly quarried.[100] Started in 1791, the quay was built under the initial direction of colliery manager William Davies, taking two or three years to complete.[101] In 1796 it was described as 'an extensive and commodious pier' and there were 'rail roads, and every other conveniency for shipping coals at a trifling expense'.[102] A weighing machine was situated at the landward end.[103] The rail road, depicted on the Ness tithe map c.1845, would have helped to minimise handling of the coal from the top of the shafts to the pier, reducing labour costs as well as damage to the newly wrought lumps.[104]

There are several possible reasons for why the new quay was built. Firstly, it may have been a response to the shifting sands and water flows in the estuary. With the prospect of the situation continuing to deteriorate, the new quay may have provided better access to the channel leading to the colliery. Secondly, increasing quantities of coal were being won at Ness rather than in Little Neston, so it made good business sense to locate the quay there;[105] this minimised transportation time and associated costs. Thirdly, the move came shortly after Lord Shrewsbury started legal action against Cottingham over royalties.[106] It may be that the irritated Earl was now also demanding payment for coal which was being carried across his foreshore to the square quay in Little Neston – a narrow strip of land seems to have been allocated for this purpose on the seaward side of a 'cop' or bank (Figure 10.5).[107] There was clearly concern about the precise location of the new structure at Ness. It was later reported that,

> When the pier ... [was] made ... Davies was anxious to keep within the [Stanley] Massey's estate, and not exceed the boundary of the Manors, and great care was taken not to go out of their own land.[108]

Despite this care, there appears to have been some argument later over whether the quay transgressed into Little Neston. As a result, following the 1822 court case between Stanley and Cottingham, the shape of the quay was altered;[109] this may explain the southward twist in the final few metres of the quay as depicted on various maps and plans (Figure 10.6).[110]

The new quay may have made loading and unloading easier and this could account for an increase in coal exports from the port of Chester at this time (Appendix V). Within a year or so there was also a sharp increase in customs duties on exports from Parkgate.[111] It seems likely that this latter increase was the result of a change in accounting practice – starting to list exports from Ness within Parkgate's duty totals – rather than simply being due to a rise in shipping of coals.[112] This change in accounting

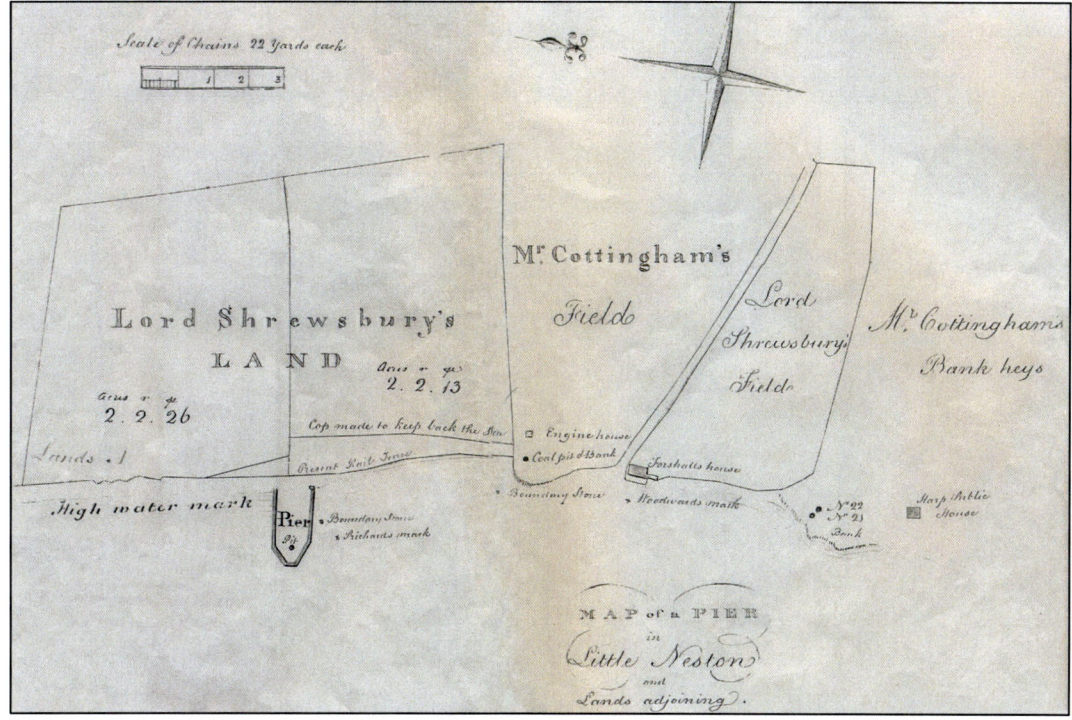

Figure 10.5: Little Neston Quay, c.1829. The quay or 'Pier' is at bottom left, with a 'Pit' shown on it. Today's Marshlands Road runs to the right of 'Mr Cottingham's Field'; the 'Harp Public House' is also shown, bottom right. Source: CALS, part of D5363 (with courtesy of CALS).

practice may have been linked to the relocation of the colliery's dedicated customs officer to Parkgate, discussed earlier in this chapter.

Little Neston Quay seems to have fallen into disrepair, but Thomas Cottingham junior attempted to reinstate the pit in 1823–4 for use in his new colliery.[113] It appears the quay was enlarged at this time, extending it to 47 yards (43 metres) long and making it trapezium-shaped at the seaward end (Figure 10.5).[114] A worker's cabin was situated at the landward end. However, the pit was soon abandoned, and the quay would have fallen into disuse as Cottingham's colliery waned.[115]

Denhall Quay remained in use as a place of loading or unloading for the increasingly infrequent vessels which made it to Ness Colliery and was still claimed to be an asset in the colliery's final decade. An 1851 advertisement for the sale of 'capital Swedish Turnips' grown in nearby Burton implied that the 'pier at Dennah Colliery' would be a good place to load the bulky vegetables for export.[116] Limestone was being imported there the same year and slate was apparently being brought in until the colliery's closure in 1855.[117] The sale advertisement for its equipment and other assets that year optimistically described the quay as 'a good shipping pier'.[118]

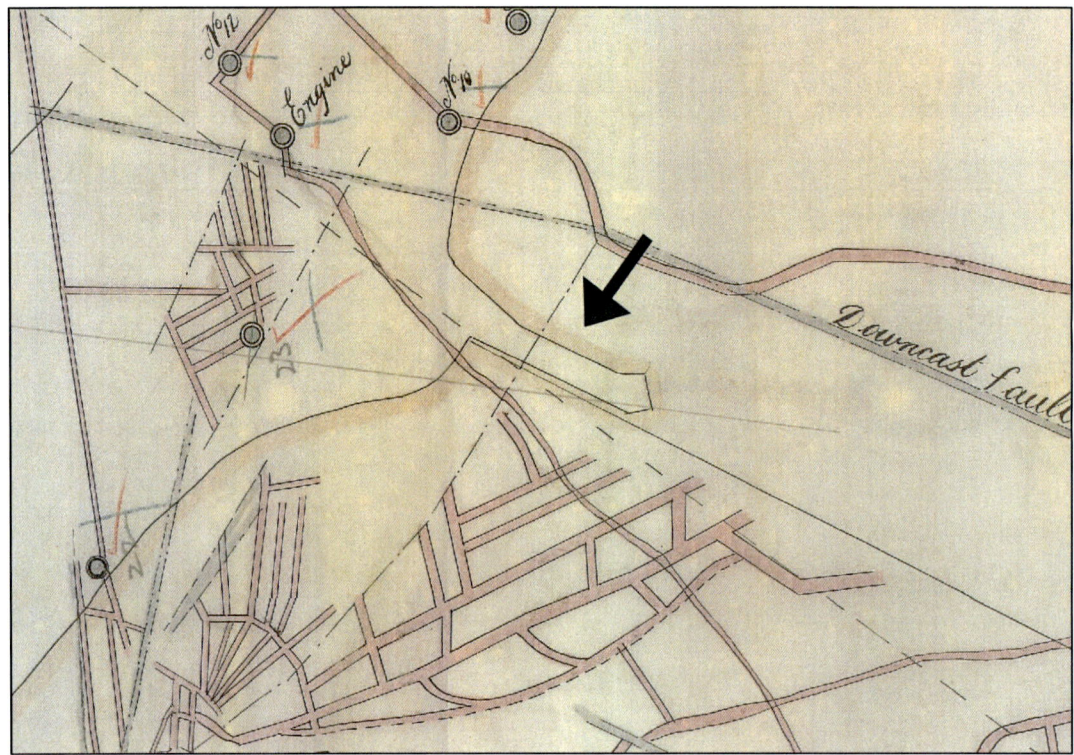

Figure 10.6: Denhall Quay, *c.*1839. The distinctive shape of the quay (marked by an arrow, oriented northwards) projects into the estuary, surrounded by various subterranean tunnels. Source: Coal Authority, 14923/3, with kind permission.

*

From piecing together the available evidence, it is clear that Ness Colliery had a leading role in the region's seasale coal trade for several decades and that, to date, the extent of this role has not been fully recognised. The scale of this activity is underlined by the supporting infrastructure put in place with a dedicated customs official appointed by the Port of Chester and the construction of two new quays. However, the Neston collieries were fighting what would ultimately be a losing battle as the diversion of the Dee took away almost all the water and, with it, the collieries' seasale business.

CHAPTER 11

THE OVERSEAS AND COASTING TRADES

The previous chapter considered the evidence for the role of Ness Colliery in the seasale coal trade of the port of Chester, a role which appears to have been largely ignored or underestimated by researchers to date. This chapter considers in more detail how that trade worked. The overseas and coasting businesses are discussed separately in terms of the ports visited, the types of vessels used, the people involved and the cargoes carried. The trade, of course, was there to meet a demand for coal, whether domestic or for industry, in different geographical markets and so comment has been included on the factors behind this demand.

As indicated in Chapter 8, this chapter concludes with a review of the marketing techniques used in both the landsale and seasale trades at the Neston collieries, bringing together content from this chapter and the previous three.

The Overseas Trade

As indicated in the previous chapter, the overseas trade comprised any journeys away from the British mainland and it appears that the opening of Ness Colliery brought about a marked and rapid increase in this trade from the port of Chester. Table 11.1 (overleaf) records the destinations of coal-carrying vessels from the port for three sample years during the period up to 1774, after which detailed customs records have not survived. Tables 11.2a and 11.2b (on p. 173) analyse various other aspects of the overseas trade in the three sample years which will be considered throughout this section.

The records show that Ireland was substantially the largest destination for Chester's coal, and this remained the case for as long as overseas trade continued. Given this significance it is worth looking in some detail at the market and how it operated.

The Coal Trade to Ireland

Coal was the largest single branch of Anglo-Irish trade in the eighteenth century and Ireland was always the principal overseas market for Neston's coal.[1] Table 11.1 shows that the large majority of coal-carrying vessels leaving the port of Chester went to Ireland, with around 60% of these going to Dublin. Ireland had very limited coal resources of its own and its mines were mostly remote from Dublin and poorly managed.[2] Thus it was almost wholly dependent on imported coal for both domestic and industrial use – primarily, as we have seen, from England (Cumberland, Lancashire and the port of Chester) but also from Scotland and South Wales.

Dublin had a voracious appetite for coal, both for industrial and, particularly, domestic use.[3] The population of Dublin was already substantial when Ness Colliery opened. The city had 100,000 inhabitants in 1750 making it the second largest English-speaking city in the world and this figure had increased to about 180,000 by 1800.[4] This concentration spurred a demand for coal for domestic use which the Irish coalfields were unable to meet.[5] Other cities and towns on the east and south coasts, which were readily accessible from Britain, also created domestic demand – but inland, rural communities were slow to move away from using turf.[6]

Table 11.1: Destinations for coal shipments exported overseas from the port of Chester, in three sample years after Ness Colliery's opening. Sources: TNA, E 190 1435/1, 1440/4, 1442/1.[7]

	Number of Shipments		
	1762	*1770*	*1774*
To Ireland			
Belfast	3	–	–
Carlingford	1	–	
Cork	1	4	2
Dingle	–	1	–
Drogheda	13	3	2
Dublin	120	131	64
Dundalk	6	–	–
Dungarvan	–	–	2
Kinsale	–	–	1
Limerick	–	1	–
Newry	5	17	11
Ross[carbery]	1	1	1
Strangford	–	10	1
Waterford	3	5	2
Wexford	19	33	26
Wicklow	–	3	4
Total to Ireland	172	209	116
To Other Destinations			
Isle of Man	30	1	14
Lisbon	–	–	1
Newfoundland	–	1	1
Oporto (Porto, Portugal)	–	–	1
South Carolina	1	–	–
Not stated	1	–	–
Total to Other Destinations	32	2	17
Total Shipments with Coal (all destinations)	204	211	133

Table 11.2a and 2b: Analysis of coal-carrying shipments exported overseas from the port of Chester in three sample years after Ness Colliery opened. Sources: as for Table 11.1.

Table 11.2a

	1762		1770		1774	
	Number of Shipments	*Percentage*	*Number of Shipments*	*Percentage*	*Number of Shipments*	*Percentage*
a) Vessels carrying *any* goods	253	–	266	–	171	–
b) Vessels carrying any coal; as a percentage of 'a'	204	80.6	211	79.3	133	77.8
c) Coal as part of a mixed load; as a percentage of 'b'	2	1.0	3	1.4	4	3.0
d) Ship's master also the merchant for the coal; as a percentage of 'b'	135	66.2	200	94.8	130	98.0

Table 11.2b

	1762	1770	1774
Total chaldrons carried in the year	7,435	8,894	5,429
Average chaldrons carried per shipment	36.4	42.2	40.8
Largest load (chaldrons)	122 (to Dublin)	127 (to Dublin)	95 (to Dublin)

Industrial demand for coal was low in the eighteenth and early nineteenth centuries compared to Britain; several factors limited Irish industrial development of which lack of raw materials was one.[8] Nevertheless, there were some early steam engines which needed fuel: the first Dublin engine was installed in an iron foundry in 1791; corn mills and breweries were to provide subsequent demand in the city, including a Boulton and Watt engine for the Guinness works.[9] Several cotton mills around Belfast were also using engines within a few years of the start of the early nineteenth century, and

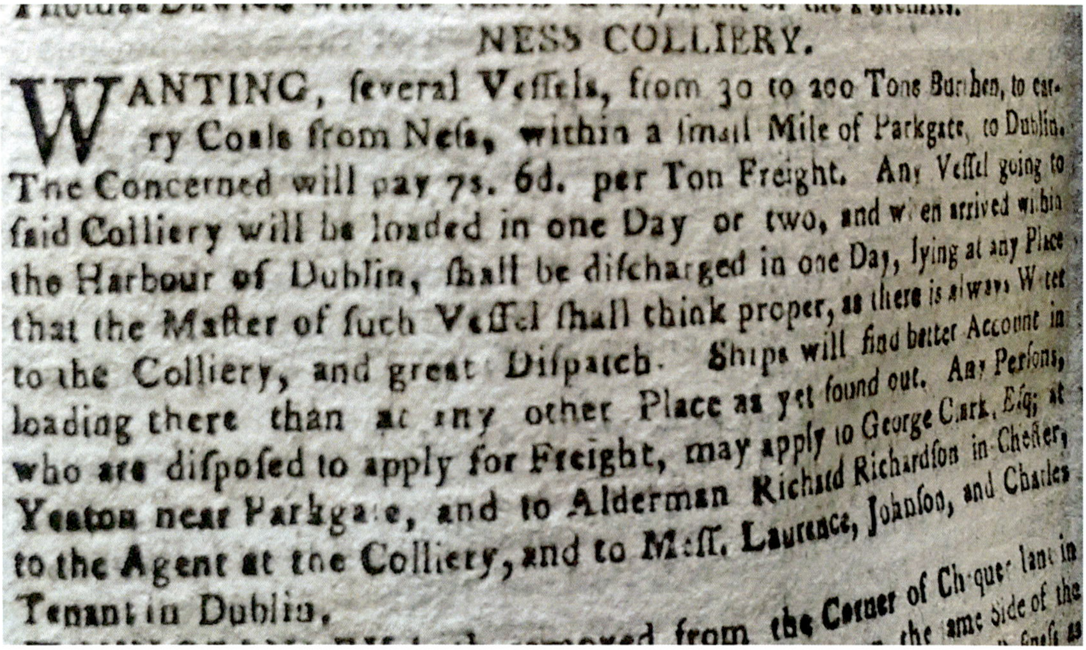

NESS COLLIERY.

WANTING, feveral Veffels, from 30 to 200 Tons Burthen, to carry Coals from Nefs, within a fmall Mile of Parkgate, to Dublin. The Concerned will pay 7s. 6d. per Ton Freight. Any Veffel going to faid Colliery will be loaded in one Day or two, and when arrived within the Harbour of Dublin, fhall be difcharged in one Day, lying at any Place that the Mafter of fuch Veffel fhall think proper, as there is always Water to the Colliery, and great Difpatch. Ships will find better Account in loading there than at any other Place as yet found out. Any Perfons, who are difpofed to apply for Freight, may apply to George Cark, Efq; at Yeaton near Parkgate, and to Alderman Richard Richardfon in Chefter, to the Agent at the Colliery, and to Meff. Laurence, Johnfon, and Charles Tenant in Dublin.

Figure 11.1: An advertisement in a 1761 Dublin newspaper for Ness Colliery's coal. This is the first known use of the name Ness Colliery and the first known advertisement relating to it. Source: *Dublin Journal*, 10 March 1761.

engines were to be found at nearby Lisburn and Bangor too, as well as at Cork in the south.[10] Industrial demand for coal also came from urban users such as ironworks, sugar-makers, glass-makers and the many brewers who did not have steam engines. These producers were largely located in maritime centres – predominantly Dublin (which, for example, had fifty-five breweries in 1804) but also Cork, Waterford and Belfast.[11]

Overall, British coal exports to Ireland almost tripled during the first forty years of Ness Colliery's operation and congestion for coal ships unloading at ports was common.[12] In the early 1760s, for example, Dublin newspapers reported large numbers of colliers (coal ships) arriving at the city – sometimes up to one hundred in just six days.[13] As with the market in Chester, the coal business was heavily intermediated meaning that this author has found no record linking Neston's coal to any specific end-user. Merchants bought the coal from, say, Ness Colliery, arranging carriage on their own or others' vessels to Ireland. While the coal could be sold direct to customers after berthing at a Dublin quay it could also be sold to intermediaries, including licensed 'factors'. One such dealer was Laurence Johnson, based on Dublin's Coal Quay, with whom Ness Colliery appears to have set up a special arrangement.[14] A Dublin newspaper advertisement (Figure 11.1) invited merchants to buy Ness's coals and transport it to Johnson who, it was claimed, would unload it within a day.[15] Johnson himself also acted as a merchant for many imported coal loads from the port of Chester – thirty-four in 1762 alone.[16]

Some of Dublin's coal ended up in the city's public coal yards. These had been established by Dublin's aldermen in the mid-eighteenth century to try to even out fluctuation in supply and demand, with the city's mayor and Lord Lieutenant having the power to intervene over pricing.[17] Fuel poverty was an enduring problem for Dubliners. Shortages or high prices could result from poor weather, which boosted demand but could make unloading on the River Liffey difficult, or from deliberate market manipulation.[18] Ships' masters and local factors might conspire to fix prices.[19] In addition, 'villainous' opportunists often sought to accumulate stocks for later release at a high price.[20] In 1761 the *Dublin Courier* reported that:

> Several worthy citizens have employed six or eight ships to bring coals from Parkgate with which they intend to stock some large coal-yards about Moss-Street and Lazors-Hill in order to prevent Forestallers of that commodity from distressing the poor in that cruel manner they have practised in every scarcity that has happened in late years.[21]

On just one occasion, in 1760, George Clarke and Co., the owners of Ness Colliery, are named as the merchant in a shipment of coal.[22] However, in the first few years of the colliery, co-owner Richard Richardson is often recorded as the merchant for coal shipments to Dublin, chartering a number of different vessels to carry the load.[23] It seems he was acting in a personal capacity rather than on behalf of the colliery as he was also separately shipping lead in large quantities to various destinations, again as the named merchant.

The coal loads over the three sample years in Table 11.2b averaged 39.7 chaldrons – about 56 tons (61 tonnes). However, these loads from Chester were small compared to the competing Whitehaven colliers. In time, vessels of 250 tons (254 tonnes) operated there – similar to those used in the substantial Newcastle–London trade – unhampered by the vagaries of the Dee which Chester's shipmasters encountered.[24]

The number of loads of coal exported *from* the port of Chester substantially exceeded the number of recorded shipments bringing goods *to* the port (Table 11.3, overleaf). Many vessels must, therefore, have arrived at the Dee empty or in ballast, i.e. carrying a heavy load of, say, sand or stone to give extra stability on their journey.[25] Limestone for burning in Wirral kilns was another weighty commodity and it also had economic value; there are a few records of imports of it from Ireland's east coast.[26] It was, of course, always likely to be more lucrative to carry payloads in both directions, when this was possible. For Irish-bound vessels this most often meant bringing back the island's principal export of linen and, in the 1760s and early 70s, animal products, particularly hides and skins, as well as grain.[27] Later, the livestock trade grew in importance. The Irish Cattle Act of 1759 opened the way for cattle imports to Britain, which had been banned for virtually all of the past ninety years, just as Ness Colliery was opening.[28] Judging by Chester's customs records, there was no immediate rush by

Table 11.3: Comparison of number of recorded shipments importing goods into, and exporting coals from, the port of Chester. Sources: as for Table 11.1.

	Number of Shipments		
	1762	*1770*	*1774*
Exporting coal to Ireland	172	209	116
Importing goods from Ireland	62	62	49
Exporting coal to elsewhere	32	2	17
Importing goods from elsewhere	9	11	19
Total exporting coal	**204**	**211**	**133**
Total importing goods	**71**	**73**	**68**

the Irish into this market but by the 1770s cattle, and also horses, were a significant aspect of Parkgate's trade. Livestock business was further encouraged by the revival of Neston Fair in 1776.[29]

Another export from Ireland was soap waste (or soap ashes), discussed in Chapter 7. 'Sopers waste' is known to have been imported by George Clarke, one of Ness Colliery's original owners, in 1762.[30] In the early nineteenth century there are many references to the Stanley estates buying quantities of up to 158 tons (172 tonnes) from the colliery, as well as directly from ships unloading on the Hooton shore of the Mersey.[31]

Despite the imbalance indicated in Table 11.3, the opportunity for Irish exports to Chester, which had a large population and was a gateway to other parts of England, meant that vessels were still less likely to be in ballast than those returning to the main source of competition for coal exports at the time, Whitehaven.[32] However, Chester's trade was to wither as Liverpool's grew and linen imports ended in 1810.[33]

Collieries were not usually involved in the onward trade in their coals.[34] The usual practice was for merchants (who were also generally the ships' masters) to buy coal from the colliery on their own account at wholesale prices and then to sell it wherever they could, for whatever profit they could make. Credit was often allowed to masters who did not have available cash. Thus, Ness Colliery's accounts for 1769–70 record ten captains who owed money, all of whom plied the Irish trade.[35] However, this was contrary to the colliery's own published credit policy. In 1763 and 1769 the proprietors of 'Ness Coal works' had joined with the proprietors of the Mostyn and Bychton collieries in Flintshire to place an advertisement in a Chester newspaper advising that 'no coals will be sold to persons without ready money';[36] exceptions had clearly been made for favoured buyers. The amounts the captains owed varied considerably with the most being £34, owed by Englefield Lloyd.

The allowance of credit indicates that Lloyd had a good relationship with the colliery. Between 1767 and 1769 he had been using his boat, the *Venus*, but he was then allowed to captain a vessel the colliery had had built for use in the Irish trade, the *Stanley Massey*.[37] The building of this ship, a two-masted brig, is referred to in the same set of accounts which record the masters' debts.[38] The *Stanley Massey* is first recorded in the Chester port books in July 1770, arriving at Chester from London – a major centre for ship-building – laden with an extraordinarily diverse range of goods.[39] Soon after, the same source details the first of several journeys with coals to Dublin, captained by Englefield Lloyd.[40]

The *Stanley Massey* illustrates the complex relationship between vessel owner, master and merchant. While a vessel might be owned by its master it was also common for it to be owned by other parties (sometimes several of them having varying proportions of the whole). In this instance, the *Stanley Massey* appears to have been owned by Ness Colliery but the master on her coal-carrying voyages was usually Englefield Lloyd; he, rather than the colliery, was also recorded as the merchant for these trips. On one occasion he was the named merchant but contracted to a different master.[41]

The reluctance of mine-owners to act as merchants was probably down to the uncertainties of the Dublin coal trade. The market was highly imperfect with little correlation between demand and supply. There were frequent gluts as well as shortages, and merchants often held off sending supplies if the price had fallen too low.[42] Overall, there was more-or-less constant low profitability.[43] Selling the coal from the pit head at a fixed price to a merchant and/or master transferred the risk of depressed Irish coal prices to him. The low profitability of the trade also meant that there were relatively few Irish ship-owners with the capital to enable them to be involved in it; the English dominated this business.[44] Table 11.2a shows that it was common for individuals to be both master and merchant on coal shipments – in 1762 this occurred in about two-thirds of cases. This percentage rose substantially over the next dozen years, perhaps as low margins squeezed out middlemen.[45]

A few weeks after her first recorded voyage, the *Stanley Massey* carried several passengers from Dublin to Parkgate.[46] The vessel appears to have run in to trouble the following year as an Irish newspaper reported she was overdue at Dublin on 10 October 1771, having sailed with passengers from Parkgate on the 6th.[47] The report 'hoped that she made the Isle of Man' and she certainly did not become a loss as she again sailed to Dublin on 30 December that year. However, this incident may well have prompted the complaint by the masters of several Parkgate-based constant trading vessels on the Dublin route, written shortly after her disappearance and published in a Chester newspaper.[48] They warned 'the Nobility, Gentry, Merchants and Traders' who were their customers that the owners and masters of vessels in the seasonal coal trade between Ness and Ireland were passing themselves off as 'Parkgate Traders', carrying passengers to their 'manifest hazard and our great disrepute'. The complainants argued that their own vessels were 'well found, manned and in right good sailing order', implying that the ships trading from Ness, such as the *Stanley Massey*, were none of these. The vessel disappears from records in 1772 so maybe she did meet an untimely end and the doubters had had a point.[49]

Prior to the October incident when she was carrying passengers, the *Stanley Massey* had made five voyages that year carrying coal.[50] If it was the target of the Parkgate operators' complaint it was not alone in carrying both passengers and coal. There are many similar examples of Parkgate ships carrying both types of load, though not necessarily at the same time. For example, the *Race Horse*, under Captain Norman did so in the 1760s.[51] So did the *Kildare* and *Nonpareil* in 1771.[52] The masters of both these vessels were amongst the signatories to the complaint in the Chester newspaper but it seems they were scrupulous in how they looked after the ships: in March 1771 the Methodist John Wesley sailed on the *Kildare* and described it as 'abundantly the best and cleanest ship which I have sailed in for many years'.[53] The vessel was a frequent coal trader to Ireland having last taken a load there four months previously.[54]

Irish vagrants, being deported from the Neston House of Correction situated by the Old Quay, were probably less welcome travellers on coal-carrying vessels. Masters were required to take them and risked a fine for failure to do so.[55] A Captain White took five vagrants on his 'Newry sloop from the colliery' in 1778 and several more were taken by a Captain Fearres on 'a sloop from ye collary' in 1781.[56] However, a Captain Terrell refused to take any men on his colliery sloop in 1783, perhaps because of trouble on a different vessel a few months previously when a 'lunatic' caused much damage.[57]

The above accounts illustrate the continuing coal trade from Ness after the final date of the surviving port books. While few such records have survived, there can be little doubt that the coal trade from the port of Chester, i.e. by this time almost wholly Ness, continued throughout the eighteenth century and into the next.[58] Indeed, as discussed in the previous chapter, by 1790 it was thought worth investing in a substantial new quay at the colliery to support this trade.

The importance of the Irish market was evident at Ness for as long as overseas shipping remained viable. Customs statistics for the port of Chester between 1791 and 1799 show that an average 5,486 chaldrons (7,928 tons/8,633 tonnes) were being exported from there annually (Appendix V) and, with little indication of trade to Ireland from Flintshire at this time, it is likely that most, if not all, of this coal came from the Cheshire colliery. The advertisement for 'coal mines' at Neston in 1795 claimed that 'great quantities [of coal] are annually wanted for Ireland', and the Irish or 'foreign' market featured in the 1812 and 1817 advertisements too.[59] The Lysons brothers, in their 1810 book on Cheshire, mentioned that Neston's coal 'is principally exported to Ireland'.[60] However, as we have seen, wider competition was fierce, notably from Cumberland which dominated the Irish trade, having little opportunity for other overseas or coastwise traffic.[61] In addition Lancashire coal, shipped via Liverpool, had grown significantly, and it could command a premium price: in 1797 a Dublin dealer was offering Neston and Whitehaven coal at 20 shillings (£1) per ton, with Wigan and Orrell coal at 24 and 25 shillings (£1.20–£1.25) respectively (there was, incidentally, no indication of any coal from Flintshire).[62] Coal from Scotland and, for buyers in southern Ireland, from South Wales also presented growing competition.[63]

The ease and frequency with which coal vessels went between Ness Colliery and Ireland was a cause of concern to a senior figure in Chester, the Rev. Peploe Ward, who was a magistrate with responsibility for the Wirral. He contacted the Home Office several times around 1800 to express his concerns.[64] This was a period of considerable tension over British rule in Ireland. The Irish Rebellion of 1798, led by republicans influenced by revolutions in France and America, had failed but considerable discontent lingered. Britain was also at war with France, which had attempted to assist the Irish revolt, and there was considerable concern about national security.[65] Thus, in 1799 Ward was very worried about 'improper intercourse' between the Wirral coast and Ireland so that it was too easy for 'traitors' to land locally. They could then blend into the local population, as local villages were 'crowded with Irish of all descriptions'. One entry route was for 'skulking passengers to get on board some of the numerous sloops or small brigs which constantly sail from different ports in Ireland to [Ness] colliery'. Ward recommended that a special constable be posted at the colliery, as well as at Dawpool and Hoylake along the coast, to prevent illicit landings.

Britain was still concerned about its defence in 1803 when a brief respite in war came to an end and Napoleon threatened invasion.[66] Young Sir Thomas Stanley took command of the newly formed Wirral troop of the Western Cheshire Yeomanry to assist in the war effort.[67] Peploe Ward, meanwhile, was still concerned about possible 'treasonable communication with the disaffected in Ireland', shortly after another failed Irish rebellion that year. He had received reports of a 'large filled caravan' (covered waggon) repeatedly visiting the colliery at night, with whatever it was carrying being loaded aboard the waiting vessels. He was also still concerned that traitors could travel easily to or from Ireland on the vessels. In his view, the customs officials stationed at Parkgate were too remote to monitor any nefarious activity; searches were 'almost impossible' as there were so many vessels coming and going each week and the outgoing ones were so laden with coals. Furthermore, the officials were open to bribery: their pay was so low that 'the timely application of a guinea shuts up their search [for] treasonable pamphlets and handbills'. (Parkgate hardly seems to have been doing its bit for the war effort: it was renowned as a haven for deserters and others looking to avoid the Liverpool press gangs which were seeking seamen as the invasion threat grew.)[68] Around this time a local fisherman reported unusual activity at Ness Colliery and, on inspection, a cargo of metal pike heads, thought to have been made in Birmingham, was found hidden amongst the coals.[69] The vessel was detained but the carter who delivered the goods made his escape. The coals were said to be bound for Holland, an unusual destination for them from Britain's west coast, and it seems likely that the pike heads were to be dropped off in Ireland en route. Pikes were a favoured weapon of insurgents; 12,000–15,000 had been seized in the attempted uprising a few weeks earlier.[70]

Customs officials may have been lax when Peploe Ward was writing but there is earlier evidence for their being assiduous in their duties. In April 1767, the *Industry* loaded coals from Ness to take to Drogheda but omitted to pay the requisite duty. This was noted by the authorities and when she came back three months later she was seized. After two months' deliberation by them she was returned; the terms of the agreement for return are not known.[71]

Surviving records from the second decade of the nineteenth century show that 'Chester River Coal' was still being advertised for sale alongside Whitehaven coal at the Dublin docks and, more specifically, coal from 'Parkgate' was still making its way to Dublin.[72] Records kept by Cumberland coal owners for the period March to December 1814 indicate forty voyages to Ireland by 'Colliers from Parkgate' with which they were in competition.[73] More than half of the loads went to Dublin, with the others going to Wicklow, Newry, Cork, Kinsale, Waterford and Baltimore. The cumulative tonnage of the vessels was 2,074 (2,107 tonnes) with the largest ones (up to 104 tons/106 tonnes) going to Dublin.

The Cumberland records give the port of registration of the vessels involved. Table 11.4 shows that Irish ships were now the main traders out of Parkgate – it seems the state of the English side of the Dee Estuary could no longer support an overseas shipping fleet.

A notable feature of the 1814 Cumberland records is the frequent reference to the vessel *Puddington*. Like the *Stanley Massey* a few decades earlier she was owned by Ness Colliery, being named after one of the Stanley family's estates. The records show

Table 11.4: Place of Registration of the various 'Colliers from Parkgate' carrying coal to Ireland, March–December 1814. Source: Cumbria Archive Service, DLONS/W7/1/131.[74]

Place of Registration	Number of Different Vessels
Ireland	14
Chester/Parkgate	2
Other England	3
Wales	4

her as the most frequently used ship on the Parkgate–Dublin route visiting the Irish city eight times in nine months.[75] However, by the end of the year she was no longer wanted and was advertised for sale as:

> The Schooner Puddington, Michael Conway Master, burthen by register 72 tons, built in 1813, drawing 7 feet of water; rigging, and other materials all in good condition.[76]

The acquisition of the *Puddington* had, perhaps, been a statement of confidence by the Stanley brothers in their colliery business at a time of high coal prices but it was, nevertheless, a curious move when the future of the course of the Dee was so uncertain. Its sale within a year or so of acquisition was, presumably, driven by a dramatic deterioration in the state of the river as far as Ness was concerned or, at least, the brothers' great pessimism about its future.

Other Overseas Markets

While Ireland was always the dominant overseas market, Table 11.1 shows that other destinations were served.

Closest to home was the Isle of Man, one of the markets mentioned in the 1812 letting advertisement for Ness Colliery.[77] The island does not have its own coal reserves so all coal needed to be imported;[78] charcoal was sometimes imported too.[79] Table 11.1 shows that the volume of shipping carrying coal there from Chester was very variable. Generally, the collieries of Cumberland dominated this market, being much better placed geographically to serve it.[80] Most of the vessels taking coal to the island arrived at the port of Chester empty or in ballast, perhaps carrying limestone. Only one vessel arrived with recorded goods (wheat) in the three sample years used in this chapter's analysis whereas forty-five had taken coals there.[81] Customs accounts for the six recorded journeys from the island to Parkgate between 1776 and 1790 indicate that cattle were then the main export.[82]

Some vessels in the port books ventured further afield, engaging in what was often termed the foreign trade. One, the *William and Edward*, part-owned by Neston brewer Joseph Hayes who was also the named merchant, sailed for Gibraltar in 1760 (having recently arrived from Ireland carrying amongst other things 'ox hoofs and bones', 'coney [rabbit] wool' and 'books not french').[83] The Chester port books show vessels also sailed with coals on one occasion to each of Lisbon, Malaga, Marseille, Bordeaux, Dunkirk and Rouen as well as several times to Oporto (Porto, Portugal).[84]

Occasionally the coal-carriers set out to cross the Atlantic. Destinations included New York (on the *Susannah* in 1760, carrying 177 chaldrons, the equal largest coal load known to have left the port of Chester), Philadelphia (*Northern Lass,* 1764), Barbados (1766 twice and 1767) and South Carolina (at least six times between 1759 and 1769).[85] A trade to Newfoundland also grew up (at least five voyages carrying coal between 1768 and 1773), largely under the direction of Chester merchant, John Rogers, in a market opened up by the conquest of Canada in the Seven Years' War.[86]

For these long-haul overseas trips, coal would primarily have been carried as ballast, occasionally alongside other goods such as lead.[87] It was the return cargoes which made these journeys worthwhile. Vessels for Spain and Portugal variously brought back wine, cork, ham, figs, oranges, lemons and 'raisins of the sun'.[88] Guernsey was another destination for Chester's coal and, in terms of trade *to* the city, was a staging post for goods from Iberia and southern France.[89]

The Newfoundland trade was largely built upon the whaling and fishing industry. Imports included fish and whale oils, cod and specifically cod's tongues (a delicacy), as well as animal skins such as otter, fox, beaver and 'cats' (presumably lynx).[90] One of the largest ships to use Parkgate was the *Fair American*. Owned by a Chester merchant Charles Goodwin she had a burthen of 200 tons or more and visited the port of Chester at least seven times between 1765 and 1775.[91] She is recorded as carrying coal on three occasions, sometimes also taking lead. She almost always made for South Carolina, with rice grown on slave plantations being a principal back-freight.[92] Often these transatlantic ships made triangular journeys, returning via Spain or Portugal where they offloaded goods and coming back to Chester with Iberian produce.[93] Boston was another stopping-off point, to load timber.[94]

The vessels in the transatlantic business were larger than those in the Irish trade. Whilst they faced thousands of miles of ocean, simply getting out of the Dee Estuary was often a significant hurdle for them. Several of the vessels taking coal from Chester had problems: the *Fair American* was driven ashore at Parkgate by high winds in 1766;[95] the *William* was damaged by 'oversetting' in the Dee when bound for South Carolina;[96] the *Nimrod* was severely damaged in 'a violent gale of wind' at Dawpool, a few miles down the Dee Estuary from Parkgate;[97] so was the 200-ton (203-tonne) *Northern Lass*, bound for Philadelphia.[98] This last incident occurred in 1764 when the Maryland-built ship was under the direction of a pilot who boarded at the same time as coal was loaded at Ness. The pilot failed to recognise the need for a large anchor to keep her under control while loading further goods at Dawpool, so that she ended up on shore, requiring much repair. She was nevertheless able to sail the following month, travelling to Dublin with coals, and was in the Caribbean the following year transporting slaves.[99] These incidents underline the hazards faced by larger vessels in the Dee Estuary and illustrate one key reason why transatlantic trade never took off from the port of Chester. The deep waters of Liverpool were much more suited to this kind of business. If vessels wanted coal as ballast, Whitehaven was another option for loading.[100]

Sailing in the Irish Sea could also be hazardous, especially because of the unpredictable weather. Thousands of ships are recorded as lost in the area during the period that Ness Colliery operated, many of which were colliers; there were numerous other unrecorded losses.[101] The incident involving the *Northern Lass* was one of several in a log recording 'Acts of Protest', i.e. captains' sworn statements to a notary following

Table 11.5: Entries in the 'Acts of Protest' relating to vessels in the overseas trade departing from Ness or Parkgate and carrying coals or firebricks, 1764–7. All the coal is likely to have come from Ness Colliery. The firebricks have also been included as there is nowhere else locally where they are likely to have been manufactured, and the *Venus*, under Captain Lloyd, was closely associated with the colliery. [102]

Date of Report	Vessel Name, Port of Registration, Master	Load (Chaldrons, unless indicated)	Sailing From/To	Cargo	Incident Summary
16/8/1764	*Northern Lass*, Dublin, Hudson	114	Ness Colliery to Philadelphia	'Part loaden' with coals. 'Rest of loading' at Dawpool.	Four oarsmen towed the vessel to Dawpool due to lack of wind. Then driven ashore there following alleged pilot error. Needed 'much repairing'.
14/3/1765	*Two Brothers*, Drogheda, Hunter	76	'Ness coal pits' to Dublin	Coals	Driven ashore at Dawpool by a gale. Cargo partly removed before she would float.
18/12/1766	*King George*, Chester, Briscoe	42	Parkgate to Dublin	Coals and merchant goods incl. beaver wool	Shipped much water off Holyhead following high seas. Returned to Parkgate with damaged cargo.
16/7/1767	*Venus*, Chester, Lloyd	70 tons (76 tonnes)	Parkgate to Dublin	Firebricks	Ship taken over by six men using 'force and violence', so prevented from proceeding on her journey.

Date of Report	Vessel Name, Port of Registration, Master	Load (Chaldrons, unless indicated)	Sailing From/To	Cargo	Incident Summary
16/10/1767	*Venus,* Chester, Lloyd	36	Parkgate to Dublin	Coals and merchant goods	Took on water following a gale and the cargo damaged.
27/10/1767	*Friend,* Newport (Monmouth.), Taylor	53	Ness Colliery to Dublin	Coals	Anchor gave way and driven ashore at Parkgate by a gale. Probably had to remove all cargo to repair.

damage to their ships or cargoes. It covers the period 1762 to 1768 and several records relate to loading of coal and other goods at Ness (or 'Parkgate'). These are summarised in Table 11.5.[103]

There are other records of accidents to ships. A great storm in October 1775 led to the loss of, or damage to, at least six Parkgate-registered vessels including the *Charming Mary* which was carrying both passengers and coals for Newry. Blown to near Blackpool, she collided with the *Trevor* which sank with the loss of thirty lives and a very valuable cargo; the *Charming Mary* was recovered.[104] The *Nonpareil* under Captain Davies, which had sometimes carried coal, was also lost in the storm with 100 people perishing.

In 1800 the Whitehaven-registered *Endeavour* left customs clearance at Parkgate bound for Ireland, laden with coal presumably from Ness. The next day she was lost off the coast of North Wales, and her crew of three perished. Her master, named Leviston, left a pregnant wife and three children.[105] Several other vessels which sailed with coals from the port of Chester in the early nineteenth century were reported to have met with accidents.[106]

Credit for the customs duty paid would be given when, as occasionally happened, vessels were unable to complete their journeys. Violent storms in late 1770 meant that several Dublin-bound vessels that had taken on coal at Ness were damaged and forced to discharge their cargoes early – the *Susannah & Maria* at Parkgate, the *Mary* at Dawpool and the *Success* at 'Ruthland' (Rhuddlan). In each case credit was given for the duty paid on the coals that had had to be unloaded.[107] The *Nimrod*, mentioned above, bound for Cork in 1773, received a similar credit.[108]

There were also several accidents at the colliery associated with sailing vessels which were probably using the Colliery Gutter to approach for loading. Chester's

Adams's Weekly Courant reported in 1773 that John Hanley drowned 'at Ness Colliery', with the coroner's report indicating that his boat had capsized.[109] Patrick Rogers, a trader from Wexford, 'drowned when his boat sank near Ness Colliery' (1776) and Daniel Garrett from the Isle of Man was accidentally 'killed while on board a vessel on the Dee near Ness Colliery' (1796).[110]

The Coasting Trade
The Nature of the Trade
Having reviewed the Neston collieries' interactions with the overseas trade we now turn to the coasting trade which differed in several respects. One key difference was that the vessels involved tended to be smaller, with considerably less coal carried on each journey. In 1762, for example, two-thirds of the vessels carried ten chaldrons (14 tons/15 tonnes) of coal or less and very few carried more than twenty chaldrons (Table 11.6b, overleaf). This compares to an average load of about 36 chaldrons in Chester's overseas trade that year with two ships carrying over 100 chaldrons. As with the overseas trade, the place of loading was almost always not named in surviving records, and the shallow draught of the coasting vessels meant that they were generally able to access any colliery on the Dee Navigation and the estuary. As such, we can usually be much less confident about identifying the Neston collieries as the source of coal in the coasting trade, although records scattered across the decades do indicate the collieries' involvement in this business throughout the period under review.

Table 11.6a shows that almost 60% of vessels leaving Chester in the coasting trade carried coal. However, another difference between the overseas and coasting trades was that it was much more common in the latter for vessels to carry mixed loads. The table shows that in around a quarter of cases where vessels carried coal coastwise they carried other goods as well; this compares to 3% or less in the case of the overseas trade. Sometimes, the range of additional goods carried coastwise was limited to one or two items. In these cases, earthenware was a common additional load suggesting that such vessels were loaded on the Dee Navigation near Buckley (Flintshire), an area which produced both goods from the local clays, and coal; an iron tramway was laid between Buckley and the riverside wharves around 1800.[111] Another commodity sometimes carried alongside coal in the early 1760s was Cheshire salt but, by the end of the decade, this was a rare cargo on the Dee.[112] Increasing volumes of salt were carried on the Weaver Navigation over the period, with the waterway providing a more direct route to carry the commodity via the Mersey to Liverpool.[113]

More often, though, vessels with mixed cargoes carried a varied range of merchandise, including coal, usually acting on behalf of a named merchant. The goods could be very diverse. For example, the *Hopewell* bound for Holyhead in July 1762 carried in addition to just over five chaldrons of coal: red and white port wine, pig iron, tobacco, copperas (for dyeing and ink), molasses, bake stones (for placing cakes on for baking in an oven), sugar, a lamp, casks of 'grocery', a bundle of whalebones, two tusks, brushes, grates, leather, hats, hops, nails, iron hoops (for barrels), and some 'manchester' (cotton). The 'grocery' might have included Cheshire cheese which was often exported from Chester. One writer has described these mixed loads as being 'as if a general shop had been bodily transported on board ship for conveyance to a more profitable district'.[114]

When carrying mixed loads it was relatively common for the vessel's master to be acting for a merchant (53.8% and 43.0% of cases in 1762 and 1770 respectively); this was especially the case where very diverse loads were involved. On occasion, Richard Richardson was one of these merchants.[115] In the instances when only coal was carried it was more normal for the master and merchant to be the same person (almost 90% of cases in 1762 and 1770). When reviewing the names of the masters of these ships it is striking how many have names of apparent Welsh origin – for example Hugh Hughes, Griffith Jones and John Morgan, or Henry Williams in the case of the *Hopewell* above –

Table 11.6a and b: Analysis of coal-carrying shipments exported coastwise from the port of Chester in the sample years of 1762 and 1770. Sources: TNA, E 190 1436/9, 1436/1, 1440/7 and 1440/12.

Table 11.6a

	1762		1770	
	Number of shipments	*Percentage*	*No. of shipments*	*Percentage*
a) Vessels carrying *any* goods	419	–	348	–
b) Vessels carrying any coal; as a percentage of 'a'	241	57.5	208	59.8
c) Coal forming part of a mixed load; as a percentage of 'b'	52	21.6	56	26.9
d) Ship's master also the merchant; as a percentage of 'b'	213	88.4	180	87.0
e) Mixed loads including coals where master and merchant were different; as a percentage of 'c'	28	53.8	24	43.0

Table 11.6b

	1762	1770
Total chaldrons carried in the year	2,257	2,295
Average chaldrons carried per vessel	9.4	10.8
Largest load (chaldrons)	50 (to Caernarfon)	38 (to Exeter)

something that is not evident in the records of the ships sailing in the overseas trade from Ness and Parkgate. So, given that the majority of coasting journeys went along the Welsh coast, it seems these were largely local men doing local trade.

The most visited Welsh ports were on the country's north and north-west coasts: Beaumaris and Caernarfon, which dominated the trade as well as Conwy, Holyhead, Pwllheli, Barmouth, Aberdyfi and Aberystwyth (Table 11.7).[116] There were also occasional longer journeys, to Cardigan and 'Milford' (Haven). Journeys north were

Table 11.7: Destinations for coal exported coastwise from the port of Chester, in two sample years after Ness Colliery's opening.[117] Sources: as for Tables 6a and b.

	Number of Shipments	
	1762	1770
To Wales		
Aberdyfi	42	7
Aberystwyth	4	23
Barmouth	2	3
Beaumaris	34	44
Caernarfon	63	61
Cardigan	3	2
Conwy	41	23
Holyhead	13	18
Milford [Haven]	5	4
Pembroke	1	–
Pwllheli	14	17
Total to Wales	**222**	**202**
To England/Scotland		
Exeter (Devon)	–	1
Kirkcudbright (D & G)	1	–
Lancaster (La.)	7	–
London	–	1
Mount's Bay (Cornwall)	–	1
Pilefowdry (Piel Island, Cumb.)	6	–
Poulton (Lancs.)	1	
Ulverston (Cumb.)	–	1
Wigtown (D & G)	–	1
Not stated/Illegible	4	1
Total to England/Scotland, or unknown	**19**	**6**
Total Shipments with Coal (all destinations)	**241**	**208**

less common but the customs records do list coal-loads bound for Lancaster, Furness, Wigtown and Kirkcudbright. Coals also occasionally found their way to various south coast ports including Exeter, Plymouth and Poole.[118] London, which was well-served by the collieries of the North East, was a rare destination for Chester's coal. Only a few such records have been found but, for example, one 1770 load was for just under 9 chaldrons in a mixed cargo which also included 20 tons (22 tonnes) of cheese, 14 bundles of tanned leather, 80 casks of lead ore and 266 iron guns (guns were a common coastwise export, presumably being manufactured at John Wilkinson's iron works at Bersham);[119] the merchant was leading Chester businessman John Hincks.[120]

It is likely that many of the vessels loading coals arrived empty or in ballast. There was little synergy between the ports shipping goods to Chester, dominated by Liverpool and London, and those wanting Chester's coal, these largely being in North Wales. Table 11.8 shows that just a handful of vessels which brought goods inwards also carried coals outwards.

However, importantly, coastwise movements of limestone were not recorded by the customs authorities, probably because it was duty free.[121] It is possible that a significant proportion of vessels coming from North Wales to Ness brought limestone for burning in local kilns.

The procedure for payment of duty on coastwise coals was not straightforward.[122] Duty was payable where the coals were unloaded. To ensure this happened the intended destination of the goods had to be declared and two bondsmen had to give a financial guarantee that the coals would go to that destination and not be surreptitiously landed without payment of duty. As evidence, a slip called a cocket (or

Table 11.8: Coastwise vessels recorded as both bringing goods to the port of Chester and carrying coals from the port. Two sample six-month periods have been used. An interval of up to one month has been assumed as indicative of the inbound and outbound sailings comprising a single return journey. The outbound shipments could be before or after the inbound one, depending on the home port of the vessel.[123] Sources: TNA, E 190 1436/1, /9, 1437/13, 1440/7, /11 and /12.

	6 July 1762–5 January 1763 (Michaelmas and Christmas Quarters)	6 July 1770–5 January 1771 (Michaelmas and Christmas Quarters)
Total inbound shipments	71	63
Inbound shipments from North Wales (included in above)	22	11
Vessels bringing above shipments and carrying coals outwards within one month.	4	5

coquet) was completed on outward clearance of the vessel from Chester. When the vessel had unloaded, a certificate was returned to the city which allowed the bond monies to be released; this return process could take months. Usually one of the bondsmen was the ship's master; in the case of the *Hopewell* above the other bondsman was George Clarke, an early owner of Ness Colliery, suggesting that the coal may have been loaded there. The bond amount could be substantial and usually seems to have been related to the value of the merchandise involved rather than the amount of duty; in the *Hopewell*'s case it was £30. Clarke acted as a bondman in a few other instances, in 1760 and 1762.[124]

Occasionally coastwise ships were forced to overseas destinations, contrary to their original plan. A £20 penalty was applied to the bondholders when, in 1766, the *Catherine* failed to unload her coal at Pwllheli. The master swore an affidavit saying that he had been forced by 'contrary winds and boisterous weather' to put into Drogheda across the Irish Sea where, 'for want of money', he had to land his cargo. The penalty was annulled.[125] Similar circumstances applied in 1762 when the *Molly and Betty* ended up in Douglas, Isle of Man en route to Lancaster.[126]

The Trade to Wales

Table 11.7 shows that, as destinations for coal from the port of Chester, the towns of North Wales dominated the coastwise entries in the port books. Much of this would have been intended for domestic use. Welsh towns, such as Conwy, Caernarfon and Beaumaris, no doubt reflected the national rise in demand for coal for use in homes. The enclosure movement in North Wales, which saw the 'waste' parcelled up and allocated to owners to bring into cultivation, also stimulated the demand for coal: there was less opportunity to take the traditional fuels of brushwood and peat from the land.[127] Coal, or slack, would also have been used for local small-scale industries such as brewing and brick-making. Furthermore, 'vast quantities' of coal were used to burn lime for agricultural use.[128] Domestic use probably accounts for the coal sent to Aberdyfi and Aberystwyth as there was little smelting done there at that time despite much mining of lead ore.[129]

However, the Chester port books give no indication of the principal users of coal in the region. These were the industries of Flintshire; any shipments to these were merely movements within the boundaries of the port of Chester and, thus, were not recorded for customs purposes. The industries were founded on North Wales' rich mineral resources – lead, zinc, copper and ironstone, as well as valuable clays. As a result, throughout the eighteenth century, ore smelting and various manufacturing operations became increasingly established in the county and these required large amounts of coal, or its derivative, coke.

Veins of lead, and to a lesser extent zinc, could be found in the Carboniferous limestone which spanned from near Prestatyn on the North Wales coast south to Minera, west of Wrexham. Lead mining had been carried out in Flintshire since Roman times and had long been a key part of the local economy.[130] Small quantities of silver were also obtained from the lead ore.[131] Zinc ores, in the forms of calamine and black jack, were mined too.[132] Throughout the early nineteenth century, Sir Thomas Stanley's Hooton estate received payments of royalties from interests it had in Flintshire lead and zinc mines at Trelogan and Porthymaen.[133] Lead smelting works operated in Flintshire, especially Bagillt, throughout the eighteenth and nineteenth centuries.[134] In the 1760s, Richard Richardson, co-proprietor at Ness Colliery and a Chester silversmith, had works at Pentrobin, between Hawarden and Buckley, to smelt lead ore from Minera.[135]

Copper was found in Snowdonia, the Llŷn Peninsula, on the Great Orme by Llandudno and, in particular, at Parys Mountain on Anglesey. A mill for manufacturing copper products, using ore smelted at St Helen's (Lancs.), was established at Greenfield, near Holywell, by the 1750s; more extensive works to process the ore from Parys Mountain were established by 1780.[136] Zinc was used with copper in brass manufacturing at Greenfield from the 1760s.[137] Many of the copper and brass goods made there were used in the slave trade.[138] In addition, twenty furnaces were in use at Amlwch, Anglesey, by the early nineteenth century to reduce the local copper ores.[139] Copper-working continued at Greenfield until 1901.[140]

The Flintshire coal mines developed rapidly under the stimulus of the local industries. A 1759 advertisement for a lease for Mostyn Colliery was able to state that it '… lies convenient for the coal trade but has a great Land Sale for ready money, and is within less than a mile of three great Smelting Works'.[141] In 1774, the writer Samuel Johnson counted nineteen industrial mills through the Greenfield Valley including copper-, brass- and iron-works.[142] The scale of local industry then was such that its smoke was said to blacken the coast road, and it was to grow even further.[143] By the end of the century the 'Copper King', Thomas Williams, was said to be using 750 chaldrons of coal (1,050 tons/1,143 tonnes) per day at Greenfield.[144] There was little use of steam engines in manufacturing in the coastal region, though; one was installed at a Bagillt lead-works in the early nineteenth century but, at Greenfield, a key attraction was the availability of a constant and substantial supply of water to power machinery.[145]

In addition to the copper- and lead-works, there were ironworks, operating at Hawarden by 1756 and expanded in the 1770s, owned by John Rigby.[146] His son, in partnership with William Hancock, bought the nearby extensive collieries of Mancot and Sandycroft by 1801, guaranteeing the ironworks' coal supply.[147] William Hancock also established a substantial pottery business at Buckley (Flintshire), where potters had been taking advantage of the combined availability of coal and clays (notably

Figure 11.2: Greenfield Dock today.

fireclay) for centuries.[148] Both Rigby and Hancock were often to supply goods to Sir Thomas Stanley.[149] As well as ironworks at Hawarden, by the early nineteenth century there were also works at Mostyn where coke ovens were installed, and at Rhuddlan on the River Clwyd.[150]

Coal or coke was not only used in the furnaces and kilns used for smelting, forging or baking, but also powered coal-hungry stationary steam engines in ore mines. An engine was installed as early as 1720 at Talargoch Lead Mine near Prestatyn and many were to follow at other lead mines. These included several used later that century by the London Lead Company, which owned a number of Flintshire mines as well as a smelting operation.[151] Coal mines, of course, also installed engines for pumping and, later, winding; they had the natural advantage of being able to use on-site fuel.

While vessels certainly took coal from Ness Colliery to supply the industries and homes of North Wales, the works could offer no particular advantage over the Flintshire collieries, unlike in the Irish trade where shallow waters prevented the larger ships from loading in Wales. Furthermore, the Flintshire collieries had industrial customers on their doorstep. By contrast, there was not a single substantial coal-using industrial site in the Neston area, or anywhere else on the Wirral, in the eighteenth or early nineteenth century. If Neston's coal was to reach large industrial users then transport costs would have to be incurred, making it less attractive. The demand from

North Wales' industry for coal from nearby collieries led Thomas Pennant, writing in 1796, to declare the state of the Flintshire mines 'to be the most flourishing I ever remember' – a remarkable turnaround from their 'low state' eighteen years earlier;[152] It was also a considerable contrast to the state of Ness Colliery which made a net loss of £5 in 1796.[153]

Despite the problems, surviving records do give occasional glimpses of Ness Colliery's involvement with trade along the Welsh coast. The register of 'Acts of Protest' – the pleas of ships' masters before a notary following an incident involving their vessel – record the running ashore at Dawpool of two vessels working in the coasting trade which had loaded at Ness in 1768.[154] The Conwy-registered *Seahorse*, bound for Rhuddlan (now in Denbighshire), was driven ashore when her anchors gave way. She was severely damaged and her cargo removed. The *Jenny* was bound for her home port of Amlwch on Anglesey and became 'much damaged'. She had loaded sugar, salt, flax and flour at Liverpool, detoured to Ness for coal, and then headed for the island. Amlwch was not yet a copper-working centre and her load indicates she was aiming to supply domestic users or small-scale manufacturers.

One industrial user was Thomas Smedley, who had a Holywell lead smelting operation. He received a vessel carrying 12 tons (13 tonnes) of coal from Ness Colliery in 1783, presumably at nearby Greenfield Dock (Figure 11.2). Smedley was unable to take it all, partly due to a delay when the boatmen got drunk and started quarrelling and fighting in the town.[155] The rest of the coal went to Mrs Vigars, a Chester-based widow who had extensive interests in the North Wales lead business.[156]

Another example of an industrial customer in the 1780s comes from a few rare surviving receipts which give interesting information on the costs involved. The Anchor Smelting Company had been established near Aberystwyth in 1786 with a view to smelting local ore to obtain lead and silver.[157] Coal was bought to heat the furnace from Liverpool, Swansea and, on at least three occasions, from Ness Colliery via the coasting vessel *Dolphin* (Figure 11.3).[158] Table 11.9 shows the costs for one load which not only included the coal itself but also customs duty, carriage and allowances for loading and unloading. In total, the extras came to more than double the cost of the coal. Anchor also sought coke from Ness Colliery in 1790, but chose to buy 'bricks' (probably firebricks) at the same time from Buckley, to be collected from 'Conners Quay' on the Dee.[159] The fact that Anchor chose its suppliers illustrates the fact that, although coal sales were generally intermediated, bigger consumers sometimes dealt direct with the collieries and arranged their own shipping.[160] The Anchor works did not survive long after these orders: it had several problems, not least its remote location from the essential materials it needed, and went out of business in 1792.

As described above, Ness Colliery had had its own vessel for the overseas trade in the 1770s, the *Stanley Massey*, and around 1809 it acquired one for the coasting business, the *Hooton*. She was a newly built galliot, costing £1,560.[161] Galliots were similar to the standard flats which were often used in the coasting trade, having two masts with a square topsail on the main mast.[162] However, the galliot did not have a keel but had a movable leeboard to assist with keeping to course.[163] The vessels were primarily designed for shallow Dutch waters and the commissioning of one by Ness Colliery appears to be a response to the increasing difficulty in negotiating local waters, driven by the River Dee Company's efforts to divert the course of the Dee. Although she had a shallow draught, the vessel was claimed to be very large. The 1812 letting advertisement for Ness Colliery described the *Hooton* as 'A new-built Galliot, burthen about 120 tons, well found and well adapted for the coasting trade' – but it is not unusual to find that ships' burthens were exaggerated in sale advertisements.

The first known reference to the *Hooton* carrying local coal was in 1809, arriving at Beaumaris from Parkgate with coals, under a Captain Hall.[164] She did not stay with the colliery for long: in 1813 she was sold off, perhaps because her size was proving problematic in the estuary's changing waters. The sale realised £1,426, thus resulting in a small loss.[165] Despite the sale, the colliery acquired the *Puddington*, of smaller burthen, in the same year. As described earlier, she primarily operated on the Dublin route but shipping notices in North Wales' newspapers show that she called at coastwise ports such as Caernarfon and Beaumaris too.[166] The colliery may have later acquired an additional vessel – the *Wirrale*. A coal-laden vessel of this name was wrecked in 1823 and she was later mentioned in colliery records as a wreck which gave rise to various costs.[167]

Table 11.9: Transcript of a receipt for sea-borne coal from Ness Colliery bought from Richard Evans, master of the Dolphin. Probert was one of the founders of the Anchor Smelting Company. The varying quantities of coal stated are evidence of the complexities brought about by lack of standardisation of measurements which included tons of 'Aberystwyth measure'. It is interesting to note the hefty rate of duty – almost six shillings (30p) per chaldron. This compares with one shilling and twopence (6p) per chaldron levied on coal for the overseas trade from 1788.[168]

Source: NLW, Powis MSS 18677.

30 May 1788 *John Probert Esq. & Co. to Richard Evans*	£	*s.*	*d.*
Paid to Mr. Wm. B. Davies of Ness Colliery for 24 tons of coal at 8/6d.	10	4	–
Paid duty for 24 chaldrons and 15 baskets and also cocket fees	6	18	9
Freight of 33 Tons from Chester	10	0	0
An allowance by loading coals		3	0
Ditto for discharging coals and also cocket fees		2	6
	27	8	3

Whilst the overseas coal trade via Parkgate had largely died by 1820, some degree of coastwise business continued for several decades with boats of shallow draught able to negotiate the Colliery Gutter on high tides. Records survive of coasting activity at Ness in every decade of the first half of the nineteenth century.[169] This includes Thomas Cottingham's plea to local customs officials for coasting vessels to be cleared outwards locally rather than having to proceed to Chester, discussed in Chapter 10. Records relating to Cottingham's business are relatively rare but feature again in the early 1830s when Cottingham's coal was the fuel of choice for one of the biggest industrial users in North Wales – the Mona Mine Company.

Mona mined copper ore on Parys Mountain, Anglesey, and smelted it at nearby Amlwch.[170] It obtained much of its coal for its furnaces from South Wales, where it had another processing works, but it also had a contract with Liverpool-based Newton Lyon and Company to supply it with coal from the Dee Estuary area.[171] The 'Lyon' in the business was Joseph Lyon, whose family was closely connected to Neston (his uncle was also named Joseph Lyon, mentioned in previous chapters).[172] Although Joseph was a Liverpool merchant he was born in Neston, lived there in the later part of his life and died there in 1844.[173]

In the early 1830s Lyon was a source of frustration to the manager of the smeltery, James Treweek, because he consistently failed to obtain coal from the Neston collieries. This was despite the view of Treweek and his experienced colleagues that Neston coal was far superior to that from the Welsh side of the Dee.[174] It was, he claimed, the best coal in the area for mixing with coal from South Wales to achieve the necessary results at the smeltery. It was also the cheapest coal available locally. Treweek wanted Lyon's vessel, the *Winefred*, to visit 'Neston or Dina' (i.e. Little Neston or Ness) but, contrary to orders, it instead usually obtained supplies from mines on the Welsh side of the river even though their produce was more expensive and, in his view, of poorer quality. The reason Lyon gave for preferring to deal with the Welsh mines was the intermittent tide at Neston which required his vessel to wait to reach or depart from the collieries.[175]

Thomas Cottingham's 'hard coal', probably from the Five-Foot seam, was particularly well regarded by Treweek, being 'most certainly better' than that from a similar seam at Mostyn.[176] There was also 'always a stack of coal' available, a point apparently indicative of Cottingham's poor sales.[177] Newton Lyon did manage to deliver about 2,800 tons (3,049 tonnes) of Little Neston coal to Mona between 1831 and 1833, perhaps making it Cottingham's biggest single customer.[178] It may be no coincidence that no coal was bought from Ness Colliery. There was clearly disdain by Lyon towards the Catholic Sir Thomas Stanley, as evidenced by a speech he gave regarding schooling in Neston (see page 229) and it is possible he sought to avoid his firm dealing with him.[179]

The last coasting vessel known to have visited Ness Colliery was the *Mary*, in 1851, with two Welsh crewmen.[180] She was recorded as lying at the quay at Ness, having brought limestone; it seems likely she then left with coal. The *Mary* was a sloop, showing that keeled boats were still able to approach the colliery, at least on occasions.

*

The surviving evidence surrounding the Neston collieries' involvement with the seasale trade is sometimes rich but more often fragmentary. Nevertheless, the material enables us to build a detailed picture of the relative importance of the overseas and coasting businesses to the collieries over time. In particular, the ever-growing demands by both industry and consumers for coal was to ensure that Neston's coal was to find its way to the hearths, furnaces and steam engines of Ireland and Wales over many decades.

* * *

Landsale and Seasale Marketing Techniques

Having reviewed the various markets for the Neston collieries' coal on land and by sea over the past four chapters, it is a suitable opportunity to consider the marketing techniques used by the businesses. The collieries offered a diverse range of products to diverse markets using diverse means. Although the evidence is fragmentary, we can recognise the use of promotional techniques which are still relevant today and to which we might now apply the label 'marketing' (although the term did not come into use in this context until the late nineteenth century).[181] Little seems to have been written about this aspect of the coal industry during the Industrial Revolution so it is useful to consider how such techniques were employed.

Newspaper advertising seems to have been little used. Relatively few people had access to newspapers, especially in rural areas, and many ordinary local folk would have been illiterate.[182] The limited use of advertising also reflects the intermediated nature of the coal business – in the seasale business it was a relatively small number of coal dealers and merchants, not the mass market, which the collieries' messages needed to target. It was these masters and merchants operating in the Irish trade which the 1761 advertisement (Figure 11.1) was aimed at; it promised them swift loading at Ness and even swifter unloading in Dublin.[183] Very occasionally, advertisements did appear which were relevant to both the public and intermediaries. In 1805, slack was advertised for sale at Ness, as was coal, slack and lime the following year.[184] These were years of low profits at the colliery suggesting they were facing difficult times, perhaps struggling to make sales.[185] The Cottinghams also occasionally advertised, promoting the coal which was available from the wharf they established in Chester.[186]

It seems that handbills or posters were sometimes used for publicity. These were mentioned by Ness Colliery's manager, James Gregory, in 1827: he had prepared

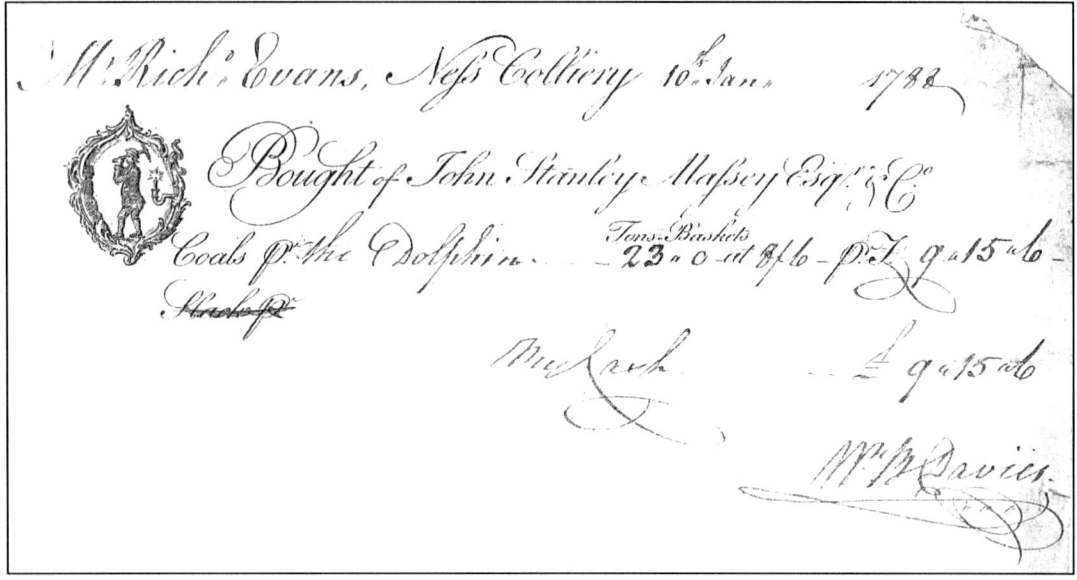

Figure 11.3: A sales receipt, with logo, from Ness Colliery in 1788. This relates to coals carried on the *Dolphin*, referred to on page 192. The logo and much of the writing were pre-printed. Source: NLW, Powis MSS, 18650. Reproduced with kind permission of the Trustees of the Powis Castle Estate.

'advertisements' which had been printed but had not yet been distributed.[187] The colliery was largely dependent on the landsale trade by this time and the material was presumably for handing to or displaying to the local public.

Given the limited evidence for written forms of publicity, it seems that word-of-mouth would have been the dominant form of communication, whether between domestic users, merchants or ships' masters. In the landsale trade, carts and other methods of distribution would have been a simple visual medium to spur such conversation. To help things, Thomas Cottingham's cart had his business's name on the side.[188]

There is one remarkable aspect to Ness Colliery's marketing: the use of dedicated, pre-printed stationery with a company logo. Three examples dated 1788 show an oval cartouche depicting a miner, pick in hand, clad in his workwear and working by candlelight (Figure 11.3; see also Figure 6.8 on p. 109).[189] This was, in effect, an effort to create a brand for Ness Colliery, distinguishing its stationery – and, by extension, the company and its products – from competitors at a glance.[190] Little published research appears to be available on eighteenth-century marketing but, while there *are* some examples of the use of distinguishing symbols – for example Wedgwood's trademark on his pottery, and the Twinings tea logo – there is little doubt that Ness Colliery's approach is highly unusual.[191] This extraordinary piece of business innovation was temporary, though. With the upheaval in the business from the mid-

1790s, pre-printed stationery of various types was retained but the distinctive logo was apparently no longer used.[192] Nevertheless, the sales vouchers the colliery issued went a little beyond the merely functional to include decorative edging (Figure 7.1 on p. 120). Little Neston Colliery, too, had its own lightly-decorated printed sales slips.[193]

CHAPTER 12

SOCIAL ASPECTS OF THE NESTON COLLIERIES

Having considered the roles and working conditions of the Neston colliers in an earlier chapter, Chapter 12 takes these human aspects of the mines further by considering the social conditions experienced by the colliers and their wives and children. This is a wide-ranging topic and includes discussion of the inter-related topics of the structure of the colliers' families and households, the health, diet and mortality of the men and their kin, and the housing conditions they experienced. There are also sections on the colliers' recreation as well as on the influence of religion and education on the mining community. The various ways in which war, which affected the country for many of Ness Colliery's first sixty years, touched the colliers is also considered. A final section considers what happened to the men and their families when the Neston collieries closed.

To give as full an understanding as possible of the life and death of Neston's colliers and their families, a comprehensive review has been undertaken of local church and chapel registers during the period of the Neston collieries' operation.[1] Information from census records for 1841, 1851 and 1861 has been incorporated in the analysis, as has data from the limited number of archival sources which mention individual workers at Neston's mines. There will have been plenty of men who, for one reason or another, do not appear in any surviving source. Nevertheless, a total of 603 workers at the Neston collieries between 1759 and 1855 have been identified in the combined sources. Of these, 547 were recorded as colliers, coal miners or similar terms throughout their working lives, or at some point(s) during it (for simplicity the term 'collier' will primarily be used for this group throughout this chapter).[2] The other men undertook supporting or ancillary roles – including management ('agents'), engineers, basket makers, brickmakers, blacksmiths and carpenters.[3] A total of 508 wives were mentioned (480 of whom were colliers' wives) and between them the couples produced a recorded 2,036 children (1,935 to colliers). Space does not permit reproduction of the relevant database here but it is available online.[4]

Analysis of the above sources forms the basis of much of the material in several sections of this chapter. It should be pointed out that there are significant challenges with using information from the various sources listed above. In church and chapel registers the type of data recorded varied greatly between institutions, time periods and individuals making the record. Records are sometimes inconsistent or incomplete. Inevitably, amongst thousands of entries, there are some apparent errors which are impossible to check from this distance in time. It should also be borne in mind that, for a variety of reasons, many baptisms, marriages or burials of local colliers or their family members do not feature in local church registers. Nevertheless, despite these limitations, the sources remain a rich source of information on the relevant population both in aggregate and at an individual level.

Marriage and Children

One point on which limited information is available in the local registers is the ages of those involved in a recorded event such as marriage. However, the limited available information suggests that Neston's colliers tended to marry relatively young. Table 12.1 shows that most first marriages occurred when the men were twenty-five or less. Grooms' average age was twenty-four; for brides it was twenty-two. This was earlier than, say, amongst Lancashire colliers, perhaps reflecting a willingness to marry and start families earlier given that the Neston women were not apparently working.[5]

The records show that it was relatively common for a couple to conceive their first child out of wedlock (Table 12.2). Almost 36% of those collier couples who married and had children at Neston had the first one baptised within eight months of marriage. Baptism data from collier families in Lancashire and Flintshire shows that it was common for there to be an interval of at least three weeks between birth and baptism, sometimes much more, so any child baptised up to eight months after marriage is likely to have been conceived before the legal union.[6] The figure of 36% is very similar to that found in larger studies relating to elsewhere in the country at the time – there was clearly little, if any, stigma at this time concerning extra-marital conception.[7] Sometimes the women in the Neston survey were several months pregnant before marriage: more than 20% of all baptisms occurred six months or less after the union.[8] In just one instance did the parish registers specifically record a child as illegitimate when apparently conceived before the parents married.[9] There are, however, few

Table 12.1: Age at first marriage, in Neston, of men who were or became local colliers, and their brides, 1759–1855. Ages and/or occupations were often unstated upon marriage so, where necessary, this information has been taken, or (for ages) inferred, from other sources concerning the individuals. Data excludes those described only as of 'full age' or '21 and upwards'. Sources: see page 198.

Age	Number of Marriages		Age	Number of Marriages	
	Groom	Bride		Groom	Bride
17	–	2	24	8	2
18	1	3	25	3	–
19	6	4	26	2	3
20	7	6	27	1	1
21	6	4	28	1	1
22	10	5	29	1	–
23	3	2	30+	4	1

Table 12.2: Interval between marriage and baptism of the first child for all couples with a recorded marriage in Neston and where the male was or became a collier, 1760–1855.[10] Sources: see page 198.

Interval Between Marriage and First Baptism	Number of Couples	Percentage of Couples Marrying and Having Children Baptised
Up to 8 months	57	35.6
9–12 months	37	23.1
13–24 months	33	20.6
Over 24 months	24	15.0
Uncertain	3	1.9
Marriage after first baptism	6	3.8
Total couples marrying and having children baptised	**160**	**100**
No recorded children in Neston	17	N/A
Total couples marrying	**177**	**N/A**

recorded cases of children being born before the parents chose to marry: only six possible instances have been identified, none of them certain.

Several couples who married locally did not apparently have children in the area. Sometimes a spouse died young; infertility is another possible cause. However, this may also be symptomatic of a wider issue: with regard to the number of children born to Neston's colliers and their wives, local parish registers almost certainly understate the number of children a couple had, for various reasons. Colliers may have had children elsewhere before coming to Neston or after leaving the town, but it is also possible their children were not registered at all. Stillbirths or babies who did not live until baptism may have been inadequately recorded, or parents may simply have chosen to avoid registration altogether.[11] It has been suggested that by the early nineteenth century as many as 30% of English births were unrecorded.[12] At Neston, comparison with census records from 1841 onwards indicate many children of colliers who did not have a recorded local baptism for some reason (reflected in Figure 6.2 on p. 92). One reason for under-recording nationally was the rise of Nonconformist religions with different baptismal practices; certainly, as discussed later, such religions did grow amongst Neston's colliers throughout the first half of the nineteenth century. Nevertheless, even allowing for these uncertainties, it is still clear that many colliers had large families, as shown in Table 12.3.

The average number of recorded children born to couples who had any at all was 4.4. In some cases, it seems that the wife was little more than a baby-making machine with up to fourteen children produced.[13] Baptisms, and presumably births, were spread

Table 12.3: Number of children born to Neston's colliers and their wives, 1759–1855. A total of 1,935 children were recorded to 438 colliers and their first and/or second wives. A further forty colliers had wives but there is no record of children. The reason for the high number of single-child couples is not obvious but possible explanations include colliers coming to work at Neston only briefly, or under-registration.[14] Sources: see page 198.

Number of Children	Number of Colliers
1	116
2	46
3	41
4	36
5	45
6	37
7	35
8	31
9	16
10	16
11	10
12	5
13	3
14	1
Total	**438**

over as many as twenty-six years, often with remarkable biennial regularity.[15] This regularity suggests that women typically breastfed their children; this usually prevents menstruation and thus would have acted as a form of contraception for twelve months or more.[16] Of course, the number of recorded children born to a collier and his wife did not necessarily mean that they brought up the same number of children. Child mortality was high and half of all couples lost at least one child; sometimes the mother died too. This subject is covered in the next section.

As noted in Chapter 6, colliery work ran in families, evidenced from a number of sources.[17] Sons followed their fathers; brothers shared their siblings' calling. Many surnames reoccurred over several generations and, while it is not always possible to pin down the precise relationships involved, it is certain that there was a significant degree of kinship in many such cases (in his study of Lancashire mines John Langton refers to there being 'dynasties' of collier families).[18] Not only did family bonds keep people together but boys who had grown up around collieries knew no other life and were ill-equipped with the skills to follow any other callings. Only twenty-six of the recorded 547 known colliers (4.8%) are known to have taken up any other form of employment while the Neston mines were still open.[19]

Figure 12.1: Chester Infirmary (left), after 1809, viewed from the city wall. Artist and date unknown. Source: 'View of General infirmary, City Gaol and walls', p2689 at Cheshire Image Bank (with courtesy of CALS).

Unsurprisingly, colliers sometimes had liaisons with local women where no permanent relationship was intended. Many illegitimate children were conceived involving colliers or colliers' daughters – a topic covered more fully later.

Health and Social Conditions

As with much else about the Neston collieries, available information on health and social conditions is fragmentary. However, the collier database interpreted in conjunction with the few surviving relevant archival sources and occasionally supplemented by descriptions of nearby contemporary collieries, gives us a good insight into the life – and death – of colliers and their families.

Chester Infirmary

One valuable and early source of insight into the colliers' health is the records of Chester Infirmary. The Infirmary had been founded in 1755 – part of growing national movement to make healthcare publicly available – and was funded by subscriptions.[20] An imposing, permanent facility was opened in 1761 which was described at the time as a 'noble square building' (Figure 12.1); it still stands, with later alterations, near the western wall of the city.[21] For two guineas each year, subscribers were allowed to nominate up to one inpatient or two outpatients for treatment – it was, effectively, an early form of medical insurance.[22] Treatment was rudimentary by today's standards but the hospital was at the forefront of medical care in its time. For example, an 'electrical machine' was bought for therapy in 1779 and, three years earlier, the Infirmary excitedly reported new techniques and equipment for 'snatching ... out of the jaws of death' the folk of North Wales and Cheshire 'falsely supposed dead by drowning, the damp of mines etc.'.[23]

Ness Colliery was a subscriber to the Infirmary from 1770 (and the colliers may have had access to treatment before then, through Richard Richardson, colliery co-owner and occasional attendee at Infirmary management board meetings).[24] This was a pioneering move – there were few early subscribers who weren't named individuals, and none of the mines in North Wales appears to have subscribed to Chester Infirmary until at least 1782.[25] Ness Colliery initially subscribed at four times the individual subscription rate, as a result of which a number of colliery workers were treated either as in- or out-patients. The subscription was reduced to five guineas from 1791 and continued at that rate for most of, if not all, the duration of the colliery.[26] Thomas Cottingham senior was also a subscriber from 1815 until his death, often paying late.[27] While the subscription is likely to have been primarily for his personal benefit, he did sponsor one man, in 1821, who probably worked at Little Neston Colliery.[28]

Records which enable named patients to be linked to Ness Colliery survive for two periods: about twenty years (with gaps) between 1759 and 1792, and from 1815 to the colliery's close (with a seven-year gap).[29] Information about inpatients' and outpatients' ages and ailments is available only for the former period. These early records list thirty-two cases from Ness Colliery; on average about six people were treated each year in the period for which most records are available (1773–7).[30] The record of illnesses and injuries for the thirty-two highlight the dangers of colliery working – Table 12.4 shows the most common 'Distemper' by far was burns; it represented one-third of cases in the period.

Other problems, each presented by a single patient, were 'Asthmatic', 'Dropsy' (oedema, or swelling from excess internal fluid), 'Spitting blood', 'Scorbutic eruptions' (spots and patches on the skin, possibly associated with scurvy), 'Bruise on his side',

Table 12.4: 'Distempers' treated in Chester Infirmary patients recommended by Ness Colliery, for which more than one case was reported. Dates and sources as per note 29.

'Distemper'	Number Treated
Burn ('in the colliery', etc.)	11
Sore (leg, knee, hand, eyes)	5
Rupture	3
Pain (stomach or bowels)	2
Fracture (leg or arm)	2
Rheumatism	2

'Gravel' (kidney stones) and 'Swelled testicle'. Some treatments went on for months but the recording of whether as an inpatient or outpatient was not always consistent. All those treated were discharged as 'Cured' except young Edward Robinson, just nineteen, who died of 'Dropsy', and John Berry who was killed by being 'Burnt in the colliery'.[31] Cure rates need to be treated with a dose of scepticism: they would be inflated by infirmaries keen to win new subscribers;[32] one collier at Ness was 'Cured' of his fractured arm within seven days!

A significant feature of Ness Colliery's infirmary subscription is that it was not confined to men. Three adult females are recorded as being treated in the early period (for long-standing 'Scorbutic eruptions', 'Pain in her bowels' and 'Sore eyes'). It is not known if they worked at the colliery or, even, if they were all related to colliers. However, having been recommended by the colliery, they must have been associated with it somehow. Clearly, working at the colliery was not a specific requirement as one infant was treated: John Smith, aged one, for a 'Rupture' in 1775. His father was presumably Edward Smith, a collier and later engineer, whose son John had been baptised the previous year. Ness Colliery continued to recommend both male and, less often, female patients until the mine closed.[33]

The availability of medical care may have been seen as a recruitment benefit at the colliery although it was never explicitly referred to in job advertisements. It probably gave the works an advantage in its early years given the lack of subscriptions by the collieries in North Wales. There was also a measure of self-interest for Ness Colliery in offering care as the sooner a miner recovered from an illness or accident, the quicker he could be back to productive work. It is noticeable that of those treated whose age is known, all except the one infant were of an age when they could still work productively – the eldest was just forty-nine.

Health and Mortality of Colliers and Their Families

The 1842 parliamentary Children's Employment Commission's reports, referred to in Chapter 6, contains many comments about the general poor health of colliers. This was perceived as deteriorating markedly over their lifetime and, by the time they were forty, they looked 'wan and emaciated'.[34] According to a surgeon working at Holywell (Flintshire):

> The chief [disease] to which they are liable [is] of the bronchi … Young persons exhibit no symptoms of the disease, but the seeds are early sown, and … miners and colliers, by the age of 40, generally become affected by chronic bronchitis, and commonly before the age of 60 fall martyrs to the disease.[35]

Examination of mortality in relation to the Neston collieries is fraught with challenges, not least because current or previous occupation of those being buried was almost never recorded in the local parish local registers, nor was age at death until about 1811.[36] Nevertheless, by various means it has been possible to identify the burial of

Table 12.5: Ages at death of males known to have been colliers at Neston, to 1855. All the men were recorded as a Neston 'collier', etc. at some point(s) in their career, although not necessarily at death. Sources: see page 198.

Age at Death	Number Recorded
Up to 10	2
11–20	3
21–30	7
31–40	8
41–50	18
51–60	18
61–70	13
71–80	17
81–90	6
91+	1
Total	**93**

scores of former colliers. In many cases their ages at death are not known, but they were often apparently young as they left behind children baptised in the previous few years; it also appears that some of their wives were pregnant, baptising children within weeks of the father's death.[37]

In ninety-three cases it has been possible to identify ages of colliers, or former colliers, at death. These are set out in Table 12.5.

The nature of the surviving records means that the table cannot claim to give a comprehensive or even representative view of the Neston colliers' mortality: for example, it probably understates deaths of younger men.[38] Nevertheless, three points stand out.

Firstly, the data confirms the tragic deaths of children, discussed in Chapter 6. Secondly, many of those identified (60%) were aged sixty or less at death. Accidents and disease had taken their toll. At first sight, the mining inspectors' comments about bronchial diseases do not seem to be strongly corroborated by causes of death recorded in Death Certificates – twenty-three have been traced so far for men known to have been colliers and who died aged sixty or less between July 1837 (when Death Certificates started to be issued) and 1855, when the colliery closed (Table 12.6, overleaf). Just four were explicitly attributed to the respiratory disease of asthma plus one who had 'inflammation on the chest'; six died in accidents. Consumption, a term usually used for what we today call tuberculosis (TB), was said to have taken another five lives.[39] TB was indeed a major killer in the nineteenth century but many British coal miners' deaths at that time were put down to TB, a symptom of which is persistent coughing, rather than the actual cause – the lung diseases of pneumoconiosis, chronic

Table 12.6: Cause of death of known Neston colliers aged sixty or less, July 1837 to May 1855. All were described at death as 'collier' or 'coal miner' except those marked * who had previously worked as colliers but were described as having other roles at death.[40] Source: Death Certificates (and other sources, see page 198).

Date of Death	Name	Age at Death	Cause of Death
6 July 1837	William Armstrong	50	Killed in an explosion
27 October 1837	Joseph Lawley	36	'Inflammation on the chest'
5 July 1838	James Lewis	38	Fell from a basket while descending a shaft
5 July 1838	Joseph Taylor	10	Fell from a basket while descending a shaft
13 October 1840	James Parr	27	'Consumption'
14 September 1841	Edward Archer	52	'Decay of nature'
28 September 1842	John Lightfoot	24	'Died by the visitation of God, To wit Epilepsy'
2 June 1843	Griffiths Littlemore	19	'Consumption of 4 months standing with Disease of the Heart'
18 March 1844	Thomas Jones	31	'Accidentally killed in a coal mine'
13 June 1844	John Hampson	30	'Consumption, one year'
1 October 1844	William Lawley	56	'Asthma and dropsy'
18 July 1845	Thomas Swift	17	'Consumption, 2 years'
19 June 1846	Charles Tunstall	36	'Fever, three weeks'
2 December 1847	Thomas Lawley*	60	'Asthma, not certified, no medical attendant'
9 November 1848	Robert Lightfoot*	59	'Asthma'
8 November 1849	William Jones	44	'Cholera'
12 October 1850	Samuel Ashbrook	42	'Consumption, 4 months'
4 December 1852	Robert Anglesey	47	'Accidentally burned in a coal pit'
11 December 1852	James Woodward*	48	'Chronic hepatitis'
20 March 1853	Robert Able	50	'Disease of the Heart, dropsy'
29 September 1853	George Gleave	52	'Asthma debility'
29 March 1854	William Roberts	50	'Scrofula debility'[41]
1 May 1855	Joseph Bartley	52	'Accidentally killed by a fall'

bronchitis or asthma.[42] The mining inspector in North Wales commented on how the constant exposure to 'foulness of the air, dust, dirt and dampness' inevitably led to colliers becoming 'asthmatic and consumptive'.[43] Understanding of diseases caused by coal mining was still in its infancy. The individuals conducting Wirral autopsies would have had very little if any experience of recognising specific mining illnesses. Many contemporary doctors rejected the idea that coal dust could cause problems; indeed, many believed that the dust might *protect* miners from TB.[44]

A third observation is that, in spite of these risks, a surprising number of men made it to an advanced age – there are records of twenty-four aged over seventy including one said to have reached his nineties. Stated ages in all sources at this time need to be treated with some caution but it is indisputable that many men made it to their sixties and beyond. The 1851 census for Ness records one man of seventy-five who was said still to be a 'coal miner'. Somehow these elderly men had survived the multiple hazards underground and on the surface which colliery work threw their way. Many would surely have had chest problems, though, through years of exposure to coal dust.[45] The Ness Colliery 'asthmatic' being treated at Chester Infirmary was just thirty-three; he was unusual in being treated there but would have shared his symptoms with many others.

Identifying deaths of colliers' wives is also challenging. Just six burials were specifically recorded as being of colliers' wives during the collieries' years of operation;[46] most, if not all, the women were young, with four having had children baptised within the previous few months. So far a further thirty-eight colliers' wives have been identified who died when they were recently married or who had borne children in the previous ten years (mostly much less than ten).[47] This represents about 7.9% of the 480 colliers' wives recorded. Several mothers died within a few months of a child's baptism; collier's wife Elizabeth Davies had a son in 1779 and both mother and son were buried within eleven days of each other early the following year.[48] The 'consumption' which took the men affected their families too: for example, Kate Ellison, a collier's wife aged forty-five, died of the disease in 1849, leaving four children, the youngest only about one year old.[49] Her exact cause of death is unclear – maybe tuberculosis or, possibly, some other respiratory disease which had been brought on by contact with the coal dust, perhaps from riddling it on the surface.

Some colliers lost two wives. One was Hugh Messham. His first wife, Jane, was around six months pregnant in March 1818 when they married.[50] He was a labourer living in Ness, perhaps working at Ness Colliery. Three months later Jane died, aged twenty-five, probably in childbirth: the child, William, was baptised on the same day as she was buried. Eight years later Hugh remarried, again to a Jane. They had at least five children and Messham was now recorded as being a collier.[51] Their first child died within a week of birth and, days after the birth of their fifth child, his second wife Jane also died. Within a year, two more of their children had been buried. There were many deaths in Neston around this time, 1837–8, probably from an outbreak of infectious diseases such as typhus or smallpox both of which were ravaging the country at this time.[52] Death seems to have stalked Messham as, in the same year as his second wife died, his candle was blamed for igniting an explosion which killed a colleague underground.[53] Messham himself, though, lived to the age of sixty-six when he died of 'asthma'.[54]

A few children had the misfortune to lose both parents, at different times and from different causes.[55] Records seldom state what happened to these children but mining communities were typically close-knit and the very real personal risks in mining meant that there was likely to be a well-developed system of mutual aid.[56] Kinship networks of extended family as well as other social connections would have been likely to ensure that some form of care was offered to the young ones left behind. The Poor Laws, discussed in the next section, were also in place to provide financial support, albeit that this was very limited.

Premature death, then, was far from unknown amongst miners and their wives at the collieries. However, it was amongst children – infants as well as older – that tragedy struck most often. The nature of the records means that the available mortality figures are almost certainly understated but they do show that at least one child in five died under the age of fifteen (388 out of 1,935 children).[57] Almost two-thirds of these deaths occurred before the child had reached its third birthday, many dying within days of birth (Table 12.7). Overall, half of all collier couples are known to have experienced the loss of one or more children.[58] Stillbirths were said to be common in Lancashire colliery communities and may have been at Neston too.[59]

Several couples lost the majority of their children. To give just one example, collier Robert Lewis and his wife Catherine had fourteen children between 1826 and 1852 of

Table 12.7: Age at death of children of men who worked as colliers at Neston.[60] A total of 1,931 children have been identified as being born to these men. A further 19 burials were recorded relating to the 101 children of men working at other colliery-related occupations.

Age at Death (years)	Number of Burials	Percentage of All Burials
0–2	246	63.7
3–5	56	14.0
6–8	23	6.0
9–11	16	4.1
12–14	7	1.8
Unknown	40	10.4
Total	**388**	**100**

whom at least nine died. These included six-week old twins who were buried on the same day. Several other men lost up to three children as well as their wives.

Sometimes a number of child deaths occurred within a short space of time. Mary, the wife of William Briscoe Davis, one-time colliery manager, bore him seven children between 1787 and 1795. Of these, four died in infancy, the first two within six weeks of each other in 1788 and the others within a fortnight in 1794. Clustering such as this is suggestive of an outbreak of disease; spikes in child mortality can be seen at various times in Neston, inevitably affecting the collieries. In 1778, smallpox, which particularly affected children, struck several villages in the Chester area.[61] In Neston, sixty-six children were recorded as being buried that year, against just seventeen the previous year. At least twenty of the children who died belonged to the colliery community; one of the colliers, James Aldcroft and his wife Margaret, lost three children.[62] They lost a further child in 1781, when the disease returned to the area.[63] Dr John Haygarth, a highly respected physician at Chester Infirmary at the time, commented that 'It is universally allowed that the … infection attacks the children of the poor people first'.[64] Measles and scarlet fever were other infectious diseases which posed a risk of death to children.[65]

For those children who survived their first few years and were able to go down the mines, it is likely that their physical development was adversely affected. Several mine inspectors across the country, including Lancashire, reported that children who worked in the pits were shorter than those of the same age who did not and that sooner or later they developed an awkward posture through constant stooping.[66] Unsurprisingly, adult colliers were also short compared to those in other occupations (although this did not prevent the men being 'strong and vigorous' and 'muscular').[67] It seems likely that both the young and old colliers in Neston shared the physical characteristics of coal miners elsewhere.

Various factors appear to have been at play here. A key one would have been the lack of vitamin D, necessary for healthy bone growth. The vitamin is usually obtained via exposure to daylight which would have been a problem for all children working underground.[68] Selection may also have been a factor with shorter men, who bred shorter children, best suited to operating in a mining environment which often required activity in confined spaces.[69] On the whole, poor diet may have been less of a factor, though: it was often (but not always) reported that colliers were reasonably well fed, at least judging by nineteenth-century records (it is, however possible that inappropriate diet in infancy and the prevalence of childhood disease which prevented adequate absorption of nutrients, adversely affected early development).[70] Inbreeding amongst colliers was also seen as a factor contributing to disease and 'deformity'.[71] In Flintshire, the inspector who gave his report to the 1842 parliamentary commission observed in collier children 'a little peculiarity … in their gait' and put any shortness down to the Welsh lack of marriage with 'foreign blood'.[72] Overall, however, the children were 'by no means an unhealthy class', he claimed.

A key factor that would have been injurious to the health of colliers and their families was poor housing. The nature of this colliers' housing is considered in more detail in a later section but it is worth stating here that the houses would have been very small and very cramped. The average collier household in the Neston area in 1841 contained six people, and households of up to eleven people are recorded (Table 12.8).[73] Such cramped conditions would have been ideal for spreading infectious diseases such as measles, smallpox and tuberculosis. In Ruabon, North Wales, a surgeon had advised that 'fever, when once in a collier's house, generally runs through all the family and, in crowded villages, through all the families'. He blamed 'the smallness of [colliers'] cottages, the want of due ventilation, [and] the total neglect of external cleanliness and drainage, the cottage floor being on a level with the ground, and pig-sty and dunghill close to the door'.[74]

Similar hygiene standards would have applied at Ness. The diarist, William Holden, writing in 1829, commented on the 'great nuisance' in most villages in the Neston area.[75] After a walk which took in Ness and the collieries he mentions:

Table 12.8: Sizes of households headed by colliers in Ness and Little Neston, 1841. 'Other Occupants' included extended family, servants and lodgers. Source: census returns, Ness and Little Neston, 1841.

Size of household (people)	Ness (Number of Households)		Little Neston (Number of Households)	
	Family (collier, wife, children)	Family and Other Occupants	Family (collier, wife, children)	Family and Other Occupants
1–2	1	1	2	2
3–4	10	8	3	2
5–6	6	5	5	5
7–8	6	9	5	6
9–10	4	2	1	1
11	–	2	–	–
Total number of households	27	27	16	16
Total occupants	149	163	90	92
Average occupants per household	5.5	6.0	5.6	5.8
Total occupants (both townships)	255 family and other occupants in 43 households			
Average occupancy	5.9			

The inhabitants heap all manner of filth before their doors in a hole dug on purpose, boys are also sent to collect the excrement left by cattle on the Roads to add to the stock, when it amounts to 'a load' they sell [it] to farmers for manure. It is needless to add the odour from such a mass of rubbish is extremely nauseous particularly in hot weather.

Hygiene standards would not have been helped if, like their Lancashire colleagues, Neston colliers and their families seldom if ever washed. As one collier put it, 'I never wash my body; I let my shirt rub the dirt off, my shirt will show that; I wash my neck and ears and face, of course'. He added that his sisters never washed their bodies either.[76]

As for the colliers' diet, it seems that in general miners were relatively well nourished – they had to be to work effectively.[77] One ready source of food would have been Ness Colliery's farm which grew grains and vegetables as well as keeping livestock. The produce was, presumably, made available for colliery households to buy, possibly at subsidised prices.[78] In addition, an area of small enclosures next to the colliery, termed 'Garden' in the 1840s, may have been used to grow saleable produce or have been rented out to colliers.[79] The colliery also took fish from nets in the estuary; shellfish and wildfowl were available too – all potential sources of protein.[80]

Some of the meals for children working in the North Wales coal pits were described in the 1842 Commission's report and showed the importance of carbohydrates to give them energy: they had a lunch of 'bread, butter, potatoes [and] a little bacon occasionally, with milk or broth'.[81] Supper was given at home in the evening and, between meals, bread and butter was eaten while working. As for animal produce, nothing went to waste if similar practice was followed to that at the Neston House of Correction at the Old Quay. There, those who needed extra fortification were given a broth made from 'sheep heads and plucks', plucks being the heart, liver and lungs of the animal.[82]

A good diet may not have always been at the forefront of colliers' minds. A Poor Law commissioner, who visited the Wirral as well as elsewhere in Cheshire and North Wales, complained that labourers who had access to cheap coal by living near mines wasted the savings on alcohol; it would not be surprising if Neston's colliers behaved in a similar way. The inspector commented: 'The advantages of cheap fuel...are exhausted by Drink. If [the labourer] was but sober his wages admit of a much-improved diet. Meal [powdered grain] might be added to his potatoe [sic] pie or fruit pie and buttermilk'.[83]

Colliers' needs for food to sustain their physical work, as well as to feed their families, would have been challenged by periodic food shortages. The key cause was poor harvests which occurred in 1766–8, 1772–4, 1794–6, 1799–1801, 1810–13 and 1816.[84] War was another factor, sometimes hindering imports.[85] A fast-growing population meant that food supplies were increasingly strained and this was at a time when more land was being given over to urbanisation and to grass to produce dairy products.[86] There were food riots in many parts of the country, including Cheshire, during the 1790s and into the early part of the next century.[87] During one two-year period – October 1798 to October 1800 – grain prices more than doubled.[88] Relief for the 'labouring poor' of Wirral, into which category some or all of Neston's colliery workers may have been regarded as falling, was organised in Neston in January 1801 due to the 'scarcity and dearness of the necessities of life'.[89] The local authorities sought to secure rice and potatoes as well as milk, curds and whey for those who were hungry.

There was unrest again during the depression following the end of the Napoleonic Wars. Popular discontent, partly prompted by the harsh economic conditions and the 1815 Corn Law, led to the 'Peterloo Massacre' at an assembly in Manchester in 1819. Fear of disturbances in west Cheshire at this time led to Sir Thomas Stanley raising a troop of Wirral Yeomanry Cavalry, in which his brother Charles was lieutenant, to guard against any agitation.[90]

Many collieries operated a 'tommy shop' (or 'truck' system), offering foodstuff to workers from company shops. The system was ripe for exploitation so that sometimes prices were inflated or pay was withheld to pay for goods – this could lead to colliers accumulating debts.[91] The tommy shop was one of the causes of a strike in some of the Flintshire collieries in 1831 and was still much complained about in 1842.[92] However no evidence has yet been found that a similar system operated at Neston.

The Poor Laws

Colliers and their families were probably regarded by many in contemporary England as part of the 'labouring poor' – those who worked with their hands and formed 'the great body of society' as the economist Adam Smith put it.[93] A common view was that, for them, low wages, menial work and dealing with the impact of fluctuating harvests and the periodic effect of war meant that poverty was their inevitable and natural condition. Thomas Robert Malthus famously claimed in his 1798 *Essay on the Principle of Population* that improving the lot of the poor would merely lead to population growth and a consequent return to poverty for them; he also believed that if the labouring poor had any spare money it would 'generally speaking [go] to the ale-house'.[94] Some contemporary thinkers, such as Edmund Burke, dismissed the term 'labouring poor' as an oxymoron – those who laboured received just reward; only those unable to work could be termed 'poor'.[95] The colliery workers of Neston were no doubt untroubled by these semantic arguments. Some of them may have been a little better paid than agricultural labourers or workers in the new 'manufactories'; they may have had a little more food in their bellies and, perhaps, access to a modest fuel allowance. But they had no wealth, few possessions and little if any discretionary income. The bottom line was that, for them, little support was available to alleviate the routine hardship of their and their families' lives.

The system instituted by the 'Old Poor Law' of 1601 was in place but relief, administered by Overseers of the Poor, was very limited and subject to local interpretation.[96] A distinction was made between the deserving and undeserving poor – it was largely just individuals who were infirm, widowed or seriously sick who were likely to be classed as the former, allowing them to receive basic assistance in money, rent or kind (such as food, fuel and clothing).[97] Recipients of relief were termed 'pauper'. The burden of support fell on the ratepayers of parishes or townships so the principle of 'settlement' applied, i.e. identifying which location had responsibility for an individual. This was usually his or her place of birth but the location could alter by, for example, the serving and completion of an apprenticeship or, for a woman, upon marriage.[98] One potential reason for parish support was for a woman to have an illegitimate child but the authorities were quick to pursue the father for maintenance in such circumstances.

As Neston's colliers were wage-earners, only a handful of individuals receiving relief are mentioned in early records relating to the Neston collieries. Some of these references are to relatively young men, hinting at disability through accident or early-onset disease, but few details have survived. One such man was Edward Davis, one of two paupers who 'suffocated in the coal pits' in 1790.[99] Davis was presumably young, having had a son baptised less than a year earlier. He and his colleague had, perhaps, previously been injured and were now doing simple underground tasks but earning too little to fully support themselves and their families. Another example of eighteenth-century poor relief relates to William Swift, one of the earliest tranche of colliers at Ness. In 1779 he was still working there but the following year his wife, Hannah, died. Within months he and his four children, the youngest around one year old, were deemed paupers; under the settlement rules they were removed the short distance to Ness to avoid being a burden on the township of Great Neston where they had been living.[100]

The story of Peter Robinson gives more insight into the forms of assistance available under the Old Poor Law. Peter's parents, John and Mary, were living in the mining village of Bagillt (Flintshire) when he was born, probably in 1763.[101] Mary died in 1770 and within three years John had moved to Little Neston, presumably to find work at Ness Colliery as it expanded.[102] However, under the settlement rules, responsibility for the pair remained with the Overseers of the Poor in their Welsh parish of Holywell. When, in 1773, fifty-four-year-old John became 'afflicted with the palsy' – perhaps some form of paralysis after an accident or stroke – the Holywell Overseers allowed him one-and-a-half guineas (£1.57½) for rent and a weekly subsistence allowance of one shilling and sixpence (7.5p). They also undertook to find an apprenticeship for Peter, aged about nine, attaching him to Hugh Maddison, Ness Colliery's basket maker. The Apprenticeship Indenture which formalised the arrangement (Figure 12.2, overleaf), stated that in return for a payment of £3,

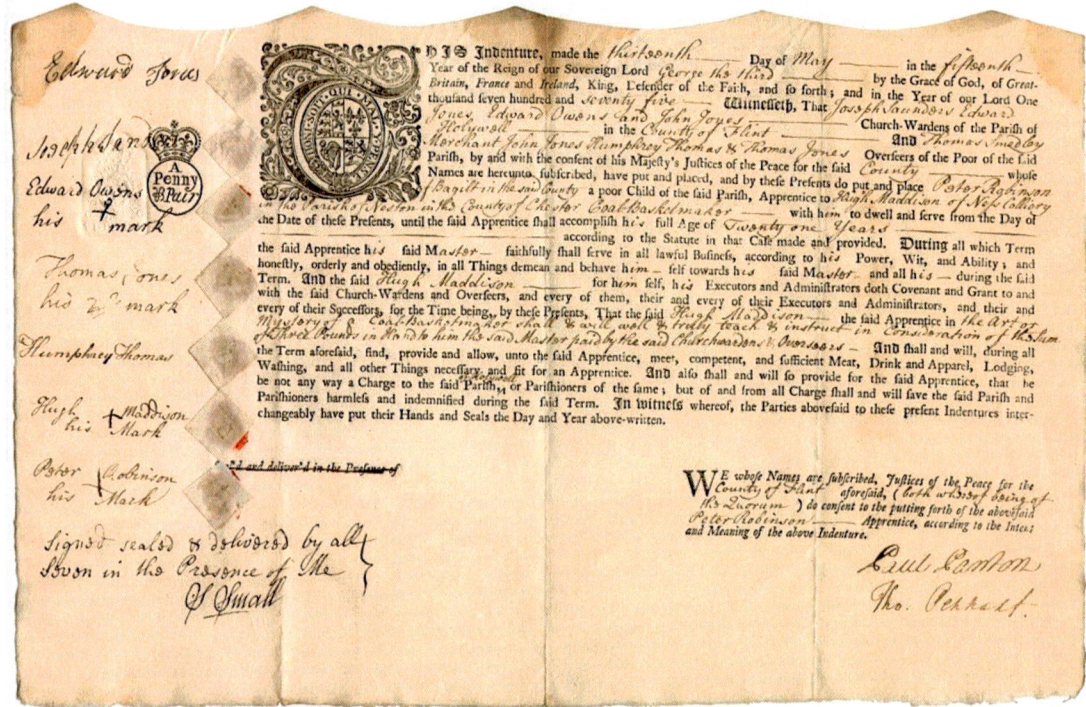

Figure 12.2: Apprenticeship indenture for Peter Robinson, 'Coal Basket-maker' at Ness Colliery, 1775. Source: NEWA, P/30/1/232/1. With kind permission of NEWA.

Maddison was to teach the 'poor child' Peter the 'art or mystery of Coal Basket-maker' until he was twenty-one. Maddison also had to provide 'sufficient Meat, Drink and Apparel, Lodging, Washing and all other Things necessary and fit for an Apprentice', thus relieving the people of Holywell of the responsibility for maintaining the child.[103] Both Peter and Maddison placed an 'X' on the document as their mark, suggesting both were illiterate.

Peter Robinson clearly learned his trade well for he was to become the basket maker at Ness Colliery.[104] Hugh Maddison, who had done the job for several years, had left by 1784 and he, his wife and five children were threatened with removal from Little Neston by the Overseer of the Poor.[105] He appealed and won but soon moved to the mining area of Prescot (Lancs.) where one of his sons, John, became a basket maker.[106]

Following criticisms of the existing system, not least the cost, the Poor Law Amendment Act of 1834 introduced a new regime. Townships and parishes were grouped into Unions overseen by an elected Board of Guardians which determined petitions for relief received from the poor. Workhouses became a central feature of the new system and were made to be deliberately unappealing to discourage feckless claims. The first chairman of the Wirral Union was Sir Thomas Stanley who, as a Whig, had supported the new Act.[107] Guardians were appointed for each township and Thomas's brother Charles took on this role for Ness. James Gregory, Ness Colliery's manager, was to become the Union's auditor and clerk.[108] A workhouse was built at Clatterbridge, using stone from Sir Thomas Stanley's quarry at Storeton, and was completed in November 1837.[109] It had a 'cheerless, prison-like appearance'.[110]

Detailed records survive of cases considered by the Wirral Union from its formation in 1836 until 1845. They show that 'indoor relief', i.e. the workhouse, was often offered to claimants – an unattractive offering of cramped conditions, separation of the sexes, menial work and poor food.[111] 'Outdoor relief', supplied to people in their homes, continued to be offered, especially for the sick and injured. Support could be temporary, longer-term or one-off – examples of the latter might include clogs and clothing, and medical equipment such as crutches or trusses. The Union's appointed surgeon occasionally also prescribed 'port wine' and gin to treat ailments![112]

Colliers or family members periodically appear in the Wirral Union records; a few examples illustrate the circumstances from which they benefited. Thomas Lawley, a collier aged fifty in 1837, had a succession of illnesses, including a 'sprained arm' and becoming 'blind in one eye'; he worked intermittently but the case of him and his family, a wife and three daughters, frequently came before the Union board, resulting in many one-off and ongoing payments.[113] He was offered a place in the workhouse but died in Little Neston in 1847 of 'asthma'.[114] John Hampson, another collier, died of 'consumption' (either tuberculosis or a mining-related disease) in 1844 after more than a year's illness.[115] During his sickness, the Wirral Union granted him two flannel waistcoats and the family, comprising his wife and three, latterly four, daughters, received relief of up to five shillings (25p) per week.[116] This was a small sum bearing in mind that colliers might be earning around twenty shillings (£1) weekly at that time.[117] It seems likely that friends and family were called on to provide additional aid. After John's death his father-in-law, a surface-worker at Ness Colliery, received Union support to raise the girls as paupers; their mother appears to have had an illegitimate daughter and moved elsewhere in Neston.[118] Mine accidents could be another reason to claim support. James Duncan was injured in this way in 1843. He was described as 'wholly disabled', probably indicating a fracture of some sort, with him and his family receiving three shillings (15p) per week for a couple of months, and two one-off payments.[119] A further form of aid was for funeral expenses: thirteen shillings (65p) was paid towards these costs when collier William Swift died of 'cancer in the right side of the abdomen' in 1845.[120]

The movement of colliers from Neston is indicated in other Wirral Union records. In a rare instance of a Neston collier who had gone to work in North Wales, John Barclay was sent back to Ness from Holywell after he broke his leg, requiring surgery. He received just three shillings (15p) per week poor relief for himself and his family of a wife and five children.[121] He later returned to Wales. As noted in Chapter 6, many other men moved to Lancashire. As they aged or became infirm, one of the townships in Neston might be required to pick up the cost of their support in Lancashire; alternatively, they were deported back to the Neston area.[122] For example, Peter Thomas and his wife had had six children in Neston parish around the turn of the century. At some point afterwards he must have moved to Tarbock from where, as a sixty-eight-year old, he was deported back to Neston in 1838 being 'unable to work'.[123] Similarly, Daniel Briscoe, aged about seventy, was removed from Whiston in 1845 and offered a place in Clatterbridge workhouse where he died six years later.[124] Meanwhile, an investigation was launched to determine why his children 'refuse to maintain their father'.

The last comment shows that families were expected to provide support to avoid the burden falling on local poor-rate payers. Ann Ken(d)rick, whose colliery-worker husband had died aged forty-six some years earlier, was refused relief in 1836 as she 'has four able-bodied sons not living with her with [a] daughter and a grandson to support her'.[125]

Illegitimacy was an inevitable part of society and, unsurprisingly, colliers or the daughters of colliers were sometimes involved. For example, the Poor Law records mention Mary Barrow who had had a 'bastard female child' in 1769. A collier, John Rowley, was said to be responsible and the Overseers of the Poor required him to make sufficient arrangements to avoid the child becoming a burden on the inhabitants of Ness.[126] The Neston parish registers are occasionally another source of information on illegitimacy but it was customary to record the mother's name rather than the father's so his identity is often unknown. In just three instances, in the 1840s, collier fathers of illegitimate children are mentioned in the local register.[127] In at least three other cases, though, the mothers of the child were said to be living at the colliery.[128] In that decade a commentary on the mining town of Flint mentioned sternly that 'fornication is common … in Flintshire, as in England, [and] assumes the form of promiscuous debauchery'.[129]

The morality of the time could split families apart. Collier's daughter Ann Littlemore, twenty-two, gave birth to a son, William, fathered by a labourer, Samuel Roscoe.[130] The child was illegitimate and the birth took place at the Wirral Union workhouse. Thereafter William was brought up in Ness by his grandparents where Ann's father, Joseph, had become an 'engine tenter'.[131] Ann, though, did not stay with her parents or son, instead becoming a house servant for the rector at Heswall who was to be a future chairman of the Wirral Union.[132] He, no doubt, would have taken a close interest in Ann's moral and religious education. Roscoe, meanwhile, was ordered to pay 1*s.* 8*d.* (8p) per week towards the child's upkeep.[133] Similarly Bridget Metcalf of Ness handed over her baby daughter to be looked after by Sarah Williams, the wife of a brickmaker at the Ness works. Williams initially received 1s. 8d. per week from the Poor Law Guardians while the father was pursued for maintenance.[134]

Occasionally, cases of orphans came before the Guardians. Mary Pulford lost both her parents – mother Anne and father Joshua who was a collier – within a week of each other in 1834 when she was just five.[135] Support was provided for her until she was twelve when a final payment of eleven shillings and sixpence (57.5p) was made to cover the cost of clothes.[136] This enabled her to enter into service, finding domestic work in a silk merchant's house.[137]

The Wirral Union record books recount many instances of men deserting their children, both inside and outside marriage. At least one story apparently had a happy ending, though: in 1837 it was reported that collier William Lea had deserted his new wife and baby, for some reason going to the mining district of Coalville, Leicestershire.[138] A warrant was issued against him by the Wirral Union and he duly returned. Surprisingly, the couple had at least five more children together.[139]

It seems that, as well as any relief available under the Poor Laws, some support was offered by Ness Colliery too. The detailed 1827 letter written by James Gregory, discussed in Chapter 6, makes reference to 'pensioners'. The number and identity of these individuals is not known but it was not uncommon in British collieries for payments to be made to widows of colliers killed in accidents or to men suffering injuries.[140] It seems likely that such payments are being referred to in the letter. As we will see in the next section, benevolence also appears to have been shown by the colliery to a widow of a collier killed in an accident in 1838.

With the levels of local poverty, the heaps of coal awaiting sale at the colliery made tempting targets for theft and several women were charged with stealing quantities of it. These included Elizabeth Edwards, a collier's wife, and Catherine Reece, wife of a Neston starch maker.[141] Both denied the charge. Witnesses called at the hearing at Neston in 1763 included collier William Kidd, the uncle of 'Emy' Lyon, the future Lady Hamilton, and the colliery 'agent' (i.e. manager) Richard Kelsall. Edwards was found not guilty but Reece was convicted and taken to Neston House of Correction, located at the Old Quay just along the shore from the colliery, to be whipped in private.[142] This was a better outcome than for Hannah Maddock, wife of a Neston labourer, in 1770. She stole 15 lbs (6.8 kg) of coal from the surface stock, and it was intimated that this was not the first time she had done so.[143] Her punishment was to be stripped from the waist up and then whipped as she walked several hundred yards from Neston Cross to Neston Bridge – humiliating as well as painful.[144] A similar punishment was given to Mary Nelson in 1784; she was whipped while being paraded half-naked through the streets of Neston on a cart after pleading guilty to theft from the colliery.[145]

Table 12.9: Place of residence for men at the time of being recorded as Neston colliers, 1760–1855. Some parish register references did not indicate a place of residence. Sources: see page 198.

Location	Number of Entries	Percentage of Total
Ness (incl. Ness Holt and Denhall)	693	60.4
Little Neston	312	27.2
Great Neston (incl. Moorside and Parkgate)	140	12.2
Burton	2	0.2
Total	**1,147**	**100**

Housing

It was usual for British colliers to live close to, or at, their place of work so one would expect to find that most of Neston's colliers lived in Ness and Little Neston rather than in the town of Neston itself.[146] Table 12.9 shows this was indeed the case, based on stated place of residence in parish registers, censuses and other sources. Most entries (60.4%) indicate that the men lived in Ness; 27.2% were in Little Neston. The general practice in the period under review was that housing was provided to colliers by mine-owners, and that a less-than-commercial rent was charged.[147] Sometimes the homes were rent-free although this might be compensation for lower wages as happened, for example, at Worsley in Lancashire.[148] Rents were certainly being charged in the 1820s at Mostyn Colliery across the Dee from Neston, with arrears deducted from wages.[149] Housing tied to a colliery was not necessarily a blessing for the workers. It created a dependency by them on owners, and eviction could be used as a threat if the workers became restive.[150]

The limited surviving records for the Neston collieries make no mention of income to the mine-owners from rentals to their workers. The earliest recruitment advertisement for Ness Colliery, in 1767, promised 'full wages' and perhaps free housing formed part of the deal offered by the colliery owners, anxious to attract plenty of good men to their new venture.

The first specific reference to local colliers' housing came in 1812 in the letting offer for Ness Colliery. The advertisement mentioned a number of buildings to be included in the arrangement including 'Agents' and Underlookers' Houses …[and] twelve Cottages for artificers and colliers.'[151] Agents and Underlookers were the highest levels of management; artificers were skilled employees such as basket or brickmakers.

At least some of these properties were probably at a site known as 'New Houses'. The buildings were first mapped in 1819, 700 yards (640 metres) east of the colliery.[152] The site is clearer on later maps, showing two terraced blocks, one apparently of eight houses and the other of four smaller buildings – maybe animal sheds.[153] The properties had gardens to the rear for growing food or grazing small animals (Figure 12.3a and b) and were located near natural water sources.[154] New Houses was the address for James Lewis who died in the tragic accident of 1838; his widow, Bridget, and children were allowed to continue to live there even though her children were almost certainly too young to work at the colliery.[155] She was still there in 1851, in one of eight or nine households, which included seven colliers and three 'brick and tile makers'.[156] One of the households contained nine people – a couple and their seven children. The buildings have since been demolished.

New Houses was typical of miners' housing, comprising groups or rows of adjoining homes.[157] It seems likely that housing of this type – albeit more rudimentary than New Houses – would have been used from Ness Colliery's early days, although relevant records have not survived. Much of this early housing would probably have been on the colliery site and some workers were still living there later. For example, in the 1828 account of a theft from the engine house, we learn that the engineer Joseph Cabry junior lived with his wife opposite one of the

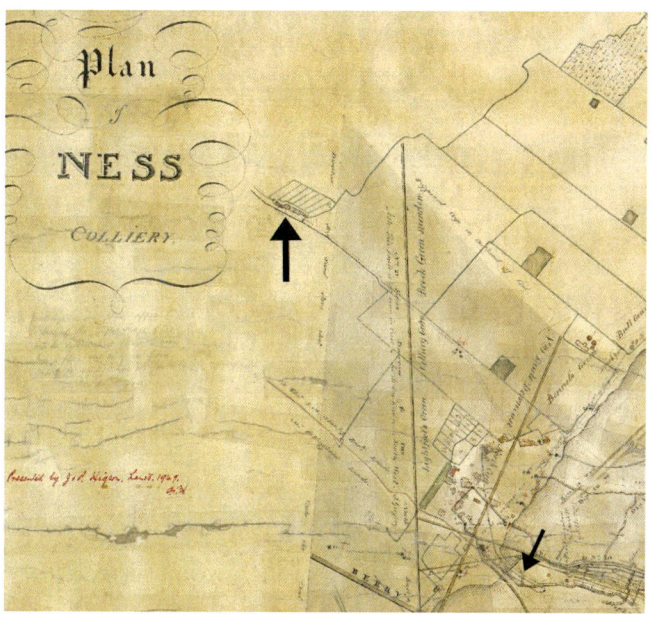

Figure 12.3a: New Houses as depicted *c*.1839 (upper arrow). To assist reader orientation, Denhall Quay is arrowed bottom right. Source: Coal Authority, 14923/4 with kind permission.

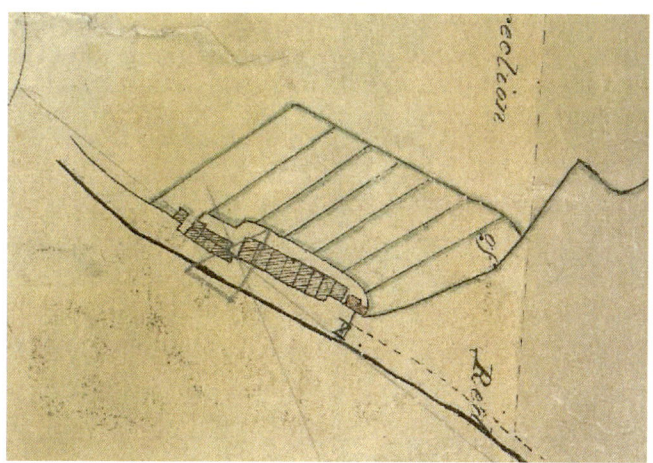

Figure 12.3b: New Houses as depicted *c*.1839. Detail from Figure 12.3a.

doors of the engine house; the 'fire man' Stephen Sharp, who looked after the engine house, lived opposite the other door.[158]

However, in the 1851 census, just six of Ness township's fifty recorded coal miners lived at the colliery; twenty-four lived in Ness village with the others scattered around the rest of the township (though none at Denhall, ensuring they were kept away from the homes of proprietor Charles Stanley and manager James Gregory). Despite the availability of New Houses, several skilled men lived at the colliery at that time – three engine operators, a basket maker and the carpenter.

Given the relative paucity of colliers' wages one would not expect them to accumulate much wealth. It is surprising therefore that one of the colliers in Little Neston was a landowner – the only such record this author has found. Thomas Cottrell was a proprietor and occupier of a small plot of land there from 1808, being recorded as a 'collier' until 1817 when he died, at a stated age of seventy-nine. His collier son, James, then took it over. Thomas Cottrell was one of the early tranche of workers at Ness Colliery and one can only speculate as to how he managed to acquire the property.[159]

Almost all the properties occupied by colliery workers in the 1840s were owned by lord of the manor, and principal local landowner, Rowland Errington, rather than by the colliery business.[160] The only significant exception was New Houses, owned by 'Charles Stanley' (as was the colliery itself). Some properties had gardens but the quality of the accommodation was in a dire state as Mortimer recorded in 1847 that,

> The village [of Ness] is one of the most miserable in the hundred, consisting of a mere mass of hovels inhabited by the colliers; the greater part of the land is of very inferior quality and much of it absolutely worthless.[161]

We can probably look to North Wales for a fuller description of the conditions. The details below come from a parliamentary education report, published the year after Mortimer's comments, and describes Rhosllanerchrugog, Wrexham (14 miles/23 km from Ness).[162] The mines of Flintshire were said to have similar social conditions and given that Ness was also said to be squalid, this is probably a fair description of housing in the Cheshire township:

> Some [cottages] consisted of a single room from 9 to 12 feet square; others have in addition a sort of lean-to, forming a separate place to sleep in. They are in general void of furniture, but in some I found a bed which is made to accommodate double numbers by arranging the occupants' feet to feet. The roofs are wattled, sometimes plastered over with mortar, sometimes bare; others are of straw, and full of large holes open to the sky, which are frequently the only means of admitting light. Each of these hovels contains on an average a family of six children, with their parents. If they comprise two rooms the parents sleep in one, and the children in the other; if there is but one room all sleep together. In either case the young people all sleep together in the same confined room regardless of age and sex.[163] [164]

Whole families of parents and their children of both sexes sleeping in one room was commonplace in the Lancashire collieries too. The inspector there for the 1842

Figure 12.4: Hooton Hall depicted just after its completion in 1778. The drawing is by Daniel Daulby, an important figure in the contemporary art world, and probably a part-owner of Ness Colliery.[164] Source: William Watts, *The Seats of the Nobility and Gentry* (London: W. Watts, 1779 reprinted as *The English Landscape Garden* (New York: Garland Publishing, 1982), Plate 13.

Children's Employment Commission commented 'There is no delicacy observed in this, which of course has a bad effect upon the morals.'[165]

It is an indication of the quality of Ness's housing that, following the closure of the colliery in 1855 and the exodus of many colliers and their families, over one quarter of the houses soon disappeared – presumably these had been little more than shacks.[166]

The Mine-Owners' Residences

Having considered the colliers' housing, it is worth contrasting this with the conditions in which the colliery owners lived.

The principal Stanley family residence was Hooton Hall which was rebuilt during the eighteenth century. It started as an imposing timber building, erected under licence from Henry VII.[167] Then in 1778 Sir William Stanley, 5th Baronet, and nephew of Ness Colliery's co-founder John Stanley Massey, commissioned a grand new neo-classical pile, with designs by the renowned Georgian architect Samuel Wyatt (Figure 12.4).[168] It was built from stone from the Stanley quarry at Storeton and had fine views over Lancashire and Cheshire.[169] There was a circular Great Staircase, said to be 'generally admired', with a skylit window above; 'Extensive offices' were attached to the main building.[170]

John would have been very familiar with both these buildings, but in about 1757, having previously been assigned the Puddington estate by his younger brother Thomas, he built Puddington Hall.[171] The date coincides with the first known borehole findings of coal at Ness and would have given John a convenient base from which to monitor the new colliery business, less than 3 miles (5 km) away. After his death it was let for a few years before becoming unoccupied for some time, though its offices remained in use.[172] Rowland Errington, John's great grandson, who took over Ness Colliery in its final year or so, apparently occupied it for a while.[173] The Hall, which was burnt down while tenanted in 1867, was a 'fine red-bricked structure' with three storeys and seventeen bedrooms.[174] Outside were a sweeping drive, formal garden, plantations, a small lake and structures including a pigeon house, coach house and dog kennels.[175] Like Hooton Hall it had fine views.[176] Two of the Hall's wings survived the fire and remain today, converted into attractive housing. Two stone driveway entrance gate posts also remain.

It appears that Sir Thomas Stanley, as 9th Baronet, preferred to live at Hooton Hall. In 1802 he invited the renowned landscape designer, Humphry Repton, to remodel the grounds.[177] His detailed drawings of the hall, and its views and grounds survive, recording the property's impressive vistas. The hall had to be sold in 1849 to pay the gambling debts of Sir Thomas's son and heir, William, who ruined the estate with his extravagance.[178] The hall has since been demolished; only its two fine lodges on Chester Road remain locally. However, eight of the hall's columns were transported to Portmeirion (Gwynedd) and four were later used in the building of the Gloriette there.[179]

Hooton and Puddington Halls, and their attached buildings and equipment, were together valued at £9,800 for insurance purposes in 1827.[180] In addition to these grand Stanley homes there was Denna House, later called Dennah Hall, owned by Charles Stanley.[181] This still stands (though much altered), just within the boundaries of Ness township and only one mile from the colliery site. The house, its high garden wall and several outbuildings were built in 1811–13 and a number of 'old pits' were filled up in the grounds.[182] The property was let to Charles Stanley on a ninety-nine-year lease.[183] It was rather less grand than the other Stanley homes but nevertheless, Mortimer, writing in 1847, after the death of Sir Thomas Stanley, starkly contrasted its location with the rest of the area:

> Denhall house, the seat of Charles Stanley, Esq. the principal proprietor of the collieries in that neighbourhood, is situated on the banks of the river; the grounds attached to the house constitute a pleasing exception to the bleak and dreary prospect of the other parts of the township.[184]

The property was described as 'Denna House and Farm' in 1813 and included a four-stalled stable and coach house.[185] There was also a vaulted wine cellar made of brick.[186] Charles was still living there in 1851 with his wife, three daughters, a governess and nine servants.[187]

The Cottinghams lived in Little Neston and, in 1783, the recently deceased Thomas Cottingham was described as having had a 'mansion-house'.[188] In about 1817, not long after his grandson, the injured Lieutenant Thomas Cottingham, came back from

Figure 12.5: Glenton House, former home to the Cottinghams.

Waterloo, a new family home was built on adjacent land on what is now Bull Hill.[189] From 1827 Thomas's wife, Sarah, would also live there. She was 'a West Indian Lady', born in Jamaica in 1790 to John Quest, who was a known slave-owner.[190] The house was called Elm Cottage, and still stands today, as Grade II listed Glenton House.[191] The property is an attractive sandstone building with a central porch of Tuscan columns (Figure 12.5). When built, it commanded fine views down the estuary and would have been very large compared to other local properties.[192] However, it was considerably less palatial than the main residences of the Stanley family.

Religion

The Church of England was, of course, the established church throughout the period under review in this book but over this time British miners were to become increasingly drawn to Nonconformist religions, such as Methodism. The traditional church was widely seen as class-based, doing little to embrace the new industrial working population.[193] Perhaps, though, Neston initially tried harder than most places as, within twenty-six years of Ness Colliery's opening, two new galleries (elevated seating platforms) were added to the parish church; at least one writer has attributed these to the swelling numbers of colliers.[194]

Neston also had a Methodist chapel where John Wesley, who often preached to colliers around the country, spoke in 1762 during one of his many journeys through the area.[195] In 1808, Neston became a station on the Methodist Circuit with an appointed missionary – it was, perhaps, no coincidence that one of the recommended appointees came from the coal mining communities of the North East, but he declined to take up the Neston post.[196] The fortunes of local Methodism fluctuated over the following years but both Little Neston and Ness were named amongst the preaching places on the region's Primitive Methodist Circuit in 1819, not least, presumably, because of their collier population.[197]

Nonconformism took a strong hold in many mining communities by the 1830s and it was certainly evident amongst the Neston coal workers then.[198] Methodist membership groups involving colliers and their wives were established in Ness and Little Neston by 1831.[199] One of the leaders was James Woodward, a collier.[200] He later recorded that an 'Independent' place of worship opened in Little Neston in 1839.[201] Methodist records three years later mention that the local 'chapel' was 'Private Property', suggesting they may have been meeting in Woodward's house.[202] By 1849 Primitive Methodists were also meeting at the home of Peter Kendrick, a colliery engineer who lived at the works.[203] He stated in the 1851 Ecclesiastical Census that an average of thirty people attended worship at his home for each morning and evening service; Woodward claimed an average of sixty at his independent chapel with a further twenty Sunday School pupils. These look reasonably healthy numbers, but they represented little more than 10% of the population of Ness and Little Neston.[204] Woodward died in 1852.[205] After the colliery closed, Kendrick was recorded as living at Buckley (Flintshire) where he was an 'engine driver and local preacher'.[206]

Coal miners had a reputation for hard drinking and various other forms of immorality. The 1842 parliamentary report on children's employment found that, for example, in Lancashire coal communities whole families gathered in the public houses on a Saturday night and were consequently in no state to 'pay attention to the Sabbath' the following day.[207] However, it was noted that for Flintshire colliers, the voice of 'dissenting' religious movements, i.e. various forms of Methodism, had been a force for good on the colliers' morals.[208] A clerk at Mostyn Colliery commented that 'All classes of labouring people are much improved of late years in their general conduct', attributing this to the church as well as to the activities of temperance societies.[209] It seems likely the Nonconformists had a similar effect on at least some colliers at Neston.

Methodism was not the only alternative to the Church of England which attracted colliery workers: both Little Neston and Ness townships also had strong Catholic connections. The Stanleys were part of a leading recusant family (i.e. Roman Catholics dissenting from the Church of England) and had chapels at Hooton and Puddington Halls.[210] At least thirty-five children of colliers were baptised at Puddington. So were all ten children of Richard Ashhurst, estate manager for the Stanley family and colliery manager for a while and also, probably, the seven children of another colliery manager, William Taylor.[211] The Shrewsburys, joint manor-holders of Little Neston and related to the Stanleys by marriage, were also Catholics, with the philanthropic 16th Earl being prominent in the religion.[212] He sponsored the building of a school on some of his land in 1840 and three years later leased it to four priests for use exclusively as a Roman Catholic church.[213] The design work was undertaken by the renowned architect Augustus Pugin, of whom the Earl was a patron; the building's unostentatious style was typical of Pugin's work at the time.[214] The church was dedicated to St Winefride – the same dedication applies to the well which was (and still is) a place of pilgrimage at Holywell, near the Flintshire collieries at Mostyn and Bagillt from where some of the Neston miners' forebears would have come. From the new church's earliest days local colliers were having their children baptised there, including Robert Lewis who had had children baptised at Puddington Hall chapel and Neston parish church as well.[215] In 1859 former mine-owner Charles Stanley was buried in the grounds of St Winefride's with the Stanley family coat of arms carved on the gravestone;[216] a stained-glass window was installed in the church in his memory (Figure 12.6).

Education

There was no formal education system in place when Ness Colliery opened in 1759; government involvement in English education would not come until the nineteenth century and, even then, it evolved only slowly.

The first school in the Neston area was established in 1610 and was funded, in part at least, by an endowment.[217] It was closed by 1779 and there is no reason to believe that any colliers' children had attended it. There was a prevailing view in the eighteenth century that for the Poor to be content they needed to be ignorant (they were considered such a distinct status in society that books of the time often capitalised the words of their description).[218] This view was bolstered towards the end of the eighteenth century by concerns that education and time to think might lead to revolution, as had occurred in France. There was a convenient economic argument against education too – children were more useful and valuable

Figure 12.6: Window depicting St Charles Borromeo at St Winefride's Roman Catholic Church, Little Neston. The window is dedicated to Charles Stanley. Borromeo was an ardent, uncompromising sixteenth-century Catholic archbishop. With kind permission of Fr Paul O'Grady.

being put to work, such as in pits, not learning. How would unpleasant work get done if people could imagine a better way of life? Ignorance was seen as bliss for everyone.

The nineteenth century saw a shift in perceptions with increasing private benevolence as a response to the poverty and misery that affected swathes of society.[219] An Anglican parish school, also known as the National School, was established in Neston in 1814. However, the location (Neston town centre) and the limited pupil places (less than 6% of the local population) suggest that there was still no particular interest in provision for colliers' children.[220] The school was funded by collections and donations and it was by similar private means that one begins to see the first indications of education for children connected to the Neston mines, through the benevolence of Sir Thomas Stanley.

Stanley's interest in education was to be long-standing, starting in his early twenties. Education at the time was very closely linked to religion in terms of the denomination of schools and, thus, what was taught there. In 1806, when he was twenty-three, Stanley donated £100 to establish one of the first Catholic charity schools in Liverpool – St Nicholas situated on Copperas Hill.[221] Subsequently the Stanley estates' accounts contain many references to donations for education costs though these were geographically scattered and, in the early years, sporadic.[222]

It is evident from Puddington estate accounts that Sir Thomas Stanley's interest in education extended to Ness. The earliest record of a payment is just 2s. 6d. (12.5p) for 'Masters at Ness Colliery' in 1810, but there is no indication of how many pupils were involved or who they were.[223] However, the Sunday School movement – which aimed to teach basic religious education and whose hours avoided interfering with children's working lives – was burgeoning at the time.[224] Three years later several local men received reimbursements for small payments to 'Masters' – recipients included William Taylor, manager at Ness Colliery, and Thomas Cottingham senior who had young children from his second marriage.[225] That year's estate accounts also record a payment for a woman to teach eleven children at a 'school' (the payment being made, incidentally, to her husband).[226] The school's location was not stated on that occasion but further payments are recorded every year until at least 1836, typically referring to, say, teaching 'ten poor children at Ness'.[227] Besides these children, a handful of other pupils who benefited from payments for schooling at Ness are named in the accounts – most seem to have been the children of men termed labourers but at least one father worked at the colliery.[228]

The Stanley estate's teaching payments were made to at least three women – Margaret Mason (from 1815 to 1823), Anne Lewis (1824 to 1846) and one or more others.[229] It seems probable that they were operating what were known as 'dame schools'. These were typically established in poor areas and were run by women, often elderly, widowed or disabled to help make ends meet.[230] Such schools aimed to teach the rudiments of learning to young children but the standard of teaching could be very

Figure 12.7: The schoolhouse at Ness, now a residence. The two-winged design went beyond the functional with decorative Flemish bond brickwork and neatly carved sandstone drip-moulding above the windows. The bricks were almost certainly made at Ness Colliery.

poor and the institutions were often viewed by parents as little more than convenient childcare facilities. Dame schools were said to be 'everywhere' in the mining areas of North Wales in the 1842 parliamentary Children's Employment Commission's report.[231]

Often dame schools operated from the instructress's homes and this may have been the case at Ness in the first few years. However, from the mid-1820s additional payments by Sir Thomas Stanley sometimes refer to a 'subscription' to the 'school' which might indicate there was then a dedicated building.[232] Numbers may well have been too large for schooling in the teacher's home by 1835 when a government education report noted that Ness contained:

> One daily school containing 42 children of both sexes, of whom the children of the poor are paid for by a gentleman, and others are instructed at the expense of their parents.[233]

The 'gentleman' was Sir Thomas Stanley and up to thirteen 'poor children', including girls, were paid for by him at any one time. It is not known when a school building was constructed but one is mapped on the edge of Ness village in 1845, with Anne Lewis still teaching there (Figure 12.7).[234] Building work was being undertaken at the school in the previous year.[235]

Figure 12.8: 'An attempt to choke John Bull with Irish-made dishes' – a satirical print from 1829 when there was much anti-Catholic sentiment in the country. Sir Thomas Stanley's Catholicism would give rise to concern over the education he was sponsoring in Ness and Little Neston. Source: British Museum, with permission.

The school was available for children of any religion. Sir Thomas Stanley had provided a school building at Eastham, an adjacent township to Hooton, in 1814 when it moved from Childer Thornton. A newspaper report stated that Stanley was happy for it to accept children of the poor regardless of denomination, 'although [the Stanley family are] Roman Catholics'.[236] This last point reflected many people's disdain, and sometimes hostility, towards Roman Catholics at the time. Anti-Catholic graffiti was even scrawled on Neston parish church in 1829, the year in which, in the face of considerable opposition, Parliament passed the Roman Catholic Relief Act (Figure 12.8).[237]

The fact that the school at Ness had only forty-two pupils suggests that sending children there was far from being an automatic choice – 131 children had been born in Ness between 1825 and 1832 which would have made them aged between three and ten in 1835.[238] As colliers made up a large proportion of the population of the township at the time it seems likely that most did not have the means to pay the fees for their children or, if they did have spare money, did not see any merit in sending them to school. Moreover, it seems that the '42 children' at the school may even have been an overstatement as a lower figure was given a few years later.

An initiative was taken in Little Neston in 1841 to address the perceived deficiencies in local moral and religious education, not least amongst colliers' children. The chairman of a newly formed committee, senior local figure Joseph Lyon, issued the following statement:

> The townships of Little Neston and Ness belong almost exclusively to Roman Catholic proprietors … whilst the resident population is almost entirely Protestant. The barren neglected condition of this district, as regards the means of moral and religious instruction, has long been a subject of loud complaint, and its natural consequences have been but too visibly developed in the general character and habits of the people. The united population of these townships is about 650, composed with few exceptions of the very lowest order of society and the only school in either is kept by a Roman Catholic, the majority of whose pupils (about 20) are the children of Protestant parents. As a more adequate remedy for this social evil, it is now proposed to erect a suitable building for a day school as soon as the necessary funds and a convenient site can be obtained and considering that a large portion of the children in this locality procure employment in the collieries at a very early age it is intended that the school be open to children of two years old and upwards.[239]

That year an infants' school was established in Little Neston probably run by collier-turned-schoolmaster, James Woodward.[240] The school at Ness continued, supported by Charles Stanley and his nephew Rowland Errington (Sir Thomas Stanley having died in 1841), but there are no further references in estate accounts to sponsoring 'poor children'.[241]

Ten years later, when the first comprehensive information is available, 106 coal miners' children were said to be 'scholars' at local schools (Table 12.10, overleaf). They started as young as two years' old and largely finished their schooling by eleven – only a handful continued beyond this age. There was apparently no material difference in the opportunities offered to boys and girls. Having said all this, care should be exercised in interpreting these figures as the term 'scholar' could encompass a wide variety of education experiences.[242] In any event, the availability of local schools did not prevent boys as young as nine from working in Neston's coal business. The children would probably also have been expected to help out on the land around harvest time.[243] Although the children may have been working, they were also available to attend Sunday School – it was claimed that seventy-three 'Sunday Scholars' attended Little Neston's Methodist chapel in the afternoon and evening on the day of the 1851 Ecclesiastical Census. It seems they were exhorted to turn out specially as the average over the previous twelve months had been just twenty!

While there were almost certainly philanthropic reasons for the Stanleys' efforts to educate a few local children, there was also a measure of self-interest for colliery

Table 12.10: Number of colliers' children aged two to fifteen described as 'scholar', or otherwise, in the 1851 census. The survey is based on all households where the head of household was a collier, coal miner or widow of one. Sources: census, Ness, Little Neston and Great Neston.

Age	'Scholar'		Colliery Worker (Male)	Not Recorded as Scholar or Colliery Worker	
	Male	Female		Male	Female
2	–	2	–	6	3
3	2	3	–	1	2
4	8	2	–	2	3
5	4	7	–	1	–
6	8	6	–	–	–
7	6	4	–	1	–
8	7	8	–	1	2
9	4	6	2	–	–
10	9	4	1	1	2
11	2	6	2	3	–
12	1	1	1	1	3
13	1	2	4	1	1
14	–	1	3	–	4
15	1	1	2	–	–
Total	53	53	15	18	20
Percentage of all children in the table	33.3	33.3	9.5	11.3	12.6

owners in educating the poor. A theme in the 1842 Children's Employment Commission's report was that it was easier to manage colliers who had had some education. The clerk to Mostyn Colliery in Flintshire, Daniel Cottrel, said that, during strikes, 'I always found those who had some education were more reasonable than others who were quite ignorant. I could talk to them with more probability of convincing them and of showing them their error; but it was useless to talk or to argue with the ignorant.' He added, 'The ignorant are less inclined to do their duty towards God and man.'[244]

What were the effects of what little learning the colliers may have had? As one indicator of literacy rates, some national studies have focused on the ability of brides and grooms to sign their own name in the parish register when they married (as opposed to just marking an 'X'). This gives an opportunity to make comparisons with Neston's colliers. Between 1760 and 1855, 177 marriages are known to have taken place in Neston involving men who were or became colliers. In these cases, just thirty-nine grooms signed – 22% of the total (Table 12.11). The equivalent figure for the brides was just fifteen (8.5%). The data shows that there was no improvement in signing rates from

Table 12.11: Numbers of grooms who were or became a collier and their brides signing marriage documents in Neston, 1760–1855 compared to grooms and brides in all Neston marriages. Source: NPR.

Status	Period	Marriages	Signed	Percentage Signing	Total Marriages	Total Number Signing	Percentage Signing
Groom: 'collier', etc.	1760–99	107	28	26.2	177	39	22.0
	1800–55	70	11	15.7			
Bride of above	1760–99	107	12	11.2	177	15	8.5
	1800–55	70	3	4.3			
Groom: all Neston	1760–99	891	462	51.9	1,558	862	55.3
	1800–55	667	400	60.0			
Bride: all Neston	1760–99	891	331	37.2	1,558	632	40.6
	1800–55	667	301	45.1			

the eighteenth to the nineteenth centuries – indeed there was a decline amongst both males and females. Certainly, by this measure, there is nothing to suggest that colliers or their families were particularly benefiting from developing education opportunities. These percentages can be compared with those for all marriages in Neston during this period: 55% of grooms signed and 41% of brides did so; nationally the equivalent figures were around 60% for men and 35% for women in 1760 with slight improvements, particularly for females, over the following ninety-five years.[245] As one might expect, the Neston colliers appear to have been considerably less educated than the general populace, a fact reflected in the disdain with which this 'lowest order of society' was viewed locally.

Recreation

Colliers typically formed fairly insular communities – the uniqueness of their type of work, their relative geographical isolation and their long hours meant they looked to each other for company.[246] They had a reputation for hard drinking (which often fuelled violence) and at Neston the colliers had plenty of options to get their ale.[247] There were many licensed beer sellers in both Ness and Little Neston in the eighteenth century, presumably partly driven by the influx of colliers, although the locations of most of the alehouses themselves are not known.[248] The Royal Oak in Little Neston and the Wheatsheaf in Ness, both of whose names live on today, were apparently operating by 1794 and 1801 respectively. The latter, which later relocated from its original position near the top of today's New Houses Lane, was owned by colliery engineer Joseph Cabry junior for many years.[249]

The pub most associated by today's locals with the collieries also still exists – the Harp, close to Denhall Quay (Figure 12.9, overleaf). The brick building was operating

Figure 12.9: The Harp Inn, some time before 1901. The building as shown here is probably little altered from when colliers were frequenting it a century or more earlier. With thanks to Susan Chambers.

as a public house by 1813 and maybe much earlier – a building was there no later than 1778.[250] The name is symbolic of Wales from where many of the early colliers came and, indeed, it was sometimes called the 'Welch Harp' [*sic*].[251] In 1813 a request was made by Ness Colliery to lease it from Thomas Cottingham for the next few years, presumably because of its importance to the colliers, but it is not clear that this went ahead.[252] The pub was referred to by a witness in the 1822 court case brought against Sir Thomas Stanley who reportedly 'saw a barrel of ale carried from the public-house to the defendant's office' to celebrate the destruction of Cottingham's tunnel.[253]

If the colliers wanted to stray further than their own townships to go drinking then nearby Neston and Parkgate had plenty of hostelries which served both the large local community as well as passing travellers and leisure visitors.[254]

An attraction said to have appealed to colliers was the local race horse meetings, held at Whitsun from 1728 until the 1850s and, in later years, in the autumn too.[255] Two different sites were used – first at Windle Hill, not far from the main road to Chester, and then, from 1829, at Parkgate.[256] For all the differences between the Stanleys and the colliers who worked for them, this was one area in which they had a shared interest. Generations of Stanley family members were ardent supporters of racing in various ways, albeit that they generally patronised society meetings such as at Chester's Roodee and at York. Nevertheless, Sir Thomas Stanley sponsored races at the Neston meetings and his brother Charles Stanley entered at least one horse in a race and maybe more.[257] One collier, Richard Blundell, was said to be a very good artist and painted some of Sir Thomas Stanley's racehorses around 1839.[258]

A fair accompanied the Neston races and activities included eating competitions, sack races and a 'grinning-match' (akin to today's 'gurning').[259] One less pleasant attraction was cockfighting, 'inseparable' from the races and said to be 'largely patronised by the colliers of Little Neston and Ness'.[260] It was probably a way to pass the time at the collieries too, as was common in Lancashire.[261] Other 'entertainment' at the fair probably included bull- and badger-baiting; the former was said to be still widely practised at fairs in Cheshire and Lancashire in 1830 but in general these activities became less popular as the nineteenth century progressed.[262]

Nothing specific is known about children's activities at the Neston collieries. However, the 1842 Children's Employment Commission's report often noted with surprise the level of energy that children had after emerging from their work in the pits. One pastime for them was football – little has changed in that respect.[263] Sometimes it was played underground when space allowed.

What interactions would the colliers have had with the wider community? As noted previously, collier communities tended to be fairly insular. Ness – both the centre of mining operations and the village itself – was over a mile (1.6 km) as the crow flies from the town of Neston. This is not a substantial distance but far enough to mean that the men and their families would have had to make a deliberate journey to mix with the locals there. There would have been little need for this. They were well served with nearby alehouses, provisions were probably largely supplied from the colliery farm and there was little else that they had the means to buy. Only local festivities such as fairs and race meetings, and church attendance for those who sought regular worship, would have necessitated venturing to the nearby town. Occasional baptisms, and to a lesser extent marriages and burials, were also reasons for colliers to venture to the church. In the late 1770s, when Ness Colliery was operating at or near its peak, almost one in five local baptisms was of a collier's child.[264]

The apparent contraction of contagious diseases such as smallpox by collier families is further evidence that the colliers did not lead an isolated existence. Nevertheless, there is little evidence that the colliers figured prominently in local consciousness – the collection for the widow of William Cottrell killed in an accident in 1815 being a notable exception.[265] Generally, though, they are likely to have been seen as a very separate community – 'the lowest order of society' as Joseph Lyon put it in 1841. William Holden had had nothing positive to say about the mining areas in his diary entries a dozen years earlier.[266] Some contemporary commentators viewed coal miners as closer to beasts and labouring machines than rational beings, even viewing them as a distinct 'race'.[267]

It is worth quoting the 1842 parliamentary commissioners' report, which commented on the behaviour of colliers until a few years previously. While the description relates to North Wales it is consistent with how Joseph Lyon had said the community in Neston's colliery townships behaved and was viewed at that time.

> The time was but a few years ago, when the colliers … were a dissipated and almost a lawless class. They spent their leisure hours, and the Sabbath in particular, in the public-houses, in noise and riot; assembling together along the road sides or sauntering in the adjacent fields. They had dog-fights, bull-baitings, and fights and broils amongst themselves. They would take delight in annoying all passers-by, and they were great trespassers on neighbouring fields and plantations. The children, following the example of parents and friends, were equally bad, and often exceeded them in mischief and vice; as for attending Divine worship or Sunday-school, such things were scarcely thought of; and swearing and profanity of all sorts were general.[268]

As noted previously, though, the report did go on to say that the men's behaviour had recently moderated with the influence of local Methodist activity.

The Impact of War

Britain was at war with France for more than half of Ness Colliery's first fifty-six years. Although all the fighting took place on foreign soil the wars were still to affect the collieries in a number of ways. In Chapter 11 it was noted how there was local concern around the turn of the century about a French-backed Irish insurgency and the indirect role Ness Colliery could be playing in facilitating it. And in Chapter 2 it was noted how, after the end of the Napoleonic Wars, Ness Colliery's poorest years were experienced as economic problems beset the country. However, war had had a more direct impact on Neston's colliers for several decades.

The Militia Act had been passed in 1757, amid growing concern about a possible French invasion. It established an armed and uniformed force of conscripts who had to serve for three years, later increased to five.[269] Every township had to provide lists of able-bodied men aged between eighteen and fifty (later reduced to forty-five) and the conscripts were then selected from the list by ballot. The men were liable to active service if required anywhere in England and had to train on Sundays and for longer periods at certain times.[270] Local men joined various companies of the Cheshire Regiment as privates, sometimes assembling at the Roodee in Chester in early summer.[271] The Act allowed the chosen men to pay a fine of £10 which exempted them from service for three years. As an alternative to serving in their own right, men had the option to pay a substitute to take their place if they could afford it.[272] In 1808 the average cost of a substitute in Cheshire was £25 11s. (£25 55p), which was probably not much different from the average annual pay for a collier at Ness.[273]

Given the numbers of colliers in the Neston area, inevitably several of them were selected for service. In the fifteen years following the colliery's opening, ten names appear on the lists of militiamen chosen by lot, half of whom paid substitutes.[274] Amongst the names are Richard Bold, selected in 1762, whose son was also to be selected in 1803; and Thomas Lyon, uncle to 'Emy' Lyon, the future Lady Hamilton, who paid for a substitute in 1770. The imposition of militia service was unpopular, leading to riots in some parts of the country.[275] It was seen as an indirect tax on the poor, the rich being little troubled by the need to pay for a substitute. Amongst senior local figures who avoided having to serve in this way were Thomas Stanley Massey, future 7th Baronet and owner of Ness Colliery, in 1780 and Thomas Cottingham senior, the future founder of Little Neston Colliery, who paid for a Chester cordwainer to take his place in 1772.[276]

As well as serving in the militia, local people took other actions to help protect the country. In 1798, there was deep concern about an imminent invasion as French troops camped on the Channel coast.[277] The national mood was captured by Samuel Taylor Coleridge in his poem 'Fears in Solitude. Written April 1798, During the Alarms of an Invasion'.[278] People 'of all rank' were expected to do their bit and voluntary collections were held across the country to send money to the Bank of England to be used in the defence of the country's 'laws, religion and constitution'.[279] The names of the donors were published in the local press: they included 'The employees at Ness Colliery' who together put in £5 14s., and two individual contributors at the colliery, Thomas Johnson and manager William Taylor, who put in half a guinea (52.5p) each.[280] Sir John Stanley Massey Stanley and his son, Thomas, had contributed £50 each to a similar collection in 1794.[281]

The Local Militia Act of 1808 reinvigorated the force as war continued to threaten the country. Although the act emphasised balloting as a recruitment method, dozens of Neston men volunteered to join in 1809.[282] These included two Littlemore brothers – Thomas and Samuel, both colliers – who joined alongside a third brother, James, also a collier, who had been chosen by ballot.[283] Three other colliers volunteered around this time with more joining later; in total, over the years, twenty-three Neston colliers are known to have been selected, or volunteered, to join the force. After the end of the Napoleonic Wars in 1815 the militia largely fell into abeyance but a Ness collier was nominated as a militiaman by ballot in 1821; he paid a Chester potter to take his place.[284]

The Aftermath of the Collieries' Closure

As Neston's two collieries closed within a decade of each other; what impact did this have on the men who worked there and their families?

It is not easy to assess the effect of the closure of Little Neston Colliery, in the mid-to late-1840s. It probably had few employees by then and most of them may simply have been assimilated into Ness Colliery's workforce, accounting, in part, for the small increase in numbers there between 1841 and 1851. However, census records do show some miners moving out of Neston around the time of Little Neston Colliery's closure. For example, collier Joseph Lewis took his wife and five of his children to work as a carter in the colliery township of Whiston (Lancs.), some time between 1841 and 1851.[285] Neston collier, John Barker, born in Flintshire, moved with his family to Wigan after 1846.[286] The most extraordinary instance of migration is Neston miner John Jones who, no later than 1850, moved to Leeds then Flint (Flintshire), Mow (east Cheshire), Castle Eden (Co. Durham), Wigan and, finally, by 1861 to Rainford, both in Lancashire – assuming the place of birth of his children reflects his own location.[287] Perhaps Jones had pit sinking skills, travelling to where there was demand.

The closure of Ness Colliery in 1855, and which was said to have had around 120 employees four years earlier, would have had a much bigger impact. This is reflected in census statistics for 1851 and 1861. The intervening period was one of continued population growth – nationally, regionally, and in Neston where the town's population grew by 15.7% (Table 12.12).[288] The trend was reflected in Little Neston, too, which grew by 13.5%. However, Ness was far more dependent on the mining business and here numbers fell by almost one quarter. Unsurprisingly, the fall was particularly marked in relation to the number of males, where there were 30% fewer.

The story behind the statistics is, again, one of migration. Colliers had particular skills and it was generally accepted that once you were a miner, you were a miner for life.[289] If the work was no longer there then it was necessary to go and find it elsewhere. Britain's insatiable demand for coal meant that there were plenty of alternative

Table 12.12: Population change in Ness, Little Neston and Great Neston townships, and the Wirral, 1851–61. Source: censuses and Rideout pp. 98–9.

		1851	*1861*	*Percentage Change 1851–61*
Ness Township	Males	234	164	-29.9
	Females	220	182	-17.3
	Total	454	346	-23.8
Little Neston Township	Males	256	281	+9.8
	Females	255	299	+17.3
	Total	511	580	+13.5
Great Neston Township	Total	1,524	1,764	+15.7
Wirral	Total	59,011	81,412	+38.0

Table 12.13: Estimates of regional and national coal mining employment, 1851 and 1861.
Source: Church, p. 189.

	1851	*1861*
Lancashire and Cheshire	32,450	46,300
North Wales	4,850	6,540
Great Britain	218,230	295,810

opportunities for employment. All coal mining regions, including Lancashire and North Wales, saw increases in employment in the coal industry in the decade in which Ness Colliery's closure fell, providing new opportunities for men with the right skills (Table 12.13).

Of the 106 men described as colliers or coal miners working in Neston in 1851, 82 were still alive and can be traced ten years later (Table 12.14, overleaf). Forty-nine of them (59.8%) were still employed in coal mining. These men were predominantly drawn to Lancashire and were joined there by dozens of other Neston-born men, boys and women who had not appeared in the 1851 census as local coal miners. These Neston emigrants went, in particular, to Rainford, Wigan, Whiston and Parr near St Helens (Figure 6.3 on p. 94). Ann Tunstall, widow of a former Neston collier, took her three sons and illegitimate daughter, also Ann, to Windle, near St Helens; all four children, including the twelve-year-old girl, were described as 'collier' in 1861.[290] Similarly, several other Neston-born females became colliers in Lancashire.[291]

A small number of men went to the mines in Staffordshire but it is curious how few became colliers in Flintshire – just two have been found to date. Given its geographical proximity and historical links with the Neston pits it might have been considered a logical destination. Even some of the men born in Flintshire and who then worked at Neston moved on to Lancashire when Ness Colliery closed.[292] The Flintshire mines were still growing so one can only speculate as to the reasons for the lack of migration to there – maybe different mining practices (the Neston men were familiar with the Lancashire System of coal working) or perhaps lingering hostility by the Welsh to an apparently less militant Cheshire workforce.[293] Concerns about the predominance of the Welsh language are less likely to have been a problem as the industrial areas of North East Wales were largely English-speaking or, at least, bilingual at this time.[294]

The fall in the number of females as well as males in Ness between 1851 and 1861 censuses suggest that many men took their wives and families with them. However, several Neston-born miners were recorded as 'lodger' in Lancashire in 1861 and it seems a number worked away, intermittently returning to their home in Neston. Three men's names were entered in the Ness census by the enumerator, Joseph Cabry junior, but then crossed out. A note was added saying these men were working in Lancashire, although their families were still in Neston. Similarly, the Little Neston census mentioned five men 'working in coal mines in Lancashire'. This practice is, presumably, the reason for ten Neston men still describing themselves as coal miners in the 1861 census; the possible opening of the Anglican Smelting, Reduction and Coal Company's operation in Little Neston around this time may also account for a brief new flurry of coal mining employment.[295] Some men were recorded as coal miners in Neston parish registers in subsequent years, either as father of a baptised child or as father of a bride or groom; three still did so in the 1871 census.

It is not possible to detail here the stories of all the colliery workers who did not become Lancashire miners but it was worthwhile giving a few examples. Three members of the Kendrick family, which had a long history of engineering at Ness, seized a growing employment opportunity of the age to become engine drivers.[296] Matthew Bates, a manager at Ness Colliery, returned to his home region of the North East to be a mining engineer.[297] However there was no further career in mining for another former manager, Isaac Jackson who had looked after Thomas Cottingham's works. Like many other former Neston mineworkers, he was described as just an 'agricultural labourer'.[298] Meanwhile ex-collier Daniel Williams settled for the simple life of a shepherd on land reclaimed from the Dee Estuary at Sealand (Flintshire).[299]

Table 12.14: Location and occupation in 1861 of men who had appeared as coal miners or colliers in the 1851 census in Great Neston, Little Neston and Ness. Source: censuses. Full location details at *nestoncollieries.org*

Location	Collier, Coal Miner, etc.	Other Role	Total
Neston	10	Agr. labourer – 16 Mason's labourer – 3 Fisherman – 2 Coal dealer – 1 Pauper – 2	34
Lancashire	30	2	32
Flintshire	2	4	6
Staffordshire	4	–	4
Cheshire	2	3	5
Yorkshire	1	–	1
Subtotal	**49**	**33**	**82**
Dead			10
Not traced			14
Total			**106**

The dispersion of Neston's colliers marked the end of the first era of mining in the area. A new beginning would come in 1875 when, once more, local men would be joined by those from Lancashire and Wales to eke a poorly-paid and dangerous living from Neston's coal.

* * *

The evidence in this chapter, drawn from diverse sources, is that the colliers of Neston led an unremittingly tough life. So did their wives and children. Poverty and disease were constant companions; death forever lurked in the shadows. There were no luxuries: after the long hours of hard toil discussed in Chapter 6, the men returned to cramped and rudimentary homes. Perhaps most strikingly, for these men and their families there was little real possibility of escape. With virtually no education and limited skills the men were destined to a life of work in an insular community of colliers. Even when such work was no longer available in Neston, the majority sought it elsewhere. The men must have had to have a fatalistic attitude, accepting the hand that life had dealt them with no real hope of anything better in the future. From a twenty-first century perspective it is easy to judge negatively the men's recourse to blood sports and their quest for solace in an ale glass. But, if we had been born into a collier's unremittingly harsh world, would we have been any different?

CHAPTER 13

THE NESTON COLLIERIES' PLACE
IN INDUSTRIAL HISTORY

This book has considered many aspects of the Neston collieries during their period of operation – a period which, as indicated in Chapter 1, largely coincided with the Industrial Revolution. With this understanding of what went on at the works, this chapter will mainly consider two key and interlinked questions: in what ways were the collieries remarkable or significant and to what extent did they reflect the events and changes that were occurring in Britain during this 'revolution'?

It may be helpful to consider briefly what is meant by the term 'Industrial Revolution'. The *Oxford English Dictionary* defines 'industrial revolution' (in lower case) as 'a rapid development of industry, chiefly as a result of the introduction of new or improved machinery and large-scale production methods'; it adds that, when spelt with capital initial letters, the term relates to this industrial development in Britain in the late eighteenth and early nineteenth centuries, before spreading elsewhere. This phrase, though, has been the subject of much debate for more than a century.

Most commentators agree that the period concerned saw profound change in Britain. Yet, many have argued that the term is misleading and even inappropriate: the changes occurring at that time extended far beyond what happened just in *industry*. In any event, was industrial change merely an outcome of *other* changes, confusing cause and effect? Thus, various schools of thought have grown up over how this 'revolution' should be interpreted, with commentators coming at developments during this period from different angles or with different points of emphasis.[1] Some have stayed close to the dictionary definition, highlighting technological innovation, in particular regarding machinery and steam engines; others have focused on industrial organisation, seeing the period as primarily one of industrialists, entrepreneurship, factories and restructuring of the workforce. Another view is that the period was one of *economic* revolution – proponents have claimed it was a time when investment, productivity and gross domestic product took off, complementing a fast-expanding population. Other interpretations have focused on the shift in importance from organic power sources (such as wood and horse power) to inorganic (coal and coke), or on changes in the political, scientific and cultural background which provided the right environment for industrial growth. Substantial social change such as in population size, the composition of the labour force and the move to urban living have also taken the argument well beyond 'mere' technical change.

In addition to these disparate views, there is argument over the word 'revolution'. It implies suddenness ('rapid', as the dictionary says) and also radical, wholesale change when the event was actually one which lasted, arguably, a century or more and which brought little tangible change to many people's lives for decades. Many parts of the country were hardly touched by industrialisation during much of this 'revolution'.[2] The North West has often been used as an example of a region transformed at this time yet the focus has largely been on the cities and towns of (historic) Lancashire and on east Cheshire. However, if ancient geological forces had not happened to deposit some coal at Neston's feet then, from an industrial perspective, the town would probably have been little different in 1800 or 1850 than in 1750. Chester had a long-term multiplicity of small-scale manufacturers but the city never burgeoned industrially. Meanwhile, the Wirral – indeed most of west Cheshire – remained predominantly rural and agricultural. Only Birkenhead at the northern end of the peninsula bucked this trend, in the last three decades of the period covered here. Of course, there may have been indirect effects of the 'revolution' on the places where new industries had not sprung up – for example, population movement, greater availability of consumer goods, changes in agricultural land use or better roads – but, at the very least, the effect of this revolution was far from uniform geographically. In recent decades it has been increasingly recognised that regional rather than national perspectives are essential to gaining a fuller understanding of the Industrial Revolution but even this level of analysis risks masking changes *within* regions.[3] (There remains, incidentally, the further problem with how a 'region' is defined – should Neston, for example, be grouped with North Wales which contained the bulk of the Flintshire Coalfield, or with Cheshire based on its county boundaries, or with Lancashire as part of the industrial North West and with which Neston had many connections? As readers will have gathered, 'west Cheshire' has often been used as the geographical unit of analysis in this book whilst hopefully recognising, where appropriate, Neston's role in other regional contexts).

This book is not the place to explore in detail the debate over the interpretation of the term 'Industrial Revolution' but readers need to be aware that the broad range of opinions about the scope of the event, and to a lesser extent its timing, informs what follows here.

Turning, then, to the role and significance of the Neston collieries in industrial history, this can be assessed at different levels – nationally, regionally and locally.

From a national perspective, it has to be conceded that the *scale* of the Neston collieries as industrial enterprises was not particularly significant. Ness Colliery was very successful for its first two or three decades and was larger than most other individual mines in south Lancashire and North Wales during this period. However, individually the mine produced a tiny percentage of national output and, even when grouped with its nearest neighbours in North Wales, it was part of the smallest region of coal production in Britain.[4] This probably accounts for why Ness Colliery has so often been overlooked in accounts of British mining history. Furthermore, in terms of industrial innovation, the Neston works almost invariably followed the trends emerging elsewhere, rather than setting them. In these respects, the Neston mines were like hundreds of other rural mines scattered across the country. This is not to say, though, that the Neston collieries were not notable in other respects.

Firstly, there were the acts of sabotage instigated by Sir Thomas Stanley in the early 1820s against Thomas Cottingham's mine – blowing them up, flooding them and maybe deliberately vandalising his engine too. Industrial sabotage was not unknown – indeed Luddism, with its deliberate breaking of factory machinery, had brought havoc to many places just a few years before – but the involvement of a British aristocrat in such shameful and discreditable activity is quite extraordinary. Secondly, the introduction of underground canals at Ness Colliery was truly remarkable. It can be argued that coal-carrying boats were very much 'old' technology and that such canals were not an idea which other collieries chose (or needed) to follow. But this means that the wholly underground canals at Neston were amongst just a handful of such arrangements in British coal mines. They were also the only ones known to have operated under an estuary or any other substantial area of water; it is an extraordinary thought that vessels were plying their way on the surface at the same time as boats were working their way through tunnels deep beneath them. The creative drive behind their introduction was, surely, indicative of this 'revolutionary' age. There is a third aspect of Neston's mines which, though not physically dramatic, nevertheless deserves recognition in British commercial history – the use of business stationery bearing an apparently unique business logo. Comment was made in Chapter 11 on the rarity of such initiatives at this time – a sign of a real innovation in a new commercially-aware age.

It is also worth mentioning that, although Ness Colliery was not large, even this provincial coal works had connections with figures who were to feature on the national stage, albeit that those connections were sometimes transitory. The engineers George and Robert Stephenson, James Brindley and the firm of Boulton and Watt all appeared in the colliery's story. In the specialised world of mine surveying Nicholas Wood, John Buddle and John Watson were renowned individuals who gave advice at Neston. In a very different context, 'Emy' Lyon, the future society darling, Emma, Lady Hamilton, should also be mentioned here, being born in Ness and the daughter of a man who was almost certainly Ness Colliery's blacksmith.

One other comment from a national perspective is that Neston's collieries also reflected events which were happening on wider political and economic stages. Wars with France impacted the mines one way or another for decades, as did concerns over events in Ireland. The impact of changing national economic circumstances as growth and recession alternated, and of fluctuations in wage rates and coal prices can all be traced at the collieries; food shortages hit the Neston area too. This was also an age of increasing scientific understanding but the collieries' story sometimes illustrates the shaky state of knowledge in some fields at this time – for example in medicine (in questionable hospital treatments and diagnoses on death) and in geology with the first, inaccurate map of the Wirral's coalfield.

The significance of the Neston collieries from a *regional* perspective can be assessed in many ways but probably the most important is that they were the first to bring to west Cheshire a central feature of the Industrial Revolution – a substantial industry powered by new technology and centred on a single site. A large workforce, almost certainly significantly bigger than any that had been assembled in the region until then, turned out industrial quantities of goods – mostly coal but other items as well. The early installation of a steam engine (one of only about 330 known to have been built in Britain by this time) is a very important milestone in the region's history and was unparalleled in the area for probably the next twenty-five years.[5] These men and machines required careful organisation on a scale hitherto unseen locally. Neston's coal industry was to wane and other industrial sites would grow elsewhere in west Cheshire but, for a while, it was surely *the* place in the region which was most indicative of the new industrial age. As such, Neston was a prime example to the citizens of Chester and the surrounding area of so much that was transforming Britain in this period – for example in entrepreneurship, technology, population mobility and social change.

The start of a new business required capital and thus the bringing together of disparate investors from Chester and the Wirral willing to share their assets and knowledge and, in turn, the risks and rewards of the business. The formation of this new business exemplified this new age of entrepreneurship which saw growing numbers of partnerships being formed.[6] The investors' capital was invested in engines and other mining equipment and machinery, in the sinking of shafts and boreholes, and in the supporting built infrastructure. As national coal mining expertise evolved over the following decades, so did what happened at Neston's mines with the utilisation of new technologies in, say, underground transport and engineering, and new mining techniques. Flirtations with the promise of canals and railways, which were to prove so important in the country's growth, can be added to the list of activities at Neston even if, ultimately, they came to nothing during the period discussed here.

As noted previously, one of the characteristics of the Industrial Revolution was the bringing together of individuals to form large workforces in a single location. Country dwellers moved to the site of newly built factories; industrial cities expanded rapidly. This was a new age of mobility and, at Neston, perhaps 180 men came to work at the new mine initially, some bringing families;[7] many other men, women and children were to come over the following decades. Thus, a substantial new community materialised almost overnight, centred on a sleepy hamlet which had previously consisted of just a few score people.

The assembling of the colliery community brought with it other social change. New systems of care began to appear at Neston – corporate subscriptions to the recently-opened Chester Infirmary gave access to treatment to colliers and, sometimes, their families; pensions were paid by Ness Colliery's owners; colliers and family members benefited from the evolving Poor Law system of relief; and Neston's miners were probably members of one or more of the new local friendly societies. The earliest societies were often a means for workers to combine to leverage their bargaining capability and such combination was demonstrated at Neston with at least one strike. Evidence for other nineteenth-century social changes can be found too, such as the growth of Nonconformist religion and the wider provision of schools and education, even if only at a rudimentary level. Meanwhile what was happening in the mines also reflected the worst aspects of industrialisation: long hours, low pay, child labour and a wholly inadequate safety regime.

It should be also be mentioned that as well as being a prime regional example of many of the changes affecting Britain at this time, the Neston collieries were also a *product* of the Industrial Revolution with its shift to using inorganic fuels. As set out in Chapter 2 it may well have been the prevailing national keenness to find coal which motivated John Stanley Massey to investigate the coal reserves beneath his land. Once new deposits were found, the surging demand for coal for domestic and industrial uses, and steadily increasing sale prices, would have helped weigh the argument for exploiting the resource even though geological conditions were not necessarily as favourable as those in, say, North Wales.[8] It was, though, pure geological chance which meant that solely this part of west Cheshire saw such industrial activity.

What about the Neston collieries' importance in terms of the region's trade? Britain was experiencing rapidly expanding demand for coal. This was both for domestic use, as the population grew and home fuel preferences changed, and also for trade users as fuel-hungry businesses manufactured a wide range of industrial and consumer goods. This demand spurred the coal trade to Wales and Ireland – Ness Colliery's two main seasale markets. The latter was particularly important to Ness Colliery but, until now, accounts of coal production around the Dee have overstated the role of the Flintshire collieries in the late eighteenth century and have failed to recognise the much greater relative contribution of Ness Colliery. The colliery's coal also occasionally found its way to more distant markets – southern Europe, North America and even the Caribbean – a small reflection of the more or less continuous growth in Britain's international trade during the eighteenth century and beyond.[9] It would be wrong to exaggerate the scale of Neston's impact on its various markets: generally, Neston's coal merely supplemented supplies that were available from elsewhere. However, from a supply-side perspective, coal which came more or less wholly from Ness formed, for a while, the largest part of Chester's overseas shipping trade. Chester itself – its people, businesses and institutions – was also an important market for Neston's coal for many decades.

The mention of Chester is a reminder of the inter-connectedness of activity amongst the industrialists, traders and landowners of the city, Neston and elsewhere around the Dee Estuary. Merchandise was making its way across the Dee from Flintshire to the Wirral – both natural resources (limestone and, sometimes, coal in competition with the Neston businesses) and also finished goods (clay wares including pottery and firebricks, iron goods and, no doubt, output from the Greenfield mills and nearby lead-works). Skilled colliery labour was also migrating to work in Neston's pits. Meanwhile, Neston's coal was finding its way to the industries and homes of Flintshire as well as further west along the Welsh coast. Richard Richardson, one of Ness Colliery's founders had mining and business interests on both sides of the water, as well as his extensive connections to Chester. The Stanleys also had lands in Flintshire and had social connections with senior landowners in the area such as the Glynnes and Mostyns. Several Neston figures had interests in businesses at the industrial hub of Greenfield. As for the shipping trade, vessels' masters, often operating for one of the region's many merchants, used a variety of places for unloading or loading in the estuary depending on the nature of their business and the state of the Dee. To complement this, a wide range of items were being brought into the area, many of them destined for Chester or inland, but including limestone, slate and soap ashes intended for the Neston collieries. All in all, there was an active and varied Dee Estuary economy and a complex, multi-layered network of relationships between parties.

The mines, of course, had an impact at *local* level too. Most of what has been said above about the regional importance is relevant here too. Neston had a 'first' and there was, presumably, some local pride in that fact if we are to believe the report that 'all Cheshire' rejoiced at the discovery of Neston's significant coal deposits in the late 1750s. This pride may well have lasted a while given Ness Colliery's success for a few decades. However, in terms of day-to-day impact locally, this was probably not as great as might first be imagined.

When Ness Colliery opened, as far as the labour supply was concerned, the need was largely for experienced colliers. This required bringing in men from elsewhere, notably Lancashire and North Wales. Fewer locals are likely to have been taken on – maybe lower numbers than Neston folk were hoping for – and any that were took the lower-skilled, less well-paid roles. Over the decades the colliers and their families formed an insular and probably fairly independent community. The colliery farm is likely to have supplied much of their food needs. Neston's clothiers and bootmakers may have had a useful new source of business but the colliers had little discretionary income and what they did have probably mostly disappeared in a handful of local hostelries. The colliers and their families sometimes interacted with local society, through church and recreation, but many locals would have viewed them with disdain and kept their distance. Over the years the building of schools and the development of new places of worship would have led to greater assimilation but one suspects that the men and their families were mostly seen as a breed apart.

The collieries' products were probably of more direct significance to local people. Its coal warmed their houses and inns and fuelled a few small businesses; its lime, soap ashes and drainage products – local evidence of the so-called 'Agricultural Revolution' – improved the land for many tenants on the Wirral; and its bricks were sometimes used in local building. In addition, a few local people earned much-needed cash by distributing these products one way or another, and a handful of local suppliers such as wheelwrights and candlemakers no doubt also found the collieries a useful source of trade.

One further question could be asked here: given the period which has been under review in the book, did the people associated with the Neston collieries feel that they were experiencing any kind of 'revolution'?

It is worth prefacing the answer with a comment that the phrase 'Industrial Revolution' was not in general use during that particular period. Occasionally, contemporary commentators did use the word 'revolution', such as Josiah Wedgwood in 1767 to describe what was happening in his own industry.[10] However, it was not until 1884 that the full phrase gained significant currency.[11] The mine-owners and colliers are very unlikely, then, to have talked about an Industrial Revolution even if they sensed they were experiencing a period of profound change.

In any event there was, arguably, only one really 'revolutionary' moment at Neston: the very opening of Ness Colliery and, in particular, the more-or-less contemporary introduction of a steam engine. This engine must have been seen as wondrous and awe-inspiring by people in the area. Admittedly, engines were established technology in Britain by 1759, even if relatively rare and rather rudimentary: many people would have heard of them, some would have seen them in other collieries where they had worked and, at the very least, smoke would have been seen from Neston across the estuary in North Wales where a few coastal mine engines had operated.[12] Nevertheless, those involved or who came to gaze must surely have felt that the introduction of an engine was a sign that a remarkable new era had reached this rural corner of England. Other than that, though, the many individual changes that local folk witnessed were small, or incremental, or largely irrelevant to their immediate lives. As one writer put it, people must have felt that 'something was happening';[13] however, at a day-to-day level, not much was. In many ways the harsh living and working conditions of 1759 were, for most of those at Ness Colliery, little different from those in 1855 when it closed. Neston's mining community was not exceptional in this regard: for most of British society there was little that was revolutionary in living standards over the period.[14] The 'hovels' of Ness were mirrored by the growing number of overcrowded slums for city-dwellers. Life probably changed more for the mine-owners who, for example, could take advantage of coal-fired central heating, improved availability of luxury goods, and better transport connections including the new railways. It is arguable, though, whether even their lives were being revolutionised.

In summary, though, while the output of the collieries at Neston was never of a nationally important scale, they nevertheless deserve to be recognised in the story of British coal mining for some remarkable events and connections to significant British figures. Furthermore, from a regional and local perspective, their significance is that *despite* being of no great scale, these works which were located in a rural backwater of Britain, devoid of any significant previous industry, exemplified in so many ways what was happening Britain at the time.

Ness Colliery, the principal mine in west Cheshire, operated for ninety-six years and was almost wholly in the hands of the Stanley family over that period. The motto of the Stanley family, often depicted with their coat of arms, is 'Sans changer' – 'without changing'. This was presumably intended to relate to the family's resolute character. It is, though, somewhat ironic, for their colliery not only had to constantly adapt and innovate but also reflected, one way or another, so much that did change in Britain during the Industrial Revolution.

EPILOGUE

The final period of coal mining at Neston from 1875 to 1927 is outside the scope of this book. However, it may be helpful to summarise events briefly.

While efforts were being made to start a colliery in Parkgate, there were also attempts to establish a combined ore smelting and coal mining business on the former site of Little Neston Colliery. This company, the Anglican Smelting, Reduction and Coal Company Limited, founded in 1858, intended to import gold ore from South America, smelting it with newly mined Neston coal.[1] It also planned to sell the coal to various markets; this was said to be 'by no means the least important part' of the undertaking.[2] Little smelting was undertaken, though, and there is no certain evidence that any coal mining ever occurred. For a number of possible reasons, the company was short-lived and was wound up in 1862.[3]

Local coal mining was, however, revived in the next decade in a move which, for the first time, would see all the remaining coal deposits on the Cheshire side of the Dee Estuary worked by a single company. Charles Mott of Birkenhead had acquired the rights from the Shrewsbury estate to extract minerals from under its land in Little Neston as well as from its portion of the 'waste' (i.e. in the estuary).[4] Mott was a director of the Great Western Railway and, as part of the arrangement, a branch line was to be allowed to be built to the colliery from the Parkgate to Hooton line which had opened in 1866.[5] This facilitated bulk transport of the coal which had become a major problem for the earlier collieries. Mott sold his interest to the newly formed Neston Colliery Company Limited, in which he was a major shareholder, and work on the first shaft started in 1875 amid much celebration.[6] The surveyor for the new works was Thomas Leacroft Cottingham, son of the final owner of Little Neston Colliery.[7] The colliery was established on the site of the former Little Neston Colliery (at the bottom of today's Marshlands Road, on the northern side), making use of the former Anglican company's buildings. Mineral rights were also obtained for extraction of coal under the two-fifths of Little Neston not owned by the Shrewsburys; a lease was soon granted, too, by Sir John Errington, Rowland's son, for the mine working to extend into Ness.[8]

Meanwhile Mott also was in negotiation with Lord Mostyn's advisers regarding the 'Parkgate Coal Field', talk of which had lingered for years. A lease was presumably entered into by the Neston Colliery Company as coal was certainly mined at Great Neston, as well as in Little Neston, in this later period.[9] The works stretched a little over half a mile (800 metres) into the former area, apparently working the seam that had been found by Mostyn's earlier boreholes but there is nothing to suggest that the coal was of any great quantity or quality.[10] A lease was entered into to work in Ness too but there was little if any real opportunity for working there – the seams had been more or less exhausted on Ness Colliery's closure in 1855 and the existing workings soon flooded.[11] There was, though, more scope in Little Neston where Cottinghams' activity had been limited to two seams; more coal was available both above and below.[12]

From the start, coal extraction at the new operation proved difficult and its variously named successors had a fitful existence which was marked by company liquidations, strikes, legal disputes and a period of virtual nationalisation during the First World War.[13] The mine was eventually given up by its owners in 1927, although informal working seems to have continued for another few months.[14]

More information on the later period of mining, including photographs and a detailed listing of the main events over the colliery's life, can be found on the *nestoncollieries.org* website.

*

In total, the life of the Neston Collieries had spanned 168 years, including a twenty-year interruption. Most of the evidence for this era of industrialisation has since been erased from the landscape. However a few clues linger, including the substantial Denhall Quay, the Harp Inn where men celebrated the sabotage of the Cottingham mine, and the subtle signs of former shafts – from both the early and later mining periods – tucked amongst the houses and leafy roads of this pleasant part of Neston.

APPENDIX I

Known Royalty Payments to the Stanley, Cottingham and Shrewsbury Estates, 1776–94

| Twelve months to end of September | Little Neston | | | Ness | Total Known Royalties (£) |
	Under Lands of Earl of Shrewsbury (£)	Under Estuary and Shore, attributed to the Cottingham estate (£)	Under Lands of the Cottingham estate (£)	Under all Stanley estate (£)	
1776	22	294	–	–	–
1777	87	207	60	274	641*
1778	10	164	–	–	–
1779	56	117	–	–	–
1780	89	138	–	–	–
1781	32	202	–	–	–
1782	53	184	–	–	–
1783	7	186	–	–	–
1784	13	129	–	258	400
1785	21	108	–	219	348
1786	39	109	–	352	500
1787	–	102	–	358	460
1788	–	–	–	409	409
1789	–	–	–	329	329
1790	–	–	–	290	290
1791	–	–	–	384	384
1792	–	–	–	470	470
1793	–	–	–	460	460
1794	–	–	–	484	484

Data is available only for the twelve-month accounting years shown; lack of data does not necessarily indicate that no royalties were paid. Royalties were payable at a rate of 10% of sales so, for example, the 1786 'Total' figure represents £5,000 of sales. The 1777 data is slightly different to that in Table 2.1 because of minor accounting adjustments made to the original sources.

*Includes an additional £13 paid to Little Neston landowner Joseph Norman.
Sources: 'Copy of Schedule', part of CALS, D5363; University of Manchester JRL, RYCH 1718 (1–4); NEWA, D/DM/452/1.

Royalties Received by the Stanley Estate, and Imputed/Actual Sales Value, 1800 to 1838

Year to Autumn ...	Royalties Received (£)	Imputed Sales (£)	Year to Autumn ...	Royalties Received (£)	Imputed/ Actual Sales (£)	Sales Volumes (Tons)
1800	146 (3 months)	1,460	1820	305	4,575	–
1801	558	5,580	1821	303	4,545	–
1802	607	6,070	1822	161	2,415	–
1803	748	7,480	1823	152	2,280	–
1804	801	8,010	1824	200	2,867*	7,608*
1805	598	5,980	1825	260	3,924*	9,634*
1806	679	6,790	1826	228	3,439*	7,690*
1807	598	5,980	1827	210	3,150	–
1808	519	5,190	1828	195	2,925	–
1809	616	6,160	1829	228	3,420	9,300*
1810	600	6,000	1830	243	3,645	–
1811	654	6,540	1831	No record	–	–
1812	616	6,160	1832	No record	–	–
1813	423	6,345	1833	No record	–	–
1814	371	5,565	1834	294	4,410	–
1815	358**	5,370	1835	254	3,810	–
1816	364**	5,460	1836	257	3,855	–
1817	311**	4,665	1837	265	3,975	–
1818	358	5,370	1838	283	4,245	–
1819	299	4,485	1839	No record		–

The imputed sales figures assume royalties at one-tenth of sales prior to 1813, and one-fifteenth from that year onwards.[1] Actual sales volumes and values for the few years for which they are known are marked *.

The dates of the accounting periods were irregular; the figures above have been based on those in the four quarters to the autumn account each year which variously fell between late September and early November. Figures marked ** have been adjusted on a pro rata basis because reporting did not match this pattern. Royalty calculations were subject to minor adjustments for 'shipping expenses' and other purposes but, for simplicity, no attempt has been made to allow for these.

In the years when sales volumes are not stated, they cannot be reliably imputed as the figures will have depended on sales prices and sales mix between different grades of coal, neither of which are known in detail and which would have constantly fluctuated, often very significantly.

The figures do not represent *total* sales values at Ness Colliery as, until about 1820, coal was also being raised by it in Little Neston. No detailed data is available but the amounts involved appear to have been relatively small.[2]

Sources: CALS, DDX 378/7, 8, 30, 31, 33; NEIMME/Wat/3/71/4.

APPENDIX II(b)

Known Royalties Received by the Stanley Estate, 1845 to 1855

Year to December	Royalties Received (£)	Year to December	Royalties Received (£)
1845	155	1851	121
1846	156	1852	?77
1847	141	1853	No record
1848	No record	1854	No record
1849	135	1855	No record
1850	No record	–	–

The limited data here is taken from photographs of part of an uncatalogued volume of Stanley Estate Accounts, 1844–56 held at CALS. The volume may contain additional information but it has not been possible to view the original. Imputed figures for sales have not been included as it is likely the royalty rate had changed from the previous figure of one-fifteenth: applying that rate would give a sales figure in, for example, 1851 of just £1,815 which seems unlikely given that around 120 men worked at the colliery then (see page 34).

APPENDIX III

References to Colliers (and a Few Other Known Colliery Workers) in Neston Parish Registers and Other Sources, 1759 to 1779

Year	Baptisms	Marriages	Burials of Colliers or a Family Member (Colliers themselves in brackets)	Total Baptism/ Burial/ Marriage Entries	Other Sources (name not in PR)	Colliers' Names Appearing for First Time (all sources)
1759	–	–	1	1	–	1
1760	2	1	1	4	–	3
1761	7	–	2 (2)	9	–	8
1762	4	–	7 (1)	11	2	7
1763	10	5	–	16	–	13
1764	10	1	–	11	–	9
1765	13	1	3 (1)	17	–	9
1766	13	1	6 (1)	20	1	8
1767	11	1	3 (1)	17	–	5
1768	17	1	3 (1)	21	1	9
1769	22	2	3 (1)	27	2	13
1770	16	–	1	17	3	8
1771	23	3	1 (1)	27	2	12
1772	25	–	1	27	1	8
1773	23	–	–	23	4	3
1774	20	–	2 (2)	22	3	6
1775	23	–		31	2	9
1776	21	1	2 (2)	24	–	9
1777	30	1	6 (6)	37	2	13
1778	15	1	10	26	–	1
1779	24	–	5	29	–	5
Total	329	23	65 (21)	417	22	159

The table shows the numbers of baptisms of children born to colliers, colliers' marriages, and burials of colliers, their wives or children during the period, as well as colliers referred to in the limited other available sources from that period. 159 workers are named in total.

Sources: NPR, Burton PR, CMLBA; CALS, MG 9/27 and 9/28, Quarter Sessions records (QJF series) and Z HI 51–53.

APPENDIX IV

Principal Chester 'Port Books' Consulted at The National Archives (E 190 series)

Year	Coastal	Overseas	Year	Coastal	Overseas
1750	1424/6 (–)	1423/12	1765	1438/2 1438/4	1438/1
1755	1429/2 (–)	1429/4	1766	(1438/6) 1439/4	1438/7
1756	1430/8 1430/5	1429/6	1767	1439/2 1439/7	1439/1
1757	1430/2 1431/9	1431/8	1768	1439/6 (1440/2)	1439/8
1758	(–) (1447/11)	1431/1	1769	1440/3 1440/9	1440/1
1759	1433/4 (1433/6)	1432/10	1770	1440/7 1440/12	1440/8
1760	1433/1 1434/7	1434/8	1771	(1440/11) (–)	1440/10
1761	(1435/4) 1435/6	1435/8	1772	(–) 1441/3	1441/1
1762	1436/9 1436/1	1436/6	1773	(–) 1442/6	1441/2
1763	1437/13 (1437/9)	1436/8	1774	1442/3 (–)	1442/1
1764	1437/11 1437/13	1437/5	1775 onwards	(–)	(–)

Coastal books cover half years (one book for the Lady Day and Midsummer Quarters, the other for the Michaelmas and Christmas Quarters); Overseas books cover full years. Years run from 6 January one year to 5 January the next but, for simplicity, dates here and throughout this book have been expressed as for the main year only e.g. 6 January 1761 to 5 January 1762 is just '1761'. Brackets indicate the book is missing or significantly illegible. No books relating to the port of Chester are available after 1774, although some books are available for the member ports of Beaumaris, Conwy and Caernarfon.

APPENDIX V

Known Seasale Shipments and Volumes of Coal from the Port of Chester, in Chaldrons, 1750–1828 (Selected Years)

	Coastwise		Overseas		Full-Year Total	
	Number of Shipments Including Coal/Total Shipments with Any Goods; Coal Shipments as Percentage of All Shipments	*Chaldrons of Coal*	*Number of Shipments Including Coal/Total Shipments with Any Goods; Coal Shipments as Percentage of All Shipments*	*Chaldrons of Coal*	*Number of Shipments Including Coal/Total Shipments with Any Goods; Coal Shipments as Percentage of All Shipments*	*Chaldrons of Coal*
1750	22/59 (Jan–Jun) 37%	286 (Jan–Jun)	64/80 80%	2,267	>86/>139 62%?	>2,553
1755	96/153 (Jan–Jun) 63%	1,006 (Jan–Jun)	53/102 52%	1,223	>149/>255 58%?	>2,229
1756	240/383 63%	2,053	42/99 42%	1,112	282/482 59%	3,165
1757	187/356 53%	1,549	44/107 41%	1,294	231/463 50%	2,843
1758	>94/165 (Jul–Dec) >57%	>572 (Jul–Dec)	19/47 40%	455	>113/>212 53%?	>1,027
1759	147/300 49%	>1,173	18/79 23%	404	165/379 43%	>1,579
1760	153/297 52%	1,272	60/103 60%	2,164	213/400 53%	3,436
1761	189/331 57%	>1350	137/187 73%	4,372	326/518 63%	>5,722
1762	241/419 58%	2,257	204/253 81%	7,435	445/672 66%	9,692
1763	>106/>239 44%?	>905	85/136 63%	2,454	>191/>375 51%?	>3,359
1764	159/297 54%	1,428	73/133 55%	2,149	232/430 54%	3,577
1765	157/332 47%	1,397	59/114 52%	2,001	216/446 48%	3,398
1766	>191/324 >59%	>2,145	72/138 52%	2,647	>263/462 >57%	>4,792
1767	180/320 56%	2,237	78/121 64%	3,011	258/441 59%	5,248

1768	>248/402 62%	>3,002	49/97 51%	1,681	>297/499 >60%	>4,683
1769	205/322 64%	2,952	127/189 67%	4,992	332/511 65%	7,944
1770	208/348 60%	2,586 '2,295'(HG*)	211/266 79%	8,894 '8,894' (HG)	419/614 68%	11,480 '11,189' (HG)
1771	>103/197 52%	>1,182	158/197 80%	6,237 '6,000+ch' (P1)	>261/394 >66%	>7,419
1772	121/197 (Jul–Dec) 61%	1,459 (Jul–Dec)	77/123 63%	2,976	>198/>320 62%?	>4,435
1773	141/205 (Jul–Dec) 69%	1,799 (Jul–Dec)	79/118 67%	2,922	>220/>323 68%?	>4,721
1774	149/255 (Jan–Jun) 58%	2,199 (Jan–Jun)	133/171 78%	5,429	>282/>426 66%?	->7,628
1776	–	–	–	'2,877ch' (P1)	–	
1786	–	–	–	'2,616ch' (P2)	–	
1790	–	–	–	1,768 (10Nch and 1,749ch)	–	1,768 + coastwise
1791	–	–	–	4,411	–	4,411 + coastwise
1792	–	–	–	5,323 (45Nch and 5,238ch)	–	5,323 + coastwise
1793	–	–	–	6,529	–	6,529 + coastwise
1794	–	–	–	4,479	–	4,479 + coastwise
1795	–	–	–	4,729	–	4,729 + coastwise
1796	–	–	–	4,915 '272' (P2)	–	4,915 + coastwise
1797	–	–	–	5,542	–	5,542 + coastwise
1798	–	–	–	6,243	–	6,243 + coastwise
1799	–	–	–	7,204	–	7,204 + coastwise

1806	–	–	–	'16,519ch' (P2)	–	
1815	–	–	226 to Ireland (40 from Parkgate)	–	>226	–
1816	–	2,574 (679t and 2,089ch)	–	19,937 (2,007t and 18,503ch)	–	22,511
1817	–	5,797 (2,136t and 4,271ch)	–	17,603 (6,267t and 13,127ch)	–	23,400
1818	–	14,020 (5,762t and 9,904ch)	–	12,861 (14,299t and 2,647ch)	–	26,881
1819	–	26,312 (36,838t)	–	9,390 (10,312t and 2,024ch)	–	35,674
1820	–	27,800 (38,920t)	–	5,656 (5,308t and 1,865ch)	–	33,456
1821	–	29,232 (40,925t)	–	3,649 (3,880t and 878ch)	–	32,881
1822	–	30,920 (43,288t)	99 to Ireland	7,117 (5,769t and 2,996ch)	>99	38,037
1823	–	35, 033 (49,046t)	–	3,707 (4,087t and 788ch)	–	38,740
1824	–	31,452 (44,033t)	–	3,706 (3,675t and 1,081ch)	–	35,158
1825	–	22,999 (32,198t)	–	5,001 (5,360t and 1,172ch)	–	28,000
1826	–	24,201 (33,882t)	–	4,059 (5,520t and 116ch)	–	28,460
1827	–	21,699 (30,378t)	–	6,847 (9,586t)	–	28,546
1828	–	26,146 (36,604t)	–	6,371 (8,919t)	–	32,517

Key:
'–' indicates that no data is available.
'>' indicates the data is incomplete as the source data is missing or significantly illegible.
'?' indicates that the figures are necessarily approximate.
'HG' – Liv. RO, Holt Gregson Papers, xix, 49.
'P1' – Pennant (1778) pp. 197–8 (no original source given).
'P2' – Pennant (1810), p. 280 (no original source given).
Data has been given for selected years before Ness Colliery's opening and for all years after opening where data is available. All available volume data has been converted into chaldrons, assuming 28 cwt/1.4 tons (t) to the Winchester chaldron (ch) and 53 cwt/2 tons 13 cwt to the Newcastle chaldron (Nch); where figures have been so computed, numbers from the original source are given in brackets. For simplicity, no attempt has been made to convert figures to tonnes. 'Years' in parliamentary and customs records ran from 6 January in one year to 5 January in the next.

Sources:
1759–74: TNA, E 190 series ('port books') – see Appendix IV. Additional sources: 'P1' – Pennant (1778) pp. 197–8 (no original source given); 'HG' – Liv. RO, Holt Gregson Papers, xix, 49.
1786: Pennant (1810), p. 280 (no original source given).
1790–9: Parl. Papers, *Report from the Committee Appointed to Consider of the Coal Trade [sic] of the United Kingdom*, Appendix 42, HOCP Vol. 132 (1800); except 'P2' which is Pennant (1810), p. 280 (the figure for 1796, for which he gives no source, is presumably an error).
1806: as for 1786.
1815: Cumbria Archive Service, DLONS/W7/1/131 and Flinn, p. 224.
1816–7: Parl. Papers, *An Account of all Coals Shipped from the Several Ports of Great Britain* (1818).
1818: Parl. Papers, *An Account of All Coals Carried Coastways as Well as Those Exported to Foreign Parts*, Paper 117 (1819).
1819–28: Parl. Papers, *Report from the Select Committee of the House of Lords Appointed to Take into Consideration the State of the Coal Trade*, Paper 9 (1830), pp. 106–27.
1822, vessel numbers: Parl. Papers, *Accounts Relating to Bonds Taken on Vessels Carrying Coals to Ireland* (1823).

APPENDIX VI

Known Seasale Volumes of Coal from the Port of Chester, 1829–55, in Tons

	Coastwise (tons)	Overseas (excl. Ireland) (tons)
1829	Not available	448
1830	Not available	252
1831	Not available	437
1832*	Not available	1,115
1833	69,346	1,291
1834	75,163	1,652
1835	79,207	1,851
1836	91,239	2,273
1837	105,656	3,175
1838	93,268	3,782
1839	88,111	3,921
1840	86,227	2,986
1841	89,477	4,310
1842	76,781	5,399
1843	68,829	4,653
1844**	70,312	2,528
1845	94,183	580
1846	96,198	1,153
1847	89,326	280
1848	100,340	Nil
1849	93,149	112
1850	95,970	2,230
1851	101,044	949
1852	85,772	1,071
1853	81,312	1,009
1854	91,469	360
1855	85,834	230

No data appears to be routinely available for shipments to Ireland. Again, for simplicity, no attempt has been made to convert figures to tonnes.

*It was reported that at Flint in 1832 570 vessels carried away 31,982 tons coastwise and 74 vessels took 4,719 tons to Ireland (Parl. Papers, *Municipal Corporations*, p. 2,684). ** Vessels were said to be taking away '50 or 60,000 tons' of coal per annum from the dock at Mostyn (Dunn, 1844, p. 135).

Sources:

1829: *An Account of the Quantity of Coals Exported from the United Kingdom in each Year, from the 5th day of January 1828 to the 5th day of January 1842*, Accounts & Papers, Paper 163 (1842)

1830–2 (overseas): *Return of the Quantities of Large and Small Coals Exported during the Year ending 5th January last*, Accounts & Papers, Paper 586 (1833)

1833–4: *Accounts and Quantity of Coals, Cinders and Culm shipped Coastways and Exported from the UK*, Paper 240 (1835)

1835: Ibid., Paper 228 (1836)

1836–7: Ibid., Paper 344 (1838)

1838–9: Ibid., Paper 283 (1840)

1840: Ibid., Paper 259 (1841)

1841–2: Ibid., Paper 322 (1843)

1843–4: Ibid., Paper 339 (1845)

1845–6: Ibid., Paper 477 (1847)

1847–8: Ibid., Paper 328 (1849)

1849: Ibid., Paper 512 (1850)

1850–1: Ibid., Paper 340 (1852)

1852–3: Ibid., Paper 472 (1854)

1854–5: Ibid., Paper 194 (1856)

GLOSSARY

Agent – manager.

Board/bord – an alternative to 'stall': see 'Pillar and stall'.

Brow – the colliery surface. A browman worked at the top of the shaft.

Burthen – the carrying capacity of a ship, usually expressed in tons.

Bushel* – a measure subdividing chaldrons. There were 36 bushels to the chaldron in the sea trade.

Cannel – a high-value hydrogen-rich form of coal.

Chaldron* – a measure of capacity for coal carried by ships. The chaldron of Winchester Measure, most widely used in the trade from Chester, was equivalent to about 28 hundredweight or 1.4 tons. A Newcastle chaldron was substantially larger, at 53 hundredweight.

Coasting/coastwise trade – shipping trade undertaken around the British coast (as opposed to 'overseas').

Collier – a) a worker in a coal mine, usually underground (see also 'miner'); b) a vessel (boat) which carried coals.

Corf (*plural:* **corves**) – wicker baskets used to convey coal underground and up to the surface.

Crowning – a collapse of the ground above mine workings.

Culm – small pieces of coal ('slack') and/or coal-dust.

Cutter – a man cutting the coal from the coal face (also 'hewer').

Dip – a downward slope in the lie of rock. The coal seams at Ness typically dipped at a gradient of one-in-six to the north-west.

Drift – an underground passage 'driven' or excavated usually horizontally, for working, exploration, ventilation, or draining.

Driver – someone employed to drive the ponies underground, usually a boy.

Flat – a type of sailing barge

Gin – generally, a mechanical winding machine, often horse-powered as opposed to steam-driven. The word is short for 'engine'.

Goaf – an area underground from which coal has been removed, and allowed to be filled by roof falls or packed-in waste material.

Hanger-on – person employed at the bottom of a shaft to attach baskets to the winding gear for hauling to the surface.

Hewer – a man cutting the coal from the coal face (also 'cutter').

Hundredweight (cwt)* – a measure of weight usually comprising, at the time under review, 120 lbs (pounds), i.e. 54.4 kg (today it is 112 lbs/50.8 kg).

Labourer – person employed to sort or move coal or perform other manual jobs. Often, but not always, the term was applied to surface workers.

Landsale – sales to customers by cart, donkey, etc.

Level – a long tunnel through the rock, used to access the coal (also 'road').

Longwall – a mining method which systematically removed all, or almost all, the coal from an area (as opposed to 'pillar and stall').

Manor – a unit of land owned by a lord consisting of land used by him and also his land tenanted by others. Originally, it was often coterminous with a township.

Miner – generally, but not always, used in eighteenth-century Flintshire and west Cheshire to describe someone digging for ore such as lead rather than coal (the latter were generally 'colliers'); became more commonly applied to coal workers in the nineteenth century. 'Collier' and 'miner' are used interchangeably in this book unless the context indicates otherwise.

Ostler – person employed to look after the horses.

Overseas trade – shipping trade undertaken from Britain across any sea, including to Ireland and the Isle of Man (as opposed to 'coasting trade').

Pillar and stall – a mining method which removed coal only from lengthwise and crosswise tunnels (stalls) leaving the coal in-between (pillars) in place (as opposed to 'longwall').

Pit – a shaft giving access to the coal seams; also, the working undertaken via a particular shaft. Sometimes used to describe a coal mine generally.

Putting – hauling coal underground, by pulling or pushing sledges or wheeled waggons.

Road – a long tunnel through the rock, used to access the coal (also 'level').

Royalty – a payment to a landowner, usually based on the value of coal sold which had been gained from under his property.

Sawney – winding gear for drawing coal from the pit; the sawney engine was the powered version.

Seasale – sales to customers by boat or ship.

Slack – small pieces of coal which were cheaper and often employed for industrial use.

Stall – see 'Pillar and stall'.

Staple – an underground shaft, linking two parts of the mine at different depths.

Strata – layers of rock e.g. coal seams.

Tenter – someone who looks after ('tends') something, usually an engine or door.

Ton* – a measure of weight, commonly comprising twenty hundredweight (cwt) but, when measuring coal, often more – up to 36 cwt. This point, and the fact that a hundredweight usually comprised 120 lbs, means that references to 'tons' in original sources need to be interpreted with care.

Township – a unit of land which formed part of a parish. Originally, the township boundary often coincided with the boundary of a manor.

Viewer – a person skilled as a colliery surveyor and engineer employed to advise on effective and efficient working of a mine.

* See Notes, page xx, for further information on the use of measures.

ENDNOTES

Prefaces
Jesse Paul, 'What is Microhistory?', *Social Evolution and History*, 17, 2 (September 2018), p. 65.

Notes
[1] NEIMME, NRO 3410/Wat/3/71/8, 12, 15, 17.
[2] John Langton, *Geographical Change and Industrial Revolution* (Cambridge: Cambridge University Press, 1979), pp. 244–7.

Chapter 1 – The Neston Collieries: A Sign of Their Times
[1] Edmond Halley, *A Synopsis of the Astronomy of Comets* (London: printed for John Senex, translated, 1705), p. 18 which said the comet would appear 'about the end of the year 1758, or beginning of 1759'. In the event, it was first seen, in Germany, on Christmas night, 1758.
[2] Sara Schechner, *Comets, Popular Culture, and the Birth of Modern Cosmology* (Princeton: Princeton University Press, 1997), p. 195. John Wesley, *The Works of John Wesley*, 17 vols (London: printed by Thomas Cordeaux, 1812), xi, p. 406. The quotation is from 1755.
[3] *Cheshire Sheaf*, 'Four Prescot Letters', 3rd series, 31 (1936), p. 62.
[4] See, for example, Charles More, *Understanding the Industrial Revolution* (Abingdon: Routledge, 2000), Chapter 1 and Joel Mokyr, *The Enlightened Economy, Britain and the Industrial Revolution 1700–1850* (London: Penguin, 2009), Chapter 5.
[5] For example, More (see note above) focuses on 1750–1850, as does *A History of Technology* (7 vols), iv, *The Industrial Revolution, c.1750 to c.1850* ed. by C. Singer, E. Holmyard, A. Hall and T. Williams (Oxford: Clarendon Press, 1958), p. 447. Thomas Ashton, *The Industrial Revolution, 1760–1830* (Oxford: Oxford University Press, 1997), in what has often been described as a 'classic' text, took a seventy-year view.
[6] E. A. Wrigley, R. S. Davies, J. E. Oeppen and R. S. Schofield, *English Population History from Family Reconstitution, 1580–1837* (Cambridge: Cambridge University Press, 1997), p. 614.
[7] The first census in 1801 shows that the population of Great Neston township was 1,486, with a further 347 in Ness and 254 in Little Neston. The second largest Wirral settlement was Tranmere with 353 (Eric Rideout, *The Growth of Wirral* (Liverpool: E. A. Bryant, 1927) p. 99).
[8] TNA, SP 36/151, f.25.
[9] See, for example, K. P. Wilson ed., *Chester Customs Accounts, 1301–1566* (Liverpool: Record Society of Lancashire and Cheshire, 1969), passim.
[10] Jane Laughton, 'The Port of Chester in the Later Middle Ages' in *'Where Deva Spreads her Wizard Stream', Trade and the Port of Chester*, ed. by Peter Carrington (Chester: Chester City Council, c.1996), pp. 66–71.
[11] Wilson, passim; Geoffrey Place, *The Rise and Fall of Parkgate* (Manchester: The Chetham Society, 1994), p. 16.
[12] Place (1994), pp. 15 and 246–7.
[13] A. Annakin-Smith, 'Neston and Parkgate: their links to the slave trade in the mid to late eighteenth century', *THSLC*, 160 (2011), pp. 29–35 and 46–7.

Chapter 1 – The Neston Collieries: A Sign of Their Times (continued)

[14] Shaun Regan, *Reading 1759: Literary Culture in Mid-Eighteenth-Century Britain and France* (Lanham, MD: Rowman and Littlefield, 2013), p. 2.

[15] For example, Basil Williams, *The Life of William Pitt, Earl of Chatham*, 2 vols (London: Longmans, Green and Co., 1914), ii, p. 1.

[16] Frank McLynn, *1759, the Year Britain Became Master of the World* (London: Jonathan Cape, 2004).

[17] Donald Woodward, 'The Port of Chester in Context 1500–1800' in *Where Deva Spreads her Wizard Stream: Trade and the Port of Chester* ed. by Peter Carrington (Chester: Chester City Council, c.1996), pp. 62–3; A. T. Thacker, 'Economic Infrastructure and Institutions: River Navigation' in *A History of the County of Chester* ed. by C. P. Lewis and A. T. Thacker, 5 vols, (London: Institute of Historical Research and others, 1987–2005), v(2) (2005), pp. 86–7.

[18] The painting is Arthur Suker's 'Neston Colliery and the River Dee' (1876) held at the Williamson Art Gallery, Birkenhead. It is reproduced, with kind permission, on the website accompanying this book.

[19] See page 143.

[20] Alan Wood, 'The Coalfields of North Wales' in *The Coalfields of Great Britain* ed. by Arthur Trueman (London: Edward Arnold, 1954), p. 245.

[21] BGS (2006), one-inch series, Sheet 96, 'Liverpool', Bedrock.

[22] Ibid. The maximum distance shown worked inland on Coal Authority plans seen by this author is 460 yards (420 metres) in the Seven-Foot seam (Coal Authority 6826). Based on a number of colliery plans, the line of the Neston Fault appears to differ from that depicted on the geological maps referenced in notes 23 and 42, especially at the northern end.

[23] BGS, Sheet 96. The sandstone is assumed to overlie Coal Measures but at great and inaccessible depth (various writers including Leonard Wills, *Concealed Coalfields* (London: Blackie, 1956), pp. 177–9).

[24] C. B. Wedd and W. King, *The Geology of the Country Around Flint, Hawarden and Caergwrle* (London: HMSO, 1924), p. 138; J. R. Davies, D. Wilson, I. T. Williamson, *Geology of the Country around Flint: Memoir for 1:50 000 Geological Sheet 108* (Keyworth: British Geological Survey, 2004), p. 135. Also known as the Denhall Fault in some sources.

[25] Wood, *Coalfields of Great Britain*, p. 250; and NEIMME/Wat/3/71/2. The stated degree of dip varies. For example, CALS, D5363, 'Little Neston Coal mines' says one-in-seven to the north and one-in-three to the west. Thomas Leacroft Cottingham in BPP [1871], *Report of the Commissioners Appointed to Inquire into the Several Matters Relating to Coal in the United Kingdom* (reprinted in Shannon, Ireland: Irish University Press, 1969), p. 374 said one-in-seven. In one area worked by Ness Colliery, the coal was said to be more 'flat', the dip being no more than one in ten (NEIMME/Wat/3/71/9).

[26] BPP [1871], p. 374.

[27] Ibid. J. H. Hanshall, *The History of the County Palatine of Chester* (Chester, c.1823), p. 70 and D. and S. Lysons, *Magna Britannia: County Palatine of Chester* (London: T. Cadell and W. Davies, 1810), ii, p. 412 claimed the distance was 1¾ miles (2.8 km) but there is no evidence for this. See also pages 32, 59 and 71.

[28] If the workings at Flint had extended the same distance under the estuary as Ness Colliery's workings did – which is unlikely – there would still have been a gap of about ¾ mile between the two set of workings. It was said that in 1842–3 the workings at the large colliery at Mostyn, where the estuary is wider than at Ness, extended only 1,000 yards (914 metres) under the Dee (Matthias Dunn, *A Treatise on the Winning and Working of Collieries* (Newcastle Upon Tyne: Matthias Dunn, 1852), p. 345). A contemporary OS map (one-inch, LXXIX (1840)), suggests those workings reached at least 1,320 yards (1,207 metres) – still a long way short of any works at Neston at any time.

[29] BGS Sheet 77 (1888); OS 25" (3rd edn, 1912), Sheet XXX.2.

[30] C. B. Wedd, B. Smith, W. Simmons and D. Wray, *The Geology of Liverpool with Wirral and Part of the Flintshire Coalfield* (London: HMSO, 1923), p. 67, attributes the missing seam to a localised 'wash-out'.

[31] NEIMME/Wat/3/71/14.

[32] Coal Authority, 14923/3. It was said to be 'eight feet thick'. This was probably the poor quality Four-Foot seam which had additional bands of cannel and bass associated with it and started at 31 yards/28 metres below the surface in Pit No. 2 (Coal Authority, 6826/1) – see note 61.

[33] NEIMME/ZA/12/278. Wedd et al., p. 68 cites the information for the three borings which was supplied by the later Wirral Colliery but at least one of the holes (the '30th') was dug by Ness Colliery (NEIMME/ZA/12/237).

[34] NEIMME/Wat/3/71/4. This issue is discussed more fully in Chapter 4.

[35] TNA, J 90/82, 30 August 1797; T&WA, DX 198/1, pp. 410 and 501; NEIMME/Wat/3/71/1–22.

[36] Wedd et al., p. 66. W. Fairley ('Practical Notes on the Geology of Wirral', *Trans. Fed. Inst. Of Mining Engineers*, 4 (1892–3), p. 322) claims '[The Coal-measures] are exposed at the surface at Ness' but this author has seen no evidence for this.

[37] NEIMME/ZA/12/236 and NEIMME/Wat/3/71/2.

[38] There is a possibility they were, however, used in adjacent Burton – see page 16.

[39] NEIMME/Wat/3/71/2; NEIMME/ZA/12/274–277.

[40] NEWA, D/M/5662, letter dated 6 April 1874.

[41] William Smith's 'A Delineation of the Strata of England and Wales and Part of Scotland': https://www.nhm.ac.uk/content/dam/nhmwww/discover/first-geological-map-of-britain/william-smith-1815-geological-map.pdf

[42] The most northerly workings on land shown on colliery plans stopped 80 yards (73 metres) south of the Old Quay. From their position it seems highly likely, though, that the Coal Measures continued under the quay before curving into the estuary as shown on the OS Geological Survey (1974), one-inch, Sheet 96, 'Liverpool', Solid.

[43] 'Copy of Answer of Deponents Massey and others', part of CALS, D5363.

[44] NEWA, D/M/5662, 'Park Gate Coal'.

[45] CALS, LUNe/6393 and 3384/53, 56 and 57.

[46] Wedd and King, p. 67; S. Lewis, *A Topographical Dictionary of Wales,* 2 vols (London: S. Lewis and Co., 1845), ii, p. 432.

[47] Wedd et al., p. 43.

Chapter 1 – The Neston Collieries: A Sign of Their Times (continued)

[48] Roy Church, *The History of the British Coal Industry,* Vol. 3, *1830–1913* (Oxford: Clarendon Press, 1983), p. 484.

[49] Wedd et al., pp. 43–4 and 170. Neston – see Table 1.1 and note 61.

[50] Wedd and King, p. 67.

[51] Thomas Pennant, *The History of the Parishes of Whiteford, and Holywell* (London: B. and J. White: 1796), pp. 134–5.

[52] Amongst many possible sources: BGS (1888), Vertical Sections, Sheet 77; Coal Authority, 8907; NEIMME/Wat/3/71/15 and 17.

[53] Coal Authority 14932/2 includes a geological section showing the Six-Foot in Little Neston, accessed from Pit No. 23. No map or plan depicts the Six-Foot in Ness, nor is there any documentary evidence for it having been worked there. NEIMME/Wat/3/71/17 refers to it in a table of strata but this probably relates to its location in Little Neston where it was being worked at the time. T&WA, DX 198/1, pp. 410 and 501 show that Ness Colliery was struggling to find the Six-Foot in Ness in 1819.

[54] See pages 42 and 55.

[55] NEIMME/Wat/3/71/15 and 17.

[56] Quality, use and depth: Wedd and King, p. 69 and NEIMME/Wat/3/71/2. Location: see Figure 4.1. Despite the stated quality rating, the Two-Foot coal was sometimes selling for more than the Five-Foot, indicating that quality varied.

[57] NRO 725 B5, p. 479, letter to C. Lloyd from William Armstrong, 14 April 1863.

[58] NEIMME/Wat/3/71/12.

[59] NEIMME/Wat/3/71/8.

[60] *Cheshire Sheaf*, 'The Old Denhall Collieries, Neston', 3rd series, 3 (1901), p. 63.

[61] CALS, D5363, 'Little Neston Coal mines'. Other known seams include the Four-Foot, about 31 yards/28 metres from the surface in Little Neston, but of 'inferior' quality and apparently never mined (Wedd et al., p. 69; shown on Coal Authority 6826/1 and BGS, Sheet 77 (1888) both of which also show several thin seams at various depths, presumably never worked); the King Seam, a thick seam worked by the later Neston Colliery but which contained many impurities (Wedd et al., pp. 69 and 170; Coal Authority 8069/1); Fairley, p. 323, suggests there were seams below the lowest worked seam, the Two-Foot; Edward Lloyd Mostyn claimed there was an upper two-foot seam at Parkgate (NEWA, D/M/5662). Thomas Leacroft Cottingham (son of the final mine-owner) mentioned several seams above and below those worked at the Neston collieries (BPP [1871], p. 374).

[62] BGS, Sheet 77 (1888).

[63] *Chester Courant*, 1 September 1812.

[64] Coal Authority, 14923/5; BGS, Sheet 77 (1888); C. E. de Rance in *The Geology of the Neighbourhoods of Flint, Mold and Ruthin* (London: HMSO, 1890), p. 99.

[65] M. W. Flinn, *The History of the British Coal Industry,* Vol. 2, *1700–1830* (Oxford: Clarendon Press, 1984), p. 9; CAS, Unerigg Colliery Book DBEN/BOX95/3540.

[66] *Chester Chronicle,* 11 December 1795; NEIMME/Wat/3/65/3 (1806).

Endnotes

⁶⁷ Peter Stanley, *The House of Stanley from the 12th Century* (Bishop Auckland: Pentland Press, 1998) gives a comprehensive account of the different branches of the family, including those at Hooton. Other sources: William Williams Mortimer, *The History of the Hundred of Wirral* (London: Whittaker and Co., 1847), pp. 245-7 and George Ormerod, *History of the County Palatine and City of Chester*, 3 vols (London: George Routledge and Sons, 2nd edn, 1882), ii, pp. 541–2 and 560. Other information – see Chapters 2 and 8.

⁶⁸ 'Sir' is an automatic addition on succeeding to a baronetcy.

⁶⁹ CALS, DDX 378/1–12, 30–33 and 41 contain numerous entries for income and expenses relating to the places mentioned in this paragraph.

⁷⁰ Langton (1979), p. 249. Bickerstaffe Colliery was offered for sale or lease in 1855, the same year that Ness Colliery was sold; enquiries were to be directed to William Stewart, the Stanleys' estate manager (*Chester Chronicle*, 17 March 1855).

⁷¹ NLW, Hawarden Deeds, 1520. See also page 33.

⁷² CALS, M/F 397, p. 486.

⁷³ Sources include *Cheshire Sheaf*, 'The Cottinghams, of Little Neston', 3rd series, 29 (1934), p. 2; *Cheshire Sheaf*, 'Some Deeds Relating to Little Neston', 3rd series, 27 (1930), p. 72; T. Hare, *Reports of Cases Adjudged in the High Court of Chancery*, (London: A. Maxwell and Son, 1845), iii, p. 627; Ormerod, ii, p. 540; NPR. Other information – see Chapters 2 and 3.

⁷⁴ 'Copy of Answer of Deponents Massey and others', part of CALS, D5363. This long document contains some factual errors so the 'Charles' reference may also be questionable.

⁷⁵ Cited as 'Collingham' in NPR but corrected to Cottingham in the Bishop's transcript.

⁷⁶ Will of Charles Cottingham, 1 October 1766 (TNA, J 90/18). See also TNA, J 90/81, 7 February 1767.

⁷⁷ Sourced from Charles Mosley, ed., 2003. *Burke's Peerage, Baronetage and Knightage*, 107th edn (Wilmington, DE: Burke's Peerage and Gentry LLC), p. 3603. Other information – see Chapters 2 and 3.

Chapter 2 – Ness Colliery: A Near-Century of Business
1 NEIMME/ZA/12/235–6.
2 Flinn, p. 71.
3 TNA, J 90/81, 13 February 1823.
4 Bangor Archives, Baron Hill MSS 6891, 'Survey of Nesse'.
5 *OED*, 'colliery'.
6 Rob Philpott, 'The Romano-British Period Resource Assessment' in *The Archaeology of North West England*, ed. by Mark Brennand, 8 (2006), 18, p. 85.
7 'Early Coal Working in the Neston Area: A Review of the Evidence' at *nestoncollieries.org*
8 NEIMME/ZA/12/235.
9 P. H. W. Booth, ed., *Burton in Wirral, A History* (Burton: Burton and South Wirral Local History Society, 1984), pp. 10 and 28.
10 For example, in 1851 the parish church paid 'Denhall Colliery' for coal (CALS, P149/9/3). OS, 25-inch, XXX.2 (1871) describes the works as 'Denhall Colliery (disused)'.
11 NEIMME/ZA/12/235 and NEIMME/Wat/3/71/1; NEIMME/Wat/35/14 mentions an undated 'Pit sunk' near 'Dinna House' (later 'Dennah Hall' and variants).

Chapter 2 – Ness Colliery: A Near-Century of Business (continued)

[12] BGS, Sheet 96; Royal Commission for Historic Monuments, *St. Andrew's Hospital, Denhall* (York: RCHM, 1998). The RCHM (p. 12) was uncertain about the origin of three hollows found close to the shore but suggested they were 'best interpreted as holes dug on a speculative basis to search for stone to rob for reuse elsewhere'. However, they do have some characteristics of bell-pits.

[13] Hatcher, pp. 188–9, gives examples suggesting they averaged about twenty feet deep; the NCM says 'up to 10 metres' (National Coal Mining Museum, 'Early Mining' (n.d.)) <https://www.ncm.org.uk/downloads/24/Early_Mining.pdf> [accessed 27 September 2018]). The depth of the seam at Burton is unknown but the possible bell-pits are downhill from where the borehole found the shallowest coal in Ness.

[14] Burton PR, 2 January 1619.

[15] J. M. Dodgson, *The Place-Names of Cheshire*, Pt. 4, (Cambridge: English Place-Names Society, 1972), p. 204.

[16] CALS, DHL 12/1 and P 149/6/1 – both pew allotments.

[17] See page 22.

[18] *Cheshire Sheaf*, (1936), p. 62. The quoted letter is dated 25 June 1760.

[19] Maurice Ridgway, *Chester Silver* (Chichester: Phillimore, 1985), p. 15. There are numerous records of Richardson's interests in North East Wales Archives and the National Library of Wales.

[20] See page 190; R. Willett, *A Memoir of Hawarden Parish* (Chester: J. Fletcher, 1822 – facsimile reprint, 1990, Library and Information Service, Cynor Sir Clwyd County Council, Clwyd), p. 107.

[21] Ridgway, p. 12.

[22] John Hatcher, *The History of the British Coal Industry*, Vol. 1, *Before 1700* (Oxford: Clarendon Press, 1993), p. 131.

[23] CALS, Z AB/4/182v.

[24] See page 166.

[25] NPR.

[26] See pages 159 and 162.

[27] CALS, QJF 191/2, 26 March.

[28] TNA, E 190 1434/1.

[29] Clarke senior's biographical information is taken from 'George Clarke' in *Cheshire Sheaf*, 1st series, 2 (1883), 101; R. H. Linaker, 'A Short Account of the Life of George Clarke, Lieutenant-Governor of New York, 1736–1745', *JCAS*, 23 (1920), pp. 55–63; and *Chester Courant*, 22 January 1760.

[30] 'George Clarke' appears in several contexts including as a named contact in a 1761 newspaper advertisement for Ness Colliery's coal (Figure 11.1) which appears to indicate he was living in Neston (*Dublin Journal*, 10 March 1761); as a bondsman for coastal shipments of coal in 1762, and importer of soap waste (see pages 176 and 189); and in CALS, QJF 191/2 as cited above.

[31] TNA, PROB 11/1037/126: will of George Clarke [junior] of Hyde, proved 6 December 1777.

[32] Ridgway, p. 12. CALS, Z TAY/2, 27 July 1761.

[33] *Cheshire Sheaf*, 'Eastgate in 1750', 3rd series, 56 (1963), p. 90.

[34] Ridgway, pp. 12, 139. The Goldsmiths' Company was officially known as 'The Worshipful Company of Goldsmiths and Watchmakers'.

[35] Joint advertisements (*Adams's Weekly Courant*, 11 October 1763 and 5, 12 and 19 December 1769) between the 'Mostyn and Bychton Coal-Works' and Ness Colliery suggest that there was a shared interest – most likely proprietorship by Richardson. He may have acquired his interest in Mostyn Colliery when it was offered for lease in 1759 (*Adams's Weekly Courant*, 12, 19, 26 June).

[36] CALS, D 4962/1, Account Book of Sir Rowland Stanley Bt.

[37] CALS, P 59/7/1, Conveyance, 3 May 1785; Letters of Administration of Thomas Whittle, 1800. He was High Constable and Bailiff for Wirral in 1768 (CALS, EJB/3/13).

[38] CALS, Will of John Oxton, 1787.

[39] He was, to give just two examples, charged with overseeing the introduction of the new 'fire engines' (in this instance, machines for fighting fires, not atmospheric engines) at Chester (CALS, Z TAB/ 7, 12 October 1759); and he was merchant for the sale of engine/machine parts – cylinders and a crank sent to Caernarfon in 1761 (TNA, E 190 1435/6, 26 September 1761). His newspaper obituary said he was a 'warm and steady promoter of arts and sciences'. See pages 148–9 re canals.

[40] TNA, J 90/82, 15 March 1822.

[41] See note 35 above, Figure 11.1, and page 203. He also sought to mediate an agreement between the beneficiaries of Charles Cottingham (d. 1766) – Thomas Cottingham and two nieces – over the colliery interest left in his will (TNA, J 90/81, 7 February 1767).

[42] See page 13.

[43] CALS, DBC 261/38, 'Cottingham v Stanley Bt.'. A document produced for the 1822 court case mentions 'The lease produced by Mr. Jones 21st May 1759' and the context implies this was the lease granted to the colliery at Ness for the mining rights on Cottingham's land. 'Mr. Jones', presumably, was the lawyer who drew up the document. '1759' is also confirmed in TNA, J 90/82, n.d.

[44] University of Manchester JRL, RYCH 1718 (1–5).

[45] Ibid.; R. Rees Rawson, 'Coal-Mining Industry of the Hawarden District', *Archaeologia Cambrensis*, 96 (1941), p. 117 says between 7% and 12% was typical in that area.

[46] The *Chester Chronicle,* 26 April 1822, states start dates by the Cottinghams of 1759, 1780 (thus apparently renewing the previous lease early) and 1814. CALS, DBC 261/38, 'Cottingham and Stanley', suggests the 1780 lease expired in 1811, which would have left a three-year gap before the next.

[47] *Adams's Weekly Courant*, 26 February 1760 and 20 January 1761 respectively.

[48] See page 148.

[49] *Dublin Journal*, 10 March 1761.

[50] CALS, PM 11/7, 'A Plan of so Much of the Lands and Premises Belonging to the River Dee Company … as lye between … Chester, Flint and Parkgate'.

[51] Peter Bell, *An Actual Survey of the Great Post Road from London to Parkgate* (London: William Faden, 1779).

[52] See Chapters 10 and 11.

[53] Pits 21 and 22 were sunk in 1770–1 (CALS, D5363, 'Copy of Answer').

Chapter 2 – Ness Colliery: A Near-Century of Business (continued)

[54] *Adams's Weekly Courant*, 5 September 1769.

[55] John Stanley Massey, Thomas Clifton, John Oxton and Thomas Whittle and Elliner Farrington [*sic*] are named in a 1775 lease (CALS, m/f 397; DSH 1453/95).

[56] CALS, m/f 397; DSH 1453/95. Ellinor (as she signed herself, although her Christian name appears in records in various other forms) was administrator for her brother's highly complex estate after he died intestate. After his death, she cared for his younger children by his first marriage (Ridgway, pp. 16, 216) and may have been granted the interest in the colliery in return. She died in 1779 and it appears that the interest in the colliery passed to her nephew Richard Richardson (IV), as he is mentioned as a proprietor of Ness Colliery in 1784 (CALS, QJB 3/14, 583). He was a goldsmith and silversmith, like his father – Ness Colliery's early co-proprietor – and in 1780–1 made a silver communion cup for Neston parish church (Ridgway, p. 181).

[57] Oxton, Whittle, Stanley Massey and Richardson are all mentioned in LA, DDCL 1065 (colliery accounts 1769–70 – see below) but not Clarke.

[58] Shafts – CALS, D5363, 1788 'Copy of Schedule to the Answer of Deponents Massey and others'; *Stanley Massey* – see page 177; horses – LA, DDCL 1065 reports eighteen horses in December 1769 and twenty-five by the following September; these accounts show bricklayers, masons, carpenters and slaters were paid, suggesting building work; engines – see page 77; CALS, Z HI/3, 2 January 1770 reported payment of the subscription due the previous March.

[59] John Richards was the 'late agent' by 1770 (LA, DDCL 1065); Small was stated as agent in *Adams's Weekly Courant*, 5, 12, 19 December 1769. Hospital – LMA, A/FH/D/04/004, passim.

[60] LA, DDCL 1065; *Adams's Weekly Courant*, 5, 12, 19 December 1769.

[61] See Chapters 10 and 11.

[62] LA, DDCL 1065. Small sections of these accounts, including some figures, have become lost due to deterioration of the paper.

[63] Some caution must be used in interpreting accounts for any colliery, especially the 'profit', as accounting practice was very different from today (see Flinn, pp. 314–16 and Mokyr (2009), pp. 351–3).

[64] University of Manchester JRL, RYCH 1718 (1–4). The period coincides with the company's financial accounting period. Figures are also available for Q4, 1777 but were distorted due to a probable accident at the colliery (see pages 111–12).

[65] 'Workmen's wages' probably including the cost of shaft-sinking. There appears to have been no distinction between capital and operational expenditure as there is in modern accounting.

[66] Annualised equivalent: £864. Flinn, p. 320; Langton (1979), p. 213.

[67] Annualised equivalent £7,192. Sales price per ton is not known and has been estimated at seven shillings (35p): six years later (Table 2.1) it was about 7/9d. (38.5p) and in the intervening period prices had risen by about 5% (Flinn, pp. 303, 306) giving a price assumption of 7/3d. (31.5p) per ton, less an adjustment for the small amount of slack sold. This is not inconsistent with Lancashire prices around this time (Langton, 1979, p. 229).

[68] University of Manchester JRL, RYCH 1718 (1–5).

[69] Langton (1979), pp. 141–5, 158, 160; Neil Raven and Jon Stobart, eds, *Towns, Regions and Industries: Urban and Industrial Change in the Midlands, c.1700–1840* (Manchester: Manchester

University Press, 2004), p. 106. However, total output from the many south-west Lancashire collieries was substantially more than in the combined Flintshire and Ness collieries.

[70] Rawson, pp. 126, 135.

[71] Mostyn Colliery was certainly quite small when Ness Colliery opened with output of no more than 5,500 tons (5,990 tonnes) p.a. (*Adams's Weekly Courant*, 26 June 1759), and this author has found no reference to it having a steam engine in the following few years which might indicate if it was large. Bychton Colliery may well also have been small, raising about 1,000 tons p.a. in 1759 (NEWA, D/NA/604). Thomas Pennant (*A Tour in Wales, 1773*, 2 vols (London: Henry Hughes, 1778), i, p. 15) mentions that these two collieries were in a 'low state' in 1773 but does then go on apparently to counter this by saying local industry was consuming 'much' coal. Bagillt Colliery had a long history of engine use (goes on apparently to counter this by saying local industry was consuming 'much' coal. Bagillt Colliery had a long history of engine use (Cultural Heritage Knowledge Exchange Hub, *Early Engine Database*, <https://coalpitheath.org.uk/engines/index.php#searchDb> [accessed 2 January 2023])) and there was a 'well-built fire engine' at Coleshill Colliery, in 1769 (*Adam's Weekly Courant*, 7 November).

[72] Pennant (1778), pp. 15–16.

[73] Small adjustments would be made to sales values before calculating royalties, for example deducting 'shipping expenses' (University of Manchester JRL, RYCH 1718 (2–5); CALS, 378/33, 18 November 1826).

[74] CALS, DDX 378/2, 1 January 1814; NEIMME/Wat/3/71/14. CALS, D5363, 'Little Neston Coal Mines' considered alternative royalty rates for that mine too.

[75] Lease date: CALS, DSH 1453/95, p. 55 (CALS, m/f 397, p. 496 incorrectly states 1774). Royalty figures: University of Manchester JRL, RYCH 1718 (2–5). Minor landholders Thomas Charnock and Joseph Norman received an additional £23 in royalties in 1777.

[76] CALS, DSH 1453/95, p. 55. The first Thomas Cottingham was lord until his death in 1783 followed by his son Thomas.

[77] CALS, D5363, letter from Joshua Small, 21 December 1781.

[78] 'Copy of Answer of Deponents Massey and others', part of CALS, D5363.

[79] *Chester Chronicle*, 26 April 1822; CALS, DBC 261/38, 'Cottingham and Stanley'.

[80] CALS, DSH 1453/95, p. 55 (July, 1794).

[81] CALS, DBC 261/38, 'Cottingham and Stanley'.

[82] Based on baptismal entries; these were the most likely type of entry to record occupations (see Figure 6.2). Recruitment: *Adams's Weekly Courant*, 1 September 1778.

[83] Birmingham City Archive, MS3147/3/400/40. See pages 79–80.

[84] Shareholders in 1787 were, apparently, Richard Richardson IV (37.5%), 'the Masseys' [*sic*] (37.5%), John Stanley (son of John Stanley Massey; 12.5%), Daniel Dawbie [*sic*] (6.25%) and Thomas Whittle (6.25%). The percentages are taken from a source without a valid reference in a short unpublished article on 'Coal Mining in the Parish of Neston' by Lyn Miles, *c*.2001. The information is, though, consistent with other known sources e.g. NEWA, D/DM/452/1, 13 April 1791 re Daniel Daulby, and the sources in notes 56 and 96. It seems likely Daulby was the man of that name who made a fine drawing of Hooton Hall in 1780 (Figure 12.4).

Chapter 2 – Ness Colliery: A Near-Century of Business (continued)

85 CALS, QDV 2/304. The firm had still been termed 'John Stanley Massey Esq. and Co.' in March 1789 (CALS, Z HI 7).

86 Quay – see pages 167–8; borehole – NEIMME/Wat/3/71/1 and 2; another borehole had been dug in 1788 (NEIMME/ZA/12/274-277).

87 See pages 55 and 141.

88 NEWA, D/DM/452/1, 25 April 1797, referring to a loan made on 10 October 1790.

89 Stanley, p. 83.

90 NEWA, D/DM/452/1, 16 June and 11 August 1798.

91 *Lloyd's Evening Post*, 3–6 October 1794; *Chester Courant*, 1 September 1795. Stanley had previously petitioned Parliament on the issue, in 1791.

92 Sir John's sons were all dead, and none of Sir Thomas's seven children had yet reached majority (Stanley, p. 83).

93 *Chester Chronicle*, 11 December 1795 (and in this and other Chester and Liverpool newspapers for several more weeks); *Chester Courant*, weekly from 9 August to 27 September 1796.

94 CALS, will of Sir Thomas Stanley Massey Stanley, 1795. The will (which makes no specific mention of the colliery) makes virtually no reference to Thomas's second son, also Thomas, and gives the executors powers to defer payments to beneficiaries until they were aged thirty.

95 CALS, DHL/54C.

96 These included Charles Stanley, a brother of Sir John, who died in 1792, and whose estate was paid £500 in 1798 for his interest in the business (LA, DDBL 54/55); and another John, brother of the elder Sir Thomas, who died in 1790. His poorly executed will took years to untangle (CALS: will and admon. of John Stanley, 1797).

97 Flinn, p. 323.

98 Ness was selling coal at 8s. 4d. per ton in April 1809 and at 18s. 8d. in 1811 (DHL 54C 29 and LA, DDBL 54/55). Trend from Flinn, p. 304.

99 CALS, DDX 378/1-12, 30–33 and 41, of which the most significant here are CALS, DDX 378/7, 8, 30, 31, 33.

100 Peak royalties to the Stanley estate came in 1804 representing £8,010 of sales (Appendix IIa). Assuming a price of 8s. 4d. (*Chester Chronicle*, 7 February 1806, the nearest available price point) this represents 19,231 tons (20,943 tonnes). Additionally, there would have been sales of a small amount of coal won from the land leased at Little Neston.

101 A. H. Dodd, 'The North Wales Coal Industry During the Industrial Revolution', *Archaeologia Cambrensis*, 84 (1929), p. 210.

102 Ibid.; Willett, p. 105.

103 Langton (1979), pp. 148–53; D. Anderson, 'Blundell's Collieries: the Progress of the Business', *THSLC*, 116 (1964), p. 113.

104 See pages 160–1.

105 Stanley, p. 84.

106 *Chester Courant*, 1 September–27 October 1812.

107 CALS, DDX 378/30, 26 October 1814, when there was an adjustment to figures relating to coal stocks on 27 February 1813 due to actions taken 'before [Sir Thomas Stanley's] intention was understood'.

[108] Thomas acquired half on 17 April 1813 (CALS, DDX 378/30). Charles paid for one quarter on 17 April 1813; the final payments were made on 24 January 1816 (NEWA, D/DM 452/1). The situation regarding the other quarter is unclear but there is no indication of any additional proprietors. Charles and Thomas were later referred to as the 'partners' in the business (CALS, DBC 261/38, 'Instructions for Indictment', 1828).

[109] CALS, DDX 378/30, 17 April 1813; NEWA, D/DM 452/1, 17 April 1813.

[110] DRO, NCB I /JB/414.

[111] The lower rate took effect from 27 February 1813 (CALS, DDX 378/2, 1 January 1814). All references to royalties prior to this date were at a 10% rate. NEIMME/Wat/3/71/14 describes Charles Stanley as 'a proprietor, having no benefit from the royalty'.

[112] *Chester Chronicle*, 26 February 1813; CALS, DDX 378/30, 17 April 1813.

[113] See page 193.

[114] CALS, DDX 378/30, 13 July 1811 and passim thereafter.

[115] CALS, QDV 2/304, Land Tax assessment. Charles is named occupier until 1832; Sir Thomas Stanley was proprietor. The lease was for ninety-nine years at £115 p.a. (CALS, DDX 378/30, 31 December 1813).

[116] Census, Ness, 1851.

[117] NEWA, D/MT/912. Mostyn's first wife was Frances Blundell, sister of William Blundell, Sir Thomas Stanley's brother-in law (i.e. husband of his sister Catherine). Thus, three notable Catholic families in the region were intertwined.

[118] NEWA, Mostyn of Talacre papers and Mostyn of Mostyn papers.

[119] Flinn, pp. 304 and 306.

[120] Flinn, p. 304; Frank O'Gorman, *The Long Eighteenth Century* (London: Arnold, 1997), p. 335.

[121] CALS, DDX 378/31, 21 January 1816 records a landsale price of 10 shillings (50p), including delivery. In 1811, the landsale price had been 18s. 8d. (93p) (LA, DDCL 1065).

[122] The price at Neston was 8s. 4d. (42p) in 1806 (*Chester Courant*, 18 February), and the same in 1823 (CALS, D5363, 'Little Neston Coal Mines').

[123] *Chester Chronicle*, 26 April 1822.

[124] Leonard Adams, *Agricultural Depression and Farm Relief in England 1813–1852* (London: Routledge, 2013), pp. 66, 151–9.

[125] Benjamin Higgins, 'Agriculture and War: A Comparison of Agricultural Conditions in the Napoleonic and World War Periods', *Agricultural History*, 14, 1 (Jan. 1940), pp. 4–5.

[126] TNA, J 90/82, 13 September 1813 which indicates the rent was to be £46 p.a. including the public house; *Chester Chronicle*, 26 April 1822.

[127] TNA, J 90/81, 11 August 1817 and J 90/82, 15 March 1822. Royalties to Cottingham dwindled to less than £50 for many years before 1821 (CALS, DBC 261/38, 'Cottingham and Stanley'); T&WA, DX 198/1, pp. 410 and 501.

[128] Coal Authority, 14923/3.

[129] T&WA, DX 198/1, pp. 410 and 501.

[130] See page 81.

[131] See pages 37–8.

Chapter 2 – Ness Colliery: A Near-Century of Business (continued)

[132] Assuming sales of £2,280 (Appendix IIa) and a prevailing mid-price of 8s. (40p) (D5363, 'Little Neston Coal Mines'), this represents 5,700 tons (6,207 tonnes) per annum or 110 tons (119 tonnes) per week.

[133] *Chester Courant*, 23 April 1822.

[134] NEIMME/ZA/12/236–7.

[135] See page 149.

[136] Tables 2.1 and 2.3.

[137] To Michaelmas 1824, £1,939 wages on £2,866 sales (68%); 1825, £2398 on £3,924 (61%) and 1826, £2,279 on sales of £3,439 (66%) (NEIMME/Wat/3/71/4).

[138] NEIMME/Wat/3/71/4; John Farey, *A Treatise on the Steam Engine* (London: Longman Rees, Orme, Brown and Green, 1827), pp. 193 and 251–2.

[139] NEIMME/Wat/3/71/1–22.

[140] NEIMME/Wat/3/71/12.

[141] Watson was a renowned freelance viewer of the time (Flinn, pp. 57–8). He was also doing work for Mostyn Colliery during some of the time he was advising Ness (NEWA, D/M/5129 (1823–9).

[142] NEIMME/Wat/3/71/2, 11, 12 and 14.

[143] See pages 9 and 32.

[144] NEIMME/Wat/3/71/11 – the price of the best coal had also been lowered the previous November.

[145] NEIMME/Wat/3/71/15.

[146] NEIMME/Wat/3/71/9.

[147] A. H. Dodd, *The Industrial Revolution in North Wales*, 3rd edn, Cardiff: University of Wales Press (1971), p. 197 makes some interesting points about such changes in attitude at the time.

[148] NEIMME/Wat/3/71/9.

[149] NEIMME/Wat/3/71/6, 8, 12, 13 and 15. See also page 68.

[150] NEIMME/Wat/3/71/2. See page 73.

[151] NEIMME/Wat/3/71/14.

[152] NEIMME/Wat/3/71/1–3.

[153] NEIMME/Wat/3/71/20.

[154] NEIMME/Wat/3/71/22.

[155] NEIMME/Wat/3/71/4, 16 and 17.

[156] NEIMME/Wat/3/71/16 and 21. Chapters 8 to 11 consider the extent of the landsale and seasale trade in more detail.

[157] NEIMME/Wat/3/71/20; Coal Authority, 14923/6.

[158] Dodd (1929), p. 210. Imputed sales at Ness in 1834 were £4,410 (Appendix IIa) – about 226 tons (246 tonnes) p.w. at the last known mid-price for coal at Ness (4½d.) in 1830 (NEIMME/Wat/3/71/19).

[159] Brian Mitchell, *Economic Development of the British Coal Industry* (Cambridge: Cambridge University Press, 1984), p. 12.

[160] TNA, HO 73/53/78, Report of Digby Neave.

[161] NEIMME/Wat/3/71/14 and 15.

162 *Sporting Magazine*, April 1820, p. 274; Stanley, p. 85.

163 *Saunders's News-Letter*, 6 February 1818; CALS, DDX 378/2, 23 December 1816; *North Wales Chronicle*, 19 May 1835. For example, Sir Thomas had given 'The Hooton Cup', run at Hoylake (*The Sporting Magazine*, Ser. 2, Vol. 5 (1832), 'Racing Calendar', p. 13). There are many references to income from horse breeding in the Hooton Estate accounts e.g. CALS, DDX 378/30, 13 March 1813.

164 NEIMME/Wat/3/71/21. Sir Thomas was married to Mary, only daughter and heiress of Sir Carnaby Haggerston, 5th Baronet, of Haggerston, Northumberland. He was probably there, but it is possible that he used the opportunity to update his knowledge of colliery practice in the region's important coalfields.

165 Georgina Battiscombe, *Mrs Gladstone, The Portrait of a Marriage* (London: Constable, 1956), p. 17. Stanley himself was High Sheriff of Cheshire in 1831–2 (*Chester Chronicle*, 6 May 1831).

166 NLW, Hawarden Deeds, 1520. Another source of royalties was Bickerstaff[e] Colliery in Lancashire (CALS, 378/7, 8 August 1834).

167 Willett, p. 104. Payments largely ceased in 1822 but two small sums were also received in 1828 (CALS, DDX 378/30 and 31).

168 For example, in the accounting year to 25 June 1814, £530 was received from Little Mountain Colliery whereas Ness paid just £371 in royalties in the year to 1 October 1814 (CALS, DDX 378/30 and 31).

169 CALS, DDX 378/30, 1 February 1814 (excluded in the £530 in note 168).

170 CALS, DDX 378/30, 6 June 1812. Another example is tiles for a barn in Storeton, paid for on 16 August 1803 (CALS, DDX 378/1).

171 *Cheshire Sheaf*, 'A Meet of Sir Thomas Stanley of Hooton's Hounds at Bidston Hill, About 1840', 3rd series, 23 (1926), p. 13.

172 CALS, Will of Thomas Massey Stanley, 1841. Curiously, there is no indication in the will that, when he died, Sir Thomas Stanley owned anything other than the whole colliery, i.e. Charles was no longer a co-proprietor. How and when this happened is unclear.

173 Errington was born Rowland Massey Stanley in 1809 but later assumed a new surname under royal licence.

174 DRO, NCB I/JB 412.

175 DRO, NCB I/JB 412–416; NEIMME/Bud/48/15, 21–22 October 1842.

176 *Mining Journal, Railway and Commercial Gazette*, 15 May 1852, p. 229.

177 1851 census, Ness, entry for James Gregory.

178 Samuel Bagshaw, *History, Gazetteer and Directory of the County Palatine of Chester* (Sheffield: Samuel Bagshaw, 1850), p. 658.

179 Church, p. 472.

180 CALS, P 149/8.

181 *Mining Journal, Railway and Commercial Gazette*, 15 May 1852, p. 229.

182 CALS, P149/8 shows Charles Stanley as the colliery owner until 1853/4, with Errington the owner in 1854/5 and 1855/6. Errington is also listed as the mine's owner in the 1854 *Reports of Inspectors of Coal Mines, June 1851–December 1853*, Report of Commissioners, Paper 1845, p. 81. Colliery manager, James Gregory, may also have had a small stake in the business, describing himself in the 1851 census as a 'colliery proprietor employing 120 men'.

Chapter 2 – Ness Colliery: A Near-Century of Business (continued)

[183] Coal Authority, 3808/1.

[184] CALS, P149/9/3, March 1855; CALS, Stanley Estate Accounts, 1844–56 (uncatalogued)**,** 26 April and 1 August 1855.

[185] *Chester Chronicle*, 23 June 1855; *Liverpool Mercury*, 29 June 1855.

[186] Two payments totalling this amount are recorded in the Puddington estate accounts for 1855, after the sale (CALS, Stanley Estate Accounts, 1844–56 (uncatalogued)). However, it has not been possible to view all of this uncatalogued item and it is possible further payments were recorded. A payment of £477 had also been received on 30 December 1854 but the purpose is not clear.

[187] BPP [1871], p. 374.

[188] NRO, 725 B5, p. 479, 14 April 1863.

[189] *Morris and Co.'s Commercial Directory and Gazetteer of Cheshire* (Nottingham: Morris and Co., 1864), p. 533.

[190] NRO 725 B5, p. 479, letter to C. Lloyd from William Armstrong, 14 April 1863.

[191] Dodd (1929), p. 216. See also Thomas Leacroft Cottingham's evidence on wasteful practice in North Wales (BPP [1871], p. 375).

Chapter 3 – Little Neston Colliery and the 'Colliery' at Parkgate

[1] *Chester Chronicle*, 21 March 1817; TNA, J 90/81, 24 February and 11 March 1817. Also TNA, J 90/18 and 19, passim. A principal creditor was Ralph Richardson, son of Ness Colliery co-founder, Richard Richardson.

[2] TNA, J 90/81, 11 and 18 August 1817, and other undated correspondence.

[3] CALS, DBC 261/38, 'Cottingham and Stanley'. The £10 one-year rent (TNA, J 90/87, Account Book 'K', 11 May 1820) seems to have been misconstrued as a new five-year lease in the *Chester Chronicle*, 26 April 1822.

[4] The first contemporary reference found to date to Thomas Cottingham senior's 'colliery' is on 14 May 1820 (TNA, J 90/82). Little Neston Colliery was initially to operate from Pit No. 21. As this was in use by the Stanleys until 1820 it seems likely Cottingham did not start before then.

[5] TNA, J 90/81, 13 February 1823; *Cheshire Sheaf* (1934), p. 3.

[6] CALS, D5363, 'Little Neston Coal Mines'.

[7] TNA, J 90/82, 14 February 1820.

[8] CALS, DBC 261/38, 'Cottingham and Stanley'.

[9] Ibid.

[10] TNA, J 90/81, 18 December 1819. Buddle was then asked to come and give a final verdict on the matter but there is no record that he did so (TNA, J 90/81, 23 December 1819).

[11] These and other details of the 1821 case are given in the report of the subsequent case in the *Chester Courant*, 23 April 1822 and *Chester Chronicle,* 26 April 1822.

[12] CALS, DBC 261/38, 'Cottingham and Stanley'.

[13] Total costs were over £639 for the case including the £100 damages (CALS, DDX 378/31, 23 April, 19 May and 3 November 1821, 5 January and 11 February 1822).

[14] DRO, NCB 1/JB 667, 25 September 1821. The unusual phrase 'knocked up' meant destroyed or 'put an end to' but this appears to have been an exaggeration as coal was being sold, albeit in limited quantities (Appendix IIa).

[15] *Chester Chronicle*, 26 April 1822.

[16] M. Lewis (2010), Researches into the Background of the 'A' Pit Railway at Newcastle NSW (unpublished), p. 47.

[17] *The Annual Register, Or a View of the History, Politics, and Literature, for the Year 1815* (London: Baldwin, Craddock and Joy, 1815), p. 288.

[18] The account of the trial is taken from lengthy reports in the *Chester Chronicle*, 26 April 1822 and the *Chester Courant,* 23 April 1822.

[19] CALS, DBC 261/38, 'Cottingham and Stanley'. The same document recounts an incident where Sir Thomas Stanley's estate manager, Richard Ashhurst, 'shook his whip' at an employee of Cottingham.

[20] TNA, J 90/82, 17 April 1822.

[21] *Chester Courant*, 23 April 1822.

[22] Assuming a mid-price of 7*s*. 6*d*. (37.5p) per ton (CALS, D5363, 'Little Neston Coal Mines').

[23] CALS, D5363, 'Little Neston Coal Mines'.

[24] Costs came to over £400 (CALS, DDX 378/31, 20 June 1822, 15, 19 and 22 February 1823).

[25] TNA, J 90/82, 18 April 1822.

[26] *Chester Courant*, 4 February 1823.

[27] TNA, J 90/81, 10 August 1822.

[28] CALS, D5363, 'Little Neston Coal Mines'.

[29] NEIMME/Wat/3/71/2.

[30] NEIMME/Wat/3/71/17.

[31] TNA, J 90/82, 6 December 1823.

[32] TNA, J 90/83, 22 February 1823.

[33] CALS, D5363 'Little Neston Coal Mines'.

[34] W. A. Scott, *Battle of Waterloo*, (London: E. Cox and Son, 1815), p. 201; *Cambridge Chronicle,* 11 March 1825; TNA, War Office: Campaign Medal and Award Rolls 1793–1949 (General Series); TNA, J 90/81, 6 December 1820 and 24 February 1822.

[35] CALS, D5363, 'Little Neston Coal Mines'; *Chester Courant*, 23 April 1822; *Cambridge Chronicle*, 11 March 1825; DBC 261/38, 'Cottingham and Stanley'.

[36] See page 55.

[37] TNA, J 90/83, 22 February 1823.

[38] CALS, D5363, 'Little Neston Coal Mines'.

[39] CALS, D5363, 'Little Neston Coal Mines'; *Morning Post*, 17 April 1829; *Chester Chronicle*, 23 April 1830. The lease was in Cottingham senior's name but assigned to Cottingham junior and Thomas Leacroft on 1 May 1827 after the father's death. Royalties were 1/7th on one piece of land and 3/50ths on the 'waste' extending into the estuary.

[40] TNA, J 90/82, 22 April 1823.

[41] TNA, J 90/19, letter, 27 May 1823.

[42] TNA, J 90/19, letter, 8 June 1825. Other papers in TNA, J 90/18 and 19 reveal John's fierce antipathy to his brother.

Chapter 3 – Little Neston Colliery and the 'Colliery' at Parkgate (continued)

[43] TNA, J 90/19, 11 July 1825. The will was not proved until 1827.

[44] The underlying data was said to be 'by no means … satisfactory' (*Chester Chronicle*, 23 April 1830).

[45] CALS, Will of Thomas Cottingham, 1825. Extensive information on the estate and its debts, before and after Thomas's death, is contained in TNA, J 90/18 and 19.

[46] 'Valuable Freehold Estate in Cheshire to be Sold by Auction', part of CALS, D5363.

[47] L. Neal, 'The Financial Crisis of 1825 and the Restructuring of the British Financial System', *Federal Reserve Bank of St. Louis Review*, 80 (1998), 3, pp. 53–76.

[48] Flinn, p. 304.

[49] List of unsold lots in TNA, J 90/18.

[50] Debt details and sale notice for 8 October in TNA, J 90/18. The sales agreed at the 1826 and 1827 auctions subsequently fell through due to uncertainty over Cottingham's legal title to the property (TNA, J 90/18, passim).

[51] TNA, J 90/83, 12 May 1827.

[52] *The Times*, 15 May 1823. Numerous sources refer to Leacroft's continuing involvement including NEIMME/Wat/3/71/17 and the *Chester Chronicle*, 23 April 1830.

[53] TNA, CUST 79/10, 24 October 1823 and J 90/81, 24 May 1827. More information on the quay – pages 167–8.

[54] BPP [1871], p. 374.

[55] *Morning Post*, 17 April 1829 which also details the 1828 case.

[56] £1,500 was the figure reported as being given in court (*Chester Courant*, 27 April 1830); John Watson, the noted viewer working for Ness Colliery, estimated the costs would have been about £1,000 and stated that the figure given in court was £1,200 (NEIMME/Wat/3/71/17); the *Morning Post* (17 April 1829) implied the figure was £1,080.

[57] *Chester Chronicle*, 23 April 1830.

[58] TNA, J 90/82, 8 July 1824.

[59] NEIMME/Wat/3/71/21.

[60] *The Times*, 17 April 1832.

[61] Papers in CALS, D5363; the *Morning Post*, 14 March 1836; *The Times*, 31 January 1843. *Reports of Cases Decided in the High Court of Chancery*, ed. by John Dunlap (New York, Gould, Banks and Co., 1843–71), pp. 627–38.

[62] He left the area for some time from about 1833 for an unknown reason but perhaps to fight his legal battles (TNA, J 90/81, 13 October 1834). Presumably Leacroft ran the business for a while.

[63] NEIMME/Wat/3/71/17.

[64] Coal Authority 14923/1 shows Cottingham's works in 1845 extending '640 yards' (585 metres), apparently crossing into Ness.

[65] Bangor Archives, Mona Mine 3207, 21 October 1831.

[66] See page 194.

[67] Parish register of St Michael's Church, Chester, 30 December 1836.

[68] Rideout, p. 82.

[69] CALS, P 149/9/2, 23 January 1842. A small further payment was made by the church to 'Cottingham for coal' in 1849. At just 6s. 10d. – less than a ton after accounting for delivery costs – it may represent clearance of a small remaining stock by the liquidator. At the same time the church paid Ness Colliery 14s. 6d. for coal. Coal Authority, 14923/1 records 'Mr Cottingham's Endway or Waggon Road in 1845' and 'Supposed [coal]face in 1845'. Coal Authority 14931/2 mentions 'Level to Cut 5 Feet coal 1845-6'. From other notes on the plan this could well be the date of survey rather than the date of working.

[70] NEWA, QS/DR/28 shows that his property was in the hands of 'the mortgagee in possession'; CALS, EDT 241/1.

[71] BPP [1871], p. 374. The case concerned was probably the one involving the estate's debts which appears to have reached its end in 1844. One other outcome appears to be that the Earl of Shrewsbury acquired Cottingham's portion of the lordship of Little Neston, becoming sole lord (Ormerod, ii, p. 540).

[72] CALS, EDT 241/1. See pages 167–8 re quay.

[73] Isaac Slater, *Directory of the Towns upon the Environs of Liverpool* (Manchester: Isaac Slater, 1844), p. 57. CALS, EDT 241/1 and 2, Little Neston Tithe Apportionment and Map (1849).

[74] The 1851 census for Little Neston describes Cottingham as 'Lieutenant, Army, Half pay. Blind'.

[75] Coal Authority, 14923/1.

[76] CALS, P149/8, Little Neston, 1848-9: Jackson was a named defaulter in relation to the parish church rate assessment; CALS, Stanley Estate Accounts, 1844–56 (uncatalogued), 28 June 1848, arrears of rent due.

[77] *Liverpool Mercury*, 18 July 1851.

[78] *Liverpool Mercury*, 15 August 1851.

[79] *Chester Chronicle* 15 May 1852, 29 May 1852.

[80] *Liverpool Mercury*, 1 June 1852; *Chester Chronicle* 29 May 1852.

[81] *Liverpool Mercury*, 1 June 1852.

[82] *Liverpool Mail*, 9 July 1853. To add insult to injury the protracted process meant that Thomas Cottingham continued to be assessed on the value of his 'coal mines' for the parish church rate assessment until 1853 (CALS, P149/8).

[83] Chandler is listed as the owner of the 'mine' at Little Neston in the surviving *Annual Reports of Inspectors of Mines* (London: HMSO) from 1855 to 1875. See also pages 48–9.

[84] Rideout, p. 82. Flooding may have been a problem, perhaps linked to the 'crownings' (Isaac Slater, *Royal National Commercial Directory of Cheshire and North Wales* (Manchester: Isaac Slater, 1869), p. 181.

[85] His monumental inscription is given in 'Glegg and Cottingham Tombstones at Neston' in *Cheshire Sheaf*, 3rd series, 6 (1906), p. 75. An article entitled 'A Neston Hero' in the *Cheshire Observer*, 14 August 1897 gives a good account of his military life.

[86] *Chester Chronicle*, 11 December 1795 (and in this and other Chester and Liverpool newspapers for several more weeks).

Chapter 3 – Little Neston Colliery and the 'Colliery' at Parkgate (continued)

[87] Davies, aka William Davis and variants, was agent (i.e. manager) between at least 1781 and 1791 at the colliery but was 'late' (i.e. former) agent in January 1792. He was a 'Grocer' the following year and in December 1795 when the advertisement appeared (all information: NPR). The reason he left Ness Colliery is unknown.

[88] CALS, Z AB/5/29. Mostyn appears to have also owned Mostyn Colliery, Flintshire (*Chester Chronicle*, 10 October 1794).

[89] *The Times*, 6 March to 16 April 1806 and others. Additional information is given in NRO Wat/3/65/3, 'Particulars of a capital extensive leasehold colliery'. Two different auction dates were given, suggesting a possible lack of interest, at least on the first occasion.

[90] *Neston 1840–1940*, ed. by Geoffrey Place (Burton and South Wirral Local History Society, 1996), p. 3.

[91] J. Hemingway, *History of the City of Chester, from its Foundation to the Present Time* (Chester: J. Fletcher, 1831), p. 238; CALS, ZCR 69/3/160 and 161. A new company, Williamson and Co., was operating in Neston around this time. Its business is unknown but it had a link to William Briscoe Davies named in the 1795 advertisement. The evidence is entirely circumstantial but there is a possibility that this business was undertaking the mining.

[92] *Chester Courant*, 12 December 1809, *Chester Chronicle*, 29 December 1809, and other editions.

[93] NEWA, D/M/5662, letter dated 6 April 1874.

[94] NEWA, D/M/5661, 'Borings at Parkgate'.

[95] *Liverpool Mercury*, 15 October 1847 and many other newspapers.

[96] Place (1994), p. 266.

[97] 'A section of the Coal Strata at Parkgate in Cheshire 1851' (Bangor, Mostyn MSS 7185), indicates two boreholes by 'Hopkins' (one of which is the cause of the constant supply of water that appears from a standpipe – actually an artesian well – on the marsh edge at the bottom of today's Moorside Lane) and two by 'Hopwood'; NEWA, D/M/5655, lease to Robert Wynne Williams dated 30 March 1852, mentions boreholes 150, 250 and 800 yards (137, 229 and 732 metres) out.

[98] For example, in newspapers across the country, including the *London Morning Post*, 8 August 1848.

[99] There are many references to 'Mr. Lancaster's borings', and undated sections depicting the coal, in Mostyn estate papers including in NEWA, D/M/5662. Mostyn later attested to these finds to a parliamentary committee (BPP [1871], p. 334).

[100] *The Mining Journal, Railway and Commercial Gazette*, 18 (1848), p. 373.

[101] *Chester Chronicle*, 17 October 1845.

[102] Place (1994), pp. 266 and 268.

[103] CALS, D 5232/7, 'Particulars of sale of the Mostyn Estate'.

[104] Place (1994), p. 266.

[105] *The Mining Journal, Railway and Commercial Gazette*, 21 (1851), p. 377. NEWA, D/M/5655, 5656, 5662 and 5666.

[106] NEWA, D/M/5661, 'Report on Coal and Ironstone Mines'.

[107] NEWA, D/M/5661, letters dated 18 June 1863 and 10 March 1864.

[108] NEWA, D/M/5661, 'Report on Coal and Ironstone Workings' mentions that there was 'no outlet [for the coal] as the gutter is silted up'.

[109] There are passing references to Chandler in Mostyn correspondence for a few years but there is no reference to him in a detailed surveyor's report dated 14 April 1863 (NRO 725 B5, p. 479, letter to C. Lloyd from William Armstrong) or thereafter.

Chapter 4 – Coal Mining and Supporting Operations

[1] Bank Hey in the Will of Charles Cottingham, 1 October 1766 (TNA, J 90/18). Later known as Bank Heys (CALS, EDT 241/2, (1849).

[2] Sources: CALS, EDT 241/2 and EDT 286/2; Coal Authority, 3808/1, 14923/1-4, 414931/2; 'Map of a Pier at Little Neston', c.1829, part of CALS, D5363; CALS, D/3884/5.

[3] NEIMME/Wat/35/18. There is, incidentally, no evidence for any significant renumbering of the pits during the colliery's lifetime.

[4] There were twenty-eight in 1822 (Stanley's agent, Robert Johnson in *Chester Courant*, 26 April) and thirty by 1826 (NEIMME/Wat/3/71/4).

[5] CALS, D5363, 'Copy of Schedule to the Answer of Deponents Massey and others'.

[6] See page 267, note 11. 'Filling up old pits' appears in CALS, DDX 378/30, 6 February 1813. However, the word 'pit' could be ambiguous sometimes referring to, say, ponds, or marl or clay pits, not necessarily coal pits.

[7] CALS, PM 11/7, 'A Plan of So Much of the Lands of the River Dee Company' (1772).

[8] Arundel Castle Manuscripts, TP 60.

[9] Coal Authority, 3808/1.

[10] LA, DDCL 1065.

[11] CALS, DBC 261/38, 'Cottingham v Stanley Bt.'.

[12] Coal Authority, 14931/2.

[13] *Chester Courant*, 1 September–27 October 1812.

[14] See page 219.

[15] The 'Counting House' is labelled on Coal Authority, 14923/1, c.1839. The accounts of the Hooton estate make several references to rent paid to it by the colliery for premises in Little Neston, e.g. CALS, DDX 378/31, 14 February 1817.

[16] *Chester Chronicle*, 9 June 1837.

[17] Pages 74 and 76–85.

[18] CALS, DBC 261/38, 'Cottingham v Stanley Bt.'.

[19] 'Information of James Gregory', CALS, DBC 261/38.

[20] CALS, DBC 261/38, 'Cottingham and Stanley'.

[21] Ibid.

[22] Coal Authority, 14923/2.

[23] For example, in LA, DDCL 1065 and NEIMME/Wat/3/71/16.

[24] LA, DDCL 1065.

[25] See page 124.

[26] *Chester Chronicle*, 26 April 1822.

[27] CALS, DBC 261/38, 'Cottingham and Stanley'.

[28] CALS, DBC 261/28, 'Cottingham v Stanley Bt.' and 'Cottingham and Stanley'.

Chapter 4 – Coal Mining and Supporting Operations (continued)

[29] CALS, DBC 261/28, 'Cottingham v Stanley Bt.'.

[30] *Chester Chronicle*, 23 June 1855.

[31] OS, two inches to one mile, Sheet 345 (1836) which refers to both a 'Colliery' at the Little Neston site and 'Denna Colliery' in Ness. The quality of the available original does not allow reproduction here.

[32] For example, TNA J 90/18, 'An Estate in Little Neston' (1826); CALS, PM 13/8a (Swire and Hutchings, 1830); CALS, PM 5.2 (Bryant, 1831).

[33] CALS, D5363, 'Little Neston Coal Mines' and 'Copy of Schedule to the Answer of Deponents Massey and others'.

[34] 'Valuable Freehold Estate in Cheshire to be Sold by Auction', part of CALS, D5363.

[35] Coal Authority, 14931/2 Coal Authority, 14931/2. Some features on this plan are dated between 1821 and 1887 and it is said to be based on 'an old plan', so it is unclear whether it represents any particular point in time.

[36] *Chester Chronicle,* 23 April 1830; Coal Authority, 14931/2. See pages 107 and 299, note 166 re reopening of the pier pit.

[37] *Chester Chronicle,* 23 April 1830; TNA, J 90/18 'An estate in Little Neston'.

[38] NEIMME/Wat/3/71/17 and 18. In 1829 a visitor to the area, referred to 'the coal pits at Denna' operating a single pit only, accessing the six-feet steam coal seam at 55 yards' depth (British Library, Add. MSS 89098, 'Diary of William Holden', 3 March 1829 (unlisted)). This is certainly untrue of Ness Colliery, as the NEIMME correspondence makes clear, and must relate to Little Neston Colliery.

[39] A report in *The Times*, 17 February 1832, relates to an attempt to work the Five-Foot seam. BPP [1871], p. 374 and Coal Authority 14931/2 both indicate working of the Six-Foot and Five-Foot implying the attempt eventually succeeded. The pit appears on many plans and was said to then be the 'only pit worked on the manor' (*Chester Chronicle*, 23 April 1830).

[40] 'Map of a Pier at Little Neston', *c*.1829, part of CALS, D5363.

[41] Arundel Castle Manuscripts, TP 60.

[42] LA, DDCL 1065.

[43] CALS, QDV 2/304. In 1789 the 'colliery lands' are mentioned for the first time in Land Tax records and are more fully recorded the following year together with part of the 'farm' and 'holding' of two individuals who had vacated them. The Land Tax records specifically refer to the 'Colliery Farm' from 1801 onwards and the contexts and amounts involved suggest that the earlier 'colliery lands' were farmland.

[44] *Chester Courant*, 9 August 1796; *Chester Chronicle*, 4 September 1812.

[45] Eleven fields totalling about 100 acres were owned and occupied by Charles Stanley on the 1845 tithe map; the colliery itself was also stated to be owned and occupied by him. For the avoidance of doubt, Ness Colliery's farm was unconnected with the later 'Colliery Farm' located at the bottom of today's Marshlands Road.

[46] See page 129.

[47] LA, DDCL 1065; *Chester Chronicle*, 23 June 1855.

[48] CALS, EDT 286/2.

49 CALS, DBC 261/38, 'Information of James Gregory', dated 1828, in which they were said to be situated between the water reservoir and the engine house, not far from the barn.

50 *Chester Chronicle*, 26 February 1813.

51 NEWA, D/DM/452, 14 April 1813.

52 CALS, DDX 378/1, 17 April 1813.

53 For example, NEIMME/Wat/3/71/4.

54 Turnip field close to the colliery mentioned in CALS, DBC 261/38, 'Cottingham and Stanley' (1821).

55 *Chester Chronicle*, 14 October 1814.

56 As happened in East Cumberland, for example (A. Harris, 'Colliery Settlements in East Cumberland', *TCWAAS*, 74 (1974), p. 124).

57 CALS, DBC 261/38, 'Cottingham and Stanley'; CALS, Stanley Estate Accounts, 1844–56 (uncatalogued), 23 December 1852.

58 Although there were fluctuations, the general trend was upwards from the 1780s and reached peaks around 1800 and 1813 (Adams, pp. 30–1).

59 *Chester Chronicle*, 8 March 1816; William Klingaman and Nicholas Klingaman, *The Year Without Summer: 1816 and the Volcano That Darkened the World and Changed History* (New York: St. Martin's Press, 2013).

60 Adams, p. 31; CALS, DDX 378/31, 28 November 1822.

61 CALS, will of Thomas Massey Stanley, 1841; *Chester Chronicle*, 6 February 1846.

62 1851 census, Ness.

63 A. R. Griffin, 'Industrial Archaeology as an Aid to the Study of Mining History', *Industrial Archaeology*, 11, 1 (February 1974), p. 16.

64 Ashton, p. 27.

65 A. Vickers, *Women working at Newbottle Colliery*, Durham County Council (n.d.) <http://www.durhamintime.org.uk/durham_miner/women_newbottle_colliery.pdf> [accessed 19 February 2019].

66 John Langton, 'People from the Pits: the Origins of Colliers in Eighteenth-Century South-West Lancashire', in *Migration, Mobility and Modernisation* ed. by David Siddle (Liverpool: Liverpool University Press, 2000), pp. 75–6.

67 TNA, HO 73/53/78, Report of Digby Neave.

68 Both University of Manchester JRL, RYCH 1718 (1–5) for 1776–7 and NEIMME/Wat/3/71/4 for 1826 include fortnightly production data for at least a year and neither shows any notable seasonal variation.

69 Full details – see *nestoncollieries.org*

70 He was baptised at Audley in 1736 (PR, St James the Great, Audley, 4 April) and married Sarah Shore from Madeley on 9 May 1755, at which time he was described as living in Flint (PR, All Saints, Madeley). His parents had moved from Audley to Buckley by 1755 (Mold PR, 19 May 1755). He was a 'collier' at Ness in 1762 and in 1763 was 'colliery agent', i.e. manager (CALS, QJF 191/2, 26 March). He apparently died the following year (NPR).

71 NPR, 17 August 1760.

72 NPR, baptisms. 'Stocks house' is recorded close to the shore in Denhall in 1826, by that time belonging to James's son Edward, also a farmer.

Chapter 4 – Coal Mining and Supporting Operations (continued)

[73] *Morning Post*, 17 April 1829.

[74] See pages 23, 29 and 34. A '30th hole' (i.e. borehole) was sunk in 1825–6 but it is not clear if this relates to the pit of that number (NEIMME/Wat/ZA/12/236–7) which was in use by 1826 (NEIMME/Wat/35/4).

[75] Flinn, pp. 71–2.

[76] NEIMME/Wat/35/2, 5 and 20.

[77] Langton (1979), p. 213.

[78] Langton (1979), pp. 213–14. An eighteenth-century document relating to Cholmondeley in Cheshire quoted £96 for 300 feet (91 metres) of boring (CALS, DCH/L/52/10) but the exact purpose is not known.

[79] Flinn, p. 74.

[80] NEIMME/Wat/35/17. Although the sandstone was reached at 12 yards depth, apparently 15 yards of walling was required.

[81] Bricks, wood or, later, cast iron were typically used for lining (Flinn, p. 76).

[82] For example, at the time of the NEIMME papers (1826–31) the principal Pits in use were 1, 10 and 28 for the Seven-Foot, Five-Foot and Two-Foot respectively but numbers 6, 8, 27 and 30 are referred to as well.

[83] T&WA, DX 198/1, p. 501.

[84] BPP [1871], p. 374. Comments by Thomas Cottingham in the 1821 court case (CALS, 261/38, 'Cottingham and Stanley') suggested levels extended about one-and-a-half miles (2.4 km) in Little Neston but there is no corroboration of this and it seems unlikely. In addition, Coal Authority 14931/2 states that the Six-Foot was 'proved 1800 yards under the river' but it is not known how, by whom or when.

[85] Coal Authority, 14923/6. C. E. de Rance, p. 99 says '2,000 yards'.

[86] *Chester Chronicle*, 23 April 1830.

[87] Another apparent pair of pits is depicted on an 1831 map by Bryant (CALS, PM 5.2) and are labelled 'Snab Pits' (by Snab Wood). They are not, though, shown on any other map or mentioned in documents so their origin and purpose is uncertain.

[88] Flinn, p. 131.

[89] Coal Authority, 14931/2.

[90] NPL, 'Mines' file.

[91] Coal Authority, 14923/1.

[92] Flinn, p. 132.

[93] For example, Coal Authority, 14923/1, 3 and 4.

[94] OS, one-inch, LXXIX (1840).

[95] Coal Authority, 14923/1 shows a pair in Little Neston described as 'staple' running between two seams. 14923/3 shows others, in Ness. No maps or documentation indicate any shafts reaching the surface offshore.

[96] Church, pp. 322–3.

[97] 'Board' often also spelt 'bord'. Robert Galloway [1898], *Annals of Coal Mining and the Coal Trade*, 2 vols (reprinted at Newton Abbott: David and Charles, 1971), ii, p. 229; BPP [1871],

p. 334; Flinn, p. 85; Matthias Dunn, *An Historical, Geological, and Descriptive View of the Coal Trade of the North of England* (Newcastle upon Tyne: Pattison and Ross, 1844), p. 135.

[98] J. Dalton in *Bell's Classical Arrangement of Fugitive Poetry*, 18 vols, ed. by John Bell (Strand: John Bell, 1789), iii, p. 50.

[99] Dunn (1844), p. 135. The point had also been made by Lord Mostyn to an 1868 meeting of the same committee (BPP [1871], p. 334). Thomas Leacroft Cottingham told the committee that the longwall system had not been used in Flintshire (ibid., pp. 374–5).

[100] B. Lewis, *Coal Mining in the Eighteenth and Nineteenth Centuries* (London: Longman, 1971), p. 42.

[101] Church, p. 333.

[103] Flinn, pp. 87–9.

[104] BPP [1871], p. 374.

[105] Langton (1979), p. 152; D. Anderson, 'Blundell's Collieries, Technical Developments 1776–1966', *THSLC*, 119 (1967), p. 123; Church, pp. 332–3.

[106] NEIMME/Wat/3/71/11. The surveyor was 'Mr. Stock', probably John Stock. The Stocks were Lancashire colliery owners, partners in 'Eccles and Stock'. Sir Thomas Stanley often bought coal from their Ashton [in Makerfield] Colliery (see page 135). Various family members (James, Thomas and John) appear in Stanley estate accounts in relation to mine surveys both at Pentrobin (Flintshire), owned and leased out by Stanley (CALS, DDX 378/30, 11 April 1812 and 9 June 1813; DDX 378/31, 4 March 1816; DDX 378/33, 8 September 1827 when John Stock was asked to advise on the 'unwrought Hollin coal') and at Ness (CALS, DDX 378/30, 9 June 1813; 378/31, 20 June 1822 and 378/8, 14 November 1837). 'Mr Stock' also undertook a survey at Little Neston Colliery in 1831 (Coal Authority, 14923/1).

[107] NEIMME/Wat/3/71/17 and 20; Coal Authority, 14923/4 and 6.

[108] NEIMME/Wat/3/71/20.

[109] NEIMME/Wat/3/71/20.

[110] NEIMME/Wat/3/71/17.

[111] BPP [1871], p. 374. Regarding the Two-foot, Coal Authority 14923/6, dated 1839, shows a complex network of pillar and stall. Coal Authority 3808/1 shows the same extent of working but almost totally devoid of pillar and stall and with some dates in the 1840s at the workings' farthest limits. It is possible this implies working back of the coal in that period. A later plan, CALS, LUNe/3384/55, includes the pillar and stall but it is not known how this plan was made.

[112] See page 35.

[113] For example, in NEIMME/Wat/3/71/6 which twice mentions safety.

[114] See pages 137–8.

[115] NEIMME/Wat/3/71/6.

[116] Flinn, p. 80.

[117] NEIMME/Wat/3/71/6.

[118] *Chester Chronicle*, 23 April 1830. Each up-brow was also termed a 'gallery'. Seventeen 'upbrows' are shown in various locations on Coal Authority, 14923/1.

[119] NEIMME/Wat/3/71/9. NEIMME/Wat/3/71/2 explains the cost of winning 211 tons (230 tonnes) of coal as being 'expensive on account of water'.

Chapter 4 – Coal Mining and Supporting Operations (continued)

[120] NEIMME/Wat/3/71/9.

[121] Flinn, p. 112.

[122] T&WA, DX 198/1, pp. 410 and 501; NEIMME/Wat/3/71/5 and 6.

[123] BPP [1871], p. 374.

[124] Ibid.

[125] BPP [1871], p. 374. The *Manchester Courier and Lancashire General Advertiser*, 31 January 1835, reported a court appearance by two beggars who claimed to have been amongst 200 men thrown out of work when the mine at Neston flooded. If this incident occurred, it could be linked to the deaths of four colliers and one of their wives in August/September 1834 (page 113). However, whilst royalty payments from Ness Colliery did fall in 1834–5 compared to the previous year (Appendix IIa), indicating lost production, the fall was not catastrophic. In any event, neither Ness Colliery nor Little Neston Colliery employed 200 people at this time; it is possible the beggars' claim was spurious.

[126] Coal Authority, 14923/1 – crownings in 1842, 1845, 1851 and 1852.

[127] Coal Authority, 8907/3. It was just such an incident that brought an end to mining at Mostyn Colliery in 1884 (NEWA, NT/1777, Papers re disaster at colliery).

[128] See Chapter 2, note 190.

Chapter 5 – Innovation: Underground Transport and Technology

[1] Waste might include coal dust, 'small coal' and pieces of other rock caught up with usable coal. The viewer, John Buddle, reckoned between 10% and 20% of coal brought to the surface was waste (Flinn, p. 32).

[2] NEIMME/Wat/3/71/15.

[3] Flinn, p. 94.

[4] Anderson (1967), p. 130.

[5] Flinn, p. 92.

[6] British Library, Add. MSS 89098, 'Diary of William Holden' (unlisted). See Chapter 4, note 38 re location.

[7] Galloway, i, p. 305; BPP [1842b], *Children's Employment Commission, Appendix to First Report of the Commissioners Mines, Pt. I* (reprinted in Shannon, Ireland: Irish University Press, 1968, Vol. 7), p. 590.

[8] Flinn, p. 94.

[9] Birmingham City Archive, MS3147/3/400/40.

[10] NEIMME/Wat/3/71/12.

[11] Ashton and Sykes, p. 62. Pennant (1796), p. 276 claims ponies were first used in Flintshire. See page 57 re use of terms 'ponies' and 'horses'.

[12] Flinn, p. 96.

[13] NEIMME/Wat/3/71/9 and /11. The boys were paid 10*d.* per day.

[14] Flinn, p. 97.

[15] Flinn, p. 95; Galloway, i, p. 324.

[16] Flinn, p. 96; R. A. Mott. 'English Waggonways of the Eighteenth Century', Pt. 1, *TNS*, 37 (1964–5), pp. 1–2.

[17] *Chester Courant*, 20 September 1796.

[18] Flinn, p. 97.

[19] NEIMME/Wat/3/71/8.

[20] *OED*, 'tram'; Flinn p. 94; Galloway, i, p. 305. Terminology could vary between locations.

[21] NEIMME/Wat/3/71/12.

[22] Ibid.

[23] NEIMME/Wat/3/71/4 and 8.

[24] NEIMME/Wat/3/71/8. Later correspondence refers to a 'waggonway' and 'waggon road' there (NEIMME/Wat/3/71/12, 15, 16, 17).

[25] NEIMME/Wat/3/71/15.

[26] NEIMME/Wat/3/71/15. This was in response to an enquiry from James Gregory, the colliery manager, about making a 'rolley road for ponies'.

[27] Mortimer, p. 246.

[28] *Chester Chronicle*, 23 June 1855.

[29] BPP [1871], p. 374.

[30] *Chester Chronicle*, 26 April 1822 and CALS, DBC 261/38, 'Cottingham and Stanley', indicate 1791 but Coal Authority 14923/1 includes the note 'Navigation by Davis, 8 Dec'r 1790'.

[31] Stephen Hughes, 'The Development of British Navigable Levels', *Journal of the Railway and Canal Historical Society*, 27, 2 (1981), pp. 2–9. More information on the various schemes can be found in Ivor Brown, 'Underground Canals in Shropshire Mines', *Bulletin of the Peak District Mines Historical Society*, 13 (1997), pp. 4, 17–23; Peter K. Roberts, 'Boat Levels Associated with Mining: I. Coal Mining', *Industrial Archaeology Review*, 5, 2 (1981a), pp. 85–95; and Mike Clarke, 'British Underground Canals associated with Mines' [trans. From the German] for Internationales Symposium 'Der Fuchsstollen in Walbrzych – ein Europaisches Technik-denkmal', 2001.

[32] Roberts (1981a), pp. 85–93; Flinn, p. 99.

[33] Roberts (1981a), pp. 85–93.

[34] Peter Roberts, 'Boat levels Associated with Mining: II. Metal Mining', *Industrial Archaeology Review*, 5, 3 (1981b), p. 204.

[35] Joseph Hayes of Neston was an initial partner in the mine, established in 1773 (Kenneth Davies, *The Greenfield Valley* (Holywell: Holywell Town Council, 1977), p. 11). DHL 52/4 (passim) mentions Neston's Joseph Lyon, and Samuel Williamson who had moved to Holywell from Neston in the 1780s, as investors (calling it the 'Holway Lead Mine'). Williamson became manager of the Parys Mine Company works at Greenfield (Pennant, 1796, p. 204). Tourists – Roberts (1981b), p. 204.

[36] Mortimer, p. 246.

[37] Coal Authority, 14923/4. *Chester Chronicle*, 26 April 1822 says '2,000 yards' – probably the direct line distance.

[38] Coal Authority, 14932/2 and 14923/4.

[39] Mortimer, p. 246.

Chapter 5 – Innovation: Underground Transport and Technology (continued)

[40] The smallest boats at Worsley are said to have carried '7 or 8 tons' (7.6–8.7 tonnes) of coal each (G. Atkinson, *The Canal Duke's Collieries* (Manchester: Neil Richardson, n.d.), pp. 24–5); the boats described at Ness carried 1,920 lbs (871 kg) assuming a hundredweight of 120 lbs. 'Long, narrow boats' were also used in the underground canal at the lead mine at Holywell (Arthur Aikin, *Journal of a Tour Through North Wales and Part of Shropshire* (London, 1797), p. 173).

[41] Mortimer, p. 246.

[42] See page 37–9.

[43] *Chester Chronicle*, 26 April 1822 records that Cottingham's claim related to trespass up to the date of the April 1822 trial.

[44] Coal Authority 14923/1 and /3.

[45] Coal Authority, 14923/4.

[46] There is, however, an 1829 reference by Ness Colliery's viewer, John Watson, to 'No. 21 Pit Navigation' in connection with drainage (NEIMME/Wat/3/71/15). This seems to be a reference to the old No. 6 Pit navigation which, some years earlier, was accessible from No. 21.

[47] Mortimer, p. 246.

[48] NEIMME/Wat/3/71/2.

[49] CALS, PM 11/7, surveyed 1770–1.

[50] CALS, DBC 261/38, 'Cottingham v Stanley Bt.'. The location is depicted on Coal Authority 14932/2.

[51] In 1776–7, annual production was probably around 22,075 tons/24,039 tonnes (Table 2.1). Assumes baskets weighed four hundredweight each (pages 72 and 80), 20 hundredweight to the ton, and 313 working days per annum (page 104). In practice, it may have required more baskets as a 'ton' could weigh up to 36 hundredweight (see Glossary).

[52] Flinn, p. 100.

[53] NEIMME/Wat/3/71/12.

[54] NEIMME/Wat/3/71/6.

[55] CALS, DBC 261/38, 'Cottingham v Stanley Bt.'.

[56] A detailed description of their use is given in CALS, DBC 261/38, 'Instructions for Indictment'.

[57] CALS, DBC 261/38, 'Brief for the Prosecution' and other documents.

[58] *Chester Courant*, 2 September 1828.

[59] Information in this paragraph from Flinn, pp. 114–16, unless indicated.

[60] J. Rhodes, 'Early Steam Engines in Flintshire', *TNS*, 41 (1968–9), pp. 217–16; The Cultural Heritage Knowledge Exchange Hub, passim. Many others had been in use in lead mines (C. Williams, *Industry in Clwyd, an Illustrated History* (Hawarden: Clwyd Record Office, 1986), p. 7).

[61] CALS, QJB 3/12.

[62] *OED*, 'engineer'.

[63] Flintshire engines: Rhodes, pp. 217–25; The Cultural Heritage Knowledge Exchange Hub, passim. Peter Ford Mason, *The Pit Sinkers of Northumberland and Durham* (Stroud: History Press, 2012), pp. 122–3 and pers. corresp. suggests Pearson married Mary Stott of a pit sinking family in 1736 at Chester-le-Street, Durham. If so, he was re-marrying at Neston, or this was his son.

[64] LA, DDCL 1065.

[65] NPR.

[66] The Cultural Heritage Knowledge Exchange Hub. The first engine in mid-Cheshire was probably erected at the saltworks at Marston in 1788 (W. Chaloner, 'The Cheshire Activities of Matthew Boulton and James Watt, of Soho, near Birmingham, 1776–1817', *TLCAS*, 61 (1951), p. 131).

[67] W. Shercliff, D. Kitching and J. Ryan, *Poynton, A Coalmining Village: Social History, Transport and Industry 1700–1939* (Poynton: W. H. Shercliff, 1983), p. 15 states that the existing engine at Norbury was being replaced in 1764. There was an 'engineer' at the colliery nine years earlier – see note 69.

[68] CALS, PM 11/7.

[69] Poynton parish register, 29 March 1755; *Manchester Mercury*, 9 October 1764.

[70] University of Manchester JRL, Legh of Lyme Muniments, Box T D, No. 1, draft lease 1 March 1795. See also Shercliff, Kitching and Ryan, p. 15.

[71] *Adams's Weekly Courant*, 5 December 1775 in which he was described as being 'late of Moncot [Mancot, Flintshire], late of Denna'.

[72] University of Manchester JRL, Legh of Lyme Muniments, Box 6, Folder 59; *Adams's Weekly Courant*, 19 December 1775.

[73] University of Manchester JRL, RYCH/1718 (1–5).

[74] The average price for coal indicated in the accounts was 8s. 6d. (42.5p) per ton; for slack it was 2s. 3d. (11p).

[75] Kanefsky (1979), p. 172. Calculation assumes seven-day operation. Twelve-hour assumption: see note 124 below.

[76] Kanefsky (1979), pp. 453–6.

[77] R. Mott, 'The Newcomen Engine in the Eighteenth Century', *TNS*, 35 (1962–3), p. 69.

[78] Flinn, p. 102.

[79] Flinn, pp. 101–2.

[80] Birmingham City Archive, MS3147/3/400/40.

[81] A. Nuvolari, B. Verspagen and N. von Tunzelmann, 'The Diffusion of the Steam Engine in Eighteenth Century Britain' *Applied Evolutionary Economics and the Knowledge-Based Economy* ed. by A. Pyka and H. Hanusch (Cheltenham: Edward Elgar, 2006), p. 194.

[82] Birmingham City Archive, MS3147/3/400/41.

[83] An octogenarian retired farmer living in one of the two buildings in the colliery area which survive from the period of Ness Colliery told this author in 2006 that a well on the east side of the building, i.e. on the *opposite* side of the building to the estuary, still had to be plugged up occasionally to prevent inundation by the highest tides. A spectacularly high tide covered some of the former colliery area in December 2013.

[84] J. Kanefsky and J. Robey say that Boulton and Watt had under 30% of the steam engine market in the last quarter of the eighteenth century ('Steam Engines in 18th Century Britain: A Quantitative Assessment', *Technology and Culture*, 21 (1980), 2, p. 185).

[85] John Goodchild, 'John Gibbons of Oswestry: an Eighteenth Century Capitalist', *Memoirs*, (Northern Mines Research Society, 1991), pp. 67, 69. Nuvolari, Verspagen and von Tunzelmann, p. 173.

[86] CALS, DBC 261/38, 'Cottingham and Stanley'.

Chapter 5 – Innovation: Underground Transport and Technology (continued)

[87] *Chester Courant*, 20 September 1796 and 1 September 1812. CALS, DDX 378/30, 17 April 1813.

[88] Institution of Mechanical Engineers, STE/1/5/2/6; Brian Lewis, *The Cabry Family* (Mold: Railway and Canal Historical Society, 1994), p. 7.

[89] W. Skeat, *George Stephenson, The Engineer and His Letters* (London: Institution of Mechanical Engineers, 1973), pp. 26–35.

[90] Institution of Mechanical Engineers, STE/1/5/2/6, 2 December 1819; *Chester Chronicle*, 26 April 1822.

[91] For Nicholas Wood: Flinn, p. 26; T&WA, DX 198/1, pp. 410, 501. For Henderson: see pages 38-40; M. Lewis, pp. 27–41. Storey: see Lionel Rolt, *George and Robert Stephenson – The Railway Revolution* (London: Longmans, 1967), p. 72; STE/1/5/2/6, 2 March 1820 and DBC 261/38, 'Cottingham v Stanley Bt.'.

[92] NEIMME/Wat/3/71/1–22.

[93] Institution of Mechanical Engineers, STE/1/5/2/6, 30 June 1824; Skeat, p. 65.

[94] CALS, DBC 261/38, 'Indictment of Charles Evans'; Institution of Mechanical Engineers, STE/1/5/2/6.

[95] IME, STE/1/5/2/6, 8 May 1825.

[96] NEIMME/Wat/3/71/9.

[97] CALS, DBC 261/38, letter dated 17 July 1828.

[98] CALS, QDV 2/304 (Land tax records) which show Cabry (senior) as living in Little Neston from 1826.

[99] CALS, DBC 261/38, letter dated 17 July 1828.

[100] See page 39.

[101] TNA, J 90/84, 22 February 1823. See also page 42.

[102] NEIMME/Wat/3/71/22.

[103] His wife, Mary, was buried 26 June 1847 (NPR). Cabry's name disappears from the parish rate assessment from 1848–9 (CALS, P 149/8). In the 1851 census he is a 'retired engineer' living with one of his daughters, Ann, in York.

[104] He owned and occupied the property, 'late of Ann Hayes' in Ness (CALS, QDV 2/304). Ann Hayes had been landlady of the pub until 1828 (CALS, QDL 2/8/12, Alesellers Recognisances). There do not appear to be any explicit references to it as a pub during the 1830s but Cabry was being called on annually to supply ale to the Stanley estate (e.g. CALS, DDX 378/7, 6 May 1834) suggesting he was still in the business. In 1842, he was described as owning a 'public house and land' (CALS, P/149/8, Church Rate Assessment). Isaac Slater (late Pigot and Co.'s), *Royal National Commercial Directory and Topography of the Counties of Chester, Cumberland, Durham, Lancaster, Northumberland, Westmoreland and York* (Manchester: Isaac Slater, 1848), p. 73, lists the Wheat Sheaf Inn [*sic*] under Cabry's name.

[105] CALS, M 5.2, Bryant 's 'Map of the County Palatine of Chester from Actual Survey' (1831). The Wheatsheaf later moved to the centre of Ness.

[106] 1841 census, Ness.

[107] NPR, 25 December 1826 (Mary), 12 October 1828 (Thomas), 27 March 1835 (Charles) and 22 September 1837 (Barbara).

[108] 1851 census, Ness: 'engineer'; 'publican' description in 1861 census.

[109] George Greenwell, *A Practical Treatise on Mine Engineering* (Newcastle: M. and M. W. Lambert, 1855), pp. 140–1. Michael Bailey, 'Robert Stephenson and Co. 1823–1829', *TNS*, 50 (1978), p. 131. It seems likely that this is the 'Iron Work' delivered to Cabry via Stephenson in Liverpool a few weeks later, referred to in a letter cited in the *Cheshire Observer*, 22 July 1893.

[110] NEIMME/Wat/3/71/9.

[111] Rolt, pp. 106–7. Robert appears to have had a failed interest in Mostyn Colliery around this time (*Cheshire Observer*, 22 July 1893).

[112] Institution of Mechanical Engineers, STE/1/5/1/10–11, 23 October and 16 November 1824.

[113] *Chester Chronicle*, 19 and 26 November 1830 and 27 May 1831.

[114] M. Lister, *The Industrial Railways of Port Sunlight and Bromborough Port* (Blandford: Oakwood Press, 1980), p. 8. Stephenson is said to have met another future renowned civil engineer, Thomas Brassey, at Storeton where he was manager (*Cheshire Sheaf*, 'Stray Notes from Neston Parish Register', 3rd series, 51 (1956), p. 24); Historic England, *Strategic Stone Study: A Building Stone Atlas of Merseyside* (2017), p. 11 <https://www2.bgs.ac.uk/mineralsuk/download/EHCountyAtlases/Merseyside_Building_Stone_Atlas.pdf > [accessed 2 January 2023]. Brassey grew up on Sir Thomas Stanley's estate at Buerton in south Cheshire; his father is sometimes mentioned in Stanley estate accounts.

[115] *Chester Chronicle*, 10 October 1834.

[116] BPP [1835], *Report from the Select Committee on Accidents in Mines* (reprinted in Shannon, Ireland: Irish University Press, 1968), p. 116.

[117] See page 33.

[118] BPP [1835], p. 82.

[119] Joseph Wright ed., *English Dialect Dictionary*, (London: Henry Frowde, 1904).

[120] NEIMME/Wat/3/71/15 and CALS, DBC 261/38, 17 July 1828.

[121] NEIMME/Wat/3/71/15.

[122] NEIMME/Wat/3/71/2.

[123] NEIMME/Wat/3/71/6.

[124] For example, in NEIMME/Wat/3/71/5, 17, 20.

[125] NEIMME/Wat/3/71/4; Farey, pp. 193 and 251–2.

[126] For example, CALS, PM 13/8a (1829) which records an 'Engine', Coal Authority 3808/1 which has an 'Engine Pit' (1839), and Coal Authority 14923/3 (1839) which has 2 x 'Engine'.

[127] DBC 261/38, 17 July 1828. Variously also spelt in contemporary records: Sharpe, Sharps and Sharpes.

[128] NEIMME/Wat/3/71/17.

[129] See Chapter 3, note 56.

[130] NEIMME/Wat/3/71/17.

[131] BPP [1871], p. 374.

[132] *Chester Chronicle*, 23 June 1855.

[133] Church, p. 318.

[134] John Langton and R. J. Morris, *Atlas of Industrialising Britain* (London: Methuen, 1986), p. 74.

[135] NRO, 725 B7, p. 139, Letter from William Armstrong to George Wythes, 17 July 1869.

Chapter 6 – The Colliery Employees and Their Working Conditions

[1] The list excludes four men termed 'miner', all with Welsh connections, who appear just once in the register and who were more likely to be ore workers or pit sinkers in Neston temporarily.

[2] The issue of under-recording is discussed more fully in Chapter 12.

[3] Burrows (also Burroughs): eight NPR entries, 4 July 1759 to 11 January 1769 (plus possible 1757 marriage as a 'servant'). Evans in Burton and Neston PRs, 10 October 1756 to 9 October 1769.

[4] Men termed 'Labourer' are, however, occasionally specifically listed in NPR as living or working at one of the collieries (in 1788, 1804, 1811, 1829, 1833 and 1839).

[5] Based on a survey of early nineteenth-century Welsh names in J. Rowlands and S. Rowlands, *The Surnames of Wales* (Federation of Family History Societies, 1996), pp. 4, 43–4. The surnames of the sixty men were amongst the twenty-two most common in Wales.

[6] For example, Wynne, Rogers and Jervas/Jarvis.

[7] Church, pp. 129–35.

[8] Julie Peakman, *Emma Hamilton* (London: Haus Publishing, 2005), p. 4. His father Thomas, brought his wife and two other children from Madeley; a fourth child, Mary Kidd – the mother of Emma Hamilton – was baptised at Hawarden on 19 May 1743. I am grateful to Dr Geoff Wright for some of this information.

[9] Dodd (1971), pp. 192–3; Willett, p. 158; T. W. Pritchard, *The Making of Buckley and District* (Wrexham: Bridge Books, 2012), p. 91.

[10] Dodd (1929), p. 205. See also Pritchard (2012), p. 91.

[11] Robinson – see page 213; Kendrick – NPR, 13 June 1764, 28 November 1789 and others, plus Hope PR, 11 December 1733; see Rowlands and Rowlands, pp. 119–20 re occurrence of 'Kendrick'; Parry – Hawarden PR, 27 August 1768, NPR, 6 October 1771 and others.

[12] NPR, 6 January 1763.

[13] Hawarden PR, 27 November 1763. The Duckworths had long-standing associations with the Hawarden pits (Pritchard (2012), p. 89).

[14] A. J. MacGregor ed., *The Alehouses and Alehouse-Keepers of Cheshire, 1629–1828* (n.p.: Caupona, 1992), p. 130.

[15] Langton (1979), pp. 154, 167.

[16] Langton (1979), p. 167.

[17] NPR, 29 March 1765.

[18] None of these surnames had any significant prior history in Neston parish. For Manchester and more on Marsh see Geoff Wright, *Emma, Lady Hamilton (1765–1815): Neston's Most Famous Daughter* (Burton and Neston History Society, n.d.), pp. 9–10. Skeath appears in Ness militia records (see pages 234–5). This unusual surname also appears in various Prescot PR and CMLBA entries, including as a collier. A William Bramhall was born at Prescot, 23 January 1731 (PR, Prescot). A collier of that name buried his son Thomas at Neston, 26 December 1759 (NPR); collier William Bramwell (a posthumous misspelling?) drowned at Ness 1761 (NPR, 19 January, *Adams's Weekly Courant*, 20 January and CALS, Z QCI/23/7) – see note 189. Thomas As(h)bury, collier of Whiston, married Elizabeth Low in 1746 (PR, All Saints, Childwall) and had several children. A couple of the same names baptised a child at Neston on 1 January 1761.

[19] Baptism of daughter, PR of St Mary the Virgin, Prescot, 5 June 1767.

[20] See page 214.

[21] Censuses, 1851 for Little Neston (Ann, widow of Thomas who had three children in Neston with one in Whiston in between) and Great Neston (Joseph – eldest son, age thirteen, born Whiston; first daughter, age eleven, and other two children born Neston).

[22] NPR, 13 April 1842.

[23] Eccles PR, 26 March 1769; NPR baptism 2 July 1769.

[24] NPR, 15 October 1758.

[25] NPR, 19 March 1762 as 'Jelico'.

[26] For example, at Wolverhampton and Bushbury (FMP).

[27] Flinn, p. 26.

[28] Pennant (1796), p. 276.

[29] J. G. Jenkins et al., eds, *A History of the County of Stafford*, 14 vols (London: Oxford University Press, 1963), viii, p. 1.

[30] See Chapter 5, note 63.

[31] Dodd (1929), pp. 220–1; Langton (2000), p. 86.

[32] *Adams's Weekly Courant*, 21 July 1767.

[33] For example, [T]Hatto-Heath Colliery near St Helens advertised for colliers, making similar promises to Ness but did not offer full wages (*Adams's Weekly Courant*, 30 January 1770).

[34] See page 203.

[35] *Adams's Weekly Courant*, 1 September 1767.

[36] See 230–1 re literacy.

[37] LA, DDCL 1065; see Table 6.4 re Hawarden details and source.

[38] Hawarden's total annual wage bill in 1770 was 'about £4,500', for 194 men. At Ness it was £3,996, i.e. 89% of Hawarden's, and this percentage has been applied to the workforce number. The figures assume the workforce composition and days-per-week worked at the collieries were similar. The wage figure for Ness may possibly, though, have been artificially inflated around this time as new pits were being dug – pay for an unknown temporary number of specialist pit sinkers may be included in the total. The workforce figure can be tested by looking at average wages. The 'daily pay' at Hawarden was said to be £16 0*s*. 6*d*., equivalent to 1*s*. 8*d*. per day per man (the Hawarden document suggests most men were earning 1*s*. 6*d*. per day but the few salaried officials would have earned considerably more and also, presumably, overtime or extra days would have been offered to the colliers from time to time). Applying these rates to the Neston salary figure, and assuming the same number of days worked as implied at Hawarden (261), gives a figure of 184 men at Neston – reasonably close to the estimated 172.

[39] See pages 191 and 243.

[40] See page 21 re annual output.

[41] The Hawarden area was said to be producing about 20,000 tons (21,780 tonnes) per annum with, apparently, 194 workers – about 103 tons (112 tonnes) per man. See also Flinn, pp. 364–5.

[42] W. Farrer and J. Brownbill, eds, *The Victoria County History of Lancaster*, 8 vols (London: Archibald Constable, 1908), ii, p. 358 mention about 300 tons (327 tonnes) per man at Worsley in 1777 although the basis of calculation is not detailed; and at Orrell near Wigan it appears to have been 318 tons (346 tonnes) per man in 1772 (Anderson, 1964, p. 74).

[43] See pages 22–3.

Chapter 6 – The Colliery Employees and Their Working Conditions (continued)

[44] *Chester Chronicle*, 26 April 1822.

[45] Census, Ness: thirty-five workers were chiefly employed in non-agricultural occupations in 1821 but seventy in 1831. Little Neston saw an increase in equivalent workers from three to fourteen.

[46] TNA, HO 73/53/78, Report of Digby Neave.

[47] Three children said to be 'assisting' their fathers, discussed later, have been included in the count.

[48] Thirty-one labourers in Ness, four in Little Neston.

[49] The 'Labourer at coal mine' has been counted in the 105.

[50] Census (1851), Ness.

[51] NPR; CALS, LGW 1/2, 3 October 1838.

[52] NPR until 30 November 1814; census, Huyton 1841; CALS, LGW 1/3, 10 January 1844 and 20 August 1845.

[53] Census, Tarbock, 1841 (Standish was a coal miner) and 1851 (Standish, now seventy-two, was a labourer).

[54] NPR, 24 May 1850; Census (Wigan) 1851 as Anglesley; Parl. Papers., *Report from the Select Committee on Coal Mines*, Committee Reports, Paper 509 (1852), p. 84; Death Certificate, 30 November 1852.

[55] Examples are John Bartley and John Hughes (both in Flint census, 1851), and William Bryan (Holywell, 1861 census). John Hampson had also spent time in Flintshire (census, Great Neston, 1851). See also page 237, and census details at *nestoncollieries.org*

[56] NEIMME/Wat/3/71/4, covering the full 1825–6 business year, indicates that labour costs of 'the brow' (excluding the accountant's salary) were 26% of overall labour costs. NEIMME/Wat/3/71/9 (two weeks in 1827) lists fifty-six underground workers and at least fifteen (27% of the total) on the surface; the latter also accounted for 27% of the costs. The percentage varied from colliery to colliery. Of the small workforce at Orrell in 1772, 40% were on the surface (D. Anderson, 'Blundell's Collieries: Wages, Disputes and Conditions of Work', *THSLC*, 117 (1965), p. 74). See also Flinn, p. 332.

[57] Joshua Small (who had kept the accounts for Chester's Foundling Hospital) was the colliery's 'agent' in 1769 (*Adams's Weekly Courant*, 19 December 1769); William Taylor, colliery agent by 1803 to 1816 was a 'Book-keeper' (CMLBA, 2 June 1799) and James Gregory was variously 'agent' and 'auditor' in the NEIMME correspondence.

[58] In 1786 the colliery had an 'underground steward', James Stock (NPR, 15 November; also 7 February 1790). John Rowland was 'Underground Agent' at Ness, *c.*1790s (TNA, J 90/82, undated/untitled note). Thomas Roberts was 'Underground Agent for Mr. Cottingham' (*Chester Chronicle*, 26 April 1822).

[59] NEIMME/Wat/3/71/9, 19 November 1827.

[60] See Appendix IIa. The letter records that 293 tons (319 tonnes) of coal were raised in the fortnight which, if production was at the same rate throughout the year, equates to 7,618 tons (8,296 tonnes).

[61] Galloway, ii, p. 372; Flinn, p. 92.

[62] Gunpowder did not, incidentally, appear as an expense in the 1769–70 accounts (LA, DDCL 1065), suggesting it was not in use then. It was apparently used at Orrell (Lancs.) for shaft-sinking by 1788 (Anderson, 1967, pp. 117–18).

[63] Hatcher, p. 380.

[64] TNA, J 90/81, 25 February 1822.

[65] Ashton and Sykes, p. 68. BPP [1842b], p. 587 states that at Killingworth, near Newcastle, cutters represented half to two-thirds of the entire workforce; at Ness they represented one-sixth.

[66] See page 69.

[67] BPP [1842c], p. 161.

[68] See, for example, Pritchard (2012), p. 91 and Flinn, p. 330.

[69] *OED*, 'hanger-on'.

[70] BPP [1842a], *Children's Employment Commission, First Report of the Commissioners: Mines* (reprinted in Shannon, Ireland: Irish University Press, 1968), p. 47.

[71] As happened in Shropshire: Barrie Trinder, *The Industrial Revolution in Shropshire*, 3rd edn, (Stroud: Phillimore, 2016), p. 164.

[72] BPP [1842c], *Children's Employment Commission, Appendix to First Report of the Commissioners: Mines, Pt. II* (reprinted in Shannon, Ireland: Irish University Press, 1968), p. 127.

[73] 110 out of the 547 men identified in Chapter 12. To give just one of many possible examples, James Lawley of Ness appears in NPR (baptisms) seven times between 1787 and 1801, being described, in sequence, as collier, labourer, collier, collier, labourer, collier and collier. There is no obvious seasonal pattern in the men's change of occupation.

[74] DBC 261/38 letter dated 17 July 1828; NEIMME/Wat/3/71/17.

[75] LA, DDCL 1065.

[76] NEWA, P/30/1/232/1. The apprenticeship is first referred to in 1773 in NEWA, P/30/1/55: Register of Holywell Children Apprenticed; the 1775 Indenture appears to formalise the agreement. See also pages 213–4.

[77] 1841 and 1851 censuses, Ness: Thomas Sharp, basket maker (mentioned as living at the colliery, 1851); 1853 'basket maker' in NPR.

[78] NPR: Thomas Lyon, 28 October 1787; James Webster, 2 July 1810 (also 'the blacksmith and gin driver' in NEIMME/Wat/3/71/9, Table 6.3) and Edward Evans 3 August 1838 and 23 July 1841.

[79] Kate Williams, *England's Mistress* (London: Arrow, 2007), p. 4; Hawarden PR, Mary Kidd baptised 19 May 1743; NPR, Samuel baptised 15 April 1764.

[80] CALS, QJF 191/2, 26 March 1763.

[81] NPR.

[82] NPR 1759–1772 in which he was variously described as living at Little Neston, Ness, Ness Holt and Neston; LA, DDCL 1065.

[83] John Cordy Jeaffreson, *Lady Hamilton and Lord Nelson, an Historical Biography*, 2 vols (London: Hurst and Blackett, 1888), ii, pp. 136–8.

[84] PR, St Mary the Virgin, Prescot. Baptismal entry 6 July 1740.

[85] Ibid., baptised 11 March 1747 (born 26 February).

Chapter 6 – The Colliery Employees and Their Working Conditions (continued)

[86] CALS, MG 9/27; NPR 29 December 1772 and 18 November 1773. He named one of his daughters Alice – his mother's name; other children were William, Thomas and Mary.

[87] NPR, 28 October 1787. He gave a statement prior to the 1821 court case (CALS, DBC 261/38 'Cottingham v Stanley Bt.'). In 1822, he was threatened with a removal order under the Poor Law from Great Neston to Little Neston (quashed on appeal in 1823; CALS, QJB 4/2), pp. 347 and 421 and died in Ness in 1826 at a stated age of eighty-one (NPR), although more probably seventy-nine based on his baptism record.

[88] K. Williams, pp. 358–62.

[89] Sir Thomas Stanley paid the colliery for smith's work at a farm in Raby on 17 November 1834 (CALS, DDX 378/7). Also, Thomas Lyon undertook work at Prenton in 1797 (CALS, DHL 52/4, 24 December). He was paid directly and it is not certain whether he was also working at the colliery at the time.

[90] One of the five, Thomas Oakes, was living at 'Little Neston Colliery' after the probable date of its closure (NPR, 10 August 1849); it seems likely the place name was being used as an address/location (as was also done in the 1850s sale advertisements) rather than as a place of employment.

[91] 'Map of a Pier in Little Neston' (part of CALS, D5363) depicts 'Forshalls house'. The property is depicted on Arundel Archives, TP60 'A Plan of Little Neston' dated 1788. 'Colliery Farm' in Historic England Archives, SC00134, 'Lord Edmund B. Talbot's Little Neston Estate' sale particulars. This is not, incidentally, the colliery's own farm discussed in Chapter 4.

[92] NPR, four baptisms between 16 October 1761 and 15 March 1767.

[93] Baptism of son, John, 27 March 1769.

[94] LA, DDCL 1065; NPR, 'labourer' on 13 March 1776 and 21 January 1781 (also 26 April 1772 – no recorded occupation).

[95] Ashton and Sykes, p. 62; Flinn p. 329.

[96] Anderson (1965), p. 109; Farrer and Brownbill, p. 358.

[97] CALS, C/10/36, DAR/D/59 and DAR/D/77/11.

[98] Ashton and Sykes, p. 134; Flinn, pp. 368 and 374–6.

[99] The combined method is mentioned in relation to both Pit Nos. 1 and 10. Metric conversion assumes 32 cwt of 120 lbs to the collier ton (NEIMME/Wat/3/71/12 and 17). This combined approach was used occasionally at Hawarden too: for example, CALS, DAR/D/59, 21 December 1771 shows James Taylor and his drawer being paid 2s. 4d. per day, plus 4d. per yard driven.

[100] A similar approach in Durham is illustrated by Dave Douglass ('The Durham Pitman' in *Miners, Quarrymen and Saltworkers*, ed. by Raphael Samuel (London: Routledge, Kegan and Paul, 1977), p. 241.

[101] They averaged 24.6 cwt per cutter-shift – less than all the figures quoted in Flinn (p. 365) such as Staffordshire in 1815 (38 cwt). Figures for Orrell Fire Engine Colliery, Lancs. in 1776 also equate to 38 cwt (of 120 lbs) per cutter-shift (Anderson, 1964, p. 74).

[102] NEIMME/Wat/3/71/9 which states the rate per yard was 20d. (8p) for 'dry narrow places' (i.e. stalls) and 3s. (15p) for 'wet narrow places' – an 80% uplift.

103 NEIMME/Wat/3/71/5 which states 10*s*. (50p) per yard for the former, 5*s*. (25p) per yard for the latter.

104 Rawson, pp. 126, 135.

105 Assuming a six-day week.

106 Based on a week of 6¼ days, the Ostlers and drivers averaged 2*s*. 2*d*. (11p); the No. 10 brow man averaged 1*s*. 10*d*. (9p) per day for six days.

107 See also BPP [1842c], p. 180.

108 NEIMME/Wat/3/71/17, 19 May 1829.

109 See, for example, NEIMME/Wat/3/71/2.

110 LA, DDCL 1065.

111 LA, DDBL 54/45.

112 Ashhurst took on managership of the colliery between 31 December 1816 and 4 February 1824 (CALS, DDX 378/31, 7 April 1817 and 29 March 1824). NEIMME/Wat/3/71/4 states payments for 'Accountants Salary' of £54 10*s*. 10*d*. in 1824 (for 1823?), £100 in 1825 covering the period 'to January 1825', but nothing indicated in 1826; the relationship between these payments, which were probably also to Ashhurst as accountant, and those to him as manager are not clear.

113 Assuming a six-day week.

114 NEIMME/Wat/3/71/11.

115 Flinn, p. 380.

116 Anderson (1964), p. 74.

117 CALS, DBC 261/38, letter dated 17 July 1828.

118 T. S. Ashton and J. Sykes, *The Coal Industry of the Eighteenth Century* (Manchester: Manchester University Press, 1964), p. 142.

119 CALS, DDX 378/30, 2 February 1805.

120 Ashton and Sykes, p. 141; Flinn, p. 379; Anderson (1965), p. 113; John Benson, *British Coalminers in the Nineteenth Century* (Harlow: Longman, 1989), pp. 64–5.

121 Wigan Archives, D Lei B/1/A/4, Book 5.

122 CALS, DAR D/59, Accounts: Hawarden coal pit.

123 For example, LA, DDCL 1065 (1769–70 accounts) and NEIMME/Wat/3/71/19 (1830).

124 Flinn, p. 369; Ashton and Sykes p. 165; Anderson (1964), p. 74.

125 Ashton and Sykes, p. 165.

126 CALS, DBC 261/38, letter dated 17 July 1828.

127 NEIMME/Wat/3/71/17.

128 Flinn, p. 369.

129 The 'Daily pay' was stated at £16 0*s*. 6*d*., and the 'Yearly pay with salaries, about £4,500 0s 0d'.

130 Ashton and Sykes, pp. 168–70.

131 NEIMME/Wat/3/71/9.

132 Flinn, pp. 368–73. Six-day weeks were the norm at Mostyn Colliery in 1825 (Lewis Jones, *The Coal Mines of Mostyn* (Rhewl: Lewis Jones 1997), p. 70).

133 Ashton and Sykes, pp. 166–7; Flinn, p. 373.

Chapter 6 – The Colliery Employees and Their Working Conditions (continued)

[134] University of Manchester JRL, RYCH/1718 (1–2); NEIMME/Wat/3/71/11, for 1826–7 and 1827–8.

[135] BPP [1842c], p. 369.

[136] E. Royston Pike, *Human Documents of the Industrial Revolution in Britain* (London: George Allen and Unwin, 1966), pp. 85, 128.

[137] BPP [1833], *First Report of the Commissioners Inquiring into the Employment of Children in Factories* (reprinted in Shannon, Ireland: Irish University Press, 1968), D.2, p. 82.

[138] BPP [1842c], p. 375. See also Peter Kirby, 'Short Stature among Coal-Mining Children: A Rejoinder', *Economic History Review*, 50, 3 (August 1997), pp. 539–40, Flinn, pp. 393–4, Dodd (1929), p. 220 and B. Lewis (1971), p. 29. Langton (2000, pp. 78–80) makes a similar point.

[139] Parl. Papers, *Second Annual Report of the Poor Law Commissioners, Appendices A–E,* Paper 595 (1836), p. 378.

[140] TNA, J 90/83, 'Labour on Land'.

[141] B. Freeman and Lt. E. S. Parry, *Historical Records of the Denbighshire Hussars Imperial Yeomanry from their Formation in 1795 till 1906* (Wrexham: Woodall, Minshall, Thomas and Co., 1909), p. 62; Emlyn Rogers, 'Labour Struggles in Flintshire', Pt. 1, *Flintshire Historical Society Publications*, 14 (1954), 47.

[142] Challinor R., *The Lancashire and Cheshire Miners* (Newcastle upon Tyne: Frank Graham, 1972), pp. 17–18; Ashton and Sykes, Ch. 6; Flinn, pp. 350–7; Langton (1979), p. 194; Anderson (1965), p. 112.

[143] E. Rogers (1954), p. 47.

[144] Challinor, pp. 23–4.

[145] NEIMME/Wat/3/71/9.

[146] Anderson (1965), p. 115; Flinn, pp. 401–5.

[147] Anderson (1965), p. 115; Flinn, p. 401.

[148] E. Rogers (1954), p. 48.

[149] Challinor, pp. 25–6; E. Rogers (1954), p. 49.

[150] Battiscombe, p. 14.

[151] *Chester Courant*, 29 November 1831.

[152] Emlyn Rogers (1955). 'Labour Struggles in Flintshire', Pt. 2, *Flintshire Historical Society Publications*, 15, p. 103; A. J. Taylor, 'The Miners' Association of Great Britain and Ireland, 1842–48: A Study in the Problem of Integration'. *Economica*, 22, No. 85 (1955), pp. 45–60; Bangor Archives, Mostyn MSS 7009; Challinor, p. 32.

[153] *Chester Chronicle*, 29 April 1842; E. Rogers (1955), pp. 103–5; Bangor Archives, Mostyn MSS, 7009.

[154] British Library, Add. MSS 89098, 29 May 1829.

[155] NEIMME/Wat/3/71/16.

[156] Dodd (1929), p. 221.

[157] Bangor Archives, Mona Mine 3216 (18 November 1831) states that 'nearly all the collieries in the River Dee are idle due to the Union Clubs'. These collieries were named as Mostyn, Bagillt, Greenfield and Flint (*Chester Chronicle*, 25 November 1831) leaving the possibility that the Neston collieries were exceptions.

[158] Flinn, pp. 426–9; Challinor, p. 22; B. Lewis (1971), p. 67.

[159] *Neston Stone Age to Steam Age,* ed. by Susan Chambers (Burton and Neston History Society, 2014), pp. 117, 213.

[160] CALS, uncatalogued: Puddington estate accounts, 1844–1856, 20 October 1853.

[161] Church, p. 582.

[162] L. J. Thomas and L. P. Thomas. *Coal Geology* (Chichester: John Wiley, 2002), p. 259; Flinn, pp. 128–9.

[163] Thomas and Thomas, p. 259.

[164] Galloway, ii, p. 34.

[165] BPP [1835], *Accidents in Mines*, p. 208. The report mentions thirty-six lives lost at Mostyn in 1806. Dodd (1929, p. 226) lists many explosions and fires occurring in North Wales between 1775 and 1849, several with multiple casualties. There had also been a major colliery fire at Flint prior to 1789 (William Camden, *Britannia*, 2nd edn (London: T. Payne and Sons, 1789), p. 592. See also Galloway, i, pp. 405, 491.

[166] *Chester Chronicle*, 7 July 1837. No. 1 Pit was said to have been 'opened' in 1837 (CALS, DDX 378/8, 4 December) – maybe actually a reopening following closure in the accident.

[167] CALS, Z HI 52, 12 August 1773.

[168] CALS, Z HI 52, 2 January 1776; NPR, 19 January 1776.

[169] NPR, 19 May 1777; CALS, Z HI 52, 26 June 1774 with two other men similarly injured. Child baptised 22 June 1777.

[170] BPP [1835], p. 82; T&WA, DX 198/1, pp. 410, 501.

[171] BPP [1835], p. 116. See page 84 re location.

[172] P. E. H. Hair, 'Mortality from Violence in British Coal-Mines, 1800–1850', *Economic History Review*, 21 (1968), p. 546.

[173] NPL, T104/1/3–5, 5 May 1790.

[174] *Chester Courant*, 20 June 1815 (mistakenly naming *Thomas* Cottrell). Further child baptised 4 February 1816 (NPR).

[175] *Chester Courant*, 20 June 1815.

[176] See pages 203–4.

[177] See page 215.

[178] Dodd (1971), p. 196; Trinder (2016), p. 165.

[179] Ashton and Sykes, p. 56; BPP [1842b], p. 545.

[180] BPP [1842c], p. 368.

[181] BPP [1842c], p. 372.

[182] NPR 7 July 1838. Thanks to Mandy Green for bringing this case to my attention; James Lewis was her great-great-great grandfather.

[183] *Chester Courant*, 22 February 1814.

[184] See, for example, several references in the 1842 Children's Employment Commission's report such as BPP [1842b], p. 196 and [1842c], pp. 63, 127, 159.

[185] A steel mill was an alternative light source but it was a far from perfect alternative.

[186] Galloway, i, p. 439; Dodd (1971), p. 196.

[187] Dodd (1971), p. 196. This was the practice in North Wales and Lancashire.

[188] There is no apparent record of his baptism so his age is not known.

Chapter 6 – The Colliery Employees and Their Working Conditions (continued)

[189] The burials on 19 January 1761 of William Bramwell and Robert Griffiths, both described as 'Collier', were also recorded but they did not apparently die at work. The following day's *Chester Courant* reported they were found drowned on the estuary's sands; see also CALS, Z QCI/23/6, 23/7.

[190] NPR: married 8 April 1776; buried 17 May 1777; child baptised 5 July 1777.

[191] University of Manchester University JRL, RYCH/1718 (3). Oddly, though, coal was still reported as being raised that week although quantities were much lower the following week, perhaps indicating some lag effect.

[192] NPR, 29 August 1834 (Thomas Fabby), 31 August 1834 (John Robinson), 4 September 1834 (Anne Pulford), 8 September 1834 (Joshua Pulford), 16 September 1834 (Thomas Roberts).

[193] See Chapter 4, note 125.

[194] BPP [1835], iii and iv. There were twenty-eight east Cheshire pits in 1855, many of which are known to have been of long standing (C. B. Phillips and J. H. Smith, *Lancashire and Cheshire from AD 1540* (Harlow: Longman, 1994), p. 181.

[195] BPP [1842a], p. 9.

[196] BPP [1842a], p. 20.

[197] *Cheshire Sheaf* (1901), p. 63.

[198] CALS, P149/11/4. See page 229.

[199] Church, pp. 191–2.

[200] Census: Ness.

[201] BPP [1842c], pp. 166–7.

[202] *OED*, 'put'; Flinn, pp. 330, 337.

[203] BPP [1842c], p. 367.

[204] BPP [1842c], p. 367.

[205] BPP [1842c], p. 165.

[206] NEIMME/Wat/3/71/6.

[207] NEIMME/Wat/3/71/12.

[208] BPP [1842c], p. 401.

[209] NEIMME/Wat/3/71/9.

[210] BPP [1842c], p. 367.

[211] BPP [1842c], p. 367; Flinn, p. 337; CALS, C/10/36 – Account: Hawarden coal pit.

[212] It is, however, possible that a male head of household was temporarily away when the census was taken.

[213] BPP [1842c], p. 367.

[214] Ibid.

[215] Flinn, pp. 333–6.

[216] P. E. H. Hair, 'The Lancashire Collier Girl', *THSLC*, 120 (1968), pp. 63–84.

[217] See page 237 and also *nestoncollieries.org*. Tunstall – NPR baptisms, 26 October 1848 (as 'Tunston'); Windle census, 1861 (incorrectly stated as age eleven).

[218] Dodd (1929), p. 216; Val Lloyd, 'Attitudes to Women at North Wales Coalmines, *c.*1840–1901' *Llafur, the Journal of the Society for the Study of Welsh Labour History*, 5, 2 (1989), pp. 7, 8, 10; BPP [1842c], p. 365.

[219] Mason, p. 73; see also B. Lewis (1971), p. 38.

[220] See page 204.

[221] Mary Price was paid on 25 November 1816, 26 January 1818, 4 October 1819, 16 May and 21 November 1820 (CALS, DDX 378/2, 4). She was wife of collier Thomas (NPR, marriage (née Cotterell), 27 April 1805; five children between 1806 and 1815). Also, Jane Ellis was paid for carting coals and gravel as well as ploughing (CALS, DDX 378/2, 27 September 1813). Catherine Oxton delivered 'Limestone, Slates, flags etc.', possibly from the colliery (CALS, DDX 378/31, 16 December 1821).

[222] CALS, P149/8/2: Nancy Matthews 14 July 1834; Jane Blundell 18 July 1835. Away from the colliery, on one occasion a woman was paid to sweep the chimney in the chancel of Burton parish church (CALS, DDX 378/33, 11 January 1829).

[223] BPP [1842a], p. 62.

Chapter 7 – The Neston Collieries' Products

[1] William Jones, *Dictionary of Industrial Archaeology* (Stroud: Sutton Publishing, 2006), p. 77; *OED*, 'coke'.

[2] Barrie Trinder, *Britain's Industrial Revolution* (Lancaster: Carnegie, 2013), p. 43; Roger Osborne, *Iron, Steam and Money* (London: Bodley Head, 2014), p. 62.

[3] NLW, Powis MSS 4102.

[4] Singer et al., p. 99.

[5] See page 192.

[6] W. Jones, p. 77.

[7] CALS, DHL 54C.

[8] *OED*, 'culm'.

[9] Wire riddles are mentioned at Ness in LA, DDCL 1065 and *Chester Chronicle*, 23 June 1855.

[10] CALS, DBC 261/38, 'Cottingham v Stanley Bt.'.

[11] *Chester Courant*, 6 August 1805, 18 February and 10 and 17 June 1806. See also Table 2.1.

[12] University of Manchester, JRL, RYCH 1718 (1–5).

[13] Ibid.

[14] CALS, DHL 54C (dated 1808–9); TNA J 90/82 (dated 1824–7).

[15] CALS, DHL 52/4, 29 October 1785.

[16] W. Jones, p. 67.

[17] University of Manchester JRL, RYCH/1718 (1–5).

[18] Contemporary local brewers, bakers and dyers can be found in NPR. Overseas: see, for example, note 79, Chapter 11.

[19] W. Jones, p. 67.

[20] W. Jones, p. 67; Flinn, pp. 240–1.

[21] Singer et al., p. 447.

[22] LA, DDCL 1065. The cost of the lime has been lost from the edge of the document.

[23] CALS, DHL 52/4, 29 October 1785.

[24] *Chester Courant*, 10 and 17 June 1806.

[25] CALS: DHL/54c; TNA, J 90/81 and J 90/82 passim; CALS, Stanley Estate Accounts, 1844–56 (uncatalogued), passim until 1 August 1855.

Chapter 7 – The Neston Collieries' Products (continued)

[26] *Chester Courant*, 7 October 1823.

[27] CALS, DHL 54C/31.

[28] For example, Mark Overton, *Agricultural Revolution in England, the Transformation of the English Economy, 1500–1850* (Cambridge: Cambridge University Press, 1996) and *The Agricultural Revolution: Changes in Agriculture, 1650–1880,* ed. by G. E. Mingay (London: Black, 1977).

[29] Henry Holland, *General View of the Agriculture of Cheshire* (London: Richard Phillips and Co. (1808), pp. 226–7; William Palin, *Cheshire Farming: A Report on the Agriculture of* Cheshire (Chester: Seacome and Prichard, 1845) p. 36; C. Stella Davies, *The Agricultural History of Cheshire 1750–1850*, Chetham Society, 3rd series, 10 (1960), p. 114.

[30] Overton, pp. 91, 108.

[31] Joan Thirsk et al., ed., *The Agrarian History of England and Wales*, 8 vols (Cambridge: Cambridge University Press, 1989), vi, p. 280.

[32] J. V. Beckett, *The Agricultural Revolution* (Oxford: Blackwell, 1990), p. 56.

[33] Rowan Patel, 'Lime Burning on Wirral: a Gazetteer of Lime Kiln Sites', *Cheshire History*, 57 (2017–18), pp. 128–56.

[34] Thirsk et al., 1989, vi, p. 280.

[35] NEIMME/Wat/3/65/9.

[36] Notice of 'Valuable Freehold Estate in Cheshire to be Sold by Auction', part of CALS, D5363.

[37] NEIMME/Wat/3/65/9 and 11.

[38] Coal Authority, 3808; CALS, EDT 286/2. By the time of the first six-inch OS map of the area, surveyed in 1869–72 (sheet XXX, published *c.*1875), these had disappeared to be replaced by a brick kiln, and two new lime kilns had been built 280 yards (256 metres) to the north-west, the remains of which still survive.

[39] *Mining Journal, Railway and Commercial Gazette,* 15 May 1852, p. 229.

[40] *Chester Chronicle,* 15 May 1852.

[41] Dodd (1971), pp. 222–3. G. Haynes-Thomas ('The Port of Chester', *TLCAS*, 59 (1947), p. 40) says that 'Conway's chief export was mountain stones; mountain stones came too from Penmaenmawr, Point of Ayr and Flint'. The Chester 'Register of Vessels Entering and Leaving the Port of Chester 1740–1769' (CALS, QDN 1/5) records limestone being carried up the Dee Navigation from various Welsh ports including Beaumaris, Llanddulas (sometimes known as 'Black and Blue'), 'Ruthland' (Rhuddlan), 'Postatyn' (presumably Prestatyn), 'Newkey' (a few miles south of Aberystwyth), and Dwyfor (Llŷn Peninsula).

[42] *North Wales Gazette*, 15 September 1814; CALS, PM 5.2 (Bryant, 1831); CALS, EDT 236/2 (Leighton tithe map, *c.*1845).

[43] *Chester Chronicle*, 10 July 1819.

44 CALS, 200585, 'The Customs Account Book of Humphrey Read'. Drogheda: Geological Survey of Ireland, *Louth – County Geological Site Report (Mell Quarry)* <https://gsi.geodata.gov.ie/downloads/Geoheritage/Reports/LH023_Mell_Quarry.pdf> [accessed 20 March 2019]; Larne: Cement Kilns, *Magheramorne Cement Kilns* <http://www.cementkilns.co.uk/cement_kiln_magheramorne.html> [accessed 20 March 2019]; Newry: A. Wilkinson, *The Newry Magazine or Literary and Political Register* (Newry: A Wilkinson, 1815), p. 119 which mentions Carlingford quarries, lying on the route from Newry.

45 CALS, EDT 286/2; Coal Authority, 14923/6.

46 Census, Ness.

47 The exact origin of Ness's slate is unknown but Haynes-Thomas, p. 40, says the towns of Caernarfon, Bangor, Amlwch, Beaumaris and Conwy regularly shipped slates to Chester. There were nine sailings carrying between 2,000 and 30,000 slates each from Aberdyfi to 'Chester' in 1791-3 (M. I. Williams. 'The Port of Aberdyfi in the 18th century', *National Library of Wales Journal*, 18 (1973), 1, pp. 95–134). Welsh port books also record slate shipments to 'Chester' e.g. TNA, E 190 1446/2 (Beaumaris), 26 May and 11 June 1789.

48 Dodd (1971), pp. 120–1. In 1790 Lord Penrhyn built Port Penrhyn to cope with the growing output.

49 *North Wales Gazette*, 29 November 1810 and 3 December 1812.

50 CALS, DBC 261/38, 'Cottingham v Stanley Bt.'.

51 CALS: DHL 54a/2 (25 December 1809 and 20 February 1811) and 54a/3; QDV 2/259 (1785); DHL 52/4. Payments were sometimes recorded as being made to William Taylor who was the colliery manager.

52 Stanley estates – see page 135; Cottinghams – TNA, J 90/82; CALS, P149/9/2, 11 April.

53 CALS, Stanley Estate Accounts, 1844–56 (uncatalogued), 26 April 1855.

54 Robin Lucas, 'The tax on bricks and tiles, 1784–1850', *Construction History*, 13 (1997), pp. 45–6. See, for example, CALS, DDX 378/8, 16 November 1836. Reusing old bricks was another option (CALS, 378/1, 18 September 1809).

55 LA, DDCL 1065.

56 Bricks feature as both an 'expense' and an asset of the colliery. The amount of expense has been lost from the edge of the page. Two bricklayers owed the colliery money implying they had bought some there.

57 Flinn, p. 76; CALS, D5363, 1788 'Copy of Schedule to the Answer of Deponents Massey and others'.

58 CALS, DHL 52/4, 29 October 1785. Timber and slates were being purchased by him at the same time (not, apparently, from Ness), presumably to be used in the same building project.

59 CALS, DDX 378/30, 17 March 1810 and DDX 378/2, 6 February 1813.

60 CALS, DDX 378/6, 17 November 1827.

61 CALS, DDX 378/2, 24 February 1815.

62 BGS, Sheet 77 (1888).

63 'Glegg Account Book and Notary's Register' (University of Liverpool Special Collections, MS.25.19). See also pages 183–4.

64 *Chester Courant*, 1 September 1812.

Chapter 7 – The Neston Collieries' Products (continued)

[65] CALS, DDX 378/2 – there are references to bricks from the colliery on 20 January and 12 December 1817 (the former delivery also appears to have included colliery-made tiles).

[66] CALS, DDX 378/4, 20 January 1822 relating to supply in 1820–1.

[67] For example, CALS, DDX 378/6, 3 December 1825 and TNA, J 90/82 (1824–7); Lucas, pp. 29–30.

[68] NPR, Thomas Shepherd, 9 September 1826.

[69] NEIMME/Wat/3/71/4 and Wat/35/14.

[70] CALS, EDT 286/2, *c*.1845.

[71] CALS, EDT 286/1.

[72] CALS, Stanley Estate Accounts, 1844–56 (uncatalogued), 1 August 1855.

[73] CALS, Stanley Estate Accounts, 1844–56 (uncatalogued), 26 April and 1 August 1855. No indication of the original brickyard appears on maps after the colliery closed although a new one had appeared, closer to the old colliery site, by 1872 (OS, 25-inch, XXX.2). Thomas Williams, Ness brickmaker, had moved to Lancashire by 1861 (census: Parr).

[74] NPR and censuses 1841 and 1851.

[75] See, for example, Flinn, pp. 237–8.

Chapter 8 – Local Trade: The Landsale Business

[1] Flinn, p. 147.

[2] Ormerod, ii, p. 354.

[3] Neston's population, including Ness, Little Neston and Leighton, at the first census in 1801, was 2,353. The next nearest was Tranmere with 353 and Birkenhead was 100. In 1821 the figures were Neston 2,532, Tranmere 825 and Birkenhead 200. By 1831, Neston had 2,863, Birkenhead 2,569 and nearby Tranmere 1,168 (Rideout, pp. 98–9).

[4] Dodd (1929), p. 209.

[5] Holland, pp. 300–1.

[6] Hanshall, p. 70. A later reference (p. 642) indicates he was writing after autumn 1822.

[7] See Table 1.1.

[8] British Library, Add. MSS 89098, 24 February 1829.

[9] *St. James's Chronicle*, 22 March 1766.

[10] Flinn, pp. 146–7.

[11] LA, DDCL 1065.

[12] John Chartres and Gerard Turnbull, 'Road Transport', in *Transport in the Industrial Revolution*, ed. by D. Aldcroft and M. Freeman (Manchester: Manchester University Press, 1983), p. 82.

[13] NEIMME/Wat/35/9.

[14] CALS, DDX 378/7, 1 April 1834.

[15] CALS, D 1841/52, 'Lease of a Tenement in Moreton'.

[16] Ormerod, ii, p. 473; *Liverpool Courier*, 4 September 1851.

[17] *Chester Courant*, 27 November 1810.

[18] Pigot and Co., *Commercial Directory, Cheshire* (n.p.: Pigot and Co., 1822), p. 20.

[19] CALS, DHL 54C/4.

[20] CALS, P149/8/2, 7/11/1837.

[21] TNA J 90/81, 82, 83, 84, passim.

[22] CALS, DHL, 52/4, 54a, 54c. Lyon died in 1809 but some records are posthumous.

[23] CALS, DHL 52/4 18 February 1798 and DHL 54A, 18 July 1807.

[24] CALS, DHL 52/4, p. 105.

[25] CALS, DDX 378/31, 21 January 1816.

[26] *North Wales Chronicle*, 30 January 1838. See also the *Morning Post*, 1 September 1841.

[27] Geoffrey Place, 'The Repatriation of Irish Vagrants from Cheshire, 1750–1815', *JCAS*, 68 (1986), pp. 125–41.

[28] CALS, QJF 191/2, 9 April 1763.

[29] CALS, QJF 198/3, 31 June [*sic*] 1770.

[30] Michael Handley, 'The Wirral Poor Law Union, 1836–1861', *TLCAS*, 104 (2008), p. 125. Workhouse examples: CALS, LGW 1/2, 15 January 1840 and 8 April 1840. Church: CALS, P149/9/2 and P149/9/3.

[31] *Morning Post*, 28 November 1833.

[32] From 1828 to 1833 the church generally paid only for carriage of coal. Records of supplies from him cease between 1833 and 1837.

[33] Lime in January 1839; slate in April 1843; bricks in 1849. Payments to Ness Colliery were often in the name of the manager, James Gregory.

[34] CALS, P149/9/3, 17 November 1849.

[35] CALS, P149/9/2, 14 July 1834.

[36] CALS, P149/9/3, 30 September 1849. From this time onwards the church was regularly buying coke from Chester.

[37] *Chester Chronicle*, 17 July 1852.

[38] *Chester Chronicle*, 3 April 1858.

[39] Booth regularly advertised his coal in the late 1850s and in the 1860s, saying it came from Blundell's Lancashire collieries in Wigan, and from Ruabon in the Denbighshire coalfield.

[40] For example, NEWA, D/M/2705 re Joseph Lyon's public brew-house and malt kiln.

[41] CALS, DDX 378/33, 28 April 1829 (bakehouse). Various surveys and inventories relating to Ness township in the seventeenth and early eighteenth centuries indicate some farms had malt kilns and this is probably true of later years too.

[42] For example, charcoal was often used in metalworking and malting (Trinder, 2013, p. 43).

[43] CALS, DHL 52/4. For example, the colliery paid off its account to the brewing business of almost £20 in 1790. Payment by ale is discussed on page 103.

[44] See page 135.

[45] *Liverpool Mercury*, 15 October 1847, and other newspapers.

[46] *The Mining Journal, Railway and Commercial Gazette*, 18 (1848), p. 373 and 21, (1851), p. 377.

[47] *Liverpool Mercury*, 14 May 1852, p. 6.

[48] CALS, DDX 378/1–8, 12, 30–31, 33; NEWA, D/DM/452/1; CALS, Stanley Estate Accounts, 1844–56 (uncatalogued).

Chapter 8 – Local Trade: The Landsale Business (continued)

[49] Locations mentioned include (a few may be coterminous, and a few relate to rented property, not owned; original spellings used): Wirral – Bebington, Benty Heath, Brimstage, Bromborow [Bromborough], Burton, Childer Thornton, Eastham, Great Meoles, Hooton, Little Sutton, Little Mollington, (Nether)Pool, Overchurch, Oldfield, Plimyard, Poulton, Rivacre, Stanney, Storeton, Thornton [Hough], Upton, Willaston, Woodchurch; North Wales – Avon Goch, Broneiron, Holywell, Porthymaen, Trefreth, Trelogan, Ysceifiog; south Cheshire – Aldford, Buerton.

[50] Locations mentioned include (N.B. as per note 49 above): Wirral – Burton, Caughall, Ledsham, Puddington, Raby, Thornton Heath; east Cheshire – Buglawton, Congleton, Great Warford, Somerford Booths; North Wales – Moor, Hawarden, Pentrobin, Saltney; Lancashire – Aughton, Bickerstaff[e], Moor Hall, Ormskirk.

[51] Coal yard: CALS, DDX 378/2, 7 December 1812; bedchamber example, CALS, DDX 378/2, 8 February 1813.

[52] Architectural Association, 'Hooton Park, in Cheshire: a seat of Sir Thomas Stanley, Bt.' by Humphry Repton (1802).

[53] Stephen Daniels, *Humphry Repton: Landscape Gardening and the Geography of Georgian England*, (New Haven, CT: Yale University Press, 1999), p. 173.

[54] CALS, DDX 378/1, 24 June 1806. There was also glazing in hothouse sheds (8 December 1806).

[55] Walter Nicol, *The Forcing, Fruit, and Kitchen Gardener*, 4th edn (Edinburgh: William Creech and others, 1809).

[56] John Claudius Loudon, *Remarks on the Construction of Hothouses* (London: printed for J. Taylor, 1817), p. 52; CALS, DDX 378/6, 8 November 1827 – James Smith was paid to sweep four hothouse flues.

[57] There are, for example, occasional instances of bricks for the Puddington estate being bought direct from the colliery e.g. CALS, DDX 378/30, 17 March 1810, 13 April 1811 and 6 February 1813.

[58] For example, CALS, DDX 378/30, 25 August 1803, (Puddington), DDX 378/1, 22 November 1804 (Hooton), 7 October 1808 (Eastham), 21 September 1811 (Childer Thornton); DDX 378/8, 14 November 1836 (Badgers Rake [Lane], near Ledsham). There was also a brick works at Bebington (DDX 378/8, 31 December 1838).

[59] CALS, DDX 378/2, 29 July 1812 and DDX 378/8, 17 May 1838.

[60] Dodd (1971), pp. 193–4.

[61] *Chester Courant*, 1 September 1812; CALS, DDX 378/6, 17 November 1827.

[62] CALS, DHL 52/4, 12 August 1785; CALS, DDX 378/30, 9 November 1811.

[63] For example, CALS, DDX 378/30 20 February and 7 August 1813.

[64] CALS, DDX 378/1, 18 September 1804 (224,500), 15 November 1805 (790,000), 25 September 1807 (333,181), 7 October 1808 (315,873), 22 November 1809 (508,470 including bricks made at Eastham too); DDX 378/30, 3 October 1806 (304,000).

[65] Historic England, List entry numbers 1115840 and 1261789. They were first mapped in 1819, by Christopher Greenwood on his 'Map of the County Palatine [of Cheshire] from an Actual Survey' (CALS, PM 13/10a). Listing particulars date them to 'the early nineteenth century'. CALS, D 293/8 (1825) shows there were originally four pairs plus other nearby buildings.

[66] CALS, DDX 378/1, 18 October 1806, 24 October 1807, 25 January 1808 and 26 January 1809.

[67] DDX 378/1, 19 December 1808 and 19 June 1809.

[68] The rectangular garden appears to be depicted on Greenwood's map of 1819 (CALS, PM 13/10a); it is more distinctive on the Hooton tithe map *c.*1850 (CALS, EDT 207/2).

[69] For example, DDX 378/1, 25 November 1801, 15 November 1802, 4 April 1804, DDX 378/4, 9 November 1818 and DDX 378/8, 8 and 23 June, 6, 20 and 27 July, 11 August and 18 September 1838.

[70] DDX 378/1, 2 March 1808, 27 February, 4 and 21 September 1811, 6 February and 11 March 1813, DDX 378/30, 22 September and 11 October 1800. 327,000 were made for the Puddington estate between 1787 and 1798 (NEWA, D/DM/452/1). It is not clear how many of these were used in the village itself; some appear to relate to the estate in Somerford Booths, east Cheshire, but others, such as those made by William Glave, probably a former collier at Ness, appear to have been used locally (16 October 1788).

[71] Chester City Council, 'Puddington, Conservation Area Appraisal, January 2008', p. 4.

[72] DDX 378/30, 25 January and 29 July 1805, and 7 June 1806.

[73] CALS, DDX 378/30, 20 and 31 December 1801, 25 January 1803, 16 and 19 October 1810, and 27 May 1812.

[74] Chester City Council, pp. 7–8 says it was built in 1830 but it appears to have been mapped by Greenwood in 1819 (CALS, PM 13/10a).

[75] CALS, DDX 378/1, 24 December 1802, 22 November 1809 and 8 November 1810; DDX 378/2, 20 August 1818 and DDX 378/4, 9 September 1818 and 9 November 1818.

[76] CALS, DDX 378/1, 21 September 1811, DDX 378/2, 22 February 1813, DDX 378/4, 3 August and 23 September 1818 and 31 July 1826.

[77] CALS, DDX 378/30, 25 August 1813; CALS, Stanley Estate Accounts, 1844–56 (uncatalogued), 7 October 1854 and 17 March 1855.

[78] Historic England List entry number 1115524.

[79] CALS, DDX 378/1, 2 and 16 July 1805. It seems likely the lodges were Hooton Hall's (which are still standing). However, they were made of sandstone so perhaps the bricks were used internally or in the adjacent grounds.

[80] CALS, DDX 378/30, 25 September 1807 and 14 February and 22 July 1809.

[81] Most years from 8 April 1801 (CALS, DDX 378/1) to 16 April 1855 (CALS, Stanley Estate Accounts, 1844–56 (uncatalogued).

[82] CALS, DDX 378/8, 4 December 1837.

[83] The total value was £265 3*s.* compared to estimated total sales of £3,975 that year (Appendix IIa).

[84] CALS, DDX 378/1, 9 April 1810 and DDX 378/8, 23 February 1838 and passim.

[85] For example, CALS, DDX 378/1, 9 April 1810 and DDX 378/8, 4 December 1837.

[86] For example, CALS, DDX 378/30, 9 July 1813 and DDX 378/7, 17 February 1836.

[87] For example, DDX 378/2, 6 August 1814, DDX 378/4, 17 January 1818 and DDX 378/8, 23 February 1838. See page 285, note 106 re surveys.

[88] CALS, DDX 378/7, 14 May 1834.

[89] CALS, DDX 378/7, 16 June 1836. N.B. coastwise coal duty had been abolished in 1831 (Ashton and Sykes, pp. 247–8).

[90] CALS, DDX 378/7, 17 February 1836.

[91] CALS, D 293/7; Architectural Association, Humphry Repton (1802).

Chapter 8 – Local Trade: The Landsale Business (continued)

[92] 8 April 1801 to 1 August 1855, excepting 1839 to 1843 for which no accounts survive (CALS, DDX 378/1 and Stanley Estate Accounts, 1844–56 (uncatalogued).

[93] CALS, DDX 378/8, 14 November 1836 to the Puddington and Hooton estates.

[94] NEIMME/Wat/3/65/15.

[95] Richard Williams, *Limekilns and Limeburning* (Princes Risborough: Shire, 2004), pp. 12–13.

[96] For example, CALS, DDX 378/1, 12 August 1805, DDX 378/2, 7 July 1816 and DDX 378/7, 17 November 1834 (at Haddon Hall Farm).

[97] CALS, DDX 378/31, 31 December 1823. James Mease, *Archives of Useful Knowledge* (Philadelphia: James Hogan 1813), p. 283.

[98] For example, CALS, DDX 378/31, 14 February 1817 and DDX 378/4, 19 June 1821.

[99] For example, loads of 54 tons/59 tonnes (CALS, DDX 378/2, 26 February 1816) 70 tons/76 tonnes (CALS, DDX 378/4, 11 September 1820) and an unspecified amount (DDX 378/6, 28 July 1828).

[100] Purchases appear in both the Puddington and Hooton estate accounts; some of the waste was carted to Eastham (CALS, DDX 378/2, 30 September 1817).

[101] For example, CALS, DDX 378/2, 12 December 1817.

[102] The last stated date of payment for soap waste was 31 October 1829 (CALS, DDX 378/12).

[103] Sarah Tarlow, *The Archaeology of Improvement, 1750–1850* (Cambridge: Cambridge University Press, 2007), p. 61.

[104] Holland, p. 210.

[105] Thomas Williams, *A Compendious Abstract of the Public General Acts Passed in 7 Geo. IV* (London, printed for Wightman and Camp, 1826), pp. 73–4; Lucas, pp. 29–30.

[106] For example, CALS, DDX 378/1, 11 July 1806 and DDX 378/30, 10 September 1813. Hancock still occasionally supplied tiles after Ness Colliery started making them.

[107] CALS, DDX 378/2, 23 July, 1 September and 5 December 1817, and 378/4, 28 September 1818. Another kiln was built at Hooton in 1819 (CALS, DDX 378/4, 29 November).

[108] CALS, DDX 378/4, 5 January 1822 relating to draining tiles and 'barn floor tiles' in 1820–1.

[109] CALS, DDX 378/7, 17 November 1834. At least 27,450 more were laid on the same farm, Lowfields, in 1835-8 (DDX, 378/7, 17 November 1835; DDX 378/8, 4 December 1837 and 31 December 1838).

[110] DDX 378/4, 7 August 1820.

[111] For example, CALS, DDX 378/2, 3 July and 1 September 1817, and DDX 378/8, 14 November 1836.

[112] CALS, DDX 378/8, 14 November 1836; CALS, EDT 335/2 (Puddington tithe map, 1839).

[113] CALS, Stanley Estate Accounts, 1844–56 (uncatalogued), 10 April and 29 May 1845; Tarlow p. 61.

[114] CALS, Stanley Estate Accounts, 1844–56 (uncatalogued), 13 April 1848.

[115] CALS, Stanley Estate Accounts, 1844–56 (uncatalogued), *passim*, detailing sales volumes and coal supplies.

[116] Palin, p. 26; C. Davies, p. 109; James Caird, *English Agriculture in 1850–51* (Longman, Brown, Green, and Longmans, 1852), pp. 256–7. Local activity: for example, CALS, Stanley Estate Accounts, 1844–56 (uncatalogued)**,** January to July, 1850, and 1852 (n.d.).

[117] For example, CALS, DDX, 378/33, 24 and 26 April 1827 and CALS, Stanley Estate Accounts, 1844–56 (uncatalogued), 23 June 1847.

[118] See, for example, CALS, DDX 378/1, 7 and 31 December 1807.

[119] CALS, DDX 387/8, 4 December.

[120] Ibid.

[121] CALS, DDX 378/2, 9 March 1812.

[122] The estates' sales of timber to the colliery in 1826–8 totalled £140; for 1834–6 it was £256 (no totals available 1831–3).

[123] For example, CALS, DDX 378/1, 28 May 1804 and DDX 378/31, 9 April 1818.

[124] For example, CALS, DDX 378/31, 9 April 1818 and 1 May 1823; Holland, pp. 197, 203–4, 326.

[125] CALS, DDX 378/2, 12 December 1817. The term 'river timber' (DDX 378/2, 19 January 1815) may relate to this use.

[126] CALS, DDX 378/6, 3 December 1825.

[127] CALS, DDX 378/1, 23 April 1803, 21 February 1806 and DDX 378/30, 6 February 1813.

[128] CALS, DDX 378/2 and 378/30, 18 February 1813. There were recorded sales between 1807 and 1830.

[129] For example, CALS, DDX 378/1, 25 May 1808 (wheat), DDX 378/31, 4 April 1818 (oats), DDX 378/6, 31 December 1823 (hay), and DDX 378/8, 14 November 1836 (potato sets).

[130] For example, CALS, DDX 378/1, 25 May 1808 and DDX 378/8, 4 December 1837 (straw); DDX 378/2, 9 January 1814 and DDX 378/33, 8 November 1828 (thatch).

[131] For example, CALS, DDX 378/30, 8 July 1808, and over 6 tons (6.5 tonnes) from Stanley's Upton Farm on 17 November 1827 (CALS, DDX 378/6).

[132] For example, CALS, DDX 378/4, 16 January 1819 (seed wheat) and 16 May 1818 (red clover seed); a mare and gelding for £50 (DDX 378/30, 19 January 1814) and a bay mare for 18 guineas in 1836 (DDX 378/8, 14 November 1836).

[133] DDX 378/8, 6 April 1839.

[134] For example, CALS, DDX 378/2, 12 December 1817 and DDX 378/8, 31 December 1838.

[135] See page 118.

[136] CALS, DDX 378/41, 'An Account of Carting or Plowing due as Boon-work'.

[137] CALS, DDX 378/6, 8 November 1828, and DDX 378/33, 8 November 1828.

[138] CALS, DDX 378/30, 20 November and 4 December 1807, 16 April 1808; DDX 378/1, 25 May 1808. Throughout the accounts, payments were generally made for goods in arrears – often substantially so. It is assumed here that profits would have been calculated based on in-year revenues.

[139] Mokyr (2009), p. 196; Stephen Roberts, *A History of Wirral* (Chichester: Phillimore, 2002), p. 147.

[140] Rideout, pp. 98–9.

[141] W. Harrison, 'Pre-Turnpike Highways in Lancashire and Cheshire', *TLCAS*, 9 (1892), p. 125.

[142] CALS, DCH/XX/4, *Act for amending and widening the Chester-Parkgate-Woodside Ferry road*.

[143] Flinn, p. 148.

Chapter 8 – Local Trade: The Landsale Business (continued)

[144] Pennant (1796), p. 51; NEWA, D/M/5300.

[145] John Stanley Massey or his estate received interest in 1788 and onwards from monies advanced to the 'Wirral Turnpike Roads' the previous year (NEWA, D/DM/452/1). Interest on this or similar loans continued to be received by the Stanleys into the 1820s (CALS, DDX 378/4, 8 August 1822).

[146] Steven Durlauf and Lawrence Blume, eds, *The New Palgrave Dictionary of Economics* (Basingstoke: Palgrave Macmillan, 2008), p. 412.

[147] The *Chester Chronicle,* 15 April 1808, advertised a forthcoming auction of the toll revenue at the 'lately erected' toll gate.

[148] CALS, QJF 206/1, 9 April 1778.

[149] Ormerod, ii, p. 406.

[150] CALS, PM 11/10, 'A New Map of the Hundred of Wirral'. The map names Philip Hervey as captain of the *King* packet ship, a post he occupied between 1790 and 1795. It also shows the route of the proposed canal between Chester and Netherpool on the Mersey, plans for which were published in 1790. The mis-location of Denhall Quay, which was probably started in 1791 (see pages 167–8), suggests a date of survey of 1790 or early 1791.

[151] See pages 167–8.

[152] In addition, 1789 Quarter Session records (CALS, QJF 217/3) record a plan for a short new stretch of road, in Puddington, signed by Thomas Stanley Massey. This *was* built.

[153] Ormerod, ii, p. 354; further acts in 1826, 1833, 1838 and 1841 as well as continuance Acts which allowed existing trusts to remain in force (G. Dodd, 'The Turnpikes of Wirral', *Journal of the North-Western Society of Industrial Archaeology and History*, 2 (1977), pp. 21–7).

Chapter 9 – Chester: Trade and the Developing Transport Network

[1] J. D. Herson, 'Late Georgian and Victorian Chester, 1762–1914' in *A History of the County of Chester*, ed. by C. P. Lewis and A. T. Thacker and others, 5 vols (London: Institute of Historical Research, , 1987–2005), v(1) (2003), p. 171.

[2] Chester – ibid. Population figures were approx. 16,095 in 1801 and 29,216 in 1851. Neston area assumed as Leighton, Ness, Great Neston and Little Neston (Rideout, pp. 98–9).

[3] The walls of many of today's listed buildings in the city dating from the late eighteenth and early nineteenth century are made wholly or partly of brick (Historic England, *National Heritage List for England* available at <https://historicengland.org.uk/listing/the-list/> [accessed 2 January 2023]).

[4] Jon Stobart, 'County, Town and Country: Three Histories of Urban Development in Eighteenth-Century Chester' in *Provincial Towns in Early Modern England and Ireland*, ed. by Peter Borsay and Lindsay Proudfoot (Oxford: Oxford University Press, 2002), pp. 188–9.

[5] Peter Carrington, *English Heritage Book of Chester* (London: Batsford/English Heritage, 1994), p. 96.

[6] Peter Broster, *The Chester Guide* (Chester: Peter Broster, 1795), pp. 73–96.

[7] Sulphur-free coal was also claimed to be available, suitable for 'smiths', from the two-foot seam at Mostyn Colliery (*Chester Courant*, 9 June 1795).

[8] Carrington, p. 96.

9 Chaloner, p. 133; CALS, Z D/HS 120.

10 R. Coppack and D. Roberts, 'Two Samuel Walkers?', *Chester Antiquary*, 1 (2003), 1; Chaloner, p. 126.

11 CALS, Z AB/4/268v; *Chester Chronicle*, 11 November 1791.

12 *Adams's Weekly Courant*, 3 September 1769.

13 NEWA, D/P/346 depicts two 'trame roads' at or near Aston and Mancot as early as 1753; see also Clwyd-Powys Archaeological Trust (n.d.) 'Ports and Harbours in North-east Wales' <http://www.cpat.org.uk/projects/longer/ports/ports.htm> [accessed 17 March 2019]; Dodd (1929), p. 208; Pritchard (2012), pp. 90, 93; James Boyd, *The Wrexham, Mold and Connah's Quay Railway* (Headington, Oxon: Oakwood Press, 1991), pp. 13–44.

14 CALS, Z AB/2/185–185v dated 1677.

15 For example, CALS, Z AB/4/141, 7 May 1751 mentions the 'coal dock' and, in 1752, Z AB/4/146 mentions that James Golborne wanted to make a road to improve access for his coal into the city. Z AB/4/149 records the authorisation of the machine, 30 November 1752.

16 CALS, Z AB/4/182 v and 216v; NLW, EJ2/1.

17 CALS, Z AB/4/268v.

18 Bagshaw, p. 111.

19 CALS, Z TAY 7, 3 November 1759 and Z TAY 2, 24 October 1761; CALS, Z TAY 2, 5 October 1761 and Z TAB/7, 23 October 1762; NPR, 11 November 1761.

20 Hemingway, pp. 235–6; Rawson, p. 131.

21 CALS, QDN 1/5, 'Register of vessels entering and leaving the port of Chester'.

22 There is no obvious explanation for this and so there is scope for further research.

23 Based on appearances in TNA, E 190 series.

24 University of Liverpool Special Collections, MS.25.19, 'Glegg account book and notary's register'. She was not specifically recorded in the Chester 'Register of Vessels', perhaps because of her accident. A similar incident happened to her the following year (see page 192).

25 Rawson, pp. 128, 132–3. Rawson details some of these river sales, which are occasionally distinguished from 'sea sales'. In 1766 Sandycroft Colliery shipped 2,206 tons (2,402 tonnes) by river, a year in which the Chester 'Register of Vessels' (CALS, QDN 1/5) states 7,815 tons (8,511 tonnes) of coal reached the city by 'Ponts and other vessels'.

26 LMA, A/FH/D/04/013/001, 'Vouchers'.

27 Gillian Pugh, *London's Forgotten Children* (Stroud: Tempus, 2007), pp. 32, 45.

28 LMA, A/FH/D/04/007 Cash Account Book.

29 LMA, A/FH/D/04/013/001 'Vouchers' and 014/001–005, 'Coal Delivery Notes'. A/FH/D/04/004, 'Copies of Letters to London Hospital', 6 September 1763.

30 LMA, A/FH/D/04/001/001 and 13/001 'Vouchers'.

31 Many delivery notes in LMA, A/FH/D/04/014/001–005 are headed 'Chester Machine'.

32 LMA, A/FH/D/04/013/001 and 014/001–005.

33 LMA, A/FH/D/04/006, (Sigismund Lane, aged ten years and seven months; and John Cheshunt, baptised 1750 (Baptism Register, Foundling Hospital, Saint Pancras, London)).

34 CALS, Z HI/5, 25 May 1779.

35 He attended six board meetings and a Special General Meeting between 21 February 1764 and 27 January 1767 (CALS, Z HI/2).

Chapter 9 – Chester: Trade and the Developing Transport Network (continued)

[36] 21 May 1782 to 27 March 1792 (CALS, Z HI/5–7).

[37] For example, CALS, Z HI/3, 24 October 1776; Z HI/5, 25 May 1779 and Z HI/7, 11 September 1792.

[38] CALS, Z HI/10.

[39] CALS, Z TAV/2/49, 10 January 1765; Z TAV/2/54; Z TAY/2; Z TAV/2/44, 22 February 1760; CALS, EDD 3/8/2, 10 October 1768; CALS, CR 65/1/7.

[40] CALS, Z TAV/7, p. 91; Z TAY/2/45 19 September 1761.

[41] LA, DDCL 1065. There were also sugar houses in Skinners Lane and Weavers Lane in the late eighteenth and early nineteenth centuries.

[42] Annakin-Smith (2011), p. 4. A good account of this sugar house is given at *Chester [Sugar Houses]* by Brian Mawer (n.d.), at <http://www.mawer.clara.net/loc-chester.html> [accessed 2 January 2023] from which the material, not otherwise referenced here, has been taken.

[43] CALS, D 5879. The Hincks accounts are very fragmented but, for example CALS, D/HINCKS/86e records stocks of 'sugar, loaves and pieces' valued at £4,817 on 9 April 1770.

[44] For example, CALS, D/HINCKS/32 shows his one-eighth share in the brig *Britannia* (which operated out of Parkgate) was worth £100. LA, DDCL 1065 records an entry for 'boatbuilding' for the colliery.

[45] John Aikin, *England Delineated, Or, A Geographical Description of Every County in England and Wales* (London: T. Bensley, 1790), p. 93.

[46] TNA, J 90/82, 31 March 1823.

[47] Edward Paget-Tomlinson, *Mersey and Weaver Flats* (Kettering: Robert Wilson, 1973).

[48] *Chester Courant,* 25 March 1823.

[49] Victoria Owens, *James Brindley's Notebooks* (Gloucester: Choir Press, 2013a), pp. 76, 83–4, 92.

[50] Christine Richardson, *James Brindley, Canal Pioneer* (Burton-on-Trent: Waterways World, 2004), pp. 43–4.

[51] Charles Hadfield, *The Canals of the West Midlands* (Newton Abbott, David and Charles, 1985), pp. 19–20; Victoria Owens, 'James Brindley's Notebooks, 1755–63: An Eighteenth-Century Engineer Writes About His Work, *IJHET*, 83 (2013b), 2, p. 236.

[52] Owens (2013a), p. 69. Gordon Emery (2005). *The Old Chester Canal* (Chester: Chester Canal Heritage Trust, 2005), p. 13.

[53] Emery, pp. 15–16, 29.

[54] CALS, Z TAV/2/55, vouchers for Chester Canal.

[55] See pages 166–7.

[56] Hadfield, p. 44.

[57] Emery, p. 135.

[58] *Chester Courant*, 16 February 1796.

[59] See page 135.

[60] Pigot and Co. [1834] *Commercial Directory for Cheshire, 1834* (reprinted Swinton: N. Richardson, 1982), p. 54; Isaac Slater (1848), p. 73.

[61] T. Barker, 'Lancashire Coal, Cheshire Salt and the Rise of Liverpool', *THSLC*, 103 (1951), pp. 94–98; Dorothy Sylvester, *A History of Cheshire* (London: Phillimore, 1980), p. 96.

[62] See *nestoncollieries.org*

[63] Bosdin Leech, *History of the Manchester Ship Canal* (Manchester and London: Sherratt and Hughes, 1907), pp. 55–62. See also page 29.

[64] British Library, *Learning: Timelines: Sources from History: The Railways* (n.d.) <http://www.bl.uk/learning/timeline/item106197.html> [accessed 2 January 2023].

[65] *Chester Courant*, 19 and 29 November 1830 and 27 May 1831. Became the Chester and Birkenhead Railway from 1837 (John Dunlap, *Report of Cases Decided in the High Court of Chancery*, xiv (New York: Gould Banks and Co, 1843), p. 778).

[66] *Chester Chronicle*, 27 May 1831.

[67] Stanley lobbied Parliament in relation to both proposals (DDX 378/33, 2 May 1831).

[68] Investment into railways during 1845–9 far exceeded that of any other five-year period between 1825 and 1869 (T. R. Gourvish, *Railways and the British Economy, 1830–1914* (Basingstoke: Macmillan, 1980), p. 12.

[69] CALS, QDP 252.

[70] *Chester Chronicle*, 17 October 1845. In error, the advertisement also stated the coalfield was at 'Denham' not 'Denhall'.

[71] CALS, QDP 266; University of Wales, Bangor, Mostyn Manuscripts 7211.

[72] *Chester Chronicle,* 13 November 1846.

[73] *Liverpool Mercury*, 15 October 1847 and many other newspapers.

[74] CALS, D5232/7, Particulars of Sale of the Mostyn Estate.

[75] Parliamentary Archives, HL/PO/PB/1/1847/10 and 11V1n266, *An Act for making a Railway from Parkgate in the Parish of Great Neston in the County of Chester to join the Chester and Birkenhead Railway in the Parish of Bebbington* [sic] *in the same County*, (1847). Edward Mostyn Lloyd Mostyn was the first of three named subscribers. The directors subsequently indicated an intention to extend the time scale by two years.

[76] *Cork Examiner*, 19 February 1849.

[77] *North Wales Chronicle*, 29 May 1849.

[78] *Morning Post*, 1 February 1851.

[79] The route of the proposed 1845 branch line from the Chester and Birkenhead Railway went to Neston town centre (CALS, QDP 242; NEWA, QS/DR/19; *Chester Chronicle*, 28 November 1845); the proposed Birkenhead and Holyhead Junction and Mold Extension Railway ran through Parkgate and across the Dee to access the Welsh coalfields, bypassing the opportunity to continue to the Neston collieries (CALS, QDP 241A; *Liverpool Mercury*, 27 June 1845). Various other schemes ran along the Wirral, passing close to Willaston in the parish of Neston.

[80] CALS, QDP 298, TNA, BT/41/839/4818 and Parliamentary Archives, HL/PO/PB/3/plan1852/H3 (1851-2); CALS, QDP 359 and Parliamentary Archives, HL/PO/PB/3/plan1859/H5 (1858-9).

[81] See page 46.

[82] *Chester Chronicle*, 15 May 1852.

[83] NEWA, D/M/5661, 'Report on Coal and Ironstone Mines'.

[84] TNA, BT 41/136/787. See Anthony Annakin-Smith, 'How South American Gold Transformed a Corner of Neston', *Cheshire History*, 61 (2021-2), pp. 202–10 for more on the Anglican Smelting, Reduction and Coal Company Limited.

[85] Parl. Papers, *Journals of the House of Commons*, 114 (1859), pp. 16, 34, 55, 136.

Chapter 9 – Chester: Trade and the Developing Transport Network (continued)

[86] CALS, QDP 387 (29 November 1861) and *Chester Chronicle,* 6 October 1866.

[87] Place (1996), p. 63.

[88] Colin Russell and John Hudson, *Early Railway Chemistry and its Legacy* (London: Royal Society for Chemistry, 2011), pp. 20, 60.

[89] Dan Bogart in *The Cambridge Economic History of Modern Britain*, ed. by Roderick Floud, Jane Humphries and Paul Johnson, 2 vols, (Cambridge: Cambridge University Press, 2014), i, Chapter 13.

Chapter 10 – The Seasale Trade: An Introduction

[1] To give examples from several otherwise excellent sources: C. Armour's thesis on 'The Trade of Chester and the State of the Dee Navigation 1600–1800' (unpublished doctoral thesis, University of London, 1956) mentions Flintshire coal several times but refers to coal from Ness just once, almost as an afterthought (p. 258; also pp. 279 and 281). Sources which make no mention of Ness include Robert Craig ('Some Aspects of the Trade and Shipping of the River Dee in the Eighteenth Century', *THSLC*, 114 (1962), pp. 99–128), P. F. Skidmore, 'The Maritime Economy of North West England in the Later Eighteenth Century' (unpublished doctoral thesis, University of Greenwich, 2009), and A. H. Dodd in both his book and article (op. cit.) which give no indication of the contribution of Ness to the stated tonnages of Chester's coal exports. Flinn's *The History of the British Coal Industry* also makes no mention of the Neston collieries, and attributes exports from Chester only to 'North Wales' (p. 223).

[2] *Coal Industry*, p. 146.

[3] Adam Smith [1776], *An Inquiry into the Nature and Causes of the Wealth of Nations* (London: Electric Book Co., *c.*2001), Bk 1, p. 36.

[4] R. C. Jarvis, 'The Head Port of Chester; and Liverpool, its Creek and Member', *THSLC*, 102 (1950), p. 83.

[5] For example, *Saunders's News-Letter* of 30 March 1784 simply reported that 'ten colliers' had arrived in Dublin the previous day.

[6] Some half-years' records for coastal business are missing; others are in very poor, sometimes illegible, condition. Armour (pp. 171–82) and D. Pope ('Shipping and Trade in the Port of Liverpool', unpublished doctoral thesis for the University of Liverpool, (1980), pp. 136–43) both give useful summaries of other potential difficulties with using the port books. However, this author has not found the problems they identify as being significant in relation to the particular records used in this study and, occasionally, the problems appear to be overstated. One issue, however, is that details of the loads carried do not always fully tally where there are entries for a voyage in both a port book and the Chester 'Register of Vessels Entering and Leaving the Port of Chester' (CALS, QDN 1/5).

[7] Woodward, p. 64; Place (1994), p. 34.

[8] G. Lloyd. 'The Canalization of the River Dee in 1737', *FHSP*, 23 (1967–8), pp. 35–41.

[9] Craig, p. 102. G. Lloyd, p. 40, states that 11,700 acres (4,735 hectares) of land have been reclaimed.

[10] British Library, S. Fearon and J. Eyes 'A Description of the Sea Coast of England and Wales' (1738).

[11] Place (1994), pp. 200–4.

[12] Thacker, pp. 86–7; P. Barfoot and J. Wilkes, *The Chester Directory and Guide,* offprint from *The Universal British Directory of Trade, Commerce and Manufacture* (Chester: printed for and sold by James Poole, 1792), pp. 724–5.

[13] Craig, pp. 102–3; Place (1994), p. 204.

[14] G. Lloyd, p. 39; Craig, p. 102; G. Hawkes, 'Shipping on the Dee: the Rise and Decline of the Creeks of the Port of Chester in the Nineteenth Century', *Maritime Wales,* 11 (1987), pp. 112–13.

[15] See pages 190–2.

[16] R. Rees Rawson, p. 133. See also Pritchard (2012), p. 93. The new roads, mentioned on pages 140 and 144, were probably another factor in the increased land sales.

[17] The rates were set in the 'River Dee Navigation Act' 17 George II *c.*28. Charges for overseas trade, based on a ship's 'burden' in tons, ranged for most goods, including coal, from 3*d.* per ton to the Isle of Man and 4*d.* to Ireland up to 1*s.* 6*d.* for many long-haul destinations. Coasting charges for most goods varied between 2*d.* and 4*d.* per ton depending on distance.

[18] CALS, QDN 1/5. The period spans the only years in which coal exports are recorded in the register after Ness Colliery opened. Six went to Dublin, three to the Isle of Man and one each to Newry and Drogheda.

[19] The average coastwise coal load of the thirty-two vessels recorded as using the Navigation in a sample year of 1767 was just 9.6 tons (10.5 tonnes) (CALS, QDN 1/5) (excluding one load of unspecified quantities of 'coals and bark', and listed in TNA, E 190 1439/7 as carrying pigs of lead instead). In another sample year, 1764, the equivalent average was eleven tons (12 tonnes).

[20] In 1767, the port books record 180 coal-carrying vessels trading coastwise from Chester (TNA, E 190 1439/2 and 7). However, only thirty-two were listed in the Chester 'Register of Vessels' (CALS, QDN 1/5) as using the Dee Navigation. While there are occasional discrepancies between the nature of the loads listed in the two sources there can be no doubt that the large majority of loads did not use the Navigation.

[21] Armour, pp. 254–5.

[22] In 1750 and 1755 there were sixteen and forty-nine shipments without coal respectively (Appendix V). There was an average of forty-nine such shipments p.a. in 1757–62 inclusive; 1758 was particularly low at twenty-eight. In 1763–7 the average figure was a little higher at fifty-five. The threat to British shipping was largely neutralised by the end of 1759.

[23] Pennant (1796), pp. 275–6. See also *Pue's Occurrences,* Dublin, 8 June 1756 and 22 January 1757. The incident allegedly led to a glut of coal to Ireland but there is no obvious increase in shipping volumes in or soon after 1756.

[24] CALS, QDN 1/5 , 'Register of vessels entering and leaving the port of Chester'.

[25] Pennant (1796), p. 134.

[26] Pennant (1778), pp. 15–16.

[27] Pennant (1778), p. 16.

[28] Pennant (1796), p. 133.

[29] Pennant (1778), p. 43.

[30] See page 167.

[31] TNA, MR 1/937/3, 'A New Chart of the West Coast of England' (London: Laurie and Whittle, 1794).

Chapter 10 – The Seasale Trade: An Introduction (continued)

[32] The Laurie and Whittle chart shows the main channel heading towards the English side just south of Flint, no depth indications on the Welsh side and different shading there from the marked navigable waters. John Evans's 'North-East Wales and the Dee Estuary' (CALS, D3968/1), also dated 1794, shows no significant channels on the Welsh side of the estuary from Flint northwards.

[33] Even allowing for the minor earlier workings at Denhall, it seems unlikely that they could have significantly accounted for the volumes of Chester's coal exports.

[34] Again, as with the previous *decline* in trade it does not appear that the Seven Years' War was a major factor as there was no significant rise in non-coal shipments from 1759.

[35] Shipments of coal from 1763–8 as a percentage of shipments of *any* goods including coal stayed in a relatively narrow range of 51% to 64%.

[36] The exceptional case is from University of Liverpool Special Collections, MS.25.19, 'Glegg Account Book and Notary's Register', 19 November 1762, re the *Judea* sailing from Bagillt to Dundalk via Parkgate.

[37] For example, TNA, CUST 39/16, Establishment List *c.*1782, lists fifteen officers at Parkgate plus John Humphreys at Ness Colliery, but just three men covering 'Baghillt', Mostyn and Flint, none of whom is linked to a specific colliery.

[38] See note 112.

[39] See, for example, *Adams's Weekly Courant,* 12 November 1771; CALS, 200585, 'The Customs Account Book, 1776-1790'; 'Captains in the Dublin Trade Living in Parkgate' in P. Broster, *The Chester Guide* (1782); and ships' masters named in the accounts for the Neston House of Correction, 1750–1799 (CALS, QSF 187–227). An apparent further sign of Flintshire's lack of overseas business is the absence of imports held 'in store' by customs officials. While hundreds of such records exist in the 1760s and 1770s in relation to named stores at Chester and, more often, Parkgate, the last such entry for Flintshire is on 14 July 1758, at Mostyn (TNA, E 190, 1432/11).

[40] Again, there is nothing to suggest war influenced this pattern significantly. John Armstrong and Philip Bagwell, 'Coastal Shipping' in *Transport in the Industrial Revolution*, ed. by D. Aldcroft and M. Freeman (Manchester: Manchester University Press, 1983), p. 146) say there is little evidence that the Seven Years' War (or the later War of American Independence) interfered with the coasting trade.

[41] TNA, HO 42/68/90, ff.223–4 (8 August 1803).

[42] Two stone causeways are depicted on Thomas Boydell's map, surveyed in 1770-1 (CALS, PM 11/7). F. Webster, 'The River Dee Reclamation and the Effect upon Navigation', *Transactions of the Liverpool Engineering Society*, 51 (1930), pp. 79–83.

[43] Boyd, pp. 35–9; G. Hawkes,' The Founder of the Port of Connah's Quay?', *FHSJ*, 32 (1989), p. 178. Another new coal business to set up around this time and keen to exploit river access was Leach and Co. in the Hawarden area in 1799 (T. W. Pritchard, *A History of the Old Parish of Hawarden* (Wrexham: Bridge Books, 2002), pp. 69–70).

[44] Exports rose 15% from 6,243 chaldrons in 1798 to 7,205 in 1799, the highest that decade (*Report from the Committee Appointed to Consider of the Coal Trade [sic] of the United Kingdom*, Appendix 42, HOCP Vol. 132 (1800).

45 C. R. Williams, 'Thomas Norbury's Letters, 1806–1822', *FHSP*, 26 (1973–4), pp. 38–51.

46 Re wharves: Flint through the Ages (n.d.). Available at Flint though the Ages, *Industry through the Ages* (n.d.), <http://www.fflint.co.uk/industry.html?> [accessed 20 March 2019]. Re Mostyn, see Patricia O'Toole, *Sea Change: History of the Port of Mostyn* (n.p.: Cheshire Country Publishing 2002), pp. 10–11, and Bangor Archives, Mostyn MSS 6980 which describes the process for creating the proposed new channel. Matthias Dunn, writing in 1844 (p. 135) refers to these early works as well as later ones to enlarge access.

47 C. R. Williams, p. 41, mentions Norbury observing a temporary halt in the movement of the channel.

48 Parl. Papers, *Tidal Harbours Commission, Second Report of the Commissioners*, Paper 692 (1846), p. 299.

49 Ibid.

50 *Chester Courant*, 18 February 1806.

51 CAS, DLONS/W7/1/131. The vessels are recorded from March to December; none are recorded in January and February, perhaps because these were generally quieter months. 226 vessels left Chester in total that year (Flinn, p. 224). See also pages 180–1.

52 Place (1994), p. 111.

53 Parl. Papers, *An Account of All Coals Carried Coastways as Well as Those Exported to Foreign Parts*, Paper 117 (1819). Chaldrons were the usual measure of sea-borne coal and related to volume rather than weight. Thus, the weight of a chaldron of Winchester measure, which was predominantly used locally, varied but averaged about 28 cwt or 1.4 tons (L. Cullen, *Anglo-Irish Trade, 1660–1800* (Manchester: Manchester University Press, 1968), p. 80). A chaldron of Newcastle measure was often used for European and transatlantic business. It was substantially larger, at 53 hundredweight (A. Velkar, *Markets and Measurements in Nineteenth Century Britain* (Cambridge: Cambridge University Press, 2012), p. 107. Confusingly, J. Nef (*The Rise of the British Coal Industry*, 2 vols (London: Frank Cass and Co.), ii, p. 370) says a chaldron was two tons and this has been used by Craig in his calculations (p. 122). However, 28 cwt seems to be more widely accepted and is consistent with the records from Anchor Smelting Co. (see Table 11.9) where 24 chaldrons equalled about 33 tons.

54 T&WA, DX 198/1, p. 410.

55 Hanshall, p. 70.

56 'Flat' is a general term for various types of barge including sailing barges (Paget-Tomlinson, 1973, p. 3).

57 Parl. Papers (1846), pp. 299–301.

58 British Library, Add. MSS 89098, 12 March 1829.

59 1929, pp. 211–2. He did, however, acknowledge that new uses for coal gave a fillip to the market.

60 Parl. Papers, *First Report of the Commissioners Appointed to Inquire into the Municipal Corporations in England and Wales*, Pt. 4, Paper 116 (1835), pp. 2,683–4.

61 Ibid.

62 Hawkes (1987), pp. 119–20; Dunn (1844), p. 135.

63 See, for example, Ashton and Sykes, pp. 247–8.

Chapter 10 – The Seasale Trade: An Introduction (continued)

[64] Duty rate taken from TNA, E 190 series, passim; different rates applied to other overseas destinations.

[65] T. W. Williams, *A Compendious Digest of the Statute Law* (London: G. Kearsley, 1787), pp. 335, 337; *Dublin Mercantile Advertiser*, 25 January 1830.

[66] The information is given in TNA, CUST 39/16, written in 1782. The exact date appears to be 5 July 1759. The '9' in the year is not well-formed and may have been taken as a '0' by some researchers, which could explain why some have attributed the opening of Ness Colliery to 1750.

[67] CALS, QDV 2/304, Ness Land Tax records show Humphreys occupying a house, land and office from 1779 (when the records start) until 1794 (record missing 1792; Humphreys absent 1793). TNA, CUST 79/18, 8 February 1831, records Parkgate as the legal quay.

[68] Land Tax records record him living in Great Neston from 1795. *The Chester Courant,* 20 September 1796, p. 4, records that vessels from the colliery were cleared out to sea at Parkgate, 'a mile distant', at that time. Nevertheless, when he died, Humphreys was still described as being 'waiter and searcher at Ness Colliery'. CALS, ZCAP 'Comptroller's Subsidy Book' suggests a change in arrangements in summer 1792 (see note 112).

[69] *Cheshire Sheaf*, 'Parkgate Custom-House', 1st Series, 2 (1883), p. 246. NPR reports he was aged eighty-two. *Chester Courant*, 11 February 1812 says eighty-seven. He had previously worked at Chester.

[70] Parl. Papers, *Accounts and Papers Relating to the Increase and Diminution of Salaries etc. in Public Offices of Britain, 1812*, Paper 112 (1813), p. 126.

[71] TNA, CUST 79/7, 8 December 1820.

[72] TNA, CUST 79/6, 28 April 1819.

[73] TNA, CUST 79/10, 24 October 1823.

[74] TNA, CUST 79/18, 8 February 1831.

[75] CALS, DDX 378/7, 3 February 1836 and 378/8, 27 January 1838.

[76] Langton (1979), p. 135.

[77] W. Enfield, *An Essay Towards the History of Leverpool* (Warrington, 1773), 'Additions' p. 3.

[78] Liverpool: Enfield, pp. 80–6 and 'Additions' p. 2. Enfield suggests 1,217 chaldrons went to other overseas destinations but the consequent total of 3,351 is slightly adrift of the source used in Table 10.1. Chester: TNA, E 190 1436/6.

[79] There is no indication from any sources of a significant increase in this trade by the 1790s. The relative insignificance of Chester is supported by the 1789 data in Table 10.2. Thomas Pennant (*Tours in Wales, With Notes,* 3 vols, (London: printed for Wilkie and Robinson, and others, 1810, iii, p. 280) suggests there was a decline in the total number of coasting vessels entered outwards from Chester (carrying all goods, not just coal) from 526 in 1771 to 402 in 1796.

[80] Cullen, pp. 82–4.

[81] Flinn, p. 222; Parl. Papers (1800), Appendix 42.

[82] Ashton and Sykes, pp. 227–9; Cullen, p. 85.

[83] Parl. Papers, *Report from the Select Committee of the House of Lords Appointed to Take into Consideration the State of the Coal Trade,* Paper 9 (1830), pp. 108–9.

[84] Cullen, pp. 85–6; Flinn, pp. 223–4.

[85] 5,892 out of 531,667 chaldrons (Parl. Papers (1830), p. 126).

[86] Dodd (1971), p. 156. Swansea journeys – see, for example, TNA, E 190 1446/2, on 26, 29, 31 May and 26 June 1789.

[87] Coal Authority, 14923/6 (1839). All detailed depictions post-date alterations probably made in the 1820s (see page 168); it is possible it was originally a different length.

[88] Place (1994), p. 16.

[89] Ibid.

[90] CALS, Z AB/4/182v, 30 November 1959.

[91] CALS, DHL 64/31; Place, (1985), p. 130.

[92] CALS, Z AB/4/185v, 209 and 209v.

[93] See pages 156–7.

[94] CALS, ZTAP/3 (City Rentals 1763–1777). A few sandstone blocks at Lightfoot's Pool by the site of the former quay hint at the beginnings of a harbour wall but there are very few of them and they cannot be dated.

[95] Arundel Castle Manuscripts, TP 60. A similar map, TP 62, is dated 1789.

[96] OS, one-inch, LXXIX (1840). Also, the 'Colliery Channel' (*Chester Chronicle*, 14 September 1838).

[97] *Williamson's Liverpool Advertiser*, 3 February 1769 re the 137-ton (139-tonne) brig *Paris Packet*; *Saunders's News-Letter*, 6 May 1794, re the Newry-registered 90-ton (91-tonne) *Peggy*.

[98] Arundel Castle Manuscripts, TP 60.

[99] CALS, Z AB/5/26, 9 December 1790. The enquiry was made by John Stanley Massey, presumably in his capacity of manorial lord.

[100] Sir Roger Mostyn made a similar purchase enquiry of the Assembly fifteen months later (CALS, Z AB/5/29) and it appears that his son Thomas went ahead with the purchase in 1799 (Rupert Morris, *Chester in the Plantagenet and Stuart Reigns* (Chester: Rupert Morris, 1893), p. 459, n. 2 incorrectly citing Sir Roger).

[101] *Chester Chronicle*, 26 April 1822 which states that the quay was built at 'about the same time' as the underground canal which was built in 1791. CALS, DBC 261/38, 'Cottingham and Stanley', *c.*13 September 1821 says the quay was built 'about thirty years ago'. Davies had left the colliery by early 1792.

[102] *Chester Courant*, 20 September 1796.

[103] Coal Authority, 14923/2.

[104] CALS, EDT 286/2.

[105] See page 23.

[106] See page 22.

[107] 'Map of a Pier at Little Neston', *c.*1829, CALS, part of D5363.

[108] *Chester Chronicle*, 26 April 1822.

[109] Bangor Archives, Baron Hill Correspondence 7312.

[110] For example, Coal Authority, 14923/4, /6.

[111] Recorded duties increased from £32 in 1791 to £193 in 1792 and £365 in 1793, remaining at high levels for the remainder of the decade (CALS, ZCAP, 'Comptroller's Subsidy Book').

Chapter 10 – The Seasale Trade: An Introduction (continued)

[112] All coal export duties listed in the Chester port books, which finish in 1774, were recorded under *Chester's* total figure for exports, not Parkgate's. This is clear even when it is known that shipments emanated from Ness Colliery. Low duty figures for Parkgate from 1776–1790 (CALS, 200585) were evidently a continuation of this practice. The figure for 1791 (note 111 above) is a further continuation, with the practice changing from the summer of 1792. The increased duty figures from summer 1792 are consistent with most, if not all, of the coal being exported from the port of Chester emanating from Ness Colliery, at the prevailing rate of duty of 1*s.* 2*d.* per chaldron.

[113] *Chester Chronicle*, 23 April 1830; CALS, D5363 'Little Neston Coal Mines' re Pit No. 1.

[114] TNA, J 90/18, (1826), 'An estate in Little Neston'; 'Map of a Pier at Little Neston', (*c.*1829), CALS, part of D5363.

[115] *Chester Chronicle*, 23 April 1830.

[116] *Chester Chronicle*, 13 December 1851.

[117] See page 123.

[118] *Chester Chronicle*, 23 June 1855.

Chapter 11 – The Overseas and Coasting Trades

[1] Cullen, p. 78.

[2] Ashton and Sykes, p. 227.

[3] Flinn, pp. 221–2.

[4] B. Cunliffe, R. Bartlett, J. Morrill, A. Briggs and J. Bourke, *The Penguin Atlas of British and Irish History* (London: Penguin, 2001), p. 146; T. Graham, 'Whitelaw's 1798 Census of Dublin', *History Ireland*, 2, 3 (Autumn 1994), pp. 10–15.

[5] Flinn, p. 448.

[6] Cullen, p. 82.

[7] 1762 is the peak year for sailings in the first few years after Ness Colliery's opening; data for 1770 provides a point of comparison with coasting trade data given later in the chapter as well as with data available for Liverpool (Table 10.1); 1774 is the last full year for which this data is available.

[8] Andy Bielenberg, *Ireland and the Industrial Revolution* (Abingdon: Routledge, 2009), p. 6.

[9] G. Bowie, Early Stationary Steam Engines in Ireland, *Industrial Archaeology Review*, 2, 2 (1978), pp. 168–74.

[10] Ibid.

[11] Carrig Building Fabric Consultants, *Dublin Historic Industry Database* (for the Geological Survey of Ireland, 2011). <https://www.gsi.ie/documents/DublinHistoricIndustryDatabaseReport.pdf> [accessed 2 January 2023]; Cullen, pp. 5–6.

[12] Cullen, pp. 79 and 126.

[13] *Dublin Courier*, 12 August 1761.

[14] *The Statutes at Large Passed in the Parliaments Held in Ireland,* (Dublin: printed by the executors of David Hay, 1782), p. 317 which lists Johnson as a dealer in 1771–2.

[15] *Dublin Journal*, 10 March 1761.

[16] TNA, E 190 1436/6.

[17] Cullen, p. 126 who states that Cork also had a public coal yard. See also *The Statutes at Large Passed in the Parliaments Held in Ireland*, (Dublin: printed by Boulter Grierson, 1769), pp. 145–6.

[18] Ibid.

[19] *Saunders's News-Letter*, 22 October 1802.

[20] The Irish newspapers frequently ran such accounts in the eighteenth and early nineteenth century, for example *Saunders's News-Letter*, 10 December 1781.

[21] *Dublin Courier*, 29 July 1761. The port book (TNA, E 190 1435/8) records a total of twenty-five ships leaving Chester with coals that month, including eight in the final week.

[22] TNA: E 190 1434/1, 15 November 1760. Also, George Clarke was merchant for imported 'sopers waste' to the port of Chester in 1762 in the *Union* (TNA, E 190 1436/6, 30 October). Laurence Johnson was merchant for the return voyage carrying coal (1 December).

[23] 1760–1762 (TNA, E 190, 1434/8, 1435/8, 1436/6, passim. His involvement seems to have faded out as Laurence Johnson's grew. He continues to appear in records from time to time, though, for example exporting both lead and coal to Dunkirk in 1765 (TNA, E 190 1438/1, 18 December). He also occasionally imported goods too e.g. linen (TNA, E 190 1436/6, 19 April 1762).

[24] J. V. Beckett, *Coal and Tobacco: The Lowthers and Economic Development in West Cumberland, 1660–1760* (Cambridge: Cambridge University Press, 1981), p. 60.

[25] This imbalance had created problems in the past with part of the Dee becoming clogged by ballast jettisoned by ships arriving from Dublin (British Library, Sloane MSS 3323 f.269). The 1733 River Dee Navigation Act imposed harsh penalties for such transgressions.

[26] See page 123.

[27] TNA, E 190 series, passim. Almost 1.4 million yards (1,280 km) of linen were imported into Chester in 1767 (Craig, p. 117).

[28] Joan Thirsk et al., ed., *The Agrarian History of England and Wales* (8 volumes) (Cambridge: Cambridge University Press, 1967–2000), 5.ii (1985), pp. 352–5.

[29] Place (1994), p. 210.

[30] TNA, E 190 1436/6, 30 October 1762.

[31] See page 136.

[32] Cullen, p. 79 states that in 1790 1,481 colliers left Dublin in ballast and it seems likely that the majority were bound for Whitehaven.

[33] Haynes-Thomas, p. 40.

[34] Cullen, p. 123.

[35] LA, DDCL 1065. All ten can be found undertaking one or more outward journeys with coals in the Chester port books for 1769 and/or for the following or preceding years and several appear in other sources associated with shipping from Parkgate, e.g. the accounts of Neston House of Correction (CALS, QJF series).

[36] *Adams's Weekly Courant*, 11 October 1763 and 5, 12 and 19 December 1769. See note 35, Chapter 2.

[37] Re Venus: *Belfast News Letter*, 8 March 1768, 12 May and 20 October 1769, and Chester port books (TNA, E 190 1439/1, 25 November 1767, 1439/8, 5 March 1768 and other entries, and 1440/5, 6 March 1769 and other entries). See also Table 11.5.

Chapter 11 – The Overseas and Coasting Trades (continued)

[38] The amount paid for 'Boatbuilding' has been lost from the edge of the document but surviving totals and other entries on the document mean that the 'boatbuilding' entry can have been for no more than £745. She is described as a brig in *Adams's Weekly Courant*, 29 May 1770. The vessel is not named in the accounts but the family name, timing and other circumstances leave little doubt that it was the *Stanley Massey*.

[39] TNA, E 190 1440/12, 12 July 1770. Thames-built vessels were termed 'river built'. Her long list of cargo included anchovies, hops, molasses, iron hoops, stationary [*sic*], books, 'british soft sope', 'oilmansware' (goods for making edible oils), gunpowder and much else.

[40] TNA, E 190 1440/6, 21 September 1770, misnamed as the *Massey Stanley*.

[41] On 26 March 1771 the vessel left Chester for Dublin with 73 chaldrons of coal. Lloyd was the named merchant but the master was William Higgins (TNA, E 190 1442/2).

[42] Cullen, pp. 119 and 128. As an example of a glut, the *Dublin Courier* reported on 1 August 1760 that sixty colliers had arrived in the previous few days which 'considerably lowered the price' of coals.

[43] Cullen, pp. 122–3.

[44] Cullen, pp. 117 and 126.

[45] Occasionally a single vessel carried coals for the master *and* for a merchant e.g. the *Britannia*, 44 and 27 chaldrons respectively (TNA, E 190 1441/1, 13 February 1772).

[46] *Hoey's Dublin Mercury*, 23 October 1770.

[47] *Belfast News Letter*, 25 October 1771.

[48] The notice, signed by eleven masters, was dated 26 October and published in *Adams's Weekly Courant* on 12 November 1771.

[49] The last known reference to her is in *Faulkner's Dublin Journal* bound for Parkgate from Dublin (9 February 1772). Whatever happened to the ship, the master appears to have survived: Englefield Lloyd – presumably the same man – was living in New Ferry, Wirral, in 1776 (*Chester Chronicle*, 14 March) and was a Neston shopkeeper when he died three years later (NPR).

[50] TNA, E 190 1442. Voyages are recorded on 22 January, 26 March, 4 May, 12 June and 25 July.

[51] *Dublin Courier*, 1 August 1760 (passengers), 12 January 1761 (coals and other goods; also in TNA, E 190 1435/1); *London Chronicle*, 3 March 1761 (passengers).

[52] Place (1994), p. 100.

[53] John Wesley, *The Works of the Rev. John Wesley, A.M.*, 14 vols, 3rd edn (London: John Mason, 1829), iii, p. 425.

[54] TNA, E 190 1440/8, 15 November 1771.

[55] Place (1994), p. 184.

[56] CALS, QJF 206/2, 2 June 1778 and QJF 210/1, 23 October 1781 (see also 14 December 1781).

[57] CALS, QJF 211/1 and 4, 15 March and 18 September 1783.

[58] Neither the Chester nor Dublin newspapers routinely recorded movements of coal-carrying vessels. There are no substantial business or customs accounts either. However intermittent references can be found in the 'Vessels Cleared Outwards' in the *Chester Chronicle* and *Adams's Weekly Courant* until about 1780, very occasionally in Irish newspapers, and in a few entries regarding the Neston House of Correction (CALS, QJF series). In addition, vessels continued to bring goods to Parkgate (CALS, 200585 covering 1776–90 and CALS, ZCAP, 'Comptroller's

Subsidy Book', April 1790 to April 1802) and it would have made sense to return with a payload whenever possible, the most readily available goods being coal.

[59] *Chester Chronicle,* 11 December 1795 (repeated in *Billinge's Liverpool Advertiser,* 11 January 1796), 4 September 1812 and 21 March 1817.

[60] Lysons and Lysons, p. 413.

[61] Cullen, pp. 82–3; Flinn, p. 223.

[62] *Saunders's News-Letter,* 24 May 1797. See also *Freeman's Journal* (Dublin), 21 October 1794 and Cullen, p. 85 re demand for Wigan coals.

[63] Flinn, pp. 223–4.

[64] Various letters from him exist at TNA, dated between 1798 and 1803. The ones cited here are HO 42/46/146 ff.312–314 (31 March 1799) and HO 42/68/90, ff.223–4 (28 August 1803). Local newspapers report Ward subscribing to other actions in 1803 intended to defend the country.

[65] Roger Knight, *Britain Against Napoleon, the Organisation of Victory* (London: Penguin, 2014), pp. 90–4.

[66] Knight, pp. 251–60.

[67] *Cheshire Sheaf,* 'Forgotten Cheshire Regiments', 3rd series, 6 (1906), pp. 107–8.

[68] Nicholas Rogers, *Resisting Napoleon: the British response to the threat of Invasion 1779–1815* (Aldershot: Ashgate, 2006), pp. 41, 46.

[69] *Morning Post,* 31 August 1803.

[70] See, for example, *Morning Post,* 2 August 1803 and 5 September 1803.

[71] TNA, E 190 1439/1, 27 October 1767.

[72] CAS, DLONS/W7/1/131; *Saunders's News-Letter,* 15 March 1815.

[73] CAS, DLONS/W7/1/131.

[74] The Irish vessels came from Arklow, Baldoyle, Baltimore, Dublin, Dungarvan, Kinsale, Newry, Ringaskiddy (Cork), Rosscarbery (Cork), Sutton (Dublin), Wicklow and even Tralee on the west coast; named Welsh ports were Aberystwyth, Beaumaris and Pwllheli; 'Other England' ports were Preston and 'Kendall' (presumably Milnthorpe). The records need to be treated with some circumspection as they contain some obvious errors, not least in relation to the port of registry of the *Puddington*. Nevertheless, the Irish domination of the port of registration appears unarguable.

[75] The *Puddington* is also recorded as carrying 40 tons (44 tonnes) of gravel from the beach at Heswall to the shore at Hooton in 1814 (CALS, DDX 378/2, 14 March).

[76] *Chester Courant,* 20 December 1814.

[77] *Chester Chronicle,* 4 September 1812.

[78] Ken Milne, *Manx Marine Environmental Assessment, Infrastructure, Energy, Mines and Minerals* (Isle of Man: Isle of Man Government, 2013), pp. 23–4.

[79] For example, TNA, E 190 1436/6, 28 October 1762.

[80] In the twelve months to 29 September 1752, forty-nine vessels from Whitehaven took coal to the Isle of Man, with eight from Mostyn, Bagillt and 'Chester' and thirteen from Liverpool (J. R. Dickinson, 'The Overseas Trade of the Isle of Man, 1576–1755', *THSLC,* 154 (2005), p. 16).

[81] TNA, E 190 1442/1, 31 August 1774.

[82] CALS, 200585.

[83] Annakin-Smith (2011), pp. 41–6; TNA, E/190/1434/8, 30 May 1761.

Chapter 11 – The Overseas and Coasting Trades (continued)

[84] TNA, E 190 series (Appendix IV): Lisbon (1774), Malaga (1764), Marseille and Dunkirk (1765), Bordeaux (with lead too, 1767), Oporto (1759 twice, 1765, 1766, 1767, 1769, 1771, 1774), and Rouen (1766). The *Chester Chronicle*, 20 December 1776, also reported a shipment of coals to Oporto.

[85] TNA, E 190 series (Appendix IV). The New York bound vessel was the *Susannah*, a prize captured from the French in 1758, and formerly called *Le Cheval Marine* (TNA, E 190 1435/8, Importations, 11 March 1761). South Carolina journeys in 1759, 1760, 1761, 1765, 1766, 1769. A further journey planned in 1770 was diverted to Newfoundland. The *Berwick* also carried 177 chaldrons, to Cork on 27 February 1766 (TNA, E 190 1438/7).

[86] TNA, E 190 series (Appendix IV) 1768, 1770, 1771, 1772, 1773.

[87] For example, TNA, E 190 1439/1, 15 April 1767 to Bordeaux. The merchant for the lead was Richard Richardson; the ship's master was merchant for the coal.

[88] TNA, E 190 1437/5, 24–25 July and 1 August 1764, 1438/1, 12 March 1765. Sometimes vessels came back via Dublin.

[89] TNA, E 190 series (Appendix IV). Outward journeys are noted in 1759, 1760 (twice), 1763 (twice), 1764, 1767. Import examples: TNA, E 190 1436/8, 15 April 1763 (cork) and E 190 1437/5, 13 April 1764 (Spanish wine and French brandy).

[90] TNA, E 190, 14401/1, 7 December 1769.

[91] Lloyd's List, 28 June 1765; TNA, E 190 1438/1, 25 August 1765 (70 ch. coal); E 190 1438/7, 20 September 1766 (45 ch. coal, and lead); 1439/3, 1 June 1767; E 190 1439/8, 17 August 1768 (inbound); E 190 1440/1, 5 October 1769 (64 ch. coal, and lead); E 190 1440/10, 13 November 1771; *Chester Chronicle*, 14 August 1775, renamed *American*. The Liverpool Plantation Register state her tonnage as '200' which would make her one of the largest known vessels to visit Parkgate; the shipping register in South Carolina, where she was built, also states 200 tons (R. N. Olsberg 'Ship Registers in the South Carolina Archives 1734–1789', *South Carolina Historical Society Magazine*, 74, 4 (Oct. 1973), 189–299, p. 223). A sailing notice (*Williamson's Liverpool Advertiser*, 16 August 1765) states her burthen as 300 tons.

[92] For example, TNA, E 190 1439/1, 1 June 1767, returning via Lisbon, and TNA, CUST 61/3, 25 March 1766.

[93] For example, the *William* returned from Newfoundland via Malaga and Barcelona, importing raisins, olive oil and wine (TNA, E 190 1440/10, June 1771).

[94] The *William* in TNA, E 190, 1440/8, 'Importations', 8 October 1770.

[95] *Lloyd's List*, 2 September 1766.

[96] TNA, E 190 14401/ 4 January 1770 and 1440/4 31 March 1770.

[97] TNA, E 190 1441/2, 22 February, 27 March and 15 October 1773. On the voyage where she was damaged she was carrying 30 chaldrons of coals intended for Cork; after repairs she re-routed for Newfoundland, carrying 63 chaldrons.

[98] *Williamson's Liverpool Advertiser*, 27 July 1764; University of Liverpool Special Collections, MS.25.19, 'Glegg Account Book and Notary's Register'. The *Northern Lass* appears to have been a rather accident-prone vessel, having lost her foremast and bowsprit in a storm in 1759 on the way to New York, and then being 'sunk' in Dublin harbour two years later (*Manchester Mercury*, 17 April 1759; *Lloyd's List*, 17 March 1761). Stated tonnage was 200 in *Williamson's Liverpool Advertiser*, 22 September 1758 but 120 in the Liverpool Plantation Register, 2 November 1758.

[99] TNA, E 190, 1437/5, 5 September 1764; TNA, CO 142/18, 9 October 1765.

[100] See, for example, the *William* (TNA, E 190 1440/10, June 1771).

[101] Bridget and Richard Larn, *Shipwreck Index of Ireland* (Redhill: Lloyds Register/Fairplay, 2002) and Richard Larn, *Shipwreck Index of the British Isles* (London: Lloyds Register of Shipping, 2000), p. 5. The Larns note (p. xii in the latter volume) that one of their primary sources, Lloyd's List, failed to record numerous losses up to 1900.

[102] The primary source used is the 'Glegg Account Book and Notary's Register' (University of Liverpool Special Collections, MS.25.19). The information has been supplemented with material from the Chester port books (TNA, E 190 series). The Glegg record usually states 'Burthen'. When this figure disagrees with the port book entry the latter has been used on the basis that this is likely to reflect the actual volume of coals carried. The complete 'Acts of Protest' cover the period 11 February 1762 to 17 February 1768. The masters' sworn statement was usually made within a few days of the relevant incident. Additionally, the master of the *Mary Ann* reported on 12 October 1764 that she had been damaged by another vessel. She was said to be sailing with 21 chaldrons of coals from Dawpool to Wexford but Dawpool was an anchorage; it seems highly probable the place of loading would have been Ness Colliery.

[103] University of Liverpool Special Collections, MS.25.19. Coastwise entries from the Acts of Protest are discussed on page 192.

[104] *Belfast News Letter*, 27 October 1775; *Chester Chronicle*, 30 October 1775. Some accounts incorrectly state the vessel to be the *Charming Molly*.

[105] *The Times*, 3 October 1800.

[106] The *Industry*, master Simpson, lost a man and boy on the sands between Parkgate and Flint (The *Cambrian*, 27 February 1808); the collier *Sedulous* was driven ashore at Parkgate with several other vessels in a severe storm (*Belfast Commercial Chronicle*, 19 October 1808); the sloop *Providence*, master Lyons, was wrecked off Bangor, Ireland (*Saunders's News-Letter*, 19 June 1811).

[107] TNA, E 190 1442/2, 16 January and 23 February 1771; E 190, 1441/1, 9 May 1772.

[108] TNA, E 190 1441/5, 15 August 1773.

[109] *Chester Courant*, 2 November 1773. CALS, Z QCI 24/24: inquest on John Handley [*sic*], 1 November 1773 which states the accident was 'near' Ness Colliery.

[110] CALS, Z QCI 25/7 and Z QCI 27/9.

[111] Rawson, p. 131; Boyd pp. 40–1.

[112] See for example TNA, E 190 1436/1, 6 August 1762 (three vessels). The record of decline is based on listings of commodities carried in the port books and the Chester 'Register of Vessels' (CALS, QDN 1/5).

[113] T. Willan, *The Navigation of the River Weaver in the Eighteenth Century*, Chetham Society, 3rd series, iii (1951), pp. 208–13.

[114] T. Willan, *The English Coasting Trade, 1600–1750* (Manchester: Manchester University Press, 1967), p. 51.

[115] For example, TNA, E 190 1438/6, 16 April 1766 which took 13 chaldrons of coal to Caernarfon plus a diverse range of other goods.

[116] Some of the coal may have been destined for smaller ports such as Amlwch, Bangor or Rhuddlan but these were listed under their superior Member Port.

Chapter 11 – The Overseas and Coasting Trades (continued)

[117] 1762 was the peak year for all shipping movements and for coal shipments out of the port of Chester after Ness Colliery opened, based on surviving customs records. 1770 is the final year for which full-year customs records survive.

[118] Other English destinations noted in the Chester port books after Ness Colliery opened include Southampton, St Ives, Falmouth and Padstow.

[119] Frank Dawson, *John Wilkinson: King of the Ironmasters* (Stroud: The History Press, 2012), p. 43.

[120] TNA, E 190 1440/7, 28 May 1770. The largest known coal load to London was 84 chaldrons on 28 October 1765 (E 190, 1438/2).

[121] Limestone is never listed as a cargo in the port books. T. W. Williams, writing in 1787 (*Compendious Digest*, p. 287), states that 'lime for the improvement of land may be carried without coquet or bond' and lists no duty rate for lime or limestone.

[122] The system is described more fully in Willan (1967), pp. 1–9.

[123] 'North Wales' has been taken to be Aberystwyth northwards. Some vessels made more than one inbound journey; each has been recorded as a separate shipment. The 1762 record of ships inbound from North Wales is skewed by an unusual surge of fifteen vessels bringing black jack (zinc ore) from Aberdyfi during July.

[124] Clarke was party to the bonds for three vessels leaving the port of Chester in January 1760 (TNA, E 190 1433/1), and three vessels to Holyhead in July and October 1762 (TNA, E 190 1436/1).

[125] TNA, E 190 1439/8, 28 March 1766.

[126] TNA, E 190 1438/3, 4 February 1762.

[127] Dodd (1971), p. 194.

[128] Pennant (1796), p. 133.

[129] W. J. Lewis, 'Some Aspects of the History of Aberystwyth', *Ceredigion: Journal of the Cardiganshire Antiquarian Society*, 3, 1–4 (1959), pp. 292, 295–6.

[130] Graham Webster, 'The Lead-Mining Industry in North Wales in Roman Times', *FHSP*, 13 (1952–3), pp. 5–34; M. Bevan-Evans, 'Gadlys and Flintshire Lead-Mining in the Eighteenth Century' Pt. 1, *FHSP*, 18 (1960), pp. 75–80.

[131] R. A. Williams, 'Hidden Bullion: Silver Production in North-East Wales', *Welsh Mines and Mining*, 2 (2012), pp. 33–44.

[132] Dodd (1971), pp. 183–8.

[133] Recorded from 16 January 1801 (CALS, DDX 378/1) to 9 January 1839 (CALS, DDX 378/8) with occasional related expenditure in between too.

[134] Bevan-Evans (1960), pp. 75–130 and M. Bevan-Evans, 'Gadlys and Flintshire Lead-Mining in the Eighteenth Century.' *FHSP*, 19 (1961), pp. 32–60; Dodd (1971), pp. 183–8.

[135] George Lloyd, 'Archaeological Notes', *FHSJ*, 19 (1961), p. 91.

[136] Kenneth Davies, 'The Eighteenth Century Copper and Brass Industries of the Greenfield Valley', *Trans. of the Honourable Society of Cymmrodorion* (1979), pp. 205, 208, 211.

[137] K. Davies (1979), p. 206.

[138] Kenneth Davies, 'Holywell and the Transatlantic Slave Trade', *FHSJ*, 40 (2015), pp. 109–40.

[139] Dodd (1971), p. 156. Coal from Golftyn, at the seaward end of the River Dee Navigation, seems to have been the fuel of choice for the Mona Mine Co. in 1791 (Anglesey Archives, WDAP/1/1, 31 March).

[140] Kenneth Davies, 'The Nineteenth Century Copper Industry in the Greenfield Valley', *Trans. Of the Honourable Society of Cymmrodorion*, (1988), p. 130.

[141] *Adams's Weekly Courant*, 12 June 1759.

[142] James Boswell, *Life of Samuel Johnson including Boswell's Journal of a tour to the Hebrides and Johnson's Diary of a journey into North Wales*, v.5, ed. by George Birkbeck Hill (Oxford: Clarendon Press, 1950), p. 441.

[143] Pennant (1778), p. 44.

[144] Dodd (1929), p. 206.

[145] *Chester Courant*, 29 November 1825. Aikin (1797), pp. 180-1, describes how 'all the mechanical power [at Greenfield] comes from the stream' and that it discharges '21 tuns of water in a minute'.

[146] Rawson, p. 130; *Chester Chronicle*, 11 April 1776.

[147] Dodd, (1929), p. 204.

[148] N. W. Jones, *The Buckley Potteries: an Assessment of Survival and Potential* (Powys: The Clwyd-Powys Archaeological Trust, 2014), pp. 5-7 and 41.

[149] See pages 33–4 and 132 for examples.

[150] Dodd, (1971), p. 148; Ray Jones, 'Industrial Landscapes of North East Wales and the Border Counties' (unpublished paper, *c.*2015?), pp. 60 and 84.

[151] R. Jones, p. 23. The work, sadly unpublished at the time of writing, includes an excellent survey of engines installed at mines in north-east Wales.

[152] Pennant (1796), p. 133; Pennant (1778), p. 16.

[153] LA, DDCL 1065.

[154] University of Liverpool Special Collections, MS.25.19, 'Glegg Account Book and Notary's Register'.

[155] CALS, ZTCP/5/106 and ZTCP/5/116.

[156] CALS, ZTCP/5/109, ZTCP/5/205 and many others.

[157] W. J. Lewis, 'The Anchor Smelting Co., Aberystwyth, 1786–1792', *Journal of the Ceredigion Antiquarian Society*, 4 (1963), pp. 129–34.

[158] Ibid.; NLW, Powis MSS 18677, 18650, 18696 and 21938.

[159] NLW, Powis MSS 4102.

[160] Dodd (1971), p. 196.

[161] LA, DDBL 54/45: Ness Colliery Summary accounts, 1795–1811' which refer to £1,560 'towards building the Galliot'.

[162] M. Stammers, *Mersey Flats and Flatmen* (Lavenham, Suffolk: Terence Dalton Limited, and Liverpool: National Museums and Galleries on Merseyside, 1993), p. 50. Another Galliot is said to have been operating between Parkgate and Dublin around this time – the *Margaret*, the first ship in the famous Bibby shipping business (E. W. Paget-Tomlinson, *Bibby Line: 175 Years of Achievement*, (Liverpool: Bibby Line, 1982), p. 55. However, this author has been unable to obtain any further information about this or other Bibby vessels which may have traded locally

Chapter 11 – The Overseas and Coasting Trades (continued)

in the first decade or so of the nineteenth century. If the information about the *Margaret* is correct it was an unusual type of vessel for overseas trading.

[163] W. Waterston, *A Cyclopaedia of Commerce, Mercantile Law, Finance, and Commercial Geography,* Edinburgh: Oliver and Boyd (1843), p. 333.

[164] *North Wales Gazette,* 6 July 1809. Hall died a couple of years later (*Lancaster Gazette,* 9 March 1811); it is not known who succeeded him as master of the *Hooton.*

[165] NEWA, D/DM/452/1, 16 October 1813. A vessel of the same name was operating on Britain's west coast from South Wales to Lancashire and across to Ireland in the 1820 and 1830s, sometimes carrying coals, but no connection to Ness Colliery or the Stanleys has been identified.

[166] *North Wales Gazette,* 4 and 11 May 1815.

[167] *Lancaster Gazette,* 23 August 1823; NEIMME/Wat/3/71/4.

[168] T. Williams, p. 335.

[169] Records not discussed here include Welsh newspaper shipping lists showing coal-carrying vessels from Ness or Parkgate to Conwy (1809 and 1810), Aberystwyth (1812, twice), Caernarfon (1808 and 1814), Beaumaris (1815); and from Caernarfon to Ness Colliery in 1840 (twice). See *nestoncollieries.org*

[170] K. Davies (1988), p. 92.

[171] K. Davies (1988), pp. 90–2.

[172] Davies' largely excellent article, *supra,* incorrectly names Joseph Lyon as Joseph Hayes Lyon. Joseph Lyon's son, Edmund Brock Lyon, was also involved with the business according to Davies (who also incorrectly says Edmund was Joseph's cousin).

[173] NPR 5 March 1780 and 26 October 1844; a newspaper report indicates he was resident in Neston no later than 1832 (*Liverpool Mercury,* 9 March 1832).

[174] Bangor Archives, Mona Mine 3204, 31 May 1831.

[175] Bangor Archives, Mona Mine, 3207, 21 October 1831.

[176] Bangor Archives, 3204, 3 June 1831.

[177] Bangor Archives, 3207 21 October 1831.

[178] Bangor Archives, Mona Mine 1098, Ledger 2. Six payments of between £45 and £352 are recorded between January 1831 and August 1833, totalling £902. This represents 2,775 tons (3,022 tonnes) at the 1831 price of 6*s.* 6*d.* (32.5p) per ton.

[179] CALS, P149/11/4. Sir Thomas Stanley did, however, occasionally buy copper wire and lead from Newton Lyon e.g. CALS, DDX 378/12, 16 June 1829, 8 May 1830 and DDX 378/7, 12 December 1834.

[180] Census, Ness.

[181] The *OED* indicates the first use of the term in this context in 1884.

[182] See pages 230–1 re literacy.

[183] *Dublin Journal,* 10 March 1761.

[184] *Chester Courant,* 6 August 1805 and 10 and 17 June 1806.

[185] LA, DDBL 54/45.

[186] TNA, J 90/82, 31 March 1823; *Chester Courant,* 25 March 1823.

[187] NEIMME/Wat/3/71/9.

188 *Chester Chronicle*, 8 March 1839.

189 NLW, Powis MSS, 18650, 18677 and 18696.

190 Brand: 'A name, term, sign, symbol, design or combination of these that identifies the products or services of one seller … and differentiates them from those of competitors' (P. Kotler et al. *Principles of Marketing*, 6th European edn (Harlow: Pearson, 2013), p. 245.

191 Neil McKendrick, 'Josiah Wedgwood and the Commercialization of the Potteries' in *The Birth of a Consumer Society: the Commercialization of Eighteenth-Century England* by N. McKendrick, J. Brewer and J. Plumb (London: Hutchinson, 1983), pp. 117–18 and 138; Twinings, *History of Twinings* (n.d.), <https://www.twinings.co.uk/about-twinings/history-of-twinings> [2 January 2023]. Neither research in multiple archives, nor specific enquiries concerning Britain's largest coal-producing region, the North East (pers. corresp. NEIMME Librarian and others, February 2019), have revealed any comparable example of logo usage.

192 Sales vouchers and receipt paperwork: CALS, DHL 54C; TNA, J 90/82.

193 TNA, J 90/82, passim.

Chapter 12 – Social Aspects of the Neston Collieries

1 Neston St Mary and St Helen parish church, Burton St Nicholas parish church, St Winefride Roman Catholic Church (from 1843) and Puddington Roman Catholic Chapel (from 1795). Cheshire Marriage Licence Bonds and Allegations also give valuable information.

2 Terms such as 'colliery banksman', 'collier's boy', 'colliery labourer' 'underground steward' and 'pitman' have been included, i.e. all those working directly with, or in close proximity to, the coal. 'Miner' has been included where the term unequivocally relates to coal. Men who were colliers at one or more points in time but who pursued other occupations before, during or after that work (notably as 'labourer', quite possibly at the colliery, but also in a few cases in other unrelated occupations) have been included in counts.

3 Five men who worked at Ness Colliery but whose role is unclear are also included.

4 See *nestoncollieries.org*

5 Langton (2000), pp. 73 and 82. See also Rhiannon Thompson, 'A Breed Apart? Class and Community in a Somerset Coal-Mining Parish, c.1750–1850', *Rural History*, 16 (2005), pp. 144–6.

6 Birth-to-baptism interval based on various Lancashire parish registers from the 1760s and Hawarden in the 1820s. Limited available data at Neston supports this too (except amongst Catholics whose children were often born and baptised on the same day).

7 Wrigley et al. (1997), p. 421 which details rates of 35–37% for most of the period under review.

8 35 out of the 160 instances of marriage and baptism – 21.8%. Again, this is similar to other research cited in the source in note 7.

9 20-week old Richard Peers was 'illegitimate' when baptised on 13 January 1845 but his parents shared the same surname by then and went on to have several more children. There is, though, no record of a marriage.

10 Figures exclude remarriages. All the men were 'collier', etc. at some point(s) at Neston.

11 E. A. Wrigley, *Poverty, Progress, and Population* (Cambridge: Cambridge University Press, 2004), p. 324.

12 J. T. Krause, 'The Changing Adequacy of English Registration, 1690–1837' in *Population in History*, ed. by D. V. Glass and D. Eversley (London: Edward Arnold, 1965), p. 392.

Chapter 12 – Social Aspects of the Neston Collieries (continued)

[13] Robert and Catherine Lewis baptised fourteen children between 1826 and 1852.

[14] All Neston-born children have been counted regardless of whether the father was termed 'collier' at the time of birth in the source record for that particular child.

[15] Numerous baptisms are recorded at two-yearly intervals. Thomas and Sarah Littlemore baptised a child every two years from 1775 to 1791 (i.e. nine children; two, maybe three or more, died as children).

[16] Wrigley et al., p. 478.

[17] Numerous instances can be gleaned from census records, occurrences of less common names in parish registers and, from 1837, in marriage register entries which record both the groom's occupation and also his father's. Other sources also occasionally give evidence e.g. CALS, MG 29/1 which records the enrolment of four Littlemore brothers, all colliers, into the Local Militia between 1809 and 1813 (see page 235, and page 340 note 283). See also, for example, Langton (2000), p. 79.

[18] Langton (2000), p. 82.

[19] Data is based on men following any later occupation, or any occupation between bouts of colliery work, other than 'labourer' which they quite possibly were undertaking at the colliery. Some of the men pursuing other occupations were described as agricultural labourers or farmers and may have been working on the colliery farm. Langton (2000, p. 79) records a similarly low percentage in eighteenth-century Lancashire – between 2 and 5%.

[20] H. Boulton, 'The Chester Infirmary', *JCAS*, 47, (1960), pp. 9–20. Paul Langford, *A Polite and Commercial People* (Oxford: Clarendon Press, 1992), pp. 134–9.

[21] British Library, Add Ms 27951, 'Journals of visits to England by an Irish clergyman in 1761 and 1772', p. 14.

[22] CALS, 229320, 'The statutes of the General Infirmary at Chester'.

[23] CALS, Z HI 4, 22 October 1776; *Chester Chronicle*, 1 November 1776.

[24] CALS, Z HI 3, 2 January 1770. Richardson attended several meetings between 1764 and 1767, presumably as a governor, entitled by subscription. In 1762 a patient from Neston was treated on the recommendation of Richardson. As Richardson had no known connections with the area other than as mine-owner, it is very likely the individual was connected with the colliery. His ailment was 'asthmatic'.

[25] Sandycroft Colliery (CALS, Z HI 5, 28 May 1782); other collieries followed. It is, however, possible that firms subscribed earlier under owners' names.

[26] CALS, Z HI 91 and 92. Records of subscriptions are unavailable between 1821–30 and from 1842.

[27] CALS, Z HI 92; TNA, J 90/82, passim.

[28] CALS, Z HI 12, 17 July 1821 – William Swift. Swift was a common surname amongst local colliers.

[29] CALS, Z HI 51 (1759–1763), 52 (1772–1778) and 53 (1782–1792), and Z HI 12 (1815–1822) and Z HI 13–16 (1829–1855).

[30] The thirty-two include three cases where Ness Colliery was almost certainly the recommender, although not specifically named. Averages: CALS, Z HI 52.

[31] Misnamed as 'James' Berry in the Infirmary records – 'John' in NPR.

[32] Roderick Floud ed., *The Economic History of Britain Since 1700*, 3 vols (Cambridge: Cambridge University Press, 1981), i, p. 214.

[33] CALS, Z HI 12–16 list thirty-nine male inpatients and eleven female (ages unknown). Charles Stanley, as opposed to 'Ness Colliery', was the named recommender from 1853.

[34] BPP [1842c], p. 375.

[35] BPP [1842c], p. 407.

[36] Other challenges include many individuals sharing surnames and/or Christian names, hindering clear identification today, and the lack of precision with which ages were sometimes remembered or recorded.

[37] For example, children of Thomas Williams (died 1776), Robert Williams (1777) and William Cottrell (1815).

[38] The principal source is NPR where colliers have primarily been identified from records of baptism of their children. Younger men who had not had children will therefore usually have been missed. Further, reasonably comprehensive recording of ages at burial did not start till around 1811 so there are good records of older men who survived until after then but not younger ones who died earlier.

[39] *OED*, 'consumption'.

[40] Lightfoot and Lawley were each 'Labourer' at death. Very unusually, Woodward was stated to be a schoolmaster in Little Neston when he died but had been a collier at least between 1826 and 1841 (NPR; 1841 census, Little Neston). Anglesey had been a Neston collier for at least fifteen years but died at Wigan – see note 54, Chapter 6.

[41] Scrofula was a form of TB creating glandular swellings.

[42] Arthur McIvor and Ronald Johnston, *Miners' Lung: A History of Dust Disease in British Coal Mining* (Abingdon: Routledge, 2016), p. 67.

[43] BPP [1842c], p. 372.

[44] McIvor and Johnston, p. 67.

[45] BPP [1842c], p. 372.

[46] Jane Jelico (1762), Jane Rowly (1765), Hannah Roberts (1770), Mary Evans (1772), Elizabeth Davies (1779), Mary Armstrong (1780).

[47] The figure includes one who died at Billinge (Lancs.) after her husband moved there when Ness Colliery closed.

[48] NPR, 11 September 1778, 7 and 18 April 1779.

[49] Death Certificate, 18 December 1849 – 'Phthisis pulmonaris'; children – NPR.

[50] All information: NPR unless stated.

[51] Census: Great Neston, 1841 records a child, Joseph, not recorded in NPR.

[52] There were 118 burials in Neston in 1837, the highest in the 1830s which averaged seventy-one burials per year. George Kohn, *Encyclopedia of Plague and Pestilence: From Ancient Times to the Present* (New York: Facts on File, 2008), pp. 52 and 107. Scarlet fever was another possibility – see note 65.

[53] *Chester Chronicle*, 7 July 1837 (as Messam).

[54] NPR, 25 November 1858; Death Certificate, 23 November 1858.

[55] Children of Thomas Fabby, James Lawley, Joshua Pulford, William Roberts and William Smith.

Chapter 12 – Social Aspects of the Neston Collieries (continued)

[56] Langton (2000), p. 76; Benson, p. 123.

[57] Throughout the NPR burial records there is often insufficient detail to firmly attribute the death of a child to a particular parent; often, ages of those buried were not recorded, especially before 1812, and the words 'Child' or 'Infant' were sometimes used as indicators but sometimes not. Problems of identification are exacerbated when common surnames are involved such as Smith, Jones and Williams. Failure to record the 331 deaths of new babies is another possible factor in under-recording. The under-15 mortality rates indicated here are somewhat lower than in Wrigley et al.'s wide study (1997, pp. 250–1) which recorded rates of between 255.9 and 301.8 per thousand during most of the period this book covers. It seems likely that, given colliers' poor domestic circumstances, the true rate of child mortality at Neston would be even higher than that in Wrigley's study which covered a broad range of parishes.

[58] 220 out of 439 collier couples – 50.1%.

[59] BPP [1842c], p. 188. A factor may have been the harshness of working lives for some Lancashire women (see D. Turner and D. Blackie, *Disability in the Industrial Revolution: Physical Impairment in British Coalmining, 1780–1880* (Manchester: Manchester University Press, 2018), p. 63) although this was not specifically mentioned in the 1842 source.

[60] 'Age' has been taken as the age stated in burial records or, if no age is stated, the interval between baptism and burial. All men were recorded as colliers, coal miners, etc. but not necessarily at the child's time of birth or burial.

[61] John Haygarth, *An Enquiry How to Prevent the Smallpox* (Chester: printed by J. Monk, 1785), p. 132.

[62] NPR, 24 and 28 September, 7 October 1778.

[63] NPR, 27 July; Haygarth, p. 113.

[64] Haygarth, p. 96.

[65] For example (from Death Certs): measles – collier's son James Burkey, age eight, 12 January 1852; scarlet fever – collier's son Thomas Miller, age six, 8 July 1837.

[66] BPP [1842a], pp. 183–6; BPP [1842b], pp. 192–3 and 212–14; BPP [1842c], pp. 65–6, 87–8 and 188.

[67] Peter Kirby, 'Causes of short stature among coal mining children, 1823–1850', *Economic History Review*, 48, 4 (1995), pp. 689–90.

[68] Kirby (1995), p. 693.

[69] Ibid. Kirby's views were, however challenged – see Jane Humphries, 'Short Stature among Coal-Mining Children: A Comment', *Economic History Review*, 50, 3 (August 1997), pp. 531–7, and Kirby's 'Rejoinder' in the same publication, pp. 538–42.

[70] Kirby (1995), pp. 690 and 695–6.

[71] Turner and Blackie, p. 58.

[72] BPP [1842c], pp. 368–9. A similar point was made in Lancashire (BPP [1842c], p. 188).

[73] William Lawley, his wife, eight children and a servant, resident in Ness.

[74] BPP [1842c], p. 370.

[75] British Library, Add. MSS 89098, 24 March 1829.

[76] BPP [1842c], p. 217.

[77] Kirby (1995), p. 690.

[78] Flinn, p. 381.

[79] Named on Ness Tithe map (CALS, EDT 286/2) *c*.1845 but depicted on earlier plans, e.g. Coal Authority, 14923/4.

[80] See page 138.

[81] BPP [1842c], p. 369.

[82] CALS, QJF 199/4, 8 October 1771.

[83] TNA, HO 73/53/78, Report of Digby Neave.

[84] S. I. Mitchell, 'Food Shortages and Public Order in Cheshire, 1757–1812', *TLCAS*, 81 (1982), p. 49; Adams, p. 152.

[85] Mokyr (2009), p. 195.

[86] Alan Booth, 'Food Riots in the North-West of England 1790–1801', *Past and Present*, 77, 1 (November 1977), p. 84.

[87] Booth, pp. 89–90; Peter Mathias, *The First Industrial Nation: An Economic History of Britain 1700–1914* (London: Routledge, 2001), p. 198.

[88] Booth, p. 89.

[89] CALS, SF/Nest/4.

[90] *Cheshire Sheaf*, (1906), p. 113.

[91] Flinn, pp. 382–3.

[92] *Chester Chronicle*, 25 November 1831 and *Chester Courant*, 29 November 1831; BPP [1842a], p. 160.

[93] Smith (*Wealth of Nations*), Bk 1, p. 118.

[94] T. R. Malthus (1803), *An Essay on the Principle of Population*, 7th edn, (London: Reeves and Turner, 1872), p. 304.

[95] Edmund Burke, *The Works of the Right Honourable Edmund Burke* (London: printed for F. and C. Rivington, 1801), pp. 293–4.

[96] Pat Thane, 'Government and Society in England and Wales, 1750–1914', in *The Cambridge Social History of Britain 1750–1950*, 3 vols., ed. by F. Thompson (Cambridge: Cambridge University Press, 1993), iii, p. 6.

[97] Steven King, *Poverty and Welfare in England, 1750–1850* (Manchester: Manchester University Press, 2000), pp. 97–9; Handley, pp. 122–3.

[98] K. Snell, *Parish and Belonging* (Cambridge: Cambridge University Press, 2006), pp. 85–6.

[99] NPR, Edward Davis and James Glaves, 5 May 1790. Also 'collier paupers' James Frumston (1789–1791) and John Thomas (1786).

[100] Birth of William (junior) 24 October 1779; burial of Hannah 17 April 1780. Poor Law removal order initiated by 3 October 1780 (CALS, QJB 3/15, pp. 180–1 and 205–6).

[101] Holywell parish register, Vol. 3, Pt. 1, 1741–1772, Peter Robinson baptised 4 December 1763. Another Peter was born to the same couple in 1755 but he apparently died in 1761.

[102] NEWA, P/30/1/55: Register of Holywell Children Apprenticed, pp. 17 and 19.

[103] NEWA, P/30/1/232/1. The apprenticeship is first referred to in 1773 in the source in note 102; the Indenture is dated 1775, maybe superseding a previous agreement.

[104] NPR, 19 February 1792. Another basket maker, John Price, was listed in NPR in 1785 and 1788.

Chapter 12 – Social Aspects of the Neston Collieries (continued)

[105] NPR, 'Labourer' 1773; 'Coal Basket-maker' in 1775, and in 1782. Removal order from Little Neston to Ness and appeal: CALS, QJF 212/2, 27 April 1784 and QJB 3/14, 13 July 1784.

[106] Parish register, St Mary the Virgin, Prescot 27 November 1785; 1851 census for Parr (Lancs.): John Maddison, age 74, 'Coal basket maker', born 'Parr Gate'.

[107] CALS, LGW 1/1, Proceedings of the Board of Guardians of the Wirral Union, 17 May 1836; Handley, p. 123.

[108] *Liverpool Mail*, 25 October 1845; censuses, Ness, 1851 and 1861.

[109] Handley, pp. 125–6.

[110] Handley, p. 126.

[111] Handley, pp. 126–7.

[112] CALS, LGW 1/1, 3 May 1837 and LGW 1/3, 25 August 1841.

[113] CALS, LGW 1/1–3, fourteen entries between 27 February 1837 and 9 August 1843.

[114] CALS, LGW 1/3, 26 July and 9 August 1843; Death Certificate, 2 December 1847.

[115] Death Certificate, 13 June 1844.

[116] CALS, LGW 1/3, seven entries between 11 January 1843 and 6 March 1844. A fourth daughter was baptised two months before he died; she died six years later.

[117] As was claimed to be the rate amongst Flintshire colliers – see page 106.

[118] Censuses, Great Neston, 1841, and 1851 (girls as Hampton); Ann Hampson baptised 13 March 1850.

[119] CALS, LGW 1/3, 27 December 1843, 10 January, 21 February and 20 March 1844.

[120] CALS, LGW 1/3, 9 July 1845, and Death Certificate.

[121] CALS, LGW 1/3, 14 May 1845 (as Barclay) and 23 July 1845 (Bartley) plus other entries; 1841 census, Flint (Barkly) and 1851 (Bartley).

[122] See, for example, CALS, LGW 1/1, 8 August 1836, Samuel and Mary White who had moved to Wigan, and Margaret Standish, widow, 10 October 1836 in Tarbock.

[123] CALS, LGW 1/2, 3 October 1838.

[124] CALS, LGW 1/3, 10 January 1844, 20 August and 29 October 1845; Bebington PR, 19 December 1850.

[125] CALS, LGW 1/1, 25 July 1836.

[126] CALS, QJF 198/4, 24 September 1770.

[127] NPR: Daniel Williams (1840), James Pie (1842, from Whiston, Lancs.) and Thomas Peers (1845; the couple went on to have several more children). Collier daughters mentioned include Mary Bold (1798), Hannah Armstrong and Elizabeth Standish (both 1818) and Martha Kendrick, age 19 (1844).

[128] Sarah Littlemore (1836), Margaret Littlemore (1854) and Sarah Newton (1855).

[129] Parl. Papers, *Reports of the Commissioners of Enquiry into the State of Education in Wales,* Papers 870–872 (1847), p. 532.

[130] NPR, 21 December 1818 and 17 January 1840.

[131] Census: Ness 1841, 1851 and 1861. Engine tenter in 1841 but 'pauper (coal miner)' by 1851.

[132] Census: Heswall cum Oldfield, 1841; CALS, LGW 1/5, 30 July 1856, Mark Coxon as chairman for the first time.

[133] CALS, LGW 1/2, 26 February and 29 April 1840.

[134] CALS, LGW 1/2, 27 November 1839; census, Ness 1841. Listed as *Rachel* Metcalf for baptism of daughter Sarah, recorded as illegitimate (NPR, 27 September 1839).

[135] NPR, 2 November 1828 and 4 and 9 September 1834.

[136] CALS, LGW 1/2–3, five entries between 4 December 1839 and 1 September 1841.

[137] Census, Lower Bebington, 1851.

[138] NPR marriage, 30 January 1836; CALS, LGW 1/1, 6 February 1837.

[139] NPR, 29 October 1843 and census, Great Neston 1841.

[140] Flinn, pp. 423–4.

[141] CALS, QJF 191/2, 24 and 26 March 1763.

[142] CALS, QJB 3/12, 19 April 1763.

[143] CALS, QJF 198/3, 8 May 1770.

[144] CALS, QJB 3/13, 10 July 1770.

[145] CALS, QJB 3/15, pp. 483 and 585, 13 July 1784.

[146] Flinn, p. 430.

[147] Flinn, pp. 429–31.

[148] Atkinson, p. 18.

[149] Bangor Archives, Mostyn MSS 6996 (dated 1824).

[150] B. Lewis (1971), p. 38.

[151] Part of CALS, D5363.

[152] CALS, PM 13/10a and PM 5/2.

[153] Coal Authority, 14923/4.

[154] A well and a spring shown on OS, 25-inch, XXX.2 (1871).

[155] See page 109 re accident. She had a girl (eight) and boys (four and under one) at the time of John's death. They were still there in 1845 (CALS, QDP 252) and in the 1851 census (but she had adopted the surname Ellison). She died in Lancashire in 1860.

[156] The census is not clear but it seems two households shared one of the properties.

[157] BPP [1842c], p. 404; Flinn p. 431–2.

[158] CALS, DBC 261/38, 'Instructions for Indictment'.

[159] CALS, QDV 2/259, Little Neston Land Tax records.

[160] Known colliers (from 1841 and/or 1851 census) as occupiers of property in Ness tithe apportionment, *c*.1845 (CALS, EDT 286/1).

[161] Mortimer, p. 246.

[162] Parl. Papers (1847), pp. 528 and 530.

[163] The conditions are similar to those provided by the Earl of Scarborough for Wearside miners in the 1770s – single storey, consisting of single room 8 feet by 9 feet, built of local stone and costing just £15 each (Flinn, p. 432).

[164] See Chapter 2, note 84 re ownership.

[165] BPP [1842c], p. 184.

[166] There were ninety-eight houses in 1851 and just seventy-one in 1861 – a 27.6% drop.

[167] Philip Sulley, *The Hundred of Wirral* (Birkenhead, 1889), pp. 224–5.

[168] Clare Hartwell, Matthew Hyde, Edward Hubbard and Nikolaus Pevsner, *Buildings of England: Cheshire* (London: Yale University Press, 2011), p. 404.

[169] Hanshall, p. 71; Sulley, pp. 224–5.

Chapter 12 – Social Aspects of the Neston Collieries (continued)

[170] CALS, DDX 378/8, 7 September 1838; Hanshall, p. 71; British Library, Add. MSS 89098, 10 March 1829.

[171] Newspaper reports the next century (e.g. *Chester Chronicle*, 14 December 1867) say 'dates on the building [appear]' to suggest a date of 1757. It seems plausible, however, that the building was *started* in response to finding new coal deposits nearby in 1757. English Heritage listing nos. 55656 and 55662 say 'c.1760'.

[172] British Library, Add. MSS 89098, 3 and 5 March 1829.

[173] *Liverpool Daily Post*, 13 December 1867.

[174] *Liverpool Mail*, 4 November 1848; *Chester Chronicle,* 14 December 1867.

[175] *Chester Courant*, 1 November 1796.

[176] British Library, Add. MSS 89098, 3 March 1829.

[177] Architectural Association, Humphry Repton (1802).

[178] Stanley, p. 85.

[179] Clive Aslet, *Villages of Britain: The Five Hundred Villages that Made the Countryside* (London: Bloomsbury, 2011), p. 503.

[180] CALS, DDX 378/7, 19 July.

[181] It was also initially called Dennah House, Dinna House and Denhall House in various maps and documents. It was considerably extended in 1831 (it has a datestone for that year and a wing appears to have been added (NEIMME/Wat/35/14; CALS, EDT 286/2) so that, by 1836 it was generally termed Denna (also Dennah and Denhall) *Hall* and the buildings 440 yards (400m) further north had become Denna House (OS, two inches to one mile, Sheet 345, 1836), occupied by colliery manager James Gregory (censuses, Ness, 1841 and 1851). This residence may, perhaps, have been upgraded from 'Denhall Cottage' (CALS, DDX 378/30, 5 December 1812 and 378/31, 13 January 1821; *Chester Chronicle*, 15 June, 1827).

[182] CALS, DDX 378/30, passim, which chronicles the construction in detail. 'Old pits': 6 February 1813.

[183] CALS, DDX 378/30, 31 December 1813.

[184] Op. cit., p. 246.

[185] CALS, QDV 2/304; *Chester Chronicle*, 11 April 1817.

[186] CALS, DDX 378/30, 2 August 1813.

[187] Census, Ness.

[188] 'Births, Marriages and Deaths (1783)', *Cheshire Sheaf*, 3rd series, 12 (1915), p. 45. However, the article states, apparently incorrectly, that Cottingham lived in Ness. NPR, on his burial, gives his place of residence as Little Neston.

[189] Susan Chambers, 'Glenton House Field – a Century of Development', *Neston Civic Society Newsletter* (1989).

[190] *Cheshire Sheaf* (1934), p. 3; parish register, St Dorothy, Jamaica, 27 September 1790; amongst Quest's slaves in 1817 were those named Liverpool, Chester and Nelson (TNA, T 71/13, Slave Register, St Dorothy).

[191] Chambers (1989).

[192] TNA, J 90/82, 28 March 1823.

193 B. Lewis (1971), p. 34.

194 Chambers (2014), p. 119 mentions new galleries *c.*1772 and 1785. Rev. Canon W. Bidlake (1935), 'Neston Church in the Eighteenth Century', *THSLC*, 87 (1935), p. 93 gives collier numbers as the reason, although giving an apparently incorrect date of 1765.

195 E. Hilditch, *Little Neston Methodist Church History* (1997), p. 6. Wesley visited Parkgate on many occasions between 1760 and 1789, en route to or from Ireland. He was known to visit colliers elsewhere e.g. at Plessey, near Newcastle; Kingswood, Bristol; Coleford, Somerset; and Jefferson, Pembrokeshire so it is possible that he had some form of contact with the colliers at Ness too, if only as listeners to his preaching.

196 Partis Haswell (or John P. Haswell, as he was known) was born in the Durham mining village of Tanfield, started training as a lawyer in Newcastle, and was recommended by preachers of the Newcastle District (F. F. Bretherton, *Early Methodism in and around Chester. 1749–1812* (Chester: Phillipson and Golder, 1903a), pp. 188–9; F. F. Bretherton, 'John Wesley's Voyages to and from Parkgate, with an Account of Early Methodism in Neston and Parkgate', *Methodist Recorder*, Winter 1903b, pp. 49–54.

197 Bretherton, (1903a), pp. 188–9; Hilditch, pp. 8–10.

198 B. Lewis (1971), p. 34.

199 CALS, CR 94/20 and 21 covering 1831–35 and 1845–47. Many names on the members' lists correspond with colliery workers in NPR and/or other sources.

200 Ibid. Listed as a collier at least between 1826 (NPR) and 1841 (census: Ness).

201 CALS, m/f 11/2, 1851 Ecclesiastical Census.

202 CALS, CR 94/25, 1842.

203 CALS, m/f 11/2, 1851 Ecclesiastical Census; NPR, 25 September 1836 and 21 December 1838.

204 See Table 12.12 for population information.

205 See Table 12.6.

206 Census for Bistre (Flintshire), 1861.

207 BPP [1842c], p. 184.

208 BPP [1842c], p. 370.

209 BPP [1842c], p. 405.

210 CALS, ERC 4.

211 Ashhurst: BPR but apparently took place at Puddington; Taylor: baptisms in Puddington RC register but his wife, Lucy's, stated maiden name of Lomas does not fit with other evidence.

212 John Stanley Massey married Mary, the sister of an early part-owner of Ness Colliery, Thomas Clifton, in 1749. Clifton's daughter, Catherine, married into the Talbot family, Earls of Shrewsbury.

213 *St. Winefride's Neston, Aspects of History* (leaflet, n.d.); CALS, m/f 11/2, 1851 Ecclesiastical Census.

214 *St. Winefride's Neston, 150 Years, 1843–1993* (n.p., 1993), p. 1.

215 Lewis had four children baptised at St Winefride's between 1844 and 1852 as well as six at Puddington (1826–1840) and four at Neston (1832–38).

216 Burial register, St Winefride, Neston, 22 November 1859.

217 Place (1996), p. 99.

218 Mary Sturt, *The Education of the People* (London: Routledge and Kegan Paul, 1967), p. 2.

Chapter 12 – Social Aspects of the Neston Collieries (continued)

[219] Sturt, p. 16; Gillian Sutherland, 'Education' in *The Cambridge Social History of Britain 1750–1950*, ed. by F. Thompson (Cambridge: Cambridge University Press, 1990), p. 127.

[220] Census, 1811 shows combined population of 2,324 in Leighton, Great Neston, Little Neston and Ness. There were 130 places (Place, 1996, p. 99).

[221] CALS, DDX 378/30, 21 February 1806.

[222] Places mentioned, starting in 1805, include Eastham and Storeton on the Wirral, Aldford in mid-Cheshire and Ysceifiog in Flintshire. See also the *Morning Post,* 1 September 1841.

[223] CALS, DDX 378/30, 30 June 1810.

[224] Flinn, p. 439; Sutherland, p. 127.

[225] CALS, DDX 378/30, 26 May 1813.

[226] CALS, DDX 378/30, 14 March 1813.

[227] CALS, DDX 378/33, 3 July 1826.

[228] For example, John Duncan, baptised son of Thomas, 3 July 1812, labourer of Ness (school entry CALS, DDX 378/31, 2 June 1824). Robert Kendrick was named as one of the pupils in November 1822 (CALS, DDX 378/31); his father, Thomas, was listed as a collier in a baptism entry for his son, George, the previous month (NPR).

[229] CALS, DDX 378/31 and 378/33, and Stanley Estate Accounts, 1844–56 (uncatalogued), passim. An unnamed school mistress is listed in the latter from 1848 with 'Miss Shea' named in 1853.

[230] Peter Kirby, *Child labour in Britain, 1750–1870* (Basingstoke: Palgrave Macmillan, 2000), p. 113; Sutherland, p. 128.

[231] BPP [1842c], p. 371.

[232] For example, CALS, DDX 378/31, 4 June 1825.

[233] Parl. Papers, *Abstract of Answers and Returns on the State of Education in England and Wales*, Vol. 1, Accounts and Papers, Paper 62, p. 80.

[234] CALS, EDT 286/1 and /2; CALS, Stanley Estate Accounts, 1844–56 (uncatalogued) 7 December 1846. Lewis died in 1848 (NPR) aged sixty-two.

[235] CALS, Stanley Estate Accounts, 1844–56 (uncatalogued), 6 April 1844.

[236] *Liverpool Mercury*, 7 December 1827.

[237] British Library, Add. MSS 89098, 13 March 1829. It was noted in the *North Wales Chronicle* (6 December 1827) that there were no celebrations in Chester to mark the twenty-first birthday of William Stanley, Sir Thomas's son and future 10th Baronet, as there had been in the villages of or near the Stanley estates. There was much ill-feeling in Chester towards Catholics in this period, including the presentation of an anti-Catholic petition to Parliament by the Anglican bishop of behalf of the city.

[238] NPR. Twenty young children were buried in that period.

[239] CALS, P149/11/4, 'Memorandum concerning the need for a school in the parish'.

[240] Place (1996), p. 100. Joseph Lyon's letter mentioned that a 'gentleman well fitted for the task' was already using a cottage for Sunday School lessons. See note 40 re Woodward's career change.

[241] Bagshaw, p. 658.

[242] Kirby (2000), p. 113.

243 CALS, P149/11/3, Little Neston National School Rules, indicates that children at the school were given a fortnight's 'vacation' to help with gleaning and this would presumably have happened in Ness too.

244 BPP [1842c], p. 405.

245 Sutherland, p. 123.

246 B. Lewis (1971), pp. 29–31.

247 Flinn, p. 440 and, for example, BPP [1842c], p. 184; Langton (2000), p. 78.

248 A. J. MacGregor ed., *The Alehouses and Alehouse-Keepers of Cheshire, 1629–1828* (n.p.: Caupona, 1992), pp. 130–1.

249 See Chapter Five, notes 104 and 108.

250 1813 – see note 252 below. The building is plotted on British Library, 'A Plan of the Township of Little Neston in the County of Chester, 1789 [from a survey made in 1778].'

251 Pigot and Co., *New Commercial Directory for the Counties of Cheshire, Derbyshire and Lancashire* (London: James Pigot, 1828, p. 46, and Pigot and Co. [1834], *Commercial Directory for Cheshire*, p. 47.

252 TNA, J 90/82, 13 September 1813 records the request of 'The Proprietors of Ness Colliery' to Thomas Cottingham to lease the public house, situated in Little Neston close to the boundary with Ness and 'occupied by Pickering', alongside their five-year lease to work coal on his land. However, an 1817 survey shows the 'Publick House and garden' in the colliery area were rented from Thomas Cottingham by a Robert Robinson (CALS, DSH 1453/20, Survey of Township of Little Neston). He was paying Cottingham £16 p.a. rent in 1819 (TNA, J 90/19, 4 August 1819) and specifically listed as the landlord of the Harp in 1822 (MacGregor, p. 130).

253 *Chester Courant*, 26 April 1822.

254 For example, there were 149 licence holders in Great Neston in the last forty years of the eighteenth century and at least twenty named alehouses between 1800 and 1828 (MacGregor, pp. 125–7).

255 Place (1996), p. 200; *Chester Chronicle*, 4 November 1837.

256 *Chester Chronicle*, 1 May 1829.

257 *Chester Courant*, 16 June 1829; CALS, DDX 378/8, 16 June 1838; *Chester Chronicle*, 24 November 1837.

258 *Cheshire Sheaf*, 'Richard Blundell, the Collier Artist of Neston', 3rd series, 3 (1901), pp. 67–9. Blundell was said to have been at the colliery sixty years previously, being recorded in 1841 as a labourer and in 1851 as a 'colliery banksman' (Great Neston censuses). He had given evidence in the 1822 court case when he was also described as a 'banksman'. He was employed by Stanley at the time of the incident but had since joined Cottingham.

259 *Chester Chronicle*, 6 June 1817.

260 Source as per note 258; see also, for example, BPP [1842b], p. 620.

261 BPP [1842c], p. 217.

262 *Cheshire Observer*, 8 September 1900; British Library, Add. MSS 89098, 30 September 1830; Benson, p. 155.

263 BPP [1842c], pp. 179 and h6.

264 NPR, 1775–1779. Total 560 baptisms to fathers with specified occupations, 108 of whom were colliers.

265 See pages 108–9.

Chapter 12 – Social Aspects of the Neston Collieries (continued)

266 British Library, Add. MSS 89098.

267 Turner and Blackie, pp. 58–9.

268 BPP [1842c], p. 370.

269 William Spencer, *Records of the Militia and Volunteer Forces, 1757–1945* (London: Public Record Office, 1997), pp. 1–3.

270 Requirements later extended to service anywhere in Britain.

271 *Adams's Weekly Courant*, 18 June 1771 and 30 June 1772.

272 J. Stevenson, *Popular Disturbances in England 1700–1832* (Abingdon: Routledge, 2014), p. 46.

273 Parl. Papers, Paper 116 (1808), 'Return of average bounty for substitutes'. 1808 collier pay data for Ness is not available but, for example, in 1827 the annualised pay of the men at Ness was around £30, and pay rates had generally risen between 1808 and 1827.

274 CALS, MG/9/27–31.

275 Stevenson, pp. 46–7.

276 CALS, MW 3/1.

277 Clive Emsley, *British Society and the French Wars* (London: Macmillan, 1979), p. 65.

278 David Fairer, *Organising Poetry: The Coleridge Circle, 1790–1798* (Oxford: Oxford University Press, 2009), Ch. 12.

279 The quotations are taken from the launch notice for the Chester 'Voluntary Contributions' scheme in the *Chester Courant*, 13 March 1798.

280 *Chester Courant*, 3 April 1798.

281 *Chester Courant,* 17 June 1794.

282 Austin Gee, *The British Volunteer Movement* (Oxford: Oxford University Press, 2003), pp. 47–8. CALS, MG 29/1.

283 A fourth collier brother, William, enrolled in 1813.

284 CALS, MG 9/30, 7 July 1821.

285 Whiston census, 1851 showing last child born at Neston in 1841.

286 Wigan census, 1851 showing last child born at Neston in 1846.

287 Rainford census, 1861 showing first child born in Leeds *c.*1850.

288 According to census data, the population of England grew by 12.2% (E. A Wrigley and R. S. Schofield, *The Population History of England, 1541–1871, a Reconstruction* (Cambridge: Cambridge University Press, 1989), p. 199).

289 BPP [1842c], pp. 184 and 371, and [1842b], p. 588.

290 Censuses for Little Neston (1851) and Windle (1861). Her age was incorrectly stated as eleven in the latter.

291 Full listing: *nestoncollieries.org*

292 For example, John Ducker (born Ewloe, Flintshire – at Parr, Lancs. 1861) and Thomas Roberts (born Northop, Flintshire – at Rainford, Lancs. 1861). Source: censuses 1851 and 1861.

293 See page 106 re militancy.

294 W. T. R. Pryce, 'Language Areas in North-East Wales, *c.*1800–1911', in *Language and Community in the Nineteenth Century*, ed. by Geraint Jenkins (Cardiff: University of Wales Press, 1998), pp. 34–42.

295 See page 248.

[296] Censuses: Peter in Holywell (Flintshire), William in Everton, Liverpool and Thomas in Willaston (Cheshire), 3 miles (5 km) from Neston.

[297] NPR, 2 December 1853; census: Ryton Woodside, 1861.

[298] Census: Little Neston, 1861.

[299] Census: Sealand, 1861.

Chapter 13 – The Neston Collieries' Place in Industrial History

[1] See summaries in, for example, Mokyr (2009), pp. 80–3; Joel Mokyr, *The British Industrial Revolution: an Economic Perspective* (Boulder: Westview, 1993), pp. 6–7; Steven King and Geoffrey Timmins, *Making Sense of the Industrial Revolution* (Manchester: Manchester University Press, 2001), pp. 10–32; and Emma Griffin, *A Short History of the British Industrial Revolution* (Basingstoke: Palgrave MacMillan, 2010), pp. 1–14.

[2] See, for example, Mokyr (2009), p. 80 and King and Timmins, Chapter 2, which discusses regional variation in the growth of industry.

[3] One influential article was Maxine Berg and Pat Hudson's 'Rehabilitating the Industrial Revolution', *Economic History Review*, 45, 1 (February 1992), p. 38.

[4] Ness Colliery was producing about 23,600 tons/23,978 tonnes of coal in 1776–7 (Table 2.1, converted to tons of 2,240 lbs to enable comparison). This would have represented under 0.3% of estimated national output of 8.8m tons/8.9m tonnes in 1775 (Flinn, p. 26). The largest of ten regions, the north-east, was producing 2.99 million tons/3.04 million tonnes, Lancashire's figure was 900,000 tons/914,000 tonnes). Flinn also gives an estimate, of inexact provenance, of 110,000 tons/111,765 tonnes for North Wales; the region had by far the lowest output of all regions in 1800, 1815 and, with one exception, 1830 too.

[5] Kanefsky (2017), p. 261.

[6] Mokyr (2009), p. 385.

[7] E. Griffin, pp. 53–6 re mobility.

[8] Prices from Flinn, pp. 303–4.

[9] Maxine Berg, *The Age of Manufactures 1700–1820*, 2nd edn (Routledge, 1994), p. 118.

[10] E. Griffin, p. 5; Mokyr (2009), p. 79.

[11] Arnold Toynbee, *Lectures on the Industrial Revolution in England* (London: Rivingtons, 1884).

[12] At Hawarden and Bagillt coal mines; also possibly visible at Trelogan lead mine, slightly inland.

[13] King and Timmins, p. 6.

[14] The question of living standards is complex and wide-ranging but can be summed up by E. Griffin's conclusion (p. 161) that 'the industrial revolution ... was not a time of rising prosperity for all, but a period of painful transition which brought few gains for the men, women and children whose back-breaking labour underpinned it'.

Epilogue

[1] TNA, BT 31/352/1280, Memorandum of Association; *Railway Record*, 7 August 1858.

[2] *Morning Chronicle*, 8 August 1859.

[3] TNA, BT 31/352/1280, Copy of Special Resolution. More information – see Annakin-Smith (2021–2).

Epilogue (continued)

[4] TNA, BT 31/2021/8751; Bangor Archives, Mostyn MSS 6959, 'Copy agreement for a lease of three fifths of the coal and cannel under … the manor of Little Neston', 25 April 1874. Benjamin Chandler was listed in official records as the mine-owner until 1875 but there is no record of any activity by him in Little Neston (see page 109).

[5] NEWA, D/M/5662, 21 August 1872; Bangor Archives, Mostyn MSS 6959.

[6] TNA, BT 31/2021/8751; *Cheshire Observer*, 3 October 1874; *Wrexham Advertiser*, 17 April 1875.

[7] *Cheshire Observer*, 28 October 1876.

[8] Arundel Archives, MD 1224, 27 April 1876; Bangor Archives, Baron Hill MSS 7311, 1 July 1876 and CALS, D 3884/5, 1 December 1880.

[9] NEWA, D/M/5662, 6 April 1874 recommended acceptance of Mott's offer but the issue had not been resolved by 11 March 1875 (also NEWA, D/M/5662).

[10] The maximum extent on any plan this author has seen went about 950 yards/850 metres into Great Neston, working the seven feet seam (CALS, LUNe/6393 and 3384/53).

[11] Boreholes – see page 48; CALS, D 3884/5, Lease for Thirty-One Years; NRO 725 B5, pp. 479–80, letter to C. Lloyd from William Armstrong, 14 April 1863. Plans from the later period of working show little, if any, activity in this area.

[12] See pages 9 and 266 note 61.

[13] Place (1996), pp. 63–71.

[14] *Birkenhead News*, 2 and 19 March 1927; Place (1996), p. 71.

Appendix II(a)

[1] See Chapter 2, note 111.

[2] CALS, DBC 261/38, 'Cottingham and Stanley' which mentions that royalties were less than £50 for many years before 1821.

BIBLIOGRAPHY

LOCATIONS OF PRIMARY SOURCES

All primary sources have been referenced in the endnotes; space does not allow the inclusion of a full listing here. Repositories from which these sources have been obtained include:

Anglesey Archives
Arundel Archives
Bangor Archives
Birmingham City Archive
The British Library
Cheshire Archives and Local Studies
The Coal Authority Records Management Service
The Common Room of the Great North (for papers of the North of England Institute of
    Mining and Mechanical Engineers)
Cumbria Archive Service
Durham Record Office
Historic England Archives
The Institution of Mechanical Engineers
The Ironbridge Gorge Museum Trust
Lancashire Archives
Liverpool Record Office
London Metropolitan Archives
Marsh's Library, Dublin
The National Archives
The National Library of Wales
The National Maritime Museum, Greenwich
North East Wales Archives
Parliamentary Archives
Tyne and Wear Archives
University of Liverpool Special Collections and Archives
University of Manchester, John Rylands Library
Wigan Archives
The Woburn Abbey Collection

Sources searched but which have yielded 'blank' returns, and those supplying copies of secondary material, have not been listed above.

SECONDARY SOURCES

Adams, Leonard, *Agricultural Depression and Farm Relief in England 1813–1852* (London: Routledge, 2013).

Aikin, John, *England Delineated, Or, A Geographical Description of Every County in England and Wales* (London: T. Bensley, 1790).

Anderson, D., 'Blundell's Collieries: The Progress of the Business', *THSLC*, 116 (1964), pp. 69–116.

Anderson, D., 'Blundell's Collieries: Wages, Disputes and Conditions of Work', *THSLC*, 117 (1965), pp. 109–43.

Anderson, D., 'Blundell's Collieries: Technical Developments, 1776–1966', *THSLC*, 119 (1967), pp. 113–79.

Annakin–Smith, Anthony, 'Neston and Parkgate: Their Links to the Slave Trade in the Mid to Late Eighteenth Century', *THSLC*, 160 (2011), pp. 27–54.

Annakin-Smith, Anthony, 'How South American Gold Transformed a Corner of Neston', *Cheshire History*, 61 (2021–2), pp. 202–10.

The Annual Register, Or a View of the History, Politics, and Literature, for the Year 1815 (London: Baldwin, Craddock & Joy, 1815).

Armour, C., 'The Trade of Chester and the State of the Dee Navigation 1600–1800' (unpublished doctoral thesis for the University of London, 1956).

Armstrong, J. and P. Bagwell, 'Coastal Shipping' in *Transport in the Industrial Revolution* ed. by D. Aldcroft and M. Freeman (Manchester: Manchester University Press, 1983), pp. 142–76.

Ashton, T. S., *The Industrial Revolution, 1760–1830* (Oxford: Oxford University Press, 1997).

Ashton, T. S. and J. Sykes, *The Coal Industry of the Eighteenth Century* (Manchester: Manchester University Press, 1964).

Aslet, Clive, *Villages of Britain: The Five Hundred Villages that Made the Countryside* (London: Bloomsbury, 2011).

Atkinson, G., *The Canal Duke's Collieries* (Manchester: Neil Richardson, n.d.).

Bagshaw, Samuel, *History, Gazetteer and Directory of the County Palatine of Chester* (Sheffield: Samuel Bagshaw, 1850).

Bailey, Michael, 'Robert Stephenson & Co. 1823–1829', *TNS*, 50 (1978), pp. 109–38.

Barfoot P. and J. Wilkes, *The Chester Directory and Guide,* offprint from *The Universal British Directory of Trade, Commerce and Manufacture* (Chester: printed for and sold by James Poole, 1792).

Barker, T., 'Lancashire Coal, Cheshire Salt and the Rise of Liverpool', *THSLC*, 103 (1951), pp. 83–101.

Battiscombe, Georgina, *Mrs Gladstone, The Portrait of a Marriage* (London: Constable, 1956).

Beckett, J. V., *Coal and Tobacco: The Lowthers and Economic Development in West Cumberland, 1660–1760* (Cambridge: Cambridge University Press, 1981).

Beckett, J. V., *The Agricultural Revolution* (Oxford: Blackwell, 1990).

Bell, Peter, *An Actual Survey of the Great Post Road from London to Parkgate* (London: William Faden, 1779).

Benson, John, *British Coalminers in the Nineteenth Century* (Harlow: Longman, 1989).

Berg, Maxine, *The Age of Manufactures 1700–1820*, 2nd edn (Routledge, 1994).

Bibliography

Berg, Maxine, and Pat Hudson 'Rehabilitating the Industrial Revolution', *Economic History Review*, 45, 1 (February 1992), pp. 24–50.

Bevan-Evans M., 'Gadlys and Flintshire Lead-Mining in the Eighteenth Century', *FHSP*, 18 (1960), pp. 75–130.

Bevan-Evans M., 'Gadlys and Flintshire Lead-Mining in the Eighteenth Century', *FHSP*, 19 (1961), pp. 32–60.

Bidlake, W., 'Neston Church in the Eighteenth Century', *THSLC*, 87 (1935), pp. 87–96.

Bielenberg, Andy, *Ireland and the Industrial Revolution* (Abingdon: Routledge, 2009).

Booth, Alan, 'Food Riots in the North-West of England 1790–1801', *Past & Present*, 77, 1 (November 1977), pp. 84–107.

Booth, P. H. W., ed., *Burton in Wirral, A History* (Burton: Burton and South Wirral Local History Society, 1984).

Boswell, James, *Life of Samuel Johnson including Boswell's Journal of a tour to the Hebrides and Johnson's Diary of a journey into North Wales*, v.5, ed. by George Birkbeck Hill (Oxford: Clarendon Press, 1950).

Boulton, H., 'The Chester Infirmary', *JCAS*, 47 (1960), pp. 9–20.

Bowie, G., 'Early Stationary Steam Engines in Ireland', *Industrial Archaeology Review*, 2, 2 (1978), pp. 168–74.

Boyd, James, *The Wrexham, Mold & Connah's Quay Railway* (Headington: Oakwood Press, 1991).

Bretherton, F. F., *Early Methodism in and Around Chester, 1749–1812*, (Chester: Phillipson & Golder, 1903a).

Bretherton, F. F., 'John Wesley's Voyages to and from Parkgate with an Account of Early Methodism in Neston and Parkgate', *Methodist Recorder*, Winter 1903b, pp. 49–54.

British Library, *Learning, Timelines, Sources from History, The Railways* (n.d.) <http://www.bl.uk/learning/timeline/item106197.html> [accessed 2 January 2023].

British Parliamentary Papers [1833], *First Report of the Commissioners Inquiring into the Employment of Children in Factories* (reprinted in Shannon, Ireland: Irish University Press, 1968).

British Parliamentary Papers [1835], *Report from the Select Committee on Accidents in Mines* (reprinted in Shannon, Ireland: Irish University Press, 1968).

British Parliamentary Papers [1842a], *Children's Employment Commission, First Report of the Commissioners Mines* (reprinted in Shannon, Ireland: Irish University Press, 1968, Vol. 6).

British Parliamentary Papers [1842b], *Children's Employment Commission, Appendix to First Report of the Commissioners Mines, Pt. I* (reprinted in Shannon, Ireland: Irish University Press, 1968, Vol. 7).

British Parliamentary Papers [1842c], *Children's Employment Commission, Appendix to First Report of the Commissioners Mines, Pt. II* (reprinted in Shannon, Ireland: Irish University Press, 1968, Vol. 8).

British Parliamentary Papers [1871], *Report of the Commissioners Appointed to Inquire into the Several Matters Relating to Coal in the United Kingdom* (reprinted in Shannon, Ireland: Irish University Press, 1969).

Broster Peter, *The Chester Guide* (Chester: P. Broster, 1782).

Broster, Peter, *The Chester Guide* (Chester: P. Broster, 1795).

Brown, Ivor, 'Underground Canals in Shropshire Mines', *Bulletin of the Peak District Mines Historical Society*, 13 (1997), 4, pp. 17–23.

Burke, Edmund, *The Works of the Right Honourable Edmund Burke* (London: printed for F. & C. Rivington, 1801).

Caird, James, *English Agriculture in 1850–51* (Longman, Brown, Green, and Longmans, 1852).

Camden, William, *Britannia*, trans. and enlarged by Richard Gough (London: T. Payne & Sons, 1789).

Carrig Building Fabric Consultants, *Dublin Historic Industry Database* (for the Geological Survey of Ireland, 2011) <https://www.gsi.ie/documents/DublinHistoricIndustryDatabaseReport.pdf> [accessed 2 January 2023].

Carrington, Peter, *The English Heritage Book of Chester* (London: B. T. Batsford/English Heritage, 1994).

Cement Kilns, *Magheramorne Cement Kilns* (n.d.), <http://www.cementkilns.co.uk/cement_kiln_magheramorne.html> [accessed 2 January 2023].

Challinor R., *The Lancashire and Cheshire Miners* (Newcastle upon Tyne: Frank Graham, 1972).

Chaloner, W., 'The Cheshire Activities of Matthew Boulton and James Watt, of Soho near Birmingham, 1776–1817', *TLCAS*, 61 (1951), pp. 121–36.

Chambers, Susan, ed., *Neston Stone Age to Steam Age* (Burton & Neston History Society, 2014).

Chambers, Susan, 'Glenton House Field – a Century of Development', *Neston Civic Society Newsletter* (1989).

Chartres, John and Gerard Turnbull, 'Road Transport' in *Transport in the Industrial Revolution* ed. by D. Aldcroft and M. Freeman, (Manchester: Manchester University Press, 1983), pp. 64–99.

Cheshire Sheaf, 'George Clarke', 1st series, 2 (1883), p. 101.

Cheshire Sheaf, 'Parkgate Custom-House', 1st Series, 2 (1883), p. 246.

Cheshire Sheaf, 'Richard Blundell, the Collier Artist of Neston', 3rd Series, 3 (1901), pp. 67–9.

Cheshire Sheaf, 'The Old Denhall Collieries, Neston', 3rd series, 3 (1901), pp. 63–4.

Cheshire Sheaf, 'Glegg and Cottingham Tombstones at Neston', 3rd series, 6 (1906), p. 75.

Cheshire Sheaf, 'Forgotten Cheshire Regiments', 3rd series, 6 (1906), pp. 102–13.

Cheshire Sheaf, 'Births Marriages and Deaths (1783)', 3rd series, 12 (1915), p. 45.

Cheshire Sheaf, 'A Meet of Sir Thomas Stanley of Hooton's Hounds at Bidston Hill, About 1840', 3rd series, 23 (1926), pp. 12–13.

Cheshire Sheaf, 'Some Deeds Relating to Little Neston', 3rd series, 27 (1930), pp. 71–2.

Cheshire Sheaf, 'The Cottinghams, of Little Neston', 3rd series, 29 (1934), pp. 2–3.

Cheshire Sheaf, 'Four Prescot Letters', 3rd series, 31 (1936), pp. 62–3.

Cheshire Sheaf, 'Stray Notes from Neston Parish Register', 3rd series, 51 (1956), p. 24.

Cheshire Sheaf, 'Eastgate in 1750', 3rd series, 56 (1963), pp. 89–90.

Chester City Council, *Puddington, Conservation Area Appraisal* (January 2008).

Church, Roy, *The History of the British Coal Industry*, Vol. 3, *1830–1913* (Oxford: Clarendon Press, 1986).

Clarke, Mike, *British Underground Canals associated with Mines* [trans from German] for Internationales Symposium 'Der Fuchsstollen in Walbrzych – ein Europaisches Technik-denkmal' (2001).

Bibliography

Clwyd–Powys Archaeological Trust, *Ports and Harbours in North-east Wales* (n.d.)
<http://www.cpat.org.uk/projects/longer/ports/ports.htm> [accessed 17 March 2019].

Coppack R. and D. Roberts, 'Two Samuel Walkers?', *Chester Antiquary*, 1 (2003), p. 1.

Craig, Robert, 'Some Aspects of the Trade and Shipping of the River Dee in the Eighteenth Century', *THSLC*, 114 (1962), pp. 99–128.

Cullen L. M., *Anglo-Irish Trade, 1660–1800* (Manchester: Manchester University Press, 1968).

Cultural Heritage Knowledge Exchange Hub, *Early Engine Database*, <https://coalpitheath.org.uk/engines/index.php#searchDb> [accessed 2 January 2023].

Cunliffe, B., R. Bartlett, J. Morrill, A. Briggs and J. Bourke, *The Penguin Atlas of British & Irish History* (London: Penguin, 2001).

Dalton J., in *Bell's Classical Arrangement of Fugitive Poetry* ed. by John Bell, 18 vols (Strand: John Bell, 1789), p. iii.

Daniels, Stephen, *Humphry Repton: Landscape Gardening and the Geography of Georgian England* (New Haven, CT: Yale University Press, 1999).

Davies, C. Stella, *The Agricultural History of Cheshire 1750–1850*, Chetham Society, 3rd series, 10 (1960).

Davies, Henry, *Coal Mining: A Reader* (Cardiff: Educational Publishing Co., 1912).

Davies, J. R., D. Wilson and I. T. Williamson, *Geology of the Country around Flint: Memoir for 1:50 000 Geological Sheet 108* (Keyworth: British Geological Survey, 2004).

Davies, Kenneth, *The Greenfield Valley* (Holywell: Holywell Town Council, 1977).

Davies, Kenneth, 'The Eighteenth Century Copper and Brass Industries of the Greenfield Valley', *Trans. of the Honourable Society of Cymmrodorion* (1979), pp. 203–32.

Davies, Kenneth, 'The Nineteenth Century Copper Industry in the Greenfield Valley', *Trans. Of the Honourable Society of Cymmrodorion* (1988), pp. 79–131.

Davies, Kenneth, 'Holywell and the Transatlantic Slave Trade', *FHSJ*, 40 (2015), pp. 109–40.

Dawson, Frank, *John Wilkinson: King of the Ironmasters* (Stroud: The History Press, 2012).

Dearne M. J. and K. Branigan, 'The Use of Coal in Roman Britain' *The Antiquaries Journal*, 75 (1995), pp. 71–105.

de Rance, C. E. in *The Geology of the Neighbourhoods of Flint, Mold and Ruthin*, ed. by A. Strahan, (London: HMSO, 1890).

Dickinson, J. R., 'The Overseas Trade of the Isle of Man, 1576-1755', *THSLC*, 154 (2005), pp. 1–30.

Dodd, A. H., 'The North Wales Coal Industry During the Industrial Revolution', *Archaeologia Cambrensis*, 84 (1929), pp. 197–228.

Dodd, A. H., *The Industrial Revolution in North Wales*, 3rd edn (Cardiff: University of Wales Press, 1971).

Dodd, G., 'The Turnpikes of Wirral', *Journal of the North Western Society for Industrial Archaeology and History*, 2 (1977), pp. 21–7.

Dodgson, J. M., *The Place-Names of Cheshire*, Pt. 4, (Cambridge: English Place-Name Society, 1972).

Douglass, Dave, 'The Durham Pitman' in *Miners, Quarrymen and Saltworkers*, ed. by Raphael Samuel (London: Routledge, Kegan and Paul, 1977).

Dunlap, John, *Report of Cases Decided in the High Court of Chancery*, xiv (New York: Gould Banks & Co, 1843).

Dunn, Matthias, *An Historical, Geological, and Descriptive View of the Coal Trade of the North of England* (Newcastle Upon Tyne: Pattison and Ross, 1844).

Dunn, Matthias, *A Treatise on the Winning and Working of Collieries* (Newcastle Upon Tyne: Matthias Dunn, 1852).

Durlauf, Stephen and Lawrence Blume, eds, *The New Palgrave Dictionary of Economics* (Basingstoke: Palgrave Macmillan, 2008).

Emery, Gordon, *The Old Chester Canal* (Chester: Chester Canal Heritage Trust, 2005).

Emsley, Clive, *British Society and the French Wars* (London: Macmillan, 1979).

Enfield, W., *An Essay Towards the History of Leverpool* (Warrington: 1773).

Fairer, David, *Organising Poetry: The Coleridge Circle, 1790–1798* (Oxford: Oxford University Press, 2009).

Fairley, W., 'Practical Notes on the Geology of Wirral', *Trans. Fed. Inst. Of Mining Engineers,* 4 (1892–3), pp. 321–8.

Farey, John, *A Treatise on the Steam Engine* (London: Longman Rees, Orme, Brown & Green, 1827).

Farrer, W. and J. Brownbill, eds, *The Victoria County History of Lancaster,* 8 vols (London: Archibald Constable, 1908), ii.

Flinn, M. W., *The History of the British Coal Industry,* Vol. 2, *1700–1830* (Oxford: Clarendon Press, 1984).

Flint through the Ages, *Industry through the Ages* (n.d.), <http://www.fflint.co.uk/industry.html?> [accessed 20 March 2019]

Floud, Roderick, ed., *Economic History of Britain Since 1800,* 3 vols (Cambridge: Cambridge University Press, 1981), i.

Freeman, B. and Lt. E. S. Parry, *Historical Records of the Denbighshire Hussars Imperial Yeomanry from their Formation in 1795 till 1906* (Wrexham: Woodall, Minshall, Thomas and Co., 1909).

Galloway, Robert [1898], *Annals of Coal Mining and the Coal Trade,* 2 vols (reprinted at Newton Abbot: David & Charles, 1971).

Gee, Austin, *The British Volunteer Movement* (Oxford: Oxford University Press, 2003).

Geological Survey of Ireland, *Louth – County Geological Site Report (Mell Quarry)* (n.d.) <https://gsi.geodata.gov.ie/downloads/Geoheritage/Reports/LH023_Mell_Quarry.pdf> [accessed 2 January 2023].

Goodchild, John, 'John Gibbons of Oswestry: An Eighteenth Century Capitalist', *Memoirs,* (Northern Mines Research Society, 1991), pp. 63–75.

Gourvish, T. R., *Railways and the British Economy, 1830–1914* (Basingstoke: Macmillan, 1980).

Graham, T., 'Whitelaw's 1798 Census of Dublin', *History Ireland,* 2, 3 (Autumn 1994), pp. 10–15.

Greenwell, George, *A Practical Treatise on Mine Engineering* (Newcastle: M. & M. W Lambert, 1855).

Griffin, A. R., 'Industrial Archaeology as an Aid to the Study of Mining History', *Industrial Archaeology,* 11, 1 (February 1974), pp. 11–28.

Griffin, Emma, *A Short History of the British Industrial Revolution* (Basingstoke: Palgrave MacMillan, 2010).

Hadfield, Charles, *The Canals of the West Midlands* (Newton Abbott: David & Charles, 1985).

Hair, P. E. H., 'The Lancashire Collier Girl', *THSLC,* 120 (1968), pp. 63–84.

Bibliography

Hair, P. E. H., 'Mortality from Violence in British Coal-Mines, 1800–1850', *Economic History Review*, 21 (1968), pp. 545–61.

Halley, Edmond, *A Synopsis of the Astronomy of Comets* (London: printed for John Senex, 1705, translated).

Handley, Michael, 'The Wirral Poor Law Union, 1836–1861', *TLCAS*, 104 (2008), pp. 119–35.

Hanshall, J. H., *The History of the County Palatine of Chester* (Chester, *c*.1823).

Hare, T., *Reports of Cases Adjudged in the High Court of Chancery*, Vol. 3 (London: A. Maxwell & Son, 1845).

Harris, A., 'Colliery Settlements in East Cumberland', *TCWAAS*, 74 (1974), pp. 118–46.

Harrison, W., 'Pre-Turnpike Highways in Lancashire and Cheshire', *TLCAS*, 9 (1892), pp. 101–34.

Hartwell, Clare, Matthew Hyde, Edward Hubbard and Nikolaus Pevsner, *Buildings of England: Cheshire* (London: Yale University Press, 2011).

Hatcher, John, *The History of the British Coal Industry,* Vol. 1, *Before 1700* (Oxford: Clarendon Press, 1993).

Hawkes, G., 'Shipping on the Dee: the rise and decline of the creeks of the port of Chester in the nineteenth century', *Maritime Wales*, 11 (1987), pp. 112–33.

Hawkes, G., 'The Founder of the Port of Connah's Quay?', *FHSJ*, 32 (1989), pp. 177–9.

Haygarth, John, *An Enquiry How to Prevent the Smallpox* (Chester: printed by J. Monk, 1785).

Haynes-Thomas, G. M., 'The Port of Chester', *TLCAS*, 59 (1947), pp. 35–40.

Hemingway, J., *History of the City of Chester, from its Foundation to the Present Time* (Chester: J. Fletcher, 1831).

Herson, J. D., 'Late Georgian and Victorian Chester, 1762–1914' in *A History of the County of Chester*, ed. by C. P. Lewis and A. T. Thacker, 5 vols (London: Institute of Historical Research and others., 1987–2005), v(1) (2003).

Higgins, Benjamin, 'Agriculture and War: A Comparison of Agricultural Conditions in the Napoleonic and World War Periods', *Agricultural History*, 14 (1940), 1, pp. 1–12.

Hilditch, E. L., *Little Neston Methodist Church History,* (Little Neston Methodist Church, 1997).

Historic England, *National Heritage List for England* available at <https://historicengland.org.uk/listing/the-list/> [accessed 15 January 2019].

Historic England, *Strategic Stone Study: A Building Stone Atlas of Merseyside* (2017), <https://www2.bgs.ac.uk/mineralsuk/download/EHCountyAtlases/Merseyside_Building_Stone_Atlas.pdf > [accessed 2 January 2023].

Holland, Henry, *General View of the Agriculture of Cheshire* (London: Richard Phillips and Co., 1808).

Hughes, S., 'The Development of British Navigational Canals', *Journal of the Railway & Canal Historical Society*, 27, 2 (July, 1981), pp. 2–9.

Humphries, Jane, 'Short Stature among Coal-Mining Children: A Comment', *Economic History Review*, 50, 3 (August 1997), pp. 531–7.

Jarvis, R. C., 'The Head Port of Chester; and Liverpool, its Creek and Member', *THSLC*, 102 (1950), pp. 69–84.

Jeaffreson, John Cordy, *Lady Hamilton and Lord Nelson, an Historical Biography*, 2 vols (London: Hurst and Blackett, 1888), ii.

Jenkins, J. G. et al., eds, *A History of the County of Stafford,* 14 vols (London: Oxford University Press, 1963), viii.

Jones, Lewis, *The Coal Mines of Mostyn* (Rhewl, Flints.: Lewis Jones, 1997).

Jones, N. W., *The Buckley Potteries: An Assessment of Survival and Potential* (Powys: The Clwyd-Powys Archaeological Trust, 2014).

Jones, Ray, 'Industrial Landscapes of North East Wales and the Border Counties' (unpublished paper, *c.*2015?).

Jones, W., *Dictionary of Industrial Archaeology* (Stroud: Sutton Publishing, 2006).

Kanefsky, John, 'The Diffusion of Power Technology in Britain, 1760–1870' (unpublished doctoral thesis for University of Exeter, 1979).

Kanefsky, John, 'Newcomen Engines Before Watt: A Quantitative Assessment', *IJHET*, 87, 2 (2017), pp. 165–75.

Kanefsky, J. and J. Robey, 'Steam Engines in 18th-Century Britain: A Quantitative Assessment.' *Technology & Culture,* 21, 2 (1980), pp. 161–86.

King, Steven, *Poverty and Welfare in England, 1750–1850* (Manchester: Manchester University Press, 2000).

King, Steven, and Geoffrey Timmins, *Making Sense of the Industrial Revolution* (Manchester: Manchester University Press, 2001).

Kirby, Peter, 'Causes of Short Stature Among Coal Mining Children, 1823–1850', *Economic History Review*, 48, 4 (1995), pp. 687–99.

Kirby, Peter, 'Short Stature Among Coal-Mining Children: A Rejoinder', *Economic History Review,* 50, 3 (August 1997), pp. 538–42.

Kirby, Peter, *Child labour in Britain, 1750–1870* (Basingstoke: Palgrave Macmillan, 2000).

Klingaman, William and Nicholas Klingaman, *The Year Without Summer: 1816 and the Volcano That Darkened the World and Changed History* (New York: St. Martin's Press, 2013).

Knight, Roger, *Britain against Napoleon, the Organisation of Victory* (London: Penguin, 2014).

Kohn, George, *Encyclopedia of Plague and Pestilence: From Ancient Times to the Present* (New York: Facts on File, 2008).

Kotler, P., et al. *Principles of Marketing*, 6th European edn (Harlow: Pearson, 2013).

Krause, J. T., 'The Changing Adequacy of English Registration, 1690–1837' in *Population in History*, ed. by D. V. Glass and D. Eversley (London: Edward Arnold, 1965), pp. 379–93.

Langford, Paul, *A Polite and Commercial People* (Oxford: Clarendon Press, 1992).

Langton, John, *Geographical Change and Industrial Revolution* (Cambridge: Cambridge University Press, 1979).

Langton, John, 'People from the Pits: The Origins of Colliers in Eighteenth-Century South-West Lancashire', in *Migration, Mobility and Modernisation*, ed. by David Siddle (Liverpool: Liverpool University Press, 2000), pp. 70–89.

Langton, John and R. J. Morris, *Atlas of Industrialising Britain* (London: Methuen, 1986).

Larn, Bridget and Richard Larn, *Shipwreck Index of the British Isles* (London: Lloyd's Register, 2000).

Larn, Bridget and Richard Larn, *Shipwreck Index of Ireland* (Redhill: Lloyd's Register/Fairplay, 2002).

Laughton, Jane, 'The Port of Chester in the Later Middle Ages' in *Where Deva Spreads her Wizard Stream: Trade and the Port of Chester*, ed. by Peter Carrington (Chester: Chester City Council, *c*.1996), pp. 66–71.

Leech, Bosdin, *History of the Manchester Ship Canal* (Manchester, London: Sherratt & Hughes, 1907).

Lewis, Brian, *Coal Mining in the Eighteenth and Nineteenth Centuries* (London: Longman Group, 1971).

Lewis, Brian, *The Cabry Family* (Mold: Railway & Canal Historical Society, 1994) .

Lewis, Michael, 'Researches into the Background of the 'A' Pit Railway at Newcastle NSW' (unpublished, 2010).

Lewis, S., *A Topographical Dictionary of Wales*, 2 vols (London: S. Lewis & Co., 1845), ii.

Lewis, W. J., 'Some Aspects of the History of Aberystwyth', *Ceredigion: Journal of the Cardiganshire Antiquarian Society*, 3, 1–4 (1959), pp. 284–302.

Lewis, W. J., 'The Anchor Smelting Co., Aberystwyth, 1786–1792', *Journal of the Ceredigion Antiquarian Society*, 4 (1963), pp. 129–35.

Linaker, R. H., 'A Short Account of the Life of George Clarke, Lieutenant-Governor of New York, 1736–1745', *JCAS*, 23 (1920), pp. 55–63.

Lister, M. D., *The Industrial Railways of Port Sunlight and Bromborough Port* (Blandford: Oakwood Press, 1980).

Lloyd, G., 'The Canalization of the River Dee in 1737', *FHSP*, 23 (1967–8), pp. 35–41.

Lloyd, George, 'Archaeological Notes', *FHSJ*, 19 (1961), p. 91.

Lloyd, Val, 'Attitudes to Women at North Wales Coalmines, *c*.1840–1901', *Llafur, the Journal of the Society for the Study of Welsh Labour History*, 5, 2 (1989), pp. 5–16.

Loudon, John Claudius, *Remarks on the Construction of Hothouses* (London: printed for J. Taylor, 1817).

Lucas, R., 'The Tax on Bricks and Tiles, 1784–1850', *Construction History*, 13 (1997), pp. 29–55.

Lysons D. and S. Lysons, *Magna Britannia, Containing the County Palatine of Chester*, 3 vols, (London: T. Cadell and W. Davies, 1806–1814), ii, Pt. 2 (1810).

MacGregor, A. J., ed., *The Alehouses and Alehouse-Keepers of Cheshire, 1629–1828* (n.p.: Caupona, 1992).

Malthus, Thomas Robert [1803], *An Essay on the Principle of Population,* 7th edn (London: Reeves and Turner, 1872).

Mason, Peter Ford, *The Pit Sinkers of Northumberland and Durham* (Stroud: The History Press, 2012).

Mathias, Peter, *The First Industrial Nation: An Economic History of Britain 1700–1914* (London: Routledge, 2001).

Mawer, Brian, *Chester [Sugar Houses]* (n.d.), at <http://www.mawer.clara.net/loc-chester.html> [accessed 2 January 2023].

McIvor, Arthur and Ronald Johnston, *Miners' Lung: A History of Dust Disease in British Coal Mining* (Abingdon: Routledge, 2016).

McKendrick, Neil, 'Josiah Wedgwood and the Commercialization of the Potteries' in N. McKendrick, J. Brewer and J. Plumb, *The Birth of a Consumer Society: The Commercialisation of Eighteenth-Century England* (London: Hutchinson, 1983), pp. 100–45.

McLynn, Frank, *1759, the Year Britain became Master of the World* (London: Jonathan Cape, 2004).

Mease, James, *Archives of Useful Knowledge* (Philadelphia, PA: James Hogan, 1813).

Milne, Ken, *Manx Marine Environmental Assessment, Infrastructure, Energy, Mines and Minerals* (Isle of Man: Isle of Man Government, 2013).

Mingay, G. E., ed., *The Agricultural Revolution: Changes in Agriculture, 1650–1880* (London: Black, 1977).

Mitchell, Brian, *Economic Development of the British Coal Industry* (Cambridge: Cambridge University Press, 1984).

Mitchell, S. I., 'Food Shortages and Public Order in Cheshire, 1757–1812', *TLCAS*, 81 (1982), pp. 42–66.

Mokyr, Joel, *The British Industrial Revolution: An Economic Perspective* (Boulder, CO: Westview, 1993).

Mokyr, Joel, *The Enlightened Economy, Britain and the Industrial Revolution 1700–1850* (London: Penguin, 2011).

More, Charles, *Understanding the Industrial Revolution* (Abingdon: Routledge, 2000).

Morris & Co., *Commercial Directory & Gazetteer of Cheshire* (Nottingham: Morris & Co., 1864).

Morris, Rupert, *Chester in the Plantagenet and Stuart Reigns* (Chester: Rupert Morris, 1893).

Mortimer, William Williams, *The History of the Hundred of Wirral* (London: Whittaker & Co, 1847).

Morton, George, *The Geology of the Country Around Liverpool* (London: George Philip & Son, 1897).

Mosley, Charles, ed., *Burke's Peerage, Baronetage and Knightage,* 107th edn (Wilmington, DE: Burke's Peerage and Gentry LLC, 2003).

Mott, R. A., 'The Newcomen Engine in the Eighteenth Century', *TNS*, 35 (1962–3), pp. 69–86.

Mott, R. A., 'English Waggonways of the Eighteenth Century', Pt.1, *TNS*, 37 (1964–5), pp. 1–33.

National Coal Mining Museum, *Early Mining* (n.d.) <https://www.ncm.org.uk/downloads/24/Early_Mining.pdf> [accessed 20 March 2019].

Neal, L., 'The Financial Crisis of 1825 and the Restructuring of the British Financial System', *Federal Reserve Bank of St. Louis Review*, 80 (1998), 3, pp. 53–76.

Nef, J. U., *The Rise of the British Coal Industry,* 2 vols (London: Frank Cass & Co., 1966), ii.

Nicol, Walter, *The Forcing, Fruit, and Kitchen Gardener*, 4th edn (Edinburgh: William Creech and others, 1809).

Nuvolari A., B. Verspagen and N. von Tunzelmann, 'The Diffusion of the Steam Engine in Eighteenth Century Britain' in *Applied Evolutionary Economics and the Knowledge-Based Economy*, ed. by A. Pyka and H. Hanusch (Cheltenham: Edward Elgar, 2006).

O'Gorman, Frank, *The Long Eighteenth Century* (London: Arnold, 1997).

Official Descriptive and Illustrated Catalogue of the Great Exhibition of the Works of Industry of All Nations, Part II, Class IX (London: Royal Commission, 1851).

Olsberg, R., 'Ship Registers in the South Carolina Archives 1734–1789', *South Carolina Historical Magazine*, 74, 4 (1973), pp. 189–299.

Ormerod, George, *The History of the County Palatine and City of Chester*, 2nd edn, Vol. II (London: George Routledge & Sons, 1882).

Osborne, Roger, *Iron, Steam and Money* (London: Bodley Head, 2014).

O'Toole, Patricia, *Sea Change: History of the Port of Mostyn* (n.p.: Cheshire County Publishing, 2002).

Bibliography

Overton, Mark, *Agricultural Revolution in England: The Transformation of the English Economy, 1500–1850* (Cambridge: Cambridge University Press, 1996).

Owens, Victoria, *James Brindley's Notebooks* (Gloucester: The Choir Press, 2013a).

Owens, Victoria, 'James Brindley's Notebooks, 1755–63: An Eighteenth-Century Engineer Writes About His Work', *IJHET*, 83 (2013b), 2, pp. 222–52.

Oxford English Dictionary (2019) <www.oed.com>

Paget-Tomlinson, Edward, *Mersey and Weaver Flats* (Kettering: Robert Wilson, 1973).

Paget-Tomlinson, E. W., *Bibby Line: 175 Years of Achievement* (Liverpool: Bibby Line, 1982).

Palin, William, *Cheshire Farming: A Report on the Agriculture of Cheshire* (Chester: Seacome & Prichard, 1845).

Parliamentary Papers (see also 'Sources', Appendix VI):

    Report from the Committee Appointed to Consider of the Coal Trade [sic] *of the United Kingdom*, Appendix 42, HOCP Vol. 132 (1800).

    Return of Average Bounty for Substitutes, Accts. & Papers, Paper 116 (1808).

    Accounts and Papers Relating to the Increase and Diminution of Salaries etc. in Public Offices of Britain, 1812, Accts. & Papers, Paper 112 (1813).

    An Account of All Coals Carried Coastways as Well as Those Exported to Foreign Parts, Accts. & Papers, Paper 117 (1819).

    Accounts Relating to Bonds Taken on Vessels Carrying Coals to Ireland, 1822, Accts. & Papers, Paper 393 (1823).

    Report from the Select Committee of the House of Lords Appointed to Take into Consideration the State of the Coal Trade, HOCP, Paper 9 (1830).

    Abstract of Answers and Returns on the State of Education in England & Wales, Vol. 1, Accts. & Papers, Paper 62 (1835).

    Second Annual Report of the Poor Law Commissioners, Appendices A-E, Committee Reports, Paper 595 (1836).

    Tidal Harbours Commission, Second Report of the Commissioners, Report of Commissioners, Paper 692 (1846).

    Reports of the Commissioners of Enquiry into the State of Education in Wales, Report of Commissioners, Papers 870–872 (1847).

    Report from the Select Committee on Coal Mines, Committee Reports, Paper 509 (1852).

    Journals of the House of Commons, Vol. 114 (1859).

Patel, Rowan, 'Lime Burning on Wirral: A Gazetteer of Lime Kiln Sites', *Cheshire History*, 57 (2017–18), pp. 128–56.

Paul, Jesse, 'What is Microhistory?', *Social Evolution and History*, 17, 2 (September 2018), pp. 64–82.

Peakman, Julie, *Emma Hamilton* (London: Haus Publishing, 2005).

Pennant, Thomas, *A Tour in Wales, MDCCLXXIII*, Vol. 1 (London: Henry Hughes, 1778).

Pennant, Thomas, *The History of the Parishes of Whiteford and Holywell* (London: B. & J. White, 1796).

Pennant, Thomas, *Tours in Wales, With Notes*, 3 vols (London: printed for Wilkie and Robinson, and others, 1810), iii.

Phillips, C. B. and J. H. Smith, *Lancashire and Cheshire from AD 1540* (Harlow: Longman, 1994).

Philpott, Rob, 'The Romano-British Period Resource Assessment' in *The Archaeology of North West England*, ed. by Mark Brennand, 8 (2006), 18, pp. 59–90.

Pigot & Co., *Commercial Directory, Cheshire* (n.p.: Pigot, 1822).

Pigot & Co., *New Commercial Directory for the Counties of Cheshire, Derbyshire and Lancashire* (London: James Pigot, 1828).

Pigot & Co. [1834], *Commercial Directory for Cheshire* (reprinted Swinton: N. Richardson, 1982).

Pike, E. Royston, *Human Documents of the Industrial Revolution in Britain* (London: George Allen and Unwin, 1966).

Place, Geoffrey, 'The Repatriation of Irish Vagrants from Cheshire, 1750–1815', *JCAS*, 68 (1985), pp. 125–41.

Place, Geoffrey, *The Rise and Fall of Parkgate* (Manchester: The Chetham Society, 1994).

Place, Geoffrey, ed., *Neston 1840–1940* (Burton and South Wirral Local History Society, 1996).

Pope, D. J., 'Shipping and Trade in the Port of Liverpool, 1783–1793' (unpublished doctoral thesis for the University of Liverpool, 1970).

Pritchard, T. W., *A History of the Old Parish of Hawarden* (Wrexham: Bridge Books, 2002).

Pritchard, T. W., *The Making of Buckley and District* (Wrexham: Bridge Books, 2012).

Pryce, W. T. R., 'Language Areas in North-East Wales, I. 1800–1911' in *Language and Community in the Nineteenth Century*, ed. by Geraint Jenkins (Cardiff: University of Wales Press, 1998), pp. 21–61.

Pugh, Gillian, *London's Forgotten Children* (Stroud: Tempus, 2007).

Raven, Neil and Jon Stobart, eds, *Towns, Regions and Industries: Urban and Industrial Change in the Midlands, c.1700–1840* (Manchester: Manchester University Press, 2004).

Rawson, R. Rees, 'The Coal-Mining Industry of the Hawarden District', *Archaeologia Cambrensis*, 96 (1941), pp. 109–35.

Regan, Shaun, *Reading 1759: Literary Culture in Mid-Eighteenth-Century Britain and France* (Lanham, MD: Rowman & Littlefield, 2013).

Rhodes, J. N., 'Early Steam Engines in Flintshire.' *TNS*, 41 (1968–9), pp. 217–26.

Richardson, Christine, *James Brindley, Canal Pioneer* (Burton-on-Trent: Waterways World, 2004).

Rideout, Eric, *The Growth of Wirral* (Liverpool: E. A. Bryant, 1927).

Ridgway, Maurice, *Chester Silver* (Chichester: Phillimore, 1985).

Roberts, Peter K., 'Boat Levels Associated with Mining: I. Coal Mining', *Industrial Archaeology Review*, 5, 2 (1981a), pp. 85–95.

Roberts, Peter K., 'Boat Levels Associated with Mining: II. Metal Mining', *Industrial Archaeology Review*, 5, 3 (1981b), pp. 203–16.

Roberts, Stephen, *A History of Wirral* (Chichester: Phillimore, 2002).

Rogers, Emlyn, 'Labour Struggles in Flintshire', Pt. 1, *Flintshire Historical Society Publications*, 14 (1954), pp. 47–71.

Rogers, Emlyn, 'Labour Struggles in Flintshire', Pt. 2, *Flintshire Historical Society Publications*, 15 (1955), pp. 102–9.

Rogers, Nicholas, *Resisting Napoleon: The British Response to the Threat of Invasion 1779–1815* (Aldershot: Ashgate, 2006).

Rolt, Lionel, *George and Robert Stephenson – The Railway Revolution* (London: Longman, 1967).

Rowlands, John and Sheila Rowlands, *The Surnames of Wales* (Birmingham: Federation of Family History Societies, 1996).

Royal Commission for Historic Monuments, *St. Andrew's Hospital, Denhall* (York: RCHM, 1998).

Russell, Colin and John Hudson, *Early Railway Chemistry and its Legacy* (London: Royal Society for Chemistry, 2011).

Schechner, Sara, *Comets, Popular Culture, and the Birth of Modern Cosmology* (Princeton: Princeton University Press, 1997).

Scott, Lieutenant-General W. A., *Battle of Waterloo* (London: E. Cox & Son, 1815).

Shercliff, W., D. Kitching and J. Ryan, *Poynton, A Coalmining Village; Social History, Transport and Industry 1700–1939* (Poynton: W. H. Shercliff, 1983).

Simonin, L., *Underground Life; Or Mines and Miners*, trans. by H. W. Bristow (London: Chapman and Hall, 1869).

Singer C., E. Holmyard, A. Hall and T. Williams, eds, *A History of Technology*, iv, *The Industrial Revolution, c.1750 to c.1850* (Oxford: Clarendon Press, 1858).

Skeat, W., *George Stephenson, The Engineer and His Letters* (London: Institution of Mechanical Engineers, 1973).

Skidmore, P. F., 'The Maritime Economy of North West England in the Later Eighteenth Century' (unpublished doctoral thesis, University of Greenwich, 2009).

Slater, Isaac, *Directory of the Towns upon the Environs of Liverpool* (Manchester: Isaac Slater, 1844).

Slater, Isaac, (late Pigot & Co.'s), *Royal National Commercial Directory and Topography of the Counties of Chester, Cumberland, Durham, Lancaster, Northumberland, Westmoreland and York* (Manchester: Isaac Slater, 1848).

Slater, Isaac, *Royal National Commercial Directory of Cheshire & North Wales* (Manchester: Isaac Slater, 1869).

Smith, Adam [1776], *An Inquiry into the Nature and Causes of the Wealth of Nations* (London: Electric Book Co., c.2001), Bk 1, p. 36.

Snell, K., *Parish and Belonging* (Cambridge: Cambridge University Press, 2006).

Spencer, William, *Records of the Militia and Volunteer Forces, 1757–1945* (London: Public Record Office, 1997).

St. Winefride's Neston, Aspects of History (Neston: St Winefride's, n.d.).

St. Winefride's Neston, 150 Years, 1843–1993 (n.p., 1993).

Stammers, M., *Mersey Flats and Flatmen* (Lavenham, Suffolk: Terence Dalton Limited, and Liverpool: National Museums and Galleries on Merseyside, 1993).

Stanley, Peter, *The House of Stanley from the 12th Century* (Bishop Auckland: Pentland Press, 1998).

The Statutes at Large Passed in the Parliaments Held in Ireland, Vol. ix (Dublin: printed by Boulter Grierson, 1769).

The Statutes at Large Passed in the Parliaments Held in Ireland (Dublin: printed by the executors of David Hay, 1782).

Stevenson, J., *Popular Disturbances in England 1700–1832* (Abingdon: Routledge, 1997).

Stobart, Jon, 'County, Town and Country: Three Histories of Urban Development in Eighteenth-Century Chester' in *Provincial Towns in Early Modern England and Ireland*, ed. by Peter Borsay and Lindsay Proudfoot (Oxford: Oxford University Press, 2002), pp. 171–94.

Sturt, Mary, *The Education of the People* (London: Routledge and Kegan Paul, 1967).

Sulley, Philip, *The Hundred of Wirral* (Birkenhead, 1889).

Sutherland, Gillian, 'Education' in *The Cambridge Social History of Britain 1750–1950*, ed. by F. Thompson (Cambridge: Cambridge University Press, 1990), pp. 119–70.

Sylvester, Dorothy, *A History of Cheshire* (London: Phillimore, 1980).

Tarlow, Sarah, *The Archaeology of Improvement, 1750–1850* (Cambridge: Cambridge University Press, 2007).

Taylor, A. J., 'The Miners' Association of Great Britain and Ireland, 1842–48: A Study in the Problem of Integration', *Economica*, 22, No. 85 (1955), pp. 45–60.

Thacker, A. T. 'Economic Infrastructure and Institutions: River Navigation' in *A History of the County of Chester*, ed. by C. P. Lewis and A. T. Thacker, 5 vols, (London: Institute of Historical Research and others, 1987–2005), v(2) (2005), pp. 83–7.

Thane, Pat, 'Government and Society in England and Wales, 1750–1914' in *The Cambridge Social History of Britain 1750–1950*, 3 vols., ed. by F. Thompson (Cambridge: Cambridge University Press, 1993), iii, pp. 1-62.

Thirsk, Joan et al., eds, *The Agrarian History of England and Wales*, (8 volumes) (Cambridge: Cambridge University Press, 1967–2000), 5.ii (1985).

Thirsk, Joan et al., eds, *The Agrarian History of England and Wales*, 8 vols (Cambridge: Cambridge University Press, 1967–2000), vi (1989).

Thomas, L. J. and L. P. Thomas, *Coal Geology* (Chichester: John Wiley, 2002).

Thompson, Rhiannon, 'A Breed Apart? Class and Community in a Somerset Coal-Mining Parish, c.1750–1850', *Rural History*, 16 (2005), pp. 137–59.

Toynbee, Arnold, *Lectures on the Industrial Revolution in England* (London: Rivingtons, 1884).

Travis, J. R., *Coal in Roman Britain*, British Archaeological Reports, British Series 468 (Oxford: John and Erica Hedges, 2008).

Trinder, Barrie, *Britain's Industrial Revolution* (Lancaster: Carnegie, 2013).

Trinder, Barrie, *The Industrial Revolution in Shropshire*, 3rd edn (Stroud: Phillimore, 2016).

Turner D. and D. Blackie, *Disability in the Industrial Revolution: Physical Impairment in British Coalmining, 1780–1880* (Manchester: Manchester University Press, 2018).

Twinings, *History of Twinings* (n.d.), <https://www.twinings.co.uk/about-twinings/history-of-twinings> [accessed 2 January 2023].

Velkar, A., *Markets and Measurements in Nineteenth Century Britain* (Cambridge: Cambridge University Press, 2012).

Vickers, A., *Women working at Newbottle Colliery*, Durham County Council (n.d.), <http://www.durhamintime.org.uk/durham_miner/women_newbottle_colliery.pdf> [accessed 19 February 2019].

Walker, George, *The Costume of Yorkshire* (London: 1814).

Waterston, W., *A Cyclopaedia of Commerce, Mercantile Law, Finance, and Commercial Geography* (Edinburgh: Oliver & Boyd, 1843).

Webster, F., 'The River Dee Reclamation and the Effect upon Navigation', *Transactions of the Liverpool Engineering Society*, 51 (1930), pp. 63–100.

Webster, Graham, 'The Lead-Mining Industry in North Wales in Roman Times', *FHSP*, 13 (1952–3), pp. 5–34.

Wedd, C. B., B. Smith, W. Simmons and D. Wray. *The Geology of Liverpool with Wirral and Part of the Flintshire Coalfield* (London: HMSO, 1923).

Wedd, C. B. and W. B. King, *The Geology of the Country around Flint, Hawarden, and Caergwrle* (London: Geological Survey, 1924).

Wesley, John, *The Works of John Wesley*, 17 vols, xi (London: printed by Thomas Cordeaux, 1812).

Wesley, John, *The Works of the Rev. John Wesley, A.M.*, 14 vols, iii, 3rd edn (London: John Mason, 1829).

Wilkinson, A., *The Newry Magazine or Literary & Political Register* (Newry: A. Wilkinson, 1815).

Bibliography

Willan, T., *The Navigation of the River Weaver in the Eighteenth Century*, Chetham Society, 3rd series, iii (1951), pp. 208–13.

Willett R., *A Memoir of Hawarden Parish, Flintshire* (Chester: J. Fletcher, 1822), facsimile reprint, 1990, by Library and Information Service, Cynor Sir Clwyd County Council, Clwyd.

Williams, Basil, *The Life of William Pitt, Earl of Chatham*, Vol. ii (London: Longmans, Green & Co., 1913).

Williams, C., *Industry in Clwyd, An Illustrated History* (Hawarden: Clwyd Record Office, 1986).

Williams, C. R., 'Thomas Norbury's Letters, 1806–1822', *FHSP*, 26 (1973–4), pp. 38–51.

Williams, Kate, *England's Mistress* (London: Arrow, 2007).

Williams, M. I. 'The Port of Aberdyfi in the 18th Century', *National Library of Wales Journal*, 18, 1 (1973), pp. 95–134.

Williams, Richard, *Limekilns and Limeburning* (Princes Risborough: Shire, 2004).

Williams, R. A., 'Hidden Bullion: Silver Production in North-East Wales', *Welsh Mines and Mining*, 2 (2012), pp. 33–44.

Williams, Thomas, *A Compendious Abstract of the Public General Acts Passed in 7 Geo. IV* (London, printed for Wightman and Camp, 1826).

Williams, T. W., *A Compendious Digest of the Statute Law* (London: G. Kearsley, 1787).

Wills, Leonard, *Concealed Coalfields: A Palaeogeographical Study of the Stratigraphy and Tectonics of Mid-England in Relation to Coal Reserves* (London: Blackie, 1956).

Wilson, K. P. ed., *Chester Customs Accounts, 1301–1566* (Liverpool: Record Society of Lancashire and Cheshire, 1969).

Wood, Alan, 'The Coalfields of North Wales' in *The Coalfields of Great Britain*, ed. by Arthur Trueman (London: Edward Arnold, 1954), pp. 244–54.

Woodward Donald, 'The Port of Chester in Context 1500–1800' in *Where Deva Spreads her Wizard Stream: Trade and the Port of Chester*, ed. by Peter Carrington (Chester: Chester City Council, c.1996), pp. 61–5.

Wright, Geoff, *Emma, Lady Hamilton (1765–1815): Neston's Most Famous Daughter* (Burton & Neston History Society, n.d.).

Wright, Joseph, ed., *English Dialect Dictionary* (London: Henry Frowde, 1904).

Wrigley, E. A., and R. S. Schofield, *The Population History of England, 1541–1871: A Reconstruction* (Cambridge: Cambridge University Press, 1989).

Wrigley E. A., R. S. Davies, J. E. Oeppen and R. S. Schofield, *English Population History from Family Reconstitution, 1580–1837* (Cambridge: Cambridge University Press, 1997).

Wrigley, E. A., *Poverty, Progress, and Population* (Cambridge: Cambridge University Press, 2004).

INDEX

Ch. (Cheshire. N.B. Wirral locations are marked as 'Wirral' but were also in Cheshire), Cumb. (Cumbria), D & G (Dumfries and Galloway), Fl. (Flintshire), Gwy. (Gwynedd), Nor. (Northumberland), La. (Lancashire), Mon. (Monmouthshire), Pemb. (Pembrokeshire), St. (Staffordshire), T & W (Tyne and Wear).
'n.'= note. '(?)' = (for individuals) identity is uncertain.
Bold = key pages. Italic numbers = illustrations.

N.B. for items with multiple entries, only the most important have been indexed. Endnote references have not been included where they are referred from an indexed entry in the main text.